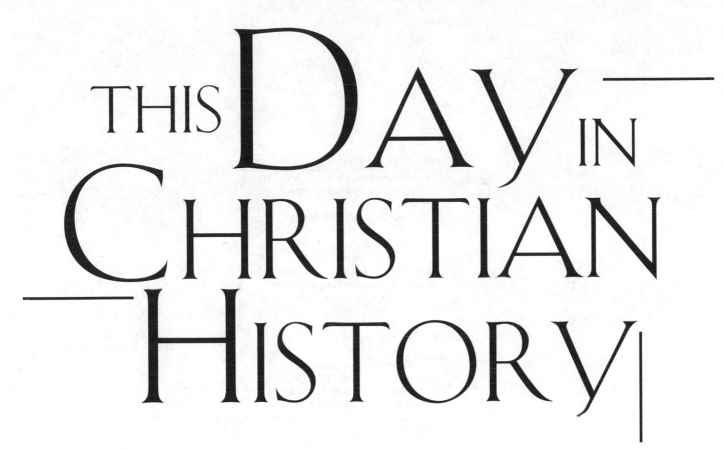

This Day in Christian History

366 Compelling Events in the History of the Church

A. Kenneth Curtis
Daniel Graves
Editors

Published by
Christian Publications, Inc.
Camp Hill, Pennsylvania
and
Christian History Institute
Worcester, Pennsylvania

CHRISTIAN PUBLICATIONS, INC.
3825 Hartzdale Drive, Camp Hill, PA 17011
www.christianpublications.com

Faithful, biblical publishing since 1883

This Day in Christian History
ISBN: 0-88965-238-4
LOC Control Number: 2004114370

Printed in Italy

05 06 07 08 09 5 4 3 2 1

Introduction

From the beginning of Creation, God has taught us to mark time—the observance of the seventh day as a day of rest, the celebration of certain feasts, the remembrance of specific acts He has done on our behalf. Thus it is part of our very nature to measure, mark and divide time, as well as to assign special significance to those measurements and divisions.

It follows, then, that from its inception, the Christian Church has attached significance to certain days, beginning with the observance of the Lord's Day on the first day of the week to celebrate the Resurrection. In the second-century document known as the *Didache*, Wednesdays and Fridays were designated as days of fasting throughout the year. They continue to be so observed in the Eastern Church.

In the Middle Ages, feasts and fasts made for a full year, with almost every day assigned to commemorate a particular saint or event in the life of the Church. Villages, towns, cities and nations lived by these Church dates. They kept people aware of who they were, of their participation in the Church and of their kinship with one another.

In keeping with this great tradition of remembrance, *This Day in Christian History* provides the reader with a compelling and interesting story for each day of the calendar year. This is done in an effort to offer a range of stories both well-known and obscure that cumulatively provide insight into the remarkably rich diversity of Christian living and experience over the centuries. In addition to the main story for each date, we have provided a list of supplemental events that took place on that day so as to widen the picture of important events in the calendar.

The thinking and planning for this book began some fifteen years ago. I had originally begun to prepare a listing of events that occurred on every calendar date with the hope that a meaningful entry could be found for every day of the year. The idea then was to use those entries as the subjects for brief radio commentaries.

In gathering our entries it would have been easy to rely on birth and death dates, but I decided to look instead for interesting and compelling happenings for each date. Further, I desired to come up with a good mix of gender, denominational and racial subjects from a wide range of time periods and places to suggest the far-reaching scope of world Christianity. Of course, it was obvious that we were limited in how far we could press this principle, since dates from the early Church and many obscure corners of the world are hard to come by.

With these goals in mind, a team of us began building the files. Historian Dr. Diana Severance gave us a major impetus forward by preparing a few sample months, which we used as a sort of template for the rest of the book. Meanwhile, researcher Ann Snyder of Christian History Institute (CHI) kept digging until she had compiled a computerized calendar to track stories and events that we might use for the project.

As you can imagine, we found we had many selections for some dates while other dates stubbornly resisted yielding any stories of the kind we sought. Activity on the project ebbed and flowed over several years until CHI Webmaster Dan Graves agreed to oversee the project and provide a daily story for our Web site. In addition, he began a thrice-weekly, free e-mail newsletter that gave little-known but fascinating stories from the annals of our Christian past. So we are most grateful to Dan, who brought the needed organization, discipline and perseverance to the task and who did the bulk of the work in preparing this volume. In fact, Dan now has three years of unduplicated articles prepared, so this book may be just the first of a series.

It is our hope and prayer that these stories provide you with a sampling that at least suggests the incredible scope and reach of the Christian message, as well as the way that God has worked through an amazing diversity of individuals and institutions in countless circumstances. This volume offers one way to take the journey through our Christian past in a go-at-your-own-pace way that we hope will stir your interest and fascination.

—Ken Curtis
Founder and President
Christian History Institute

Please Note: You can find more information on many of the main subjects found in *This Day in Christian History* by using the search engine on the CHI Web site at: www.chinstitute.org.

A Significant First on the First

David Nasmith's heart was broken. Nineteenth-century Scotland was rich in industry, but when twenty-seven-year-old Nasmith looked around his native Glasgow, it was not wealth he saw, but poverty: spiritual poverty. He said:

> Although this city is highly favored with religious privileges yet there are thousands who know as little of the Gospel as if it never had been preached in their land . . . they are living as careless as if they were never to be called to account. There are thousands of families where the name of God is never mentioned except when it is taken in vain . . . a vast number of the poor have never been taught to read.

The churches of Glasgow sat right in the middle of the city's poorest neighborhoods, but they might as well have been located on Mars for all the impact they had on their neighbors.

Others may have looked at the situation and thrown up their hands in defeat, but Nasmith was no idle talker: He was a person who got things done. In fact, at the age of fourteen he began distributing Bibles to people too poor to buy their own. In 1824, he founded the Young Men's Society for Religious Improvement. That led him to wonder what would happen if all of Glasgow's churches, all of its helping agencies, and any other Christians who cared to, were to band together to reach the city with the gospel.

So on this day in 1826, David Nasmith opened the world's first city mission in Glasgow, Scotland. The mission was also the first interdenominational agency in the world whose aim was to take the gospel to all of the citizens in its area of operation. Nasmith's organization addressed both the spiritual and physical needs of the people. The organization handed out gospel literature and held services, but it also obtained medical care for the poor, providing the kind of public health services that governments did not yet offer. The mission's workers also opened schools, visited prisoners and went to court with those who ran afoul of the law.

Nasmith's idea appealed to Christians everywhere. City missions sprang up all across the world. Nasmith himself founded several in Britain, France, Ireland and the United States.

Nasmith died on Christmas day thirteen years after he made his great innovation. He was just forty years old and as poor as a church mouse. However, he left a rich legacy that has resulted in hundreds of city missions worldwide.

David Nasmith was on the cutting edge of outreach, with Glasgow as his target. (Burger, Delores T. *Women Who Changed the Heart of the City: The Untold Story of the City Rescue Mission Movement*. Grand Rapids: Kregel Publications, 1997.)

Other Events

379 (probable date): Basil the Great, pioneer in founding church-run hospitals and schools, died.

1519: Reformation began in Switzerland when a young priest named Ulrich Zwingli started preaching through the Bible.

1585: Giovanni Gabrieli became the principle organist of St. Marks Cathedral in Venice. His innovations fostered a revolution in church and secular music and led to the development of the concerto form.

1901: In an all-night service at which she and other students prayed to receive the Holy Spirit, Agnes Ozman spoke in tongues at Bethel Bible School in Topeka, Kansas, setting off a chain of similar occurrences first at Bethel and then throughout the United States.

1922: Edith Stein was baptized. A top-ranking German philosopher, Stein converted from Judaism to Catholic Christianity and died a martyr under Hitler. "One can only learn the 'science of the cross' if one feels the cross in one's own person," she wrote.

St. Marks, Venice. (Evelyn, John. *Diary and Correspondence of John Evelyn*. London: Henry G. Bohn, 1859.)

January 2

Making Waves

Studying radio waves at the Marconi Institute. (Bucher, Elmer E. *Wireless Experimenter's Manual*. New York: Wireless Press, 1920.)

The first person to suspect the existence of radio waves was the Christian physicist James Clerk Maxwell. His studies of light led him to the development of the electromagnetic theory on a mathematical basis. In 1865 he proved mathematically the possibility of radio waves. Around 1885, the German scientist Heinrich Rudolf Hertz actually produced and detected radio waves at a distance of approximately one yard. By 1890, Édouard Branley had converted incoming radio signals to direct current, an important development in radio reception. Guglielmo Marconi combined the equipment of Hertz and Branley (and some say he stole the ideas of Nikola Tesla) to transmit a radio signal across the Atlantic in 1901.

The development of radio was very much an international effort, which seems fitting in light of its international reach. Public radio broadcasts began on November 2, 1920. Station KDKA of Pittsburgh advertised that it would broadcast the Harding-Cox election returns. Few people had the equipment to enjoy the results, but a precedent was set. The scheduling of radio broadcasts opened up a whole new world of communication opportunities.

On this day, January 2, in 1921, just two months to the day after its first broadcast, KDKA aired the first religious service in the history of radio. The program was undertaken by the Westinghouse-owned radio station to test its ability to do a remote broadcast far from a radio studio. Pittsburgh's Calvary Episcopal Church was chosen because one of the Westinghouse engineers, Fletcher Hallock, happened to be a member of the choir and made the arrangements. The bulletin announced that "an interesting arrangement has been made for tonight's service. There will be special Christmas carols and Gounod's magnificent *Credo* by the choir. Mr. Whittemore will preach a New Year's sermon." The broadcast covered a radius of more than a thousand miles. Technicians (one a Jew, another a Catholic) were outfitted with choir robes in order to keep them from distracting the congregation. Rev. Lewis B. Whittemore, junior pastor, preached, because the senior pastor was leery of the new medium.

KDKA soon offered a regular Sunday evening service from Calvary Episcopal Church. The senior pastor, Rev. Edwin Van Ettin, overcame his initial reluctance to become the weekly speaker. Regular broadcasts continued through 1962.

In no other country of the world has religious broadcasting taken such hold as in the United States. Curiously enough in light of the huge radio ministries that exist today, radio was viewed by many ministers in those days as a frivolity if not an outright evil. They resisted using the medium to spread the gospel. But others, such as Paul Radar, Chicago's pioneer Christian broadcaster, jumped at the chance and founded WJBT (Where Jesus Blesses Thousands). The growth of religious programming led to the formation of the National Religious Broadcasters on September 21, 1944, at a convention in Chicago's Moody Memorial Church.

Today, radio is a powerful means of reaching people for Christ, especially those trapped in nations where preaching the gospel is not allowed. Radio knows no walls or fences.

Edward Perronet, author of "All Hail the Power of Jesus' Name," a favorite hymn for worship. (Courtesy of cyberhymnal.org. Available online at: <http://www.cyberhymnal.org/bio/p/e/perronet_e.htm>.)

Other Events

Annual: This day is set aside to honor those who died as martyrs for their Scriptures. According to the Saxon historian Bede, hundreds of people were slaughtered in 286 by imperial order for refusing to surrender their bits of Scripture at the place later known as Lichfield, meaning "field of corpses," because of the event.

1792: Edward Perronet died. He worked with the Methodists and was the author of the popular hymn "All Hail the Power of Jesus' Name."

1930: Newlyweds Mr. and Mrs. George Roffe, Christian and Missionary Alliance workers, arrived in the Laotian kingdom of Luang Prabang to begin mission work, having traveled twenty-two days under torturous and dangerous conditions, with little knowledge of the local languages. "Some three days in plank canoes we negotiated boiling rapids and swift currents . . . that twenty-two-day trek was not all travel. Each time we had to recruit carriers, horses, boats and boatmen; each time we had to wait for the uncertain schedule of a mail truck our journey was inevitably broken for a day or two."

A Workaholic Reformer for Denmark

3

When Martin Luther's Reformation began in Germany, it was inevitable that his ideas would seep through the cracks in the borders into neighboring Scandinavia. The most vigilant efforts of government and Church could not stop German ideas, books and preachers from slipping into Denmark.

A shoemaker's son was the chief agent of reform in Denmark. Peder Palladius was still a student when Reformation ideas arrived in his country. He found himself agreeing with the Reformation call to a life of faith grounded on the Word of God alone. The writings of Melanchthon, composer of the first treatise on evangelical doctrine, drew Palladius as flowers draw bees.

Denmark fought a civil war over the Reformation in 1533 when Denmark's Catholics revolted at the prospect of a Protestant king. Duke Christian defeated them and was crowned King Christian III. He asked the Catholic Church to pay his war debts, but it refused, so he locked up the bishops, blaming them for the rebellion. (When he later released them, some joined his side.) Christian III was so reform-minded that he sometimes even climbed into the pulpit himself. Remarkably tolerant for those times, he pensioned off Catholic churchmen who refused to join the Reformation.

In 1537 the Danish Church broke completely with Rome. King Christian deliberately had Johann Bugenhagen consecrate several bishops outside of the apostolic succession. Palladius had just completed his doctoral exams at Wittenberg, the center of Lutheran thought in Germany. Christian III summoned the scholar and appointed him to the highest Church office in Denmark, superintendent of Zealand. At the same time, Palladius was ordered to hold another influential position: theology professor at the University of Copenhagen.

Palladius showed everyone what a bishop should be. Not only did he visit all of the 390 parishes under his oversight, but he also held hundreds of seminars, preached, taught at the university and wrote books that explained complicated theology so simply that the common folk could understand it.

The hard-working bishop also prepared a liturgy in the Danish language. Of course, some Danes didn't want to become Lutherans. Palladius instructed their bishops to accept this hesitancy with patience and educate the people in the new doctrine.

When Palladius died, on this day in 1560 (as it is thought), he left behind a lasting legacy of devotional and professional writings. His life had been so zealous that the new generation eagerly studied his works to imitate him. Not bad for a shoemaker's son.

Peder Palladius, reformer of Denmark. (Fabricius, A. *Illustreret Danmarkshistorie for Folket*. Kjobenhavn: Rittendorf and Auguurd, 1854-5.)

Other Events

Annual: The feast day of Genevieve, whom legend says saved Paris several times, is celebrated. On one occasion she called the city to prayer, averting an attack by Atilla II. Holy even as a child, she was dedicated for Christ's service by a passing bishop, represented in the detail from this painting by Puvis de Chavannes (at right).

1521: Pope Leo X excommunicated German reformer Martin Luther a second time. Luther had refused to be silenced from speaking out against a number of abuses in the Church and had developed an independent theology despite an earlier, conditional excommunication.

1918: Annie Sherwood Hawks, the Baptist hymn writer who wrote "I Need Thee Every Hour," died.

1984: Dr. Jacob Gartenhouse, founder and first president of International Jewish Missions, died.

Young Genevieve is dedicated for service. (Bell, Mrs. Arthur. *Saints in Christian Art*. London: George Bell, 1901-4.)

Young Nazi guard. (Courtesy of Trinity Films/Gateway Films.)

JANUARY

4 Muzzled but Protesting

Adolf Hitler's Nazi regime in Germany has been denounced as one of the most heinous in all of history. Yet when it first came to power, it was welcomed by many German church members. Hitler replaced the decadent Weimar Republic that had produced a literature and art of despair. Large numbers of Germans hoped that he would bring spiritual renewal because he talked about German history and traditions.

Most of the churches in Germany were Lutheran and organized by provinces. A movement began to nationalize the Church under a single Reichs-bishop. This was actually a trick to bring the Church under Nazi control. In May 1933 the constitution for a unified national Church was produced. The so-called "German Christians" elected Ludwig Müller, a fervent Nazi, to head the Church. In July, two restrictions were placed on the clergy: (1) A clergyman must be politically reliable; and (2) he must accept the superiority of the Aryans.

Hundreds of clergy accepted these demands, but a small group of Church leaders did not. They openly opposed those "German Christians" who accepted the government's terms. These dissidents insisted that the Church must obey Christ apart from political influence. In September 1933 Martin Niemöller sent a letter to all German pastors, inviting them to join a Pastor's Emergency League to oppose the Unified Church. Karl Barth and Dietrich Bonhoeffer were among those who joined him.

In October, Niemöller asked pastors to take a pledge to be bound by the Scriptures and the old confessions of faith. They pledged themselves to protest certain violations of the faith, to stand with the persecuted and to acknowledge that Aryanism (with its claim of racial superiority) was a violation of Reformation and Christian teaching.

Theologian Karl Barth, world-famous for a commentary on Paul's letter to the Romans, issued a refutation of Unified Church doctrines and *Fundamentals*, a paper against the teaching of the "German Christians." He said that the source of all of the errors of the "German Christians" was that they gave German nationality, history and politics equal weight with Scripture. Many pastors resigned from the Nazi's Unified Church after Barth pointed this out.

On this day in 1934, Reichs-bishop Müller issued a decree, which he claimed was needed to restore order in the German Evangelical Church. This decree became known as the "Muzzling Order," because it forbade ministers to say anything in their sermons about the Church controversy. But faithful ministers could not allow themselves to be kept out of politics by such an order—not when politics violated the deepest principles of their faith. In fact, the very day that Müller issued his decree, 320 elders and pastors were already gathered at Barmen, calling themselves the First Free Reformed Synod. They accepted Barth's "Declaration on the Correct Understanding of the Reformation Confessions in the Evangelical Church."

More meetings were held in the months that followed. In April, pastors who opposed Hitler formed the Confessing Church. It included Lutheran, Reformed and United churches. The Confessing Church was named so because it clung to the Church's great historical confessions of faith.

The Confessing Church stood almost alone in Germany against Nazi falsehood during the terrible years of the Third Reich. Because of their boldness, its leaders paid a steep price. Niemöller went to prison. Bonhoeffer was hanged.

J.P. Morgan, financier. (Courtesy of the University of Texas collection of public domain portraits on the Web.)

Other Events

1913: J. Pierpoint Morgan, one of the richest men in the United States, confessed his faith in Christ in the will that he drew up on this day:

> I commit my soul into the hands of my Savior, full of confidence that having redeemed it and washed it with his most precious blood, he will present it faultless before the throne of my heavenly Father. . . . I entreat my children to maintain and defend, at all hazard, and at any cost of personal sacrifice, the blessed doctrine of complete atonement for sin through the blood of Jesus Christ, once offered, and through that alone.

1985: Shenouda III returned to Cairo from exile to lead the Coptic Church. Egyptian President Anwar Sadat had banished Shenouda for his outspokenness against Islamic persecution of Christians.

1988: A group of Christian women gathered to form the Hong Kong Women's Christian Council in response to the pending reoccupation of Hong Kong by the People's Republic of China in 1997.

Organizing the Rapidly Growing Methodist Movement

Muscle builders and pregnant women know that anyone whose body grows too fast is liable to get stretch marks. Organizations that grow too rapidly can get stretch marks too. That was the case with the Welsh Methodists in the early 1740s. Converts were coming in so fast that leaders were unsure of how to cope with the growing number of "societies." The problem needed immediate attention. Field preacher Howel Harris wrote to George Whitefield, pleading for guidance. "We are all like little children, not knowing what to do," he said.

Eight Methodist leaders gathered in Waterford, South Wales, on this day in 1743 to hold the first Calvinist Methodist Conference. The best known of the eight attending leaders was the evangelist George Whitefield, whose preaching on both sides of the Atlantic converted thousands to Christ. Whitefield had an extraordinary voice that could be heard without amplifiers by up to 40,000 people. Crowds hung on his words, which were accompanied by dramatic gestures and deep emotion. As chosen moderator of the Waterford conference, Whitefield preached both morning and evening.

Three other clergymen were also present at that January 5 meeting: Daniel Rowlands, John Powell and William Williams. Rowlands was considered superior even to Whitefield in his ability to set forth the meaning of the Bible. He had formed several societies of new converts that he watched over with tender care. Of Powell we know little save that he was an attendee at this meeting. More is known about Williams, the third clergyman present that day. When Williams was converted at the age of twenty-one, he gave up his medical studies to enter the ministry. He was ordained as a deacon by the Church of England and became a notable preacher. He is also known for writing the popular hymn "Guide Me, O Thou Great Jehovah."

There were lay preachers at the first Calvinist Methodist Conference as well. Chief among them was Howel Harris, whose enthusiasm had originally sparked the Welsh revival. John Cennick, a colleague of Harris's, was also an attendee. On one occasion, while they were preaching in Swindon, London, Cennick and Harris were attacked. "Mr. Goddard, a leading gentleman of the town, lent the mob his guns, halberd and engine [water pump] and bade them use us as badly as they could, only not kill us," recounted Cennick.

The conference proved to be harmonious. Guided by Whitefield, the eight leaders drew up regulations for their association. Ordained ministers were appointed to be overseers, each with a district under him. Lay workers throughout Wales were appointed to fill two newly created offices: superintendent and exhorter. Exhorters were of two sorts: public (those who spoke to large crowds) and private (those who worked best with small groups and in homes). Each exhorter was put in charge of twelve to fourteen societies. Duties and terms of admission were set for the offices.

The conference established its headquarters at Moorfields Tabernacle, a London church built by Whitefield in 1741 that had often served as his base of operations when he was in England. A regular schedule of local and regional conferences was also established during the meeting.

The Waterford meeting. (Hyde, A.B. *Story of Methodism*. Greenfield, MA: Willey and Co., 1887.)

Whitefield's ideas were soon picked up by another Methodist organization. John Wesley held his first Methodist conference eighteen months later, and his followers adopted a similar setup to that which had been established during the trailblazing meeting at Waterford.

Other Events

1527: Felix Manz became the first Anabaptist martyr when he was executed by drowning. The Anabaptists refused to baptize their children until they were old enough to understand that the rite unites one with Christ, who takes away our sins by His death (represented by the water) and resurrects us to a new life (represented by coming out of the water).

1943: George Washington Carver, who overcame the adversity of being born a slave to become a leading American educator and scientist, died on this day. He was noted for his deep faith and humility and for his lively Bible lessons.

George Washington Carver livened his Sunday school classes with science experiments. (Courtesy of the Christian History Institute archives.)

January 6

So Persuasive He Got Himself "Exiled"

Columns in lovely St. Sophia. Theophylact bemoaned leaving this culture behind. (Oman, C.W.C. *Story of the Byzantine Empire*. New York: Putnam's Sons, 1892.)

Can you make too good an impression on someone important? Theophylact may have thought so. On this day in 1088, he gave an enthusiastic speech before Alexius, emperor of Byzantium, in which he warmly praised the emperor and his mother Anna Dalassena. He crowed over the emperor's conquest of parts of the Balkans. The emperor was a diplomat and a servant of the Church, said Theophylact.

His speech had unintended effects. Evidently the emperor was pleased. In Byzantium (the eastern half of the old Roman Empire), church posts were under government control and they were often given as rewards. The emperor promoted Theophylact to be archbishop of Ohrid in Bulgaria.

For Theophylact, who was a cultured man, the promotion was like a sentence of exile. In Constantinople there were libraries, palaces and shimmering architecture. There he taught the sons of important men. He even taught Prince Constantine Doukas, who was expected to become emperor one day, and he was a friend to the boy's beautiful mother, Maria of Alania. A transfer to Bulgaria meant that he would have to leave all of that, and his many friends, behind. Like many other Byzantines, he considered Ohrid a barbarian backwater. But churchmen were civil servants who had to go wherever the emperor ordered, so Theophylact went to Ohrid.

Theophylact may not have been thrilled with his new appointment, but neither were the people of Ohrid. Byzantium's conquest of Bulgaria still rankled Ohrid, and Theophylact's appointment rubbed salt in the wounds of their defeat. Formerly, the Bulgarians had had their own patriarch so, resentful of their loss of independence, they greeted their new archbishop with jeers and insults. They were not consoled by the fact that the emperor had given local bishops the privilege of consecrating Theophylact or that the emperor had confirmed that Bulgaria's Church would be independent of the patriarch of Constantinople. As far as they were concerned, Theophylact was an outsider, and they knew that he was expected do his part to keep Bulgaria glued to the empire.

Theophylact did not like Bulgaria, which he called "of all provinces of the empire, the most pitiable." He was homesick and begged his friends to help get him released from the place. After a visit home, he wrote, "So I return to the Bulgarians, I who am a true Constantinopolitan and, strange though it is, a Bulgarian." Yet he had compassion on Bulgaria's poor. In several letters he pleaded for tax relief and pointed out that one child in five was seized to be sold into slavery as payment for taxes. He urged a show of mercy "lest the patience of the poor be finally exhausted."

One way that Theophylact tried to forget his homesickness was to write. He had 130 of his letters published. The letters are difficult to understand today because he wrote in a "puzzle" style. Even so, they capture bits of Byzantine and Bulgarian history that are useful to historians. He came to love Slavic literature and Slavic Church heroes and wrote about the life of St. Clement of Ohrid and of the fifteen martyrs buried at Strumitsa, not far from Ohrid. In "exile," he also wrote commentaries on Paul's epistles and the Gospels.

Amazingly, 400 years later, Theophylact's January 6 speech was still generating fallout. A German scholar named Erasmus discovered the archbishop's writings and borrowed some of Theophylact's ideas for a satire called *Praise of Folly*. That book, by poking fun at wrongs in the Church and society, helped bring about the Protestant Reformation in Europe.

Alexander Whyte, author and finest preacher of Victorian Scotland. (Barbour, G.F. *The Life of Alexander Whyte*. London: Hodder and Stoughton, 1925.)

Other Events

386: Siricus, bishop of Rome, held a synod at Rome with eighty bishops, an event that bolsters papal claims to Roman primacy.

1579: The Union of Arras was formed in the Netherlands when Catholics, outraged by Calvinist destruction of their churches and images, returned to Spanish control.

1850: Charles Spurgeon was converted. He went into an almost empty church on a snowy night and was confronted with the gospel by an ill-prepared deacon.

1921: Alexander Whyte, regarded as the finest preacher of the Free Church of Scotland, died. He was also the author of *Bible Characters*.

1948: Janani Luwum was converted to Christianity in Uganda. Determined to live a godly life, he immediately asked his family to pray that he wouldn't backslide. Eventually he became archbishop of Uganda and was butchered by the brutal dictator Idi Amin.

1964: Pope Paul VI visited the Holy Land. In Jerusalem, he met with the Orthodox patriarch of Constantinople, Athenagoras, in a move that was widely heralded as a step toward the reconciliation of the Orthodox and Roman Catholic Churches, which had separated in the eleventh century.

Writings with Power to Help

When you open a Bible, you see at once that it is one long book made up of many shorter books. Do you wonder how people decided which books should be in the Bible? It was important for Christians to know which works were true Scriptures and which weren't. For one thing, they needed to know what teachings they should follow. For another, they needed to know what writings they should protect if they had to, because they didn't want to be tortured or killed for trying to save a book that wasn't God's Word. About 130 years after Christ's resurrection, bishops began listing the writings that they regarded as Scripture. Their lists, while similar, did not always agree with one another.

At the beginning of the year 367, Athanasius, bishop of Alexandria, sat down to write an Easter letter to his church. He wrote these "festal" letters every year to put his people into the right frame of mind for celebrating Easter.

That year, he saw that Church people were being confused by books that claimed to be Scripture but weren't. For instance, they might wonder if the Epistle of Barnabas was to be obeyed. Or they might fall for the Gospel of Peter by the Gnostics, a group who claimed secret knowledge of God. Peter's name was assigned to the work to give it creditability, but it was not written by the Apostle. Athanasius realized that the best defense against error was a clear understanding of Scripture, but which writings were actually Scripture? In his festal letter dated this day in 367, he wrote:

> Inasmuch as some have taken in hand to draw up for themselves an arrangement of the so-called apocryphal books and to intersperse them with the divinely inspired Scripture . . . it has seemed good to me . . . to set forth in order the books which are included in the canon and have been delivered to us with accreditation that they are divine.

The Church already accepted the books of the Jewish Scripture as inspired by the Holy Spirit. These became our Old Testament. The Church also agreed that books and letters written by the apostles or by writers under the apostles' direct influence were probably Scripture, if the books had been used for a long time by the Church. These became our New Testament. Athanasius thought it best to list the trustworthy books so that the common people would not be led astray by the false teachings of other works. He was the first man to compile a list of New Testament books as we know them.

Athanasius had a high regard for Scripture. He wrote:

> These are fountains of salvation, that they who thirst may be satisfied with the living words that they contain. . . . Let no man add to these, neither let him take ought from these. For concerning these the Lord put to shame the Sadducees, and said, "Ye do err, not knowing the Scriptures." And he reproved the Jews, saying, "Search the Scriptures, for these are they that testify of me."

The famed Lighthouse of Pharos was already 200 years old in Athanasius's day. (Adams, W.H. Davenport. *Egypt Past and Present*. London: Thomas Nelson, 1894.)

As bishop of the prominent city of Alexandria, Athanasius became well-known. Much of his life was spent battling Arianism, a heresy that denied Christ's divinity. His strong convictions got him into trouble with the emperor, and he was exiled five times. Each time, the Egyptians welcomed him back.

Because of his influence, Athanasius's list of books helped to settle the question of which books do and don't belong in the Bible. People recognized the truth of what the great bishop wrote. The books of the Bible are not God's Word because Athanasius said so; they are in the Bible because the majority of Christians recognized their wisdom as coming from God. Athanasius was confirming the conviction and practice of the early Christian churches across the empire.

Other Events

312 (probable date): Lucian, presbyter of Antioch, was tried and executed in Nicomedia during the last great persecution in the Roman Empire.

1715: François Fenelon, the mild and holy archbishop of Cambrai, died on this day. He was beloved by both Catholics and Protestants for his spiritual writings on love and perfection.

1865: William Bradbury, composer of the tune "Jesus Loves Me" and many other hymns, died.

1867: James Edmeston died. He wrote 2,000 hymns, among them "Lead Us, Heavenly Father," and "Savior, Breathe an Evening Blessing."

1893: Edith Warner arrived at Onitsha (now in Nigeria) to begin a life work as a missionary-educator.

1902: Hyman Jedidiah Appleman, a Jew, was born in Russia. He became an evangelist in the United States.

1952: Janos Peter took Andor Engedi's place as head of the Reformed Church in Communist Hungary. Engedi had resigned rather than yield key points to the government.

Mild Fenelon. (Courtesy of the Christian History Institute archives.)

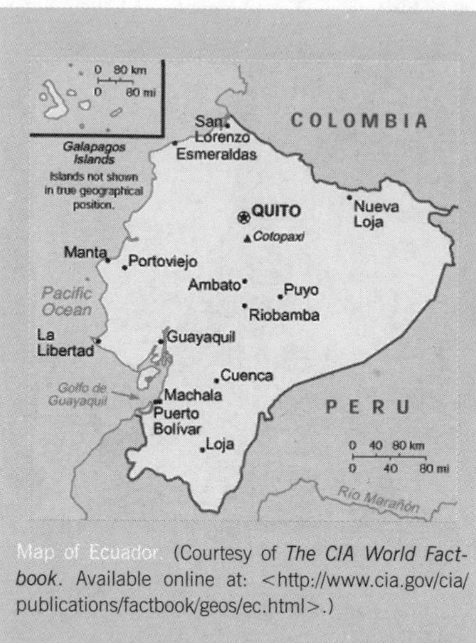

Map of Ecuador. (Courtesy of *The CIA World Factbook*. Available online at: <http://www.cia.gov/cia/publications/factbook/geos/ec.html>.)

January 8

Death in the Jungle

The five men on "Palm Beach," a strip of sand on the Curaray River, Ecuador, knew that there was danger. But they took the risk, hoping to make friendly contact with the Auca (Waodani) Indians. Missionaries Ed McCulley, Nate Saint, Jim Elliot, Pete Fleming and Roger Youderian had landed on the makeshift airstrip in their "modern missionary mule" (a Piper Cruiser).

Back at Shell Mera on this day in 1956, Marj Saint awaited word from her husband and the other missionaries. The shortwave radio crackled. She listened as her husband, Nate, told her that "a commission of ten" was on its way from "Terminal City." "Looks like they'll be here for the early afternoon service. Pray for us. This is the day! We'll contact you next at 4:30." Excitement was intense. Months of efforts were about to bear fruit. The "commission" was a group of Auca men. "Terminal City" was the code name the missionaries had given an Auca village that they had spotted from the air. Saint spoke in code words because he did not want Ecuadorians with guns wrecking the mission's friendly overtures to the Aucas. The Aucas were sturdy forest dwellers who fiercely resisted all efforts to subdue them, killing many people who ventured into their territory. Saint had first spotted one of their villages from the air on September 19, 1955.

On October 1, the missionaries developed a plan for reaching the Auca. McCulley, Saint and others gathered at Shell Mera and talked into the wee hours of the morning, huddled over maps, establishing their strategy. What they decided to do was fly over the villages and lower gifts to the people. They used a public-address system to repeat friendly phrases that Jim had collected from an Auca woman living on a nearby plantation. Soon large numbers of Aucas were converging for the gift drops. Finally the day came when the villagers tied a gift to the line in return. It was a feathered headdress.

Next, a landing spot had to be found. One of the sandbars on the Curaray River would have to do. Saint found a good one about four-and-a-half miles from Terminal City. Finally, on January 3, Saint and McCulley landed. The sand proved softer than they had thought, but by letting air out of the tires, takeoff was possible. Saint ferried the men and the supplies to the camp. The men erected a prefabricated tree house and shouted friendly words into the bush. Four days later an Auca man and two women appeared. Then on January 8, several Auca were spotted heading to "Palm Beach."

The time for the planned radio contact rolled around. Eagerly Marj switched on her radio back at the base. Nothing! Had the men been invited to the Auca houses? She waited. There was no sound. The minutes passed and lengthened into hours. Silence.

Johnny Keenan flew over Palm Beach on Monday morning. He reported to Marj that he had spotted Saint's plane, stripped of its fabric. On Wednesday he saw the first of the bodies from the air. Then another. Soon it was evident that all five men were dead.

Jim Elliot once said, "When it comes time to die, make sure that all you have to do is die." The five men on the beach had been ready to die, and their deaths were not in vain.

Through the efforts of the widows of the five men killed on "Palm Beach" that day, the Aucas discovered Christian forgiveness. The day came when they invited missionaries to work among them and explained that they had killed the five men out of fear, thinking they were cannibals. The same Aucas who killed the men who had come to bring them the gospel are now believers in the Lord. Some even died as martyrs themselves, carrying the gospel to other Indians in Ecuador.

Pope Celestine III, who confirmed the new military order of the Teutonic Knights. (Montor, Chevalier Artaud de. *Lives and Times of the Popes*. New York: Catholic Publication Society of America, 1911.)

Other Events

1198: Pope Celestine III died. He confirmed the new military order of the Teutonic Knights, dealt mildly with the cruel emperor Henry VI of Germany (whom he crowned) but excommunicated Duke Leopold of Austria, who imprisoned Richard I "the Lionheart" of England.

1198: Lothair of Segnei was elected as Pope Innocent III on the same day that Celestine III died. He made strong claims for papal power and was the first to consistently wear the title "Vicar of Christ." Under him, the papacy reached its peak in the Middle Ages.

1539: Tjard Reynders was executed for the desperate "crime" of sheltering the gentle and holy Anabaptist leader Menno Simons.

1672: Quaker Elizabeth Hooten, possibly the first modern woman preacher, died on this day.

1958: The Church of Christ in Africa, an independent black church, was registered by the government of Kenya.

An Urgent Call to Assemble Saves the Swedish Reformation

Would you die for your faith? Many ordinary sixteenth-century Europeans did just that. England's Queen Mary executed hundreds of Protestants, and even more died in her prisons because of their faith. Horrible atrocities were perpetrated against many Protestants, from France to the Netherlands. In some areas, Protestants retaliated with similar atrocities. Across Europe, blood flowed in battles between Catholics and Protestants.

In 1593, the Swedes had reason to suspect that their turn was coming. Lutheranism had gained a firm hold over the minds of the Swedish people. They were concerned about the results of a Catholic monarch taking over the country. Sigismund III of Poland was in line to become Sweden's next monarch. An ardent Catholic, he had already pushed the Protestant Reformation out of Poland. And he was on his way to Stockholm with 20,000 crowns (a valuable coin) in his pocket, a gift from the pope to restore Catholicism to Sweden.

In Sweden, a small group of Lutheran leaders discussed the potential danger to Swedish Protestants. They thought they saw a way to prevent disaster. With the help of Charles, duke of Sudermania (Finland) and the Protestant uncle of Sigismund III, they went into action.

On this day in 1593, messengers raced into the Swedish countryside with an urgent summons for all Protestant clergy to assemble at Uppsala within a month. Uppsala, a few miles north of Stockholm, had once been a Viking burial ground but now was home to Sweden's archbishops, who since 1531 had been Lutheran.

Scores of churchmen heeded the call. By the time the diet (a formal meeting of provincial leaders) began on March 1, 306, clergymen had assembled. Members of the Council of State were also in attendance. On March 10, the assembly decreed that all future monarchs of Sweden must be Lutheran. The Lutheran Augsburg Confession was declared to be the only legal, binding confession for the Swedish Church, its subjects and its rulers. Before Sigismund could land in Stockholm, Charles was chosen Regent of Sweden and head of the Council of State.

Sigismund wanted to keep both Poland and Sweden but could hardly be a Catholic in one country and a Lutheran in the other. His Jesuit confessors urged him to subscribe to the Augsburg Confession. Subsequently, Sigismund swore to uphold the decision of Uppsala and was then crowned as the ruler of Sweden in 1594. His coronation oath included a promise to preserve the Swedish Church. He immediately broke his word, appointing a Catholic governor to Stockholm, founding Catholic schools and ruling Sweden through Polish Catholics.

Sweden's parliament confirmed Charles as regent, and he would govern when Sigismund returned to Poland. After Sigismund sailed away late in 1594, Sweden's peasants petitioned for a single king, saying Sigismund had forfeited his right to rule by going against the Augsburg Confession. Charles was unwilling to lead a revolution, and Sigismund might have remained king (in name at least) except that he raised an army to attack his own country. In response to the threat, Charles met Sigismund near Linköping between Vattern and the eastern coast in 1597 and routed him.

The Swedes made Charles their king. The Swedish Church remained independent of Rome. Charles's son, Gustavus Adolphus, became one of the greatest of the Protestant generals and saved their cause during the Thirty Years' War that soon enveloped Europe.

Gustavus Adolphus inherited Sweden's throne due to the decision at Uppsala. (Gindely, Anton. *History of the Thirty Years' War*. New York: Putnam, 1884.)

Other Events

1522: For the first time in 200 years, a non-Italian pope took office. Dutchman Adrian Dedel took the office, calling himself Adrian VI. He was also the last non-Italian pope to sit in office until the twentieth century.

1765: Samuel Stillman was installed as pastor of Boston's First Baptist Church. An influential pastor, he called for separation of Church and state in a 1799 sermon.

1944: Edward Martin, a convict on a Virginia chain gang, converted to faith in Christ. Earlier, he had escaped from his chain gang. A reward of only $10 was posted for his capture, dead or alive, so worthless was he considered. Nevertheless, he was eventually captured. As he lived out his sentence, his sister's roommate wrote him letters containing Scripture verses. Martin answered every letter and read the camp Bible. After his conversion, his transformation was so complete that one of the guards recommended him for parole. Following his parole, he married the letter-writer Miss Alfreda Enders, served as a foreign missionary and founded Hope Aglow ministries to serve convicts.

1947: Japan's Christian Layman's Association was formed under Dr. S. Uzawa, former president of the Japanese bar association, and Dr. T. Yamamoto, a prominent scientist.

Samuel Stillman called for a bill of rights. (Armitage, Thomas. *A History of the Baptists: Traced by Their Principles and Practices, From the Time of our Lord and Saviour Jesus Christ to the Present*. New York: Bryan, Taylor and Co., 1893.)

Cardinal Ximenez, who funded the first printed polyglot translation of the Bible. (MacNutt, Francis. *Augustus Bartholomew de las Casas: His Life, His Apostolate, and His Writings*. New York: Putnam, 1909.)

January 10

Many Versions Inside One Cover

Maybe you've skimmed down the columns of one of those Bibles that has four—or even as many as eight—translations side-by-side. It is interesting to compare their wording, isn't it? Such Bibles are useful for study, especially if they give the original Greek or Hebrew. We call them *polyglot* Bibles, and they help us to capture the meaning of the original words of Scripture.

Polyglot means "many languages." The first polyglot Bible was compiled in the third century by the famous Alexandrian theologian Origen. The first polyglot Bible ever printed was the Complutesian Polyglot, which was produced in sixteenth-century Spain. It is called Complutesian from Complutum, the original Roman name of Acalá, the place where it was printed.

The Complutesian Polyglot was paid for by wealthy Cardinal Ximenez, the stern inquisitor of Spain. Although rich, Ximenez chose to live as a simple Franciscan friar. The pope himself had to order Ximenez to accept the position of archbishop of Toledo. A man of great ability, Ximenez founded the University of Acalá, defeated the Moors at Oran, North Africa, and governed Spain during absences of the royal family. Had Julius II (and later Leo X) listened to Ximenez, Martin Luther's Reformation might never have happened, for the cardinal protested the infamous indulgences that triggered the split in the Church. As head of the infamous Spanish Inquisition, Ximenez restricted the scope and actions of its officers, but thousands of people suffered its cruelties all the same.

Ximenez appointed Diego Lopez de Zunga to head up the work on the expensive polyglot project. It ended up costing what would be about $500,000 today. The Old Testament ran to four volumes. Jerome's Latin Vulgate was sandwiched between the Hebrew text and the Septuagint (the Greek version of the Old Testament). For the Pentateuch (the five books of Moses) the arrangers also provided an Aramaic translation. In the preface to the polyglot, Ximenez said he hoped it would assist scholars in determining the correct interpretation of Scripture. He pointed out that while the "meaning of heavenly wisdom" can be found in any language, the true meaning of Scripture cannot "be understood in any way other than from the very fount of the original language."

According to the colophon of the first volume of the polyglot (a colophon is an inscription placed at the end of a book or manuscript telling about its production), it was issued on this day in 1514, more than three years before Luther tacked his ninety-five theses to the church door. The sixth volume did not come off the press until 1517.

Pope Leo X had been slow to approve the huge project. Also, the fact that Erasmus had been given express permission by Emperor Maximillian to print Greek New Testaments also impeded publication. The official publication date of the entire Complutesian Polyglot Bible was not until 1522, several years after Ximenez died. Begun in 1502, it had taken twenty years to publish. It stands as a monument of Renaissance Bible scholarship.

An artist's conception of Blessed Pope Gregory X. (Montor, Chevalier Artaud de. *Lives and Times of the Popes*. New York: Catholic Publication Society of America, 1911.)

Other Events

1276: Blessed Pope Gregory X died. When he was consecrated, the papacy had been vacant for three years while political powers wrangled. Gregory, who had not even been a priest, established peace between Europe's rulers and recognized Rudolf of Hapsburg as emperor.

1858: Francis Havergal wrote the hymn "I Gave My Life for Thee" after seeing Sternberg's painting *Ecce Homo* under which was the inscription "This have I done for thee; what hast thou done for me?" Thinking her words very poor, she threw the poem in the stove. It fell away from the flame and was rescued. When her father saw the words, he immediately composed a tune for them.

1863: Lyman Beecher, famed anti-Unitarian preacher and father of Harriet Beecher Stowe, who wrote the novel *Uncle Tom's Cabin*, died.

1915: Missionary Mary Slessor held her last church service. Three days later she died in Nigeria, having done much to end age-old cruelties such as the exposure of twins in the jungle and trials by ordeal.

Only One Day of School a Week?

"Yeah! No school!" Most kids jump for joy when school is cancelled because of inclement weather or other circumstances outside of the school's control. For one day, students are free of books and blackboards.

In 1790, many children had no school to hate. They worked six days a week in factories and never learned to read or write. Christian leaders in England and America thought this a tragic and unacceptable fact. They knew that those children would lose opportunities in life because of their lack of education. They also realized that as the children grew older they would be better workers if they could write letters and figure bills and that they would be better Christians if they could read the Bible.

Sunday was the one day that the children had free. If they were to attend classes, it would have to be then. Here and there, concerned Christians opened Sunday schools. However, these schools were not very effective because each one worked independently.

In Gloucester, England, around 1780, someone griped to Robert Raikes that children were rough and rowdy on Sunday. Raikes was a newspaper publisher, and the person who had complained to Raikes expected that he would write an editorial calling for more policemen to help keep the children in line. Instead, he rented a room on a street that had the rowdiest kids and hired four teachers. He paid children a penny each (which would be about fifty cents today) to come to class. Churchgoers said Raikes was wasting his time. Friends referred to "Bobby Wild Goose and his ragged regiment." But Raikes stuck to his plan. Three years later, when he was sure that his experiment had succeeded, Raikes published a newspaper story about it.

At that time, William Fox, a wealthy London merchant, was looking for a way to educate the poor so that they could read the Bible. After reading Raikes's story, he formed a Sunday school society to help spread Raikes's ideas. The ideas traveled to America, where the first American Sunday school was begun in Virginia in 1785 when William Elliot taught his own children and slaves. His school was a great step, but hundreds more were needed, as well as money to pay teachers.

On this day in 1791, a group of concerned Philadelphians met to do something about education. Among them were Bishop William White, doctors Benjamin Rush and William Currie, the Quaker Joseph Sharpless, two merchants, Thomas Pym Cope, Thomas Mendenhall, other Quakers and Matthew Carey, a Catholic publisher.

Sunday, said the men, ought to be devoted to religious improvement for both adults and children, but instead it was being used by many children for "wicked" purposes. In their opinion, "the establishment of first-day or Sunday schools in this city would be of essential advantage to the rising generation."

They formed the First Day Society to promote Sunday schools in Philadelphia, electing Bishop White as its president. White had been one of those who took the lead in organizing the Episcopal Church when America became an independent nation. He wrote histories, revised the Episcopalian prayer book and served as a chaplain to Congress. For forty-six years he directed the First Day Society. The society rented rooms and opened its first school that March with John Ely and John Poor as teachers. Over the next nine years, the First Day Society enrolled 2,127 pupils and raised thousands of dollars.

Other Events

1817: Timothy Dwight of Yale, who stood strong for sound doctrine and wrote the hymn "I Love Thy Kingdom, Lord," died on this day.

1869: Rev. Kelly Lowe organized the first African-American Sunday school in Springfield Baptist Church in Augusta, Georgia.

1919: H.J. Heinz, the food manufacturer, gave testimony to Christ in his last will and testament, which he dictated to his attorney on this day. "I have been wonderfully sustained by my faith in God," he said.

William White headed the First Day Society for forty-six years. (Perry, William Stevens. *The Episcopate in America*. New York: Christian Literature, 1895.)

Sunday schools began to pop up everywhere. As a result, fewer children attended the First Day Society's schools. When that happened, the Society shared its money with the newer Sunday schools. Eventually, the government took over education and Sunday schools became less important than they had been in the general education of children.

Dr. Timothy Dwight stood for sound doctrine. (Ninde, Edward S. *The Story of the American Hymn*. New York: Abingdon, 1921.)

Death of Aelred

Aelred left his job as a steward to the kings of Scotland and became a monk. (Baring-Gould, S. *Lives of the Saints*. Edinburgh: John Grant, 1914.)

History is full of surprising connections. One of them ties this day's notable Christian figure to the future of the throne of Scotland. Aelred was born in 1109, the son of a priest with court connections (in those days, English priests often married). Aelred spent time at the court of King David I of Scotland, where he was liked so well that he was appointed to the influential position of steward of Scotland.

But Aelred longed for the religious life. King David would have awarded the gifted young man a bishop's see (seat of authority), but Aelred refused. Instead, he chose to become a Cistercian monk. But his abilities made him master even there. In 1146, he was elected abbot of Rievaulx. This made him the superior of a community of at least 150 monks and head of all the Cistercian abbots in England.

Aelred must have been a man of strong determination, for, despite illness, he traveled often, hearing cases and attending conferences. On top of this, he wrote extensively. When his old friend, King David I of Scotland, died, Aelred penned an account of David's life. Aelred also wrote about the life of another king, Edward the Confessor, an act prompted by the removal of Edward's remains to the rebuilt Westminster Chapel.

Aelred wrote popular devotional and ascetic works that are often compared with the writings of Bernard of Clairvaux. He also reworked Cicero's essay "On Friendship," extending the Roman's teachings with concepts of Christian brotherly love. And, of course, he preached. Many of his sermons still exist. Evidently, his words had the power to stir souls. When Aelred undertook a missionary trip to Galloway, its Pictish king was so moved by the preacher's words that he became a monk.

When Aelred resigned the stewardship of Scotland, history was changed. David awarded the vacant position to Walter Fitzalan, who assumed the title "First High Steward." His son Alan succeeded him as steward. The job remained in the direct family line, and the Stewards of Scotland sometimes performed notable service for the crown. Six generations later, through intermarriage with the family of Robert the Bruce, one of the steward's sons, Robert, became King Robert II of Scotland, the first of the Stewart (or Stuart) line.

Aelred could foresee none of this, of course, when he obeyed his conscience and turned to the Church. On this day in 1167, Aelred died. A feast day is celebrated in his honor on this day.

Henry Alford wrote the thanksgiving hymn "Come, Ye Thankful People, Come." (Hare, Augustus J.C. *Biographical Sketches*. London: George Allen, 1895.)

Other Events

1871: Hymn writer and scholar Henry Alford died. His *Expositor's Greek Bible* was a notable work, and he authored the popular hymn "Come, Ye Thankful People, Come."

1943: Medical doctor Howard Atwood Kelly died this day. One of the famed original Johns Hopkins Four, he was noted for his evangelical activities as well as for pioneering the use of radium treatment for cancer. He wrote *A Scientific Man and the Bible* and *How I Study the Bible*, as well as treatises on Maryland snakes and medical works.

1958: The last broadcast of the *Old Fashioned Radio Hour* from the Municipal Auditorium in Long Beach, California, was titled "Seven Marvels of Mercy." The program then moved to a Hollywood studio.

It's Only Fair to Explain

On this day in 1547, the Council of Trent approved a decree on justification (the way God puts us right with Him when we have sinned). It took council members months of hard work and was extremely difficult to assemble.

The Council of Trent (named for the Italian city where the council was held) came about largely because Martin Luther had protested that the Roman Catholic Church was corrupt. Christians were taught things that had no support in Scripture, such as that they could buy indulgences to get the souls of loved ones out of purgatory. Against this, Luther argued that justification is by faith alone.

The popes saw that Luther's argument needed to be addressed, but they had trouble assembling enough bishops to hold a council. Twenty years passed. When a council finally met at Trent, it was because Emperor Charles V, who ruled much of Europe, insisted on it. He thought that the best chance of winning the Protestants back to Catholicism was for the Church to clean up its act. The pope did not agree. He saw Protestant ideas as heresy and wanted to define Catholic doctrine and condemn the Protestants as heretics. The council finally did a bit of both, switching back and forth between theology and reform.

Justification was the toughest theological question that the council tackled. A few bishops wanted to condemn Luther's views without any explanation, but the rest felt that if they were going to condemn someone else's theology, they should explain why. They knew that it was going to be hard to do, because Catholics themselves did not fully agree on justification.

In addition to the theological disagreements, there were also personality clashes that made it hard for the council to reach an agreement. Some council members even resorted to name-calling and physical violence. For instance, Sanfelice overheard Grechetto mutter that he was either a knave or a fool. Sanfelice asked Grechetto what he had said. Grechetto repeated his remark aloud. Sanfelice seized Grechetto by the beard and shook him so hard that hair came out in Sanfelice's hand. Sanfelice was locked up and excommunicated, but Grechetto pleaded for his liberty.

Officials put six questions to the council: 1) What is meant by justification? 2) What brings it about: What is God's part and what is man's? 3) What does it mean to say that a man is saved by faith? 4) Do works play a role before and after justification, and what is the role of the sacraments? 5) Describe the process of justification, what precedes, accompanies and follows it. 6) What proofs support Catholic doctrine?

Another question also arose: Is it possible to know with certainty that one is saved? It took sixteen congregations (meetings in which each bishop stated his opinion and cast a vote) to reach a decree. The Doctrine of Justification was issued as sixteen chapters followed by thirty-three binding statements or canons aimed against Protestant ideas.

The Council of Trent tackled the issue of justification in response to Protestant assertions that were contrary to contemporary Catholic beliefs. (Robinson, James Harvey. *Medieval and Modern Times*. Boston: Ginn and Co., 1919.)

Despite the council's strong statements against Protestant ideas, it is obvious that the council read and were influenced by Luther's works. The council decided that grace is necessary at each step of justification. However, man's free will must cooperate. Justification is more than forgiveness of sins, they said: It is God's ongoing process of making a person new and good. They also stated that faith is not the only condition of salvation, although it is its beginning, foundation and root. In order for the grace of justification to grow, we must obey God's commands. The council also decided that justification can be lost by certain sins and that no man can be sure that he is saved.

Other Events

1501: The world's first hymnbook in a living European language other than Latin was issued by Bohemian followers of Jan Hus on this day. It was printed in Prague and had just eighty-nine hymns.

1691: George Fox, founder of the Society of Friends (Quakers), died this day.

1817: Robert Moffat reached Cape Town on this day. Because of his limited education, the London Missionary Society had been reluctant to send him, but he nevertheless proved himself by translating the New Testament into Bechwanas within ten years. He also demonstrated that Christian missions could succeed in Africa through persistence and patience. He was the mentor and father-in-law of David Livingstone.

1887: Athlete C.T. Studd wrote checks giving away his birthday inheritance to Christian ministries, believing that he could not live a life of faith unless he did so.

1915: Missionary Mary Slessor, who braved many dangers to bring the gospel and justice to the Africans she loved, died on this day.

Bold Mary Slessor. (Livingstone, W.P. *Mary Slessor of Calabar*. London: Hodder and Stoughton, 1917.)

JANUARY

14

Valdés Published His Dialogue and Then Ran for His Life

Charles V. The fact that Valdés's brother was secretary for this emperor did not protect him from the Inquisition. (Ruoff, Henry W. *Masters of Achievement: The World's Greatest Leaders in Literature, Art, Religion, Philosophy, Science, Politics and Industry*. Buffalo, NY: The Frontier Press Company, 1910.)

The sixteenth century was a time of great Church reform in Europe. The newly invented printing press allowed many from within the Church to make a pubic call for it to clean up its act. Martin Luther set reform blazing in Germany with pamphlets and a German Bible. William Tyndale issued the Bible and many booklets in English and died for it. John Calvin published a powerful theological work that won millions of followers. The very air seemed charged with new learning. Spain too had its champion of reformation: a freshman at the University of Alcalá named Juan Valdés.

Valdés was just eighteen years old on this day in 1529 when his *Dialogue on Christian Doctrine* was published. A professor cautioned Valdés to make a few changes so that the work would not rouse the wrath of the Inquisition. Valdés agreed and made some changes, but even so, the book was strongly Protestant in tone. It was the first popular Protestant catechism. (Luther did not issue his long and short catechisms until later the same year.)

The impetus behind the writing of the *Dialogue* was Valdés's lament over the deep doctrinal ignorance of the priests. He determined to remedy that in the writing of the *Dialogue*. It is written as a conversation. According to its story line, a friend invites a simple, ignorant priest to visit the well-known historical archbishop Don Fray Pedro de Alba. The priest is told that Fray Pedro will answer his questions and explain doctrine to him. The simple priest, his friend and Fray Pedro talk to each other. Fray Pedro holds faith high—like the reformers did:

> The faith and trust that we put in Jesus Christ throws out all trust in our own wisdom, justice, and virtue, because it shows us that if Jesus Christ would not have died for us, neither ourselves nor any other creature could give us true happiness.

Fray Pedro does not care for devotions to Mary or the saints. He says that prayers should be modeled on the Lord's Prayer:

> In this prayer our Lord Jesus Christ teaches us how we ought to pray. And by its own example the prayer teaches us that it should be brief in words, but abundant in content. . . .

Although the Roman Catholic Church teaches that there are seven sacraments, Fray Pedro mentions only the same two that Protestants accept: baptism and the Lord's Supper.

The *Dialogue* caught on in Spain. The inquisitor of Navarre, Sancho Carranza de Miranda, was so impressed with the book that he bought several copies and distributed them among his friends. But in 1531 the book fell under suspicion of heresy. It was placed on the Catholic Index of Prohibited Books. The *Dialogue*'s printer was examined for heresy, and action was started against both Valdés and his brother, Alfonso, secretary to Emperor Charles V. Every copy of the *Dialogue* was ordered confiscated, and the Inquisition gathered them up. Valdés ran for his life. Soon the *Dialogue* could not be found in Spain, or anywhere else for that matter, except a single copy, which fortunately reached Portugal before the recall. If that had not survived, we would not know what the *Dialogue* contained.

Valdés settled in Naples, Italy, where he wrote more books. Agreeing with the reformers in many things, he said that we are obliged only to keep the commandments of God, not those of the Church, such as going to confession once a year or attending mass every week. He emphasized faith: "And I think that a man may know when he has inward confidence in God by what he discovers of his outward reliance upon God." But Valdés also criticized the reformers for breaking from the Catholic Church.

He died in 1541, still a Catholic. His books attracted many followers. A Spanish reformation movement appeared, but the Inquisition soon stamped it out. Many other catechisms were written after the *Dialogue*, some of them imitating it.

Macrina, grandmother of St. Basil the Great. (Courtesy of the Christian History Institute archives.)

OTHER EVENTS

Annual: The feast of St. Macrina is celebrated on this day. She was the grandmother of St. Basil the Great, St. Gregory of Nyssa—two significant churchmen and theologians of the early Church—and their sister Macrina.

1236: Rastko (St. Sava) died on this day. He became a monk and rose to be the archbishop of the Balkans. Over the years, thousands of people visited his tomb to be cured of various ailments until a Turkish ruler ended the pilgrimages by destroying the site.

1753: George Berkeley, famed immaterialist philosopher and Anglican bishop, died on this day. His immaterialism was developed to counter the ideas of John Locke, which Berkeley believed were tending toward Deism.

1886: John Mott heard cricket-hero-turned-missionary C.T. Studd speak and it changed his life. He became a notable evangelist himself.

Salem Repents of Witch Trials

In 1697, five years after the Salem witch trials, the town of Salem and the Massachusetts Bay Colony passed a resolution proclaiming that this day, January 15, would be a day of fasting and repentance before God for the tragic error and folly of the trials. The resolution was adopted so God's people could offer up prayers for God to help them in their errors and keep them from repeating such sins. Among the reasons for the day of fasting given by the resolution were:

> So all of God's people may offer up fervent supplications unto him, that all iniquity may be put away, which hath stirred God's holy jealousy against this land; that he would show us what we know not, and help us, wherein we have done amiss, to do so no more. . . .

Judge Samuel Sewell and those who had served as jurors in the trials all confessed their errors and prayed for God's forgiveness and guidance in the future. Indeed, Judge Sewell, who had presided over many of the capital judgments, published a written confession acknowledging his own "blame and shame."

The witch trials, a senseless, isolated and unbiblical miscarriage of justice, left an unfair stain on the reputation of all of Puritan New England. Over 150 suspected witches were imprisoned, and 19 were hanged during a few frenzied months of 1692. Most of the accused were women and social misfits. Sad to say, only a few of Salem's townspeople opposed preacher Samuel Parris, who encouraged the proceedings.

The hysteria began when two children had fits and claimed they were bewitched, naming people of the town whose spirits they said they had seen. The evidence presented was usually groundless accusation, scapegoating or the product of mass suggestion. At the trials, no evidence of Satan worship or the practice of witchcraft was presented. Breaking with precedent, the court did not require two witnesses or even a showing that the accused had committed any acts. It was enough if a witness had seen a ghostly form that resembled one of the accused.

Some Puritan clergy recognized that the real evil was in the accusers rather than in those accused of witchcraft. Increase Mather spoke out strongly against the trials, calling for implementation of the biblical principle of two or three witnesses. Such was the prestige of Mather that the trials quickly ended. Today we look back on the whole episode as a tragic example of misdirected zeal.

Parris was driven from the village for his role in the trials. In 1710 the legislature reversed some of the convictions, and in the following years compensation was given to the families of the accused witches.

A "witch" hanging at Salem. (Northrop, Henry Davenport. *New Century History of Our Country and Its Island Possessions*. Chicago: American Educational League, 1900.)

Other Events

345: Tradition says Paul of Thebes died on this day at the remarkable age of over 130 years. He was the first known Christian hermit, having fled to the desert to escape persecution, and he was the friend and inspiration of Anthony of Egypt, the originator of Christian monasticism.

1549: Anabaptist Elizabeth Dirks was arrested on this day. She made a strong confession of her faith under torture before her execution.

1951: Harry Ironside died on this day in New Zealand. The notable dispensationalist preacher and author was laid aside at birth as dead. An hour later a nurse detected a pulse and saved his life. His father died while Ironside was a child, and his mother reared him, teaching him to read the Bible. By age fourteen he had read it through fourteen times! He served as pastor of Chicago's Moody Memorial Church for eighteen years.

1984: Billy Graham preached before Queen Elizabeth II of England at her request.

1985: Businessman Lance B. Latham died on this day. He was instrumental in founding Awana, New Tribes and other Christian endeavors.

Paul and Anthony, founders of Egyptian monasticism. (Bell, Mrs. Arthur. *Saints in Christian Art*. London: George Bell, 1901-4.)

Bible Reading Outlawed

Thomas Jefferson wrote the Statute of Virginia for Religious Freedom but also deleted passages from his Bible that he thought were not authentic. (Lord, John. *Beacon Lights of History*. New York: James Clarke, 1886.)

How much are your ears worth? What about your tongue? Some insurance policies have clauses that award damages for lost fingers, eyes and other vulnerable body parts. What value would you place on such vital body parts?

For many centuries, people lost their ears and tongues for their faith. This was the result of Church monopolies. A government would choose a single denomination for its territory and then tax everyone to support it. Governments preferred to have just one Church, because a single Church was easier to oversee.

These "established" Churches were often opposed to reforms because they feared that changes to the status quo might jeopardize their privileges. Authorities were severe with anyone who threatened Church monopolies. A man might have his tongue cut off for preaching without a license. An ordinary citizen might lose his ears for listening to unapproved preaching. In the worst cases, people were burned to death for teaching children the Ten Commandments or the Lord's Prayer.

Charles P. Chiniquy, Catholic priest turned Protestant evangelist. (Hendrickson, Ford. *Martyrs and Witnesses*. Detroit: Protestant Missionary Pub. Co., 1917.)

Religious authorities were concerned that if laity had direct access to the Scriptures they would misinterpret them and it would open the door to spiritual and civic anarchy. For centuries, the Roman Catholic Church blocked ordinary people from reading Scripture in their own language. Even Protestant governments tried to keep the Bible away from the common man. For example, on this day in 1543, nine years after King Henry VIII became the head of the Church of England, Parliament passed a law making it illegal for any "women or artificer's prentices, journeymen, serving men of the degree of yeomen, or under, husbandmen or laborers to read the New Testament in English."

For a long time the common people were only allowed to hear the portions of Scripture that the Churches wanted them to hear. The law was eventually revoked, but even after commoners won the right to read the Bible, the established Church still held great sway in many countries. Germany and Sweden chose Lutheranism as the denomination for their state Churches. England had the Church of England. In Massachusetts, the Puritans were so concerned with maintaining their monopoly that they were very severe with Baptists and Quakers who dared to believe differently, jailing them, whipping them, exiling them and even hanging them. In Virginia, Anglican priests did not hesitate to demand that the authorities jail Baptist preachers who competed with their monopoly.

Thomas Jefferson, then governor of Virginia, was disgusted. For seven years, sometimes allied with Baptists and Presbyterians, he battled to pass an act in his state that would establish complete freedom of religion. He argued against many of the policies and practices that had come about because of the monopolies of established churches. He argued that "to compel a man to furnish contributions of money for the propagation of opinions which he disbelieves, is sinful and tyrannical." He also argued that if an office or position of authority was made available only if people would hold or renounce certain ideas, it would encourage men to betray themselves for money. "Truth," he said, "is great and will prevail if left to herself. . . ." He also felt that no one should be punished by the government for his religious beliefs and that people should be free to spread their own religious opinions. Jefferson did not argue that religion should be suppressed but only that the state must not make any form of it mandatory.

The Statute of Virginia for Religious Freedom was finally passed on this day in 1786, 243 years to the day after Parliament passed its act making Bible reading illegal for commoners. So proud was Jefferson of his role in obtaining this piece of legislation that he wanted his tombstone to read: "Author of the Declaration of Independence, Founder of the University of Virginia, and Author of the Statute of Virginia for Religious Freedom."

Other Events

1545: Georg Spalatin, Martin Luther's friend at the court of Frederick the Wise, died on this day. Luther wrote him more than 400 letters.

1899: Charles P. Chiniquy died on this day. As a Catholic priest in Illinois, he ran afoul of Church and civil authorities, which resulted in a trial at which Abraham Lincoln defended him. Chiniquy resigned rather than submit to his bishop. He was excommunicated and then converted to Protestantism. He spun an absurd conspiracy theory that claimed vengeful Jesuits were behind Lincoln's assassination.

1965: Harriet Beardsley, missionary to India, died on this day. She once stared down a tiger for an hour, praying that it wouldn't pounce! It left without harming her or anyone else.

1994: Timothy van Dyke and Steve Welsh, missionaries with New Tribes Mission in Colombia, were taken at gunpoint on a Sunday morning. Both were killed by their captors a year-and-a-half later on June 19, 1995.

January 17

Hampton Court's Good Result

In 1604, when James VI of Scotland rode south to London and the coronation that would make him James I of England, Puritans presented him with a petition pleading for freedom from man-made rites and worship ceremonies. Since over 1,000 reform leaders signed this "Millenary" petition, James could not well ignore it. He called for a conference of churchmen and theologians to be held at the royal palace of Hampton Court. His attitude toward the event was signaled by the wording of the summons: "for the hearing, and for the determining, things *pretended* to be amiss in the Church" (italics are the emphasis of the author).

The Puritans thought that the Church of England had kept too many Catholic practices. They wanted Church government put in the hands of the people rather than a hierarchy of bishops and archbishops. But the Puritans weren't going to get their wish. The king made that plain at Hampton Court. He recognized the democratic tendencies of Puritanism and suspected that if the people got rid of the bishops, they might want to get rid of their king as well.

James and the Puritans did agree on one thing at Hampton, however. When Dr. John Rainolds, president of Corpus Christi College, Oxford, proposed a new translation of the English Bible, he found James enthusiastic. The king detested the Geneva Bible, the most popular translation in use in England at the time. He considered its margin notes "very partial, untrue, seditious, and savoring too much of dangerous and seditious conceits." In other words, the Geneva Bible did not support his theory that kings have a divine right to rule, even if they behave badly. James wanted a Bible free of political and theological notes.

And so, on this day in 1604, the motion was carried "that a translation be made of the whole Bible, as consonant as can be to the original Hebrew and Greek; and this to be set out and printed, without any marginal notes. . . ."

Forty-seven of England's top Bible scholars were appointed to do the work. In an effort to diminish bias, Anglicans and Puritans were included in the mix. King James himself organized the task. The translators were counted off into six panels (three for the Old Testament, two for the New Testament and one for the Apocrypha). They were charged to stick as close to the earlier Bible translation as accuracy would allow but to take into account even earlier versions as well. In the end, about seventy percent of the wording was borrowed from William Tyndale's vivid translation. Each translator was assigned a portion of Scripture. He had to present his work to his group for approval. Each book was then sent to the five other groups for review and criticism. With this procedure, each book was scrutinized by every member of the team. A committee of twelve—two from each team—made a final review.

King James I. (Jesse, John Heneage. *Memoirs of the Court of England During the Reign of the Stuarts, Including the Protectorate*. London: Henry G. Bohn, 1857.)

By 1611, the translation was complete, but it was years before this version of the Bible was generally accepted. Readers who had memorized Scripture from earlier versions hesitated to accept new wordings. One scholar opposed it on the grounds that he was preparing a better version! Others complained that it was not consistent and that there were spelling errors.

Because of James's strong support of the 1611 translation, it is called the "Authorized Version" (in America, the "King James Version"). In time it became the most beloved English translation, its powerful rhythms and pleasing phrases shaping the language of the Bible-reading public. Even today, a few denominations consider it virtually inspired and the only acceptable translation for reading and study.

Other Events

356: St. Anthony of Egypt, a desert father, died on this day. He is credited as being the founder of monasticism. He gave up his inheritance as a young man when he fell under conviction. Anthony's piety inspired others to join him in renouncing material possessions in order to focus on spiritual matters. People from all over Egypt came to obtain counsel from the holy monk. The press of visitors was so great that he had to seek even wilder places to find time for reflection.

1377: Pope Gregory XI returned the papacy to Rome. For years the popes had resided at Avignon, France. Gregory was the last Avignon pope. He made a noteworthy but unsuccessful effort to heal the schism between the eastern and western halves of Christendom.

1530: The first book of William Tyndale's English Old Testament came off the press.

1853: Harry Monroe was born in Exeter, New Hampshire. He ran off with a circus as a boy, became an outlaw and an alcoholic. After his conversion at the Pacific Garden Mission, a rescue work, in Chicago, he immediately joined its work. He wrote, "Tell the converts all over the world, whose lives I have been able to touch, to be faithful to Christ, who has saved them."

Anthony of Egypt, founder of monasticism, depicted battling demons. (Bell, Mrs. Arthur. *Saints in Christian Art*. London: George Bell, 1901-4.)

January

18

First Armenian Church in the United States

An Armenian cathedral. (Rohrbach, Paul. *Armenian*. Stuttgart: J. Englehorns Nachf., 1919.)

On this day in 1891, the first Armenian church in the United States was consecrated in Worcester, Massachusetts. It is surprising that the Armenian Church was so slow in taking hold on American shores since individual Armenians began arriving in America as early as 1618. Today there are 1 million Armenians in the United States and Canada.

According to tradition, apostles Thaddeus and Bartholomew were the first to bring the gospel to Armenia. They laid the groundwork, but Christianity really took hold when Gregory the Illuminator (enlightener) came up from Caesarea and influenced the conversion and baptism of King Tiridates III. Tiridates made Christianity the official state religion around the turn of the fourth century. As early as 303, Gregory built the mother church at Etchmiadzin in Armenia, and a distinctive Christian culture began to flourish.

Inspirational Andrew Murray. (Meyer, F.B. *Winter in South Africa*. London: National Council of Evangelical Free Churches, 1914.)

In 374, the fiercely independent Armenian Church announced its autonomy when it refused to submit to reforms proposed by the current bishop of Caesarea. However, the Armenian Church continued to use the Greek and Syriac languages in worship because Armenia had no system of writing. Early in the fifth century, a monk named Mesrob gave his nation an alphabet of thirty-six characters. As a result of Mesrob's work, the Bible was translated into the local language and Armenian literature flourished.

The Armenian Church experienced a time of intense activity and rapid development, and then its progress was interrupted. Persia conquered Armenia, and a decree went out in AD 450 requiring all Christians to convert to Zoroastrianism. For thirty years the Armenians battled heroically to preserve their faith, and finally a weary Persian government agreed to peace.

Thereafter, Armenia experienced many ups and downs. At times it flourished as an independent nation. At other times it was under the heel of foreign oppressors. Islam and Communism both persecuted the Armenian people fiercely.

In the 1880s and '90s, many Armenians fled to the New World to escape being massacred by the Ottoman Turks. Once the Armenians reached America, they often made arrangements with local denominations (especially the Episcopalians) to use their facilities for their worship services. Finally, in 1898 the Armenian Church was officially organized.

The Armenian population in the United States and Canada took a great leap between 1915 and 1923 when more Armenians fled their country as Young Turks massacred, tortured, starved or exiled virtually the entire remaining Christian population. Although 1.5 million Christians died, the Turkish government denies that these atrocities ever took place.

Other Events

1525: Even before their first baptism took place, the Anabaptists were threatened with exile by Protestant reformers in Zurich, Switzerland. Instead of being exiled, Anabaptists were soon killed.

1678: James Mitchell, a Scottish Covenanter, was executed for having tried to assassinate Anglican Archbishop James Sharp, who was butchering Covenanters.

1875: Joseph P. Webster died on this day in Manchester, New York. He is remembered as the composer of the hymn "In the Sweet Bye and Bye."

1917: Andrew Murray, pastor, inspirational author and founder of a seminary in South Africa, died on this day.

1951: Amy Carmichael, who rescued children from temple prostitution in India, died on this day. When neuralgia left her bedridden, she wrote inspirational books.

Questions and Answers

If your work required you to multiply numbers such as 6 x 7 or 8 x 9, you would save a lot of time by memorizing the multiplication table. Some things must be memorized to be really useful—such as the multiplication table or the common formulas of physics. The same is true of a catechism.

A catechism sets out the core beliefs of a Church. It is usually arranged in the form of questions and answers for easy memorization. It might ask, "What is true faith?" and answer:

> True faith is not only a knowledge and conviction that everything God reveals in His Word is true; it is also a deep-rooted assurance created in me by the Holy Spirit through the gospel, that, out of sheer grace earned for us by Christ, not only others, but I too, have had my sins forgiven, have been made forever right with God, and have been granted salvation.

If what you believe is important to you, a catechism can be as helpful as a multiplication table and a good deal more comforting. One of the best-known catechisms of all time is the Heidelberg Catechism. It is named for the German city where it was prepared by theologians from the University of Heidelberg. Elector Frederick III, a friend of the Protestant Reformation, requested that a catechism be developed. He hoped the new catechism would secure harmony among Protestants in his territories and strengthen the hold of the Reformed faith on his provinces. He himself wrote the preface of the Catechism, which was dated this day, January 19, 1563. The Heidelberg Catechism is used by the Reformed Church today. Hundreds of thousands of people have memorized it and live by its teachings.

The Catechism presents 129 questions with their answers, backed up by more than 700 Bible references. The authors said they wanted it to be an echo of the Bible. Frederick pointed out in his preface that the references had been selected "with great pains" to give the best possible authority to the Catechism's claims. A nice thing about the Catechism is that it is written in a very personal manner, using the words *I*, *me* and *my* in its answers.

The Heidelberg Catechism wasn't the first of its kind. Zecharias Ursinus, the twenty-eight-year-old theology professor who drew up the content of the Catechism, borrowed the theological ideas from an earlier catechism by John Calvin and the arrangement of its questions from Martin Luther. Frederick's court preacher, twenty-six-year-old Caspar Olevianus, was involved in the final composition and editing of the work, which the University of Heidelberg's theologians approved.

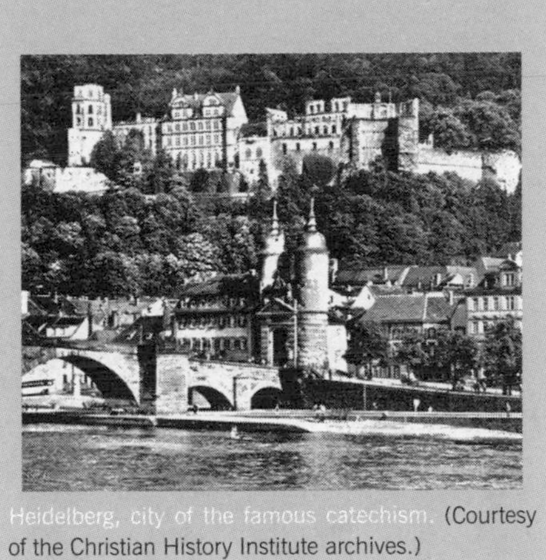

Heidelberg, city of the famous catechism. (Courtesy of the Christian History Institute archives.)

Later, someone divided the Heidelberg Catechism into fifty-two parts, one for each week of the year, so that it could be easily studied in the Church. Pastors were expected to preach a sermon on the appropriate question every Sunday afternoon.

Soon after it was written, the Heidelberg Catechism was translated into Dutch. The Dutch heartily endorsed it at four different synods. The Dutch Reformed Church is now one of the strongest branches of the Reformed Church.

The influence of the Heidelberg Catechism did not end with the Dutch. On November 5, 1647, when the Westminster Assembly of Divines presented their Shorter Catechism to the English House of Commons for approval, it was based in part on the famous Heidelberg text.

Other Events

973: Pope Benedict VI was consecrated on this day. The hand-picked choice of Emperor Otho I, Benedict was not well-received by the citizens of Rome and was strangled by an antipope.

1523: Ulrich Zwingli published his sixty-seven articles on this day, an important step in the reformation of Switzerland. The articles rejected the authority of the pope, made Scripture the sole authority for faith and denied the sacrifice of mass, invocation to saints and clerical celibacy.

1565: Diego Laynez, the second general of the Jesuits, died on this day.

1852: The crew of the British ship *Dido* found Captain Gardiner and his team of missionaries dead in Patagonia, the first of fourteen missionaries who would die before the first Patagonian was won to Christ.

1861: On this day, Albert B. Simpson fasted, prayed and wrote out a dedication of himself to God. Simpson went on to found The Christian and Missionary Alliance and what is now known as Nyack College.

1897: Melvin Ernest Trotter, a hopeless drunk, was converted on this day. Brokenhearted at his failures and the pain he caused his wife, he hopped a freight car to Chicago on a bitterly cold night, intending to buy himself one last drink and drown himself in Lake Michigan. But he heard the gospel preached at the Pacific Garden Mission and found Christ sufficient to keep him from ever drinking again. He founded sixty-seven rescue missions to help others as desperate as he himself had been.

Benedict VI was strangled by an antipope. (Montor, Chevalier Artaud de. *Lives and Times of the Popes*. New York: Catholic Publication Society of America, 1911.)

An artist's representation of the martyr bishop Fabian. (Montor, Chevalier Artaud de. *Lives and Times of the Popes*. New York: Catholic Publication Society of America, 1911.)

January 20

Fabian, the First Christian Martyr Under Decius

In Rome, there is a very old slab of stone on which worn Greek letters are still visible. Translated, they read, "Fabian, bishop, martyr." Fabian had been the bishop of Rome (pope) for fourteen years when the Roman emperor Decius made up his mind to destroy the unpopular Christian Church. On this day in 250, the prominent and holy Fabian died for his faith.

According to tradition, Fabian was the first person killed in the savage onslaught, which was the first persecution to include the entire Roman Empire. The bishop is said to have died bravely, setting an example for his entire flock. Unfortunately, we have no details of how he died or what he said at his death. In art, he is often shown being beheaded.

That Fabian was bishop at all is curious. When Bishop Anteras died in 236, Fabian was a farmer who came to Rome to observe the choice of a successor. Needless to say, no one in the assembly gave a thought to the layman. No one, that is, until a surprising event took place.

The early Church historian Eusebius, writing almost a hundred years after Fabian's death, reported that suddenly a dove flew into the room and landed on the farmer's head. The assembly took this as a sign from God, for had not a dove also descended on Christ at His baptism? Fabian was immediately chosen for the vacant position.

Fabian proved to be a good leader. He battled a North African heresy and appointed seven men to collect the records of recent martyrs. He also honored the bones of two Roman bishops, Pontian and Hippolytus, who had died in exile in Sardinia's mines. He organized Rome under seven deacons. Later reports say he sent St. Denis and six other missionaries to help with the evangelization of Gaul (France).

Fabian also wrote letters. At least three of them survive. As the following excerpt from one of those surviving letters shows, he was a man concerned about the spread of faith and the preservation of Church discipline.

> We beseech you also to be zealous in praying in your pious supplications, that our God and Lord Jesus Christ, who will have all men to be saved, and no one to perish, may, by His vast omnipotence, cause their hearts to turn again to sound doctrine and to the Catholic faith, in order that they may be recovered from the toils of the devil who are held captive by him, and be united with the children of our mother the Church.

Fabian's most notable action was to willingly lay down his life for Christ. In this he became a heroic example for a Church that had grown soft during a time of peace. Two early Christian writers of renown, St. Cyprian and St. Jerome, affirmed that Fabian died a martyr.

Sebastian survived an onslaught of arrows only to be beaten to death. (Bell, Mrs. Arthur. *Saints in Christian Art*. London: George Bell, 1901-4.)

Other Events

Annual: St. Sebastian, who survived being shot full of arrows for his faith but then was beaten to death at Emperor Decian's orders, is remembered on this day.

524: Bishop Simeon of Beth Ashram, in the region of Arabia, traveled from the Lakhmid capital Hirta d Na'man and recorded several martyrdoms there, especially those of holy women.

1541: A popular meeting in Geneva, Switzerland, ratified John Calvin's plan of organization for the moral rule of the city.

1569: Miles Coverdale died on this day. He edited one of the first complete English-language translations of the Bible, which became the first Bible with royal authorization.

1637: Rev. John Wheelwright of Boston preached a sermon in support of Anne Hutchinson's theory of grace. Puritan leaders convicted him of contempt and sedition for it.

1951: Ethelwyn Taylor, author of the hymn "Calvary Covers It All," died on this day. She was active in the Pacific Garden Mission.

1952: Bishop Anton Vouk of Yugoslavia was ambushed, doused with gasoline and set on fire, probably by government hit men. By quick action he managed to save his life.

January 21

Baby Steps

On this day in 1525, the Church changed because of a baby.

The Protestant Reformation in Europe had brought with it new interpretations of the Bible. When Reformers gained control of governments, they replaced Roman Catholic churches with Reformed churches. For the most part, everyone within such a jurisdiction was expected to belong to the new faith, just as he had belonged to the old. Newborn babies were baptized into the Reformed Church and became members simply by being born in their community, much as a person becomes a citizen of the United States by being born there.

Reformation had been brought to Zurich under the Bible-centered teaching of Ulrich Zwingli. The Zurich City Council and most Christians supported his reforms. However, when a small, eager group of Zwingli's supporters looked into the Bible, they found a wide difference between the primitive churches of the first century and the big state churches of the sixteenth. They became convinced that the Church wasn't intended to include everyone in a community, but only those who really follow Christ. This observance brought them to the question: How can a baby join a church, then, when it knows only how to cry and eat?

These Christians believed that true baptism required a person to be old enough to understand the meaning of baptism. Among this group of Zwingli's followers were Georg Blaurock, Conrad Grebel and Felix Manz. When Grebel's wife had a baby, the couple decided not to baptize their child although authorities said they must. The Zurich City Council handled this civil disobedience the same way they would have handled an appeal for trash pickup: On January 17, 1525, they held a public debate on the issue. The people's representatives heard both sides and voted for baby baptism.

The Council ordered that the "radicals" must no longer meet together or teach their opinions to others and that all families must baptize their children within eight days of the decision or leave Zurich.

The deadline was running out. The group of "radicals" decided that they must do something. Trudging through the wind and snow on that chilly night, they gathered at Felix Manz's house to decide their course of action. Their meeting was "illegal," of course, but the little group was sure that the government had no right to dictate religious beliefs. It was a radical idea at that time, but once they grasped it, they knew there was no turning back.

They talked and prayed. When they rose from their knees, Blaurock had made up his mind. He asked Grebel to baptize him in the "apostolic" manner, upon confession of faith. Grebel did, and then Blaurock baptized all who were willing. Thus, the Anabaptist movement was born. *Anabaptist* means "rebaptizer." It was a name given to the group in mockery by their enemies.

The Anabaptists obeyed the Zurich council and moved out of town. They started their own Church, free of state ties, and preached to others in Zurich. To the authorities this was rebellion and they jailed the offenders. When released, the men preached again. Many Anabaptist leaders, including Manz and Blaurock, were executed. The bold stand of those men changed the entire Church, but only after much blood had been poured out as a result of one group trying to control other people's faith.

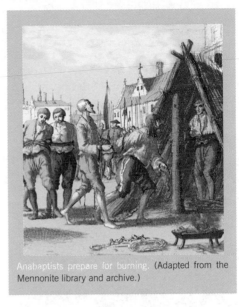

Anabaptists prepare for burning. (Adapted from the Mennonite library and archive.)

Mennonites, Hutterites and the Amish are the direct offspring of the early Anabaptist movement. Baptists and many other groups baptize a person only if he or she is old enough to understand the meaning of the act and can make a confession of Christ. But all denominations have benefited by the Grebels' decision not to baptize their baby. Thanks to their stand, most Protestant churches now act on the principle of separation of Church and state, although around the world governments often try to impose their stamp on the Church.

Other Events

1118: Pope Paschal died on this day. During his troubled pontificate, he was taken captive by Holy Roman Emperor Henry V, who extorted concessions from Paschal.

1217: Matthew Paris is remembered as a monk who chronicled English history.

1560: John Jewel was consecrated as bishop of Salisbury on this day. He was the leading defender of Anglicanism in his day.

1621: The *Mayflower* company gathered on shore in the New World for their first preaching service.

1956: Elders of the Little Flock (China) and twenty-eight other Christian leaders in Shanghai were arrested. They had carried on church work after Pastor Watchman Nee was imprisoned.

Matthew Paris in his own representation of himself at Mary's feet. (Green, John Richard. *A Short History of the English People*. New York: Harper & Brothers, 1893-5.)

Sarah Doremus was so active with missions that she became known as the "Mother of Missions." (Courtesy of the Christian History Institute archives.)

Mother of Missions

One day a friend met Sarah Doremus, seemingly unaccompanied, at a Dwight L. Moody meeting in New York and asked, "Are you here alone?"

"No, I am never alone," replied Doremus. She meant that she had taken God as her continual companion—and it showed.

Sarah Platt Doremus was married to a wealthy man, and she used their wealth and social position to involve herself in many activities aimed at promoting the gospel, easing physical distress and setting people's lives right. In addition to raising her eight children, she led an organization to return women prisoners into society, managed a tract society, organized relief for Christian Greeks oppressed by Muslim Turks, distributed Bibles to the destitute, founded a self-help organization and cooperated with efforts to create a children's hospital and a separate women's hospital in New York state. During the Civil War, she helped distribute supplies among city hospitals.

Doremus was also involved in the creation of women's mission societies. In 1834 Rev. David Abeel, a missionary to China from the Reformed Church in America (Doremus's denomination) told of Chinese women who wanted "female men" to come and share their Christianity with them. Doremus was especially moved by this plea, but there was intense opposition to single women being missionaries, and the early organization that she created was not particularly successful.

The effort that made her famous, however, was her work with the Woman's Union Missionary Society of America, founded in 1860. The Society was the first organization created solely to provide a means for single women to become overseas missionaries. Doremus became its first president and operated a branch out of her New York home. So many missionaries came and went from her home that she became known as the "Mother of Missions." Over a period of approximately twenty years, the society supported over 100 missionaries at twelve stations.

Doremus continued her philanthropic pursuits well into old age. Then, on this day in 1877, she died as the result of a fall.

The church that was erected in honor of Madagascar's martyrs. (Dennis, James S. *Christian Missions and Social Progress*. New York: Fleming H. Revell Co., 1897-1906.)

Other Events

1867: Ambatonakanga Memorial Church was opened on this day in Madagascar in honor of Christians martyred under the cruel Queen Ranavalona.

1876: John Dykes, who wrote the well-known hymn tunes for "Holy, Holy, Holy" and "Jesus, the Very Thought of Thee," died on this day.

1922: Pope Benedict XV died on this day. He kept the papacy neutral during World War I and offered to broker peace. United States President Woodrow Wilson rejected the offer but incorporated some of the pope's ideas in his fourteen-point peace plan.

1976: Louis Talbott, Bible expositor, conference speaker and long-time pastor of Los Angeles's Church of the Open Door, died on this day. He roused mission interest through showing black-and-white films in the days before television came into wide use.

Leading Mathematician Defends Jansenism

January 23

"How wrong we were! I only had my eyes opened yesterday." With those words begins one of Christianity's best-known religious satires, the *Provincial Letters*. The first of the letters appeared in Paris on this day in 1656.

But who wrote the letters? No one was saying, and with good reason. There was danger in speaking up. The author would probably be labeled as a heretic and excommunicated. Imprisonment and torture were distinct possibilities.

Years later, the identity of the author of the *Provincial Letters* became known: It was the brilliant French mathematician Blaise Pascal. Until then, it had seemed that Pascal's genius lay entirely in science. At sixteen he published a groundbreaking work on the geometry of cones; at nineteen he invented a primitive calculator. Next he proved that, since atmosphere has weight, its pressure varies according to altitude, and he showed that vacuum is possible. He proved that pressure on the surface of a fluid is transmitted equally to every point in a fluid. Thanks to Pascal, we have syringes and the hydraulic lift. He also helped create probability theory.

But Pascal was not just a scientist; he was a Christian too. A near-death experience had shaken him up and he interpreted it as a warning from God to set his mind on spiritual things. His interest in probability theory led him to invent an argument that is known as Pascal's Wager. The stakes of life are so high, he said, that we should gamble on God's existence. We have nothing to lose if it turns out that God does not exist, but everything to gain or lose if He *does* exist.

Pascal would have preferred certainty over probability in matters of faith but concluded that it could not be had. In his words, "The heart has its reasons which reason does not know at all." Attracted to the Jansenists because he loved those whom he was acquainted with (his own sister was a Jansenist) and because he admired their puritanical lifestyle, Pascal became their defender. The *Provincial Letters* were the result.

Why did the letters create such a fuss? With the coming of the Protestant Reformation to Europe, many Frenchmen became Calvinists. Their theology emphasized man's corruption, his inability to save himself from sin and his need of God's grace at every stage of conversion. In opposing the Calvinists, the Jesuits took a more cheerful view of man's interaction with God, putting heavy emphasis on human works and free will. They used a system called *casuistry* to decide right from wrong.

Cornelius Jansen, Catholic bishop of Ypres, Belgium (then part of France), felt the Jesuits went too easy on sin while neglecting the importance of grace. He made his point in a book about Augustine of Hippo, the Church's top authority on grace. The pope condemned Jansen's book. After Jansen's death, one of his admirers, Antoine Arnauld, defended the Jansenists.

Nuns of Port Royale, the Jansenist center. (Jameson, Mrs. *Legends of the Monastic Orders*. London: Longmans, Green, and Co., 1872.)

It was soon clear that Arnauld would be disgraced. At that point, Pascal's *Provincial Letters* appeared, taking the Jansenist side of the argument. Pascal invented a character who wrote as if he were a perplexed bystander searching for truth in the quarrel. To make this character seem real, Pascal wrote French the way common people spoke it. No French writer had done this so well before, and the letters gave French prose new power.

Pascal's imaginary letter writer exposed the double standards and clever word play of many theologians. By digging up absurd examples of Jesuit casuistry, he unfairly made it appear that all Jesuits winked at sin. Pascal was not able to save Arnauld from disgrace, but his letters won sympathy for the Jansenists and changed French literature forever.

Other Events

1755: John William Fletcher was converted on this day. He was an Anglican influenced by Methodists, and he defended the Arminian theology.

1875: Charles Kingsley, rector of the Church of England and author of *Westward Ho*, died on this day. He was heavily engaged in the religious controversies and movements of his day.

1890: Neesima Shimeta, a Japanese evangelist, died on this day. He was so determined to find out more about the gospel that he escaped from Japan (a capital offense), came to America and received a grounding in the gospel. Back in Japan, he founded a Christian school.

1918: The Soviets separated Church and state on this day. The Russian Orthodox Church had played an important role in politics for centuries.

1945: Helmuth James von Moltke, international lawyer who used his position to relieve Jews, was executed on this day by the Nazis. They told him, "The only trouble with you is you are a Christian."

1950: *Caritas* (relief) offices were taken over by Polish Communists, who charged the Church organization with irregularities in order to put a stop to its ministries.

Neesima Shimeta risked death to learn more about the Christian faith. (Dennis, James S. *Christian Missions and Social Progress*. New York: Fleming H. Revell Co., 1897-1906.)

Irene Ferrel, a Baptist Mid-Missions worker, died in a revolt in the Congo (now the Democratic Republic of the Congo). (Courtesy of Baptist Mid-Missions from Hege, Ruth. *We Two Alone: Attack and Rescue in the Congo*. Belfast, Ireland/Greenville, SC: Emerald House, 1997. Used by permission of Bill Smallman.)

January 24

The Warning Came Too Late

"We fear the beating of the drum for classes is inciting the *Jeunesse*," Nkedi, the Congolese director of the Baptist primary school in Mangungu, said with concern. The *Jeunesse* ("youth") were rebels, notorious for massacres and tortures. They had forced all of the village schools to close. The "beating of the drum" (the Congo school bell) was a daily reminder to the terrorists that the mission school was still operating. This spelled danger, for the Marxist guerrillas considered Christianity their most formidable competitor.

Standing in the shade in front of their house, missionaries Irene Ferrel and Ruth Hege listened with sympathy as the teachers agreed with Nkedi that the school should be closed for a couple of weeks until the threat passed. As they talked, the whir of an airplane was heard. They all ran together as the pilot flung out something that trailed a white bandage. It fell into nearby bushes. Attached was a note.

Opening the letter with trembling fingers, Ferrel read, "Are you in trouble? All missionaries have been evacuated from Mukedi. Kandala Station burned and missionaries evacuated." The note asked them to signal their intentions: "If you want to be evacuated, sit on the ground. We will send a helicopter for you." The red-and-white plane circled back to get their response. There was no time to weigh options. "Lord, lead us," they gasped. They did not want to abandon the African Christians, and yet, as the only two white women in the region, they stuck out as targets, inviting attack.

Hand-in-hand, Ferrel and Hege walked to the clearing and sat. The plane dipped a wing to show that their reply was understood and then zipped away. It was three o'clock on January 24, 1964, in the Congo (what is now known as the Democratic Republic of the Congo). There was no time to lose. No doubt the helicopter would be winging toward them within the hour. "We will be back," they promised their loyal Congolese friends, and they hurried to wrap up final details.

Evening brought no helicopter. The village Christians gathered for a farewell service. When the meeting broke up at midnight, Luka, one of the local pastors, offered to stay outside the house to wait for the plane. The missionaries were grateful. They knew their converts were tactfully offering what little protection they could.

Exhausted from the day's events, Hege went to bed. Suddenly, the night air carried urgent cries—Luka and others were shouting a warning. There was the sound of running feet. Shrieks and the crash of broken glass plainly told that the *Jeunesse* had come. Hege leaped up and jerked on her clothes. She rushed to Ferrel's room.

The *Jeunesse* poured into the house, looting everything, even grabbing Hege's shoes out of her hand. Shoving, pulling, shouting, the drug-crazed bandits dragged the two women fifty feet across the lawn. Hege's skirt was ripped from her with such violence she was almost flung to the ground. She thanked God that she and Ferrel were still together. Then an arrow hurtled toward them and plunged into Ferrel's throat. "I am finished," gasped Ferrel. She took one step and fell. She became Baptist Mid-Missions' only martyr of the twentieth century.

Wounded by a blow from behind, Hege cried out Ferrel's name, collapsed beside her and passed out. Because Hege was bloody and motionless, the *Jeunesse* thought she was dead. When they left, she crawled to a hiding place and survived the following four days of threats and terror before her rescue by helicopter. Pastors Luka and Zechariah, who shielded her, were later tortured but escaped and hid in the forest.

John Albert Broadus, conscientious teacher. (Armitage, Thomas. *A History of the Baptists: Traced by Their Principles and Practices, From the Time of Our Lord and Saviour Jesus Christ to the Present*. New York: Bryan, Taylor and Co., 1893.)

Other Events

1722: Edward Wigglesworth became Hollis Professor of Divinity at Harvard. Although claiming to be an orthodox Calvinist, he actually tended toward Unitarianism.

1827: John Albert Broadus was born on this day in Blue Ridge, Virginia. He was converted at age sixteen and was ordained in 1850. Following the Civil War, when the South was in great economic depression, he taught in a new seminary that had only seven students. He had just one student in his homiletics class—and that student was blind! For that one blind student, Dr. Broadus prepared a textbook, *Preparation and Delivery of Sermons*, which was still in use for many years afterward. His faithful teaching influenced literally thousands of young preachers.

1990: "The Bible has come!" yelled 5,000 men who were gathered for a big celebration in the Moni tribe in the highlands of Irian Jaya, Indonesia. Bill and Grace Cutts, missionaries under The Christian and Missionary Alliance, had spent their lives learning the language, preaching the gospel and translating the Bible into the Moni language. The work of evangelizing the 25,000 members of this tribe had been long and difficult but very worthwhile. A huge feast was planned, and when the plane landed with the books, there was great rejoicing.

January 25

Formation of a Mission Society

John Veniaminov was the Paul Bunyan of the Christian world. He was a tall tale of a man at six-feet-three-inches tall with the burly build of an ox. And, like the Paul Bunyan of legend, Veniaminov was a tireless worker capable of great feats who was always clever enough to contrive a way around any problem. He had a practical genius for blacksmithing, brickmaking, carpentering, clockmaking, furniture building and construction. He used these skills well in his service to the Church.

In 1823, when Veniaminov was still a priest in Irkutsk, where he had married Catherine Sharina and taken his training at the Russian Orthodox Seminary, his superior, Bishop Michael Burdakov, asked Veniaminov to go to the Aleutian Islands of Alaska. Thirty years earlier, Russians had begun converting the Indians native to the islands, but their mission collapsed when the monks died or retired. Someone new was needed to take over the work. Although reluctant at first, Veniaminov finally relented.

There was no trans-Siberian railroad or steamship to speed the young family to its destination. It took them fourteen months to reach windswept Unalaska Island. There they found that they had neither a parsonage nor a church. Despite the serious lack of amenities, Veniaminov put aside all plans to build a house and a chapel (and a meteorological station) in order to focus on evangelizing the Aleuts.

The Aleuts knew little of Christianity beyond baptism. But Veniaminov was delighted with their attitude, saying, "The most inexhaustible preacher might well be worn out before their attention and their eager desire to hear the Word of God began to fail." He learned the Unanagan language, invented an alphabet for it, opened a school and translated the Gospel of Matthew.

Somehow he also found time to write. He wrote *Notes on the Island of Unalaska* and a catechism called *A Guide to the Kingdom of Heaven*. Peering across the sea, the giant missionary saw spiritual and human need everywhere and set out to meet it. During the four warm months of each year, he crammed his large frame into a kayak for fourteen hours or more a day, paddling to the islands of his parish.

Later, he and his family moved to the city of Sitka, learned the Tlingit language, opened an orphanage and built a cathedral with icons so beautiful that visitors were said to catch their breath upon seeing them.

In 1839, Veniaminov approached the Holy Synod in St. Petersburg, leaving Catherine with her family in Irkutsk. When he had explained the needs of Alaska to the Church leaders, they appointed him bishop of the Aleutians, Kamchatka and the Kurile Islands. However, Veniaminov's joy at the appointment was crushed by the news that Catherine had died during his absence. He returned to Sitka and set up a seminary to train priests. He also traveled across his whole diocese, even to the farthest boundaries north of Siberia. Later, he was made archbishop, and the provinces of Yakutsk and Amur were added to his care.

At the age of seventy Veniaminov retired—or so he thought. The metropolitan of Moscow, the highest figure in the Russian Orthodox Church, died. At the urging of what seemed like the entire Church, Veniaminov took his place. During his eleven years in Moscow, Veniaminov made missions a priority, saying that every Christian has a missionary obligation.

An Orthodox church in Sitka, Alaska, reminds us of the influence of Russian missionary Veniaminov. (Jackson, Sheldon. *Alaska and Missions on the North Pacific Coast*. New York: Dodd, Mead, 1880.)

With his support, the Orthodox Missionary Society was born on this day in 1870. One of its first missionaries was Nikolai, who did impressive work in Japan. Veniaminov also set up a committee to offer good pay and pensions for priests who volunteered for at least ten years of service in Siberia. Many fine priests signed on.

In 1977 Veniaminov was canonized as the "Apostle to America." Two years later Alaska celebrated the bicentennial of his birth. A hymn in his honor has these words: "Rejoice! O holy Father Innocent, Equal to the Apostles and Enlightener of North America."

Other Events

1523: On this day, Ulrich Zwingli's doctrine was debated and affirmed by city hall in Zurich.

1532: Pope Clement VII rebuked Henry VIII of England for his divorce from Catherine of Aragon.

1631: Marie de L'incarnation entered the Ursuline convent of Tours. Later she founded what is now the oldest North American convent school.

1707: The papal legate Charles Maillard de Tournon threatened excommunication of Catholic missionaries in China if they did not forbid sacrifice to ancestors.

1980: Bill Miller, son of the atheist Madelyn Murray O'Hair, was converted on this day. His mother used him as a test case to ban Bible reading from US schools. Miller wrote, "I had heard many times in various churches that all one needed to do was to admit guilt and ask Jesus in. I had not made that one step, to ask Him into my heart. I knew I must take that step, and I did so that night. God was no longer a distant, impersonal 'force.' I now knew Him in a personal way."

Clement VII rebuked Henry VIII of England for his divorce from Catherine of Aragon. (Bezold, Friedrich von. *Geschichte der Deutschen Reformation*. Berlin: Grote, 1890.)

Bossuet vs. Jouarre

Bishop Bossuet has been called the "Pope of France." He was a player in most of the key religious issues of his day. (Courtesy of the University of Texas collection of public domain portraits on the Web.)

What authority should women exercise in the Church? This has been a highly charged issue throughout Church history. In medieval times, some abbesses were granted a great deal of power and were allowed to take tithes, judge civil disputes and command neighboring monks.

One abbey with such powers was Jouarre in France. Jouarre was founded under the inspiration of a visit by Columban, the sixth-century Irish monk who dotted Europe with monasteries. Relatives of the nobleman and clergy with whom Columban stayed founded male and female abbeys at Jouarre near the river Marne. The female house was predominant, and its abbesses enjoyed autonomy from the nearby bishop of Meaux, answering directly to the pope instead. The monks who lived at Jouarre and later at nearby Rebais, were under the jurisdiction of the abbesses of Jouarre.

Five hundred years after the founding of the abbey, the bishop of Meaux contested the right of the abbey to control the local churches, clergy and people. Pope Honarius II ruled in favor of the bishop, but Jouarre presented a strong defense and Innocent II later reversed the decision. The sparring between Jouarre and the bishopric continued for almost a century. Abbess Eustache was forced to publicly submit to the bishop of Meaux. Her successor, Agnes I, refused to swear her oath to the bishop, however, and was excommunicated. The next abbess, Agnes II, traveled to Rome bearing documents that proved the abbey's historical exemption from the bishop's rule. Pope Innocent III was convinced and restored Jouarre's ancient rights. The matter was rested until after the Protestant Reformation when the Roman Catholic Church cracked down on independents. Jouarre's nemesis was the new bishop of Meaux, Jacques Benigne Bossuet, sometimes called the "Pope of France."

Bossuet's eloquent histories and sermons ornament the literature of his age, and his deeds show that he was active in the ecclesiastical and political affairs of the day. He squelched the Jansenists and was a driving force behind the Four Articles that rejected papal dominion over the French Church, asserting the ancient "Gallican liberties," which in essence limited papal authority to spiritual matters, leaving administrative matters in the hands of the Church of France.

When he was appointed bishop of Meaux in 1681, a showdown with Jouarre loomed. Seizing on weaknesses in the throne (which was dependent on Bossuet as champion of Gallican rights) and the papacy (which was hesitant to interfere in the French Church because of the Gallican controversy), Bossuet accused the abbey of simony (the attempt to buy spiritual office). Five hundred years earlier, as a gesture of peace, Jouarre sent a gift of grain to the bishop of Meaux. According to Bossuet, Jouarre bought its rights with that gift. The charge was so absurd that it quickly collapsed. So Bossuet shifted his ground, claiming that the abbey's privileges were not authentic. Even if authentic, he argued (probably incorrectly), the councils of Trent and Vienna had revoked such privileges. Jouarre defended itself vigorously, showing that as late as 1631 Parliament had confirmed its rights. But Jouarre argued in vain.

On this day in 1690, the men won the skirmish; the judges ruled in Bossuet's favor. A month later Bossuet led his followers to the abbey and demanded entrance. He was barred. On March 2, he again sought submission from Jouarre. The following day he forced the locks, entered and celebrated mass in the chapel, dressed in the splendid vestments of a bishop. Henrietta of Lorraine, the reigning abbess, resigned. The next abbess, Marguerite de Rohan, submitted to Bossuet but refused consecration at his hands, waiting ten years to receive it from his successor.

Pius IV ratified the decrees of Trent. (Montor, Chevalier Artaud de. *Lives and Times of the Popes*. New York: Catholic Publication Society of America, 1911.)

Other Events

1564: Pope Pius IV issued the bull *Benedictus Deus*, ratifying the decrees of the Council of Trent. Since these included doctrines that Protestants could not accept, reconciliation between the Protestant and Catholic Churches became more difficult.

1800: John Oncken was born on this day in Varel, Germany. After his conversion to the Baptist faith, he became an evangelist to eastern Europe and Russia.

1977: Allan Grant Mcintosh, pioneer African missionary, died on this day. A Canadian, he was decorated for bravery in World War I. After he joined the African Inland Mission, he worked in the region that is now the Democratic Republic of the Congo.

1991: Rev. Everett C. Eck, retired Christian and Missionary Alliance missionary to Chili and Colombia, South America, died on this day. Born in Dover, New Jersey, he graduated from Nyack College, and in 1939 he married Catherine Ellen Wagoner. The couple were dedicated musicians and developed the music of the Chilean evangelical Church.

Henry and Hildebrand Duke It Out

JANUARY 27

In a close boxing bout, first one boxer is on the ropes and then the other. Neither competitor is able to deliver a knockout punch. Round after round, the match remains in doubt.

Such was the struggle between Henry IV, Holy Roman Emperor, and Pope Gregory VII (Hildebrand). Henry inherited his throne in 1065 when he was fifteen. From the first, he faced rebellion, and in 1073 the Saxons destroyed several churches. Henry accused them of sacrilege, and Pope Gregory VII, who wanted to remain on good terms with Henry, condemned them. Round one goes to Henry.

Historically, the Roman emperors had required the Church to obtain imperial consent before confirming a pope. However, when Hildebrand took the office he did not seek the usual approval, and Henry was too weak to insist. By petitioning the pope to condemn the Saxons, Henry had effectively admitted that his consent was not needed to ratify Hildebrand's confirmation as pope. Round two to the pope.

The Saxons offered to make reparations for the churches and the castles they had destroyed, but in 1075 Henry defeated them in a surprise attack. He imprisoned many nobles and some bishops and installed his own bishops without Hildebrand's approval. Round three, King Henry.

Hildebrand's bishops were in prison, and Henry was selling bishoprics to new bishops and investing them with the spiritual insignia of their office. Hildebrand took Henry to task and demanded proof of his obedience to the Church. Round four to the pope.

Henry summoned the German bishops to the city of Worms. On this day in 1076, twenty-four bishops "deposed" Hildebrand. According to their allegations, Hildebrand had sworn never to become pope, had been elected unlawfully, had dealt high-handedly toward bishops in four nations, was accepting the counsel of women and had violated an election decree that had been established in 1059. The bishops of Lombard approved the German vote. Henry addressed a letter to the pope with these stinging words: "Henry, not by usurpation, but by God's holy ordinance, King, to Hildebrand, not Pope, but false monk." He demanded that Hildebrand relinquish the papacy. "Step down, step down, thou eternally damned." Round five, King Henry.

Hildebrand convened a council of his supporting bishops. Scarcely had they met when a priest named Roland rode up, bearing a message from Henry. Hildebrand was commanded to step down and his bishops told to appear before the king to elect a new pope. Infuriated, the bishops leaped up, drawing their swords so they might hack Roland to pieces, but Hildebrand shielded Roland with his own body. Hildebrand excommunicated Henry and absolved Henry's subjects of loyalty to the king. For the better part of a year, Henry struggled to hang on to his kingdom, but the next January he gave in and appeared barefoot in the snow at Canossa, Italy, in token of submission, requesting that the pope absolve him. After making him wait three days, Hildebrand restored Henry's kingly privileges but imposed severe penance. Round six, Pope Hildebrand.

Henry IV stood barefoot and humiliated in the snow at Canossa. He regained power only to lash back at Pope Gregory VII. (Ruoff, Henry W. *Masters of Achievement: The World's Greatest Leaders in Literature, Art, Religion, Philosophy, Science, Politics and Industry*. Buffalo, NY: The Frontier Press Company, 1910.)

Hildebrand's penalties embittered Henry and he summarily ignored them. In retaliation, the pope induced Rudolf of Swabia (a German duchy) to revolt against Henry. Henry gathered an Italian army and killed Rudolf. Round seven, King Henry.

Once again Hildebrand excommunicated Henry, so round eight goes to Pope Hildebrand. The king and the pope were tied four to four.

Henry struck back with fury, marching into Italy, deposing Hildebrand and capturing Rome. He appointed his own pope, Clement, who repaid the favor by crowning Henry as Holy Roman Emperor. Round nine, Henry.

Henry may have won the bout with Hildebrand, but he did not land the last blow. In 1105, his own son forced Henry from the throne. The once-fearsome emperor died neglected and alone.

Sergius II faced Muslim advance. (Montor, Chevalier Artaud de. *Lives and Times of the Popes*. New York: Catholic Publication Society of America, 1911.)

Other Events

847: Pope Sergius II died on this day. During his papacy, the Saracens (Muslims) plundered the region around Rome.

1302: Dante's sentence of exile from Florence reached him. It is possible that he sought solace in writing his epic, *The Divine Comedy*. The great poet believed in Christ and that at the Resurrection "at the last trump every saint shall rise out of the grave, ready with voice new-fleshed to carol Alleluia to the skies."

1521: The Diet of Worms met to deal with Martin Luther, who was agitating for the reform of the Roman Catholic Church. Luther arrived later.

1978: Twenty-nine adult Christians were seized by Ugandan chiefs in the Masaka district. They were forced to crawl on their hands and knees and were beaten. They were held for six days and used the opportunity to witness about Christ to their fellow prisoners.

Reuben A. Torrey, who led Oswald J. Smith to Christ in Toronto. (Courtesy of The Sword of the Lord from Torrey, R.A. *Apostle of Certainty*. Murfreesboro, TN: Sword of the Lord Publishers, 1976. Used by permission of Terry Frala.)

January 28

Oswald's Legs Turned to Lead

The hall was packed with over 3,000 people night after night, with hundreds turned away. Evangelist R.A. Torrey and song leader Charles M. Alexander were holding meetings for spiritual awakening in Toronto's Massey Hall. Those turned away must have been sorely disappointed, for some of them had traveled up to 200 miles to hear Torrey, who created such a stir that the newspapers printed his entire sermons. Reading the newspaper accounts of the meetings, Oswald and Ernie Smith of Cody's Corners, Ontario, ninety miles from Toronto, were stirred too. They asked their mother if they could go to the meetings. She said "yes" and immediately wrote to Torrey and asked him to pray that her boys would become Christians.

Walt Whitman came to Moody's evangelistic meeting to mock. (Whitman, Walt. *The Gathering of the Forces*. New York: G.P. Putnam's Sons, 1920.)

Off went Oswald and Ernie to Toronto. They got off the train and went directly to their Aunt Phoebe's house, where they asked for directions to Massey Hall. A streetcar deposited them beside a great crowd that was waiting for the doors to open. Elbowing their way to the front of the throng, Ernie and Oswald found themselves almost lifted off their feet when the doors were opened and the mass surged into the hall.

Oswald was awestruck. In his sixteen years he had never been inside so large a building. Massey Hall's second- and third-floor balconies amazed him. He was fascinated by the building, by the music, by Alexander waving his arms as he led the singing and by Torrey's preaching. The boys made a point not to miss even one of the eight meetings that Torrey conducted in Toronto.

Having heard Torrey's messages, Ernie and Oswald made up their minds quite deliberately to give their lives to Christ. They went to the second-to-last meeting, held on this day in 1906, with that intention. The meeting was especially for boys.

Once again the hall was packed. Oswald remembered that Torrey preached from Isaiah 53:5, changing the word *our* to *my*: "He was wounded for [my] transgressions, he was bruised for [my] iniquities: the chastisement of [my] peace was upon him; and with his stripes [I am] healed" (KJV). Torrey gave the altar call by ages, beginning with those twenty-five and over and lowering the age until Oswald was included. Oswald meant to go forward. "But to my amazement," he recalled, "I was turned to a chunk of lead." He could not move until Ernie nudged him and broke the spell.

Soberly Oswald stepped toward the front. Dr. Torrey gripped Oswald's hand for a moment and then sent him to the basement, where a worker explained the way of salvation. The worker left, believing that Oswald was converted, but the boy experienced nothing and continued to sit there.

> Then suddenly it happened. I cannot explain it even today. I just bowed my head, put my face between my hands and in a moment the tears gushed through my fingers and fell on the chair, and there stole into my boyish heart a realization of the fact that the great change had taken place. Christ had entered and I was a new creature. I had been born again. There was no excitement, no unusual feeling, but I knew that something had happened and that ever after all life would be different.

He called it the greatest event of his life.

When Oswald returned home, his one petition was "Lord, what will you have me do?" He read the Bible and prayed that he might become an evangelist. With his mother's help, he started a Sunday school. He sang hymns while walking on the railroad tracks near his home, and he preached sermons alone in his bed at night.

In time, Oswald became a notable preacher. He founded his first church, the Alliance Tabernacle, in 1921, and later pastored the People's Church of Toronto, which was highly supportive of missions and one of the largest Protestant congregations in the world. His books on Christian living were read by hundreds of thousands. What he had seen Torrey do, Oswald J. Smith did too.

Other Events

1560: John a Lasco (Laski), a Polish reformer, died on this day. He had trained for the priesthood but, sickened by corruption in the Church, became a Calvinist reformer instead.

1877: Dwight L. Moody's evangelistic campaign in Boston opened. Poet Walt Whitman attended and mocked it afterward.

1896: Joseph Barnby, who wrote the tunes to such beloved hymns as "Just As I Am" and "When Morning Gilds the Skies," died on this day.

1856: Reuben Archer Torrey was born on this day in Hoboken, New Jersey. He was ordained in the Congregational Church and served at various times as an evangelist, president of Moody Bible Institute, dean of the Bible Institute of Los Angeles and the founder of the Montrose Bible Conference. Many use his often-reprinted Bible study aid entitled *What the Bible Teaches*. He died in 1928 and was buried at Montrose.

JANUARY 29

If Only Gildas Had Told Us More

Ancient Church history is like a slice of Swiss cheese with more than the usual number of holes. Historian Hugh Ross Williamson wrote, "For every relevant fact that can be discovered, there are ten thousand that cannot." What we don't know is far greater than what we do. Even what we "know" is often too little cheese and too many holes.

For instance, the only eyewitness to write the story of the fall of the Britons—the British Celts—was a man named Gildas. He told how the Romans abandoned England, how one Briton imported the first Saxons to fight his battles and how they subsequently seized Britain for themselves. The Britons, led by Ambrosius Aurelianus, recovered for a short time, temporarily stopping the Saxon drive. But in the end, the Britons were driven into Wales and Cornwall in western England. The pagan Anglo-Saxons became the rulers of the land, which took their name, Angland (England).

Gildas was not a trained historian. His book *The Destruction of Britain* leaves out just about everything we'd really like to know. Although that was the era of the legendary King Arthur, Gildas never mentioned him. In fact, he ignored all too many names and dates. Mostly he was concerned with showing how the sins of the clergy and nobles weakened the Celts and made them easy for the Saxons to defeat. The conquest of his country left Gildas gloomy. He was like Jeremiah, who wept over the decline and fall of Jerusalem.

Who was this British Jeremiah? We have as few hard facts of Gildas's own life as we do for the history of his time. He was born the same year that the Britons defeated the Saxon invaders at Badon Hill under King Arthur. But since no one can say for sure what year that was, the best guess of scholars is 516. We aren't sure where Gildas grew up, either, but some say it was in Strathclyde, Scotland. It is thought that Gildas joined the Church, most likely as a monk, but even that is not certain.

Usually, if we have no other date for a well-known man of the Dark Ages, we at least know when he died. With Gildas, we aren't even sure of that. It is thought that he died on this day in 570, because it is his feast day and Welsh chronicles suggest the year was 570. Apart from that we have no interesting details such as what he died of or whether it was in sunny day or gloomy night.

Gildas may have been a friend of St. Brigid, who founded Kildare and became the patroness of Ireland and of scholars. After spending time in Ireland, Gildas moved to France. It is almost certain that he founded the monastery of St. Gildas at Ruys, in Breton, because a monk there claimed so in a biography of Gildas that he wrote. The people of Brittany considered Gildas a saint and gave his name to a second monastery that was built later.

Friends urged Gildas to write the story of the ruin of his people. At first he refused, because he had no documents to work from. Later, he relented and began work on his manuscript. Even then, he had to rely too heavily on vague reports written by foreigners.

Kit's Coty House, an ancient British ruin near Addington, England. Ruins such as these were already legendary when Gildas wrote his history. (Green, John Richard. *A Short History of the English People*. New York: Harper & Brothers, 1893-5.)

Although we wish there was more cheese and fewer holes in Gildas's book, we can be glad for what he did write, for the information he gives is certainly better than none at all. A much more famous monk, the Venerable Bede, who was born 100 years after it is supposed that Gildas died, used Gildas's writings to prepare the first great history of England. To this day, histories of England glean what they can from Gildas's writings to fill out our spotty knowledge of his era. Monks like Gildas preserved much of what we know about early Church history.

Remember too that Gildas isn't the only man with gaps in his story. Multiply Gildas many times over and you can see how hard the job of the early Church historian is.

Other Events

1523: The "First Disputation" was held in Zurich. Radical reformers and moderates adopted a similar line against the Roman Catholic Church, but Ulrich Zwingli chafed at any "Donatist" (stern and rigid) approach.

1739: Thomas Shepherd, who wrote the hymn "Must Jesus Bear the Cross Alone?", died on this day.

1880: Frederick Oakley, who is most famous for translating the hymn "Adeste Fidelis" from Latin into English, died on this day. We sing it as "O, Come, All Ye Faithful."

1917: Stephen Merritt died on this day. He had made himself an authority on the work of the Holy Spirit. A young African man named Sammy Morris traveled to America to learn about the Spirit from Merritt. Merritt attempted to show Morris the buildings of New York, but Morris asked him to stop the carriage and to pray. He said he came to learn about the Holy Spirit, not about the big buildings in a busy port!

1949: Part of the convent of Santo Domingo in Guatemala was given to a secular charity as the government continued to nationalize Church property.

Ulrich Zwingli, reformer of Zurich, Switzerland. (McGiffert, Arthur Cushman. *Martin Luther, the Man and His Work*. New York: The Century Co., 1911.)

King Charles I of England on the scaffold. His religious squabbles with Parliament were largely responsible for his death. (Ruoff, Henry W. *Masters of Achievement: The World's Greatest Leaders in Literature, Art, Religion, Philosophy, Science, Politics and Industry*. Buffalo, NY: The Frontier Press Company, 1910.)

January 30

King Charles Bends His Neck with Grace

This day in 1649 was so bitterly cold that the Thames froze over. King Charles I of England was afraid that he might shiver as he stood on the scaffold and the people would think he was trembling from fear, so he donned an extra shirt. He chose his other clothes with care so that he might look his best. "I do not fear death," he said. "Death is not terrible to me. I bless my God I am prepared."

Despite the errors that brought Charles to the scaffold on this day, there is no denying his adherence to the forms of faith. He knelt in prayer every morning of his reign, even on hunting days, and kept a prayer book by his bedside.

What led this apparently religious man to such a grievous fate? Charles could not get along with Parliament. During his reign, every Parliament sought to rebuke him before giving him money, and so he quickly dissolved them. The third Parliament, aggrieved by Charles's high-handed actions, forced Charles to sign a "petition of right," a statement of civil liberties, before he dissolved it. He levied taxes without parliamentary approval and then dissolved the fourth Parliament when it opposed the taxes. Then Charles decided to rule without any Parliament at all, and he did so for eleven years. To raise money, he taxed ships.

Charles raised Bishop William Laud to the powerful Star Chamber and Court of Commissions, from where Laud oppressed the king's opponents. Charles had long wanted to compel the Presbyterian Scots to accept a liturgy based on that of the Church of England, so Laud tried to force a new prayer book on Scotland. Great numbers of Scots pledged to resist the changes. These "Covenanters" defeated Charles in battle.

Again Charles called a session of Parliament. It would not give him money until it stated the nation's grievances, so Charles dissolved it. But after another defeat in Scotland, his financial straits forced him to call a Parliament in November 1640. This was the famous Long Parliament that impeached and executed Archbishop Laud. The House of Commons prepared a Grand Remonstrance against Charles. In retaliation, he entered Parliament with an armed force to arrest five of its members. The House of Commons called out London's militia for protection.

With the smell of war in the air, the queen fled to the Netherlands and Charles left for York, where noblemen gathered at his side. The Puritans, who had suffered much at Laud's hands, took Parliament's side, and civil war ensued. After five years of war, Charles fell into Parliament's hands. He escaped and rallied the Scots to his cause, but Oliver Cromwell defeated them and Charles was again made the prisoner of Parliament.

The House of Commons appointed a commission of sixty-seven men to try Charles for his crimes. Most members of Parliament were opposed to killing the king. In fact, when the death sentence was passed, only half of the commissioners were present—and some of them balked at signing the sentence. There was great difficulty finding an executioner who would carry out the sentence.

However, Cromwell overcame these and other obstacles, and Charles was brought out to be executed. The king had planned to speak to the crowd before he died, but barriers around the scaffold prevented the people from seeing him. A bystander felt the edge of the axe, and Charles pleaded that he not dull the blade. To the fifteen men who were within earshot, he read his last speech. Turning to Bishop Juxson, he said, "Remember," and gave the bishop his bedside prayer book. Then he tucked his hair under a white cap so that it might not impede the blade. "I am going from a corruptible to an incorruptible crown, where no disturbance can be," said the king.

The executioner asked Charles to pardon him for the act he was about to commit, but Charles said, "The king cannot pardon a subject who willfully sheds his blood," then added, "I pray you, do not put me to pain." Charles prayed a last prayer and then lay down flat with his neck on the block. The crowd saw the axe flash high and heard its thud. With a single voice, they groaned. Their willful but brave king was dead.

Bathild, slave queen of France. (Baring-Gould, S. *Lives of the Saints*. Edinburgh: John Grant, 1914.)

Other Events

680: Bathild, a slave girl who became the queen of France, died on this day. To escape an unwanted marriage, she smeared her face with ash and worked the dirtiest jobs. When King Clovis married her, she used all of her energies to do good, especially fighting slavery.

1592: Clement VIII was elected pope; his revised Vulgate Bible was used by the Church for 300 years.

1630: John Brebeuf pronounced his final vows as a Jesuit. In preparation, he devoted himself to Ignatius's *Spiritual Exercises*, writing later, "I felt within myself an overpowering desire of suffering something for Christ." He was tortured to death by the Iroquois in Canada.

1956: About 22,500 members of China's Little Flock (formerly led by Watchman Nee) were forced to attend a mass denunciation because of their faith.

JANUARY 31

The Death of John Mott

In his last public appearance, Methodist layman John Mott said, "While life lasts, I am an evangelist."

Mott played a strategic role in world evangelism and the unification of divided denominations. He died at the age of eighty-nine on this day in 1955 in Orlando, Florida. He had told a reporter some years earlier that death was just a place to change trains. A few days before his death, he sent a message to the World Council of Churches, saying, "Old things are passing away. All things may become new. Not by magic, nor by wishful thinking, but by self-sacrifice and the will to bring them about in the name of Jesus Christ."

Mott's life epitomized the will to bring about new things in the name of Jesus Christ. Sixty-nine years before his death, on January 14, 1886, twenty-year-old Mott had walked late into a meeting at Cornell University and heard C.T. Studd say, "Seekest thou great things for thyself? Seek them not. Seek ye first the kingdom of God."

Mott couldn't sleep all that night, and he later set up a meeting with Studd so they could have a private talk. That encounter changed Mott's life—and the world. Mott demonstrated a living faith in Christ and became a notable evangelist, a YMCA leader and a cofounder of the Student Volunteer Mission. He labored to pull all Christians together to win the world for Christ in his generation.

In fact, in 1900 he published the book *The Evangelization of the World in This Generation*, which became a challenge for the young men and women of his day to attempt to win the world for Christ. In the book Mott showed first of all what he meant by evangelization—letting the whole world hear the news about Christ—and he demonstrated from Scripture that God expected no less. Admitting that there were serious difficulties involved in world evangelization, he nonetheless insisted that the job could be done. He reminded his readers of what Christians in the earliest days of the Church had accomplished and showed striking examples from more recent times. He asserted that, given modern technology, even more could be accomplished.

Mott's influence was enormous. It is impossible to say how many people he inspired to go into missions. He was a major force in the ecumenical (Church cooperation) movement. In 1910, he helped organize a major conference in Edinburgh for the purpose of uniting Christians behind world evangelism. "The church is confronted today, as in no preceding generation, with a literally worldwide opportunity to make Christ known," he told the 1,200 delegates who were there as representatives of at least 160 mission boards and societies.

Mott became so well-known that heads of state greeted him by name. Even while still in his thirties, he was considered the Protestants' leading statesman. At the age of eighty-one he was awarded one of the highest honors given on earth: the Nobel Peace Prize.

John Mott. (Copyright © 2002 The Nobel Foundation. Used by permission of Lorenette Gozzo.)

Church historian Kenneth Latourette described Mott as one of the outstanding leaders of the entire history of Christianity. He achieved what he did at an enormous expenditure of energy, paying personal attention to hundreds of letters, remaining in nonstop prayer and working endlessly to promote world evangelism.

OTHER EVENTS

Annual: The feast of St. Marcella, a woman who studied with St. Jerome (translator of the Vulgate Latin Bible) and used his name as a cover for her original ideas, is celebrated on this day.

1561: Menno Simons died on this day. This gentle Anabaptist leader gave his name to the Mennonites. Surprisingly, considering the bounties on his head, he died a natural death.

1607: William Bishop and twelve leading priests repudiated the use of forced political conversions in England, having seen that they were counterproductive during the martyrdoms that took place in the Catholic Queen Mary's reign.

1686: King Louis XIV of France issued an edict to burn Waldensian churches to the ground. The group had been founded by Peter Waldo around 1200.

1968: On the Friday of the Tet Offensive, several Christians, including missionaries and many indigenous Vietnamese, were massacred by the Vietcong.

Peter Waldo left everything to preach the gospel and founded the Waldensian movement, which was severely persecuted. (Courtesy of the Christian History Institute archives.)

Not Dangerous at First

Erasmus, the greatest scholar of his day, loaded the cannon that Martin Luther fired, ramming two shots into the barrel that was the Reformation. The first shot was a satire entitled *Praise of Folly,* which poked fun at the errors of Christian Europe. For example, Erasmus reminded his readers that Peter said to the Lord, "We have left everything for you." But the character Folly boasts that, thanks to her influence, "there is scarcely any kind of people who live more at their ease" than the successors of the apostles.

The second shot was Erasmus's Greek New Testament. For centuries, Jerome's Latin translation, the Vulgate, was the Bible of the Church. However, Jerome's translation had deficiencies. Recognizing that fact, Erasmus reconstructed the original New Testament as best he could from Greek texts. He printed the Greek text in one column, and in a parallel column he provided a new Latin translation. What is more—and this could have cost him his life—he added over a thousand notes that pointed out the Church's errors in interpreting the Bible. He attacked Rome's refusal to let priests marry despite the fact that some openly lived with mistresses, and he denied that the popes had all the rights that they claimed. The scholar also challenged prayers to the saints, indulgences and relic worship.

After years of work, Erasmus was ready to release his book, but he was unsure of how to do so without getting into trouble. One way was to link the New Testament with some great man's name. And so, on this day in 1516, Erasmus dedicated his New Testament to Pope Leo X. (He had gotten the pope's permission to do so the year before.) In a soothing letter written to Leo a few months later, Erasmus assured the pope that he meant no harm. "We do not intend to tear up the old and commonly accepted edition [the Vulgate], but amend it where it is corrupt, and make it clear where it is obscure." And, just in case the authorities should be angry with Erasmus's work, Erasmus pointed out that the ideas in his translation were not new with him. He quoted the greatest Church fathers in support of his corrections, knowing that it would be a lot harder for Rome to argue with dead heroes than with him.

Since Erasmus did not have access to the oldest New Testament manuscripts, his translation did have faults. Nonetheless, it was such an improvement over the old version that Martin Luther, William Tyndale and other Protestants based their vernacular versions on it. In addition, they based some of their work on Erasmus's calls for reform.

The result was that the reformers broke away from the Roman Catholic Church. For a time Erasmus and Luther remained friends, but Erasmus disliked Luther's violent words

Erasmus plying his powerful pen. His scholarship and wit sparked Church reform. (McGiffert, Arthur Cushman. *Martin Luther, the Man and His Work*. New York: The Century Co., 1911.)

and Luther called Erasmus vicious names, such as "secret atheist." Soon Erasmus was in grave danger from both camps: Protestants said he held on to too much that was Catholic; the Catholics threatened him because they claimed he was wrecking the Church. In fact, Erasmus had to flee from Catholics in Louvain to escape being burned to death at the stake.

We do not often hear about Erasmus anymore, even though Anabaptists, Zwinglians and Lutherans have all claimed to be his true children. It is certain, though, that his translation of the Bible and his wit helped to form the Reformation.

Other Events

772: Adrian I was named pope on this day. When the Lombards threatened to take him in chains, he appealed to Charlemagne, who rescued him, thus strengthening the special relationship between the Church and the Franks.

1567: Frisian and Flemish Mennonites met to patch up their differences, but the Frisians offered to help the Flemish off their knees, "for they were more in the wrong." This dig worsened the split.

1822: Mother Anne-Marie "Nanette" Javouhey sailed to Senegal as a missionary. Her extraordinary vitality and power caused the king of France to remark "There goes a great man."

1842: The king of Prussia visited an English jail with Elizabeth Fry to observe her innovative methods of dealing with prisoners.

1862: Missionary James Stewart met his hero, missionary-explorer David Livingstone, in the heart of Africa. He soon decided that Livingstone's methods were not for him and founded an educational center known as Lovedale.

1933: Nazi resister Dietrich Bonhoeffer gave a radio speech warning about the consequences of putting blind trust in any man (i.e., Hitler). Studio executives cut out the warning. Bonhoeffer was later executed by the Nazis for his opposition to their regime.

Elizabeth Fry showed the king of Prussia her work on this day. (Hare, Augustus J.C. *The Gurneys of Earlham*. London: George Allen, 1895.)

2

A Fat, Barefoot Ambassador Headed East

The Polos receive a gift at the court of Kublai Khan, one of several Mongol rulers whose names became widely notorious in Europe. (Courtesy of the Christian History Institute archives.)

For centuries, Europe lived with almost no knowledge of the huge realms of East Asia. But a Mongol chieftain named Genghis Khan knocked on Europe's door and changed that. Genghis Khan's hordes slaughtered so many people in such horrible ways that Europeans could no longer ignore the East. Also, the way east was open because the Islamic nations, which had formerly blocked Christian movement, had been broken by the Mongol invasions.

Carpini da Plano Carpini was a fat, sixty-year-old Franciscan friar whom Pope Innocent IV summoned to carry a message to the great khan. Although Carpini seemed an unlikely choice for such a mission, the pope knew him as a zealous preacher, a good organizer and a shrewd judge of people, which made him the ideal candidate for the position of courier.

In the letter that Carpini carried, the pope urged the khan not to attack Europe lest he fall under divine wrath. In addition to delivering the letter, Carpini had been instructed to keep his eyes open and pick up whatever knowledge he could obtain about the Mongols, particularly about their intentions regarding Europe. Barefoot (because he was a begging friar), Carpini set out with a small company for the heart of Mongol Asia on this day in 1245. The early parts of the journey were not hard. Because they went as begging friars and papal couriers, Carpini and his companions received great courtesy in Christian lands. But the Asian stages of the journey were every bit as difficult as expected. The little party of Christians was exposed to every kind of bad weather, days of hunger, attacks by bandits, forced marches, threats and long waits at the hands of suspicious men. Without a good interpreter, Carpini was hard pressed to make himself understood.

Evidences of recent Mongol ferocity were everywhere, a grim reminder to the travelers of the terrors the Christians might face. "[We] found many skulls and bones of dead men lying upon the earth like a dunghill," the brave friar wrote. When Carpini reached a Mongol camp on the Volga River, an under-khan named Batu sent him forward by way of the imperial post system. Carpini's progress was swift, because the imperial post changed horses as many as six times a day. The khan needed to know what was taking place in his vast realm.

The post took Carpini across Asia, above the Aral and Caspian Seas and almost to Karakoram, where Güyük Khan was about to be crowned emperor. Güyük kept the insignificant Christian ambassador cooling his heels, but Carpini spent the time well, creating a family tree of the khans that was remarkable for its accuracy. The genealogy needed only slight modification when new details came to light 600 years later. Carpini also gathered material for a report on the land and its rulers.

When he finally met the khan, Carpini tried to convert him to Christianity. Courtiers pretended the great ruler was considering the faith, but in the end the khan refused baptism. He sent Carpini back with a message for the pope.

The return journey was even more difficult than the initial journey had been. The land was buried in snowdrifts, and the company spent nights without shelter on the open steppes of Asia. They traveled all winter and did not reach Kiev until June 1247. The people of Kiev greeted Carpini as a man risen from the dead.

In Güyük Khan's reply to the pope's missive, the pope was ordered to present himself at the Mongol court at the head of all of his kings:

> [I]f you disregard the command of God and disobey Our instructions, We shall look upon you as Our enemy. Whoever recognizes and submits to the Son of God and Lord of the World, the Great Khan, will be saved, whoever refuses submission will be wiped out.

Those words were not very comforting, but even so the pope had no intention of complying. So for decades Europe lived in terror of another Mongol invasion. Fortunately, it never came.

Carpini da Plano Carpini was later made an archbishop. He lived to be sixty-seven.

George Whitefield, Methodist revival leader in colonial America. (Perry, William Stevens. *The History of the American Episcopal Church: 1587-1883.* Boston: J.R. Osgood, 1885.)

Other Events

1257: On this day, Bonaventure became general of the Franciscan order. The order had already begun to move away from the simplicity that marked its early years under Francis.

1738: George Whitefield sailed for Georgia on this day. He preached the gospel throughout the American colonies and was one of the key individuals behind the Great Awakening.

1864: On this day Fanny Crosby was introduced to William Bradbury and his studio, marking the commencement of her hymn-writing ministry.

He'd Rather Have Been a Missionary

If you have ever been pushed forward to speak for a group when you just wanted to go unnoticed, you have an idea of how Gregory felt on this day in 590. Bishop Pelagius II was dead, and a successor was needed. All eyes turned to one man: Gregory. He was elected unanimously.

Now, if there was anything Gregory did not want, it was to be pope. He had experience in governing men, and the job looked impossible to him. The government of Rome was unstable, and its responsibilities were falling on the Church. Famine, plague and war raged in the countryside. Lombards, Franks and Imperial troops pillaged the starving land. Who in his right mind would want to deal with that? Legend says he tried to escape from Rome by hiding in a basket. In fact, if Gregory had had his way, he would not even have been in Rome when Pelagius died.

Gregory was born into a noble family around 540. He served as a prefect of Rome, presiding over the senate and providing for the city's defense, food supply and finances. Later, he became one of the seven cardinal deacons of the Church. Pelagius made him *nuncio* (highest ranking papal legate) to the imperial court of Constantinople, where Gregory met Maurice, the future emperor. On his return to Rome from Constantinople, Gregory saw fair-haired Saxon lads being sold as slaves in the market. Told they were "Angles," he replied, "not Angles—angels!" His heart went out to them, and he got the pope's permission to carry the gospel to Britain and slipped out of town. Riots resulted, and he was recalled to Rome. Pelagius died soon afterward, and Gregory was thrust into his place.

Gregory still had one hope of squirming off the hook: The emperor had to approve Gregory's election, and there was a chance he might veto it. But the emperor approved, and on September 3, 590, Gregory was consecrated as pope. All winter long, his letters grumbled at the heavy load that had been piled upon his unwilling back. The job was every bit as hard as he had expected. He had to feed starving Rome, and it was he, not the Italian civil leaders, who had to negotiate with the Lombard invaders.

The Church was the biggest landlord in Italy, and Gregory spent much of his precious time reforming the practices that prevailed on the lands, both to make them more profitable and to relieve the peasants who were often badly treated. His strong sense of justice caused him to protect their rights although he must have been sorely tempted to wring every possible coin from them. The papal estates provided the revenues from which he funded his widespread assistance to the needy and paid off attacking armies. Perhaps it was with all this work in mind that Gregory nicknamed himself "Servant of the Servants of God."

Over time Gregory did become reconciled to his task. He became one of the most notable men of the medieval era and his books helped form the mind-set of the Middle Ages. By means of Scripture studies and popular works, he urged men to contemplate eternity. His *Pastoral Care* became a textbook for kings and bishops:

> Every preacher should give forth a sound more by his deeds than by his words, and rather by good living imprint footsteps for men to follow than by speaking show them the way to walk in.

Alfred the Great of England not only followed Gregory's wise advice but also translated it into the Saxon tongue. Alfred felt he owed a great debt to Gregory because, even in the midst of all his cares, Gregory did not forget the Saxons. He sent the monk Augustine as a missionary to them, and that is how, centuries later, Alfred reaped the inheritance of Christianity.

Gregory's name is often associated with the arts. He is especially known for his standardization of plainsong, which is now called Gregorian chant. He encouraged art in the Church in order to portray the story of Christ for people who could not read.

When the patriarch of Constantinople adopted the title "Ecumenical Patriarch," Gregory objected. To elevate one bishop over all others was to degrade the others, he said. This was ironic, because his success as an administrator helped make the bishops of Rome—the popes—far more powerful than the other patriarchs and led them to make greater claims than the others dreamed of making.

Gregory the Great accepted the papacy reluctantly but transformed the Church with his energy and commonsense reforms. (Barry, William. *Story of the Nations: Papal Monarchy*. Whitefish, MT: Kessinger Publishing, 1911.)

Other Events

865: Ansgar, a Frankish missionary to Denmark and Sweden who overcame formidable odds in his efforts to organize the Scandinavian Church, died on this day.

1943: Four chaplains selflessly helped men to safety, losing their own lives when the Allied troopship *Dorchester* was torpedoed and sank.

1949: The trial of Cardinal Mindszenty of Hungary by the Communist regime began. He had resisted their efforts to bind the hands of the Catholic Church and was forced to pay the price for his resistance.

Ansgar evangelized Scandinavia, but the work did not last. (Boyesen, Hjalmar Hjorth. *The Story of Norway*. New York/London: G.P. Putnam's Sons, 1886.)

4 The First of Many Martyrs

John Rogers at the stake committed his spirit to the Lord and washed his hands in the flames as if he could not feel them. (Chester, Joseph Lemuel. *John Rogers: The Compiler of the First Authorized English Bible*. London: Longman, Green, Longman and Roberts, 1861.)

On this day in 1555, John Rogers was bound to a stake at Smithfield, England, and burned to death. His wife and children were among the onlookers. What monstrous crime had earned him this cruel death?

Rogers was born around 1500. He was educated at Cambridge, became a Catholic priest and was given a Church position at the time that the Protestant Reformation was in full swing. His conscience later told him that certain teachings of the Catholic Church were wrong, and he resigned, moving to Antwerp, Holland, where he ministered to English merchants.

In Holland, he became friends with William Tyndale, a reformer who was translating the Bible into English. Tyndale converted Rogers to Protestant views. Rogers got married. Nine months later, Tyndale went to prison and was executed as a heretic. But Tyndale had left a precious manuscript in Rogers's keeping: his English translation of the books from Joshua to Chronicles, which had not yet been printed.

Rogers was determined to see that Tyndale's valuable work was not lost. For the next twelve months he labored to put together a complete Bible. Its text was based on Tyndale's and Coverdale's work, and its 2,000 notes were borrowed from the writings of other reformers. For obvious reasons, Tyndale's name could not go on the Bible, and Rogers could not claim the work as his own, so he used a pseudonym: Thomas Matthews. When Bishop Cranmer saw the new Bible, he was so excited he asked Chancellor Thomas Cromwell to see if the king would license it. Henry VIII did, and the Matthew Bible became the first officially authorized version in the English language.

After sickly Edward VI became king, Rogers returned to England. He was given a high position in the Church of England. Regrettably, he was one of those who agreed to allow the insane woman, Joan of Kent, to be burned to death even though he had been urged to show her mercy because some day he might need it himself.

Edward VI died, and Mary, a Roman Catholic, became queen. Rogers preached a stirring message, urging his congregation to remain loyal to the Reformation principles that they had been taught. Catholic bishops questioned Rogers about this sermon, but he answered so well that he was released.

However, when a Catholic was appointed to speak at Paul's Cross, churchgoers rioted. The mayor was present and could not restore order. Bishop Bonner, an eminent supporter of Queen Mary, was attacked. Rogers shouted to the crowd to calm down and helped hustle Bonner to safety. The Queen's council was upset, and they told the mayor to prove he could keep order or he would lose his office. Instead of arresting the real culprits, the mayor seized Rogers and some others. Rogers spent over a year in prison and was questioned about his beliefs by Lord Chancellor Stephen Gardiner. At his last examination he said, "I have a true spirit, agreeing to and obeying the Word of God. I would further have said that I was never the worse, but the better to be earnest in a just and true cause, and in my master Christ's matters; but I could not be heard."

When the sentence of death was passed, Rogers begged Gardiner to let him speak a few words with his wife. Gardiner refused, telling Rogers he was not legally married because he had once been a priest. However, as Rogers walked to the stake, singing psalms, his wife met him at the roadside, holding their youngest baby, whom he had never met.

At the stake, Rogers was offered a pardon if only he would recant his beliefs and return to the Roman Catholic Church. He refused. The fire was lit, and Rogers washed his hands in the flames as though he did not feel them. He was the first of many martyrs during Mary's reign.

Adoniram Judson Gordon sweat so badly under the angry eyes of his students that he had to change his shirt. (Gordon, Ernest B. *Adoniram Judson Gordon: A Biography*. New York: Garland, 1896.)

Other Events

856: Rhabanus Maurus, one of the great Christian encyclopedists, died on this day. He was among the most learned men of his day.

1787: Bishop William White of Pennsylvania was consecrated in the apostolic succession of the Church of England for the United States, allowing the US Church to function independently of its English parent. The denomination became known as the Episcopal Church.

1798: Elizabeth Fry of the Society of Friends (Quakers) converted to Christ. She became a notable prison reformer.

1873: George Bennard was born in Youngstown, Ohio. He became an American Methodist evangelist and penned over 300 gospel songs. He is remembered today for one in particular: "The Old Rugged Cross."

1884: Veteran pastor A.J. Gordon wrote his wife a letter saying he had faced his toughest day ever. He had preached at Princeton before an angry group of students who had been compelled to attend chapel—attendance had formerly been voluntary. Gordon sweat so badly while preaching that he had to change his shirt.

A Deadly Mix

Mix together arrogance, greed, shipwreck, earthquake, national rivalries and Japanese fears and you have a deadly brew. On this day in 1597, General Toyotomi Hideyoshi crucified six Franciscan friars, seventeen Japanese converts and three Jesuits because of that mixture.

Hideyoshi had risen from humble origins to become the leader of Japan. He completed the unification of the nation. As his strength increased, so did his ambition. It seemed possible to him that he might even bring China under his heel. He attacked Korea to gain a foothold on the mainland, but then China entered the war and Hideyoshi's troops were beaten. He needed more money to finance his campaign. About that same time, an earthquake ruined his lovely new palace and he needed money to rebuild it.

When Franciscan friars came to Japan from the Spanish controlled Philippines, Hideyoshi was happy to talk with them and allow them to operate a mission in Japan, even though Christianity was illegal at that time. His reasons were economic: He hoped that by allowing the Spanish ships to join in the trade business with China, it would introduce competition into the market. At that time, the Portuguese had a lock on Japan's trade with China. By allowing the Spanish to enter the market, he hoped the prices would be brought down.

Jesuits who had been working in Japan for a while urged the Franciscans to walk softly and convert Christians quietly, for they had learned through hard experience that the Japanese were not to be won by brashness. The Franciscans, however, boasted of their success with Hideyoshi and celebrated mass openly. They accused the Jesuits of cowardice for wearing Japanese clothes. The Jesuit father Valignano warned that trouble would follow such brazen actions.

No one could have foreseen the exact circumstances that would prove his words true. The *San Felice*, a Spanish galleon leaving Manila with a cargo valued at more than 1.5 million silver *pesos*, was driven off-course by a typhoon. It broke up off the coast of Japan, and a local samurai appropriated the cargo. The Franciscans took the matter up with general Hideyoshi.

Hideyoshi coveted the treasure for himself. At the same time, he did not want to ruin the prospect of trade relations with the Spanish. So he smiled, made promises and waited. His indecisiveness proved costly to the Christians.

While Hideyoshi procrastinated, his mood changed. According to the Portuguese, this was because the Spanish pilot of the *San Felice* boasted of the greatness of the Spanish king. However, the Spanish said the tide turned because the Portuguese denounced them. Others say that Hideyoshi realized that Christianity was impeding the establishment of his absolute control over the Japanese people.

Whatever the truth, Hideyoshi ordered the execution of all Christians, including the Jesuits. After he thought it over, however, he decided the Jesuits were too useful for trade to kill, so he spared most of them.

Hideyoshi ordered the executions of twenty-six Christians. (Brinkley, F. *History of the Japanese People From the Earliest Times to the End of the Meiji Era*. New York: Encyclopedia Britannica, 1915.)

During thirty days of torments, which included having their left ears cut off, the Christians were marched to Nagasaki. On this cold February morning, the twenty-six brave martyrs were publicly humiliated and crucified. Some sang hymns. From his cross, Paul Miki, a Japanese convert, preached:

> I have committed no crime, and the only reason why I am put to death is that I have been teaching the doctrine of Our Lord Jesus Christ. I am very happy to die for such a cause, and see my death as a great blessing from the Lord. At this critical time you can rest assured that I will not try to deceive you, I want to stress and make it unmistakably clear that man can find no way to salvation other than the Christian way.

Other Events

1631: Roger Williams arrived in America on this day. His appeals for separation of Church and state led to his expulsion from Massachusetts and to the founding of Rhode Island. Williams became the first of America's Baptist leaders.

1705: Philip Spener, who founded the Lutheran reform movement known as Pietism, died on this day. Spener emphasized a deep relationship with Jesus Christ and love toward others. He wrote evangelical books and helped found the University of Halle.

1835: On this day, Daniel Lindley first saw Africa through the mist. He became a notable missionary in South Africa, straining to convert both the Zulu and Boer peoples. He helped preserve Zulu lands from being gobbled up by white settlers.

1885: The Cambridge Seven, a group of upper-class Englishmen, set off as missionaries to China.

1900: Pandit Kharak Singh died. In a desperate search for truth, he had tried to drown himself in the sacred Ganges. Then he heard Christ's words, "Come unto me, all ye that labour and are heavy laden, and I will give you rest" (Matthew 11:28, KJV). He was transformed and preached the gospel throughout northern India.

Roger Williams was an American original. (McLean, Archibald. *Epoch Makers of Modern Missions*. Cincinnati: Fleming H. Revell Co., 1912.)

6 First Spanish *Auto-da-Fé*

Spanish *auto-da-fé* shows "penitents" marching around an arena. (Sabatini, Rafael. *Torquemada and the Spanish Inquisition: A History*. New York: Houghton Mifflin Co., 1924.)

Spain's name is forever linked with the Inquisition, but it did not actually begin there. Pope Innocent III and Pope Gregory IX established the dreaded institution in the thirteenth century to combat heresy in Italy, France and Germany. What made the Inquisition so terrible was the severity of both the questioning and the punishment, as well as the lack of rights granted to the accused. Those who "snitched" on them could do so secretly, but a victim could not challenge the witnesses against him or her.

When Isabella and Ferdinand united Spain in 1479, a fear of revolt made them paranoid. Thus, when the queen's confessor, Tomás de Torquemada, who was of Jewish origin himself, whispered into her ear that Christianized Jews were secretly practicing their Hebrew faith and corrupting good Christians, Isabella was horrified and frightened. She asked the pope for permission to establish an inquisition in Spain. Permission was granted.

Julius I fought any suggestion that Christ was created. (Montor, Chevalier Artaud de. *Lives and Times of the Popes*. New York: Catholic Publication Society of America, 1911.)

Under the rigors of sadistic torture, suspects often incriminated other people. These in turn accused almost anyone they could think of just to please their captors and reduce their own torment. Every confession added to the alarm of the Catholic king and queen because it suggested widespread corruption of the Christian faith. Soon the burning began.

The first Spanish *auto-da-fé*, or "act of faith," was held on this day in 1481, when six men and six women who had refused to repent of alleged backsliding were burned at the stake. Those deaths were just the beginning. In the first 12 years of the Spanish Inquisition, 13,000 "heretics" were tried. Hundreds perished at the stake. Dressed in penitents' gowns, they were marched in processionals to the stake and urged to repent even as they were bound. Those who confessed were strangled before the fire was lit. Those who refused to admit wrongdoing or those who defiantly clung to their "heresy" were burned alive.

The Inquisition ran for 327 years in Spain. It was not abolished until 1808, during the brief reign of Joseph Bonaparte. In the 3 centuries of the Inquisition, close to 32,000 people perished in the flames. About 300,000 others were forced to make some kind of reconciliation with the Church. Incredible as it may seem, King Ferdinand VII reestablished the Inquisition in 1814. But six years later, a revolution swept it away—hopefully forever.

The practices of the Inquisition were not restricted to Europe. Spain exported it to the New World, where, in the beginning of the sixteenth century, men and women in Mexico and Peru were burned for their supposed heresies. Portuguese priests also operated an inquisition in Goa, India.

It is impossible to see Christ winning followers by such means. As John Jortin, an eighteenth-century English preacher and historian wrote:

> To banish, imprison, plunder, starve, hang and burn me for religion is not the Gospel of Christ but the policy of the devil—Christ never used anything that looked like force or violence but once, and that was to drive bad men out of the temple, not to drive them in.

Other Events

337: St. Julius I began his reign as Catholic pope. He was firm in his opposition to Arianism, which sought to diminish Christ.

1564: John Calvin preached his last sermon. As he spoke, his mouth filled with blood and he had to leave the pulpit.

1749: Isaac Backus, a Baptist leader, was threatened with jail if he did not pay the state Church tax in Massachusetts. Someone else paid it for him, but Backus lobbied powerfully for separation of Church and state.

1992: Dedicated Christian and Missionary Alliance missionary Robert Revel Hess died. Hess, with his wife, served for twenty-eight years in the Philippines. During World War II, his entire family was incarcerated by the Japanese. His son was born in prison. Hess was later rescued and returned to active ministry.

Savonarola Burned Lewd Works of Art

Savonarola slipped out of his home in Ferrara without saying good-bye to his parents. The twenty-three-year-old left secretly because he feared that his family would not approve of what he was doing. He had become convinced of the reality of an afterlife that would bring everyone either dismal doom or glorious salvation, so he threw aside years of medical and philosophical education to join the Dominicans.

When he began to preach, his strong sense of right drove him to denounce the sins of the day. At first his sermons were too scholarly for the masses, but he soon simplified them. Large audiences heard him utter dark prophecies about the future of Italy and compare the Church to a prostitute.

Savonarola became abbot of San Marco at Florence. His allies formed a republic, and soon gangs of Dominicans roamed the streets, enforcing a dress code and begging for food. Savonarola denounced the sins of corrupt Pope Alexander VI and called on Europe's leaders to throw the pontiff out of office.

Alexander plotted to bring down the friar, but he knew that he could bide his time, for he realized that sooner or later Florence would turn against Savonarola.

For the time being, however, Savonarola rode high in public opinion. No building could hold the thousands who thronged to hear his sermons. He called on the Florentines to burn all books, paintings, carvings and any other luxury that drew their hearts away from God. Florence listened. On this day in 1497, Savonarola consigned the follies of the city to a great "bonfire of the vanities." Dirty pictures, gambling tables, books and art went up in smoke. Savonarola especially loathed paintings that made the Madonna, in his opinion, look like a whore.

But in 1498 the situation changed. Although some of Savonarola's predictions came true, others proved false. Bad decisions, not all Savonarola's, brought the city to the brink of starvation. Its money chests were empty. Alexander VI threatened an interdict (which would cut off all religious functions from the people).

The people of Florence turned against the preacher. A Franciscan challenged Savonarola to an ordeal by fire. Savonarola's disciple, Domenico da Pescia, accepted in his place. Crowds gathered to watch, but the Franciscan chickened out. Cheated of their spectacle, the crowds blamed Savonarola. The next day he was arrested.

Between April 9 and May 23, Church authorities tortured Savonarola again and again and forced him to recant. Each time, when he recovered from the torment, he ate his words—the last time with such fury that his interrogators became frightened of him. On May 22 he was interrogated one last time. His interrogators saw that he could not be moved, so they sent him back to his cell in shackles and sentenced him to death.

The sentence was carried out on May 23. As he went to the scaffold, did Savonarola remember the words of a sermon he had once preached on how to prepare for death?

Savonarola preaching in fiery style. (Lord, John. *Beacon Lights of History*. New York: James Clarke, 1886.)

> First, run to Christ Crucified and behold His loving kindness: He willingly was crucified and died in order to save you. Trust that if you run to Him with a contrite heart, He will help you, even if you have committed a thousand sins.

It seems so, for he prayed, "O Lord, a thousand times have You wiped out my iniquity. I do not rely on my own justification, but on Thy mercy."

Savonarola and two other friars were first hung and then burned. As the reformer's body was dumped into the fire, scoffers shouted, "If you can work miracles, work one now!" His hand flew up, two fingers extended, as if he was blessing the crowd. The crowd panicked and fled from the square, crushing several children to death.

Other Events

543: According to a story told by Pope St. Gregory the Great, St. Scholastica, the twin sister of St. Benedict, founder of the Benedictines, had a premonition of her death while her brother was visiting her on this day. She had founded a convent five miles from her brother's famed monastery. She asked him to stay with her as her death approached, but he refused. Not to be defeated, she lowered her eyes in prayer. A severe thunderstorm developed, preventing Benedict from departing. St. Scholastica died three days later.

561: Pope Pelagius II died. He protested when a council gave the patriarch of Constantinople the title "Universal Bishop." (Note: This is not the Pelagius whose doctrine of salvation was condemned by Augustine and the Church.)

1528: The Swiss canton of Bern embraced the Reformation with an official mandate following twenty days of public disputation. Five years earlier, preachers had been ordered to teach only what they could prove from Scripture. The Reformation was supported by the middle class and magistrates.

Scholastica, Benedict's twin. (Courtesy of the Christian History Institute archives.)

Paul may have sailed this day. (Baring-Gould, S. *Lives of the Saints*. Edinburgh: John Grant, 1914.)

February 8

Paul Sails from Malta—Maybe

Dating the events that are related in the New Testament is a tricky business that has many potential pitfalls. Controversy swirls around any attempt to tie a calendar date to a specific event in the lives of Christ, Paul or other biblical figures. Scholars are always delighted when they can link an event from the Gospels or the Acts of the Apostles with a date that can be determined from non-biblical sources. It helps them to fit the events together chronologically.

Because we are given so much detail about Paul, not only by Luke but by Paul himself in his letters, historians have many facts that they can attempt to tie in with ancient writings and archaeological finds. We know, for example, that Paul was brought before Gallio in the year that Gallio was proconsul of Achaia. We know that Paul met Priscilla and Aquilla after they had been expelled from Rome. We know also that he stood before Festus in Festus's first year as governor of Judea. If dates for those events can be determined, a rough outline of Paul's movements may be sketched out.

According to Jack Finegan's reckoning in the *Handbook of Biblical Chronology*, Paul was converted in the year 36. For years he preached the gospel, always going to Jews first, and when the majority rejected him, turning to the Gentiles. His gospel taught salvation by faith in the crucified and resurrected Christ, whom he had seen with his own eyes. As he told the Corinthians, "I determined not to know any thing among you, save Jesus Christ, and him crucified" (1 Corinthians 2:2, KJV).

Despite great adversity, Paul carried the gospel through Asia Minor and southern Europe. In fact, Europe is Christian today in large measure because of Paul's zeal. Eventually Paul was arrested in Jerusalem, where he was imprisoned for several years. He finally appealed to Caesar for his release, which was his right as a Roman citizen. As a result of the appeal, he was shipped off to Rome under guard, probably in the year 57. On the way, he and his companions were wrecked on the island of Malta, where they wintered in the custody of Roman soldiers.

On this day in the year 58, Paul may have sailed from Malta. Pliny tells us in his *Natural History* (an early encyclopedic work) that February 8 was the date when spring opened the seas to voyagers. If the sailors who manned the ship that Paul sailed on acted on the traditional date, we may actually have pinned down an exact moment in Paul's life. But with the evidence we have today we cannot know for certain. Even the year is conjectural.

Pius IX didn't back the war with Austria. (McGovern, James J. *The Life and Life-Work of Pope Leo XIII*. Chicago: Monarch Books, 1903.)

Other Events

1587: Mary Queen of Scots was beheaded for entering into treasonous plots against Elizabeth I. Although this was a political act, it had religious ripples because some Roman Catholics had favored removing Elizabeth and placing Mary on the English throne.

1716: Peter the Great of Russia implemented a new law requiring confession to the Orthodox Church once a year.

1849: Three years into the reign of Pope Pius IX, the Italian state took away the pope's temporal powers because he had refused to throw the papacy's weight behind a war against Austria. The Church was accused of interfering in European politics and of enslaving the serfs on its papal estates.

1958: Bishop Tang of Canton, China, was arrested for refusing to join China's Communist-controlled Patriotic movement.

"Old Eloquence" Awarded the Presidency

The election of 1824 had given none of the three candidates a majority vote. Who would be the next President of the United States? Under the Constitution, the House of Representatives must decide the matter.

On this day in 1825, they did. After Henry Clay threw his support to John Quincy Adams in a secret deal that raised howls of corruption by the supporters of Andrew Jackson, the House chose Adams. He was the first President's son to become President himself. (George W. Bush was the second.)

Before holding America's highest office, Adams had been a lawyer, senator, diplomat and secretary of state. That a man of such firm faith could be elected to such an important governmental role is a reflection of America's religious roots. If Christianity is proven by character, Adams was surely a Christian. He was a stubborn man whose motto was "watch and pray" and who spoke openly of his trust in God. But it was not for this that he won the nickname "Old Eloquence." Rather, it was for championing principle and attacking the institution of slavery.

He was an unyielding patriarch, tough as the granite of his native New England. He prayed daily. He also read several chapters of the Bible (in the original Hebrew and Greek) and drew strength from them every day. Not content merely to read, however, he acted on what he read. So often did he put principle before party that he became highly unpopular with those of his own followers who wanted to reap the spoils of their political victory.

Adams did not let his unpopularity alter his course. As he said in a letter to his father:

> The Sermon on the Mount commends me to lay up for myself treasures, not on earth, but in Heaven. My hopes of a future life are all founded upon the Gospel of Christ.

Christ was central to Adams' theology. He had walked for a time with the Unitarians, a sect that denied the full divinity of Christ. But his reading of the Bible eventually convinced him that Unitarian doctrine was false. He embraced the traditional Christian position that Jesus is God incarnate and our only path to salvation.

His father held a view that diminished Christ. With characteristic honesty, Adams Quincy tried to change his father's mind, writing:

> I find in the New Testament Jesus Christ accosted in His own presence by one of His disciples as God, without disclaiming the appellation . . . I see him named in the great prophecy of Isaiah concerning him to be the mighty God.

After his single term as President, Adams returned to Congress.

John Quincy Adams served one term as President of the United States. He was known as "Old Eloquence" in part because of his pleas for integrity. (Wildman, Edwin. *The Builders of America*. Boston: L.C. Page & Company, 1925.)

Other Events

1119: Calixtus II became pope. By negotiating the Concordat of Worms, he resolved a long-running quarrel with the Holy Roman Empire over lay investiture, determining that the Church, not politicians, should name bishops.

1555: During the reign of Queen Mary, John Hooper, formerly bishop of Gloucester, then of Worcester, was burned at the stake in England on a charge of heresy. Several years before, he had embraced Protestant views and married.

1709: The Wesley home burned. John was nearly killed. Afterward, he always referred to himself as a brand plucked from a burning fire.

1958: David Wilkerson decided to sell his TV and pray for two hours a night. Soon afterward, the Lord led him to begin work with New York gangs. He wrote *The Cross and the Switchblade* and other books telling his story.

John Wesley rescued from his burning home. (Hyde, A.B. *Story of Methodism*. Greenfield, MA: Willey and Co., 1887.)

Prior to the passing of laws allowing common people to read the Bible, believers were forced to read the Bible in secret. (Armitage, Thomas. *A History of the Baptists: Traced by Their Principles and Practices, From the Time of Our Lord and Saviour Jesus Christ to the Present*. New York: Bryan, Taylor and Co., 1893.)

February 10

The Bible Makes the Newspapers

Can you imagine the announcement of a new version of the Bible stirring up so much interest that your local newspaper felt obliged to print the entire text of the New Testament? That actually happened in the nineteenth century. What an improvement from the days when common people had to read Bibles secretly for dread of religious authorities!

A Bible version long in use can become cherished through familiarity. Today, when we have almost too many versions, it can be difficult for us to understand the excitement that was caused when the Authorized (King James) Version, long venerated by the English-speaking world, was revised. Three million copies of the New Testament sold within a year, and the full text was printed in two Chicago newspapers within two days of its reaching the United States. That is the kind of interest the Word of God generated back then!

When the Authorized Version was first compiled, it was based on earlier English translations, all of which traced back to Tyndale's translation, whose New Testament was in turn translated directly from the Greek text of Erasmus. In truth, the Authorized Version cannot really be called a translation at all since the compilers simply made a choice of words between existing English versions, with few other changes.

After the making of the King James Version, several Greek texts came to light, all older than Erasmus's manuscript. Among these were the Sinaitic, Vatican and Alexandrian manuscripts. A manuscript of the Septuagint (the early Jewish translation of the Old Testament into Greek) also turned up. Each of these finds underscored the need for revisions in the accepted text to bring it into closer conformity with the original.

Although scholars agreed that the King James was inaccurate in some details (but not in any essential doctrine or important emphasis), laymen were unwilling to part with its familiar words and phrases. And, of course, men remembered the fierce battles by which the Bible had been won, often over the ashes of martyrs. Probably no single "correction" of the King James Version caused as much outrage as that of Isaiah 7:14. In the King James it reads, "Behold, a virgin shall conceive, and bear a son, and shall call his name Immanuel." The Revised Version substituted "young woman" for "virgin."

Apart from the understandable upset over this lapse, the opposition to the Revised Version was ironic, for the King James itself had been greeted with just such grumbles in its own day. But the King James Version's musical prose soon earned it the status of a literary masterpiece. In fact, no one can say how greatly its cadences have molded the English tongue.

As a concession to those who loved the beauty of the old King James language, the revisers retained much of it. In fact, they sometimes opted for idioms predating even Shakespeare. The revised translation was not a modern-language version by any stretch of the imagination. It had, however, solved some textual problems. And, despite criticism, tens of thousands of copies were sold immediately upon its publication.

On this day in 1899, use of the Revised Version was authorized as the standard for the Church of England. However, the English psalter stayed with Coverdale's translation of the psalms, because a long tradition of music had been set to them. The Revised Standard Version is a later revision of the Revised Version.

Johann Mayer, a.k.a. Eck. (Bezold. *Geschichte der Deutschen Reformation*. Berlin: Grote, 1890.)

Other Events

1543: Johann Mayer, known as "Johann Eck," died. He was a champion of Catholicism against Martin Luther.

1787: Charles Chauncy, an American clergyman who condemned the Great Awakening as emotional extravagance, died.

1829: Pope Leo XII died. He was a strong opponent of secret societies such as the Freemasons. Through his warm personality, statesmanship and encyclicals (papal letters to the bishops of the Church), he raised the prestige of the papacy.

1927: John Sung, a Chinese student in the United States, gave up his desire to live after having studied many world religions and finding them all empty. On this night he was overwhelmed with a vision of Christ. He then denounced Henry Emerson Fosdick for having caused him to lose his faith earlier. School authorities pulled strings and had Sung committed to a lunatic asylum for six months. Upon his release, he returned to China, where he became a great evangelist.

1939: Pope Pius XI died. He had negotiated the restoration of papal authority over the Vatican city. During his pontificate, an agreement with Mexico ended persecution of the Roman Catholic Church in that nation. He issued a record number of more than twenty encyclicals.

1973: During the terror-filled reign of Ugandan dictator Idi Amin, several Christians were shot in a stadium in Kabale, Uganda.

1977: Ugandan bishops bravely protested Idi Amin's persecution of the Church and the mistreatment of his people.

World's Smallest State Established

The story of the papacy in the 1800s was one of riches to rags. When Pope Pius IX was crowned in 1846, the Church owned the Papal States: 17,000 square miles of Italian territory as well as parts of Rome. When Pius IX died, he was a prisoner of the vatican and the papal lands were gone.

For over 1,000 years the Church had been the biggest landlord in Italy. Under a good administrator like Gregory the Great, the lands were well-managed and the peasants were cared for. Under other popes, however, conditions were sometimes quite different: Peasants were oppressed, power was abused (prisons in the Papal States held thousands of political prisoners) and the Church often meddled unhealthily in Italian politics. Popes like Julius II were warriors rather than "fishers of men" or pastors. Others, like Pius IX, faced serious dilemmas, such as whether they should exercise military force against other Catholics or not.

In Pius IX's case, his refusal to send troops from the Papal States to fight Catholic Austrians demonstrated the incompatibility of a moral papacy with the exercise of political power. When Italy lost its war against Austria, mobs turned against the pope and he was forced to flee to the kingdom of Naples. On February 9, 1849, the Italians declared a Republic, headed by the revolutionary leader Giuseppe Mazzini. After various shifts of control, Italy completed the takeover of papal lands in 1870. The newly consolidated Italian nation took away the Vatican's status as a separate nation. For its part, the Vatican, which had always dealt directly with foreign powers, continued to receive foreign ambassadors. An uneasy coexistence developed between Church and state.

At times, the Italian government seemed to be just waiting for an excuse to pounce upon Vatican City and impose police rule. As a case in point, when Leo XIII became pope, the secular authorities made it clear they would not protect the Vatican from riots. They allowed hoodlums to smash the windows of any house that displayed lights in celebration of the new pope.

Despite the hardships it endured, it is arguable that the loss of lands was good for the Church. Deprived of lands, papal leaders could, and to a large extent did, concentrate more on spiritual and moral issues. In his encyclical on faith and religion, *Qui Pluribus,* Pius wrote:

> So when we reflect on the most serious duties of the supreme apostolate, especially in a period of great instability, we would simply have fallen into great sadness did we not place all our hope in God who is our Saviour. For He never abandons those who hope in Him.

In 1929, Mussolini needed the support of Catholics if he was to consolidate his power base. He sought an agreement with the Church. Under the agreement, Italy recognized the sovereign status of the Vatican. On this day in 1929, the 109 acres of Vatican City became the smallest nation in the world and was placed completely under the jurisdiction of the pope. The Italian authorities promised they would no longer interfere with the Vatican's internal affairs.

The Vatican. (Begni, Ernesto. *Vatican: Its History—Its Treasures*. New York: Letters and Arts Pub. Co., 1914.)

During World War II the independence of the Vatican was of considerable significance to Jewish and Allied fugitives. Church agents, acting covertly from the Vatican, rescued many who would otherwise have perished. Today, its independence allows the Vatican to negotiate with the nations and religions of the world. It even has observer status at the United Nations.

Other Events

1302: King Philip IV "the Fair" of France publicly burned the papal bull *Ausculta Fili,* which excommunicated him. He was a cruel man who grasped for gold and debased the French coinage. He retaliated against the papal bull by having Pope Boniface VIII seized and imprisoned.

1526: Martin Luther's books were burned by Roman Catholic authorities at St. Pauls, London. "Little" Bilney, who won Hugh Latimer to Christ, was forced to abjure at that time.

1858: Marie-Bernarde Soubirous, a misused fourteen-year-old peasant girl, told her parents she had seen the apparition of a lovely woman at the grotto of the rocks in Lourdes. Later, she said that the woman was the Virgin Mary. Then a spring mysteriously appeared at the site, where no water had flowed before. When the story got around, Lourdes became a center for healing, and it receives hundreds of thousands of visitors a year.

1888: John Smith Moffat, a missionary and an agent of empire builder Cecil Rhodes, for whom Rhodesia (now Zimbabwe) was named, made a treaty with the African king Lobengula. By this treaty the Matabele people came under British protection. This close relationship between missionaries and colonialists both helped and hindered the spread of the gospel.

The Grotto at Lourdes. An image of Mary has been installed. (Boissarie, Prosper Gustave. *Die Grosse Heilung von Lourdes*. Luxemburg: J.P. Baustert; Cincinnati: Kommissionsverlag Benziger, 1902.)

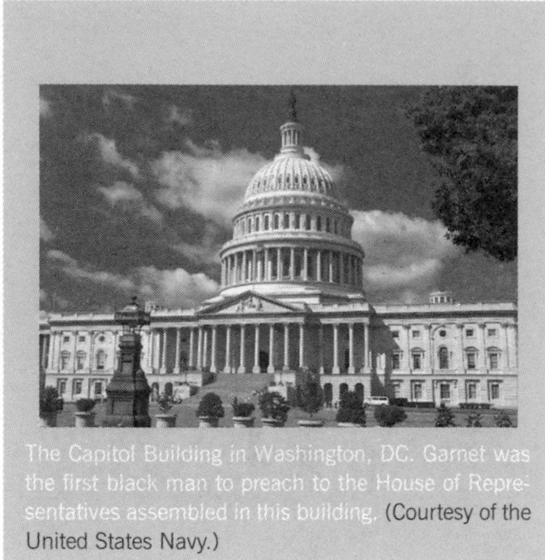

The Capitol Building in Washington, DC. Garnet was the first black man to preach to the House of Representatives assembled in this building. (Courtesy of the United States Navy.)

February 12

First Black Man to Preach to the US House of Representatives

Presbyterian minister Henry Highland Garnet was the first African American to preach a sermon in the House of Representatives.

On this day in 1865, the galleries of the United States House of Representatives were packed. African Americans and Caucasians alike vied for a place from which they might observe and share in the historic moment. For the first time in the history of the Republic, a black man—and an ex-slave at that—was about to address the House of Representatives.

President Lincoln had asked Garnet to deliver a sermon in the United States House of Representatives. Other national leaders added their encouragement. Now Garnet stood poised to give one of the two most important speeches of his life. He had delivered the other speech twenty-two years earlier, in 1843.

Garnet was born a slave in Maryland in 1815. With the help of Quakers, nine-year-old Garnet escaped with his father and other family members. Eventually the fugitives settled in New York, where Garnet received an education. Unable to find work, he went to sea. On his return from a voyage to Cuba, he found that his home had been raided by slave hunters and his sister had been seized. His father had escaped by leaping from an upstairs window. Furious, the boy bought a bowie knife and stalked the streets, bent on revenge. However, his friends coaxed him to lie low.

In 1835, Garnet was given another reason to be angry. He and thirteen other black students were admitted to Noyes Academy in Canaan, New Hampshire. On July 4, they spoke up for the abolition of slavery. This angered local Caucasians, and in retaliation they dragged the schoolhouse into a swamp. Garnet was seriously ill, but he was forced to flee all the same. He crossed the mountains into New York, where he took a steamboat to safety. His friends spread their coats on the deck to cushion him during the trip. He was bedridden for two months.

Afterward, he was invited to study for the ministry. Even before his ordination, he began to pastor a church. Eventually, he became a Presbyterian missionary to Jamaica.

It was at the Negro National Convention in Buffalo, New York, in 1843 that Garnet made the first speech that brought him to national attention. He called on America's 4 million slaves to revolt. "You had far better all die—die immediately—than live as slaves," he cried. "If you must bleed, let it all come at once—rather die freemen, than live to be the slaves." He went on to state that slaves were not allowed to keep God's laws and therefore they must throw off the wicked system that oppressed them.

In his second important speech, standing in the House of Representatives, Garnet compared those who kept slaves to the Pharisees whom Jesus charged with laying heavy burdens on others while refusing to lift a finger themselves. He exclaimed,

> Great God! I would as soon attempt to enslave Gabriel or Michael as to enslave a man made in the image of God, and for whom Christ died. Slavery is snatching man from the high place to which he was lifted by the hand of God, and dragging him down to the level of the brute creation, where he is made to be the companion of the horse and the fellow of the ox.

Garnet died in Liberia in 1882, where he had joined those who advocated the establishment of a state of free African Americans there.

Franz Joseph Haydn professed to be a Christian and wrote works with Christian themes. (Haddne, J. Cuthbert. *Haydn*. London: J.M. Dent and Sons, Ltd; New York: E.P. Dutton and Co., Inc., 1902.)

Other Events

1049: St. Leo IX was consecrated pope. He instituted Church reforms and attempted to end simony (the practice of buying religious office). Using tours and synods, he spread his ideas quite effectively.

1111: Henry V renounced investiture with the treaty of Sutri. The insistence of emperors and kings to a right to appoint bishops had long been a thorn of contention between Church and state.

1797: "The Emperor's Hymn" (Austrian national anthem) was first sung at Emperor Francis II's fifth birthday. Set to music by Franz Joseph Haydn, it is the tune to which we sing the hymn "Glorious Things of Thee Are Spoken." Haydn, a professing Christian who lived openly in adultery, wrote many works with Christian themes, such as the oratorio *The Creation*.

1878: Scotsman Alexander Duff died. Despite ill health, he spent many years as the Church of Scotland's first missionary to India. He had been shipwrecked on arriving to India and had lost all his books and clothes. However, his Bible, wrapped in a package, floated ashore. The very next day, Duff began a Bible class with five boys. Within a week it had grown to 300. A few years later a church of 1,000 members stood on the very spot where he had first preached. When forced to return to Scotland because of ailments, Duff continued to promote missions.

Glorious Revolution

An extraordinary event occurred in the year 1689: William III of Orange took the British throne in a bloodless revolution.

King James II had not hesitated to exert his royal authority as he saw fit. The problem was that the Roman Catholic king used his powers to browbeat Anglicans and raise Catholics to positions of authority.

On this day in 1689, Parliament granted the throne to William with certain religious and civil conditions:

> Whereas the late King James II . . . did endeavor to subvert and extirpate the Protestant religion, and the laws and liberties of this kingdom . . . [we] do resolve that William and Mary, Prince and Princess of Orange, be declared King and Queen of England.

James might have kept his throne if he'd been more merciful to rebels early in his reign and more accommodating to the interests of his people. Protestantism was firmly entrenched, and the English had no desire to return to the Catholicism whose hierarchy seemed contradictory to the democratic ideals of their short experience with a liberating parliamentary system. For those churchgoers who thought about it, a return to Catholicism seemed a return from a gospel of faith to a life of works. Liberties were still scarce enough that people prized those they had won, and not least of those was the principle that the king could not ride roughshod over Parliament.

James had a knack for rousing suspicion. He raised a personal army of 13,000 men, which was perceived as a threat to Parliament, and he accepted subsidies from Louis XIV, the Catholic king of France. Jeffries, a cruel and dishonest man, was his leading judge, and James made him a lord. James forbade clergymen to preach on certain political topics and arrested John Sharp when he gave a sermon on the motives of converts.

At that time, the universities of Cambridge and Oxford were training grounds for Anglican priests. Even knowing that, James tried to force Cambridge to accept a Roman Catholic student. The schoolmen resisted, and James became furious. He then tried to usurp Magdalen College's longstanding right to elect its own president and compel them to accept a Roman Catholic as head of the school. Again the schoolmen balked. The situation worsened when Anglican churchmen refused to read James's Declaration of Indulgence from their pulpits. The Declaration was an excellent grant of religious liberty, but it was seen as an attempt to defy Parliament. James brought four Anglicans to trial for their refusal of the Declaration, but the jury acquitted them.

William III. Disgruntled with King James II, Parliament invited William and Mary to accept the English throne. (Green, John Richard. *A Short History of the English People*. New York: Harper & Brothers, 1893-5.)

What finally brought James down was the birth of his son. Rather than face the prospect of a Catholic heir, the English decided to replace James with a Protestant. They contacted his daughter Mary and son-in-law, William, who accepted the offer of the crown. William was made king under the Declaration of Right. That declaration "forever" barred anyone of the Roman Catholic faith from possessing the English throne.

Other Events

962: Otho I, Germanic emperor, issued privileges to the Roman Catholic Church. He was in a position to do so because he had been generally victorious in a long succession of wars.

1199: Stephen I, ruler of the Serbs and Bosnians, died. His son was the famous St. Sava. Three years before his death, Stephen relinquished his power and joined Sava in a monastery at Mount Athos.

1633: Galileo, an old man, arrived in Rome on a litter to answer charges before the Inquisition. He recanted his scientific views, and his judges placed him under house arrest.

1793: Pietist Christian Friedrich Schwartz, "Apostle of India," died. He left the University of Halle for the mission field, where he died. So great was his influence that the rajah of Tanjore erected a monument to him.

1926: In a move to reduce the influence of its Church, Mexico deported foreign monks and nuns.

Galileo Galilei's notorious confrontation with the Church occurred on this day. (Lord, John. *Beacon Lights of History*. New York: James Clarke, 1886.)

February

14 Cyril Destined for Lasting Fame

Cyril and Methodius, the brothers who brought Christianity to the Slavs. (Baring-Gould, S. *Lives of the Saints*. Edinburgh: John Grant, 1914.)

When Cyril died on this day in 869, he left behind one of the greatest legacies any man has been graced to give the world. His influence and that of his brother Methodius reverberates down to our own day. So lasting is their imprint that the two are called "the Apostles of the Slavs."

Around 860, Rastislav, a prince of the Moravians, requested that the Byzantine emperor send someone to teach his people about Christ. The Byzantine patriarch Photius delegated the noble-born brothers Cyril and Methodius to the task.

They were a logical choice. Both were learned and pious. They were inhabitants of Thessalonica, Greece, and they were no strangers to eastern Europe. Furthermore, they had carried out diplomatic missions for Byzantium with the Abassid Caliph and with the Khazars. As if that were not enough, Cyril was a professor of some standing at the University of Constantinople and had won the nickname "the Philosopher."

The brothers were of Slavic origin themselves, so they knew the language and began developing a special alphabet to capture its sounds. This Glagolitic script was based on the Greek alphabet and was developed by followers into the Cyrillic, which became the alphabet of learning and commerce in eastern Europe.

Using this script, the brothers translated Scripture, Church liturgy and other writings into the Slavic tongue. These old Church writings taught salvation through faith in Christ to the people in a voice they could understand, and Christianity spread among the Slavic peoples as a result.

For a time, Magyar invasions and German opposition wiped out the religious gains the brothers had made, but not the alphabet or the writings. Disciples transplanted Christianity to Bulgaria and carried the precious translations south with them. When Vladimir of Russia converted to Christianity a century later, he adopted the Orthodox faith. Copies of the brothers' translations and writings made their way to his court, where they influenced the Russian Church for many centuries. A variation of Cyrillic script became the alphabet of Russia.

German bishops of the Roman Catholic Church had criticized the brothers and argued that the Slavs should use Roman-style worship. Cyril and Methodius traveled west to defend their practices. Pope Hadrian II accepted their work with enthusiasm, but this did not please the Germans.

In the end, the Germans got their way. When Methodius returned to Moravia as a papal legate, he was consecrated an archbishop. The Germans, however, seized him. After a trial that violated Church law, they imprisoned him for three years in a monastery. It took the intervention of a pope to free him. He died on April 6, 884, fifteen years after his brother.

In his commemoration of the eleventh century of Cyril and Methodius's work, Pope John Paul II said:

> We can look in a new way—a more mature and profound way—at these two holy figures, now separated from us by eleven centuries. And we can read in their lives and apostolic activity the elements that the wisdom of divine Providence placed in them, so that they might be revealed with fresh fullness in our own age and might bear new fruits.

Benedict VIII. (Montor, Chevalier Artaud de. *Lives and Times of the Popes*. New York: Catholic Publication Society of America, 1911.)

Other Events

270: According to tradition, this was the day Valentine was beheaded. No one knows for sure which Valentine is meant (there are three in the Church calendar) or how his name became connected to love letters.

1014: Pope Benedict VIII crowned Henry II as Holy Roman Emperor. A layman who became pope, Benedict was forced on the Church by the powerful house of Tusculum, which controlled Rome. He defeated the Saracens and prohibited clergy marriages.

1130: Pope Honorius II died. At his accession, two popes had been elected. Both resigned and Honorius was reelected. He restored discipline to the monastic houses of Cluny and Monte Cassino and achieved reconciliation with major European powers.

1556: Thomas Cranmer, archbishop of Canterbury, was degraded from his office with humiliating ceremonies. In due course, he was burned as a heretic by the Roman Catholics after he renounced the pope as "Christ's enemy and anti-Christ, with all his false doctrine."

1953: Bishop Andrew Kagura of Kenya was martyred for his outspokenness against the Mau Mau revolutionaries.

Baptism of a Grand Duke

By 1386 only one European people remained largely without Christian influence: the Lithuanians. They were a fierce people without fixed boundaries who at times controlled large tracts of eastern Europe. The gospel had been brought to Lithuania fifty years before but had never taken root. The country's eventual conversion is an interesting story.

Jogaila (or Jagiello), grand duke of the Lithuanians, was battling the Teutonic Knights, a quasi-Christian order. These knights had originated as military nurses in a crusader hospital in Jerusalem but became the terror of eastern Europe upon their return there. Although their mission was to fight infidels, they turned their weapons against Christians also, seizing whatever lands they could and reducing freemen to serfs. Among the lands they controlled were Estonia, Livonia, Prussia and East Pomerania.

The knights repeatedly assaulted Lithuania and were repulsed. Lithuania was a significant power at the time: It controlled eastern Europe from the Baltic to the Black Sea and stretched eastward almost to Moscow. Jogaila looked about for an ally. Poland, having suffered so much from the knights, seemed the natural choice for an alliance. The Poles were agreeable on one condition: Jogaila must convert to Christianity. And so, on this day in 1386, Jogaila was baptized, taking the name Ladislas. When he returned to Lithuania he was accompanied by many priests.

Jogaila's conversion is important for several reasons: 1) It marked the end of established paganism in Europe; 2) the see at Vilnius, which still exists, was founded as a result; and 3) as part of the deal with Poland, Jogaila married Jadwiga (Hedwig), the heiress of Poland's throne. He was an illiterate, thirty-six-year-old, recently converted heathen, and she was a highly literate sixteen-year-old who had been raised solidly Catholic and had been "ruler" of Poland since the age of eleven. Despite their disparate backgrounds, however, they managed to rule well together. Under Ladislas and his offspring, Poland became a Christian commonwealth and enjoyed a rare century of peace. The Jogaila dynasty eventually ruled Hungary and Bohemia as well.

The combined might of Lithuania and Poland destroyed the Teutonic Knights, although the masterful king did not bring this about until 1410 in the Battle at Tannenberg. Armies of 100,000 men each clashed that day. The Teutonic Knights left behind 18,000 dead, 14,000 captives and their grand master. It was the beginning of the end of the troublesome order.

A statue commemorating Jogaila, the grand duke of Lithuania, who converted to Christianity in order to assume the throne of Poland and who brought Lithuania into the Christian fold. (Slocombe, G.E. *Poland*. London: T.C. & E.C. Jack, Limited; New York: Frederick A. Stokes Co., 1916.)

Other Events

1145: Pope Lucius II died. Unsuccessful in quelling local riots, he was killed when struck by a paving stone that was hurled at him while he led troops against a mob.

1730: Thomas Bray died on this day. He founded the Society for Promoting Christian Knowledge, organized the Anglican Church of Maryland and secured a charter for the Society for the Propagation of the Gospel in Foreign Parts.

1776: On his wedding day, James Taylor, the grandfather of Hudson Taylor, the founder of the China Inland Mission, converted to Christianity.

1865: Nicholas Wiseman, a Catholic educator and spokesman, died on this day. His writings helped lower British distrust of Catholic political ideas.

1905: Lew Wallace, author of *Ben Hur*, a famous novel on the life of Christ, died.

1977: Ponsiano Lwakatale, a Ugandan pastor, was miraculously saved from death at the hands of a Ugandan chief who tried to kill him. The chief raised his spear, Christians prayed, and the chief was unable to drive the spear through the pastor.

Lew Wallace, war hero and author of the famous novel *Ben Hur*. (Wallace, Lewis. *The Story of American Heroism: Thrilling Narratives of Personal Adventures During the Great Civil War as Told by The Medal Winners and Roll of Honor Men*. Philadelphia: Calvert & Co., 1897.)

Melanchthon, Luther's number-two man. (McGiffert, Arthur Cushman. *Martin Luther, the Man and His Work*. New York: The Century Co., 1911.)

FEBRUARY

16

Who Would Have Thought?

On this day in 1497 was born a man of peace into an age of conflict, a reasoner into a world of passion. His birth name was Philip Schwarzerd, which means "black earth," and in Latin is *Melanchthon*. At the age of ten, Philip was orphaned, and his grandmother took him in. Famed German humanist Johannes Reuchlin was his grand uncle.

Like his grand uncle, Melanchthon was a good scholar. He entered the University of Heidelberg at the age of twelve. Two years later he graduated with his bachelor's degree. He tutored while adding to his knowledge of Greek. Soon afterward he entered the University of Tübingen, where he received his master's degree. After he graduated, he was awarded a position as professor of Greek at Wittenberg. As such, he could not fail to meet Martin Luther, who was stirring the cauldron of the Christian world.

Melanchthon was ripe for reform. Having read Erasmus's Greek Testament, he was convinced that salvation must be by faith rather than works. He backed Luther in public dispute. Not content to argue orally, Melanchthon also defended his position in writing. With careful reasoning he clarified what the Reformation was all about. Others called him the brains behind the movement.

Because he was a peaceable man, Melanchthon was the natural person for Luther to ask to prepare a statement to deliver to Emperor Charles V. Charles had summoned the German Diet to settle the nation's religious differences and prepare a defense against the Turks, who were then threatening Europe. Melanchthon's statement was conciliatory:

> [W]e offer, in this matter of religion, the Confession of our preachers and of ourselves, showing what manner of doctrine from the Holy Scriptures and the pure Word of God has been up to this time . . . taught in our churches.

Twenty-one points emphasized doctrines on which both sides were largely agreed:

> [T]he Word, that is, the Son of God, did assume the human nature in the womb of the blessed Virgin Mary, so that there are two natures, the divine and the human, inseparably enjoined in one Person, one Christ, true God and true man, who was born of the Virgin Mary, truly suffered, was crucified, dead, and buried, that He might reconcile the Father unto us, and be a sacrifice, not only for original guilt, but also for all actual sins of men.

Seven points addressed differences between Catholics and Protestants. The key difference was that justification of the soul is by faith alone. Known as the Augsburg Confession, it remains a basic statement of Lutheran doctrine.

Rome rejected the Confession. Melanchthon continued to strive for a formula that would be acceptable to all sides, feeling strongly that the Church must not remain divided. But his voice of reason was lost in the roar of the day. Even Luther turned on the mild scholar because Melanchthon would not accept the great reformer's vehement position on the Sacrament. Luther blasted his quiet friend mercilessly. On his death bed, Luther felt remorse for this. "Dear Philip, I confess to have gone too far in the affair of the Sacrament," he wrote.

Melanchthon lived for several years after Luther died, steadily teaching at Wittenberg but too often ignored by the radicals who pushed to the front of the Protestant movement. In the end, his quiet soul longed for death as a way to escape the "frenzy of theologians." Nonetheless, his Augsburg Confession remained one of the few writings mutually respected by the quarreling reformers.

Cardinal Wolsey was asked to select the new abbot of Glastonbury. (Besant, Sir Walter. *London in the Time of the Tudors*. London: A. & C. Black, 1904.)

Other Events

1525: Richard Bere, abbot of Glastonbury, died. The monks asked Cardinal Richard Wolsey to choose their next abbot. Some days later, with the approval of the king, Wolsey appointed Richard Whiting. About a decade later, after the king had begun dissolving the monasteries, he executed Whiting for treason.

1801: The African Methodist Episcopal Zion Church (AMEZ) was incorporated as a denomination separate from its parent organization, the Methodist Episcopal Church. The racist practices of most existing churches led African-American groups to separate themselves from Caucasians.

1910: Robert T. Ketcham was converted under the ministry of Harry S. Tillis. After his conversion, he became a preacher and a key leader in forming the General Association of Regular Baptist Churches. He also edited their magazine, the *Baptist Bulletin*.

1921: Rev. Jason Lee was accepted by the United States House of Representatives as Oregon's greatest hero at the state of Oregon's request. Lee had labored hard for Oregon statehood, even making a transcontinental trip to testify in Washington, DC. He helped form the state's first provisional government.

The Waldensians Are Finally Relieved

Each year, on the evening of February 16, bonfires are lit on mountainsides in the north of Italy. These are a harbinger of the joyous worship services and festivities that will fill the following day. The Waldensians have reason to be glad: This day, February 17 marks the anniversary of the day in 1858 when they finally received a guarantee of civil and religious rights.

This relief had been long in coming. The Waldensian saga began in 1176. A rich merchant, Peter Waldo, heard the words of Christ to the rich young ruler: "Go, sell everything you have and give to the poor, and you will have treasure in heaven. Then come, follow me" (Mark 10:21). After hearing those words, Waldo determined to do just that. He provided for his wife, placed his daughters in a nunnery and sold his property and distributed it among the poor.

His first effort was to hire two priests to translate parts of the Scriptures into French. He memorized large portions of this translation and began to preach among the people, urging them to imitate Christ's voluntary poverty. As quickly as he made followers he sent them out by twos with the Scriptures and his message of poverty. Disgusted with voluptuous Rome, the Waldensians denounced man-made feasts. They rejected three Catholic sacraments but kept baptism, absolution, confession and the Eucharist. Like the Quakers of later years, they refused to take oaths.

Waldensians renounced altars, church buildings, holy water, indulgences and all the paraphernalia and trappings of the established Church. They denied the theology of purgatory. The local archbishop, stung by the implied rebuke, excommunicated Waldo. Waldo appealed to Pope Alexander III. Alexander was sympathetic and said Waldensians could preach with the permission of local bishops. Of course, such permission was not forthcoming.

With or without permission, Waldo and his followers continued to preach, converting souls over a wide area. Waldensians became one of the most widespread nonconformist groups of the Middle Ages. Its adherents were excommunicated and butchered. Over a course of 682 years they were forced to flee across Europe or hide in caves, and they were persecuted, hunted and exterminated like vermin. With the coming of the Reformation, many joined the Protestants. Survivors gathered in 1561 and pledged themselves to adhere to the Scriptures. Eventually, they were reduced by persecution to only a few thousand individuals. They had been allowed refuge in Switzerland, but they pined for their Italian homeland and in 1689 made a "glorious return." Not until the Italian revolutions of the mid-nineteenth century destroyed the power of the popes were the Waldensians, who were dwelling in alpine valleys of northern Italy, guaranteed their rights. After centuries of persecution, it is little wonder that the Waldensians celebrate their relief with bonfires, worship services and festivities.

Four hundred Waldensians who had taken refuge in this cave of Mount Pelvoux, in the Alps, were martyred. Their persecutors piled firewood at the cave entrance and smothered the Waldensians with smoke. They speared any who tried to run out. (Armitage, Thomas. *A History of the Baptists: Traced by Their Principles and Practices, From the Time of our Lord and Saviour Jesus Christ to the Present*. New York: Bryan, Taylor and Co., 1893.)

Other Events

1600: Giordano Bruno was burned to death by Roman Catholic authorities for his belief in multiple inhabited worlds and a number of other ideas deemed heretical.

1905: A joint resolution by the chambers of the United States Congress named Francis Willard one of America's greatest women on this day, the seventh anniversary of her death. A statue of the Christian leader was unveiled.

1912: "Praying Hyde," an intercessor for India, shouted praise to Jesus in the Punjab language.

1926: Doctor Kao was arrested. An enthusiastic, faith-filled Chinese Christian, he won many to Christ, especially in the city of Gan-djou. His stand against wrongdoing in high places led to his arrest.

1977: Ugandan radio announced the death of outspoken Archbishop Luwun. He allegedly died in a car accident, but his death was actually at the hands of Idi Amin. He had been arrested and was severely beaten before his "accident."

Bruno was burned for his views. (Chamberlain, Houston Stewart. *Immanuel Kant: A Study and a Comparison with Goete, Leonardo da Vinci, Bruno, Plato and Descartes*. London/New York: John Lane Co., 1914.)

Pilgrim's burden falls off at the foot of the cross as he begins his adventure toward the Celestial City. (Godolphin, Mary. *Pilgrim's Progress in Words of One Syllable*. New York: George Routledge, 1899.)

FEBRUARY

18

Every Pilgrim's Story Is Published

On this day in 1678, the most popular book in the Christian world, next to the Bible, was published. It is a story of fantastic creatures and deadly dangers. In his many adventures, the hero battles with a raging dragon, flounders in a bog from which he is unable to extricate himself and is chained in a castle, hostage to despair.

The book is *Pilgrim's Progress*, authored by John Bunyan while he lay in prison for preaching without a license. Since its publication, it has never been out of print. The book made Bunyan famous in his own day and has been a help to Christians for centuries since.

The hero is a pilgrim, a man named Christian, whom Bunyan introduces to us as one searching for truth and for relief from a terrible load he carries on his back. This load is sin, and as Christian reaches the foot of Christ's cross, the load tumbles off. Freed, Christian hastens by a path narrow and hard toward an eternal city. Along the way he meets a great variety of vividly described individuals, some who help and some who hinder him. And of course, there are giants and dragons that are part of an almost medieval panoply of fearsome or winsome dangers. Christian encounters Doubting Castle, the Valley of Shadow and Vanity Fair, all of which he must pass on his way to the Celestial City.

The book is rich in allegory, and many of its phrases have come into common use. We speak of a "slough of despond," of "bearing a burden of sin," of "crossing the river of death." In addition to the allegorical phrasings, the narrative itself is larded with many biblical quotes. In the margins, Bunyan cited Scripture references.

Not only English-speaking Christians but also those from the rest of the world have benefited from the tale. Often it is the first book missionaries translate when they complete the Bible in a native language. It has been translated into African, European and Asian tongues. Surprisingly, the Chinese Communist government also printed the book, and 200,000 copies sold out in 3 days.

Bunyan's pilgrim and all of the others who reach the Celestial City steadfastly hold one belief: that salvation is of Christ alone. As Hopeful says:

> I believed that . . . without the righteousness of this Christ all the world could not save me; and therefore thought I to myself, If I leave off [praying to know Christ], I die, and can but die at the Throne of Grace. And withal, this came into my mind, If it tarry, wait for it, because it will surely come, it will not tarry. So I continued praying until the Father showed me his Son.

This is the essential Christian gospel. Bunyan's pilgrim made it safely to the Celestial City by heeding and believing that message and so shall all who believe.

Crusaders and Saracens fight. (Archer, T.A. *The Crusades: The Story of the Latin Kingdom of Jerusalem*. New York: G.P. Putnam's Sons, 1895.)

Other Events

1229: Jerusalem was surrendered to crusaders following negotiations by Frederick II.

1546: Martin Luther died. More than any other man, he initiated and represented the Protestant Reformation.

1688: Quakers and Moravians united in Pennsylvania to write the Germantown Protest, America's first formal protest against slavery.

1856: Hatt-I-Humayun, an edict by the Ottoman sultan, guaranteed Christian rights in the Turkish empire.

1874: William Sandys died. He had been admitted to the bar at age twenty-two and became a lawyer. He promoted the use of Christmas carols and wrote one of the best loved of them all: "The First Noel."

Celebrating the Memory of Armenian Monk Mesrob

The monk Mesrob belongs on any list of the ten greatest men of Armenian history. One Catholic historian wrote of him, saying:

> To Mesrob we owe the preservation of the language and literature of Armenia; but for his work, the people would have been absorbed by the Persians and Syrians, and would have disappeared like so many nations of the East.

But Mesrob's importance goes beyond that. Thanks to the alphabet that he invented and the schools that he founded, old versions of the Bible and of other early Christian writings, which otherwise would have been lost, were preserved. Mesrob is remembered in Church calendars on this day, January 19.

Mesrob was born in Armenia around the year 361. He became a master of several languages. Since the Armenian language had no written alphabet, Mesrob was employed as a secretary to his king, translating his orders into Greek, Persian and Syriac so that as many people as possible could understand them.

Evidently, despite his success as a civil servant, Mesrob felt something was lacking in his life. He decided that he wanted to work directly for God, so he became a monk, took holy orders and withdrew to a monastery, where he deliberately subjected himself to suffering in order to harden his body, firm up his mind and deepen his spiritual determination. Then he went out to preach. Although he won many converts, he had great difficulty teaching them and helping them grow in their faith because there was no Christian literature written in their language. So, with financial backing from the king and phonetic help from others, Mesrob created an alphabet of thirty-six letters to represent the complex sounds of the Armenian tongue.

Armenia became a battleground between the clashing Roman and Persian empires. In Mesrob's lifetime, the foreign powers split his country between them. Historians agree that Mesrob's invention of the alphabet saved Armenia and gave it a national spirit all its own.

The Bible was soon translated into Armenian, and many other books were written or translated using the new script. The result was a body of national literature that inspired Armenian Christians and held them together when outside forces threatened to destroy them.

Mesrob, who lived on the Persian side of Armenia, got permission to preach and teach on the Roman side. He worked among the Georgians, Albanians and Aghouanghks as well, adapting his alphabet to their languages. He also planned for the future and not only preached the gospel but also built schools and appointed men to continue his work after him. Like the Apostle Paul in Asia Minor, he later went back and visited the churches he had founded as a way of strengthening them in their faith.

When he died in 441, all recognized that a great man had passed from the face of the earth. His body was laid in the crypt of the church at Oshakan. A beautiful cathedral now marks the spot.

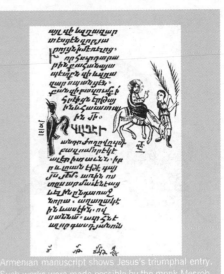

Armenian manuscript shows Jesus's triumphal entry. Such works were made possible by the monk Mesrob. (Rohrbach, Paul. *Armenmien*. Stuttgart: J. Englehorns Nachf., 1919.)

Other Events

842: Icons were returned to the graceful Hagia Sophia, the most important church of the Byzantine Empire, after the controversy over them had come full circle.

1473: Astronomer Nicolaus Copernicus was born on this day in Poland. He served for most of his life as a churchman and did not publish his "heliocentric" theory of the solar system until just before his death. It was condemned by both Catholics and Protestants but eventually revolutionized astronomy.

1568: Miles Coverdale, an early translator of the Bible into the English language and the first to issue a complete Bible, died on this day. He was also the editor of the Great Bible. During Queen Mary's reign, Coverdale fled to Europe, where he assisted in the translation of the Geneva Bible.

1948: John Trever, working at the American University of Beirut, became the first American scholar to see the Dead Sea Scrolls, conveyed to him by Father Boutris Sowmy of the Orthodox Church.

Nicolaus Copernicus, a churchman and advocate of a heliocentric solar system. (Ruoff, Henry W. *Masters of Achievement: The World's Greatest Leaders in Literature, Art, Religion, Philosophy, Science, Politics and Industry*. Buffalo, NY: The Frontier Press Company, 1910.)

20

Forbidden to Preach

Pastor Samuel Rutherford became highly influential when he turned his acute intelligence to the consideration of political theory. (Smellie, Alexander. *Men of the Covenant*. Edinburgh: The Banner of Truth Trust, 1903.)

On this day in 1636, Samuel Rutherford was banned from his church, forbidden to preach anywhere in his land and confined to the town of Aberdeen, Scotland. He had already endured the deaths of his wife and children as well as his own illness. It seemed that outside forces were determined to keep him down.

Rutherford lived in a time of religious persecution in Britain, with the government closely dictating what people should believe. While many British subjects were fleeing to America to escape persecution, Rutherford stayed and fought his spiritual battles in Scotland. He had been assigned to the rural county parish of Anwoth, which had a small congregation that was scattered among the surrounding farms. Though his congregation was small, Rutherford was a devoted pastor who rose at 3 a.m. to pray, study and care for the spiritual needs of his congregation.

What got him into trouble was his book *Apology of Divine Grace*, which challenged the spreading notion that righteousness could be based on human works. This book offended powerful Archbishop Laud, who controlled the established Church. So, Rutherford was put out of his church.

The discouraged preacher felt abandoned by God and useless. Thinking the matter through, however, he came to a hard-won conclusion: "Duties are ours, the events are the Lord's." However long the Lord chose to restrict him to Aberdeen, Rutherford would not question Him. In a letter to the congregation at Anwoth, Rutherford wrote, "It is not for us to set an hour-glass to the Creator of time."

Rutherford may not have been allowed to preach, but he could still write. The hundreds of letters he wrote to members of his congregation at Anwoth and to other Christians were full of encouragement and loving devotion to Christ. They bubble with anticipation of the coming of Christ or, as he put it, the "Marriage Supper of the Lamb." Little did he suspect that those letters would one day be acclaimed as a masterpiece.

After a year and a half of exile in Aberdeen, Rutherford resumed preaching and teaching. During the 1640s he represented the Church of Scotland in the Westminster Assembly in London, where he was a major author of the Shorter Catechism, with its famous beginning, "What is the chief end of man?"

While serving the assembly, Rutherford wrote *Lex Rex*, or *The Law of the Prince*, a book that declared that God alone has absolute authority and that even kings must obey the law. The premise that all government leaders are responsible to a law higher than themselves was central to the formation of the United States government.

When Charles II became king of England, *Lex Rex* was burned by the public hangman, and Rutherford was summoned to appear before Parliament under charges of treason. Rutherford replied from his deathbed, saying, "I have got a summons already before a superior judge and judicatory, and I behoove to answer my first summons, and ere your day come I will be where few kings and great folks come."

After Rutherford's death, his letters were published. Charles Haddon Spurgeon, one of the greatest preachers and writers of all time, said of Rutherford's letters, "[L]et the world know that Spurgeon held Rutherford's letters to be the nearest thing to inspiration which can be found in all the writings of mere man."

Ex-slave and abolitionist Frederick Douglass. (Courtesy of the University of Texas collection of public domain portraits on the Web.)

Other Events

1878: Leo XIII ascended to the papacy. He was a reform-minded pope who issued an encyclical against the African slave trade and founded the Catholic University in Washington, DC.

1895: Frederick Douglass, an escaped slave, author, acquaintance of President Lincoln, United States ambassador and Christian, died on this day.

1949: Two hundred thousand Romans gathered in St. Peter's Square to affirm their loyalty to the Church in light of developments against the faith in Communist nations.

1950: A United States court issued a permanent injunction (Cadmon vs. Kenyon) against the union that became the United Churches in Christ. The United Churches in Christ won an appeal in 1952.

February 21

Execution of a Jesuit Poet

The death of Robert Southwell on this day, February 21, in 1595, emphasizes the fact that neither high birth, sincerity, poetic gifts nor a sweet disposition can protect one from persecution.

Chances are that if you have seen Southwell's name at all, it has been attached to the poem "The Burning Babe" in an anthology of English literature. The Christmas babe is Christ, who says:

> My faultless breast the furnace is;
> The fuel, wounding thorns;
> Love is the fire, and sighs the smoke;
> The ashes, shames and scorns.

Southwell's poems were read by Shakespeare himself, and Ben Jonson said he would gladly destroy many of his own if he might thereby have written Southwell's best.

The author of "The Burning Babe" was born in England around 1561 to an old Catholic family. His grandfather had been a prominent man in Henry VIII's court, and the family remained among the elite of the land. So beautiful was he as a boy that a gypsy stole him; he was quickly recovered. He grew up to be a short, handsome man with gray eyes and red hair.

Even as a child, Southwell was distinguished by his attraction to Catholicism. Protestantism had come to England, and it was actually a crime for any Englishman who had been ordained as a Catholic priest to remain in England for more than forty days at a time.

In order to keep the faith alive, William Allen had opened a school at Douai, where he made a Catholic translation of the Bible, the well-known Douai version. Southwell attended Allen's school and asked to be admitted into the Jesuit order. At first the Jesuits refused his application, but eventually his earnest appeals moved them to accept him. He was ordained a priest in 1584. Two years later, at his own request, he was sent as a missionary to England, well knowing the dangers he faced.

Southwell's arrival in England was reported to the authorities. For six years they kept him under surveillance. He assumed the last name Cotton and found employment as a chaplain to Lady Arundel. Although he lived mostly in London, he traveled in disguise and preached secretly throughout England.

His downfall and capture came about when Anne Bellamy, a Catholic girl, betrayed him into the clutches of Richard Topcliffe, a notorious agent of the anti-Catholic persecution.

Southwell remained in prison for three years. He was tortured thirteen times, but he nonetheless refused to reveal the names of fellow Catholics. During his incarceration, he was allowed to write. His works had already circulated widely and seen print, although their authorship was not well-known. Now he added to them poems intended to sustain himself and comfort his fellow prisoners.

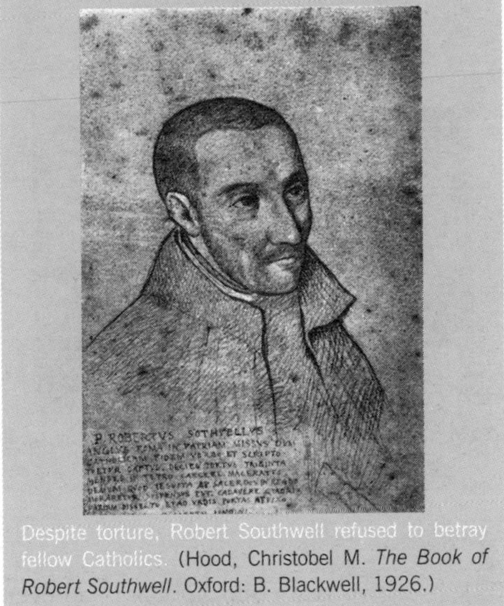

Despite torture, Robert Southwell refused to betray fellow Catholics. (Hood, Christobel M. *The Book of Robert Southwell*. Oxford: B. Blackwell, 1926.)

On this day in 1595, Southwell was brought to Tyburn, where he was hanged and then quartered for treason, although no treasonous word or act had been shown against him. It was enough that he held a variation of the Christian faith that was then unpopular in England.

Other Events

891: Pope Stephen VI crowned Guido, duke of Spoleto, as king of Italy, acting as the power-broker between Guido and Berengarius of Friuli.

1076: A letter from Holy Roman Emperor Henry IV reached Pope Hildebrand as he sat in council. Some of the bishops with him leaped up, drawing their swords and screaming for the messenger's blood, but Hildebrand interposed his own body to protect the man.

1173: Thomas à Becket, former archbishop of Canterbury, was canonized. He had been murdered three years earlier by knights of King Henry II of England.

1945: Eric Liddell died in a Japanese prison camp. He was the Scottish runner who broke the world record and took the Olympic gold in a race he was not considered likely to win. His story was told in the film *Chariots of Fire*. Before, during and after his Olympic victory, his life was dedicated to God's work.

Eric Liddell breaks the tape in a 1923 victory. (Courtesy of the Christian History Institute archives.)

February

22 Billy Graham Takes a Bombshell

Billy Graham preaching. (Courtesy of the Billy Graham Evangelical Society.)

For two years Billy Graham had been planning a Greater London Crusade, intended to kick off on March 1, 1954. The crusade had become the greatest test of his ministry up to that point. The British were suspicious of the Yank and his "hot gospel." An Anglican bishop predicted that Graham would return to America with his tail between his legs. Even Graham's backers were uneasy, thinking that nothing could shake spiritually dull England. Present the crusade in outlying regions first, they urged. Graham refused, saying that God did not need a pilot program.

Difficulties mounted. The crusade committee had trouble booking an auditorium. They finally settled on Harringay Arena, a location that past speakers had seldom been able to fill for two nights in a row. Funds were short. During the crusade, Graham and his coworkers took pay cuts. At times Graham faltered. At one point he said, "To go to London for a campaign is indeed frightening and humbling. If anything is done for Christ, it will have to be the Lord's doing." Bob Jones, Sr., accused Graham of attempting the London crusade as a matter of pride.

Despite the opposition that he faced, Graham sailed for England. Aboard ship on this day in 1954, he was handed a telegram. It read:

> A Labor Member of Parliament announced today that he would challenge in Commons the admission of Billy Graham to England on the grounds the American evangelist was interfering in British politics under the guise of religion.

The problem had been caused by a crusade brochure that had referred to the woes brought on by socialism. The Labor Party had seen the brochure and had taken it as a political attack.

The London media demanded Graham's scalp. Lukewarm supporters backpedaled. For a moment Graham thought the crusade was ruined. Yet, since God had led him that far, he decided he would go on. Meanwhile, he sent an apology to the Labor Party.

When he disembarked in Britain Graham was mobbed by hostile reporters. He said he believed that God was going to pour out revival upon England. As he passed through customs, an agent thanked him for coming. So did a cab driver. Graham's spirits lifted.

Nonetheless, he was all nerves before the first meeting, shaking like a leaf. He spent the day on his knees. A senator called to withdraw his promised attendance at the first meeting. Someone called to announce that only 2,000 people had shown up at the 11,000-seat arena. Again Graham dropped to his knees.

In the end, the negative publicity his crusade had received proved to be a blessing. Not only did the first night attract crowds, but for three months the arena was jammed at every service. Wherever Graham went he was mobbed by crowds. Extra meetings had to be scheduled. Londoners began singing hymns in the subways.

Altogether, over 2 million people attended the meetings. Thousands came to Christ. Winston Churchill met Graham and privately heard the gospel message from him, a message Graham never ceased to preach:

> [M]an cannot renew himself. God created us. Only God can recreate us. Only God can give us the new birth we so desperately want and need.

The Greater London Crusade did much to establish Graham's international ministry, which continued to expand over the next four decades.

Pope Gregory VII "Hildebrand." (Montor, Chevalier Artaud de. *Lives and Times of the Popes*. New York: Catholic Publication Society of America, 1911.)

Other Events

1076: Hildebrand, Pope Gregory VII, excommunicated all who attended the Diet of Worms, which deposed him at the instigation of Holy Roman Emperor Henry IV.

1198: Pope Innocent III, who would make some of the strongest claims for the papacy of the Middle Ages, was consecrated this day. He had been chosen in January of the same year.

1901: Charles and Lettie Cowman arrived in Tokyo, Japan. Charles wrote in his notebook, "A new era in our lives. New responsibilities, new hopes, new avenues of thought, new subjects for prayer. Oh, for faith, unyielding faith! My soul yearns for a close alliance with God." The Cowmans helped to form the Oriental Mission Society.

1954: TransWorld Radio went on the air in Tangier, Morocco, broadcasting in Spanish across the Strait of Gibralter to Spain. Paul E. Freed founded the ministry as International Evangelism, Inc.

FEBRUARY 23

Testified to His Faith with His Life

Toward the end of the first century, or perhaps even at the beginning of the second century, the Apostle John died after years of ministry to the churches of Asia Minor in the region that is now occupied by Turkey. John was the last of the original apostles, but the truths of Christianity did not die with him. His spiritual children continued to stand firm in their faith in Christ as the Son of God, whom John had heard, seen and even touched (see 1 John 1:1-2).

One of John's spiritual sons, Polycarp, was born around the year 69. He lived in Smyrna and learned much by listening to John. Polycarp became a leader of the church at Smyrna, and in many ways his character reflected that of his teacher. He had the same noble Christian spirit, full of gentleness yet inflexible in speaking out against error.

The church at Smyrna, of which Polycarp was the bishop, was one of those addressed by Christ in the Revelation. Christ told them that persecution was about to come upon them and promised a crown of life to those who were faithful unto death (see Revelation 2:8-11). The promise was undoubtedly repeated over and over by Polycarp to encourage faithful Christians as the Romans hauled them off to face wild beasts or death by fire.

When the authorities searched for Polycarp, his friends persuaded him to leave the city and hide in a farmhouse. There he spent much time in prayer. A letter written by the church of Smyrna told that:

> [W]hile praying [Polycarp] fell into a trance three days before his capture; and he saw his pillow burning with fire. And he turned and said to those that were with him, "It must be that I shall be burned alive."
>
> When his pursuers were on his track he went to another farmhouse. Finding him gone they put two slave boys to the torture, and one of them betrayed his place of concealment. Herod, head of the police, sent a body of men to arrest him on Friday evening. Escape was still possible, but the old man refused to flee, saying, "The will of God be done." He came down to meet his pursuers, conversed affably with them, and ordered food to be set before them. While they were eating he prayed, "Remembering all, high and low, who at any time had come in his way, and the Catholic Church throughout the world." Then he was led away.

The proconsul (a high magistrate) ordered Polycarp to renounce Christ and give obedience to Caesar as Lord. Polycarp answered:

> Eighty and six years have I served Christ, nor has He ever done me any harm. How, then, could I blaspheme my King who saved me? You threaten the fire that burns for an hour and then is quenched; but you know not of the fire of the judgment to come, and the fire of eternal punishment. Bring what you will.

Polycarp, the last of those personally taught by the apostles, was burned at the stake on this day in the year 155. As the Lord required, Polycarp was faithful unto death; he did so in expectation that he would receive a crown of life from Christ.

Smyrna as seen from the sea in the late nineteenth century. (Ballie, E.C.C., Mrs. *Sail to Smyrna*. London: Longmans, Green, 1873.)

Other Events

1855: John Bright, a Quaker Parliamentarian in England, made on this day a passionate appeal for peace in what has been called his most eloquent speech.

1982: The US Supreme Court ruled that the Amish must pay taxes (US vs. Lee). According to the ruling, state demands supersede conscientious objections against the manner in which taxes are collected and spent.

John Bright brought Quaker ideas of social justice to the British Parliament. (Smith, George Barnett. *The Life and Speeches of the Right Hon. John Bright, M.P.* London: Hodder and Stoughton, 1881.)

Pope Gregory XIII took forceful action to bring the calendar back into line with the equinoxes. The calendar was then in error by ten days. (Montor, Chevalier Artaud de. *Lives and Times of the Popes*. New York: Catholic Publication Society of America, 1911.)

February 24

"Give Us Back Our Eleven Days!"

"Give us back our eleven days!" shouted the protesters.

The Julian calendar, which had been promulgated by Julius Caesar, made the year too long by several minutes, resulting in the calendar being displaced by 3 full days every 400 years. In 1582 it was out of sequence with the equinoxes by ten days and fourteen days out of synch with Caesar's original calendar. Several Church councils had discussed the issue.

Gregory XIII was an energetic pope. He had long been active in Church affairs and was a patron of education. He was not one to let the matter slide. He determined to correct the problem and, acting on the recommendations of a special council, Gregory issued a bull on this day in 1582 requiring all Catholic countries to follow October 4 with October 15 that year. To illiterate people, it seemed as if their days had actually been stolen from them.

Although the papal commission, advised by Jesuit scientist Christopher Clavius, is generally credited with aiding the pope in making the reform, a similar plan had actually been proposed by brilliant Bishop Robert Grosseteste of England 300 years earlier. This fact was not generally known and resulted in an irony. The English, afraid of appearing to give too much deference to the pope by adopting his calendar, refused the Gregorian correction and stuck with the Julian calendar for another two centuries, oblivious to the fact that the change had originally been the proposal of their own native son, Grosseteste.

At any rate, Britain and its American colonies did not change calendars until 1752. By then the Julian calendar was eleven days out of date. The common people were angry at having those days "stolen" from them and took to the streets in protest. In one of his satirical paintings, the great British painter William Hogarth showed a man getting drunk beside a poster demanding back the days.

The revision of the calendar was intended primarily for the benefit of the Church, which needed to plot the variable date of Easter. No teaching, not even of Christ's birth as a man, is more important than that of Easter and, since it is a variable date, fixing it with accuracy was essential to the Church. Easter is the most important feast because it is the observance and celebration of Christ's sacrifice for our salvation. Christ suffered for our sins, died on the cross, was buried and rose again from the dead. When His followers found the tomb empty and Christ afterward appeared to His disciples, mankind was given a new and happier hope than ever before known, for the same power that raised Christ from the dead will raise those who believe in Him. Paul summed up the principles involved when he wrote, "If Christ has not been raised, your faith is futile; you are still in your sins" (1 Corinthians 15:17).

Gregory's calendar reform, which was concerned primarily with an issue of faith, became significant to the entire world. Through conquests and business dealings, the Gregorian, or Western, calendar became the international standard and is now used wherever world trade is conducted.

Because the Gregorian calendar was a Christian contrivance, some nations balked at accepting it. Cultures such as China had calendars that went back several millennia, and they did not want to break from those long-standing traditions. Other nations did not like the idea of following the lead of the West. Consequently, nations such as China, Japan and Russia did not adopt the Gregorian calendar until the twentieth century. Then the need for a standardized calendar became overwhelming. The dominance of the West, the scientific superiority it then enjoyed and the lack of a universally recognized alternative made the adoption of the Gregorian calendar inevitable.

Francis of Assisi heard a life-changing message on this day. (Bell, Mrs. Arthur. *Saints in Christian Art*. London: George Bell, 1901-4.)

Other Events

1208 (or 1209): Francis of Assisi heard Matthew 10:7-10 preached. It is a passage in which Jesus tells his disciples to go out and preach that the kingdom of God is at hand, to heal the sick and to trust God for their needs. His obedience to that passage led to the founding of the Franciscan order.

1527: A group of Anabaptists under Michael Sattler developed articles of faith, including details of the Lord's Supper, passive obedience and adult baptism. These are known as the Schleitheim Articles.

1833: Eugene Casalis arrived in Cape Town, South Africa. He became a notable missionary in Basutoland (now known as the Kingdom of Lesotho). His Morija station became the headquarters for French Reformed work in South Africa.

1915: Amanda Smith, the ex-slave who became a world evangelist and wrote a compelling autobiography, died on this day.

1949: Weary of resistance from believers, Bulgaria's atheistic Communist government passed a law naming the Bulgarian Orthodox Church the traditional Church of Bulgaria.

Deaconess Elizabeth Fedde

On April 8, 1883, Elizabeth Fedde began a journal. She wrote:

> I came here to New York and was received by my brother-in-law, with whom I have lived for three weeks. During that time I have gone around to become a bit acquainted and have made some house visits and sick calls (ten in all).

The year before, thirty-two-year-old Fedde had been serving as a deaconess (essentially a nurse with spiritual duties) in her native Norway. She had pioneered in Tromsø, a harsh region, under primitive conditions. But on her birthday on Christmas day in 1882, she opened a letter from her brother-in-law. It dared her to undertake a work among Norwegian seamen in New York's busy port. She accepted the challenge.

Once in America, Fedde wasted no time. With the help of Pastor Mortensen, pastor of the Norwegian Seamen's Mission Church, she established the Norwegian Relief Society just nine days after arriving in New York City. She began her work by visiting the sick and distressed. As her diary tells it:

> Spent some time with a distressed woman who was disturbed about her family's wandering on the broad road away from the Father's house. God grant that she herself may come with a whole heart to You so that she can witness about You to her own!

During her first two years in her new land, Fedde ran a small, three-room boarding house for Norwegian sailors. Then she opened a deaconess school in Brooklyn and a nine-bed hospital. Many successful years later the hospital became the Lutheran Medical Center.

Fedde's success led others to request her assistance. In 1888 she answered one such call and left New York for two years to open a deaconess training center and hospital in Minneapolis, Minnesota. She also helped plan a hospital for Chicago.

Her diary reveals that she was a woman who worked herself to the bone for the kingdom of God and who was filled with prayer for the salvation of others. For instance, in October 1884 she wrote, "I found a sick person with whom God's spirit works hard and I believe truly that You, Lord, will have the victory." More often she grieved to see so little spiritual fruit. At the end of 1884 she wrote:

> This month is gone and with it the old year full of trouble and suffering. Little accomplished for the Kingdom of God. Sin and shame, blame and guilt.

Immigrants' Hospital. In her diary, Elizabeth Fedde mentioned working here. (Richmond, J.F. *New York and Its Institutions, 1609-1872: A Library of Information, Pertaining to the Great Metropolis, Past and Present*. New York: E.B. Treat, 1872.)

Fedde's choice to go to America was not without personal cost. She had left behind a man who desired to marry her. After thirteen years of work in the United States, she returned to Norway late in 1896. There she married the patiently waiting Ola Slettebø, who gave her a home when she was "worn out." She died in Norway on this day in 1921.

Elsie Smith, director of pastoral care at Lutheran Medical Center, summed up Fedde's contribution with these words: "She came before Lady Liberty [did]. I like to say she was the first lady in the harbor. She was a beacon of hope."

Other Events

1296: The papal bull *Clericis Laicos* forbade ecclesiastics to pay taxes to temporal powers.

1796: Samuel Seabury, first bishop of the Protestant Episcopal Church (formerly the Church of England) in the United States, died. Many lies were told about him because he was loyal to Britain during the Revolutionary War. His efforts to rebuild the denomination were hampered by American suspicions.

1912: A three-religion conference held in Japan included Shinto, Buddhism and Christianity but, surprisingly, not the long-established Confucian faith.

1940: Mary Mills Patrick died. She was a gifted woman who had been sent as a missionary to Turkey to teach at the "Home School." She did far more: With the help of the American philanthropist Caroline Borden, Patrick turned the school into Constantinople Women's College. She kept it open through two wars and a revolution. Believing in the equality of the sexes, she was absolutely determined that the institution would be no mere finishing school. Consequently, its female students were provided with teaching on all sorts of useful trades, including dentistry and medicine.

All this was at a time when most schools in Britain and the United States still rejected female applicants. The Constantinople Women's College still exists today as a part of Roberts College, which serves both men and women.

Samuel Seabury, an unjustly reviled bishop. (Perry, William Stevens. *The Episcopate in America*. New York: Christian Literature, 1895.)

Chrysostom reading. (Bell, Mrs. Arthur. *Saints in Christian Art*. London: George Bell, 1901-4.)

February

26

Compelled to Become Bishop of Constantinople

John Chrysostom resisted and pleaded, but the Imperial messengers were deaf to his pleas. They had their secret orders, and he was coming with them whether he wished it or not. Outside Antioch they transferred him into a royal chariot and rode for Constantinople.

There, in the capital of the Roman Empire, he learned the truth. He had been chosen to be bishop of the imperial city, a position he never wanted but for which many others were fiercely vying. His heart must have sunk as he realized that those who did not win the position would form implacable resentments against him. But what could he do? The imperial apparatus had brought about his elevation, and he was helpless before it. So on this day in 398, Chrysostom unwillingly became bishop of Constantinople.

Chrysostom's widowed mother reared him and taught him about Christianity, hoping that one day he would work for the Church. But Chrysostom intended to go into law. So his mother, trusting God for the outcome, sent Chrysostom to study with Libanius, the great pagan rhetorician of the day. As he learned about the law, Chrysostom's conscience began to trouble him. He learned that lawyers must constantly take oaths, and that conflicted with his mother's teaching that oath taking was wrong. Furthermore, through the influence of saintly Bishop Meletius, Chrysostom was attracted to Christ.

Chrysostom was later converted and baptized, but he resisted becoming a bishop. Instead, he spent four years in the desert and two as a hermit in study of Scripture and in austerities. Filled with knowledge of Scripture, he finally agreed to be made a deacon in 381 and a priest in 386. His eloquent preaching won him the name Chrysostom, which means "Golden tongue." Many of his sermons still exist in written form today.

Less than a year after becoming a deacon, Chrysostom rose to special attention. Taxes had been raised in Antioch, and the populace rioted. Would the emperor punish the city? In Thessalonica a few years earlier, Theodosius slaughtered 7,000 in an amphitheater for rebellion. While Bishop Flavian rushed to Constantinople to plead for Antioch, Chrysostom preached a series of sermons to the terrified populace. Death stared the people in the face as they awaited the emperor's sentence. Chrysostom's fierce attacks on sin cut their consciences. Many confessed their sins and repented, and the emperor pardoned the people.

Chrysostom's brilliant preaching made him famous. When the court in Constantinople could not agree on any of the rival candidates for the position of bishop of Constantinople, Chrysostom's fame brought him to imperial attention.

Once in Constantinople, Chrysostom continued his attacks on sin. The empress Eudoxia felt some of these sermons were directed toward her. The emperor also was unhappy with Chrysostom because he felt Chrysostom had been forced on him by court intrigue. The imperial pair teamed up with Patriarch Theophilus of Alexandria to have Chrysostom deposed on trumped-up charges by a synod of enemy bishops in 403. Chrysostom was exiled, but the people of Constantinople were so violent in their rage over Chrysostom's exile that the terrified empress quickly ordered him brought back.

However, when Chrysostom spoke out against excessive ceremonies held in honor of a new statue erected to the empress, Eudoxia became so furious that she ordered the bishops to exile Chrysostom again. This time it was permanent. He died on a forced march that was taking him further away from the court that had made him its bishop in the first place.

Suffering under Queen Ranavalona I of Madagascar. (Mears, John W. *The Story of Madagascar*. Philadelphia: Presbyterian Board of Publication, 1873.)

Other Events

1816: The rules and constitution of the New York Sunday School Union Society were perfected this day. Rev. Dr. John Mason presented a powerful and eloquent appeal about the purpose of the society.

1835: Ranavalona I, queen of Madagascar, forbade the preaching of the gospel. Eventually many Christians were imprisoned or martyred under her cruel regime.

1950: Harry Lauder, a Scottish comedian and singer whose talents and war service to his nation earned him a knighthood, died on this day. One day he received a telegram that his son had been killed on the battlefield. This almost unhinged his mind until he learned that the boy had become a Christian. Knowing that the boy was alive with Christ lifted Lauder from despair. He exclaimed, "I would that I could picture to you the joy that lies in the assurance of seeing my boy again."

Birth of the Reforming Raven

Anthony Rabe was born at Warburg Castle in Eisenach, Germany, on this day in 1501. He became a humanist scholar and adopted a Latin form for his last name that meant "Raven." And so we know him as Anthony Corvinus.

In time, Corvinus became a monk and at first wanted nothing to do with the new ideas that were being put forth by Martin Luther. But upon reading the great reformer's works and observing his bold stand at the Diet of Worms, Corvinus changed his mind. He even sent Luther a keg of beer for his refreshment!

Corvinus was ousted from his monastery because of his Lutheran leanings. He became an enthusiastic supporter of the Reformation and preached in Goettingen, Northeim, Hildesheim and Calenberg.

The task he had set himself was a dangerous one, for at that time Reformation preachers were often hunted men, and threats of heavy penalties hung over their heads. Corvinus, however, won the confidence of Landgrave Philip of Hesse. (A landgrave is a high-level count.) During most of the 1530s, Corvinus was at the landgrave's side. Philip consulted him on many occasions, and Corvinus attended almost all of the important conferences of the early Reformation.

Philip granted Corvinus permission to preach in Goettingen and Hanover. Previously, efforts to take the gospel there had resulted in the preachers being hunted, but Corvinus enjoyed considerable success.

The Duchess Elizabeth, governing for her underage son, Erich, supported the Reformation. She wrote Luther to ask for assistance, and in response he sent Corvinus. This cleared the way for the gospel in the southern part of Lower Saxony. Corvinus also brought the Reformation to Northeim, which had seemed a stronghold for the Catholics.

To this point, Corvinus had met with little direct opposition to his spreading of the gospel. During this time, Emperor Charles arranged for a temporary doctrinal formula called the Augsburg Interim. The Interim made a few concessions to the Lutheran position, allowing the clergy to marry and permitting the cup as well as the bread in communion. But for most reformers, these concessions did not go far enough. In their minds, the real issues were things such as penances, confessions and the doctrine of justification. So, Corvinus opposed the Augsburg Interim. The duke of Goettingen-Kalenberg, however, sided with Rome and was angered by Corvinus's resistance to the Interim. The duke threw Corvinus into prison, where he suffered for almost three years.

Anthony Corvinus, from an old woodcut. (Bainton, Roland Herbert. *Women of the Reformation, from Spain to Scandinavia*. Minneapolis, MN: Augsburg Pub. House, 1977.)

His health deteriorated as a result of his extended incarceration, and he died just a few months after his release in April 1553. He had been "a true and faithful Lutheran Christian." His motto in his last years was "My hope is Christ."

Corvinus was not a particularly famous person, but his life shows how the Reformation spread, carried forward by many willing hands.

Other Events

1536: The Helvetian Confession was drawn up by Heinrich Bullinger in an attempt to settle dogmatic controversies between the Lutherans and the Zwinglians. It did not succeed in its purpose.

1547: Vittoria Colonna, a minor poetess whose correspondence and poems of faith inspired the great sculptor Michelangelo, died on this day.

1706: John Evelyn, the famous English diarist, died. His life and the pages of his diary show that he feared God. For example, he described his horror at hearing some lawyers discuss ways in which they had bilked clients. Evelyn wrote, "This they made but a jest, but God is not mocked."

1764: Rome condemned the book *The Status of the Church and the Lawful Power of the Roman Pontiff* by Fabrionius (his real name was John Nicholas von Hontheim). It called for councils to have authority over popes and claimed that popes had usurped authority throughout history.

1893: Benjamin T. Roberts, founder of the Free Methodist denomination, died. Converted at the age of twenty, he pastored several Methodist churches until he was expelled from the conference for criticizing the Methodists for departing from truths they had earlier held.

John Evelyn, the famous English diarist. (Evelyn, John. *Diary and Correspondence of John Evelyn*. London: Henry G. Bohn, 1859.)

Ambrose bars Theodosius from church for ordering a massacre. (Lord, John. *Beacon Lights of History*. New York: James Clarke, 1886.)

February 28

Theodosius's Edict Blurs Boundaries

There have been many turning points in Church history. One of the most significant of those turning points is one that is probably little known by most Christians.

After Emperor Constantine's conversion, he officially legitimized Christianity in the Edict of Milan. Soon thereafter, Christians in the Roman Empire became divided between Arianism (which denies the full divinity of Christ) and Trinitarianism (which sees God as three persons in one). The first universal Church council, held at Nicea in 325, resisted Arianism, and all but three of its bishops voted for a Trinitarian creed.

Shortly after Theodosius became emperor, he ended the Arian dispute by the simple expedient of issuing an edict on this day in 380. The edict commanded that everyone become a Christian—but not just any kind of Christian: a Catholic Christian. Catholic Christians, the edict said, held the Father, Son and Holy Spirit to be one Godhead and equal in majesty. This, of course, was the essential position of the Nicene Creed, which was the product of the council held at Nicea in 325. Theodosius's decision may well have been the result of his upbringing in a Christian home (it appears he was the first emperor to enjoy that distinction). He did not always act like a Christian, however, as was shown when he massacred 7,000 people during a revolt in Thessalonica.

Theodosius was about to take the field against the Goths but decided to be baptized first. As he ascended from the font, he dictated the solemn words of his decree:

> It is our pleasure that all the nations which are governed by our clemency and moderation should steadfastly adhere to the religion which was taught by St. Peter to the Romans, which faithful tradition has preserved, and which is now professed by the pontiff Damasus, and by Peter, bishop of Alexandria, a man of apostolic holiness. According to the discipline of the apostles, and the doctrine of the Gospel, let us believe the sole deity of the Father, the Son, and the Holy Ghost, under an equal majesty and a pious Trinity. We authorise the followers of this doctrine to assume the title of Catholic Christians; and as we judge that all others are extravagant madmen, we brand them with the infamous name of Heretics, and declare that their conventicles shall no longer usurp the respectable appellation of churches. Besides the condemnation of Divine justice, they must expect to suffer the severe penalties, which our authority, guided by heavenly wisdom, shall think proper to inflict upon them.

The following year, Theodosius issued another edict, specifically requiring worship of the one God according to the Nicene Creed. He deposed Demophilus of Constantinople, an Arian bishop, and replaced him with a Trinitarian.

The passing of those laws (Theodosian Codes 16.1.2 and 16.5.6) was significant for many reasons. They mark the first time the state coerced people to become Christians. They made Catholic Christianity the official dogma of the Church and suppressed the Arian factions. They established a pattern of using the apparatus of the state to suppress diversity of religious opinion, a pattern that would become more pronounced as Theodosius's reign progressed. Before all was done, pagans, Arians, Manichees (those who believed that life was essentially a struggle between good and evil) and Jews would be persecuted by Christians. However, many of these churchgoers did not follow Christ out of zeal but because it was politically prudent.

In 381 Theodosius called a council of bishops, which met at Constantinople. It reaffirmed and smoothed out the Creed of Nicea. Theodosius may soon have lamented the power his edicts awarded the Church, however, for in 388 he was forbidden the sacraments for eight months until he publicly humbled himself for the atrocious massacre at Thessalonica. Nonetheless, the edicts became part of the foundation of Church power in the Middle Ages.

George Wishart, mentor of the Scottish Reformation. (Courtesy of the Christian History Institute archives.)

Other Events

1546: George Wishart was arrested and burned the next day in Scotland for his Reformation beliefs.

1551: Martin Bucer died. Although he left no church named after himself, he was one of the steadiest and best-known reformers of the day.

1638: The National Covenant was signed in Scotland in the Greyfriars churchyard of Edinburgh, giving rise to the Covenanter movement of the Scottish Presbyterians.

1909: Pastor Zamora announced the formation of La Iglesia Evangelica Metodista las Islas Filipinas, an independent national Filipino church that became very successful.

February 29

Rumania's "Prisoner Number One"

On this day in 1948, a beautiful Sunday morning, Pastor Richard Wurmbrand of Rumania set out on foot for church. He never arrived. For eight-and-a-half years his wife and son did not know where he was or even if he was alive or dead. "Ex-prisoners" assured Wurmbrand's wife, Sabina, that they had witnessed her husband's funeral in a Communist prison. Sabina was heartbroken, and yet she doubted the word of those men, suspecting that they might be agents of the government.

Wurmbrand's disappearance was expected. Anyone who acted contrary to the Communist regime that held Rumania in its fist could expect imprisonment or death. One might say he had asked for it, but he didn't do so without a good reason. At a "Congress of Cults" held by the Communist government, religious leaders stepped forward to swear loyalty to the new regime. Sabina asked Wurmbrand to "wipe the shame from the face of Jesus." Wurmbrand replied that if he stepped forward, she would no longer have a husband. "I don't need a coward for a husband," she answered. And so Wurmbrand stepped forward and told the 4,000 delegates that their duty as Christians was to glorify God and Christ alone.

He returned home to lead an underground church and promote the gospel among Rumania's Russian invaders. He smuggled Bibles, disguised as Communist propaganda, into Russia. And then he disappeared.

What had actually happened? As Wurmbrand walked to church, a van full of secret police stopped in front of him. Four men jumped out and hustled him inside. He was taken to their headquarters and later locked in a solitary cell, where he was designated "Prisoner Number One." His years of imprisonment consisted of a ceaseless round of torture and brainwashing. For seventeen hours a day, repetitious phrases were dinned into his ears: "Communism is good." "Christianity is stupid!" "Give up. Give up!" Over the years, his body was repeatedly cut and burned. His jailers also broke many of his bones, including four of his vertebrae. When asked later about what he had endured, he replied, "I prefer not to speak about those [tortures] through which I have passed. When I do, I cannot sleep at night. It is too painful." Miraculously, despite all of the hardships he endured, he survived. Other martyrs did not.

Eight-and-a-half years later, in 1956, Wurmbrand was released. During that time, Sabina had been brutalized in prison for three years, and their nine-year-old son, Mihai, was treated as an orphan. Upon their release, the Wurmbrands immediately recommenced underground work. Wurmbrand was taken again to prison and was not released until 1964. In 1965, Western churches ransomed Wurmbrand from Rumania for $10,000.

Wurmbrand and his wife immediately spoke out for those still suffering in Communist hands. Wurmbrand was asked to testify before the United States Senate. He displayed the eighteen holes cut in his body. Afterward, he was invited to speak before hundreds of groups. By 1967, "Prisoner Number One" had incorporated a mission organization known as the Voice of the Martyrs, an organization dedicated to assisting those who suffer for Christ throughout the world.

He and his wife were able to survive their ordeal through the power of love. Wurmbrand wrote:

Richard Wurmbrand suffered dreadfully in his eight-and-a-half years in Rumanian torture cells, but love triumphed over pain after his bold testimony for Christ made him a prisoner. (Courtesy of Voice of the Martyrs archives. Used by permission.)

If the heart is cleansed by the love of Jesus Christ and if the heart loves Him, you can resist all tortures. What would a loving bride not do for a loving bridegroom? What would a loving mother not do for her child? If you love Christ as Mary did, who had Christ as a baby in her arms, if you love Jesus as a bride loves her bridegroom, then you can resist such tortures. God will judge us not according to how much we endured, but how much we could love. I am a witness for the Christians in Communist prisons that they could love. They could love God and men.

Other Events

1604: John Whitgift died. He was an Anglican archbishop who crowned James I king of England and who sat in the Hampton Court Conference, which authorized the King James Version of the Bible. On the darker side, he violently suppressed Puritanism.

1692: The Salem witch trials began with just two accusations, but before all was done, many people were executed. The hysteria of this time exerted a strong influence on American art and literature.

1960: Thomas Obediah Chisolm, Methodist editor of the *Pentecostal Herald* and author of such hymns as "Great Is Thy Faithfulness," "O to Be Like Thee" and "Living for Jesus a Life that Is True," died on this day

John Whitgift. (McKilliam, A.E. *Chronicle of the Archbishops of Canterbury*. Cambridge, England: James Clarke & Co., 1913.)

March 1

Alone Among 500 Million Souls

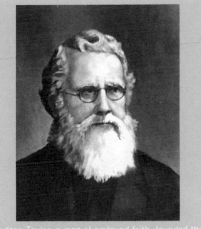

"My feelings on stepping ashore I cannot attempt to describe. My heart felt as though it had not room and must burst its bonds, while tears of gratitude and thankfulness fell from my eyes." So wrote Hudson Taylor of the moment of his landing at Shanghai, China, on this day, at 5 p.m., in 1854.

For years Taylor's heart had burned with desire to carry the gospel to China. He had exerted every ounce of his energy for that moment. Through weary struggles, bouts of depression, danger of shipwreck, heart-wrenching separation from his family, isolation from other Englishmen and hours of intense prayer, he had persevered to step upon that shore.

He did not know a soul nor where to turn, although he had a letter to a missionary who was already established in China. But Taylor had learned much about trusting the Lord, and that night his trust was not misplaced. Guided by an invisible hand, he found his way to a mission compound, where he was kindly received.

Nothing worked out according to his expectations. His first six months in China were dreary and lonely. His income was tiny, and he could do little. Civil war began the week he arrived. He was unable to rent a house as he had hoped, so he had to impose on his kindly hosts.

There was one thing he could do, though: study Chinese. He flung himself into language study, neglecting even his devotions. Not only did he learn the language, but he made up his mind to adopt native dress. He wrote:

> I had better tell you at once that on Thursday last at 11 p.m. I resigned my locks to the barber, dyed my hair a good black, and in the morning had a proper queue plaited in with my own, and a quantity of heavy silk to lengthen it out according to Chinese custom.

It was his hope to establish a thoroughly native Church. The Chinese, he felt, had little to do with Christianity because they hated foreign ways.

His methods proved successful. In time he broke gracefully away from his English board and founded the China Inland Mission, which was based wholly on faith. He did not tell others of his financial needs, instead trusting that the Lord would provide whatever was needed. He said:

> Want of trust is at the root of almost all our sins and all our weaknesses; and how shall we escape it but by looking to Him and observing all His faithfulness?

He prayed specifically for his needs and for other missionaries to be sent to China. One year he prayed for seventy missionaries; the Lord sent seventy-six. Another year he asked for 100 and got 102. He was thankful for the provisions of the Lord but still felt there was a need for even more missionaries:

Hudson Taylor, a man of profound faith, founded the China Inland Mission. (Courtesy of the Christian History Institute archives.)

> Last week I was at Taiping. . . . My heart was greatly moved by the crowds that literally filled the streets for two or three miles. . . . I was constrained to retire to the city wall and cry to God to have mercy on the people, to open their hearts and give us an entrance among them.

Chinese Christianity grew slowly. For many years, the number of Protestants hung at barely a million. Later, under savage persecution, Christianity flourished. Today the Chinese Church is one of the fastest growing in the world, with about eight percent of the nation claiming allegiance to Christ.

Many Chinese Christians owe their first contact with the gospel to the evangelism of men such as Hudson Taylor. When he stepped in faith onto Shanghai's soil, he became one of the greatest missionaries the world has known.

Other Events

492: Pope Felix III died. He excommunicated Acacius, patriarch of Constantinople, for the heresy of Monophysitism (belief that Christ had only one nature, the divine).

499: Pope St. Symmachus held a synod that issued new rules on papal elections. His own election had been disputed, and King Theodoric the Great of the Ostrogoths had sided against him.

1562: Huguenots were massacred by Catholics at Vassy, France, in disregard of an edict of tolerance.

1587: Peter Wentworth, member of the English parliament, challenged Queen Elizabeth I about England's right to control Church affairs. He lost the battle.

1767: The Jesuits were expelled from Spain. King Carlos III wrote:

> I charge the provincials, presidents, rectors, and other superiors of the Society of Jesus to accept these provisions punctually, and in carrying them out the Jesuits shall be treated with the greatest regard, attention, honesty, and assistance, so that in every respect the action taken may be in conformity with my sovereign intentions.

1815: Georgetown, the first Catholic university in the United States, was granted a charter by President James Madison.

Felix III. (Montor, Chevalier Artaud de. *Lives and Times of the Popes*. New York: Catholic Publication Society of America, 1911.)

March 2

Australia Adopts a Constitution with God in It

Map of Australia. (Courtesy of the CIA World Factbook. Available online at: <http://www.cia.gov/cia/publications/factbook/geos/as.html>.)

Church bells rang when Australia adopted its constitution in July of 1900. And well they might: Consensus had been difficult to obtain. The hard work and the petitions, prayers and initiatives of churchgoers had helped to make the federation a reality.

One of the fights Christians had helped win was over a proposal to include a reference to God in the constitution's preamble. Early in the constitutional discussions, Patrick Glynn, a Roman Catholic delegate, proposed that the preamble include the words "invoking Divine Providence." Australia's secularists did not like this. They wanted no reference to God in the document, and neither did the unpopular Seventh Day Adventists, who feared that religious language could be used against them.

On the whole, however, the delegates favored Glynn's proposal. It was batted about, and different wording was suggested. Churches got involved and huge petitions were gathered, pressuring the delegates to make mention of God. The churches collected so many signatures that some political leaders became convinced the constitution could never be approved without a reference to the Creator.

On this day in 1898, Glynn said, "I beg to move: That the following words be inserted after the word 'Constitution' (line 2)—'humbly relying on the blessing of Almighty God.' "

Sir John Downer backed him, saying:

> I don't know whether it has occurred to Honorable Members that the Christian religion is a portion of the English Constitution. . . . It is part of the Law of England which I think we undoubtedly brought with us when we settled these colonies.

Secularists jeered in the last session when the majority of delegates voted to honor God. The wording that was finally adopted was as follows:

> Whereas the people of New South Wales, Victoria, South Australia, Queensland, and Tasmania, humbly relying on the blessing of Almighty God, have agreed to unite in one indissoluble Federal Commonwealth under the Crown of the United Kingdom of Great Britain and Ireland.

As small as that remembrance of God was, Christians cheered.

The constitution promised religious protection by prohibiting the government from establishing a religion or imposing religious tests on citizens' activities. It also guaranteed religious freedom.

As for Glynn, in the middle of one of the sessions, he dashed off a proposal of marriage to a woman he had met just once, three years before. She accepted by telegram, and they married within a week.

Samuel Chapman Armstrong. (Dunning, Albert E. *Congregationalists in America: A Popular History of Their Origin, Belief, Polity, Growth and Work*. New York: J.A. Hill, 1894.)

Other Events

1791: John Wesley, founder of the Wesleyan Methodists, died on this day.

1811: John S.B. Monsell was born in Londonderry, Ireland. Educated at Trinity College, Dublin, he was ordained in 1834 and became a vicar in England. To correct a lack of praise in worship ("we sing, not as we should sing to Him who is chief among ten thousand and altogether lovely"), he composed 300 hymns. Some hymn books still carry "Light of the World, We Hail Thee," "Fight the Good Fight with all Thy Might," and "Sing to the Lord of the Harvest." Oddly enough, Monsell was killed when a stone fell from the roof of a church that was under repair.

1867: Howard Normal and Theological Institute became The Howard University, which was its fourth name in three months. The school, located in Washington, DC, was chartered by Samuel Chapman Armstrong, son of a Hawaiian missionary. Armstrong had become aware of the crying need for African-American education while heading a "colored" regiment in the Civil War. His creed was not elaborate: "Simply to Thy cross I cling is enough for me."

Dissolved in the Divine?

When Simplicius became bishop of Rome on this day in 468, it seemed most likely that any troubles he might face would come from the western half of the disintegrating Roman Empire. There, Vandals, Visigoths and Franks had replaced Roman power with their own and for thirteen years had ruled the Western empire through puppet emperors. Furthermore, Odovakar, a Herulian (one of the Teutonic tribes) and an Arian, seized power in Rome. Despite these omens, however, it was the East that gave Simplicius problems.

Odovakar treated the Catholic Church with respect, and conditions remained stable in the West. In the East, however, the climate was not so stable. A usurper, Basiliscus, drove Emperor Zeno from the throne. In order to hold on to his newly acquired position, Basiliscus needed Monophysite support, so he placed members of the sect in key religious positions.

Monophysitism began as the Orthodox response to Nestorianism. Nestorius refused to call Mary the "Mother of God," for, said he, the child in her womb was thoroughly human. In contradistinction to this, the Monophysites taught that Christ's human nature was dissolved in his divine nature. Eventually the Church balanced the two ideas at the Council of Chalcedon in 451 by declaring Christ both truly God and truly man.

Instead of resolving the issue, however, the council's ruling became grounds for further fighting. The Monophysites refused to accept defeat. Basiliscus, with the agreement of 500 bishops, ordered the acts of Chalcedon burned. Simplicius defended Bishop Acacius of Constantinople, who sturdily resisted the Monophysite error.

Simplicius wrote letters to the major people involved in the conflict and made every effort to maintain the Catholic dogma and the definitions of the Council of Chalcedon. He insisted that Rome, successor to Peter, held the truth.

In Alexandria, Egypt, the controversy became fierce, and the rival factions began torturing and killing each other. A Monophysite monk, operating under the name Timothy the Cat, had the patriarch of Alexandria butchered three days before Easter, consigning his corpse to flames and triumphantly seizing his position.

Eventually, Emperor Zeno regained his throne and ousted the Monophysite bishops. But, having learned the power of the Monophysites, he determined to arrange a compromise. This compromise, named the *Henoticon*, was worded vaguely enough to escape the charge of heresy while leaving the Monophysites enough leeway to retain their views. It carefully avoided using the Catholic formula

An artist's conception of Pope Saint Simplicius I. (Montor, Chevalier Artaud de. *Lives and Times of the Popes*. New York: Catholic Publication Society of America, 1911.)

"one Christ in two natures" and accepted only the first three ecumenical councils, even going so far as to speak disrespectfully of the Chalcedon council.

However, compromise was not possible. It was determined that unless Christ is God, He cannot redeem us; and unless He is truly man, He cannot stand as a representative in our place. Simplicius's defense of this principle as it had been laid down at the Council of Chalcedon ensured that the Orthodox view of Christ was retained in the West. However, not everyone accepted Simplicius's view, and in fact some Eastern sects remain Monophysite to this day.

As a historical sidelight, Simplicius is said to have been the first pope to convert Rome's public buildings into churches.

Other Events

1256: Pope Alexander IV ordered the University of Paris to give the doctor of theology degree to the Dominican Thomas Aquinas, asserting that Aquinas had earned it. University masters balked at awarding it because the Dominicans would not take an oath related to university autonomy.

1835: Fanny Crosby left home to attend a school for the blind. She was very nervous but determined, and she soon proved to be an outstanding success. We remember her as a hymn writer.

1889: John Wood, Anglican theologian and naturalist, died. His many books popularized the study of nature.

1929: M.R. DeHaan announced that he was forming the Calvary Undenominational Church following the resignation of seventeen members from the Calvary Reformed Church he pastored in Grand Rapids, Michigan. DeHaan is best known for the Radio Bible Class and the devotional aid *Our Daily Bread*.

1933: The Navigators, a group whose work began among sailors, formed under the leadership of Dawson E. Trotman. Ten years later, on the same day in 1943, it was officially incorporated. Its founder was known as the "Apostle of Follow-up," for he refused to lead men to salvation and then neglect them. The Navigators remain committed to Christian discipleship today.

Fanny Crosby as a young girl. In middle age, she became a hymn writer and produced many favorites. (Crosby, Frances Jane. *Memories of Eighty Years*. Boston, MA: James H. Earle & Company, 1906.)

March 4

A Broken Leg Saves a Life

Gilpin narrowly escaped being among the martyrs who died at Smithfield during Mary's reign. (Besant, Sir Walter. *London in the Time of the Tudors*. London: A. & C. Black, 1904.)

Have you ever heard of a broken leg saving someone's life? Well, it is likely that it did for Bernard Gilpin. In 1558 Bishop Edmund Bonner had summoned Gilpin to London to answer for his doctrine, but Gilpin met with an accident on the way and was allowed some time to recuperate before he answered the bishop's summons. Queen Mary died before Gilpin could finish his journey, and with the accession of the Protestant queen, Elizabeth I, Gilpin escaped the "tender mercies" of the bishop's court.

In an age of cruelty and intolerance, Gilpin stood out as an unusually merciful and giving man. On one occasion, he saw a poor farmer's horse drop dead at the plow. Gilpin immediately dismounted from his own horse and presented it to the man. More than once he warmed some beggar or another by stripping off his own cloak and giving it to the poor fellow. On Sundays he fed everyone in his parish at his own expense. When he founded a grammar school, he personally defrayed the cost of attendance for poorer lads.

Gilpin was exposed to Erasmus's teachings when he attended Queens College at Oxford, and he gradually moved toward Reformation views. However, like many men of the day, he had difficulty convincing himself to take the new oath of ordination. He could not subscribe wholeheartedly to either Roman Catholic or Church of England doctrines. In Gilpin's view, Protestants "were not able to give any firm and solid reason of the separation [from Rome] besides this, to wit, that the Pope is antichrist."

After traveling abroad for a time, he was appointed by his friend and great uncle, Bishop Tunstall, to the parish of Houghton le Spring. Jealousy earned Gilpin many enemies, for his parish was large and its rectory the size of a bishop's mansion.

It was at Houghton that Gilpin obtained his name, the "Apostle of the North." He pitied the ignorance of the common people and rode, even in the bitter winter months, to preach in districts that were without pastors. These were rough areas where duels were common.

Through his ministrations and by distributing alms among the poor, Gilpin exerted great influence on Northumberland and Yorkshire. The people adored him. On the other hand, the clerics resented him and denounced him as a heretic. Bishop Tunstall ordered him left alone, saying, "[H]e has more learning than you all." The envious group then forwarded thirty-two charges to Bishop Bonner, who summoned Gilpin for an inquiry. That is when he broke his leg.

After Elizabeth's ascension to the throne brought with it the ascendancy of the Protestants, Gilpin was offered high positions within the Church. He rejected them with humility. He continued to wrestle hard with his conscience before accepting Church of England orders. At one point he was forced to preach a sermon against his will, and he boldly censured his own bishop. The bishop followed him home, pleading for forgiveness. He probably got it, for Gilpin seemed always ready to forgive. In fact, when rebels plundered and burned his house and barn, he pleaded with the authorities to spare their lives.

Gilpin had escaped Bonner's wrath in 1558, but death still found him in the end. He was knocked down by an ox in the market, and he did not recover. He died on this day in 1583. Two biographies were written about his life by admiring contemporaries, one a family member, the other a former pupil who had become a bishop.

William Penn. (Northrop, Henry Davenport. *New Century History of Our Country and Its Island Possessions*. Chicago: American Educational League, 1900.)

Other Events

561: Pope Pelagius I died. Few clergy attended his consecration. During his troubled papacy, dissension raged over the Three Chapters heresy and Monophysitism. On the home front, Pelagius's personal negotiations won concessions from the Goths who besieged Rome.

1681: William Penn was given the charter to land in America by King Charles II of England. When Penn protested King Charles's intention to call the colony "Pennsylvania," supposing it was an honor to himself, Charles smoothly put Penn in his place, making him appear proud by saying the honor was for Penn's father, an admiral. The charter is dated February 28.

1766: Naphtali Daggett became the divinity professor at Yale.

1840: James Garfield converted to Christianity. He was twenty when he was baptized by the disciples of Christ. His faith remained with him throughout the Civil War and into his presidency and upheld him as he lay dying from the bullet of an assassin.

1963: The missionary Gaspar Makil, his young daughter, Janie, and Elwood Jacobson were killed by the Vietcong.

America's First Religious Journal 5

Christianity is a historical religion. It is not just that Christianity has a history, but that Christianity recognizes that history is a record of God's works throughout time. Both the Old and the New Testament Scriptures are full of history, and Christians throughout the centuries have written histories to record God's dealings with men. In America, the first religious journal published was *The Christian History*, which was first printed by Thomas Prince on this day in 1743.

Prince, born in Sandwich, Massachusetts, in 1687, became a Congregational minister. After spending two years ministering in the West Indies and England, he returned to Massachusetts and became copastor of Boston's Old South Church, where he remained until his death forty years later. Prince and his wife were active in the Puritan social life of Boston.

In the 1740s, Prince was a strong supporter of the revival movement known as the Great Awakening. He invited the English evangelist George Whitefield to preach in Boston and became a leading "New Light" (the name adopted by supporters of the Great Awakening), cheering on the revival.

Prince also saw the importance of the history of current events. In 1736, he had written a chronological history of New England based on a collection of over 1,500 works. In 1743 he established *The Christian History* to report on the revivals sweeping America and Europe. He hoped the publication would encourage enthusiasm for the things of Christ. He asked pastors to communicate their experiences to him so that he could use the stories in the publication. Jonathan Edwards, who in effect brought the Great Awakening to New England, sent Prince a description of changes that were taking place in Northampton:

> There has been vastly more religion kept up in the town, among all sorts of persons, in religious exercises, and in common conversation, than used to be before: there has remain'd a more general seriousness and decency in attending the publick worship; there has been a very great alteration among the youth of the town, with respect to revelling, frolicking, profane and unclean conversation, and lewd songs: instances of fornication have been very rare: there has also been a great alteration amongst both old and young with respect to tavern-haunting. I suppose the town has been in no measure so free of vice in these respects, for any long time together, for this sixty years, as it has been this nine years past. There has also been an evident alteration with respect to a charitable spirit to the poor.

The Christian History ran for only two years. However, Prince was so influential that Princeton, Massachusetts, was named after him.

Thomas Prince, pioneer of American religious journalism. (Avery, Elroy McKendree. *History of the United States and Its People: From Their Earliest Records to the Present Time*. Cleveland, OH: The Burrows Brothers Company, 1904.)

Other Events

1558: Anabaptist Thomas von Imbroich was just twenty-five when an executioner lopped off his head at Köln am Rhein. Like many other Anabaptists, he went bravely to his death, which was at the hands of "Christians" who could not tolerate differences of opinion. The young man had founded many congregations of believers outside of the established Church and written a confession of faith for them. As he faced execution, he was bold:

> I am willing and ready, both to live or to die. I do not care what happens to me. God will not let me down. I am comforted and in good spirits while yet on the earth. God gives me friendly assurance, and my heart is encouraged through my brothers.

1797: Henry Nott arrived in Tahiti, which, owing to the savagery of its people, was no island paradise at the time. Twenty-two years passed before Nott made his first convert.

1835: William McKendree, the first American-born bishop of the Methodist Church, died on this day. Bishop Francis Asbury consecrated him in 1808.

William McKendree, first American-born bishop of the Methodist Church. (Asbury, Francis. *The Heart of Asbury's Journal*. New York: Eaton & Mains; Cincinnati: Jennings & Graham, 1904.)

March

6

Delivering Children from the Horrors of the Temple

Amy Carmichael with Lola and Leela, two of the Indian children who sheltered with her at Dohnavur. (Houghton, Frank. *Amy Carmichael of Dohnavur: A Story of a Lover and Her Beloved*. London: S.P.C.K., 1953.)

Amy Carmichael was a kidnapper—many times over, in fact! On this day in 1901, she sheltered her first temple runaway, a young girl who had been dedicated to the Hindu gods and forced into prostitution to earn money for the priests. Technically, that made Amy a kidnapper. Over the years, Amy rescued many other children, often at the cost of extreme exhaustion and personal danger.

Irish-born Amy was a most unlikely heroine. She suffered neuralgia, a disease of the nerves that made her whole body weak and achy and put her in bed for weeks on end. Friends thought she was foolish when she announced she was going to be a missionary. They predicted that she would soon be back in England for keeps. But Amy was sure that God had called her to go overseas.

When Amy was a child, her mother told her that if Amy prayed, the Lord would answer. So Amy prayed that God would change her brown eyes to blue. In the morning she jumped out of bed and ran to the mirror. Mrs. Carmichael heard Amy wail in disappointment. It took Mrs. Carmichael several minutes of careful explanation before Amy understood that "no" was an answer too. God meant Amy to have brown eyes for a reason, explained Mrs. Carmichael. Amy wasn't so sure. Smiling Irish blue would always be her favorite color, even if God said "no."

As a youth Amy thought she was a Christian, but an evangelist showed her that she needed to make a personal commitment to Christ. She gave her heart to Jesus, and service for Him became the center and passion of her life.

The year that Amy's father died unexpectedly, Amy started classes and prayer groups for Belfast ragamuffins. She also began a Sunday work with the "shawlies." These were factory girls so poor that they could not afford hats to wear to church and wore shawls instead. Respectable people didn't want anything to do with them, but Amy saw that they needed Christ just the same as their supposed "betters." So many shawlies attended Amy's classes that she had to find a building large enough to hold the more than 300 attendees.

The Carmichaels lost all their money through financial reverses, and a change became necessary. Mrs. Carmichael decided to move to England and work for a family member there. Amy and one of her sisters joined her. The family member asked Amy to teach his mill workers about Christ, and Amy threw herself into the work. However, she was constantly sick with neuralgia and had to lie in bed for days at a time. It soon became clear that she must give up the work.

Faith and circumstances eventually led Amy to India, where she began her rescue work with small children who were forced to prostitute in Hindu temples.

> Sometimes it was as if I saw the Lord Jesus Christ kneeling alone, as He knelt long ago under the olive trees. . . . And the only thing that one who cared could do, was to go softly and kneel down beside Him, so that He would not be alone in His sorrow over the little children.

Dressed in a sari, her skin stained brown, Amy could pass as a Hindu. Now she understood why God had given her brown eyes. Blue eyes would have been a dead giveaway!

When she rescued five-year-old Kohila, the child's guardians wanted the child back. Amy refused to return the little girl to certain abuse. Instead, she arranged for her to "disappear" to a safe place. The plot was discovered and charges were brought against Amy. She faced a seven-year prison term.

But Amy did not go to prison. A telegram arrived on February 7, 1914, saying, "Criminal case dismissed." No explanation was ever forthcoming, but Amy had no doubt that the Lord had had a hand in the decision.

Michelangelo's *Pieta*, one of his most famous religious sculptures. (LaFarge, John. *Great Masters*. New York: McClure Phillips Co., 1903.)

Other Events

766: Saint Chrodegang, bishop of Metz, died. He was a member of the French nobility and authored the religious rule *Vita Canonica* for his clergymen. He was a man of great ability and charity and served as bishop at the same time that he was Pépin's prime minister.

1475: "Today March 6, 1475, a child of the male sex has been born to me and I have named him Michelangelo," wrote the great artist's father. "He was born on Monday between 4 and 5 in the morning, at Caprese, where I am the Podestà." Michelangelo produced much Christian art.

1858: The Missionary Society of St. Paul the Apostle (the Paulists) was founded by Isaac Hecker and his companions. Its purpose was to convert Americans to Roman Catholicism, for Hecker viewed the United States as a mission field comparable to any other. The Paulists became highly successful. They made strong use of print media.

1919: Julia Johnston, author of the hymn "Marvelous Grace of Our Loving Lord," died this day.

What's a Bible Worth to You?

By the early 1800s Wales had experienced revival. One thing, however, was lacking: There were not enough Bibles for everyone.

Fifteen-year-old Mary Jones saved the money she had made from tending chickens and doing other odd jobs for six years so that she could purchase a Bible. When she had enough, she walked twenty-five miles to see Rev. Thomas Charles, who was said to sell Bibles in the Welsh tongue. The good man had just sold his last copy, but the buyer had not picked it up yet. Charles was so impressed with Jones that he gave that copy to her. He would find another copy for the other buyer.

Thomas Charles was a notable figure in the Welsh revival. In 1802, perhaps stirred by Jones's hunger for the Word, he visited the Religious Tract Society in London and pleaded with them to supply him with Scriptures. The society had to turn him away: Providing Bibles just was not in their job description. However, as society members discussed the request, Rev. Joseph Hughes said, "A society might be formed for the purpose [of distributing Bibles]—and if for Wales, why not for the Kingdom; why not for the whole world?"

Why not indeed? Fifteen months later, the spark of Hughes's suggestion became reality. On this day in 1804, The British and Foreign Bible Society was formed to publish, distribute and translate the Bible. It was the first of many similar organizations that would be formed throughout the world.

Key supporters of the young society were members of the Clapham sect, those well-placed evangelicals who did so much to improve society in the late eighteenth and early nineteenth centuries. Among them were William Wilberforce, Zachary Macauley and Hannah More.

The society represented a wide spectrum of Christian life in Britain and refused to distribute or print Bibles with notes. They felt that too often Bibles had been printed with barbed comments aimed at other Christian sects.

The British and Foreign Bible Society began an immediate and useful work, not only publishing and distributing their own translations of the Bible but also supporting other translators. The trailblazing missionary William Carey was funded by the society in his translation work. When Robert Morrison, the first Protestant missionary to China, began to translate the Bible into Chinese, he was generously assisted by the society. So was Henry Martyn, missionary to India, who worked on a Persian translation. The society's influence spread as far away as the Cook Islands in the Pacific, where it funded a translation of the Bible into the Rarotongan language. In fact, wherever Christian missions spread around the globe, the society could be found, lending a hand with the Scripture work.

Within 100 years The British and Foreign Bible Society had distributed over 200 million pieces of literature. By 1962 four-fifths of the inhabitants of the globe had the Bible in their own tongue, although 2,000 or more languages still remained without any translation.

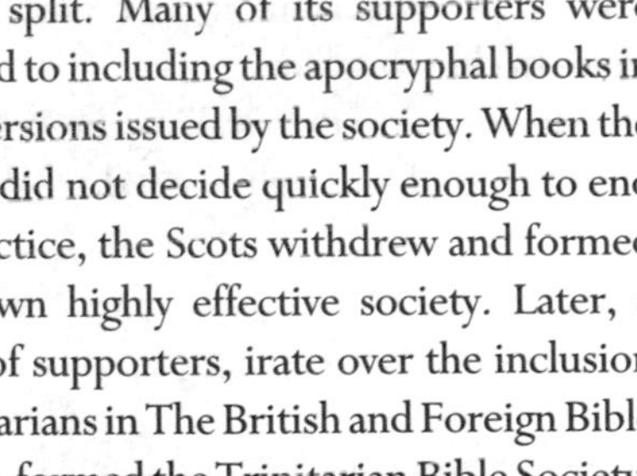

The Bible Society headquarters in 1910. (Loftie, W.J. *London City: Its History, Streets, Traffic, Buildings and People*. London: The Leadenhall Press, 1891.)

From the start The British and Foreign Bible Society let missionaries do their own translation. The societies with whom they worked trained their own workers. The society made no attempt to dominate or direct the process. Auxiliaries to the main society quickly sprang up. In just ten years, sixty-nine other Bible organizations had formed.

But twenty years after its formation, the society split. Many of its supporters were opposed to including the apocryphal books in Bible versions issued by the society. When the society did not decide quickly enough to end the practice, the Scots withdrew and formed their own highly effective society. Later, a group of supporters, irate over the inclusion of Unitarians in The British and Foreign Bible Society, formed the Trinitarian Bible Society.

Other Events

202: Perpetua was flogged and run through the throat with a sword in the arena of Carthage. She suffered martyrdom with her slave Felicitas and other Christians. Perpetua's boldness encouraged the rest to remain steadfast. Both women had infants and were pressured to recant for the sake of their children, but both refused. It is thought that Perpetua was the first Christian female author.

1274: St. Thomas Aquinas died. Thomism, his philosophy, remains the basis for much Catholic theology.

1526: Zurich authorities sentenced Conrad Grebel and other Anabaptists to life imprisonment for their faith.

1799: In a message issued this day, the second President of the United States, John Adams, called for a day of national fasting to be held on the twenty-fifth day of April, urging every citizen to devote the time to the

> sacred duties of religion, in public and in private that they call to mind our numerous offenses against the most high God, confess them before Him with the sincerest penitence, implore his pardoning mercy, through the Great Mediator and Redeemer [Jesus Christ], for our past transgressions.

1964: Pope Paul VI celebrated mass in the Italian language, facing his congregation, signaling a new day; usually priests faced away and used Latin.

Perpetua and Felicitas die. (Courtesy of the Christian History Institute archives.)

How Dare You Deny Our Faith?

Mieczyslaw I, the first Polish prince to be baptized. (Missalet, Don Erich. *Konigreich Polen*. Bielefeld: Velhagen & Klasing, 1915.)

In 1945 the Soviets seized control of Poland and imposed their atheistic Communist regime on the nation. Despite the fact that ninety percent of the Polish people considered themselves Roman Catholics, the new government stripped the Church of its legal status. Religious symbols were banned from public places.

However, after the election of Pope John Paul II in 1978, Poland enjoyed greater religious freedom than most eastern European states of that time. When Pope John Paul II visited his homeland, he drew millions of Poles to church rallies.

In response to these rallies, the Polish government evidently felt a need to show the Church who was boss. They demanded that all crosses be taken down from public buildings. Only one school obeyed. Others reasoned that the schools belonged to Poland and Poland was Catholic; therefore, the crosses should and would remain. "There is no Poland without the cross," said one priest, alluding to Poland's 1,000-year history of Christianity.

Christianity had first been introduced in Poland in the tenth century. Prince Mieczyslaw I was baptized in 966. In subsequent years, the Church survived persecution, civil war, the Reformation and partition by its neighbors. Almost a millennium later, the Soviets controlled the nation, and the Church became a rallying point for those who rejected Communism, including many Polish youth.

Riot police were sent to the Staszic Agricultural College when two-thirds of the students staged a sit-in to protest the removal of seven crosses from the campus. Within days, thousands of Polish students were involved in demonstrations across the nation. On this day in 1984, 3,000 young students protested, waving crucifixes in the air.

The government tried to force the parents of seniors who were attending the Agricultural College to sign forms acknowledging that schools were secular in nature. They were told that if they did not sign the forms, the students would not be allowed to graduate. Most parents refused, and the Church applauded their determination. For most Poles, the pronouncements of the Church had more real authority than those of a brutal, atheistic regime that had forfeited its right to rule by demanding the violation of conscience and the repudiation of the man whom even some secularists acknowledge was the greatest individual in history—Jesus Christ.

The parents' stand was successful. Eventually the government retreated, although it still held to its premise that the schools were secular and shouldn't be allowed to display crosses.

Ultimately, even before the Communist regime was overthrown, Bibles were permitted in the classroom. Evangelistic meetings were held openly. As has happened so many times since He walked on earth, Christ overcame the world.

Controversial Henry Ward Beecher. (Kennedy, James H. *American Nation, Vol. 1*. Cleveland, OH: Williams Publishing Company, 1892.)

Other Events

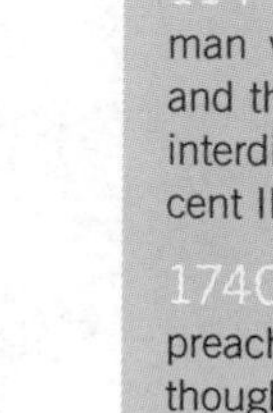

1144: Pope Celestine II died. He was a learned man who had been a pupil of the philosopher and theologian Peter Abelard. Celestine lifted the interdict that had been placed on France by Innocent II.

1740: Presbyterian minister Gilbert Tennent preached a sermon in answer to clergymen who thought that George Whitefield's revival services were too emotional. Tennent saw a different danger: "For I am verily persuaded the generality of preachers talk of an unknown and unfelt Christ; and the reason why congregations have been so dead is because they have had dead men preaching to them.

He went on to say that New England churchgoers were like sheep without shepherds and that their pastors were too often without personal knowledge of Christ. These remarks outraged Presbyterians. His synod reproved him. In response, Tennent and other New Brunswick preachers withdrew from the Presbyterian association.

For the next seventeen years, Presbyterians were divided into New Lights, those who desired a more experiential interpretation of the Christian life, and the Old Lights, those who believed that adherence to orthodoxy was more important than Christian living. Near the end of his life, Tennent tried to unite the factions.

1887: Henry Ward Beecher, son of Lyman Beecher and brother of Harriet Beecher Stowe, died on this day. His dramatic flair, popular writing style and willingness to tackle tough issues made him a leading spokesman of the day. However, he slipped into Unitarian thought, denying Christ's divinity, and was brought to trial for alienating the affections of another man's wife. The charge was not proved against him.

Naked for Christ in a Frozen Swamp

If you think it is hard to crawl out of a warm bed on an icy morning and drop your feet onto a cold floor, how would you like to stand barefoot on a frozen pond in winter? Ice fisherman bundle up in warm clothes and appreciate the shelter of a fishing hut. Stop and think, then, what it would feel like to be stripped stark naked in the dead of winter and forced to stand out on a frozen lake. That is what happened to forty Christians on this day in 320 (the date is based on long-standing tradition).

When Licinus was Roman emperor, the empire was threatened on three sides at once. He saw the pacifism of Christians as a threat to his kingdom and ordered all Christians to renounce their faith on pain of death. Forty soldiers of the twelfth legion, stationed at Sevastia (now Sivas, Turkey) refused. These men, who hailed from various countries, were chained, beaten with stones and imprisoned. When this did not compel them to renounce their faith, stronger measures were taken against them.

The soldiers were stripped naked and forced, in darkness, onto the ice of a frozen pond in Sevastia. Baths of hot water were placed around them as a temptation to renounce their faith. All they had to do was give in and they could be warm again. The temptation must have been great, for it was very cold. Instead, the forty men huddled together on the ice and sang hymns. The hardened soldiers who had brought the men there could not have failed to admire the pluck of their former comrades.

According to tradition, one of the men guarding the naked victims said he saw a heavenly light surrounding the men and glorious crowns on the heads of all but one. As the night progressed, voices dropped out of the singing: The men were dying. Then a noise was heard. The nerve of one of the Christians had cracked, and he had crawled off the pond to a warm bath. Distressed by this desertion and impressed by the fortitude of the remaining Christians, the pagan guard who had seen the heavenly light threw off his own clothes and marched out to join the martyrs.

When day dawned, a few of the Christians were still alive. The guards went onto the lake and broke the legs of all but one of the ex-soldiers to hasten their deaths. The dying men commended their souls to God. The Romans had spared that one soldier this brutal treatment because the soldier, Meliton, was young and strong, and they hoped he might survive and forsake his faith. It is said his mother stood nearby. A Christian herself, and fearing lest he should buckle, she urged him to hold out:

> Behold, Christ is invisibly standing by to help you. A little bit more, my child, and you shall never be grieved or tired again. All the tortures are past, all the hardship you have conquered with your courage. Joy shall receive you after this, pleasure, comfort, elation, other goods, which you shall enjoy reigning with Christ and being an ambassador to Him for me, your mother.

(It is at this point in the story that it becomes difficult to determine true fact from elements of legend. However the events actually unfolded, it is a story worth telling, so we will continue with it as it has been told through the ages.)

The forty martyrs. (Traditional icon. Courtesy of the Christian History Institute archives.)

When the soldiers piled the bodies onto carts but left Meliton, hoping he would live and recant, his mother lifted the young man to her shoulders and ran after the carts, believing she would see her son alive when she had seen him dead for Christ.

The soldiers lit a great fire and burned the bodies of the martyrs. Then they threw the ashes and all remaining fragments into the river because they wanted to prevent Christians from making relics of them. However, their plan was thwarted by nature itself, for remains of the brave men tumbled together at a waterfall, and local Christians recovered fragments and dedicated churches to house the remains.

Other Events

395: Gregory of Nyssa, an outstanding bishop in Cappadocia (a region of what is now Turkey), died on this day. Gregory was influential in developing the theology of the Trinity. He was one of those who recorded the story of the forty martyrs who froze to death in Sevastia.

1074: Pope Gregory VII ordered married priests and those who had bought their offices to cease from their duties.

1118: Gelasius II was ordained a priest, and on the next day, pope. Emperor Henry V seized him and set up an antipope, but rioting mobs forced the emperor to release Gelasius. Gelasius fled, was consecrated and then excommunicated Henry. Gelasius eventually died in France, where he had retired for protection.

1931: World Radio Missionary Fellowship was incorporated by Clarence W. Jones and Reuben Larson in Lima, Ohio. It became a far-reaching radio ministry, broadcasting the gospel to many nations.

Pope Gelasius II, whose papacy struggled against Holy Roman Emperor Henry V. (Montor, Chevalier Artaud de. *Lives and Times of the Popes*. New York: Catholic Publication Society of America, 1911.)

John Newton, slaver turned parson. (Courtesy of the Christian History Institute archives.)

MARCH 10

Out of a Stormy Sea and a Stormier Heart

To be at sea in a storm on a sturdy ocean liner can be thrilling. But, as John Newton discovered, facing a storm in a sailing vessel that is not seaworthy can be terrifying. The ship in which Newton sailed was in disrepair, and its sails and rigging were worn.

One night he was wakened by a violent wave crashing against the vessel. Water filled his cabin. Hurrying above, he found that timbers had been ripped away from the ship's structure. The entire crew was in terrible danger as the ship plunged through a furious storm. Men desperately tried to pump the water out of the ship. Clothes and bedding were stuffed into holes and boards were nailed over them. Newton joined those at the pumps.

When he became too exhausted to pump any longer, he was lashed to the wheel and told to steer the ship. The storm raged on and on. It was bitterly cold, the more so since the men had few clothes left. In this desperate moment Newton turned his eyes back over his life. Raised to the age of seven by a Christian mother, he had sought the Lord with fasts and prayers, but failing to find God he had become bitter. He grew into a hard man who often mocked God. He was considered desperately wicked even by his godless shipmates. Despite this, however, the Lord had preserved him through many dangers, including a stint as a servant on the west coast of Africa.

The strange thing was that in his heart he believed Christianity to be true. However, this brought him no consolation. Reflecting about his experience on the storm-tossed ship, Newton said, "I concluded my sins were too great to be forgiven. I waited with fear and impatience to receive my doom." But soon he heard the glad news that the ship was freed of water.

> I began to pray . . . to think of that Jesus that I had so often derided; I recollected His death: a death for sins not His own, but, as I remembered, for the sake of those who should put their trust in Him.

On this day in 1747, a day he ever after observed, Newton realized he needed a Savior to intercede for him with God. He snatched a free moment during the tumult to open the Bible and began to read. Though the storm raged on for days, Newton spent every free moment in the Scripture and praying for guidance. Hungry, cold, exhausted, the men managed to keep the ship afloat. Only one man died of exhaustion. Not knowing of Newton's change of heart, the captain muttered that Newton ought to be thrown overboard like Jonah, thinking that Newton's wickedness was the cause of all their misery. Finally they reached Ireland.

By then Newton was convinced the Lord had reached down and delivered his soul. The story of the Prodigal Son seemed to exactly fit his case. He never turned back from that day of salvation.

Not realizing that the slave trade was a sin, however, Newton worked for six more years as a slaver. But his attitude was softer and he showed kindness to the slaves he transported. He even held worship services for his men and wrote hymns for them.

Eventually he woke up to the fact that slavery was wrong and became an abolitionist and a minister. Reflecting back upon his hard life, he wrote one of the world's most loved hymns:

> Amazing grace, how sweet the sound
> That saved a wretch like me!
> I once was lost, but now am found;
> Was blind, but now I see.

George Müller, faith advocate and prayer warrior. (Pitman, Mrs. E.R. *George Müller and Andrew Reed*. London: Cassell & Son, Ltd., 1885.)

Other Events

1528: Balthasar Hubmaier, an Anabaptist leader, was burned at the stake as a martyr. He was considered by his enemies to be the most important of the Anabaptists. He argued for religious toleration and the restrained and judicious use of the sword.

1774: The Reformed Presbyterian Church Evangelical Synod was formed. It never became a large denomination but clung to the Westminster Confession and catechisms when some other larger, "mainstream" Presbyterian churches were slipping away from them.

1880: The Salvation Army landed in New York. The following day an issue of the *New York Tribune* reported that seven women and one man had come as "Missionaries to America." The Salvation Army, which had begun several years before in England, quickly grew to have several hundred American branches with thousands of workers.

1898: George Müller of Bristol died. Müller was an advocate of faith, and he diligently prayed for the money to operate orphanages. Speaking of his conversion, he said,

> [A] great love for Christ filled my soul. That was more than fifty years ago. I loved Jesus Christ then, but I loved him more the year after and more the year after that and more every year since. How much I love Him now I could not begin to tell you. Jesus Christ is my great and glorious and adorable God and Savior, whose love fills my soul.

A Master Revives a Master

It is clear from his music that Johann Sebastian Bach believed in the Resurrection. For example, the "Crucifixus" of his *Mass in B Minor* ends with low-register voices to suggest Christ going down into the grave, and the next chorus breaks forth in joy to express His resurrection.

Bach's music went through a resurrection of its own. Virtually forgotten at his death, the bulk of his work lay neglected for almost a century. In fact, his work was valued so little that fish at market were wrapped in Bach manuscripts.

Bach's life was defined by poverty, but his music was rich. Every form that he touched, he improved. He perfected the "well-tempered" scale which, by dividing every octave into twelve equal distances, allowed any key on the organ to start a scale. His keyboard technique used all five fingers of each hand where three had previously been the norm. His works *The Well-Tempered Clavier* and *Art of the Fugue* trained musicians such as Beethoven, who said: "He should not be called Bach [brook] but Meer [sea]."

Every manuscript that Bach wrote was dedicated to Christ. Throughout their pages appear cryptic abbreviations such as "I.N.J." standing for *In Nomine Jesu*, that is, "In the Name of Jesus." According to Bach, music's aim and purpose is to glorify God and provide recreation for the mind. "Where this is not observed there will be no real music but only devilish hubbub."

He poured a new depth of emotion into his music. For example, his portrayals of Christ's passion gain power by making frequent use of dissonance. Combining expressive melodies with a rhythmic bass line, he conveyed, according to Bach scholar and enthusiast William H. Scheide, "the union of the divine and human in the person of Christ."

That such work fell into neglect was regrettable. His genius was not recognized in his time. Shortly after Bach died, one burgomaster (chief magistrate) remarked unfeelingly, "The school needed a cantor [choir leader] and not a Kapellmeister [director]." For fifty years after his death, no Bach piece was published separately on its own merits.

Bach's revival was largely due to the efforts of Felix Mendelssohn, a composer whose family had converted from Judaism to Christianity. Mendelssohn was in awe of Bach, Mozart and Beethoven and in love with music. He said:

> People often complain that music is too ambiguous, that what they should be thinking as they hear it is unclear. . . . With me it is exactly the reverse. . . . The thoughts which are expressed to me by music that I love are not too indefinite to be put into words, but on the contrary, too definite.

He arranged to have Bach's *St. Matthew Passion* played on this day in 1829, almost exactly a century from the date of its first, long-forgotten performance. Mendelssohn himself conducted the performance.

Felix Mendelssohn with his beloved sister Fanny, a composer in her own right. (Rowlands, Walter. *Among the Great Masters of Music: Scenes in the Lives of Famous Musicians*. Boston: D. Estes & Co., 1900.)

"Never," wrote one participant, "have I known any performance so consecrated by one united sympathy." The concert was sold out, and more than 1,000 people were unable to get tickets. Two additional concerts were scheduled at once. So great was the sensation caused by the work that composer Hector Berlioz marveled, "There is but one god—Bach, and Mendelssohn, his prophet."

Today many consider Bach the greatest composer who ever lived because of his originality and technical mastery. His work might never have been recognized had it not been for Mendelssohn's efforts.

Mendelssohn was a great composer in his own right. He wrote his first mature work, the "Overture" to *A Midsummer Night's Dream* at the age of seventeen. His oratorio *Elijah* is his own monument to faith. He died at thirty-six, worn out from overwork.

Other Events

1095: The Council of Rockingham opened to decide whether Anselm could keep allegiance to both the king and Pope Urban, whom the king had not yet accepted. Virtually all of England's churchmen sided with the king against Anselm.

1559: Reform-minded mobs burned churches in Perth, Scotland, and told their friars that there must be no more mass.

1870: The Martyrs Memorial at Smithfield, England, was inaugurated. Many Christians were executed at Smithfield over the years.

1888: Samuel Zwemer, who would become the "Apostle to Islam," preached his first public sermon to an African-American congregation in Michigan.

1897: Henry Drummond, noted for his popular Christian writings, died on this day. *The Greatest Thing in the World* was the most popular and enduring of his writings, and *Natural Law in the Spiritual World* was the most controversial. "I discovered myself enunciating Spiritual Law in the exact terms of Biology and Physics," he wrote. But he himself quickly became dissatisfied with the work, sensing that its assumptions could not be established.

Henry Drummond, notable Christian writer. (Smith, George Adam. *The Life of Henry Drummond*. New York: Doubleday & McClure Co., 1898.)

MARCH 12

Jews Complete New Temple

Herod's temple. (Courtesy of Datafoto.)

In 539 BC, Babylon fell to a coalition of Medes and Persians. The new rulers of the Mideast made it their policy to restore captives to their respective homelands. Among those captives were the Jews. They returned to Judah with permission to rebuild their temple. However, seventeen years after their return, construction still languished. So God raised up the prophets Haggai and Zechariah to rebuke this neglectful behavior.

In 520 Haggai, speaking words from the Lord, asked, "Is it a time for you yourselves to live in your paneled houses, while this house lies in ruins?" (1:4, NRSV). Through Haggai, the Lord spoke to the Jews about how they had fared since their return:

> You have sown much, and harvested little; you eat, but you never have enough; you drink, but you never have your fill; you clothe yourselves, but no one is warm; and you that earn wages earn wages to put them into a bag with holes. (Haggai 1:6, NRSV)

Haggai announced that God wanted the Jews to bring wood and rebuild His house.

Judah's political and religious leaders listened. Under their leadership, the remnant of Jews who had returned to Israel rebuilt God's house. According to Jack Finegan's *Handbook of Biblical Chronology,* they completed their construction of the temple on this day in 515 BC.

It apparently wasn't much to look at, for the Lord asked them:

> Who is left among you that saw this house in its former glory? How does it look to you now? Is it not in your sight as nothing? (2:3, NRSV)

He told them that they should not think that way, for His Spirit was with them. He also told them that:

> In a little while, I will shake the heavens and the earth and the sea and the dry land; and I will shake all the nations, so that the treasure of all nations shall come, and I will fill this house with splendor. . . . The latter splendor of this house shall be greater than the former . . . and in this place I will give prosperity. (2:6-7, 9, NRSV)

The temple was destroyed and was rebuilt again by Herod the Great, who restored it in stone and covered it with gold. It was that temple that Christ visited, bringing it glory. A generation after Christ's death and resurrection, Herod's temple was cast down by the Romans. A mosque now stands on its platform.

Haggai also prophesied that all the nations would bring their treasures to the temple. That event has not been fulfilled. It awaits yet another temple when Christ returns.

The little *Mayflower* served as quarters for the Pilgrims for several months after their arrival in the New World. (Courtesy of the Christian History Institute archives.)

OTHER EVENTS

604: Pope Gregory the Great died on this day. He left a lasting mark on the Middle Ages with his musical reforms, political leadership, pastoral counsel and superstitious tales.

1112: At the Church of St. John, Lateran, Paschal II renounced an agreement that he had made with Holy Roman Emperor Henry V and required his bishops to sign the repudiation.

1607: Paul Gerhardt was born near Wittenberg in Saxony, Germany. Despite a life of distress (four of his five children died and he was ousted from his pastorate for refusing to compromise his faith) he wrote over 130 hymns, including "O Sacred Head, Now Wounded."

1621: The Pilgrims, refugees from religious persecution in England, finally left the little ship *Mayflower*, on which they had lived for many months after their arrival in New England.

1875: John McCloskey was named the first Roman Catholic cardinal of the United States.

"Let There Be Peace"

Seldom in history have counsels of peace prevailed. Seldom has faith intervened in history to bring a peaceful solution to an international crisis. In the early 1900s, however, that rarity occurred.

Argentina and Chile were rattling sabers at each other. They were disputing the placement of the boundary in the Andes that separated the two nations, one claiming that the line should be drawn at the watershed, the other that it should be at the highest point of the range. The debate became heated, and war threatened in 1902.

The people of the Andes are by and large Roman Catholics. In November of 1900, Pope Leo XIII issued an encyclical that called for consecration of the entire world to Christ the Redeemer. Remembering Leo's call, both Argentine and Chilean Christians urged their respective governments to settle matters amicably.

Leo's encyclical said:

> The common welfare, then, urgently demands a return to Him from whom we should never have gone astray; to Him who is the Way, the Truth, and the Life—and this on the part not only of individuals but of society as a whole. We must restore Christ to this His own rightful possession. All elements of the national life must be made to drink in the Life which proceedeth from Him—legislation, political institutions, education, marriage and family life, capital and labor. Everyone must see that the very growth of civilization which is so ardently desired depends greatly upon this, since it is fed and grows not so much by material wealth and prosperity, as by the spiritual qualities of morality and virtue. . . . The world has heard enough of the so-called "rights of man." Let it hear something of the rights of God. That the time is suitable is proved by the very general revival of religious feeling already referred to, and especially that devotion towards Our Savior of which there are so many indications, and which, please God, we shall hand on to the New Century as a pledge of happier times to come.

The governments of Argentina and Chile listened to their citizens and agreed to submit the matter for arbitration. Arbitrating the Northern end of the line was the United States ambassador. Arbitrating the Southern end was King Edward VII of England. War was averted when both sides accepted the arbitration results in 1903.

As happy as this outcome was, it is not the end of the story. Monsignor Marcolino del Carmel Benavente, the bishop of San Juan, suggested the erection of a statue to remind the people of Christ's words, "And I, if I be lifted up from the earth, will draw all men unto me" (John 12:32, KJV). The statue would remind all that they should be consecrated to mutual understanding. Thus was born the concept of the Christ of the Andes.

Leo XIII. His 1900 encyclical *Tametsi*, on Jesus Christ the Redeemer, helped avert war in South America. (McGovern, James J. *The Life and Life-Work of Pope Leo XIII*. Chicago: Monarch Books, 1903.)

Tourists traveling the Pan American highway can see the result—a twenty-six-foot-tall bronze image of Christ holding out His right hand in blessing over the disputant nations. His left hand clings to a cross. Under His feet is the Western Hemisphere. The cross is located at a level of 13,000 feet in the Uspallata Pass and stands against the backdrop of Mount Aconcagua, which rises another 13,000 feet above the statue. This is the highest readily accessible point on the boundary between the two nations.

Sculptor Mateo Alonso modeled the work. Señora Angela de Oliveira Cézar de Costa raised the financing. Workmen melted down old cannons to make the casting.

The statue was dedicated on this day in 1904.

Other Events

1271: Gregory X entered Rome a few days before his consecration as pope. The papacy had been vacant for three years because of a serious division among the cardinals. Gregory had been on a pilgrimage to the Holy Land when he was elected to the position. As pope, he succeeded in bringing peace to Europe's rulers.

1455: Pope Calixtus III issued the bull *Inter Caetera*, giving jurisdiction of Africa and southern Asia to the grand master of the *Militia Christi*.

1569: Roman Catholics defeated the Huguenots at Jarnac, France. Condé, the Huguenot leader, was killed.

1660: A severe law against the Society of Friends (Quakers) was passed in Virginia. The law called them unreasonable and turbulent and charged them with publishing lies, miracles and false visions.

1892: Charles Henry Packhurst preached his famous documented sermon against Tammany Hall corruption in New York, helping to bring about reform in the city.

1925: Tennessee's Butler Bill prohibited the teaching of evolution in its public schools. This ban led to the Scopes Monkey trial in which William Jennings Bryan prosecuted John Thomas Scopes (who was found guilty of violating the law).

William Jennings Bryan, who prosecuted the Scopes Monkey Trial. (Bryan, Mary Baird. *The Memoirs of William Jennings Bryan*. Dayton, TN: Bryan Memorial Univ., 1925.)

March 14

Cult of Myths and Blood

Hitler. (Courtesy of Ann Snyder.)

Hitler came to power in 1933. That same year, the Vatican signed a concordat with the Reich in order to protect the interests of the Catholic Church and its people. Hitler observed it as faithfully as he observed his other treaties, which is to say, when it suited him. By 1937 the concordat had broken down.

Pope Pius XI was alarmed by the unreasonable claims of the Nazis and by their disrespect for the Church. The Nazis restricted Catholic schools and presses and destroyed Catholic organizations throughout Germany piece-by-piece.

In response, the pope issued an encyclical on this day in 1937. The encyclical was smuggled into Germany and read on Palm Sunday from every Catholic pulpit. Fortunately, not a single copy came to the Nazis' attention beforehand. "*Mit brennender sorge* . . ." it began:

> With burning concern and mounting consternation we have been observing for some time now the cross carried by the church in Germany and the increasingly difficult situation of those men and women who have kept the faith.

The pope claimed that the failure of the concordat was not the fault of the Church:

> Anyone who still has within him the slightest feeling for truth . . . will have to admit that in these difficult and eventful years which have followed the Concordat, every one of our words and every one of our deeds have been regulated by loyalty to the agreement. . . . He will, however, also have to note with consternation . . . how for the other side [the Nazis] it has become the unwritten law of their conduct to misconstrue, evade, undermine, and in the end more or less openly violate the treaty.

The encyclical especially urged Catholics to resist the idolatrous cults of state and race:

> Race, nation, state . . . all have an essential and honorable place within the secular order. To abstract them . . . from the earthly scale of values and make them the supreme norm of all values, including religious ones . . . is to be guilty of perverting and falsifying the order of things created and commanded by God.

The pope warned against accepting the dark and impersonal gods of pre-Christian Germany:

> Our God is the personal God, supernatural, omnipotent, infinitely perfect, one in the Trinity of Persons, tri-personal in the unity of divine essence, the Creator of all existence, Lord, King and ultimate Consummator of the history of the world, who will not, and cannot, tolerate a rival god by His side.

He went on to say that the German nation must work for the common good: "Society was intended by the Creator for the full development of individual possibilities." Sounding very much like the Presbyterian reformers, he wrote:

> The believer has an absolute right to profess his Faith and live according to its dictates. Laws which impede this profession and practice of Faith are against the natural law.

The pope denied the legality of the Nazi policy of forced school enrollments:

> Conscientious parents, aware of their educational duties, have a primal and original right to determine that the children which God has given them should be educated in the spirit of true faith.

Although buoyed by the pope's words and encouraged to stand firm in their faith, many Catholics suffered greatly during Hitler's regime.

Basel, Switzerland, passed a harsh law against Anabaptists. (Armitage, Thomas. *A History of the Baptists: Traced by Their Principles and Practices, From the Time of our Lord and Saviour Jesus Christ to the Present*. New York: Bryan, Taylor and Co., 1893.)

Other Events

1528: The Protestant city of Basel, Switzerland, passed a law that all Anabaptists and other religious dissenters who did not forsake their "errors" were to be fined £5; so were any who gave them aid.

1643: The English parliament granted a charter to Roger Williams to found Rhode Island, the first colony in America to allow freedom of religion.

1873: A 200-year-old edict against Christianity was revoked in Japan after Commodore Perry of the United States forced the nation to open its ports. Western diplomats had complained of the mistreatment of Christians.

1948: Gustav Tuurs was placed at the head of the Latvian Lutheran Church after other leaders were exiled or sent to prison by the Communist regime.

1951: The Rumanian National Catholic Church, a government entity, took over all of Rumania's Roman Catholic Church establishments in the continuing effort of Communists to control the Church.

March 15

Money for Leo's Coffers Sparks a Split in Christendom

When warlike Pope Julius II died in 1513, his successor, Giovanni de' Medici, took the name Pope Leo X. Julius had loved a fight, but Leo preferred fun. In fact, his aptitude for self-indulgence helped destroy the unity of the Christian Church in Europe.

From birth Leo had been earmarked for the Church. At the age of seven he was made a monk. By thirteen he was a cardinal. In between, the boy served as an abbot. He became pope before turning forty.

Despite, or perhaps because of, the austerity of his upbringing, he had developed costly tastes. As pope, he was only too happy to spend lavishly on himself and extravagant entertainment. Humanists with scanty morals swarmed the papal court, where wit mattered more than witness. Plays and shows, ballets and games abounded. Few hunts were turned down. Eminent artists such as Raphael lived off the papal treasury. Julius had left a full treasury; Leo drained it in eight short years.

St. Peter's Basilica was being rebuilt, but there was no money. Leo decided to solve the problem in time-honored fashion. On this day in 1517, he declared that anyone who contributed financially to the rebuilding of the cathedral would be granted indulgence from sins. Here is how the indulgence read:

> May our Lord Jesus Christ have mercy on thee, and absolve thee by the merits of His most holy passion. And I, by His authority, that of His blessed Apostles Peter and Paul, and of the most holy Pope, granted and committed to me in these parts, do absolve thee, first from all ecclesiastical censures, in whatever manner they may have been incurred, and then from all thy sins, transgressions, and excesses, how enormous soever they may be, even from such as are reserved for the cognizance of the Holy See; and as far as the Keys of the Holy Church extend, I remit to you all punishment which you deserve in purgatory on their account, and I restore you to the holy sacraments of the Church . . . and to that innocence and purity which you possessed at baptism; so that when you die the gates of punishment shall be shut, and the gates of the paradise of delight shall be opened; and if you shall not die at present, this grace shall remain in full force when you are at the point of death. In the name of the Father, and of the Son, and of the Holy Ghost.

Sent to preach the indulgence in Germany was a Dominican named Tetzel. Tetzel's words promised that the indulgence even covered future sins.

Frederick the Wise refused to allow the indulgence to be preached in Saxony. He was reluctant to allow Saxon coin to leave his already depleted realm. Tetzel came as near the border as he could. Folk from Wittenberg crossed over and bought the prized papers.

After the excitement over the indulgences died down, a few of those who had purchased them began to doubt that the guarantees were really good. They began to wonder if they had been conned out of their hard-earned money. Some of them solicited the opinion of a middle-aged monk named Martin Luther.

Luther refused to confirm the value of the writs. Instead, following common practice, he posted theses for debate on the door of Wittenberg Castle Church where the crowds could see them.

Raphael's famous portrait of Leo X, shown flanked by his nephews. (Potter, Mary Knight. *Art of the Vatican: Being a Brief History of the Palace, and an Account of the Principal Art Treasures Within Its Walls*. Boston: L.C. Page & Co., 1903.)

The result of his actions is well-known. From those ninety-five theses the Reformation was born. Leo X rejected the merits of Luther's protest. Luther went on to proclaim the doctrine of justification by faith, stating that God's free gift of pardon in Christ—nothing else—covered our sin.

Other Events

1711: Eusebio Kino collapsed and died. He was a notable Jesuit missionary to what is now New Mexico, Arizona and the southwestern United States.

1841: The teaching of the Tractarians, a group of High Church Anglicans, was condemned by Oxford University, which said that their interpretation of the Thirty-Nine Articles of the Anglican faith was in error. Some of the Tractarians later joined the Roman Catholic Church. Among the Tractarians was Edmund Pusey, well-known defender of the Tractarian society.

Edmund Pusey, one of the Tractarians. (Liddon, Henry Parry. *Life of Edward Bouverie Pusey*. London: Longmans, 1894.)

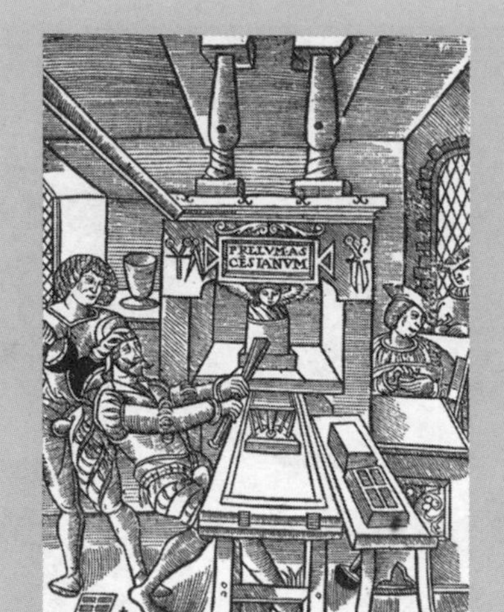

Printers with an early press. (Bouchot, Henri. *The Book, Its Printers, Illustrators and Binders from Gutenberg to the Present Time*. London: H. Grevel & Co., 1890.)

MARCH 16

Banning Pornography—and Heretic Pens

Throughout history, many nations have found it desirable to impose censorship. The Church too has engaged in this practice.

With the emergence of the printing press, a new danger to Christian unity and holiness arose. Most early books were of a devout or educational nature. Indeed, the Bible itself was among Gutenberg's first printing projects. However, the serious tone of early printings could not endure forever. Within a mere sixty years of the invention of movable type, printed pornography had entered the market.

In response to this danger, the 1515 session of the Fifth Lateran Council decreed that books should no longer be printed without ecclesiastical examination and consent. Every book published was to feature a license to print. The service would be rendered free by the Church. Each bishop automatically became censor for his diocese.

Of course, pornography wasn't the only reading material affected by the decree. Whether the churchmen realized it or not, their ruling had more sinister implications. Various Church authorities had already declared on several occasions that Scripture should not be placed in the hands of the laity in their native languages. Thus the council was effectively ensuring that there would be serious impediments to producing vernacular Bibles that might feed men's souls or fuel agitation for reform.

Martin Luther's theses were still two years away, so the council could not have had him in mind. But the memory of the work of John Wycliffe and Jan Hus must certainly have lingered. Even without the benefit of the press, the reform-oriented ideas of those popular preachers had taken strong root in England and Bohemia. The manuscripts of both had been burned by an angry Roman Catholic Church, and so had Hus himself. If Wycliffe escaped the same fate, it was only because powerful friends protected him. His bones were later dug up, burned to ashes and cast on water. The Catholic Church realized that if writings like those by Wycliffe and Hus were to reach the market in thousands of identical copies instead of in a trickle of laboriously hand-copied rarities it could have serious trouble on its hands.

The decree was largely unenforceable, however. A few short years after the pronouncement of the decree, Luther posted his ninety-five theses and made masterful use of the new print technology to spread his theories across the breadth of Europe. His was possibly Christendom's first media publicity campaign, although Erasmus certainly had shown the way in pre-Reformation Europe.

Under the protection of German princes, Luther could get away with printing his ideas. Other reformers, such as William Tyndale, however, were forced to resort to secret printing and pious smuggling. Clearly the underground press is no new phenomenon.

The Fifth Lateran Council broke up on this day in 1517. As history shows, its decree was unable to prevent the spread of religious and scientific ideas. And as for pornography—regrettably, its growth was not stunted in the least.

Bust of Jean de Brebeuf, in the Hotel Dieu, Quebec. The heroic Jesuit was martyred in 1649. (Parkman, Francis. *The Jesuits in North America in the Seventeenth Century*. Boston: Little, Brown, and Company, 1897.)

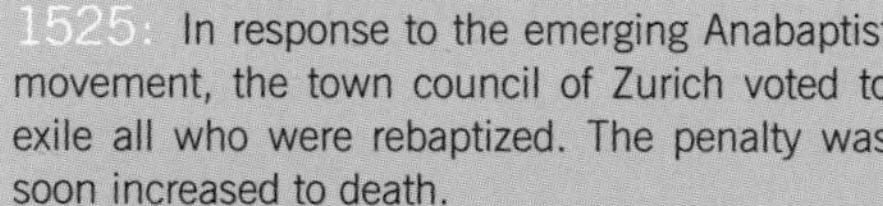

Other Events

1525: In response to the emerging Anabaptist movement, the town council of Zurich voted to exile all who were rebaptized. The penalty was soon increased to death.

1649: Jean de Brebeuf was tortured and martyred by Iroquois Indians. Brebeuf had been an extraordinary Jesuit who had suffered great privation to bring the gospel to the Indians of North America. He remained to give the last rites to the Indians of a Huron village that was under attack. Boiling water was poured on his head in mockery of baptism, his lips and tongue were torn off and fire was applied to him.

1889: Alfred Edersheim, famed for his in-depth study of the *Life and Times of Jesus the Messiah*, died on this day.

1950: The Social Unity Party of East Germany (SED) announced that its atheistic youth dedications would no longer be required. These were a secular attempt to displace Christian practices. SED soon reneged on the promise and tried again to compel the secular dedications.

MARCH 17

Tepid Office Holder? Not Chalmers!

When the Church becomes a state-supported official institution, churchmen often tend to become tepid officeholders. Such was the case in the early nineteenth century. The zeal that had characterized many Scottish clergymen at the time of John Knox had become diluted.

As hard as it is to believe today, the majority of nineteenth-century Scotland's preachers resisted Sunday schools, saying the schools would put ideas in the heads of poor children. They also rejected giving religious instruction to the industrial poor on the grounds that to do so was cutting across class barriers. Missions were absurd, they said, and they blocked them for many years. Rather than create charitable structures to help the poor, they preferred to tax citizens for the purpose of raising money. They also said that churchgoers should not be given the right to veto the assignment of a particular clergyman to their parish.

On this day in 1780, a man was born whose every fiber would rebel against a lukewarm Church. Thomas Chalmers, the sixth child in his family, would grow up to blaze like a nova in Scotland. From childhood he wanted to be a minister. At the same time, he was fascinated with science and mathematics. He studied and taught both. He was ordained in 1803, and then he experienced a spiritual transformation in 1810 after reading an evangelical book. From then on, his zeal could not be tamed. Wherever there was a physical or spiritual need, he pressed for an evangelical answer.

Chalmers created relief for the poor. He supported the veto act, which would allow individual churches to refuse a minister they did not want. He created a system of delegation and evangelized the areas worst hit by industrial overcrowding. He taught at St. Andrew's and created Sunday schools to teach the poor to read. Above all, he led the fight to reform the Scottish Church.

Over a period of years, the Popular Party, of which Chalmers was a leader, gained a majority in the Church. It promptly passed a veto act. The Moderates just as promptly challenged it and had it declared illegal. In response, Chalmers led 450 ministers out of the Church of Scotland and with them created the Free Church.

The regular clergy were state-funded, but that obviously would not be the case for the pastors of the Free Church. So, Chalmers employed his mathematical skill to show that if each parishioner gave just pennies a week, a fund could be sustained that would provide each pastor with a livable stipend. He threw his immense energy into the scheme, and the preachers were supported at a higher income than he had estimated.

Thomas Chalmers, the energetic leader of the Free Church of Scotland. (Hanna, William. *Memoirs of the Life and Writings of Thomas Chalmers, D.D., LL.D.* New York: Harper & Brothers, 1852.)

He also helped establish a system of schools for the parishioners. At the same time he served as professor of divinity and as principal of the Free Church's newly created college in Edinburgh.

Eventually the Church of Scotland saw the light and changed its policies. It gave its churches the right to veto, and its clergy relinquished their state stipends.

Other Events

461: Possible date for the death of St. Patrick, who evangelized Ireland after escaping years of slavery there.

1649: Gabriel Lalemant died as the sun came up, after a night of terrible torture by Iroquois Indians. The brave young Jesuit had been ordered to flee by his superior, Jean de Brebeuf, when the Indians attacked, but he pleaded to be allowed to give absolution to the Huron Christians under his care. Brebeuf, who died at the hands of the Iroquois, gave him permission.

1737: The first St. Patrick's Day celebration was held in America.

1856: Ex-slave Amanda Smith was converted. She went to a cellar to pray, saying she'd be saved or die. Afterward, she became a world-renowned evangelist and missionary.

1865: While worshipping in Tokyo, M. Bernard Petitjean was approached by a Japanese man who whispered to him that he too was a Christian. Under intense persecution and without a known scrap of Scripture, Christianity had survived in Japan for 200 years as a secret faith.

1960: Bishop Kung Ping Mei of Shanghai, China, was sentenced to life imprisonment for refusing to head the Communists' church "reform" movement.

Saint Patrick of Ireland. (Baring-Gould, S. *Lives of the Saints*. Edinburgh: John Grant, 1914.)

Fra Angelico. (Villari, Pasquale. *Life and Times of Girolamo Savonarola*. New York: C. Scribner's Sons, 1888.)

March 18

It Was Said He Painted on His Knees

As a kid you were probably scolded if you painted on the walls. Rather than getting in trouble for painting on walls, Guido di Pietro was praised when he did. He was a painter of gorgeous frescoes (paintings in fresh plaster) that are admired to this day.

When Guido di Pietro became a Dominican friar at Fiesole, a town in Florence, he changed his name to Giovanni (John) and became known as Fra Giovanni da Fiesole. Italians called him "Beato," which means "Blessed One." But the name we know him by today was given to him as a tribute fourteen years after his death: Fra Angelico. It means "angelic brother." The people who knew him said that Angelico took his vows as a friar seriously. Purity of form and space characterized his art; purity of soul characterized his life.

His first efforts in art were as an illuminator of manuscripts. Later he moved to larger forms. The landscapes in his backgrounds are said to capture depth and perspective as well as any from the artists of the early Renaissance. Supposedly Angelico never painted without first praying, and he is said to have wept whenever he painted Christ. "To paint Christ one must know Him," he said. His *Lamentation Over the Dead Christ* is too tranquil to seem real but creates an illusion of timeless rapture.

His paintings are not so much mystic as educational, which was in keeping with the intent of the Dominicans, who were a teaching order. Although Angelico kept traditional symbols such as haloes in his paintings, his work moved firmly into the Renaissance with rich colors and figures that were elaborately grouped.

Wherever he resided—Cortona, Fiesole, San Marco or Rome—Angelico left frescoes and paintings. When the decayed monastery at San Marco in Florence was restored by the Dominicans, Angelico and his pupils painted fifty frescoes throughout the building as aids to contemplation. His most famous works are there. The figures are lyrical—tender, even—as in *The Annunciation*. The angel is gracious, feminine, not at all fearsome and yet is the center of light in the room. By contrast, Mary's face is a study in consternation.

In his painting of altarpieces, Fra Angelico created the form known as *Sacra Conversazione*, which is a grouping of saints in conversation around Mary, the mother of Jesus. As his fame as an artist spread, he was called to Rome to decorate the Vatican. Most of the frescoes he created in the eternal city have perished with the walls on which they were rendered. Among those that remain are scenes from the lives of St. Lawrence and St. Stephen.

Thanks to Fra Angelico, the Vatican possesses portraits of some of his contemporaries, as well as depictions of famous churchmen such as Thomas Aquinas and Albertus Magnus.

Angelico died in Rome on this day in 1455. He and Fra Filippo Lippi are considered the two greatest artists of their generation.

The Nazarenes and Pre-Raphaelites, two nineteenth-century schools of art, imitated Angelico, often adding more sentimentality to their works. As long as works of art are remembered, Fra Angelico's Christian paintings will live with them.

Gregory III looked north and west. (Montor, Chevalier Artaud de. *Lives and Times of the Popes*. New York: Catholic Publication Society of America, 1911.)

Other Events

731: St. Gregory III was consecrated pope. By appealing to Charles Martel for aid against the Lombards, he increased Rome's reliance on the Franks. He supported Boniface's mission to the Germans.

1123: The First Lateran Council began. It offered an indulgence to crusaders, repealed consecrations made by antipope Burdin and confirmed an agreement with Holy Roman Emperor Henry V.

1227: Pope Honorius III, who fostered learning by granting privileges to the universities of Paris and Bologna, died on this day. Although a strong advocate of crusades against Islam and the Albigenses heretics, he was called the "Great Pacificator" for bringing peace to much of Christendom. He confirmed the Carmelite, Franciscan and Dominican orders.

1314: Thirty-nine Knights Templar were burned at the stake in Paris. Under torture they confessed to fictional crimes.

1582: Juan Jaireguy attempted to assassinate William of Orange, Protestant leader of the Netherlands' resistance to Catholic Spain.

1979: The Nakasero Three, two laymen and a laywoman, were arrested for evangelizing on Uganda's roads. For a week they were starved, beaten and tortured, and the woman was forced to undress publicly.

Preaching to the Fishes

19

An often-painted story from the Middle Ages shows St. Anthony of Padua preaching to fish. When he was rejected by a group of heretics, he said he would go preach to the fish instead, for they would listen! Sure enough, the fish stood on their tails in the water and heard Anthony out. The astonished heretics who witnessed the event became converts.

Born Ferdinand de Boullion, he took the name "Anthony" when he became a monk. The martyrdom of five priests by Muslims challenged him to become a missionary, and he decided that he too would spend his life for Christ. He sailed to Morocco but fell seriously ill on the journey. When he did not recover after several weeks, he was recalled to his native Portugal. But during the trip, a storm blew his ship to Sicily. He decided that rather than return in defeat to Portugal, he would instead proceed on to Italy.

The Franciscans' fourth general chapter met in 1220. On May 30 of that year, Anthony, still weak from his recent illness, met St. Francis of Assisi. Francis approved of the young monk's determination not to return to Portugal. But Francis's appeal for one of the Franciscan houses to accept Anthony met silence. No one wanted the sickly friar. So Anthony was assigned the lowly task of caring for six elderly lay brothers at Monte Paolo.

On this day in 1221, Anthony's circumstances changed. New friars were to be ordained at Forli. Anthony was summoned by his superior, Father Gratian. At such ordinations it was customary to present an address on the high calling of the priestly office. The responsibility was Gratian's, but for some reason he had come unprepared. And so Gratian turned to Anthony. Anthony protested, saying that he was not prepared to speak and that his recent experiences had fitted him for the kitchen, not the pulpit.

Father Gratian ordered Anthony into the pulpit. Gratian even assigned the text: "[Christ] became obedient unto death, even the death of the cross" (Philippians 2:8, KJV). Trembling, Anthony rose to obey. At first his voice was low, but as he spoke, it gathered strength. Those who heard him sensed the power of the Holy Spirit.

After that first address, never again did Anthony labor in obscurity. He preached in Bologna, Toulouse, Montpellier, Florence and Padua. Next to Francis, he became the most famous Franciscan in history.

If half of the miracles attributed to him actually happened, they mark him as a man of extraordinary faith. It is said that during one of his sermons, every man present heard him in his own language, just as at Pentecost. In a well-attested miracle, Francis, who was many miles away, appeared on the platform beside Anthony.

The miracles that were supposed to have accompanied Anthony's work may have brought him renown, but it was his teachings that truly affected his listeners. His teaching was lively and often cut through high concepts such as forgiveness and brought them to a level that could be understood by even the most common of listeners.

Anthony of Padua is said to have worked many wonders that led to the conversion of numbers of heretics. (Jameson, Mrs. *Legends of the Monastic Orders*. London: Longmans, Green, and Co., 1872.)

Toward the end of his life, Anthony resided in Padua. He led a revival there, speaking outdoors to crowds of as many as 30,000 people. So holy was his life, and so extraordinary the signs of power that attended it, that less than a year after his death in 1231 he was canonized.

Other Events

1227: Ugolino, Gregory IX, was chosen pope. He formed an alliance against Holy Roman Emperor Henry II, attempted to restore unity with the Christians of the East and instigated the collection and organization of the decretals (early papal rulings).

1263: Hugh of St. Clair died. He compiled the first known Bible concordance and divided Scripture into its present chapters. Hugh was also the first Dominican cardinal.

1972: Crushed beneath the grinding heel of Communism, Lithuania's Catholic Christians determined to make the West aware of their plight. On this day they began to publish a journal, *The Chronicle of the Catholic Church in Lithuania*, documenting governmental abuses against the Church. Examples include a seventy-year-old woman sentenced to a year in prison for teaching children the Lord's Prayer and the sending of a man to a psychiatric prison for making a cross. At Loyola University in Chicago, the *Chronicle* was translated into Spanish, French and English. Where Christ reigns in hearts, faith threatens godless governments—and they know it.

Gregory IX restored and organized. (Montor, Chevalier Artaud de. *Lives and Times of the Popes*. New York: Catholic Publication Society of America, 1911.)

20

Catherine of Genoa Discovers God's Love

Catherine of Genoa. (Staley, Edgcumbe. *Heroines of Genoa and the Rivieras*. London: T.W. Laurie, 1911.)

Catherine of Genoa was desperately unhappy. As a girl she had wanted to become a nun, but she was told she was too young. Then when she was sixteen, her parents forced her to marry a young nobleman, Giuliano Adorno. It proved to be an ill-suited match. Adorno did not care for the things of God, and he also squandered his family funds, ruining them financially.

Catherine drifted into a life of small diversions to take her mind off of her unhappy marriage. If she attended church it was more out of habit and duty than out of adoration for her Creator. Nonetheless, she prayed desperately for relief. Her sister, who was a nun, urged Catherine to go to confession at her convent. Catherine agreed, although she didn't really want to do so. Her sister said, "At least go to obtain the blessing of our confessor." He was reputed to be a holy man.

On this day in 1473, miserable, twenty-six-year-old Catherine knelt in the confessional. At that moment she experienced an overpowering sense of her faults and of the world's misery due to its sin against the goodness of God. She believed that she saw her soul as God saw it. The experience was so overwhelming that she all but swooned. Transported by love for God, she repeated to herself again and again, "No more world, no more sin." The confessor, unaware of the experience she was undergoing, excused himself so he could take care of another matter. When he returned, Catherine said, "With your consent, Father, I will leave my confession till another time."

From that day forward to the end of her life, Catherine lived in an unusually heightened spiritual state, which she expressed as including a sense of God's holiness burning away her dross. She partook of the sacraments almost daily. Her condition has been described in terms of pathological psychology, but if this is all her transformation amounted to, its effects are hard to explain. She succeeded in converting her playboy husband: Giuliano died a penitent, turning from frivolity to care for the sick at a hospital in Genoa.

Catherine wrote about her experiences, likening them to purgatory. Purgatory, she said, is actually a happy state, for the rust of sin that covers a soul is burned away so that it can more and more see the sight which above all others a good soul desires: The sight of God. Catherine also wrote a dialogue of her soul with the world in which she showed the dangers faced by a soul caught up in worldliness. Her works became popular, although the parts about purgatory had no scriptural warrant.

Cuthbert died this day. (Craik, George L., Charles MacFarlane, et al. *The Pictorial History of England: Being a History of the People, as Well as a History of the Kingdom*. New York: Harper & Brothers, 1846-8.)

Other Events

687: Cuthbert, a zealous saint of Northumbria, England, died. He had served as bishop of Hexham and then as bishop of Lindisfarne. The beautiful Lindisfarne Gospels were prepared in his honor.

1202: Joachim of Fiore, a mystic who wrote on Bible prophecy and founded a strict abbey, died. He viewed history as falling into three dispensations, one of which was yet to come.

1415: Antipope John XXIII fled the Council of Constance dressed as a groom, terrified lest he be made to stand trial for his many crimes. He was captured, deposed and imprisoned.

1531: Sicke Freerks was executed for being rebaptized. His Anabaptist testimony greatly impressed Menno Simons, founder of the Mennonites, and was a factor in Simons' conversion to a living faith.

1799: William Cowper wrote the pathetic poem "Castaway," believing that God had rejected him. He died apparently still believing this.

1858: Johannes Gossner died in Berlin. A convert from Catholicism to Protestantism, he was influential in evangelizing Russia and founded an international mission, which took his name.

1973: John Sanford, missionary pilot, crashed and died in Rwanda.

Death of Monastic Innovator Benedict of Nursia

"For God's sake he deliberately chose the hardships of life and the weariness of labor." So wrote Pope Gregory I about Benedict of Nursia. Benedict was born into a well-to-do family in sixth-century Italy. At a young age he became appalled at the degeneracy of Rome, so he renounced wealth, the love of women, the bustle of the city and the promise of power in order to seek God. He left his childhood home, taking with him only the servant who had nursed him as a child. Later, he left even her behind when he sought to escape the notoriety caused by a miracle he had purportedly worked.

Benedict settled in a cave below a monastery in the mountains. For three years he remained there, praying, meditating and maturing. The monks brought him food at set times. When their abbot died, they pleaded with Benedict to take his place. Benedict hesitated, knowing that the monks did not live as he would like and would not be a good match for him. But their pleas prevailed over his hesitation. Soon both sides regretted the new arrangement. After the lukewarm monks tried to poison Benedict, he went back to his cave.

Benedict's saintly character and miracles attracted followers, and he eventually opened several small monasteries in the valley and wrote his rule for monastic life. This rule, as the Catholic Encyclopedia notes, "holds the first place among monastic legislative codes, and was by far the most important factor in the organization and spread of monasticism in the West."

Benedict's rule saw work as a means to godliness. It emphasized prayer and practicing God's presence, provided a simple form of government and called on the monks to live with as few worldly goods as possible.

The rule, while recognizing the importance of love for God, seemed to expect salvation through self-denial and pious practices more than through Christ, although at one point Benedict pointed the monks to the ultimate goal of sharing in the sufferings of Christ:

> But as we advance in the religious life and faith, we shall run the way of God's commandments with expanded hearts and unspeakable sweetness of love; so that, never departing from His guidance, and persevering in the monastery in His doctrine till death, we may by patience share in the sufferings of Christ, and be found worthy to be co-heirs with Him of His kingdom.

Near the end of his life, Benedict had a vision in which he saw God's glory. In the vision the whole world seemed to be gathered under a beam of heavenly light. Benedict also foresaw his own death. Six days before he died, he ordered his tomb opened. After that, he fell into a shaking fever and became weak. Then:

> [U]pon the sixth day, he commanded his monks to carry him into the oratory, where he did arm himself, receiving the body and blood of our Savior Christ; and having his weak body held up between the hands of his disciples, he stood with his own hands lifted up to heaven; and as he was in that manner praying, he gave up the ghost.

Tradition says that he died at Monte Cassino on this day in 547. However, the dates of his life remain unclear.

Other Events

1098: The Citeaux monastery was founded in France as home to the Cistercians, a new, influential reform order.

1556: Anglican archbishop Thomas Cranmer was burned alive. He chose at the last to stand by his Protestant beliefs. He was one of many martyrs from Queen Mary Tudor's reign. He burned off his hand first because with it he had signed a recantation that he regretted.

1564: Five Augustinian friars sailed to evangelize the Philippine Islands. There is still a strong Roman Catholic presence in the Philippines to this day.

1799: Joseph Bullen was commissioned as a missionary to American Indians by his Presbyterian congregation. He became known as the "Father of Mississippi Presbyterianism."

Benedict of Nursia, who set the tone for much of European monasticism. (Bell, Mrs. Arthur. *Saints in Christian Art*. London: George Bell, 1901-4.)

Pope Gregory I's life overlapped Benedict's, and he greatly admired the monastic founder. Gregory helped to spread the Benedictine movement throughout Europe. It became an essential feature of the Middle Ages. In 1965 Pope Paul VI proclaimed Benedict the patron saint of Europe.

Thomas Cranmer at the stake. (Besant, Sir Walter. *London in the Time of the Tudors*. London: A. & C. Black, 1904.)

An artist's conception of Gutenberg. (Bouchot, Henri. *The Book, Its Printers, Illustrators and Binders from Gutenberg to the Present Time*. London: H. Grevel & Co., 1890.)

MARCH 22

Most Famous Printer

Johann Gutenberg became incredibly famous thanks to his world-changing invention of the printing press, but even so, we know next to nothing about him. Even the pictures we have of him are merely artists' conceptions. Although we can pinpoint the month and day of his death, we aren't sure of the year. All the same, if you appreciate books, you owe a debt to this extraordinary inventor.

Gutenberg was the first person in history to actually print books from movable type. However, the original idea may not have been his. A silversmith named Waldvogel taught "artificial writing" at Avignon as early as 1444, using steel alphabets and an iron-screw press. However, it does not seem that he was able to overcome the obstacles, including the development of an oil-based ink, which Gutenberg shrewdly mastered at great personal cost.

As a goldsmith, Gutenberg had the technical training to accomplish the project and was able to fund his own early experiments. But eventually he needed capital, and that proved to be his downfall. He took Johann Fust of Mainz as his partner. Gutenberg was excessively secretive about his invention, and in the end, Fust sued him.

It is one of the great ironies of history that Gutenberg was unable to profit from his invention. His creditors foreclosed on him just when success was within his grasp. The man who more than anyone else brought about the print revolution was forced to answer in court like any other debtor. As a result of the trial, Fust was awarded most of Gutenberg's equipment and the stock of Latin Bibles he had printed.

Today, Gutenberg's few surviving Bibles are worth millions of dollars. And yet, we don't know for sure when his first Bible was published. Some popular chronologies say it happened on this day in 1457. However, this must be wrong, because copies already existed when Fust sued Gutenberg in 1455.

Gutenberg's Bible was in Latin, the language of the Church. Today we are used to elegant and "clean" typefaces, but Gutenberg printed his text in the thick and elaborate Gothic style familiar to readers of medieval manuscripts. His Bible was printed in 3 volumes with a total of 1,282 unnumbered pages.

After he lost his lawsuit, Gutenberg continued to print. However, he dreamed of making his books as beautiful as the illuminated manuscripts of the day and it just wasn't feasible then. Practical printers, who cared less about aesthetics and more about production, got the customers, leaving Gutenberg with little or no income.

In his old age, Gutenberg was very poor. Archbishop Adolf of Nassau took pity on the old man and gave him an appointment at his court that at least fed and clothed him.

Modern site of Nicea. (Courtesy of the Christian History Institute archives.)

OTHER EVENTS

325: On this day the Council of Nicea decided that Easter must fall between March 22 and April 25 each year.

1621: Hugo Grotius spent an hour on his knees in prayer, then crept into a book crate and escaped from prison. He was in prison because he had stood with Barnevelt and other Arminian leaders during Holland's internal squabbles.

1638: Anne Hutchinson was pronounced a liar, excommunicated and banished from Massachusetts. The woman had dared to teach men and to promote religious ideas that affronted the leading pastors of the colony.

1758: Jonathan Edwards, called "the greatest philosopher-theologian yet to grace the American scene," died on this day. He died from a live-virus smallpox vaccination after serving just one month as president of Princeton.

Verification from Beneath Ruins

The simple spade has been responsible for exploding more clever theories about history and confirming more ancient writings than any other tool used by man.

You can "prove" just about anything on paper if you don't have hard evidence to set you straight. For instance, Aristotle reasoned that women had less teeth than men, but an inspection of a few people's mouths proves otherwise. Others have made logical cases for a flat earth, an eternal universe, even that the bumblebee cannot fly because it breaks the laws of aerodynamics. In each of these cases, however, hard evidence tells a different story.

Throughout 1898 and the early part of 1899, Robert Koldewey, a brilliant architect and archaeologist, reconnoitered the ancient city of Babylon. He knew that he was about to be named to head a dig of the ancient city and he was "scoping out" the areas that he wanted to begin digging in first.

The real work began after he received official authorization to go ahead with the dig. On this day in 1899, Koldewey began excavation in earnest on the east side of the mound of Kasr. With 200 men digging, the excavation went swiftly, and Koldewey was soon writing excitedly of great finds. He uncovered the enormous walls of Babylon, so wide four spans of horses could drive abreast atop it. This was evidence of the fact that Babylon had been enormous, larger than any other citadel known to history. Not only this, but it was built of fired brick, not crumbly, sun-baked clay, and the bricks were stamped with Nebuchadnezzar's name.

In another section of the dig, Koldewey unearthed the base of a tower. King Nabopolassar had inscribed on it:

> At that time Marduk [the god] commanded me to build the Tower of Babel which had become weakened by time and fallen into disrepair.

Wherever Koldewey turned his spade, he turned up verification of much that the Bible had to say about the great kings and empires that had once existed in the Middle East.

Koldewey also verified some of the writings of Josephus. The Jewish historian had mentioned the hanging gardens of Babylon, and, lo and behold, hardworking Koldewey had unearthed the stone arches that had supported the impressive gardens.

The archaeological team shipped the Gate of Ishtar from the Processional Way of Marduk to Germany. The Processional Way was the street that served as Babylon's defensive entrance. Forty-foot walls lined with 120 stone reliefs of fierce lions rose up on either side of the sunken road.

They also shipped many other objects to Germany, among them a basket full of 300 cuneiform tablets. These were administrative tablets taken from an outbuilding some distance from the Ishtar gate. Upon initial investigation it seemed that there was nothing much of interest to be found in the tablets. It was not until after 1933 that anyone bothered to fully decipher the bureaucratic texts. But then E.F. Weidener, a translator, announced an electrifying find: The tablets contained a record that directly corroborated Scripture.

According to the Bible, King Jehoiachin of Judah was taken into captivity around 600 BC (see 2 Kings 24:8-12 for an account). A later passage says that after a period of suffering, the Babylonian ruler, who was then Evil Merodach, lifted up the former king of Israel and

> Jehoiachin put aside his prison clothes and for the rest of his life ate regularly at the king's table. Day by day the king gave Jehoiachin a regular allowance as long as he lived. (2 Kings 25:29-30)

There, in cuneiform, was verification of the biblical text, listing the supplies given to King Jehoiachin of Judah. It was a very welcome discovery, for critics had long scoffed that the Bible was unhistorical. Koldewey had dug up more than Babylon: He had dug up priceless data that would help us confirm and better understand God's Word.

A bas relief on one of the walls that Koldewey exposed in Babylon. (Koldewey, Robert. *Das Wieder Erstehende Babylon*. Leipzig: J.C. Hinrichs, 1913.)

Other Events

1324: Pope John XXII excommunicated Lewis of Bavaria for exercising imperial power when ordered not to. The influential scholar William of Occam supported Lewis.

1534: Henry VIII of England's marriage to his late brother's wife, Catherine of Aragon, was declared valid by the pope. Henry broke with Rome in order to obtain a divorce and a male heir.

1858: John Paton was ordained in Scotland. His first mission work was in the slums of his own nation. But it is for his work among the cannibals of New Hebrides that he is known.

1948: Berdyaev, an existentialist philosopher of Christianity and a critic of almost every major system of modern thought, died on this day. His own theories were largely based on German idealism.

Catherine of Aragon, the lovely woman whose inability to bear a son led Henry VIII to seek a divorce. (Courtesy of the University of Texas collection of public domain portraits on the Web.)

John Endicott, who was responsible for Leddra's execution. (Holder, Charles Frederick. *The Quakers in Great Britain and America: The Religious and Political History of the Society of Friends from the Seventeenth to the Twentieth Century*. New York: Nuner, 1913.)

March 24

William Leddra, Last of the Quakers Executed in Boston for His Faith

William Leddra stood at the foot of the tree where he was to be hanged. As his arms were being tied, he said, "For bearing my testimony for the Lord against deceivers and the deceived, I am brought here to suffer." His final words were, "Lord Jesus, receive my spirit." A few moments later, on this day in 1661, he became the last Quaker to swing in Boston for the crime of returning from banishment.

From the first, Quakers who landed in Massachusetts were arrested, beaten and banished. Some were lashed behind carts, others taken deep into the forest and abandoned, still others branded with "H" for "heretic." Some had their tongues bored with hot irons and others had their ears cut off. When such severity did not stop them from preaching pacifism and insisting that Christ could be known intimately as a friend without the need of religious rituals, Governor John Endicott pushed for the death penalty. Between 1659 and 1661, four Quakers were hung in Boston. These unfortunates were Marmaduke Stephenson, William Robinson, Mary Dyer—and William Leddra.

Leddra was a man of pure character. Even the court acknowledged that it "found nothing evil" in him. Yet he was beaten and banished for preaching in Massachusetts. When he dared to return in 1660, Puritan authorities arrested him. The charges against him were typical: He had sympathized with the Quakers who were executed before him, he had refused to remove his hat and he used the words *thee* and *thou*, which, to a Quaker, implied the equality of all people.

After his arrest, Leddra lay in an unheated prison cell all that winter. On the last day of his life, he was chained to a log in a dark cell, and he wrote to his wife:

> Most Dear and Inwardly Beloved,
> The sweet influences of the Morning Star, like a flood distilling into my innocent habitation, hath filled me with the joy of [God] in the beauty of holiness, that my spirit is, as if it did not inhabit a tabernacle of clay. . . . Oh! My Beloved, I have waited as a dove at the windows of the ark, and I have stood still in that watch . . . wherein my heart did rejoice, that I might in the love and life speak a few words to you sealed with the Spirit of Promise, that the taste thereof might be a savor of life to your life, and a testimony in you, of my innocent death.

Despite the fact that the court could not produce any hard evidence against Leddra, he was still hung. Robert Harper, a prominent Quaker in Boston, caught Leddra's body under the scaffold when the hangman cut it down. For this sign of respect toward his dead friend, Harper and his wife were banished. Another Quaker, Edward Wharton helped bury the body. Shortly after Leddra's death, King Charles II put a stop to the executions.

Ida Scudder with women she trained. (Courtesy of Vellore Christian Medical College Board, Inc. Used by permission of Willie Salmond.)

Other Events

1208: Pope Innocent III placed England under interdict because John Lackland opposed the pope's choice of archbishop.

1396: Walter Hilton, English mystic who wrote "The Ladder of Perfection," died on this day.

1816: Francis Asbury preached his last sermon in Richmond, Virginia. He had been instrumental in organizing the Methodist Church in America and had become responsible for thousands of souls.

1922: Ida Scudder rejoiced as her first class of Indian female doctors graduated. The standards for passing had been set so high that she had feared none of the women would pass. All fourteen did, whereas less than half of the male applicants did. Scudder educated Indian women doctors in order to meet the desperate medical needs of the nation's women. Vellore Hospital, which she founded, remains a tribute to her faith.

How Many Popes Allowed?

On September 13, 1376, when good-natured Pope Gregory XI reached the door of his Avignon palace, he found his father stretched there in his path. The Count de Beaufort was determined to keep his son from moving the papacy from France back to Rome. Gregory XI, who knew he had hesitated too long already, stepped over his father. With that step the papal court began its journey back to its traditional residence.

The French government, which had borrowed heavily from the papacy to finance its Hundred Years War against England, was loath to see the pontiff depart. If the financial rewards of controlling the papacy had been great, the political leverage had been greater. They had gotten used to having things their way. After all, eighty-four percent of all cardinals nominated during the Avignon years had been, much to the distress of the Italians, Frenchmen.

Gregory succeeded in moving the papal see back to Rome, but that did not do much to end the animosity between the French and the Italians. Then Gregory died in 1378, and a new pope was to be elected. While Italian mobs raged outside, demanding an Italian pope, an overwhelmingly French conclave elected Bartolomeo Prignano to the position. Despite the public uprising, the cardinals assured the world that the election had been free.

Prignano called himself Urban VI. Almost immediately, he tongue-lashed the bishops and cardinals in a humiliating manner. He would reform the Church, he said, and end its French dominance. Embittered by his haughtiness, the cardinals and bishops announced to a surprised Christendom that the election had actually been made under duress after all. They declared the election of Urban VI invalid and elected a second pope. Robert of Geneva became Clement VII and took up residence in Avignon, France.

There were now two popes. The Papal Schism had begun. Nations had to decide which religious leader they favored. As might be expected, the choices fell along the lines of international alliances. France, Naples, Scotland and Spain held Clement VII to be the true pope. Bohemia, England, Flanders, Germany, Hungary, Italy, Poland and Portugal sided with Urban VI. Each side cut the other off from the Church and declared rival weddings, baptisms and penances null and void.

Clement and Urban died and others took their positions. Additional complications arose when the French successor to the papacy, Benedict XIII, was renounced by France and was forced to flee to Spain. The situation was becoming even more absurd. Several cardinals called for a Church council. Although popes often denied that councils had authority over them, it was clear to all that only a fully representative council could end the impasse. On this day in 1409, the council met at Pisa, Italy. It deposed the rival popes and elected a third, who called himself Alexander V. But, since neither of the other two leaders accepted the council's authority, there were now three popes instead of two!

Alexander V died almost as soon as he was elected, and the council chose another pope, who called himself John XXIII. (He is now reckoned among the antipopes.) He was a man of shameful habits, but he still managed to justify the council of Pisa's existence by taking a step that brought about a resolution.

Pope Urban VI angered the cardinals with his haughtiness. (Montor, Chevalier Artaud de. *Lives and Times of the Popes*. New York: Catholic Publication Society of America, 1911.)

He called the Council of Constance. Approximately 5,000 churchmen attended. They deposed all the rival claimants, including John himself (among the many allegations brought against him was that he had seduced over 200 women), and elected Pope Martin V. All of Christendom accepted the new pope, and the Papal Schism was at an end.

In spite of its role in bringing an end to the embarrassing schism, the council of Pisa was never recognized by the Church.

Other Events

1525: The Anabaptist leader Conrad Grebel, who had been exiled from Zurich, arrived at St. Gall, Switzerland. Hundreds flocked to hear him preach and to be baptized.

1586: Margaret Clitherow, a Catholic, was crushed to death by English Protestants for harboring Roman Catholic priests and converting others to Catholicism. She went to death speaking of her love for Jesus.

1632: Antoine Daniel sailed from France to New France (Canada), where he became one of eight Jesuits martyred while conducting missionary work among Indians.

1634: The first colony of over 200 Catholics and Protestants arrived on the Potomac to settle Maryland, a British colony founded by the Catholic Lord Baltimore. One of their first acts was to celebrate Annunciation Day.

A worship service of the first Maryland settlers. (Andrews, Matthew Page. *Tercentenary History of Maryland*. Chicago/Baltimore: The S.J. Clarke Pub. Co., 1925.)

Stephen III, first to administer papal lands. (Montor, Chevalier Artaud de. *Lives and Times of the Popes*. New York: Catholic Publication Society of America, 1911.)

March 26

The First Papal Monarch Looks North and West

Stephen II died of apoplexy after the shortest pontificate in history: three days. On this day in 752 (or perhaps a few days later—records are a bit sketchy), a Roman deacon became Stephen III. (Because of Stephen II's short reign, he is sometimes not numbered with the popes. Stephen III then becomes Stephen II. For our purposes we will refer to him as Stephen III.)

Stephen III's papacy was highly significant. Up until his reign, popes had exercised little temporal power, but because the emperors in Constantinople had practically abandoned Italy, popes increasingly had to fill the vacuum of power. In this way they came to possess lands. Stephen became the first papal monarch when Ravenna was placed under his control by Pépin the Short of France.

That Pépin was in a position to award these lands is the significant fact of Stephen's reign. The Lombards had invaded Italy, seized Ravenna and set their eyes toward Rome. Stephen paid handsomely for a peace treaty with the Lombards, but it was a shaky sort of truce. King Aisulf of the Lombards wasn't one to put much stock in his own oaths, especially when he knew that there was loot to grab.

Seeing that no help was coming from Constantinople—the emperor had his hands full with the Bulgarians and Saracens—and afraid of losing his holdings, Stephen made a personal trip to France to seek assistance from Pépin (or Pippin). Dressed in black robes and with ashes on his head, the pope knelt before Pépin and pleaded for assistance. "Save St. Peter," he implored. Pépin agreed. In return, Stephen crowned Pépin king and his sons Charles and Carloman became royal heirs. (Charles, of course, is better known to history as Charlemagne.)

Pépin led a Frankish army into Italy and forced the Lombards to abandon their conquests. But as soon as the Franks pulled back across the Alps, the Lombards marched forth again. They seized all the territory Pépin had taken and blockaded Rome. Stephen wrote entreaty after entreaty to Pépin, finally appealing to him in the name of St. Peter.

At last Pépin acted. When his armies drew near, the Lombards purred as if they hadn't a ferocious bone in them. This time they remained quiet for a while, but Aisulf was preparing a third attack on Rome when he died.

Acting on a spurious document known as the Donation of Constantine, Pépin handed Ravenna to Stephen. He recognized Stephen and his successors as "Protectors of the Romans." Thus the Papal States were born. A pope had become a king, had tied the papacy to France and had given ecclesiastical sanction to a man who would become one of the greatest emperors of Christendom: Charlemagne, who eventually had to rescue the popes from the Lombards again.

The papal lands brought their own grief. The pope found he could not protect them, and the Lombards seized parts of them back. Stephen appointed Sergius, archbishop of Ravenna, as governor of the papal lands. Sergius rebelled and had to be subdued and brought to Rome where a stern eye could be kept on him.

In 757 Stephen died. He had little inkling of how greatly he had changed the course of Europe and of the Church. Left to himself, he would have been content to practice virtue and distribute charitable gifts to Rome's poor.

Bishop François Laval. (Avery, Elroy McKendree. *History of the United States and Its People: From Their Earliest Records to the Present Time*. Cleveland, OH: The Burrows Brothers Company, 1904.)

Other Events

685: At the urging of King Ecgfrith, Cuthbert was consecrated bishop of Lindisfarne. He is remembered as one of the most beloved saints of English history. Later, when Lindisfarne Isle fell under Viking threat, the monks buried Cuthbert's body in Durham, where many miraculous cures were attributed to his remains.

1663: Bishop François Laval obtained permission to establish a Canadian theological seminary. This continues today under the name Laval University.

1723: The first performance of Bach's *St. John Passion* took place on Good Friday in the Thomas Church of Leipzig, Germany.

1775: Henry Alline was converted. He became a leader of the Canadian "New Light" movement and went on to become the "Apostle of Nova Scotia." After his early death, his followers soon fell into disarray.

1957: Dr. Basil W. Miller founded the Basil Miller Foundation, now known as the World-Wide Mission.

Lillian Trasher Ordered Out of Egypt

The Egyptian civilization is one of the most ancient in the world. Yet a Christian woman of the early twentieth century became known as the "Mother of the Nile." What did Lillian Trasher do to win that accolade?

Trasher was born in Boston to a Quaker family. After the Civil War, the family moved to Georgia. Although she left a fine Boston home for a cash-strapped farm, Trasher delighted in the change, flourishing despite hard work and an occasional lack of food. Some of their Georgian neighbors told her that she could have a true relationship with Christ, and she believed them. As a young girl, she went into the woods near her home and prayed, "Lord, I want to be your little girl." Then she added bold words: "Lord, if ever I can do anything for You, just let me know and I'll do it."

After failing to get a newspaper job that she really wanted (she was hired, but the staff mistakenly told her the job had been given to someone else) she served in a North Carolina orphanage that operated on faith principles. She met a man named Tom and felt sure he was to be her husband. Ten days before their planned wedding date, Trasher went to hear a missionary from India speak and knew God meant for her to be a missionary. Sobbing bitterly, she abandoned her marriage plans and told Tom she was going to Africa.

The church she attended couldn't support her financially, so she sold all of her belongings and raised money to go overseas. She ended up with only $18, but it was enough to start her at least partway on her journey. Through the provision of the Lord, she eventually made it to Egypt in 1910.

The needs of the people of Egypt, particularly the children, nearly overwhelmed Trasher. She began taking in orphaned children, depending on the Lord for the provision of food or money to feed all of them. She ate the poorest food, including *Besara*, a cereal she detested. As she traveled throughout the country seeking donations, she was often forced to sleep in jails when she could not find a place to stay.

She continued traveling throughout Egypt, more often receiving more children rather than the donations of food and money that she was seeking. Finally, she announced that God was going to build a great Christian orphanage in Egypt, one that would operate by faith.

God was indeed going to do that, but first Egypt entered a period of political turmoil. The British ordered Trasher out of the country. On this day in 1919, she stood at the rail of the ship that was taking her back to America and wept, "Egypt, I love you!" Vowing she would return, she sailed back to the United States, where the newly formed Assemblies of God took her to heart.

The mosque of Kait Bey, Cairo, Egypt. (Barry, John Patrick. *At the Gates of the East*. London/New York/ Bombay: Longmans, Green, and Co., 1906.)

She returned to Egypt in 1920 and promised the Lord she'd take whomever He sent to her orphanage, telling Him that it was up to Him to provide the money. She kept her word, and God kept His. The orphanage grew and flourished under the care of both Trasher and the Lord. By 1960, when Trasher was 73 years old, there were 1,200 children living at the orphanage. Trasher became known as the "Mother of the Nile" and was famous worldwide.

Other Events

1329: In the constitution *In Agro Dominico*, Pope John XXII condemned twenty-eight propositions of Meister Eckhart, a Dominican mystic.

1416: Francis of Paola, founder of the Minims, was born on this day. The Minims are an order of friars who practice humility as their chief virtue.

1536: The first Helvetic Confession was signed. It temporarily defined the Swiss Protestant faith, but unhappiness with its Lutheran tone prevented its widespread acceptance.

1549: Elizabeth Dirks, a staunch Anabaptist, was drowned in a bag after suffering severe torture, which included the application of thumb screws until blood spouted out of her fingers. She never betrayed her faith or named anyone who had worshiped with her.

1555: In England during the reign of Queen Mary, William Hunter, a believer in the Lord Jesus Christ, was burned to death because he was unwilling to compromise with the religious powers of the day. He was just nineteen years old. With his last words, he forgave those who officiated at his execution.

1991: Lynda and Ralph Bethea, Southern Baptist missionaries, were attacked and beaten in Kenya. Lynda died. Ralph reminded reporters that more people suffer such tragedies in the average American city in a week than in all of Kenya in a month.

Francis of Paola, founder of the Minims. (Baring-Gould, S. *Lives of the Saints*. Edinburgh: John Grant, 1914.)

March 28

Teacher on the Run

Comenius leads his battered Brethren out of Bohemia into Poland in 1628. The refugees stopped to pray for a hidden seed. (Courtesy of the Christian History Institute archives.)

Teachers today sometimes experience serious difficulties in overcrowded, understaffed classrooms. Jan Amos Comenius had it even tougher than teachers do today: Most of the time he had no classroom at all, and he was often in danger of arrest when he visited his pupils. In spite of these difficulties, however, his ideas—such as graded curricula, pictures in children's textbooks and hands-on learning—transformed education.

Comenius was born on this day in 1592. When he was older, he studied under the innovative educator and encyclopedist Johann Alsted and became a man of immense learning like his teacher. His insights actually took him beyond his master.

Teresa of Avila remains one of the most popular saints. (Colvill, Helen Hester. *St. Theresa of Spain*. New York: Dutton, 1909.)

Comenius was destined to spend much of his life in flight from savage persecution. When the Thirty Years' War broke out in 1618, Bohemia officially became Catholic again. Bohemian Protestants known as the Unity of the Brethren, who were followers of Jan Hus, were ordered to leave the nation. Many left, but Comenius, recently appointed school principal and pastor by the Brethren, remained in hiding for seven years in Bohemia, trying to minister to the scattered remnant of his flock. Eventually he left his native land with a small band of the Brethren, never to return. The Brethren later settled in Leszno, Poland. In Poland, Comenius wrote several textbooks on education. These were so original that they won him the name "Father of Modern Education."

What made his ideas so original? To begin with, he saw children through Christ's eyes, as precious gifts from God to be cherished rather than annoyances to be suppressed. He felt that children were important because they could become joint heirs of Christ just as much as their parents. Someday they may rule in the kingdom of God and judge the very devils. However unimportant they seemed, they were actually of inestimable importance. Therefore, children were to be treated as if they were more precious than gold and should be showered with love.

According to Comenius, it followed, then, that educational material should be adapted to children's ability to learn. He reasoned that since a combination of words and pictures is more powerful than either alone, the two should be united in children's texts. Curricula should move from simpler to more complex, with plenty of repetition and review so that little learners could gain mastery of it. He taught that children should never be punished for failing, but rather helped and encouraged. He thought that the subjects taught should have practical use and that wherever possible, demonstration and direct observation should be the norm.

Like modern educators, Comenius used pictures, maps, charts and other visual aids. He even brought drama into the classroom. In his system, there were four grades, equivalent to preschool, grade school, high school and college. He was also an advocate of continuing education, believing that learning should be a lifelong process. He saw the right kind of education as Christ-centered and pansophist, which meant that he thought that spiritual, philosophical and scientific learning should be integrated. He hoped that through education mankind might be changed for the better.

If Comenius's ideas sound highly modern, it is because it took centuries before they were applied. It has taken the world a long time to catch up with Comenius. Students of his writings say that there are still more good ideas to be mined from them that would benefit education in our age.

Other Events

519: Pope St. Hormisdas's legates accepted the Church of Constantinople back into fellowship after the Acacian (Monophysite) Schism.

1288: Bar Sauma, Nestorian emissary from the Mongol court, attended Easter services in Rome. He was a Marco Polo in reverse.

1515: Teresa of Avila was born. She was a Carmelite nun and became one of the most popular Catholic saints.

1937: Billy Graham preached his first sermon—actually four sermons in eight minutes—at the insistence of Rev. John Minder, who sensed potential in the young man.

March 29

A Record of Unfavorable Wind and Other Interesting Details

"Anno Domini 1630, March 29, Monday. [Easter Monday.] Riding at the Cowes, near the Isle of Wight, in the *Arbella*, a ship of three hundred and fifty tons . . ." So begins one of the most famous journals ever written, a journal that remains a treasure of information for historians of New England.

John Winthrop, the writer of the journal, was a well-educated, upper-class Englishman. He was a successful lawyer but left that career to join the Massachusetts Bay Company. Motivating his decision was a personal inclination toward Puritanism and distress over the religious condition of Europe. Puritans believed that the Church of England was cluttered with leftover practices from Roman Catholicism, and they wanted those practices eliminated.

As the journal tells it, the company sailed on this day in 1630 from Cowes to Yarmouth. Unable to catch a satisfactory wind, however, the ship was back at Cowes by Sunday, the fourth of April.

Eventually, the Puritans reached Massachusetts. For nine years, Winthrop served as a somewhat dictatorial governor and for ten years as deputy governor. He was impeached once, but he escaped censure. According to his journal, he asked leave to speak, saying:

> I am well satisfied; I was publicly charged and I am publicly and legally acquitted, which is all I did expect or desire. And though this be sufficient for my justification before men, yet not so before God, who has seen so much amiss in my dispensations (and even in this affair) as calls me to be humble.

Since, on the whole, he was humble, tactful and moderate, even his critics were willing to vote for him again. His legal experience and years of managing an English manor had made him a capable leader. He generally lived out the brotherly love and intense religiosity that he advocated in his *Model of Christian Charity*.

In the *Model*, he told his readers that they were to be an example to the world, "a city on a hill." They had entered a contract with God and must remain true or be perjurers and fall under God's judgment. The only way to avoid shipwreck of their enterprise was

> to follow the counsel of Micah, to do justly, to love mercy, to walk humbly with our God. For this end we must be knit together in this work as one man, we must entertain each other in brotherly affection . . . we must delight in each other, make others' conditions our own, rejoice together, mourn together. . . . So shall we keep the unity of the spirit in the bond of peace.

He maintained that there were two kinds of liberty. The first was a natural liberty, the liberty that enables a person to do good or evil. It always tends toward corruption, he said, until it reaches a point at which it cannot endure any restraint, however just. The other liberty is internal and moral, the liberty of love such as a wife has under her husband and the Church has under the authority of Christ.

John Winthrop's journal is a valuable record in the history of the Puritans. (Northrop, Henry Davenport. *New Century History of Our Country and Its Island Possessions*. Chicago: American Educational League, 1900.)

Yet despite his talk of "brotherly affection," Winthrop presided over the court that banished Anne Hutchinson. Were his actions inconsistent with his beliefs? Not in his mind. To him it was wrong to allow non-Puritans to subvert the community that God had so graciously given them and therefore the "heretical" and irritating Anne had to go. He felt that her treatment was in keeping with his theory.

Winthrop is often considered to have been one of the most influential citizens of early America. His journal, which he maintained sporadically until 1649, was published in 1908 as *The History of New England from 1630 to 1649* and is considered to be one of the most valuable sources of American history.

Other Events

1058: Pope Stephen X died on this day. He ruled for barely a year but in that time witnessed with sadness the solidification of the split between eastern and Western Christianity.

1549: The first Jesuits arrived in Brazil under father Manuel de Nobrega. Catholicism remains the dominant religion of the nation to this day.

1788: Charles Wesley died. He wrote many hymns, such as "Come, Thou Long-Expected Jesus," "Hark, the Herald Angels Sing" and "Christ the Lord Is Risen Today."

1790: Pope Pius VI took a stand against the false ideas of the French Revolution, which exalted mankind and reason above God while butchering any individual who stood in the way of the revolution.

1866: John Keble, poet and high churchman, died. He wrote several of the "Tracts for the Times" for the Tractarians and a volume of poetry, *The Christian Year*.

1887: Ray Palmer, hymn writer, died. His most famous song is "My Faith Looks Up to Thee."

...rench Revo-
...Artaud de. *Lives*
...ew York: Catholic
...rica, 1911.)

Thomas Cranmer didn't want to be archbishop. The job cost him his life. (Courtesy of the Christian History Institute archives.)

March 30

He Got the Job He Didn't Want

When Thomas Cranmer learned he had been named archbishop of Canterbury by King Henry VIII, he balked. At the time, he was visiting Germany to promote the king's interest in a divorce, so he dawdled there for seven weeks before going back to England.

Cranmer had first come to the king's attention when, in conversation with two of Henry's men, he had suggested that the universities could just as well settle the question as the pope. Henry swore Cranmer had "the right sow by the ear." He earmarked the priest to become archbishop of Canterbury, England's highest religious post. Cranmer was consecrated on this day in 1533.

At the time of Cranmer's appointment, the English Church was in a turmoil over the question of Henry's desired divorce from Catherine. Having failed to give him a male heir, the queen, once so charming to Henry, was now repugnant to him. Yet he could not get the pope to agree to an annulment. However, believing himself subject to the king, Cranmer promptly granted Henry the annulment he so desired.

Throughout his tenure as archbishop, Cranmer would do pretty much whatever the king commanded. Henry's continual shifts of policy and ever-changing wants and desires often made Cranmer appear wishy-washy. For example, under Henry's direction, he ruled Henry's eventual marriage to Anne of Cleve lawful and then six months later annulled it as unlawful.

Cranmer had already been leaning toward Protestantism before his appointment as archbishop, and he soon became the chief architect of the English Reformation. He urged the king to place Bibles in England's churches, and Henry ordered it done. Cranmer wrote the first *Book of Common Prayer*, penning such beautiful wording as:

> Hear, beloved, forasmuch as our duty is to render to Almighty God our heavenly father most hearty thanks, for that he hath given his son our savior Jesus Christ, not only to die for us, but also to be our spiritual food and sustenance.

In only a few things did he resist Henry. At no little jeopardy to himself, he pleaded for the lives of the Roman Catholics Thomas More and Bishop Fisher. He balked at Henry's Six Articles, which would have brought back into the Church some of the Roman practices that had so recently been jettisoned.

By twisting and turning, Cranmer escaped execution under Henry. Henry trusted Cranmer above all of his other prelates. In fact, as the king lay on his deathbed, he clung to Cranmer's hand.

Under Henry's successor, King Edward, Cranmer pushed Protestant reforms forward, helping draft doctrines that became the basis for the Church of England's Thirty-Nine Articles.

Pressured by the nation's top civil leaders, Cranmer reluctantly supported Protestant Lady Jane Gray to succeed Edward. It was not to be. Catherine and Henry's daughter, Mary, a Catholic, took the throne and charged Cranmer with treason and heresy. Fearing death, he recanted his Protestant opinions. When he learned he was to burn anyway, he publicly renounced his recantation, saying, "As for the pope, I refuse him, as Christ's enemy and Antichrist, with all his false doctrine."

When the fire was lit, he held in the flames the hand that had signed the recantation, burning it off before the fire touched the rest of his body, saying, "This unworthy right hand." As death approached he repeated several times, "Lord Jesus, receive my spirit."

Pius V, who organized the Ho... the Turks. (Montor, Chevalier Ar... and Times of the Popes. New Yor... Publication Society of America, 1911.)

Other Events

1544: Bartholome de Las Casas was consecrated bishop. He championed the American Indians, often failing in the short term because of his unworkable communist schemes but winning ...the long run because of his love.

... Robert Farrar, bishop of St. David's ...Wales, was martyred on this day. ...fty-six charges on which he ... but he was burned any- ...authorities for his defense

War as Love

> This is an age like no other that has gone before; a new abundance of divine mercy comes down from heaven; blessed are those who are alive in this year pleasing to the Lord, this year of remission, this year of veritable jubilee. I tell you, the Lord has not done this for any other generation before, nor has he lavished on our fathers a gift of grace so copious.

What was this opportunity, this gift of grace, that was lavished on wicked men? It was a chance to join the Second Crusade and receive indulgence for past sins. The preacher was Bernard of Clairvaux. The place was Vézelay. The date was this day, March 31, 1146.

St. Bernard had permission from Pope Eugenius III to preach the new crusade. After the Muslim capture of Edessa's "Christian" fort, Europeans were nervous that Islam would retake the Holy Land. With this in mind, Bernard said that a terrible judgment faced those who did not take up the cross of the crusade. In a field outside Vézelay he read the pope's encyclical and then preached a stirring sermon. "This is a plan not made by man, but coming from heaven and proceeding from the heart of divine love," he assured his listeners.

Thousands flocked to join the expedition. Perjurers, murderers and thieves came, eager to earn indulgences for their sins. The following year, Bernard gave another reason why men ought to fight for the Holy Land: Muslims, he said, accused Jesus of being an impostor who claimed to be God when He was not.

> Any man among you who is His vassal ought to rise up to defend his Lord from the infamous accusation of treachery; he should go to the sure fight, where to win will be glorious and where to die will be gain.

The Second Crusade failed miserably. It did not even retake Edessa. Bernard's extravagant claims were harshly criticized. In response, he claimed that for the crusaders, just as it was with the Hebrews of the Old Testament, their sins were the cause of their misfortunes and miseries.

Bernard is remembered for his essay "On Loving God." In the essay, he points out that even the natural man ought to love God with his whole being out of mere gratitude. "For who else gives food to all who eat, sight to all who see, and air to all who breathe?" He went on to say that the faithful have even greater reason to love God, for they "know how totally they need Jesus and Him crucified."

Bernard with the Virgin Mary in a vision. (Bell, Mrs. Arthur. *Saints in Christian Art*. London: George Bell, 1901-4.)

> O wretched slaves of Mammon, you cannot glory in the Cross of our Lord Jesus Christ while you trust in treasures laid up on earth: you cannot taste and see how gracious the Lord is, while you are hungering for gold. . . But the believing soul longs and faints for God; she rests sweetly in the contemplation of Him.

Of all the medieval saints, Bernard was one of the greatest and is respected to this day by Protestant and Catholic alike.

Other Events

1492: The Spanish Inquisition was extended by Ferdinand and Isabella to banish Jews in addition to all Protestants.

1534: The lower house of the English parliament voted 34-4 that the Roman bishop had no more authority over England than any other bishop.

1631: John Donne, mystical churchman and poet, died on this day.

1982: An official Chinese Communist Party (CCP) memo concerning religious policy was smuggled into Hong Kong. It read:

1. Atheistic Marxism is the ideological foundation of CCP policy.
2. Religion will ultimately disappear, but freedom of religious belief is to be tolerated within strict limits.

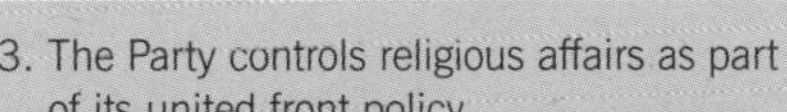

3. The Party controls religious affairs as part of its united front policy.
4. The organs to implement Party policy are the patriotic religious organizations.
5. Only places of worship and religious personnel supervised by these organizations are tolerated. Independent religious activity is largely prohibited.
6. Younger patriotic religious personnel are to be trained in accordance with CCP policy.
7. Internationally, the religious organizations are to fulfill Party goals in making friends and influencing people. Foreign religious infiltration is to be resisted especially by the Vatican and Protestant missions.

Ferdinand and Isabella. (Prescott, William Hickling. *Historia del Reinado de Los Reyes Catolicos, Don Fernando y Doña Isabel*. Madrid: Imprenta de Gaspar y Roig, 1855.)

Most Beautiful Human Soul

In every era individuals emerge whose voice, character, personality and ideals captivate those around them. On this day in 1872, such a one drew his last breath.

Frederick Denison Maurice was the "most beautiful human soul" that novelist Charles Kingsley had known. "Oh, he was the prophet, he was the prophet!" exclaimed Thomas Hughes, another novelist. A third acquaintance spoke of Maurice as the most Christlike individual he had ever met.

Maurice died of overwork. He had written books and pamphlets, edited newspapers, preached, attended the sick and taught in both traditional and workingmen's schools all of his life. Despite physical weakness, he rose early each day and did not slack his pace until after evening dinner. Even as a boy he spent little time on amusement. The Bible, histories and grown-ups' meetings occupied his childhood leisure.

Unfortunately, the atmosphere of his childhood home was strained. His father was an avowed Unitarian, a man of such determined principle that he once rejected an estate rather than change his deviant doctrine. For a long time, Maurice's mother was a Unitarian also, but the death of a sister caused her to reevaluate her thinking, and she eventually joined the Church of England.

The arguments between his parents were painful to Maurice. He himself converted to the Church of England and was baptized in 1831. By 1834 he had taken his orders in the Church. But the Church's doctrine was never entirely a comfortable fit for him. His ideas were broad and inclusive and often got him into hot water.

Although shy, he attracted an impressive group of contemporaries into his circle. The two famous novelists quoted earlier were among them, and so was James Clerk Maxwell, one of the greatest physicists before Einstein. At Cambridge, Maurice formed the Apostles' Club, a group of young men who were eager to bring about personal and social reform. Maxwell became a member of the club and lectured without pay to workingmen who were the beneficiaries of some of the club's time and efforts.

Maurice contended that society could only be transformed through the incarnation of Christ. He felt that Christians must become "socialists," that is, socially active, and socialists must become Christians. He was a founder and the chief voice of England's Christian Socialists. He edited their newspaper, *The Athenaeum*.

In an effort to put his ideas into practice, he created institutions for workers, such as the Workingman's College. Education, he believed, could do much to set society right. He was a trained lawyer and helped secure the passage of a bill through Parliament that gave legal status to cooperatives. This was a big boost to workers who sought to unite.

F.D. Maurice, workingman's friend, was beloved by his generation. (Brookfield, Frances M. *The Cambridge "Apostles"*. New York: C. Scribner's Sons, 1906.)

His many efforts strained his health. He found it necessary to resign positions and became depressed as the responsibility fell off of him. His body, weary beyond its capacity, failed him, and he passed away at the age of sixty-six.

Other Events

1572: William of Orange and his "Sea Beggars" launched an offensive against Philip II of Spain and the duke of Alva, who had oppressed the Netherlands with great cruelty. The oppression was due in part to religious differences because much of the Netherlands had accepted the Reformation while Spain had remained Roman Catholic.

1718: Burkhard Freystein, a German lawyer and public official who also wrote hymns, died. His best hymn was "Rise, My Soul, to Watch and Pray." One line warned that "Satan's prey oft are they who secure are sleeping."

1815: William Chalmers Burns was born in Dun, Scotland. Converted to Christianity at the age of sixteen, he went on to study divinity at Glasgow University. After being licensed to preach in 1839, he sought permission to go as a missionary to India. However, a mighty revival began under him before he could go overseas, so he stayed to preach in Scotland. Eight years later, the English Presbyterians made him their first missionary to China. It was six years before he made his first recruit. He worked with Hudson Taylor, who said, "Never had I such a spiritual father as Mr. Burns." A fellow missionary once described Burns as "the holiest man alive."

1860: Jonathan Goble and his wife, workers with a Baptist mission, arrived at Kanagawa, Japan, becoming some of the first Protestant missionaries to enter Japan. Goble invented the rickshaw.

1940: The Religious Organization Bill in Japan required each denomination to send a representative to the government. Because of its ancient culture, Japan had been, and remained, largely closed to Christianity.

Sea Beggars' medals. (Putnam, Ruth. *William the Silent, Prince of Orange*. New York/London: G.P. Putnam's Sons, 1895.)

APRIL

2 Edmund of Abingdon Consecrated Archbishop of Canterbury

Edmund of Abingdon. (Baring-Gould, S. *Lives of the Saints*. Edinburgh: John Grant, 1914.)

Edmund of Abingdon, archbishop of Canterbury, had a motto: *Caclum dives ingredi*, which means "to enter heaven rich." It was a pun on his family name of Rich.

Edmund's parents were deeply religious folk who, after the fashion of the time, imposed daily penances upon themselves. Their interest in spiritual matters spilled over onto Edmund. As a youth studying at the newly formed Oxford University, he believed he had literally encountered Jesus while he was walking alone in a field one evening. Ever afterward, Edmund made a special gesture of remembrance of that experience by vowing to remain chaste.

Edmund learned well at Oxford and became a doctor of divinity. Soon he became a teacher, lecturing at the universities of Oxford and Paris. In fact, he was the first person to teach the works of Aristotle at his alma mater. On both sides of the channel he was held in high esteem for his holiness. At night, he spent more time in prayer than in sleep. His preaching was so dynamic that he was commissioned to preach the Sixth Crusade.

On this day in 1234, Edmund was consecrated archbishop of Canterbury. The position brought him much conflict with King Henry III of England. Henry was a corrupt man who refused to allow Edmund to fill Church vacancies. Meanwhile, the king pocketed the Church money that would have gone to those positions.

Despite the difficulties caused by the king, Edmund struggled to clean up the Church and restore its rights. In 1236 he issued a series of "constitutions" (some of which were still in force in the twentieth century), but England's corrupt churchmen refused to be reigned in. He also worked with a coalition of barons to try to reduce the power of Henry's foreign-born favorites.

Edmund wrote to Pope Gregory IX for help over the issue of the Church vacancies, but Gregory failed to resolve the situation. In fact, the representative the pope had sent to deal with the matter fell under Henry's power, and vacancies continued to pile up.

Caught in a difficult position, Edmund decided to flee from England. He retired to Pontigny, France, where he died in 1240. Edmund was so admired that his final resting place became a popular destination for pilgrims.

Voltaire, best known of the philosophers who sought to suppress the Jesuits. (Courtesy of the University of Texas collection of public domain portraits on the Web.)

OTHER EVENTS

1767: Sealed letters from the emperor were opened throughout Spain, and the next morning every Jesuit in the realm was arrested, placed aboard a ship and sent out of the country. Influential men such as Voltaire actively sought to suppress the Jesuits.

1894: William D. Longstaff, the Englishman who wrote the hymn "Take Time to Be Holy," died on this day. Longstaff was a philanthropist and the friend of D.L. Moody and Ira Sankey.

1914: Pentecostals met in Hot Springs, Arkansas. Their ten-day conference led to the formation of the Assemblies of God denomination.

1952: Samuel Zwemer, "Apostle to Islam," died on this day. He cofounded the Arabian Mission and served it as missionary, field evaluator and author for many years.

1978: Canon Mary Simpson of New York became the first woman to preach in Westminster Abbey. Traditionally women had not been permitted to preach in the Church of England.

"Sons of Perdition"?

We think of democratic ideas such as the division of powers in government and the separation of Church and state as modern innovations. You may have been told that these concepts are derived from John Locke's famous eighteenth-century treatises on civil government or possibly from Samuel Rutherford's seventeenth-century *Lex Rex*. But in fact, the ideas go back further than that: The theorist Marsilius of Padua made a strong case for them in the fourteenth century.

Marsilius was troubled by the conditions in the Italy of his day and concluded that the popes were to blame for much of its misery. Excommunication and interdict had interfered with lawful governments, he alleged, subjecting Italy to crime, wars, corruption and many other blights. In his book *Defensor Pacis*, Marsilius insisted that the state should run its own affairs without interference from the Church.

In describing his concept of the ideal state, Marsilius noted that there were two kinds of government: that which rules with the consent of the people and that which rules without. He stated that the latter was tyranny and that government is best when it not only rules with the consent of the people, but also by election.

If he had his way, people would elect both their council (a congress or parliament) and their ruler (Americans call him "president"). Marsilius stopped short of a full separation of powers, however, for he made judges an appendage of executive authority.

Like the reformers who came after him, Marsilius argued that popes have no scriptural basis for their authority. Christ claimed no earthly power for himself, saying, "My kingdom is not of this world" (John 18:36), and Marsilius thought popes should take the same attitude. Throughout his writings, Marsilius assumed that the Scriptures alone are the rule of faith, stating that neither Church councils nor popes could replace biblical authority. The spirit of true Christianity is service, observed Marsilius, yet popes lorded their power over nations, interfering and bringing chaos. (Of course, they also settled disputes and sometimes had been the only authority available to meet Italian crises, but he didn't say much about that).

Such an attack on the claims of the Church could not be ignored. Marsilius's book was completed on June 24, 1324, and within two years he and his collaborator, John of Jandun, were forced to flee Paris and seek asylum in Bavaria.

On this day in 1327, the pope issued a bull denouncing the pair as "sons of perdition and fruits of malediction." Clearly the top churchman did not like what he had read. To make sure no one missed the point, Rome condemned the work again on April 27.

Lewis of Bavaria protected Marsilius. When Ludwig invaded Rome and deposed Pope John XXII, Ludwig took Marsilius with him and made Marsilius vicar of Rome. Marsilius vigorously persecuted those clergy who remained loyal to John, proving that he too needed checks and balances, just as his theory taught. Apparently it was easier to preach than to practice.

Pope John XXII, who declared Marsilius and Jadun "sons of perdition." (Montor, Chevalier Artaud de. *Lives and Times of the Popes*. New York: Catholic Publication Society of America, 1911.)

During Marsilius's lifetime *Defensor Pacis* was virtually ignored. After his death, however, it assumed more importance. According to the *Catholic Encyclopedia*, "Marsilius certainly selected for emphasis just those ideas that would become important in the future." Copies of the book survived their double condemnation, and it was printed in 1517, the same year, incidentally, that Martin Luther posted his ninety-five theses. In fact, Luther was accused of resurrecting Marsilius's ideas. It is obvious that the condemnation of such a work rarely destroys its influence. In fact, the English reformers Thomas Cranmer and Richard Hooker studied the work when constituting the English Church.

Other Events

1507: Martin Luther was ordained, seemingly just one monk among many. But ten years later he proved to be less than run-of-the-mill.

1646: Presbyterianism was established as the official religion of Britain by order of the English parliament. Presbyterians dominated Parliament at the time. Although Oliver Cromwell opposed this legislation, it was in effect during his rule as protector.

1769: Protestant mystic Gerhard Tersteegen died. A German pietist, he devoted his life to ministering to others and writing hymns.

1826: Reginald Heber died on this day. The next year, his *Hymns* were published, encouraging more hymn use in the Church of England. Among his contributions were "Holy, Holy, Holy" and "From Greenland's Icy Mountains."

1851: John J. Hughes became the first archbishop of New York City. During the Civil War he supported Lincoln and personally appealed for an end to the draft riots. His influence was especially strong among Catholic immigrants.

1950: Ira B. Wilson, who wrote the hymn "Make Me a Blessing," died.

Oliver Cromwell, a leader of England's Puritans. (Daniels, W.H. *Illustrated History of Methodism in Great Britain and America, From the Days of the Wesleys to the Present Time*. New York: Phillips & Hunt, 1880.)

Isidore, the learned bishop of Seville, shown reading. He compiled an influential encyclopedia. (Bell, Mrs. Arthur. *Saints in Christian Art*. London: George Bell, 1901-4.)

A Record of All There Was to Know

Isidore, bishop of Seville, lived in an age when ancient science was fast being forgotten in Europe. To preserve that knowledge and keep it from slipping completely away, he collected it into twenty volumes called *The Etymologies*. This encyclopedia, arranged by topic, was better organized than Pliny's, the last great encyclopedia before it, although just as full of errors. So popular was Isidore's work that parts of over 1,000 copies of the manuscript survived 1,400 years after it was produced.

Isidore was educated by his brother, Leander, and by monks. The thinking of the day was largely analogical rather than analytical. Isidore imbibed this view with all its limitations. It goes without saying that his science held nothing new, for he shared with alchemists a belief in the existence of four fundamental qualities: coldness, dryness, wetness and hotness. Dealing with scriptural numbers, he became mystical and fanciful.

At the root of Isidore's concern for science was his desire to reform the Church through discipline and the establishment of schools. Isidore considered liberal arts and secular learning the foundation for Christian education. He borrowed freely from the pagans, especially from Latin sources. He thought the ideal monastic community should include a library complete with secular works—although he said it would be better to be without the knowledge in such books than to be misled by their heretical contents. His Christian sources included Boethius and Augustine of Hippo.

Isidore sought to convert Jews and defended Christ's divinity against attacks by the Arians. Typical of Isidore's thinking is this quote from his maxims:

> Learning unsupported by grace may get into our ears; it never reaches the heart. But when God's grace touches our innermost minds to bring understanding, his word which has been received by the ear sinks deep into the heart.

Isidore wrote little that was original. To glean the learning of the past was enough of a job for a man in his position. He assembled *The Etymologies* in spite of the heavy spiritual and administrative duties that fell upon him after he became archbishop in 599, taking over when his older brother, Leander, died. The work may not have entailed a great deal of creativity on Isidore's part, but it did prove to be very useful to the Middle Ages. Rhabanus Maurus, for example, drew heavily on Isidore's work in preparing his own encyclopedia. In England, the Venerable Bede consulted Isidore's work, and Aldhelm, whom people from both Ireland and the Continent sought for wisdom, cited him. Without Isidore's efforts, the medieval world would have been bereft of a great deal of knowledge. *The Etymologies*, incomplete at his death on this day in 636, was edited and issued by his friend and disciple, Bishop Braulio.

Isidore's work demonstrates the high sense of responsibility that many theologians have exhibited toward the preservation of learning. Modern scholars find Isidore's writings useful for pinning down technical meanings of Latin terms and find his histories of the Goths and Vandals invaluable.

James II. His offer of religious toleration met with disapproval because it circumvented Parliament. (Cheyney, Edward Potts. *A Short History of England*. Boston/New York: Ginn and Co., 1932.)

Other Events

397: Ambrose, bishop of Milan, one of the Latin church fathers, died on this day. He led Augustine of Hippo to Christ and resisted the Roman Emperor Theodosius. Typical of Ambrose's thought is this excerpt:

> Who can be weary following Jesus? For he himself says: "Come to me, all you who labor and are burdened and I will give you rest." Let us then always follow Jesus and never falter, for if we follow him we never fail because he gives his strength to his followers. The nearer you are to this strength, the stronger you will be.

896: Pope Formosus died. He crowned Arnulf king of the Franks in a dispute with Emperor Guido. Formosus was exhumed and his corpse given a mock trial by Pope Stephen VII. He was reburied with full honors in St. Peter's the following year.

1660: Charles II of England issued the Declaration of Breda, saying he was ready to grant liberty of tender consciences in religion, to pardon all former enemies of the House of Stuart and to govern in cooperation with Parliament. He was crowned king of England a few weeks later and subsequently broke those promises.

1687: James II of England issued a declaration of religious tolerance. This was out of turn since he failed to consult Parliament. Even the beneficiaries of the declaration were displeased.

April 5

Princess Matoaka: A Marriage of Races

On this day in 1614, a marriage of two races took place. From the Algonquin Indians came Princess Matoaka, known as Rebecca after her baptism. From the English came John Rolfe, a tobacco planter and gentleman. The wedding took place in Jamestown, Virginia. The bride's two brothers and an uncle stood for her. The marriage initiated a period of friendly relations between Indians and colonists.

The story behind the marriage is more complicated than the above summary would have you believe. Matoaka, or Pocahontas, which means "princess," the daughter of chief Powhatan, befriended the invaders of her land. Through her, it is said, the Jamestown settlers obtained food until they acquired the means to survive on their own. Pocahontas was about ten at the time. John Smith later claimed that Pocahontas had saved him from having his brains clubbed out during his captivity with the Indians, but the story was probably concocted to tickle the ears of the English who fussed over Pocahontas—then Lady Rebecca Rolfe—when she visited England.

In 1613, Captain Samuel Argall seized the Indian princess in a raid, planning to exchange her for British prisoners held by the Indians. Taken to Henrico, Virginia, she was instructed in Christianity by Rolfe, who fell in love with her. Rolfe longed to spread the gospel to the Indians

> on whose faces a good Christian cannot look without sorrow, pity and commiseration; seeing they bear the image of our heavenly Creator, and we and they come from the same mold.

He hesitated to marry Pocahontas, however, thinking it would be a sin for him, just as it was for an Israelite to marry a Canaanite. He decided that as a laborer in the Lord's vineyard, he would try to bring her to the Lord. Then, after Pocahontas was converted and baptized, Rolfe married her with her father's permission.

American legend neglects these details of her story, and as a result, popular accounts impress a residue of semi-Christian ideals upon a pseudo-historical event.

Pocahontas. (Lossing, Benson J. *Eminent Americans*. New York: Hovendon Company, 1890.)

Other Events

1419: St. Vincent Ferrer, considered one of the great preachers of his day, died.

1621: The *Mayflower* sailed home, leaving the Pilgrims in New England, where many died over the winter.

1796: Singing "Jesus, I Long for Thy Blessed Communion" as he worked, Hans Nielsen Hague suddenly overflowed with joy. He left home to spread the gospel throughout Norway, traveling 10,000 miles to preach, sparking renewal wherever he went and suffering imprisonment ten times.

1811: Robert Raikes, one of the founders of the modern Sunday school movement, died on this day.

1887: Roman Catholic historian Lord Acton wrote his famous mot: "Power corrupts; absolute power corrupts absolutely" in a letter to his friend Mandell Creighton. Acton balked at the doctrine of papal infallibility.

1943: Dietrich Bonhoeffer, author of *The Cost of Discipleship*, was arrested by the Nazis, whom he had resisted. He would be hanged in prison.

1956: The ruins of Ulrich Zwingli's church in Magdeburg were blown up by the East Germans, despite protests. The building, dating back to 1028, had been damaged in the war, but the church was planning to rebuild it.

Lord Acton, historian of the church. (Acton, John Emerich. *Lord Acton and His Circle*. London: G. Allen, 1906.)

April

6 Death of One of the Milk People

Ivan Prokhanov (or Prokhanoff) died in exile for spreading the gospel. (Prokhanoff, I.S. *In the Cauldron of Russia*. New York: All-Russian Evangelical Christian Union, 1933.)

The Molokans were a Russian sect that was formed during the late eighteenth century. Molokans believed that the Bible was the soul's guide for salvation and rejected the rituals, icons, fasts, ornate churches and the veneration of relics that were common in the Orthodox Church. They were called Molokans or "milk people" because they drank milk instead of observing Orthodox fasts. The government sent many Molokans to the Caucasus, a region in eastern Europe and western Asia between the Black Sea and the Caspian Sea. One such family was the Prokhanovs. In 1869, Ivan Prokhanov was born into this heritage.

When he was about ten years old, Prokhanov fainted and lay lifeless. A doctor pronounced him dead, and he was placed in a coffin. But as the elders read the Bible over him, preparing to bury him, Prokhanov opened his eyes and began to cry. In later life, he thought:

> Surely the power of the Omnipotent appointed me to live and to solve a special problem set by Him for my life; another power, the power of death, wanted to cut my life short in its very beginning, but the power of the Omnipotent overcame . . . and I was left to be on earth.

Remembrance of this helped him whenever he became depressed.

Prokhanov read Voltaire and Rousseau and became confused about the purpose of life. In 1886, he took up a New Testament and saw Christ's claim: "I am the way and the truth and the life. No one comes to the Father except through me" (John 14:6). He also read Paul's words: "For to me, to live is Christ and to die is gain" (Philippians 1:21). He sought forgiveness for his unbelief and thanked God for salvation.

Prokhanov wanted to be useful to the Russian people. So, like the Apostle Paul, he resolved to provide for his own needs while engaging in Christian work. And so he studied mechanical engineering at the Institute of Technology in St. Petersburg. At the same time, he taught children and preached. His preaching and teaching had to be kept secret, because religious gatherings were illegal outside the Orthodox Church.

Prokhanov was convinced that the Russian people needed spiritual reform more than anything else. He wrote:

> No social or political reforms could prove successful unless a moral and spiritual reform in the people themselves was first realized.

In an effort to reach the Russian people with the gospel, he published an illegal Christian magazine. At one point, he had to flee to the West because he was close to being caught by Church authorities. When he returned, he served as an engineer for Westinghouse Electric Company by day and as an evangelist and hymn writer by night. He established a Bible school and organized youth groups. Often he did not get to bed until 2 a.m. Twice he was imprisoned for his faith.

Beginning in 1905, Russia enjoyed several years of religious freedom. Prokhanov served as president of the All-Russian Evangelical Christian Union.

Two years before his death he wrote:

> As I look back, analyzing the events of the past fifteen years, I cannot but see that every incident, every hindrance, even persecution and imprisonments, served definitely and positively for the growth of the Evangelical Christian Movement in Russia.

He died in exile on this day in 1924 in Berlin.

Famed engraver and painter Albrecht Dürer was noted for his religious spirit and admiration of Luther. (Bezold, Friedrich von. *Geschichte der Deutschen Reformation*. Berlin: Grote, 1890.)

Other Events

885: Methodius, who, with his brother Cyril, evangelized the Balkans, died on this day.

1199: Death of England's King Richard I, the "Lionhearted." As one of the three leaders of the Third Crusade, Richard negotiated Christian access to Jerusalem. He died at the age of forty-one.

1252: Peter Martyr died on this day under an assassin's axe after vehemently preaching against the Cathars and other heretics.

1415: The Council of Constance issued a decree declaring its authority over popes. The question troubled the Church for many years. Is a Church council supreme, or is the pope? In the end, the popes won the dispute.

1528: The famed engraver Albrecht Dürer died on this day. Although an admirer of Luther, it is doubtful that he ever converted from Roman Catholicism to Lutheranism.

1593: John Greenwood and Henry Barrow, nonconformists who denied that the Church of England had biblical authority, were martyred on this day.

No More Contrary Winds

Francis Xavier was born into a noble family. As he grew up he showed brilliant promise. At a young age, he became a professor at the College of Beauvais in Paris. While there he met Ignatius Loyola.

Loyola had recently undergone a conversion experience and turned from his life as a grandee (nobleman) to being a wholehearted servant of Christ. Xavier disliked him from the start, but Loyola's persistent goodness toward the young teacher changed his mind. Xavier abandoned his professorship and bound himself to evangelism, poverty, chastity and obedience. He was propelled into a life of prodigious labor for Christ. With a few other companions, Loyola and Xavier founded the Society of Jesus, more commonly known as the Jesuits. At first they hoped to carry the gospel to Islamic peoples, but that hope did not develop into practical application. The pope, however, employed the Jesuits throughout Europe in responsible positions. True to their mission, they labored in prisons among the needy and with the sick.

It was at that time that King John III of Portugal asked the pope for missionaries to evangelize his far eastern possessions. Because no one else was available, Xavier was chosen to go. He departed at once for Portugal. There he met the king, who begged Xavier to visit all of his oriental possessions, report on the state of religion and do all he could to bring Christianity to the lost.

For three weeks, contrary winds kept Xavier from sailing. Finally, on this day in 1541, the wind turned, and the command was given for all those who were sailing to go aboard. Before the ship departed, monks brought out a pulpit and Xavier preached to the people on the shore, many of whom were there to say farewell to loved ones. As he finished preaching, word was brought to him of a youth who had been mortally wounded in a duel. Xavier hurried to the young man's side and pleaded with him to forgive the man who had wounded him. The dying duelist was unwilling. "Would you pardon him if God granted you life?" asked Xavier. "Yes," whispered the dying youth. "Then you will recover," said Xavier, and the young man did.

Xavier, who at the time of his departure was thirty-five, never saw Europe again. Obedient to his promise to King John, he traveled throughout Asia, preaching the gospel. His labors were herculean. In 10 years, he traveled 9,000 miles, a considerable feat in those days of primitive transportation. He brought the gospel to more than 50 kingdoms and baptized as many as 1 million converts. Xavier was the first to plant the gospel in Japan. The church he started there was later strengthened by other missionaries and endured three centuries of persecution without access to the Bible or priests. In the nineteenth century, 25,000 Christians remained on the islands.

Xavier's thoughts were lofty:

Thou, O my Jesus,
Thou didst me
Upon the Cross embrace,
For me didst bear the nails, the spear
And manifold disgrace,
And griefs and torments numberless,
And seat of agony—
Yea death itself: and all for me,
Who wast thine enemy.
Then why, O blessed Jesus Christ,
Should I not love thee well?
Not for the sake of winning heaven
Nor of escaping hell!
Not from the hope of gaining aught,
Not seeking a reward
But as Thyself hast loved me
O ever loving Lord!
So would I love Thee, dearest Lord,
And in Thy praise will sing:
Solely because Thou art my God,
And my most loving King.

His holy zeal attracted converts wherever he went. Hundreds of churches sprang up in his path. He died at the age of forty-six, worn out from his labors. Pope Gregory XV canonized him as a saint. He is remembered as the "Apostle of the Indies."

Francis Xavier, who carried the gospel to millions in Asia. (Nicolini, G.B. *History of the Jesuits: Their Origin, Progress, Doctrines and Designs*. London: George Bell and Sons, 1879.)

Other Events

30: Only two dates for Christ's death can be reconciled with the Bible and all other sources. This day is considered one of two likely choices.

1028: Benedict VIII, the first Tusculan pope, died. He crowned Henry II emperor. He was a layman when his powerful family placed him on the papal throne, but he did justice to the position.

1628: The New Amsterdam Reformed Church was organized under minister Jonas Michaelius, bringing the Reformed faith to Dutch North America.

1966: Emil Brunner, an influential theologian, died on this day. His thinking was influenced by existentialism and Martin Buber's I-Thou philosophy. Brunner wrote, "The true Word of God is not the Bible, but Jesus Christ."

The crucifixion. (Bell, Mrs. Arthur. *Saints in Christian Art*. London: George Bell, 1901-4.)

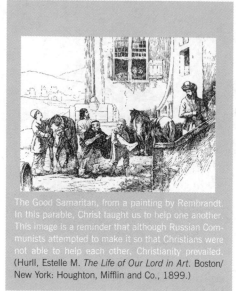

The Good Samaritan, from a painting by Rembrandt. In this parable, Christ taught us to help one another. This image is a reminder that although Russian Communists attempted to make it so that Christians were not able to help each other, Christianity prevailed. (Hurll, Estelle M. *The Life of Our Lord in Art*. Boston/ New York: Houghton, Mifflin and Co., 1899.)

From Fear of Conscience

Tyrants fear faith. Their deepest dread is of a religion that teaches people to obey conscience. They have good reason: No world system can stand the scrutiny of biblical faith. Wherever Scripture has liberated minds, laws have been transformed and governments forced to yield or fall. For example, in early centuries Christian tenacity compelled Roman emperor Galerius to issue an edict of tolerance ending the Diocletian persecutions. Quaker determination moved England to allow individuals to practice conscientious objection to war. Baptist die-hards were largely responsible for adding the Bill of Rights to the United States Constitution.

Communism can be viewed as one such tyrannical governing power. The atheistic tenets of Communism are diametrically opposed to faith, therefore when the Communists came to power in Russia, they tried very hard to wipe Christianity out. On January 23, 1918, the Bolsheviks issued a decree separating Church and state. This was welcomed by evangelical Christians, who had suffered terribly under Orthodox persecution. Under Lenin, the Bolshevik leader, a certain amount of freedom was allowed to Christians. However, that changed after his death.

After Lenin's death, the Communist Party became much less tolerant of religion. The teaching of religion in schools, private or public, was prohibited. The Soviet constitution favored atheism but did not come right out and prohibit the practice of other religions: "Freedom of religious worship and *freedom of anti-religious propaganda* are recognized for all citizens." Church buildings were confiscated by the state and then rented back for sums beyond the ability of congregations to pay. House churches were outlawed. Bible printing became illegal. Preachers were denied ration cards and were told that they were "nonproductive citizens." If congregations wished to support their pastors, they first had to pay an exorbitant tax that was greater than the minister's salary. The Russian people in general were poor and could not afford to do this. Christians who refused to obey the laws were sent to labor camps, where many died. Every impediment to worship that could be contrived was introduced.

In spite of this, pockets of faith survived. "Suffering is testimony to Jesus," said the Christians. Rather than pray that their sufferings be relieved, they prayed for strength to bear them.

On this day in 1929, a new and terrible regulation came into force. It was aimed directly at activities and beliefs that gave evangelicals their edge: love and outreach. The new regulation stated:

> Religious associations may not (a) create mutual credit societies, cooperative or commercial undertakings, or in general, use property at their disposal for other than religious purposes; (b) give material help to their members; (c) organize for children, young people and women special prayer or other meetings, circles, groups, departments for biblical or literary study, sewing, working or the teaching of religion, etc., excursions, children's playgrounds, libraries, reading rooms, sanatoria, or medical care. Only books necessary for the cult may be kept in the prayer buildings and premises.

So much did the Communists fear the power of Christianity that they even tried to strip it of the most common expression of humanity—a helping hand stretched out to a brother or sister in need.

James Chalmers investigates idols and skulls. The missionary-adventurer perished in New Guinea when he was clubbed and eaten by cannibals. (Lambert, John C. *The Romance of Missionary Heroism*. London: Seeley, 1907.)

Other Events

1498: Savonarola, a Florentine reformer, was arrested. His friars fought fiercely despite his pleas that they not take up the sword.

1546: The Council of Trent adopted the Vulgate as the only valid Latin text for the Roman Catholic Church. Scholars and reformers had charged that the Latin translation, made in 405 by Jerome, was faulty.

1685: Lo Wen-Tsao became the first native Catholic bishop of China.

1868: George Matheson, a blind hymn writer, was ordained pastor of Clydesdale parish of Innellan in Argyllshire, Scotland. He wrote the hymn "O Love That Will Not Let Me Go."

1901: Missionaries James Chalmers and Oliver Tomkins, along with several natives who accompanied them, were martyred on the Fly River in New Guinea. They were visiting a previously unreached tribe. Later, investigators learned that they were clubbed, chopped up, boiled and eaten.

The Birth of a New Denomination

No one accomplishes anything worthwhile without overcoming difficulties. In becoming America's first black bishop, Richard Allen triumphed over formidable odds. He was born a slave. This meant he had to fight racism and inequity every step of his way. He did not automatically receive an education. Whatever he undertook required his master's permission. Slavery's cruelties touched his life: To pay debts, Allen's master sold off Allen's mother and three of her children. Allen never heard from them again.

At the age of seventeen, Allen met Christ:

> I was awakened and brought to see myself, poor, wretched and undone, and without the mercy of God must be lost. Shortly after, I obtained mercy through the blood of Christ. . . . I was tempted to believe there was no mercy for me. I cried to the Lord day and night . . . all of a sudden my dungeon shook, and glory to God, I cried. My soul was filled. I cried, enough for me—the Savior died.

He saw himself as a human being loved by God, and it transformed his outlook. He became a member of the Methodist Episcopal Church and began preaching in 1780.

To prove the merits of Christianity to his master, Allen worked twice as hard. His master fell under conviction, but indebtedness did not permit him to free Allen outright. However, he was able to offer to let Allen buy his freedom. So, by working evening and weekend jobs, Allen saved up the necessary funds. Meanwhile, an inward urge propelled him to educate himself, and somehow he found the time. By 1782 he had become licensed to preach. Four years later he bought his freedom.

From Delaware, where he had been a slave, he moved to Philadelphia. While a member of St. George's Methodist Church, Allen was allowed to preach to African Americans at 5 a.m. meetings. However, racism reared its ugly head even in the Church. One day Allen and his close friend, Absalom Jones, were dragged from the altar, where they had knelt to pray alongside whites. Allen and Jones left St. George's Methodist, taking their fellow African-American worshippers with them.

Allen decided to form an independent Methodist body. The result was the Bethel Church, formed in 1787 in Philadelphia. By 1791 Bethel Church still did not have its own building, so Allen established "the Blacksmith Shop Meeting House" by purchasing an abandoned blacksmith shop from a man named Sims and moving it to a plot of ground on Sixth Street between Lombard and Pine Streets. It became the first church for African Americans in America. Methodist Bishop Francis Asbury dedicated the structure in 1794 and ordained Allen a deacon in 1799.

African-American churches across the eastern United States organized themselves into a new denomination, the African Methodist Episcopal Church, on this day in 1816. Allen Allen was elected their bishop, becoming the first black bishop of the United States.

Richard Allen, an ex-slave, was the first black bishop in the United States. (Courtesy of the Christian History Institute archives.)

Allen helped to organize the Free African Society, an association that fostered self-help and self-dependence for black people. He valued education highly and founded several schools. He also operated a station on the Underground Railroad for escaping slaves. This work was continued by Bethel Church until the Emancipation Proclamation freed the remaining slaves.

Humble before Christ, Allen was charitable even to the Caucasians who oppressed him. His story is one of great adversities boldly overcome in the strength of Christ. He died on March 26, 1831.

Other Events

30: Only a couple of dates fit all of the known limits and evidence for Christ's resurrection. This is one of them.

715: Pope Constantine, a Syrian by birth, died on this day. He visited Constantinople at the command of Justinian. The pope feared for his life but was received graciously and returned safely to Rome.

1045: Pope St. Leo IX died. He was admired for his efforts to end the practice of simony (the buying of religious offices). When he led an army against German foes, he was captured and held prisoner for ten months.

1321: Jordan Catalini's Franciscan companions were martyred at Thana near modern-day Bombay (Mumbai), India.

1906: Holiness minister William Seymour of Los Angeles experienced a "baptism of the Spirit" marked by speaking in tongues. Thus began the three-year "Azusa Street Revival," a landmark for Pentecostalism.

1945: Deitrich Bonhoeffer was hanged, just days before Allied armies liberated the German prison camp at Buchenwald. He had been an outspoken critic of Hitler's godless regime.

Pope Leo IX was admired for his efforts to end the sale of Church positions. (Montor, Chevalier Artaud de. *Lives and Times of the Popes*. New York: Catholic Publication Society of America, 1911.)

The "Nestorian Stone," dating from 781, was found in Sigan Fu, North China. It conveys the essential gospel in Chinese characters, as well as a history of the planting of the Christian Church there. (Parker, Edward Harper. *China and Religion*. London: John Murray, 1905.)

April 10

A Tale of Contrary Errors

On this day in 428, Nestorius was consecrated bishop of Constantinople. His elevation to this influential position had profound repercussions for the Church.

Nestorius was a firm opponent of the Arian heresy. Arians taught that Christ was a created being. To refute this, Nestorius argued that the Godhead joined with the human rather as a man enters a tent or puts on clothes. Apparently, Nestorius saw Christ as a conjunction of two natures so distinct as to be different persons who had merged.

Nestorius refused to call Mary *Theotokos*, that is, "Mother of God," saying that the child she bore was very human. He thought that Jesus's human acts and sufferings were of his human nature, not his Godhead. To say Mary was the mother of God was to say God had once been a few hours old. "God is not a baby two or three months old," he argued.

Nestorius never denied that Christ was divine. On the contrary, it was to protect Christ's divinity that he argued as he did, lest it be lost in worship of the human child. He believed that the divine nature could not be born of a woman. Nestorius's refusal to use the term *Theotokos*, "Mother of God," led to a big argument. He pointed out that the apostles and early Church fathers had never employed the word. However, he was unable to clarify what he meant in such a way as to bring into focus the Jesus we know from Scripture who is completely and truly both God and man.

Cyril, the patriarch of Alexandria, condemned Nestorius's works by issuing twelve anathemas against him. Nestorius responded in kind against Cyril. The two men were harsh individuals, and it soon became apparent that there was no chance of reconciliation. And so Emperor Theodosius II called a council at Ephesus in 431 to settle the question. Theodore of Mopsuestia held the Nestorian position. The "Mother of God" camp was represented by Cyril, Pope Celestine and Theodosius.

The Council opened under Cyril before Nestorius and his supporters arrived in an effort to depose Nestorius before the Syrians could reach the council. Rome backed Cyril's move, and Nestorius was subsequently stripped of his position and sent into exile. Cyril has been criticized for being "high-handed" and serving as both accuser and judge. Since there had been other misunderstandings between Alexandria and Constantinople, the decision was not impartial.

Although there is doubt today that Nestorius was a heretic, Cyril and other fathers felt that Nestorianism attacked a basic dogma of the Church—the very nature of Christ Himself. They reacted accordingly. However, Nestorius's followers did not yield. In regions controlled by Persia they formed their own Church. It became a strong body that evangelized as far east as China. Nestorian churches appeared in Arabia, India, Tibet, Malabar, Turkostan and Cyprus. Many exist to this day, especially in Iraq. Some of these groups joined the Catholic Church around the sixteenth century.

Two years after Nestorius was stripped of his powers, a council gathered at Chalcedon. The assembled bishops declared that Christ was two natures in one person:

> We all with one voice confess our Lord Jesus Christ one and the same Son, at once complete in manhood, truly God and truly man, consisting of a reasonable soul and body; of one substance with the Father as regards His Godhead, of one substance with us as regards His manhood, like us in all things, apart from sin.

Brahms, whose *Requiem* was a triumphant masterpiece of Christian music. (Erb, J. Lawrence. *Brahms*. London: J.M. Dent & Co.; New York: E.P. Dutton & Co., 1905.)

Other Events

419: St. Boniface entered Rome to the cheers of the populace who supported his papacy against antipope Eulalius. Emperor Honorius had to decide between the two claimants.

1512: The Fifth Lateran Council began, running to March 1517, and declared that the soul is immortal. It also invalidated anti-papal decrees formulated at the Pisa council.

1829: William Booth was born. A Methodist, Booth founded the Salvation Army to reach out to those who were missed by the churches. He worked in the slums, offering breakfasts and other assistance for the needy, often accompanied by brass bands. The Salvation Army observes this day as Founder's Day.

1868: Brahms' *A German Requiem* was first performed. It has been described as music not for the dead but for the living. Although he was known to be a religious man, there is no evidence that he embraced Christianity.

1952: Watchman Nee, a Chinese Christian, was arrested. He was well-known in the West for his writings such as *Sit, Walk, Stand* and *The Normal Christian Life*.

APRIL

11

Do Too Many Architects Spoil the Cathedral?

The walls of the old church were veined with cracks. Churchmen feared it might collapse and kill the worshippers within. Pope Nicholas V was worried enough that he summoned two famous architects with orders to strengthen the historic building. Alberti and Rossellino looked it over and came up with a plan for new walls. St. Peter's Basilica, first constructed by Constantine the Great, needed to be shored up.

The basilica sat on the site where tradition says that Apostle Peter was buried after being executed in the year 67. As early as the year 90, an oratory had memorialized the spot.

The work on the building was just begun when Nicholas died. Succeeding popes let the project lapse for various reasons. Not until Julius II became pope was the project revived. Julius threw out halfway measures and made up his mind to replace the basilica completely. He appointed Donato Bramante as architect. Bramante drew up huge plans and outraged traditionalists by unceremoniously ripping down the old building. "He should at least have disassembled the old columns," they sputtered. Bramante went ahead with excavation.

On this day in 1506 (there is some disagreement about this date), Pope Julius laid the foundation stone. The elderly pontiff descended deep into the earth on a wobbly rope ladder to perform the honor. Lack of funds slowed construction. Leo X replaced Julius in 1513 and, after Bramante's death in 1514, made Raphael the chief architect.

Again, work progressed slowly due to lack of funds. Raphael never completed the project. Sangello, Peruzzi, Vignola and Bernini, among others, also served as architects at one time or another. Eventually Michelangelo was put in charge. By then, the great sculptor was in his seventies. He redrew the plans. By the time he died in 1564, the shell of the dome was complete.

The great cathedral was not finished until 1626, 120 years after Julius laid the first stone. Carlo Maderna completed the façade. Men in those times projected their schemes across centuries. It is one of the most admirable characteristics of the Church that confidently expected the Body of Christ to survive all vicissitudes.

Neither Bramante's plans nor Michelangelo's were followed. Consequently, the finished building was a series of compromises. Despite this it came forth with grandeur, covering four acres of land, its vast interior gloriously decorated. St. Peter, who admired Herod's temple in Jerusalem, might have been astonished at this triumph of religious architecture.

St. Peter's Cathedral needed shoring up. Instead, it was rebuilt. (Barrows, John Henry, ed. *The World's Parliament of Religions*. Chicago: Parliament Pub. Co., 1893.)

OTHER EVENTS

627: Hilda of Whitby was baptized. She was one of England's most influential women of the Middle Ages. She founded the Whitby Monastery, discovered the early English poet Caedmon and trained five bishops.

1079: Stanislaus, the bishop of Krakow, Poland, was martyred. King Boleslaw II called him a traitor. Stanislaus had excommunicated the evil king, nicknamed "the cruel."

1567: Thomas Aquinas, probably the greatest Christian philosopher of the Middle Ages, was elevated to the status of doctor of the Church.

1836: George Müller opened his first orphanage in Bristol, taking in twenty-six waifs. Forty years later, his orphanages housed 2,000 children. Their needs were met not by public appeals, but by private prayer.

1861: Sarah Doremus became the first president of the Women's Union Missionary Society of America for Heathen Lands. She would be known as the "Mother of Missions."

Ruins at Whitby. (Lefroy, W. Charles. *Ruined Abbeys of Yorkshire*. London: Seeley and Co., 1891.)

Japanese medieval warriors. (Northrop, Henry Davenport. *The Flowery Kingdom and the Land of the Mikado, or, China, Japan and Corea*. Toronto: Winston, Phillips, 1894.)

April 12

Final Assault on the Rebel Fortress at Hara

Would you revolt over eggplant? Well, in November 1637, Japanese peasants of the Shimabara peninsula and the Amakusa islands did. After the revolt, a commission looked into the events and concluded that the rebellion occurred because the prince of Karatsu was more tyrannical than most. In addition to the usual taxes, he had added surcharges to the produce of poor farmers, which included the best tobacco leaves and the number of eggplants they produced. To this unbearable tax burden he added cruelty and torture.

Because the peninsula and the Amakusa islands were more isolated than the rest of Japan, Christianity made greater headway there and much of the population became Christians. The new Christians, with more zeal than understanding, were filled with Messianic hope, and as a result they joined the rebellion against the prince. It may have seemed like a good idea at the time, but it proved costly to the future of the faith in the islands of the rising sun.

The lords of Nagasaki, who had recently departed for Edo (Tokyo), rushed back to defend the city from the rebellion. In December, a force of 3,000 men stormed Amakusa; all but 200 died in the offensive. During the fight, Christians waved banners and shouted the names of Jesus and Mary. Afterward, they tore down Japanese religious symbols and raised Christian ones in their place.

The invocation of Jesus and Mary did not bring victory in the next battle, however. Only about 1,000 people survived the second battle. Those survivors fled to join 35,000 rebels in Shimabara. The rebels assaulted the principle government fortress and almost captured it. They failed, however, and holed up in the Hara fortress.

The rebels were led by Masuda Shiro, a brilliant lad about sixteen years old, who went by the Christian name Jerome or Jeronimo. Aided by the severely cold weather, they inflicted major defeats on the government forces. In one night sally alone, they killed 2,000 of the government's 100,000 troops. Despite the advantage of greater gun power, such as cannons, the government could not dislodge the rebels and lost over 8,000 men in January and February. The rebels lost hardly a soul. Japan asked a Dutch ship to shell the Hara Fortress, which it did, but to little effect. They lost two of their own men to rebel sharpshooters.

But the end was inevitable. Having held out for four months, the rebels ran low on food. Deserters reported this to the government. Encouraged by the news, government forces began an all-out assault on the fortress on this day in 1638. It took them three days to overcome the desperate rebels. Afterward, Christianity was banned from Japan more strictly than ever as a troublesome religion.

Julius I. (Montor, Chevalier Artaud de. *Lives and Times of the Popes*. New York: Catholic Publication Society of America, 1911.)

Other Events

352: Pope St. Julius died on this day. He was a staunch defender of Athanasius of Alexandria, and once gave him asylum when the Arians drove him into exile.

366: Pope Liberius died. It is said he was restored from exile by swearing to a heretical Arian creed. Under threat, he also agreed to allow Athanasius of Alexandria to be deposed.

1204: In three days of looting, the Fourth Crusade sacked the Christian city of Constantinople. The attack ended any hope of reunifying eastern and western Christendom.

1850: Adoniram Judson, Baptist missionary pioneer to Burma, died on this day. He translated the Bible into Burmese. At his death, he was on a voyage in an attempt to regain his health and overcome depression that made him doubt his salvation.

1978: Two hundred Makarere Church people were arrested in Uganda under Idi Amin's cruel regime.

April 13

Sing Hallelujah! Handel's Masterpiece

At twelve noon on this day in 1742, the world first heard the lovely strains of the overture of the most famous oratorio ever written. There has not been a year since then that George Frederick Handel's *Messiah*, with its memorable arias and majestic choruses, has not been performed in a concert hall somewhere.

The performance took place in Dublin, in the Fishamble Street Musick Hall. Dubliners received it with enthusiasm. The *Dublin Gazette* wrote, "The best judges allowed it to be the most finished piece of music," and "Words are wanting to express the exquisite delight it afforded." Two years later, annual performances were established in Dublin. London, however, did not receive the oratorio as readily. Because of criticism, it did not catch on in the capital until 1749.

Handel had turned to oratorios, most of them on religious themes, only after he could not make a go of opera with his English audiences. *Messiah* was special even within the genre of the oratorio. Handel deliberately wrote it so that it could be performed by as few as four singers with strings, continuo (bass line played by keyboard or stringed instrument), two drums and two trumpets. The idea was to produce a work that could be staged almost anywhere. This was a great boon to Handel, who was often near destitution. A piece like *Messiah*, which could be performed by small ensembles, offered more than the usual number of opportunities to raise desperately needed cash.

Charles Jennens pulled together the text of *Messiah* from fragments of Scripture relating to Christ. The power of the Scriptures comes by laying them forth almost as translated (he used more than one translation where it suited his purpose), joining them so that they built on and clarified one another without comment. Old and New Testament passages that belonged together were put side-by-side.

Where Jennens modified passages, he did so to make them scan better and to keep the texts in the third person throughout. Handel, who claimed to know the Bible as well as any bishop, made a few alterations himself. Jennens, a devout Anglican, intended through his libretto to challenge the Deists, who denied Christ's divinity: "And His name shall be calléd, Wonderful, Counselor, the Mighty God, the Everlasting Father, the Prince of Peace."

He certainly succeeded in presenting his challenge, for *Messiah* portrays Christ as Son of God, the fulfillment of prophecy, Savior of the world and coming King. John Newton, slaver turned Anglican clergyman, preached fifty sermons on the text. Although Newton preached his series as a rebuke to those who glorified the music above God's Word, he said the piece covered all the principle truths of the gospel. That Jennens fused the words together without once backtracking or repeating a passage demonstrates a great deal of perfectionism.

Handel brought the whole to magnificent completion, writing the work in twenty-three fervent days despite having already suffered a stroke. The music often rises to great loveliness and power. Passion builds until the climactic Hallelujah chorus: "Hallelujah, Hallelujah, For the Lord God Omnipotent reigneth." Of this chorus, Handel said in his broken English, "I did think I did see all heaven before me and the great God Himself!"

George Frederick Handel wrote *Messiah* in twenty-three intense days. (Bourne, C.E. *The Great Composers or Stories of the Lives of Eminent Musicians*. London: S. Sonnenschein, Lowery & Co., 1887.)

Other Events

799: Paulus Diaconis, a monk, died. Diaconis was called to Charlemagne's court, where he compiled a book of homilies from the Church fathers that received wide circulation throughout the empire. He prepared an accurate and useful history of the Lombards and wrote other historical and religious works.

1055: Victor II, a reform-minded pope, was enthroned. Holy Roman Emperor Henry II opposed his friend's election because he didn't want to lose Victor as a counselor.

1059: In an attempt to normalize papal elections, Pope Nicholas II issued a decree limiting electors to cardinals.

1598: King Henry IV, whose mother, Jeanne d'Albret, was a prominent French Protestant (Huguenot), issued an edict in Nantes granting toleration to the Huguenots.

1829: In an Emancipation Act, the English Parliament granted freedom of religion to Roman Catholics after 200 years of suppression. Within a few weeks, a Catholic was elected to Parliament.

1950: Monasteries and convents in Czechoslovakia were attacked by Communists this night, and their monks and nuns were carted off.

1986: Pope John Paul II visited a synagogue in Rome as a goodwill gesture toward Jews. His visit was the first recorded instance of a pope visiting a Jewish house of worship.

Nantes. (Courtesy of the Christian History Institute archives.)

Icon in the cupola of the Cathedral of St. Sophia, Novgorod. (Meakin, Annette M.B. *Russia: Travels and Studies*. Philadelphia: J.B. Lipincott Co., 1906.)

APRIL

14

The Flame of Genius

Archpriest Petrovich Avvakum was appalled. The Russian Orthodox Church had a new overbearing patriarch—Nikon—a zealot who wanted to incorporate changes borrowed from the Roman Church into the Russian Orthodox liturgy. As Avvakum and many others saw it, these changes threatened the purity of the old faith. Their protests were met with cruelty. Tsarevna Sof'ya decreed that "Old Believers," as those of the unaltered Russian Orthodox persuasion were called, were to be tortured, and any who remained "obstinate" were to be burnt to death.

Avvakum became the spokesman for the Old Believers. Fortunately for Russia, he was not sentenced to death at once but instead was chained, imprisoned, beaten, spat upon and exiled to Siberia. He and his family survived by eating offal that wolves had rejected. Two of his sons died under the brutal conditions. When he was forced to join an expedition to Amur under a brutal leader, Avvakum spoke out against the cruelty. For this he was flogged and chained to a barge overnight in a cold, autumn downpour. Then the faithful witness was thrown naked into a cell, but, he said, "God kept me warm without clothes!"

He began to wonder what use his protest against the liturgical changes was. The new formulas spread no matter what he said. He asked his wife, Gospozha, if she thought he should continue to speak or if he should instead hold his peace. "You have tied me down," he said, thinking of her sufferings and those of his children.

"Lord have mercy, what are you saying Petrovich?" the good woman replied. "I and the children bless you. Dare to preach God's word as heretofore and do not feel anxious about us; so long as God wills it, we shall live together, and if we are parted, remember us in your prayers. Christ will not abandon us!" Shaking off his temporary "blindness of discouragement," Avvakum renewed his preaching.

For all her faith, his wife still could not help asking her husband, "How long will this suffering last, Archpriest?"

"Till death," he answered.

Sighing, she said, "So be it, Petrovich; let us trudge on."

And trudge on they did. While imprisoned, Avvakum wrote hundreds of pages of doctrine. He also produced an autobiography, the first in Russian history. Written in zestful, contemporary Russian, it is considered a milestone of the language, much as Pascal's *Provincial Letters* are for French and Chaucer's *Canterbury Tales* are for the English:

> When I was a Dauria and I labored as a fisherman, I went in winter to my children, and I went along the lake on show-shoes; there was no snow but great frosts and the ice froze well-nigh the thickness of a man. I began to want to drink, and I suffered much from thirst. I couldn't go on, I was midway in the lake, I couldn't get to the water; the lake was eight versts [long]. I began to look up to heaven and to say, "O Lord, you caused water to flow in the desert for the thirsty people of Israel, then and now you are! Give me to drink by whatever means seems good to you. . . ." The ice gave a crack beneath me and split up to either side across the whole lake and came together again. . . . God had left me a small hole in the ice, and I, falling down, slaked my thirst. And I wept and was glad, praising God.

Thousands of the Old Believers were executed. In 1682, a council ordered Avvakum burned too. On this day in 1682, at Czar Theodore's order, Avvakum and his fellow prisoners were locked in a log cabin and burned alive. Thus perished in flame a spiritual hero and literary genius whose remembrance endures to this day.

And what became of faithful Gospozha? She and one of their sons were buried alive for their faith.

Magellan lands in the Philippines. (Woodburn, James Albert and Thomas Francis Moran. *Introduction to American History*. New York/ Chicago: Longmans, Green and Co., 1916.)

Other Events

1521: After landing in the Philippines, Spanish explorer Ferdinand Magellan began giving Christian instruction and baptism to more than 800 Filipinos.

1570: The Consensus of Sendomir unified the Lutherans, Calvinists and Moravians of Poland.

1950: Mitsuo Fuchida, the Japanese commander who led the World War II attack on Pearl Harbor, converted to Christianity.

1950: Agreement was reached between the Catholic Church and the Communist government of Poland. The agreement included nineteen articles and a protocol.

1951: Bishop Francis X. Ford was arrested by the Chinese Communists as they cracked down on the Church. Accused of espionage and the recruitment of resistance forces, he was executed a few months later. Many other Catholics were arrested around this time as well.

John Harper Preached as *Titanic* Sank

The clear April night sky was filled with sparkling stars as the largest and finest steamship in the world sped through the calm waters of the icy North Atlantic. Many of the passengers had gone to bed, but some were still in the lounges, enjoying the *Titanic*'s many luxuries. No one was alarmed by the slight jar felt around 11:15 p.m., but many noticed when they no longer felt the vibration of the engines.

The crew of the *Titanic* had ignored iceberg warnings and had the ship steaming full speed ahead. Suddenly, the great vessel struck a large iceberg, which ripped the ship's side open. Within fifteen minutes the captain realized the danger of the situation, and he had the wireless operator put out a call for assistance. Lifeboats were quickly made ready, and women and children were ordered to get into them first (Christian culture had stamped the ideas of chivalry into men, making them willing to give up their lives for women and children). There were twelve honeymooning couples onboard the ship. Though all of the new wives were saved, only one of the husbands survived.

The captain ordered the band to play to keep up the spirits of the passengers. It began playing a rag-time tune, but the musicians soon changed to playing hymns.

There were only twenty lifeboats on the huge ocean liner—barely enough for one-third of the passengers and crew. Not even all of them could be lowered. All eighty-five of the ship's engineers continued to work to keep the ship afloat as long as possible. At the end, many people knelt together in prayer until the waters covered them.

Throughout the mournful evacuation, as loved ones were tearfully separated, the band continued to play. There is some dispute about what was played that night. Several people in the lifeboats heard "Nearer, My God, to Thee."

One of the passengers traveling on the ship was evangelist John Harper. He put his six-year-old daughter into a life boat and then ran through the ship warning others of the danger and talking to them about the eternal destiny of their souls. When he was finally forced to jump into the icy water, he clung to a piece of wreckage and asked another man, "Are you saved?" When the man answered "no," Harper said to him, "Believe on the Lord Jesus Christ and you will be saved."

When the *Titanic* sank early in the morning on this day in 1912, Harper was among the 1,522 people who died. The band went down with the ship. The last hymn they played was "Autumn," which concludes with the prayer:

Hold me up in mighty waters
Keep my eyes on things above,
Righteousness, divine Atonement,
Peace, and everlasting Love.

WHITE STAR—AMERICAN LINE
SOUTHAMPTON—NEW YORK SERVICE
"TITANIC"
SOUTHAMPTON TO NEW YORK
ON HER MAIDEN VOYAGE
On WEDNESDAY, April 10th, 1912, at noon
Calling at Cherbourg and Queenstown
LOADING BERTH—WHITE STAR DOCK
DISCHARGING BERTH—NEW YORK CITY

Titanic poster. (Courtesy of the Christian History Institute archives.)

Other Events

1729: Bach produced his *St. Matthew Passion* for its first and only performance during his lifetime (unless it was also performed in 1727 as some scholars think). The piece is considered his greatest work, possibly the pinnacle of Baroque music because it fused spirituality and art. Even Nietzsche praised it for having the power to convey the gospel afresh to one who had forgotten it.

1950: Thirty-six leading members of religious orders in Hungary sent a protest letter to their government for abuses done to their orders.

1958: Dayuma, an Auca woman, was baptized. Her people had killed the missionaries who came to bring them the gospel.

1983: Corrie Ten Boom died on this day, her ninety-first birthday. She protected Jews from the Nazis and was incarcerated in a concentration camp. After the war, she became an internationally known evangelist.

Johann Sebastian Bach, who found ways to express the gospel in music. (Courtesy of the University of Texas collection of public domain portraits on the Web.)

16 A Controversial Nominee and the Three Chapters Controversy

Emperor Justinian, whose edict on the Three Chapters caused Pelagius so much embarrassment. (Diehl, Charles. *Études Byzantines: Introduction à L'histoire de Byzance*. New York: B. Franklin, 1905.)

Following the death of Pope Vigilius in June 555, the Western Church was without a replacement for several months. On the third of March in 556, Pelagius*, a Roman from a noble and wealthy family, was named to succeed him. He was already an old man when he became bishop of Rome and patriarch of the West. He was elevated to the papal throne on this day in 556. Three bishops were needed for the ceremony, but only two were willing to serve, so a priest representing the bishop of Ostia aided them in the ceremony.

Why this reluctance to elevate a man to the papacy? The answer would soon appear.

After his elevation, Pelagius stood before the crowd in St. Peter's Basilica and affirmed the decisions of the first four ecumenical councils. Then, with cross and Bible in his hands, he astounded the crowd by assuring them that he had nothing to do with the death of any man. He was referring to the death of his predecessor, Pope Vigilius, whom he had once branded as a turncoat for at first opposing and then agreeing to Emperor Justinian's opposition to the Three Chapters.

The Three Chapters were three writings condemned by the emperor in an edict in the years 543 to 544. The condemned works were by Theodore of Mopsuestia, by Theodoret (writing against Cyril of Alexandria) and a letter by Ibas of Edessa to a heretic named Maris. All three contained statements that could be interpreted as Nestorian. The Nestorians supposedly reduced Christ's divinity when they said Mary was the mother only of our Savior as a man, not as God.

Since nothing had been condemned by the Council of Chalcedon, which dealt with the Nestorian issue, many Christians were reluctant to condemn these writings. However, Justinian wanted them condemned because they offended the Monophysites, a powerful group of theologians who argued that Christ had only one nature. Justinian was trying to pacify them.

The Eastern bishops signed Justinian's ban, albeit under protest, but the West would not sign it. As a result, Justinian had Vigilius arrested in 545 and detained in Sicily for a while. Then he was brought to Constantinople, where he excommunicated Patriarch Menas, who turned around and did the same to him. But because Vigilius resisted the imperial decision, his life was endangered and he was forced to flee at least once.

Vigilius finally accepted the imperial decision. The Fifth Ecumenical Council (the second Council of Constantinople) then condemned the Three Chapters. The council was held under Eutychius, archbishop of Constantinople, Vigilius, bishop of Rome, and Emperor Justinian. It was attended by 165 fathers of the Church.

Pelagius inherited some of the strife that marked Vigilius's career, and when he agreed to accept the council's decision, the sees of Aquileia and Milan renounced communion with him. However, before his death in 561, he accomplished much good by relieving poverty and starvation, ransoming prisoners of war and overhauling the papal finances. He was buried in St. Peter's.

* This Pelagius is not the same Pelagius for whom the so-called "Pelagianism heresy" was named and which was condemned at the third Ecumenical Council, held in Ephesus in 431.

John Paton. (Johnston, Julia H. *Fifty Missionary Heroes Every Boy and Girl Should Know*. New York/Chicago: Fleming H. Revell Company, 1913.)

Other Events

1858: John Paton and his wife sailed from Scotland to become missionaries in the New Hebrides. His wife soon died with their infant son, both of whom Paton buried by himself. "But for Jesus and his fellowship, I must have gone mad beside that grave and died," he wrote.

1905: A Tolerance Manifesto gave Russian evangelicals a measure of freedom. Their faith was strongly opposed by the reigning Orthodox Church.

More Than Just Surviving

What would happen to the Christians? They were so few in number and knew so little about Christ. The missionaries lifted their hearts in prayer as Italian soldiers forced them away from their Ethiopian converts.

It was on this day in 1937 that Italian soldiers had come to take all Protestant missionaries out of the Wallamo region of Ethiopia. A year earlier, on May 5, 1936, Addis Ababa, the capital of Ethiopia, had fallen to Mussolini's invading armies. Ethiopian Emperor Haile Selassie had to flee. Barefoot Ethiopian soldiers bravely resisted against tanks and mustard gas, but the better-equipped Italians won.

Soon the victors came for the missionaries, who left just forty-eight baptized Christians behind them in Wallamo. The converts had the Gospel of Mark and a few other passages of Scripture in their language, but few knew enough to read even that. Several of the Christians already knew firsthand what persecution was like, having experienced it from heathen neighbors. The missionaries prayed constantly for their converted friends.

On May 5, 1941, five years to the day that he had left Ethiopia, Haile Selassie returned. The missionaries eagerly returned to the capital as well, but they were unsure of what they would find. Reports reached them from Wallamo: Not only had the Church survived; it had grown. Not only had it grown; it had grown to more than 200 times its original size. The 48 believers had become 10,000!

They confessed that their secret was the Holy Spirit, who guided them in their suffering. Cheerful and forgiving under enemy savagery, they proved that their faith was genuine. They sang songs with encouraging words: "If we have little trouble here, we will have little reward there. We will reign."

They were beaten, tortured and killed, yet they stood fast, heroes of God. They even sang when told to tear their church down—and as they cheerfully obeyed. One of their leaders, Toro, was thrown facedown in the mud of a jail cell and beaten with a hippo-hide whip. "Where is the God who can deliver you out of our hands?" he was asked.

"My God is able to deliver me—if He chooses—and if not, He has promised to take me to heaven to be with Him there." Soon afterward, a terrible storm blew off the prison roof and melted its mud bricks. The guards were terrified. They pleaded with Toro to pray for them and then released him! But other Christians died of cold at night in the unheated cells.

In some jails, the Protestants perceived the persecution as motivated not by politics but by differences in religious faith, since Catholic priests promised them freedom if only they would kiss the crucifixes held up to them. To the Wallamo, this seemed like idolatry, and they refused freedom at that price. Their faith and courage in the face of persecution attracted others to Christ.

Adoua Church, Ethiopia. (Bent, J. Theodore. *The Sacred City of the Ethiopians*. London/New York: Longmans, Green, and Co., 1893.)

The missionaries rejoiced at hearing of the continued faith of their Ethiopian friends. Upon their return, their main work consisted of clearing up a few misunderstandings of Scripture, translating the rest of the Bible into the native language, educating the converts and adding structure to a national Church that was struggling to organize itself.

Other Events

326: St. Alexander died. He was appointed to the patriarchate of Alexandria instead of Arius, who denied Christ's divinity. Alexander was kind to Arius, even while supporting Athanasius, the defender of the Trinity.

341: Simeon, bishop of Seleucia Ktesiphon (located south of Baghdad), was executed for refusing to levy an extra war tax on his church people. He was one of many Persian martyrs.

858: Pope Benedict III died. Emperors Lothaire and Louis II had confirmed Anastasius in his place, but popular protest brought Benedict back.

1640: Robert Torkillus of Sweden became the first Lutheran pastor to arrive in the American colonies when he landed in Delaware.

1713: William Law was suspended from his pulpit for nonconformist views. He is famed as the author of *A Serious Call to a Devout and Holy Life* and a later book entitled *The Power of the Spirit*.

1912: The International Conference of the Negro began. Although not explicitly Christian, out of it came a renewed impulse to reach Africa for Christ.

Benedict III was the popular favorite for pope. (Montor, Chevalier Artaud de. *Lives and Times of the Popes*. New York: Catholic Publication Society of America, 1911.)

Luther in 1546. (McGiffert, Arthur Cushman. *Martin Luther, the Man and His Work*. New York: The Century Co., 1911.)

APRIL 18

Most Noble Protestant Words: "Here I Stand"

Since your majesty and your lordships desire a simple reply, I will answer without horns and without teeth. Unless I am convicted by Scripture and plain reason—I do not accept the authority of popes and councils for they have contradicted each other—my conscience is captive to the Word of God. I cannot and I will not recant anything, for to go against conscience is neither right not safe. Here I stand, I cannot do otherwise, God help me. Amen.

According to early printed reports, this was Martin Luther's reply at the Diet (Congress) of Worms when he was urged to recant. These are perhaps the most notable words spoken in the Reformation. On this day in 1521, he uttered the memorable lines in German and then, upon request, repeated their gist in Latin for those who did not understand his first recitation. He was sweating, said witnesses. With a gesture of victory, he slipped out of the room.

Frederick the Wise, Luther's supporter, was uneasy. He was unsure whether the Scriptures condemned Luther or not. "He is too daring for me," the elector admitted. Nonetheless, on the next day, when asked to stand against Luther with the emperor, he did not sign the condemnation, although it was endorsed by four other electors.

As for the emperor, he reasoned that a single friar who went contrary to the whole Church could not possibly be right. He was descended from a long line of Christian emperors, and he felt that to accept Luther's view was to betray the faith of his fathers. He vowed to take prompt action against Luther, but since Luther had been given safe conduct to Worms, he would allow him to depart in safety.

Luther did not leave Worms at once. For several days a committee reasoned with him, begging him not to tear the Church in two. They pointed out that war would surely come to Germany if the Church were to split. Also, there was the possibility that Melanchthon, his beloved coworker, might be killed. Luther could not help but be moved, but his determination held, for he knew that the truths he had discovered in God's Word must be followed whatever the cost.

There is some dispute as to whether or not Luther actually said, "Here I stand. I cannot do otherwise." Although the earliest printed versions of his speech contain these lines, the official transcripts do not. Whether spoken or not, the words convey the brave monk's attitude. When Luther left Worms, the Reformation was irrevocable.

Martin Luther was at his noblest at Worms. His bold words have stirred men's imaginations throughout subsequent centuries. They have also been seen as a landmark in the unfolding of Western and religious individualism.

John Foxe, author of the *Book of Martyrs*. (Courtesy of the Christian History Institute archives.)

Other Events

246 (probable date): Cyprian of Carthage was baptized. Cyprian was a notable North African bishop who wrote about the unity of the Church. He died a martyr.

1161: Theobald, archbishop of Canterbury, died. He had been chosen as archbishop in 1138 for his meekness, and he remained a moderate churchman for most of his life. However, he disobeyed an order by King Stephen not to attend a council in Reims. He also refused to crown Stephen's son, Eustace, and crowned Henry II instead. His successor was Thomas à Becket.

1587: John Foxe died on this day. He wrote an influential history of England, which put a strongly Protestant slant on his nation's history. *Acts and Monuments* is popularly known as *Foxe's Book of Martyrs*.

1870: Isabella Thoburn opened her school, one of the first for the women of India. Seven frightened girls were coaxed into attending. Their priests had warned them that the gods would destroy them if they gained education.

1874: David Livingstone's remains were interred at Westminster Abbey in London. The explorer-missionary had died in Africa.

Papal Pawn of Powers

John, who was pope from 523 to 526, did not want to go to Constantinople. But Theodoric, the Gothic ruler of Italy, insisted that he must. An Arian (a heretical group that denied the divinity of Christ), Theodoric had become suspicious of a recent thaw between the Church in Rome and the Church in Constantinople.

Not long before Theodoric decided to send John to Constantinople, the bishops in the two halves of the empire had been at odds. The root of the earlier coolness had been the *Henoticon*, a statement of faith that had been carefully crafted by Bishop Acacius for Emperor Zeno. The *Henoticon* was intended to allow the Monophysite heresy to persist without seeming to violate orthodox doctrine on Christ. Most Eastern bishops had accepted it, but the Western bishops, led by Rome, had repudiated it. The *Henoticon*, while safely avoiding outright heresy, did so only by ignoring important distinctions between Christ's Godhead and manhood, distinctions made at the Council of Chalcedon. The wounds of this disagreement were no longer raw, and the healing made Theodoric suspicious.

Theodoric was also furious with the new emperor, Justin, because he had deprived Arians of their churches in the eastern half of the empire. Theodoric thought this was just plain wrong. "To pretend to dominion over the conscience is to usurp the prerogative of God," he wrote. Justin didn't think so: In his view, a smoothly functioning society required unity of belief.

Theodoric ordered John to travel to Constantinople and convince the emperor to restore the Arian churches. John protested, saying that he was committed to stamping out heresy, not pleading for it! Theodoric hinted darkly that he might go to war against Justin on behalf of the Arians if John did not obey.

Reluctantly, John began the wearisome, dangerous voyage to Constantinople. As he neared the capital, he was hailed with joy by great crowds. When he was twelve miles outside of the capital, clergy greeted him with crosses and candles. Justin himself seemed glad that John had come and met him with high honors.

The high point of John's journey came on this day in 526. He was invited to conduct the liturgy in Constantinople's gloriously decorated cathedral, the Santa Sophia. (The Hagia Sophia of Justinian had not been built yet.) With oriental splendor, John crowned Justin emperor and, as part of the ceremony, Eastern bishops vowed their loyalty.

As delightful as these ceremonies were, they didn't make the Arian problem go away. Theodoric would still expect a favorable report when John returned. Justin, of course, had no intention of meeting Theodoric's demands, so he sent John away empty-handed.

Pope John I in an artist's conception. (Montor, Chevalier Artaud de. *Lives and Times of the Popes*. New York: Catholic Publication Society of America, 1911.)

Back John traveled. He cannot have expected a hearty welcome from Theodoric, nor did he get it. The king flung him into prison in Ravenna. John had nothing to look forward to but misery. While John had been traveling, Theodoric had tortured and beheaded the philosopher-theologian Boethius, a firm believer in the Trinity, as well as a senator.

Theodoric was spared the trouble of ordering John's execution, however. Worn out with travel and the hardships of prison, John died. The Church later canonized him as a saint and a martyr.

Other Events

Annual: Feast day of St. Alphege, archbishop of Canterbury. He refused ransom when captured by the Danes, saying England was too poor to afford it. The Danes martyred him.

1529: In response to the decision of the German diet of Speyer to stay the growth of the new religion of Protestantism, five princes joined with fourteen cities to protest on this day. The name Protestant came from that protest.

1560: Melanchthon, the influential reformer and friend of Martin Luther, died on this day. He wrote the Lutheran Augsburg Confession.

1824: Johannes Gossner gave his last Russian sermon. Originally a German Roman Catholic, he began preaching evangelistic messages until he was driven out of his native land by Jesuits. Traveling to Russia, he preached to large crowds before an Orthodox backlash forced him out of the country.

1959: The Coptic (Egyptian) Church chose its 116th patriarch, Kyrillos VI.

An elderly Melanchthon shortly before his death. (Bezold, Friedrich von. *Geschichte der Deutschen Reformation*. Berlin: Grote, 1890.)

A scene from the Inquisition. (Hendrickson, Ford. *Martyrs and Witnesses*. Detroit: Protestant Missionary Pub. Co., 1917.)

April 20

Domini Canes: "God's Dogs"

Two of the darkest blots on Christian history are the witch hunts of medieval Europe and the horrors employed by the Inquisition. No one knows for sure how many people suffered at the hands of the Inquisition, but the lowest estimates place the number in the tens of thousands. To most churchmen and governments it seemed self-evident that orthodoxy must be preserved, whatever the price. (It is worth remembering that the Roman Church was not alone in this attitude: Protestants have also persecuted when their churches became state institutions.)

Early Christians such as Tertullian, Origen and Cyprian rejected violence as a way to force people to become Christians or remain faithful to truth. The Christian apologist Lactantius wrote in 308:

Cabral took possession of Brazil with religious ceremonies. (Fonseca, Faustino da. *A Descoberta do Brazil*. Lisboa: Typographia de Empreza do jornal O Século, 1900.)

> [N]othing is so important as religion, and one must defend it at any cost. . . . It is true that it must be protected, but by dying for it, not by killing others; by long-suffering, not by violence; by faith, not by crime.

However, even good men can be led astray by political pressures and misguided zeal. The kings and emperors of the time wanted something done about the new religious ideas that were threatening the unity of their lands. Add to that Pope Gregory IX's strong feelings about heresy and you get the Inquisition. Gregory created the Inquisition in 1227 when he appointed a board of inquisitors to sit against heresy in Florence. Shortly afterward, he expanded the operation to include a larger region because movements that the Church defined as heretical were becoming strong in Italy, France and the Balkans.

By 1231, Gregory had issued formal rules for his inquisitors. He intended the Inquisition to be for the salvation, coercion and punishment of erring Catholics only. Jews, Muslims and other non-Christians were not to be touched. The Inquisition would inquire into the spread of heresy, summon suspected heretics before tribunals and punish the faithless so as to convert and save their souls. It was aimed primarily at the growing numbers of Waldensians and Albigenses. Torture would be allowed, as it had been under Roman law. Gregory appointed the brutal former heretic Robert le Bougre as his inquisitor in France. Le Bougre once burned 180 individuals at the stake in 1 day and performed so many other atrocities that he was finally recalled and put in prison for life.

On this day in 1233 (this date is not certain), by papal bull, Gregory placed the operation of the Inquisition largely into the hands of the Dominicans, although the Franciscans were also involved. The Dominicans were the obvious choice for the role because: 1) They were still new and popular; 2) their purpose was to employ the power of reason in support of faith.

The methods employed by Dominic's order were not gentle. About twenty years after the Inquisition began, inquisitors started to make heavy use of torture. Popes might instruct the inquisitors "not to punish the wicked so as to hurt the innocent," but, men being what they are, the tendency was to exceed rules that limited torture.

Many Dominicans never participated in the Inquisition. Others were mild in their measures. Some resigned rather than do the brutal work. Nonetheless, the good name of the Dominicans was forever stained by their participation in this cruel activity. Before long the order became popularly known as *Domini Canes*, Latin for "God's Dogs."

Other Events

1500: Pedro Cabral took possession of Brazil for Portugal with religious ceremonies this Easter Monday.

1558: Johannes Bugenhagen, a coworker of Martin Luther's, professor at Wittenberg and key reformer, died on this day. He helped Luther translate the Bible into German and did another translation into Low German.

1884: Leo XIII issued the encyclical *Humanum Genus* against the Masonic order.

1946: The Lutheran bishops' conference of the United Evangelical Lutheran Church in Germany issued a protest to the Communist government against ongoing persecution.

1999: At a Colorado school, several children were killed by classmates in an incident known as the Columbine shooting. Among those killed was a Christian girl who answered "yes" when asked point-blank if she believed in God.

Proving That Which It Is Said Cannot Be Proven

When St. Anselm died on this day in 1109, the Church lost a great mind and England a zealous reformer. Anselm won a name as a reformer because he attempted to end abuses such as the slave trade. He urged the holding of regular synods and, while he was archbishop, enforced clerical celibacy within his see. Through his learning and methodology, he became one of the creators of scholasticism. But his most notable gift to history was what has become known as the *ontological proof for the existence of God*.

Can the existence of God be proven? Anselm thought so. Modern philosophers and theologians disagree. However, it is Anselm's argument, the ontological proof, which remains the slipperiest for modern logic to deal with and is thought to be impossible to refute.

Anselm's argument went something like this: When we discuss the existence of God, we define Him as a perfect being, greater than anything else that can be conceived. If God does not exist, then the name "God" refers to an imaginary being. This makes the definition of "God" contradictory, for to be real, to be living, to have power is greater than to be imaginary. It is clear that the word *God* cannot be discussed as defined if He does not exist, because He must be conceived as really existing in order for Him to be greater than anything else, for a God who does not exist is not greater than anything else.

In short, no philosopher can legitimately argue that God does not exist if he defines "God" as a perfect being that is greater than any that can be imagined; for to be perfect, God must have real existence. Those who acknowledge that He exists do not have a problem with self-contradiction when they affirm His existence, whereas those who deny His existence do. Since we can indeed raise the question of God's existence and argue the point, then God must exist.

As archbishop of Canterbury, the zealous Anselm struggled with King William for Church rights. As a result of the struggle, he was exiled. As a theologian, the holy Anselm is remembered for his book *Why Did God Become Man?* In it he argued that each of us has run up such a debt of sin that there is no way we can repay God. Christ, as infinite God, has merit enough and plenty to spare to pay our debts. Anselm argued that we must first believe in order to understand. In modern terms we might say that truth only begins to come clear when one is committed to it: You cannot see around a bend in a trail unless you walk toward it.

Anslem was more than a philosopher. He was a mystic who panted for union with God:

> Be it mine to look up to Your light, even from afar, even from the depths. Teach me to seek You and reveal Yourself to me when I seek You, for I cannot seek You unless You teach me, nor find You unless you reveal yourself. . . . O supreme and unapproachable light, O holy and blessed Trinity, how far You are from me who is so near you. How far are You removed from my vision, although I am so near yours! Everywhere You are wholly present and I see You not. In you I move and in You I have my being and cannot come to You. You are within me and about me and I feel You not.

St. Anslem's ontological proof for the existence of God remains difficult, if not impossible, to prove or refute. (McKilliam, A.E. *Chronicle of the Archbishops of Canterbury*. Cambridge, England: James Clarke & Co., 1913.)

Anselm died surrounded by friends who placed his body in ashes on the floor. He was probably canonized in 1494, although there is debate as to whether this occurred at all. His beatific status aside, Anselm will long be remembered as the author of the ontological proof.

Other Events

1073: Pope Alexander II died. He became the first pope elected under the new electoral system by the college of cardinals.

1142: Peter Abelard died on this day. His conceptualism (a way of describing how the mind knows ideas) tried to resolve differences between two schools of philosophy called Nominalism and Realism. But Abelard may be better remembered as the man who seduced his student Heloise than as a thinker who tried to ground theology in reason. He was often accused of heresy, but he remained one of the most popular teachers of his day and was a cofounder of schools that were later incorporated into the University of Paris.

1621: William Bradford was chosen governor of Massachusetts when John Carver died.

1855: Dwight L. Moody was converted to Christianity. His Sunday school teacher, Edward Kimball, said, "My plea was a very weak one, but I was sincere." Moody became a powerful evangelist.

Peter Abelard teaching in the Paraclete. (Lord, John. *Beacon Lights of History*. New York: James Clarke, 1886.)

Jan Hus. (Lutzow, Count. *The Life and Times of Master Jan Hus*. New York/London: AMS Press, Inc., 1909.)

APRIL 22

The Council of Constance and Hus

For thirty-three years, Christendom had suffered from the Papal Schism. Both popes in Rome and popes in Avignon claimed to be the legitimate successors of Peter. A council held at Pisa that was intended to end the schism actually ended up worsening the problem by creating a third pope. When Sigismund became emperor in 1411, he had had enough. He ordered one of the papal claimants, Pope John XXIII, to call a council. John did so reluctantly, dragging his heels as long as he dared. He did not convoke the council until November 1414. He called 18,000 churchmen from all over Europe to attend. Their retinues and camp followers (including 1,500 prostitutes) swelled the population of little Constance (now in the Grand Duchy of Baden), the site of the council.

Even though he was the one who had called the council, John had no desire to be subjected to its scrutiny, so he fled, dressed as a groom, hoping to escape censure for his crimes. It seems that he thought that by leaving he would remove the council's authority. In this he was mistaken. The prelates simply declared themselves under the direct authority of Christ and declared that everyone, even the real pope, whoever he might be, was bound to obey the council's authority in matters of faith.

The bishops deposed Pope John. The charges against him included theft, lechery, paganism, lying, simony and treachery. John accepted the decree and was imprisoned until 1418.

Jan Hus had voluntarily appeared before the bishops to persuade them to legitimize his Bohemian reforms. Although he arrived under promise of safe conduct from the emperor, who had said, "Even if he had killed my own brother . . . he must be safe while he is at Constance," Hus was seized and imprisoned by the bishop of Constance. When told he must recant, he refused: "I would not for a chapel full of gold, recede from the truth."

That done, the council turned its fury upon Hus. On July 6, 1415, the council condemned him "unanimously" as a heretic. (Since each of the four "nations" was given only one vote, unanimous meant four votes. Individuals within the delegations may have disagreed.) Hus was burned to death the same day. Before his execution he said:

> God is my witness that the evidence against me is false. I have never taught nor preached except with the one intention of winning men, if possible, from their sins. Today I will gladly die.

Also, since Hus's teachings were based on the work of English reformer John Wycliffe, the council proceeded to condemn Wycliffe as well, even ordering his bones dug up and burned. The following year, Jerome of Prague was sentenced to Hus's fate by the assembled bishops.

Angered by the actions of the council, Bohemia revolted from the Church and remained Hussite for 200 years until Catholicism was forcibly restored by the Hapsburgs. Germany and England were dissatisfied with the council's determinations as well and demanded reforms. The council evaded their issues.

On this day in 1418, the council declared itself dissolved. It had achieved its main end: the removal of the three rival popes and election of another, Martin V. The new pope, who owed his papacy to the council's authority to depose popes, immediately rejected any council's right to depose a pope.

Johann Sebastian Bach, who created a new music after the Reformation. (Bourne, C.E. *The Great Composers or Stories of the Lives of Eminent Musicians*. London: S. Sonnenschein, Lowery & Co., 1887.)

Other Events

536: Pope St. Agapetus died in the eastern empire, where he had gone in a vain attempt to prevent General Belisarius from coming to Italy. He failed at that but succeeded in moving Justinian away from the Monophysite heresy. After his death, his body was brought back to Rome.

1538: John Calvin and William Farel were fired by the town council of Geneva and ordered to leave the city within three days. The day before they had refused to administer the Lord's Supper unless the townsfolk repented.

1723: J.S. Bach was elected cantor of St. Thomas in Leipzig. This was the last post that he held before his death. Bach had a rule never to convert Christian works to secular use, although he often converted secular works to Christian use.

1987: Dr. J. Edwin Orr died on this day. He was a historian of revivals and showed that no revival ever began without prayer.

Most Important Day to Christianity

APRIL 23

The three Marys at the tomb of the risen Christ. (Bell, Mrs. Arthur. *Saints in Christian Art*. London: George Bell, 1901-4.)

Many scholars believe that Christ died and rose from the dead again in AD 30 (see our April 7 story). Others prefer a date in AD 33, although champions of several other dates can also be found. If the events recorded in the Gospels took place in AD 33, then this day in the year 33 is the probable date for Christ's resurrection.

The witness of the Christian Church and of convinced believers across the centuries has affirmed that without the Resurrection, there could be no Christianity. The cross of Christ makes no sense without His triumphant restoration to life, for it is the Resurrection tht explains His death as a sacrifice for sins. It is the Resurrection that proves Christ was no liar. It is the Resurrection that gives us hope of a new, eternal life, showing to us that as Christ rose, so will we.

The Resurrection is the one fact that the apostles and the early Church constantly held forth as the vindication of their message. It is the oldest traceable doctrine of the early Christian liturgy. Even notable anti-Christian scholars admit that the early Church held the Resurrection as fact, however much those same scholars hope to show that the Church was mistaken in its belief.

The records we have tell us that Christ was buried, His tomb sealed and soldiers posted around it. At about dawn of the first day of the new week (Sunday), there was an earthquake because an angel came down from heaven and rolled back the stone. The guards were so frightened that they fell senseless to the ground. At that time, some of Christ's female followers were on their way to the tomb to anoint His body. They were no doubt wondering how they would roll away the stone. Imagine their surprise when they found it rolled back and Christ's body gone! Thinking that His body had been removed, they began weeping. One of them asked a gardener if he knew where the body had been taken. Then she recognized the "gardener" as Jesus himself.

The women rushed back to tell the disciples what they had witnessed. Peter and John raced to the tomb and found that all was as the women had said. An angel assured the men that Christ was indeed risen (see Matthew 28:1-20; Mark 16:1-20; Luke 24:1-49; John 20:1-30). Afterward, Jesus appeared several times to His disciples and to His brother James.

All arguments against the Resurrection must deal with the eyewitness testimony of the early disciples, the great Church that sprang from it, the witness of changed lives around the world and the empty tomb. Modern dimensional mathematics suggests the plausibility of Christ's appearances, and modern physics demonstrates the necessity of additional dimensions, bringing the account into the sphere of scientific plausibility.

The Church has historically insisted that our Christian life would be impossible without the Resurrection, for through it Christ has removed the sting of death from all those who believe in Him (see 1 Corinthians 15:54-57).

Other Events

1616: William Shakespeare died. The great poet-playwright quoted from or alluded to the Bible hundreds of times in his plays and other works.

1849: The young Fyodor Dostoevsky was arrested and accused of plotting to overthrow the Russian government. After a terrifying appearance at a fake execution, he was exiled to Siberia, where he took comfort in the Bible. Later he wove Christian themes into his novels.

1950: Lutheran Bishop Otto Dibelius of Germany issued a protest against teaching materialism as a substitute for religion in state-sponsored youth movements.

1959: The Communists of Poland confiscated Church properties. The congregations were required to lease the properties back for their use.

1960: Japanese Christian Socialist Toyohiko Kagawa died on this day. Kagawa sought to literally apply Christ's words by embracing the lowest orders and slum populace.

1982: Cameron Townsend, founder of Wycliffe Bible Translators, died. Wycliffe Bible Translators is one of the world's largest missions organizations.

William Shakespeare was born (in 1564) and died (in 1616) on this day, April 23. (Courtesy of the University of Texas collection of public domain portraits on the Web.)

April

24

Clearing the Way for Freedom of Thought

Reuchlin's battle to preserve Jewish writings helped win freedom of thought. (Hirsch, Samuel Abraham. *A Book of Essays.* London: Published for the Jewish Historical Society by Macmillan, 1905.)

Some legal cases are so important that they have everyone holding their breath as they wait for the outcome. Such was the case when the future of European scholarship hinged on a ruling regarding the intellectual giant Johann Reuchlin.

A man of lowly birth, Reuchlin's talent for singing brought him to the attention of the Margrave of Baden, a member of the German nobility, who made him a companion of the margrave's son. In love with learning as well as with song, the singer made the most of the advantages offered by his new position and pursued an education for himself. Languages were his forte. He wrote the first Latin dictionary to be published in Germany and also prepared a work on Greek grammar. But Hebrew was his dearest love. He ferreted out the rules of Israel's ancient language by studying Hebrew texts and by conversing with every rabbi he met. His authority on the language became widely recognized.

Reuchlin's reputation was nearly the cause of his ruin. Two bigots, a converted Jew and a Dominican inquisitor, had obtained an order from Emperor Maximillian to burn all Hebrew works except the Old Testament, charging that they were full of errors and blasphemies. Before the edict could be carried out, however, the emperor had second thoughts and consulted the greatest Hebrew scholar of the day: Reuchlin.

Reuchlin urged that the Jewish books be preserved as aids to study and as examples of errors against which champions of the faith might joust. It was his opinion that to destroy the books would give ammunition to the Church's enemies. On Reuchlin's word, the emperor revoked his order.

The Dominicans were furious. Selecting passages from Reuchlin's writings, they tried to prove that he was a heretic. It is, in fact, possible that he was one, for he seemed to expect salvation through Kabbalistic practices rather than by relying on Christ's atoning blood. The Inquisition summoned him and ordered his writings to be burned. Sympathetic scholars appealed to Leo X on Reuchlin's behalf. The pope referred the matter to the bishop of Spires, whose tribunal heard the issue. On this day in 1514, the tribunal declared Reuchlin not guilty. It was a great victory for freedom of learning.

However, the Dominicans were not so easily brushed off. They incited the faculties at Cologne, Erfurt, Louvain, Mainz and Paris to condemn Reuchlin's writings. Thus armed, they approached Pope Leo X. Leo hesitated, uncertain whether he should try to win the thanks of the scholars by protecting the Jewish books or whether he should try to placate the clerics by condemning Reuchlin. He appointed a commission to help him in the decision. The commission backed Reuchlin, but still Leo hesitated. At last he decided to suspend judgment. This in itself was a victory for Reuchlin, since it meant his studies could continue and the Hebrew books wouldn't be burned. The cause of the embattled scholar became the cause of other innovators of the time period. Reuchlin's nephew, Melanchthon, rejoiced. Erasmus praised him.

Then in 1517 Martin Luther posted his ninety-five theses. "Thanks be to God," said the weary Reuchlin. "At last they have found a man who will give them so much to do that they will be compelled to let my old age end in peace."

Thanks to Reuchlin, the Talmud and Kabbala were preserved. Luther used Reuchlin's Hebrew grammar and studies to aid him in his translation of the Old Testament. Reuchlin's influence assured Melanchthon a position among the top scholars of the day and sent him on his way to fame in the Reformation.

Nicholas I. (Montor, Chevalier Artaud de. *Lives and Times of the Popes.* New York: Catholic Publication Society of America, 1911.)

Other Events

858: St. Nicholas I the Great was elected pope. He ruled firmly and fairly at a time of serious crisis when Charlemagne's empire was disintegrating because of wars between his heirs.

1547: The German Protestant Schmalkaldic League was routed by Roman Catholic emperor Charles V at Muhlberg.

1585: Pope Sixtus V was elected. He administered stern justice, clearing the countryside of brigands that had flourished under his predecessors. He also founded the Vatican library and a number of colleges.

1901: All evangelical missionaries to the Philippines gathered to discuss ways to achieve unity in their work. The meeting lasted through April 26.

1920: Hymn writer Eliza E. Hewitt died on this day. In addition to writing such hymns as "More About Jesus," "Sing the Wondrous Love of Jesus" and "Sunshine in My Soul," she was a Sunday school leader in a Presbyterian church.

April 25

Raised to New Life

"And we were baptized and all anxiety for our past life vanished away." With these joyous words Augustine recorded his entrance into the Church on this day in 387.

It had taken Augustine thirty-three years to get to the public confession of Christ that was represented by his baptism. He was born in North Africa in 354 to a Christian mother and a pagan father. He became a student in Carthage at twelve years of age. At sixteen, he began to teach grammar.

While he was young, he became promiscuous. He tells in his famous *Autobiography* that he boasted of sins he had not had the opportunity to commit, rather than seem to have fallen behind his peers.

His mother, Monica, was determined to see him converted. He was equally determined to have his pleasures. He took a mistress, and she bore him a son, whom they named Adeodatus, which means "Gift of God." For a while Augustine resented the lad but soon became inseparable from him.

When he was twenty-nine, Augustine's restless spirit drove him to Italy. His mother decided to accompany him so that her prayers might be reinforced by her presence. But Augustine gave her the slip, sailing away while she knelt praying in a chapel.

In Rome he taught rhetoric for a year, but was cheated of his fees. And so he looked for a more fertile field of labor and settled on Milan. His mother caught up with him and prevailed upon him to attend the church of St. Ambrose. Augustine found that Christian singing moved him deeply, and in spite of himself he began to drift toward his mother's faith. He found the writings of the Apostle Paul deeply stirring and more satisfying than the cool abstractions of philosophy. He wrestled with deep conviction but was unable to yield himself to God because of his strong attachment to the flesh.

Finally he reached a day when his inner struggles were too great to bear. He tried reading Scripture but abandoned the effort. Unable to act on the truth he knew, he began to weep and threw himself behind a fig tree. "How long, O Lord," he cried. And his heart answered "Why not now?" A child's singsong voice came clearly to him, repeating over and over, "Take it and read it." It seemed a message from God. Augustine snatched up the Bible and read Paul's words:

> Let us behave decently . . . not in orgies and drunkenness, not in sexual immorality and debauchery, not in dissension and jealousy. Rather, clothe yourselves with the Lord Jesus Christ, and do not think about how to gratify the desires of the sinful nature. (Romans 13:13-14)

Augustine writing. (Ruoff, Henry W. *Masters of Achievement: The World's Greatest Leaders in Literature, Art, Religion, Philosophy, Science, Politics and Industry.* Buffalo, NY: The Frontier Press Company, 1910.)

Faith flooded in upon him. He immediately thrust aside the sins of the flesh that had held him in bondage. "But this faith would not let me be at ease about my past sins, since these had not yet been forgiven me by means of your baptism." He entered the water and was relieved.

After his mother's death, Augustine returned to Africa, where he founded a monastery and became bishop of Hippo and a brilliant and prolific theologian. More than any other man, his imprint was stamped upon the medieval Church.

Other Events

799: Pope St. Leo III's eyes were stabbed and his tongue torn out in a conspiracy by the nephews of an earlier pope. He recovered and crowned Charlemagne emperor.

974: Ratherius, who raised a ruckus to end clergy marriages, died on this day.

1475: A young Savonarola left home and walked to Bologna, taking the family Bible with him. He became a monk and later a reformer. He was eventually martyred for his faith.

1800: William Cowper, a depressed but original poet and hymn writer, died. He is remembered for his friendship with ex-slaver John Newton and for his hymn "There Is a Fountain Filled with Blood."

1879: Joseph Barber Lightfoot, considered the greatest biblical scholar of his day, was consecrated as bishop of Durham. He was a godly man and became one of the greatest bishops of the day.

1911: A rare Gutenberg Bible sold for $50,000, the equivalent of at least $500,000 today.

William Cowper, poet and hymn writer, is considered the first of the English Romantic period poets. (Bruce, J. *Cowper's Poetic Works*, 1910.)

Transubstantiation: Body and Blood

Cesar Franck at the organ. The notable French composer suffered ridicule for his belief in transubstantiation. (Mason, Daniel Gregory. *From Grieg to Brahms: Studies of Some Modern Composers and Their Art.* New York: The Outlook Company, 1902.)

It is thought that the first person to write a book exclusively on the Eucharist was Paschasius Radbertus in 831. The book was called *On the Body and Blood of the Lord*. Although he did not use the term, he taught transubstantiation, the belief that the substance of the bread and wine used in the Eucharist service really become, by faith, Christ's body and blood.

Radbertus took a literal, as opposed to a symbolic, view of Christ's words, "This is my body, which is broken for you" (1 Corinthians 11:24, KJV). In his book he very quickly made his main point and hammered it home through many arguments. He said, "Yet these [the bread and wine] must be believed to be fully, after the consecration, nothing but Christ's flesh and blood." In Radbertus's view, God miraculously creates the physical, historical body of Christ in the Eucharist any time the loaf is consecrated:

> That in truth the body and blood are created by the consecration, no one doubts who believes the divine words when the Truth says: "For my flesh is real food and my blood is real drink" (John 6:55).

Radbertus emphasized mystical union with Christ through the partaking of the Eucharist. He pointed out that Christ taught, "Whoever eats my flesh and drinks my blood remains in me, and I in him" (John 6:56). Radbertus felt that the Eucharist, if taken in a worthy spirit, unites the believer with Christ.

Contemporaries criticized the abbot's view as too crude and materialistic. Most argued for a more symbolic interpretation of the body and blood. Radbertus defended his views in a famous letter in which he attempted to show that he was in agreement with the writings of the Church fathers. He was a well-read scholar and was therefore eminently capable of putting up a stout defense.

Radbertus's work might not have achieved the influence it did but for the fact that it was circulated under the name of St. Augustine of Hippo. This gave it credibility since Radbertus himself was just an obscure Benedictine monk. He must have had considerable ability, however, for although he was but a deacon, he was chosen to be abbot of Corbie. He sought to reform the abbey but resigned in 851 when his changes were rejected. He was active in church synods and as a writer. He lived for some years at St. Riquier, in northern France, after his resignation from Corbie. Radbertus died on this day in 856 at Corbie, to which he had returned a short time before.

Radbertus's work paved the way for other scholars who would further develop the concept of transubstantiation. Berengar of Tours developed concepts similar to Radbertus's in the eleventh century. The word *transubstantiation* was in widespread use in the West by the later part of the twelfth century. Belief in transubstantiation was defined at the Lateran Council of 1215. Thomas Aquinas and his use of Aristotelian physics in the thirteenth century furthered the formulation of the theory. The Council of Trent (1545-1563) reaffirmed the doctrine. It was one of the main issues that separated Protestants from Catholics, because most Protestants interpreted the Eucharist differently.

Despite the Catholic Church's affirmation of the doctrine, most other churches rejected the idea of transubstantiation. As such, those who held the view often endured ridicule. But, despite the ridicule, there was one man of note who would not be budged from the Catholic position. Famed French composer and organist Cesar Franck, known as "Father Seraphicus" for his serene and gentle character, was mocked for his belief in the doctrine of transubstantiation.

Lorenzo the Magnificent, one of the two Medici brothers who were attacked on Easter Sunday in 1396, survived the plot to kill him; his brother Giuliano did not. (Villari, Pasquale. *Life and Times of Girolamo Savonarola*. New York: C. Scribner's Sons, 1888.)

Other Events

1396: St. Stephen of Perm, who converted the heathen Zyrian tribes of the Ural Mountains in Russia, died on this day.

1478: As they were entering church to celebrate Easter mass, two Medici brothers were attacked by the pope's men, with the pope's knowledge. The Medici and Pazzi families were quarreling over which would handle Vatican banking. The pope wanted to drop the Medicis and install his own favorites.

1877: Minnesotans observed a statewide day of prayer to implore the Lord to remove a plague of grasshoppers. Grasshoppers had devastated the land in 1876. The prayer did not seem to work. Warm temperatures over the next two days caused millions of larvae to wiggle to life. But a plunge in temperature on the fourth day froze and killed all of the newly hatched wrigglers.

April 27

Paradise Lost, the Ten Pound Epic

On this day in 1667, the most magnificent epic in the English language was sold: John Milton conveyed the rights for *Paradise Lost* to Samuel Simmons.

Although Milton was well-known, the sale roused little notice, and the book went for a pittance. *Paradise Lost* was not actually published until August 20 of the same year and was not an immediate bestseller. But in time, it became ranked by hosts of readers as next only to the Bible.

The blind poet's lofty narrative was told in twelve books. In those twelve volumes, Milton dealt with the highest dramatic events known: the rebellion of Satan and the fall of man. He showed Adam and Eve naïve of evil and delighting in the garden, their sin and consequent woe and God's promise of eventual restoration of all things through Jesus Christ.

Milton presented his epic in blank verse, knowing that rhymes would make it trite and tire his readers' ears. He felt that the majesty of iambic pentameter would best suit his conception. Theological truths that would not easily bear rhyme would work well with alliteration (repeating stressed consonants)—if it wasn't overdone. For example, God says of Adam and Eve:

> [T]hey themselves decreed
> their own revolt, not I. If I foreknew,
> Foreknowledge had no influence on their fault.

It is remarked that Milton achieved his finest effects when depicting the rebel Satan. As a Puritan, Milton had participated in the revolt against Charles I; no doubt this helped him frame the sentiments he ascribed to Satan: "Better to reign in Hell than serve in Heav'n." Try as he would to pervert God's purpose, however, Satan was ultimately thwarted; evil was transformed by God into means for good:

> Who seeks to lessen thee,
> against his purpose serves
> To manifest the more thy might: his evil
> Thou usest, and from thence creat'st more good.

Had Milton meditated on Joseph's words before he wrote this? Joseph's brothers had sold him into slavery, and when Joseph, after rising to power, confronted them, he said, "You intended to harm me, but God intended it for good to accomplish what is now being done, the saving of many lives" (Genesis 50:20).

Milton's daughters read to him. (Ruoff, Henry W. *Masters of Achievement: The World's Greatest Leaders in Literature, Art, Religion, Philosophy, Science, Politics and Industry*. Buffalo, NY: The Frontier Press Company, 1910.)

Paradise Lost, a work of unparalleled genius, earned Milton £5 with a promise of £5 more at publication and £5 for each reprinting. According to the agreement into which he entered that April, the number of copies to be printed with each impression was limited:

> [The] impression shall be accounted to be ended when thirteen hundred books of the said whole copy, or manuscript imprinted shall be sold or retailed off to particular reading customers.

Millions have sold since.

Other Events

304: Pollio was burned to death in Gibalea (which is now Vinkovce, Hungary) after declaring his Christianity before a judge. Nothing else is known about him.

1539: Latin-American bishops Zumairaga, Zarate and Vasco de Qiroga drew up the chapters of the ecclesiastical commission of 1539.

1541: Three Protestant and three Catholic theologians met at the Council of Ratisbon in Germany to see if differences between their faiths could be worked out. The conference ended in failure.

1594: The body of St. Sava was burned by order of the vizier of the Turks. Sava's relics had been a popular attraction for Christians.

1775: Peter Bohler, the Moravian missionary who had much to do with leading John Wesley into a deeper Christianity, died on this day.

1950: A Communist-controlled National Catholic Church was created in Rumania under the direction of Andreas Agotha, whom Rome promptly excommunicated.

1960: Police in Nowa Huta, Poland, tried to remove a cross from a clearing in the center of the town. Women protested. Men joined to protect the women from police brutality. Riots developed, and the Communist headquarters was burned.

Ratisbon Cathedral Well. (Baring-Gould, S. *Lives of the Saints*. Edinburgh: John Grant, 1914.)

The distinctive spire of Salisbury Cathedral has often been depicted in paintings. (Hyde, A.G. *George Herbert and His Times*. London: Methuen, 1906.)

April

28 Laying Foundation Stones for a Distinctive Spire

John Constable and Joseph Turner portrayed the Salisbury Cathedral many times in paintings, as did lesser artists. Because of its distinctive cross-tipped spire, straining to a point 404 feet in the air, people who otherwise know little of architecture are able to recognize it. It may even be more widely recognized than England's other great monument: St. Paul's Cathedral.

The Salisbury Cathedral, located in Old Sarum, England, is one of the most beautiful pieces of architecture to be spawned by Christianity. Unlike most other medieval cathedrals, Salisbury was built in a single century. Bishop Poore laid the first five stones on this day in 1220, one each for himself, Archbishop Stephen Langton, Pope Honorius III, Earl William and Countess Ela of Salisbury. By 1237, the choir and east transepts were built, and by 1258 the nave and main transepts had been completed. The plans and their implementation experienced few alterations. Consequently, Salisbury has more unity of design than most English cathedrals of the period.

The designer of the cathedral is not known. Historian Paul Johnson suggests that Elias of Dereham and Nicholas of Ely combined their talents. At any rate, Bishop Poore was the motivating force behind the project. He obtained the papal authority to build the cathedral and found a location for it. A different location had actually been picked out prior to Poore's involvement, but the new structure would have had to be accommodated to old foundations and would not have achieved the charm that is unique to its design.

Salisbury Cathedral was designed in the Early English Gothic style, which employs pointed arches, slender vertical piers, buttresses and diagonals in an effort to reach an austere effect. It was shaped as a cross, ever the symbol of Christian faith. Its interior was well-lighted. The flying buttresses (outside arches) were later additions that were made necessary because of the one major change made to the original conception.

The original plan called for a low tower. However, 110 years after the first stone was laid, the height of the tower was doubled. Richard of Farleigh designed the octagonal spire that now completes the whole, making it the second tallest tower in Europe. The addition of the spire added so much weight that the crossing piers bent. It was no wonder since the piers had to support almost 6,500 tons! Consequently, new supports, the flying buttresses, had to be added.

The cathedrals of Europe are symbols of intense faith, for it took a great deal of faith to start building such a structure, particularly since most were not completed in one generation—or even in two. Their spires, straining toward heaven, are standing prayers to God. In their windows we read the gospel story. Ornaments remind us of the lurking powers of hell. Salisbury Cathedral remains a beautiful testimony to the faith of the time.

Julius III was pope when Sullaqa submitted a statement on behalf of the Uniate Nestorians. (Montor, Chevalier Artaud de. *Lives and Times of the Popes*. New York: Catholic Publication Society of America, 1911.)

Other Events

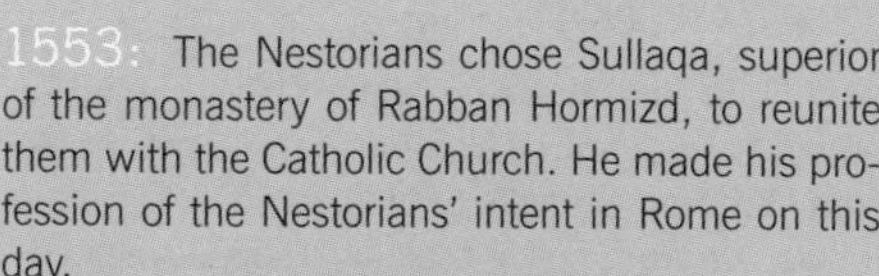

1553: The Nestorians chose Sullaqa, superior of the monastery of Rabban Hormizd, to reunite them with the Catholic Church. He made his profession of the Nestorians' intent in Rome on this day.

1841: The Roman Catholic missionary Pierre Chanel died a martyr in Tonga, where he had gone despite strong Protestant resistance. He was working on an island that had been unreached by Protestants.

1872: Francis Havergal wrote her hymn "Lord, Speak to Me that I May Speak" in Winterdyne, England. It first appeared in a leaflet with the title "A Worker's Prayer."

1911: Thousands of Genevans demonstrated for five hours against a religiously inspired ban on gambling. A shocked Karl Barth was appalled at their mindless slogans and came out in support of the ban.

1955: Christian and Missionary Alliance pilot Albert Lewis died when his seaplane crashed in the pass leading into the Baliem Valley in Irian Jaya (then known as Nederlands, New Guinea). Ten thousand souls came to Christ, owing in part to Lewis's supportive ministry.

APRIL 29

Joan of Arc Turns Tide of French-English War

Throughout much of the fourteenth and fifteenth centuries, the English fought the French in an attempt to claim France as their own. The English had the upper hand until Joan of Arc appeared.

Joan was a simple and pious peasant girl who wove and spun. She began to see heavenly beings and hear their voices, which told her that deliverance would come to France through her. The voices sent her to the nearest French bastion, but when she appeared before him her pleas were ignored. Eventually, Joan convinced local authorities that she was for real. One thing led to another and she ended up picking the disguised dauphin out of a crowd of courtiers. She also made prophecies, which were recorded in a letter written from Lyons on April 22, 1429. Those prophecies came true.

One of her predictions was that she would save besieged Orleans, an area that was crucial to the defense of France. On this day in 1429, a rapid march brought Joan of Arc, accompanied by French forces, to the city of Orleans. It was the turning point of the Hundred Years' War. The English retreated the next day, but as it was Sunday, Joan forbid the French to pursue them. Within a few days, the English garrisons around Orleans had all been captured. Joan was wounded in the fighting, which was also as she had predicted.

Charles, the irresolute dauphin, had to be coaxed into action. Joan convinced him to undertake various moves, which he did halfheartedly. A dramatic French victory at Pasay opened the way for Charles to retake Reims. Again Joan had difficulty convincing him to take the logical step of having himself crowned, but he finally acquiesced. Then she knelt before him and called him king.

The voices told her that she had less than a year left for her work. Those succeeding months proved to be frustrating for her. The king and his advisors lacked the boldness to pursue the advantages Joan had gained for the French. A feeble attempt to retake Paris failed. Not long afterward, Joan was captured by the English, who brought charges of witchcraft against her. Determined to find grounds for executing her, they had a group of high-powered theologians browbeat her and did not allow her any legal counsel.

As could be expected with such a stacked trial, Joan was convicted of practicing witchcraft. In a moment when her terror overcame her, she recanted with the caveat that she did so only as far as it was God's will. Her persecutors soon entrapped her with accusations.

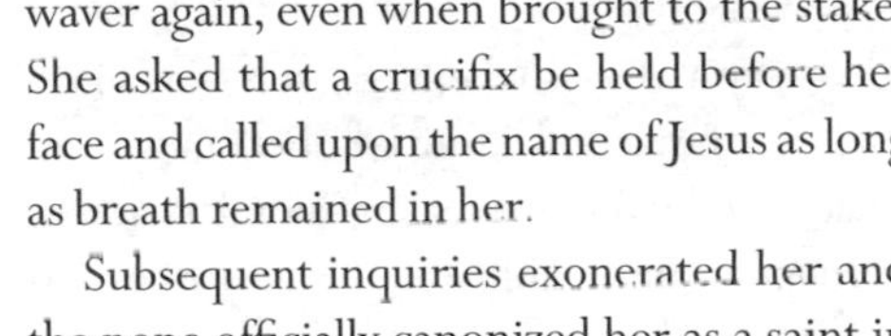

Joan of Arc heard voices. (Lord, John. *Beacon Lights of History*. New York: James Clarke, 1886.)

Quickly she regained her courage and did not waver again, even when brought to the stake. She asked that a crucifix be held before her face and called upon the name of Jesus as long as breath remained in her.

Subsequent inquiries exonerated her and the pope officially canonized her as a saint in 1920.

OTHER EVENTS

1380: Catherine of Siena, Dominican tertiary and mystic, died in Rome. She had a strong influence on world events through correspondence with the notables of her day.

1525: Fray Pedro de Cordoba died. He was a mentor to Las Casas, the "Father of the Indians."

1607: The first Anglican church was established in the American colonies, at Cape Henry, Virginia.

1882: John Nelson Darby died in Bournemouth, England. He was founder of the Plymouth Brethren movement and exerted a strong, worldwide influence on dispensationalism (the teaching that God deals differently with people in different eras, or dispensations) and modern ideas about the second coming of Christ. In the United States, many of Darby's ideas were popularized in the notes of the Scofield Bible.

1933: Dawson Trotman began his work with Navy men. The work led to the formation of the Navigators, a discipleship organization.

1945: Five hundred Greek Catholic clergymen in the cathedral at Lwow, Poland, were surrounded by police and arrested. Many were shot.

Catherine of Siena swoons in religious ecstasy. (Jameson, Mrs. *Legends of the Monastic Orders*. London: Longmans, Green, and Co., 1872.)

Emperor Diocletian. Galerius pushed him to persecute Christians. (Firth, John B. *Constantine the Great: The Reorganisation of the Empire and the Triumph of the Church*. New York/London: G.P. Putnam's Sons, 1905.)

APRIL 30

Galerius Issues a Toleration Edict as He Dies

Sometimes when a person stares into the face of eternity, he becomes more religious or makes moral changes, perhaps hoping to influence his future beyond the grave. This may have been the case with Roman Emperor Galerius when he issued an Edict of Toleration on this day in 311.

Galerius, the son of a Greek shepherd who became a Roman soldier, rose in power and authority to become a junior ruler under Diocletian. It was Galerius who instigated Emperor Diocletian's persecution of Christians in 303 by convincing Diocletian that Christians were dangerous enemies of the empire.

Galerius himself issued an edict in 304 requiring everyone in the empire to sacrifice to the gods of the empire on pain of death or forced labor. Leading churchmen were imprisoned, precious Bible manuscripts were destroyed and hundreds of Christians were executed as a result of his edict.

When Diocletian abdicated, Galerius became senior emperor in 305. He continued his cruel persecution, which was so widespread and intense that it became known as the Great Persecution. However, Christianity simply would not go away. Even Galerius recognized the impossibility of snuffing out the illegal religion.

Then he became ill. A Christian writer named Lactantius said that Galerius's body rotted and was eaten by maggots while he writhed in agony. Evidently Galerius's conscience connected his persecution of Christians with his miserable condition. He apparently saw his illness as a judgment from the Christian God, for from his sickbed he issued an Edict of Toleration that mentioned only Christians.

The edict began by justifying the murders that had been committed under his original edict:

> Amongst our other measures for the advantage of the Empire, we have hitherto endeavored to bring all things into conformity with the ancient laws and public order of the Romans. We have been especially anxious that even the Christians, who have abandoned the religion of their ancestors, should return to reason.

Noting that some Christians had betrayed their faith out of fear while others endured torture, Galerius decided illogically that:

> [W]e, with our wonted clemency, have judged it wise to extend a pardon even to these men and permit them once more to become Christians and reestablish their places of meeting.

Galerius added:

> [I]t should be the duty of the Christians, in view of our clemency [mercy], to pray to their god for our welfare, for that of the Empire, and for their own, so that the Empire may remain intact in all its parts, and that they themselves may live safely in their habitations.

Prayer seems to be the point of the proclamation. Galerius wanted Christian prayers. Did he hope for a miracle? If so, he was disappointed. He died a week after issuing the edict.

His successor, Emperor Maximinus, tried to counteract the edict but did not succeed to any great extent during his short reign. The Great Persecution of Christians had ended.

Sir Thomas More, who opposed James Bainham. (Pollard, Albert Frederick. *Thomas Cranmer and the English Reformation*. London: Putnam's 1905.)

OTHER EVENTS

418: Pelagians were banished from Rome by imperial edict as a great threat to peace, apparently for teaching that men can save themselves.

1532: James Bainham, a Lollard (a follower of the teachings of John Wycliffe) barrister (lawyer), was burned at the stake in Smithfield. He had been tied to a tree and whipped by Sir Thomas More, recanted his faith, was fined and then withdrew his recantation.

1658: Marguerite Bourgeoys established the first uncloistered Catholic missionary community in the new world at Ville Marie, Canada.

1854: James Montgomery, who for many years was Scotland's sole Moravian pastor, died on this day. Twice he went to prison for expressing his social views too freely in his newspaper, the *Sheffield Iris*. He was the author of many hymns, and he helped win acceptance for hymn singing in the Anglican Church. His best-known hymn was the Christmas carol "Angels from the Realms of Glory."

Raised Up to Remake English Morals

God raised up Mr. Addison and his associates to lash the prevailing vices and ridiculous and profane customs of this country, and to show the excellence of Christ and Christian institutions.

To win such praise from John Wesley, Joseph Addison must have been a good influence indeed.

God "raised up" Addison on this day in 1672. He was born in England near Amesbury in Wiltshire, in the heart of Old Wessex, not far from the Avon River. His health at birth did not give much assurance that he would survive long, so he was baptized the same day. Despite his early poor health, he survived and grew into a young man, surrounded by strong moral influences. He was related to clergymen on both sides of his family. His mother was sister to the bishop of Bristol, and his father became dean of Lichfield while Joseph was a youngster. Richard Steele visited the Addison home and considered its air of affectionate peace worthy of writing about in an issue of *The Tatler*.

Addison became one of the great stylists of the English language. His Latin poetry was also among the best written by an Englishman. But his real fame comes from the periodicals he and Richard Steele produced together: *The Tatler*, *The Spectator* and *The Guardian*.

The papers enjoyed a wide readership. Addison's stated purpose in *The Tatler* was "to enliven morality with wit, and to temper wit with morality." The papers introduced the middle-class readership to recent developments in philosophy and literature. It is said that Addison and Steele's works in the three papers were responsible for raising the general cultural level of the English middle class.

One of the most popular sections of the papers was Addison's tales about a fictional character named Sir Roger de Coverly. Lively anecdotes about him exposed folly and suggested better behavior:

> My friend Sir Roger has often told me, with a great deal of mirth, that at his first coming to his estate, he found three parts of his house altogether useless: that the best room in it had the reputation of being haunted, and by that means was locked up; that noises had been heard in his long gallery, so that he could not get a servant to enter it after eight o'clock at night; that the door of one of his chambers was nailed up, because there went a story in the family that a butler had formerly hanged himself in it; and that his mother, who lived to a great age, had shut up half the rooms in the house, in which either her husband, a son, or daughter had died. The knight, seeing his habitation reduced to so small a compass and himself in a manner shut out of his own house . . . ordered all the apartments to be flung open and exorcised by his chaplain, who lay in every room one after another, and by that means dissipated the fears which had so long reigned in the family.
>
> I should not have been thus particular upon these ridiculous horrors, did not I find them to very much prevail in all parts of the country.

Although he trained to become a priest, Addison never became one. It would have been a difficult path for him, for he was painfully shy. Instead of preaching to the public in a church, the press became his pulpit. In addition to his satires, Addison wrote hymns such as "When All Thy Mercies, O My God":

> When all Thy mercies, O my God,
> My rising soul surveys,
> Transported with the view, I'm lost
> in wonder, love and praise.

On his deathbed, Addison was calm and courageous. He urged his nephew to "see how a Christian can die." The excellence of his writing ensures that his memory will not perish soon, for his essays are often included in anthologies of English literature.

Joseph Addison. (Aikin, Lucy. *The Life of Joseph Addison*. London: Longman, Brown, Green, and Longmans, 1843.)

Other Events

1551: The eleventh session of the Council of Trent opened. The council, which began in December 1545, was interrupted so many times as it dealt with deep issues that it took eighteen years to accomplish its work on the Counter-Reformation, finally closing in December 1563.

1873: Missionary-explorer David Livingstone died in Africa near Lake Bangweolo (now within Zambia).

1939: The popular radio series *Back to the Bible* began broadcasting.

David Livingstone died in Africa. (Courtesy of the Christian History Institute archives.)

May 2

Practical Bishop of African Methodists

William Taylor, Methodist bishop of Africa, after a long and adventurous life. (Taylor, William. *The Story of My Life: An Account of What I Have Thought and Said and Done in My Ministry of More Than Fifty-Three Years in Christian Lands and Among the Heathen*. New York: Hunt & Eaton, 1895.)

William Taylor was born in Virginia on this day in 1821. He made his mark as a Methodist circuit rider and a missionary. The mark he made as a child, however, was probably not much different than that of other boys of his day.

There was the time, for instance, when three-year-old Taylor saw a large cluster of bees hanging down from the front of his grandfather's hive:

> I said, "Ah, my sweeties, I'll fix you." So I got an empty horn of a cow and filled it with water and dashed it on the bees. They resented it and speared me most unmercifully. The lesson I learned was to attend to my own business and not meddle with the affairs of other folks.

Before Taylor was ten, his grandmother taught him the Lord's Prayer and explained that he could be a son of God. He longed for the relationship but did not know how to get it. Overhearing the story of a poor black man who had gotten salvation, Taylor wondered why he could not do the same:

> But soon after, as I sat one night by the kitchen fire, the Spirit of the Lord came on me and I found myself suddenly weeping aloud and confessing my sins to God in detail, as I could recall them, and begged him for Jesus' sake to forgive them, with all I could not remember; and I found myself trusting in Jesus that it would all be so, and in a few minutes my heart was filled with peace and love, not the shadow of a doubt remaining.

After his conversion, Taylor backslid. Satan, he perceived, told him there was no longer forgiveness for him, and for years he lived in dread and misery. But then, when he was a teen, he was restored to Christ, and he became so joyful that he felt he had to tell others. It was the beginning of a long life of evangelism.

Taylor's greatest torment was to go up to perfect strangers and speak to them about their souls, but he did it until he learned better methods. One technique that he learned was to join the people at their work—even log-rolling—win their confidence with his brawn and then invite them to hear him preach.

Taylor rode circuits in Virginia and Maryland. In 1849 he accepted an appointment to California and journeyed there with Annie Kimberlie, his wife, and their two children. When they reached California they lived for a fortnight in the open air before someone relented and took them in. Taylor cut trees and built a home while at the same time he ministered to California's gamblers, gold diggers and sick.

Annie was four-and-a-half years younger than her husband but looked younger still. People often mistook them for father and daughter. Although deeply in love, they were often separated for years at a time while he led revival meetings and mission work around the world. It was Taylor's contention that if whalers could leave their families for three years to gather blubber, he could do no less for the greater treasure of souls.

Taylor's labors took him to every continent. He preached in Canada, Australia, Africa, India, Britain and South America. Wherever he went, hundreds turned to Christ. He became bishop of Africa. With wry humor, he remarked that if he disposed to lay a scheme for killing bishops decently, he would advise that by all means they avoid the highlands of Liberia and remain on the deadly malaria-infested coast.

William Taylor urged that missions be self-supporting. By his hard work, he showed how they might become so. Taylor University in Upland, Indiana, is named for him.

Elizabeth Barrett Browning. (Whiting, Lilian. *Women Who Have Ennobled Life*. Philadelphia: American Sunday School Union, 1915.)

Other Events

373: Bishop Athanasius of Alexandria died on this day. Athanasius not only defended the theology of the Trinity but was the first to list the New Testament canon as we have it. He was exiled many times but remarked, "If the world goes against truth, then Athanasius goes against the world."

1550: Joan Boucher was burned to death in England for denying that the Virgin Mary was sinless. The minister who preached at her execution made so many errors in his sermon that she told him, "Go read the Bible."

1559: After serving a stint as a prisoner in the French galleys, John Knox reached Edinburgh to lead the Reformation in Scotland.

1913: The love letters of the Christian poet Robert Browning to Elizabeth Barrett were sold. Browning inspired Elizabeth to rise from her sick-bed through a faith expressed in terms of positive thinking. They married. He was distressed when she dabbled in spiritualism.

1982: Ailing Pastor Lin Xiangao was arrested in Guangzhou, China, for holding house-church services despite a government ban.

Sailing Toward Hard Work

On the west coast of Greenland, in the tundra zone about 150 miles south of the Arctic Circle, a new colony was being built. Europeans had established a presence in Greenland as early as 980 under Eric the Red. Severe winters and the problems of maintaining trade caused the colony to perish 400 years later. In 1722, the Danes reestablished that presence. The leader of the expedition was not a Dane, however. He was a tough-skinned Norwegian named Hans Egede. More important than his heritage, however, was his calling: He was a Christian missionary.

As eighteenth-century Protestantism slowly developed a commitment to missions, the little nation of Denmark was among the first Protestant countries to recognize the urgency of spreading the gospel. They founded a mission school in 1714. Among the missions-minded was their ruler, King Frederick IV, who had been influenced by the Lutheran reform movement known as Pietism. Frederick strongly supported the proposals of the Norwegian Hans Egede. So, backed by the king, Egede and his wife, Gertrude, sailed on this day in 1721 for the inhospitable regions of the north.

Greenland, the world's largest island, is a harsh land. No settlement is possible except along the coasts, for the interior is ice-covered year round. In spite of all of its ice, Greenland's northern regions are more arid than the driest Sahara, receiving less than five inches of precipitation a year. The southern coasts, on the other hand, receive thirty inches. There, grasses and even some trees—alder, birch and willow—grow.

Hans Egede found both winter and summer beautiful despite the low average temperatures and the pale sun that never rose very high in the sky. In 1722 he founded a colony and named it Godthåb. Known as Nuuk today, it is the capital of the nation. From this base he preached to the Eskimos but saw few indications of success.

Superstition ran deep in the hardy Indians native to the land, and they could not be weaned from their *angakut* (soothsayers). The problems of teaching Christianity were compounded by Egede's difficulties in mastering the Eskimo language. It seemed to have few words with which to express Christian concepts. Despite this, he attempted to produce a translation of the New Testament in the Eskimos' language. Adding to all these barriers was his own temperament, which tended to be harsh and overbearing. He dearly loved the people, but, like many other Christians, he did not know how to express those sentiments in human terms.

Gertrude Egede tends sick Eskimos in Greenland. (*Lives of Missionaries, Greenland: Hans Egede, Mathew Stach and His Associates*. London: Society for Promoting Christian Knowledge, 1860s.)

That changed in 1733 when a smallpox epidemic swept the island. Egede and his wife poured themselves heart and soul into caring for the dying Greenlanders, who saw Christlikeness in their behavior. "You have been kinder to us than we have been to one another," exclaimed one. Egede's wife was so exhausted by her efforts that she died shortly after the epidemic passed. Egede returned to Denmark in 1736.

His son, Paul, who had been raised among the Eskimos, took over the work, mastered the language, completed the translation of the New Testament that his father had started and witnessed revival. His father rejoiced to see his son reap where he himself had sown.

Other Events

996: Gregory V became the first German pope. He was a nephew of emperor Otto III, whom he crowned. During an absence from Rome, rivals set up an antipope, but Gregory was able to overthrow him. There was a suspicion of foul play when Gregory died suddenly.

1512: The Fifth Lateran Council opened. Called by Pope Julius II, it was not accepted as legitimate by the French Church because it denied their claim to ancient liberties.

1738: Evangelist George Whitefield arrived in America, where he preached thousands of outdoor sermons. Whitefield described the theme of his sermons in these words: "Oh, the righteousness of Jesus Christ! I must be excused if I mention it in almost all my sermons!"

1832: Edward Irving was barred from his Presbyterian church, where he honored "prophets" and tongues-speakers. Later he was stripped of his ordination because of faulty teachings on the nature of Christ.

Gregory V, first German pope, in an artist's conception. (Montor, Chevalier Artaud de. *Lives and Times of the Popes*. New York: Catholic Publication Society of America, 1911.)

4

Irrevocable Decision to Join Outcasts

The young Damien. (Clifford, Edward. *Father Damien: A Journey from Cashmere to His Home in Hawaii.* London: Macmillan and Co., 1889.)

"I am ready to be buried alive with those poor wretches." The man who said this was Father Damien. The wretches he spoke of were the miserable sufferers of leprosy on Molokai Island. Leprosy was the curse of the Hawaiian archipelago, which was so blessed in other ways. People with the disease were isolated on the peninsula of Molokai. The disease causes nerves to die and leads to damage of the body's extremities. Leprosy was so feared that the Hawaiian government made it illegal for anyone landing on the peninsula to return to the other islands. Damien knew that if he went, he would not be allowed to return. On this day in 1873, he made an irrevocable decision: He would confront the gates of hell.

Conditions on the island were bestial. Beautiful young girls in whom leprosy had just been discovered were raped by demon-faced men in the stages of final decay. Victims of the dreadful disease threw weaker victims out of the huts to die. Not that the huts were wonderful: They were hideous with disease and despair. Most of the wretched men and women reeked of decaying flesh.

Damien turned white as a sheet as he landed on the beach. Yet he prayed to be able to see Christ in the ghastly forms before him. Given one last chance to leave, he refused. He had volunteered for hell, and he intended to civilize it.

The son of a Flemish farmer, Damien had entered the priesthood with great fervor. His very presence in Hawaii was the result of his constant appeals to his supervisor to let him go. Once there, he proved himself a determined evangelist.

Nothing he had done before could compare with the efforts he now made. Although water was plentiful in the mountains, there was little in the settlement, so Damien organized daily bucket brigades. Later he constructed a channel that diverted a stream of water to the very doorsteps of the unhealthy town. He developed farms. The apathetic lepers had neglected even this simple attempt to make themselves self-sufficient. He burned the worst houses and scoured out those that could be salvaged. Saw and axe in hand, he built new houses. He laid out a cemetery, stating that from that point on, anyone who died would be properly buried. He prepared a dump and cleaned up the village and its land. He shut down alcohol stills.

And he told his decaying audience about Christ. His cheerful conversation led dozens to turn to Christ. The same men who had been stealing from dying outcasts or dumping them into ditches to die asked for baptism.

Jealous Hawaiian authorities and Protestant missionaries, who had done little for the outcasts, spread scandalous stories about Damien. But he labored on.

Twelve years after he arrived on the island, Damien discovered that his own feet were leprous. Four years later he was dead. His quiet heroism won worldwide renown. It brought new donations to help the leper colony and a staff of nurses and other helpers. By his gruesome living death, Damien assaulted the gates of hell.

Alexander IV, spiritually sound but politically inept. (Montor, Chevalier Artaud de. *Lives and Times of the Popes*. New York: Catholic Publication Society of America, 1911.)

Other Events

1256: With the bull *Licet Ecclesiae Catholicae*, Pope Alexander IV founded the order of Hermits of St. Augustine, also known as Augustinians.

1453: Patriarch Yohannis XI, one of a long line of patriarchs in the Ethiopian Coptic Church, died on this day.

1493: Pope Alexander VI issued a bull on the West Indies, drawing a line of demarcation between the colonial possessions of Spain and Portugal.

1521: Martin Luther arrived at Wartburg after having been kidnapped for his own protection by German ruler Frederick the Wise on his way home from the Diet (Congress) of Worms. During his months there, Luther translated the Bible into German.

1535: King Henry VIII of England had several Carthusian monks hanged, drawn and quartered in London for refusing to submit to him as head of the Church.

1923: W. Robertson Nicoll died. The sickly scholar was in bed for much of his life but read two books a day and wrote the *Expositor's Bible*.

Throwing Down the Gauntlet

May 5

Just as the opponents of the arch-heretic Arius acknowledged his purity of life, so did critics of William Ellery Channing admit they could find little to fault in his personal conduct. His theology, however, was another matter.

As a youth Channing was serious-minded with a bent toward religious and moral readings. When he reached young adulthood, he decided to become a minister and subjected his body to severe austerities. He was courteous, gentle and refined. Although he became the focus of a great religious controversy, his writings were calm and cool. On the moral issues of the day, he took a clear stand. He hated slavery but was opposed to any practical means to overthrow it. He spoke against war and urged against the annexation of Texas. He supported Horace Mann's educational efforts and was a champion of American literature.

After completing his ministerial studies, Channing was installed in 1803 as pastor of the Federal Street Church in Boston. Puritan Calvinism was the reigning theological system of New England, but many ministers, Channing among them, were not in step with it. He said, "Calvinism owes its perpetuity to the influence of fear in paralyzing the moral nature." If it were up to him, man's head and heart would be the final test of truth.

To attack Calvinist theology was heresy in New England. Calvinists recognized that a "head and heart" religion not firmly based on God's Word would lead to the denial of Christ's divinity. The Calvinists demanded the expulsion of Arians and Socinians from their midst because both groups denied the divinity of Christ.

Channing met the Calvinists head-on. At the ordination of a protégé, Jared Sparks, held on this day in 1819, Channing delivered the speech that separated the Unitarians from the Calvinists and soon made them an independent denomination. The first half of his speech defended the use of human reason in interpreting Scripture. His arguments ignored the role of the Holy Spirit in illuminating Scripture. In the second half of the speech, he sported the results of his new theology of the unaided human mind. Not surprisingly, the doctrine of the Trinity was the first to go. "We object to the doctrine of the Trinity, that it subverts the unity of God," he said.

In rejecting the Trinity, the Unitarians rejected many other Christian doctrines as well. Channing expressed these views forthrightly in his speech: Christ was not both God and man nor a member of the Godhead; the vicarious atonement of Christ for sin was absurd; election by grace was a preposterous notion; and so on. In short, Channing renounced virtually every doctrine that is fundamental to the Christian religion.

Channing, a "Rational Christian" or Unitarian, who challenged the Trinity. (Lossing, Benson J. *Eminent Americans*. New York: Hovendon Company, 1890.)

Ironically, his decision to dump the Trinity for the sake of reason came just as breakthroughs in infinity mathematics and concepts of multi-dimensionality helped some to find it more reasonable than ever to believe in the Trinity.

Channing's ideas were trumpeted by liberals for many generations and some are held to this day.

Other Events

321: Emperor Constantine, unable to subdue the Donatists, gave them grudging tolerance. The Donatists, a North African sect, split from the Catholic Church because they insisted that those who had betrayed Christ and the Scripture could not lightly be readmitted to the Church. Bishops consecrated by former traitors were not in the apostolic succession, they said, and so they set up their own succession.

553: The Council of Constantinople II began. Under Emperor Justinian, who was manipulated by his wife, Theodora, it issued a ruling favorable to the Monophysite heresy.

1525: Frederick the Wise, benefactor of Martin Luther and the Reformation, died.

1910: Alexander Maclaren, a Baptist preacher with a worldwide reputation for his sermons and writings, died on this day. He refused to write out his sermons so that the Holy Spirit would have free play when he spoke. During singing, he sat with the congregation, observing that he wanted to "join the praise, not lead it."

Theodora, wife of Emperor Justinian. She favored the Monophysite heresy. (Oman, C.W.C. *Story of the Byzantine Empire*. New York: Putnam's Sons, 1892.)

Alfred the Great ensured the preservation of Christianity in England. (Courtesy of the University of Texas collection of public domain portraits on the Web.)

May

6 Christianity Survives a Crisis in the Kingdom

At Ethandún (probably the present-day Edington in Wiltshire), Dane met Saxon in war, pagan challenging Christian. The battle, which took place on this day in 878, ensured that Christianity survived in England. As with every major battle, the events preceding and following Ethandún were as important as the battle itself. In fact, the battle was merely the turning point, the moment of crisis.

Alfred, leader of the Saxons, stood to lose everything. Vikings had been attacking the British Isles for many years; Northumbria, East Anglia and Mercia had already fallen. By 877 the kingdom of Wessex alone resisted the invaders. Danish leader Guthrum made peace with Alfred. But then, in a treacherous winter attack, he drove Alfred from his throne. It seemed the Danes had triumphed. They most likely expected Alfred to flee overseas, as other kings and nobles had done in the past. Christianity would be forced underground, civilization would take a beating and the Saxons would be slaves.

But Alfred didn't run. He didn't go overseas but instead hid on the Isle of Athelny in Somerset. With the coming of spring, he sent secret messengers to summon the remaining Saxons to Egbert's Stone. The thanes responded readily, weeping with joy when they saw their king, for he seemed to them as one raised from the dead. Once they had all gathered, Alfred led them to confront Guthrum.

The armies met at Ethandún. Surprisingly, Guthrum, with his professional soldiers and confidence of previous battles won, was the loser. He fled to his fortress at Reading, pursued by the Saxons. For once, Alfred had sufficient arms and men to destroy his enemy. Instead of decimating the Danes, he offered Guthrum peace and baptized him along with thirty of his pirate earls. For twelve days he catechized the new converts in the peace of Christ and then let them go.

For the most part, Guthrum kept the peace. He did join a band of Danish raiders some years later, but by then Alfred had developed a system of forts and levies that secured England, and the raiders posed little threat.

Alfred had done more than win just one battle: He had begun the unification of England, which was later completed under his son Edward. A wise treaty with the Danes reduced feuds. No wonder Alfred is called "Great," the only English monarch to have received that title.

Alfred also earned another title: He was called the "Father of the English language." War had destroyed learning in England. He could have despaired and left the work to others, but instead, he heeded his own wise counsel:

> No man may do aught of good unless God work with him. And yet no one should be idle and not attempt something in proportion to the powers which God gives him.

He could have tried to rebuild Latin learning, but that would have taken generations. He was deeply concerned for the souls of his people, so he turned to the homely Anglo-Saxon language instead, realizing that it would take less time to create a new system of learning than to try to revive the old. His creation of an English-language literature and educational system united his people around a few well-selected texts. He himself learned Latin and spearheaded the drive to translate the psalms, Gregory's *Pastoral Care*, Orosius's *Geography*, Boethius's *The Consolation of Philosophy* and other works.

Because of Alfred, England possessed a native and wholly Christian literature long before other Western countries.

Amalia Gallitzin had a strong influence on her son. (Heyden, Thomas. *A Memoir on the Life and Character of the Rev. Prince Demetrius a de Gallitzin*. Baltimore, MD: John Murphy & Co., 1869.)

Other Events

1312: The Council of Vienne ended. It was called chiefly to suppress the Knights Templar at the insistence of Philip IV of France. Philip made sure he got his way by appearing outside the city with an army.

1527: Charles V's out-of-hand army entered Rome, killing, looting, raping and torturing. Pope Clement VII barely escaped with his life. The tragedy followed a prophecy by a beggar-preacher that Rome would be destroyed for Clement's sins.

1746: William Tennent died on this day. He opened what was called a "log-college," and his zealous students played a key role in the Great Awakening and in founding the school that became Princeton Theological Seminary.

1840: Father Demetrius A. Gallitzin, "Apostle of the Alleghenies," died. He emigrated to the US from Russia, converted to Catholicism, studied at Baltimore Seminary and spent the bulk of his life establishing churches in the Allegheny Mountains. He had been strongly influenced by his zealously religious mother, Amalia, who had brought many to a belief in Catholicism.

1986: The first American Indian Roman Catholic bishop, Donald E. Pelotte, was ordained in Gallup, New Mexico.

Before Marco Polo

Everyone, it seems, has heard of Marco Polo and his journey to far-off China. But on this day in 1253, a year before Polo was even born, a courageous monk from Flanders, William of Ruisbroek, left Constantinople on his own trip to the Far East. William visited the court of the Great Khan Mangu in the very heart of Mongolia.

From the start, his efforts were intended to be evangelistic. Louis IX, the saintly king of France, heard that the Mongolian under-khan, Sartak, son of Batu, was a Christian. He determined to contact and encourage his distant brother in the faith. William, a Franciscan friar, was the man Louis chose for the job. Accompanied by Bartholomew of Cremona (a fellow friar) and a few others, William left for Sartak's kingdom, hoping to establish a mission work there.

Much to William's surprise, however, Sartak proved to be no Christian. William and his companions suddenly found their mission stretched well beyond their expectations. They were ordered to visit Batu, father of Sartak. And so the two Franciscans traveled up the Volga River to Batu's camp. Batu sent them on to Mongolia with two Nestorian priests and a guide. The little party crossed Russia and Mongolia in the depths of winter and arrived in Karakoram in January 1254.

Other Europeans, captives of war, were already present in the city. Nestorian Christians had long since penetrated the region with the good news of Christ's reconciliation of mankind to God. Their ministry had little effect, perhaps because (according to William's report) they habitually became drunk on wine rather than on the Holy Spirit.

William met the khan, discussed theology in his presence and was allowed to preach. Once he became vehement in his preaching and upset the khan. Nevertheless, William survived at the Mongol court for eight months, apparently without serious threat to his person. In that time he converted and baptized sixty Mongolians.

In August, William left the khan's court, bearing a letter from Mangu, the great khan, demanding submission of all Western kings as well as the pope. The khan claimed that God had appointed him master of the world and not even mighty seas and high mountains would prevent him from conquering the West.

William of Ruisbroek arrived at Acre, a Syrian seaport in the Mediterranean, in May of 1255, bearing the khan's grandiose proclamation. He forwarded it to King Louis with a careful and accurate report of what he had seen and experienced during his journey. The report included the best descriptions of Asia to have reached Europe up to that point. In its pages were also suggestions for further mission work, but nothing was done with them.

Genghis Khan—the name means "Greatest of All Rulers"—created the Mongol power base. This is an artist's reconstruction of his inauguration. (Abbott, Jacob. *History of Genghis Khan*. New York: Harper, 1899.)

Other Events

1274: The Council of Lyons II met. The council was supposed to promote plans to reunite the Eastern and Western Churches, but nothing came of it.

1794: French revolutionaries proclaimed the worship of a "supreme being," a Deist god.

1823: A group of Russian Orthodox missionaries left Irkust to evangelize the Aleutian Islands and Alaska.

1844: Protestants burned dozens of Irish Catholic homes and the St. Augustine Church in Kensington, a suburb of Philadelphia. The action was in retaliation for the killing of one of their own by a Catholic the day before during an ill-advised rally in the Irish streets. Protestants were outraged that Catholics would not participate in school Bible reading (the Catholics believed that Church leaders, not individuals, should interpret Scripture). In defense of their property, Catholics killed several more Protestants as the riot progressed.

1859: Guido Verbeck and his bride, Maria, destined for Shanghai, sailed from New York aboard the *Surprise*. With them were Rev. and Mrs. Brown and the medical missionary Duane B. Simmons and his wife. Verbeck was so notable a missionary that the Japanese honored him highly.

Guido Verbeck sailed for Japan, where he made a lasting impression for Christ. (Dennis, James S. *Christian Missions and Social Progress*. New York: Fleming H. Revell Co., 1897-1906.)

Jacobus Arminius. Holland divided over his theories on predestination. (Daniels, W.H. *Illustrated History of Methodism in Great Britain and America, From the Days of the Wesleys to the Present Time*. New York: Phillips & Hunt, 1880.)

May 8

Is Grace Irresistible and Who Is Elect?

On this day in 1603, after a lengthy exchange of letters, the curators and burgomasters of Leiden officially appointed Jacobus Arminius professor of theology at their university. When he was first proposed for the position, Arminius did not think he would take it because he had formed loving ties with his flock in Amsterdam, where he had served for fifteen years. His working relationship with Amsterdam's authorities was also good, and he seldom found it necessary to oppose them for the sake of conscience. Furthermore, he found theological researches a hindrance to his growth in personal sanctity. But perhaps the biggest obstacle to his moving to Leiden was a lifelong contract with Amsterdam from which he could not just walk away.

The possibility of appointment to Leiden raised the question of his orthodoxy, particularly in regard to his interpretation of the seventh chapter of Paul's letter to the Romans. Calvin and Beza taught that the chapter referred to a regenerate man. Arminius held that it was the description of an unrepentant person. This raised opposition, although his chief opponent in Leiden, Franciscus Gomarus, confessed he had never read Arminius's work. After Arminius explained his views, Gomarus agreed they were a defensible interpretation, although he preferred Calvin's. Arminius showed that his position had been held by a score of eminent theologians from Church history. Everyone was satisfied.

Arminius's appointment cleared its last hurdle when Amsterdam graciously released him from his contract. The city even promised to provide his wife with a pension on the event of his death and gave their favored son a substantial parting gift.

Arminius had not escaped controversy, however. At Leiden he became embroiled in theological arguments that he would rather have avoided. The lecture schedule required him to speak on predestination, a topic on which his views differed from that of strict Calvinists. Arminius decided to reduce conflict by building his lecture almost entirely out of Scripture, adding the least amount of commentary he could get away with. However, Arminius's careful pastiche of Scripture quotes did not follow the Calvinist line, and subsequently the Calvinists challenged him. Strict Calvinists believe Christ died only for the elect; Arminius said Christ died for all. He also said that everyone has genuine free will and that grace is resistible. Strict Calvinist views seemed to take away free will because they said grace was not resistible.

Arminius tried hard to keep peace, even deliberately withholding some of his views. He tested each of his views to make sure none nullified the doctrine of salvation by faith. Furthermore, he was careful to avoid anything that smacked of Pelagianism (the teaching that man can save himself). He never denied predestination.

The controversy became hot, so hot in fact that the Dutch nation split into Arminian and Calvinist factions. The Calvinists soon got the upper hand.

After his death, the Synod of Dort condemned Arminius's views—or at least the theology derived from them. But in 1795 the Dutch Church admitted Arminianism was a legitimate interpretation of Scripture. Today Protestant groups are often categorized as Arminian or Calvinist.

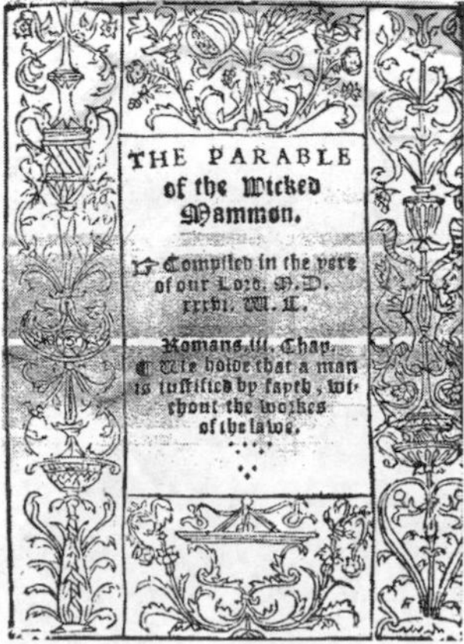

THE PARABLE
of the Wicked
Mammon.

Compiled in the yere
of our Lord. M.D.
xxvi. W.T.

Romans.iii. Chap.
We holde that a man
is iustified by fayth, without the workes
of the lawe.

A facsimile of the front page of Tyndale's *Parable of Wicked Mammon*, published in the 1500s. Because such books were illegal, the authors and publishers did not provide publisher and city information.

Other Events

1528: William Tyndale's *Parable of Wicked Mammon* was printed. At the time Tyndale was a fugitive on the Continent, so he smuggled the book into England through merchant friends.

1814: The East India Company consecrated Thomas Middleton privately as the first bishop of Calcutta; the company feared outrage from Hindus if the event were publicized.

1920: H.G.C. Moule died on this day. He was a prominent Anglican bishop who published many respected Bible works.

1979: The Communist regime in Poland forbade Pope John Paul II to attend the feast of St. Stanislaus.

MAY 9

President Woodrow Wilson Proclaimed Mother's Day

Ana M. Jarvis was deeply attached to her mother, Mrs. Ana Reese Jarvis. Mrs. Jarvis had taught in a Methodist Sunday school in Grafton, West Virginia.

She died in 1905. Two years later, the Sunday school superintendent of her Grafton congregation asked Ana to help him arrange a memorial for her mother because she had been highly influential in his church. This got Ana thinking. It seemed to her that children often did not do enough to show their mothers that they appreciated them while their mothers were still alive.

Grafton held its special service on the second Sunday of May in 1907, which was the anniversary of Mrs. Jarvis's death. The following year, Ana convinced her own church in Philadelphia to hold a Mother's Day service on May 10. Ana supplied the church with white carnations, which had been her mother's favorite flower.

After that, Ana wrote thousands of letters and held many interviews to promote a national Mother's Day. She enlisted friends to help in the effort as well.

It took them six years, but in the end they succeeded. On May 8, 1914, both houses of the United States Congress passed resolutions establishing an annual Mother's Day observance. Acting on the authority of that resolution, President Wilson, on this day in 1914, issued a proclamation regarding Mother's Day:

> Now, therefore, I, Woodrow Wilson, President of the United States of America, by virtue of the authority vested in me by the said Joint Resolution, do hereby direct the government officials to display the United States flag on all government buildings and do invite the people of the United States to display the flag at their homes or other suitable places on the second Sunday in May as a public expression of our love and reverence for the mothers of our country.

Today, Mother's Day is not celebrated so much with flags as with gifts, cards, hugs, thank yous and other tokens of affection.

Thanks to the efforts of one Christian woman, Mother's Day is observed everywhere in the United States on the second Sunday of May. Several other countries—Christian and non-Christian alike—celebrate the holiday on that day as well, including Australia, Belgium, Canada, China, Denmark, Finland, Italy, Japan, Mexico, Turkey and parts of Africa and South America. In some countries, the appreciation lasts for two days.

Woodrow Wilson. (Courtesy of the University of Texas collection of public domain portraits on the Web.)

Other Events

1087: Blessed Victor III was enthroned as pope. He had refused the office for a year after his election; when he finally relented and accepted the post, his papacy lasted for only a few months.

1619: The Synod of Dort in the Netherlands ended. It condemned the Remonstrant position (Arminianism) and banished forty-five ministers who had signed the Arminian Articles of the Remonstrance.

1707: Composer and organist Dietrich Buxtehude died on this day. Johann Sebastian Bach once walked many miles to hear Buxtehude play.

1760: Count Nikolaus von Zinzendorf, the Pietist leader of the Moravians, died on this day. He died quoting a Scripture about peace.

1848: Andrew Murray was ordained on his twentieth birthday. He became a notable educator of Christians in South Africa and the author of books on Christian living.

Victor III, who refused the papacy for over a year. (Montor, Chevalier Artaud de. *Lives and Times of the Popes*. New York: Catholic Publication Society of America, 1911.)

May 10

Hard Delivery, but Worth It

Dr. Karl Barth and Dr. Emil Brunner relaxing between sessions of the First Assembly of the World Council of Churches. (Courtesy of World Council of Churches.)

On this day in 1886, at about 5 a.m. on a Monday, Anna Katherina Sartorius Barth delivered a son after a long and hard labor. Karl Barth was born at home on 42 Grellingerstrasse in Basle, Switzerland, with an aunt attending. Although both parents were born and raised in Basle, they had only recently returned to the city when Barth's father, Johann Friedrich Barth, accepted a pastorate there. Barth's father was an earnest, outspoken preacher, much respected by his congregation. His son would follow in his footsteps and later become one of the best-known theologians of the twentieth century.

After a happy childhood in Basle and Bern, Barth attended the universities of Bern, Berlin, Tübingen and Marburg. Beginning in 1909 he pastored for many years, and even after he had become a famed professor at the universities of Göttingen, Münster and Bonn, he held that the essential task of theology was preaching. His theology, he said, grew out of his first pastorate in Safenwil, where he carefully crafted his sermons each week. At that time he was a liberal who even went so far as to publicly praise the German preacher and theologian Friedrich Schleiermacher and to make speeches for the Religious Socialists.

Barth's friend Thurneysen said to him, "What we need for preaching, instruction and pastoral care is a 'wholly other' theological foundation." For some reason the words stuck in Barth's mind. Although he had usually focused his sermons around a Scripture verse, for the first time he really became aware of the Bible. He began to study Paul's epistle to the Romans.

Unlike many religious thinkers of the twentieth century, who synthesized Christianity with other beliefs, Barth refused any "insights" borrowed from world religions on the grounds that other religions are man's attempt to reach God, whereas Christianity is God's act of reaching down to humans through Christ Jesus. He held that Christianity is not man's discovery but God's revelation.

As Barth saw it, God's revelation is not just intellectual:

> The revelation which has taken place in Christ is not the communication of a formula about the world, the possession of which enables one to be at rest, but the power of God which sets us in motion, the creation of a new cosmos.

Originally he drafted his book on Romans only for himself and a close circle of friends. The first printing, published in 1918, consisted of only 1,000 copies, which sold slowly. Barth's *The Epistle to the Romans* took theologians back to the great doctrines of Augustine and the Reformation: salvation, sin, God's judgment and Christ's return. It became one of the most influential works of twentieth-century theology and made Barth famous.

Later, Barth wrote *Church Dogmatics* and other theological works. Perhaps his most practical contribution was the *Barmen Declaration*, which called Christians back to the historical truths of their doctrine at a time when Hitler loyalists within the national Church were warping the faith into a parody that applauded his killer regime and allowed Hitler to dictate in matters of religion. When Barth refused to take an oath of unconditional allegiance to Hitler, he was expelled from his professorship at Bonn.

Agapetus II. (Montor, Chevalier Artaud de. *Lives and Times of the Popes*. New York: Catholic Publication Society of America, 1911.)

Other Events

Annual: The feast day of St. Comgall, who is credited with founding Irish monasticism, is celebrated on this day. Irish monks are credited with preserving civilization in the darkest of the Middle Ages.

946: Agapetus II was consecrated pope. A tyrant reigned at the time and Agapetus had little power, but he planned the evangelization of Europe and persuaded Otho I to invade Italy.

1887: Ian Keith Falconer, a British subject carrying the gospel to Aden, a city in what is now Yemen, was martyred. He said:

> While vast continents are shrouded in almost utter darkness, and hundreds of millions suffer the horrors of heathenism and Islam, the burden of proof rests upon you to show that the circumstances wherein God has placed you were meant by Him to keep you out of the foreign field.

1939: After 109 years of separation, the Methodist Episcopal Church in America, the Methodist Protestant Church and the Methodist Episcopal Church reunited in the United States.

From Many, One

Hundreds of thousands of immigrants arrived in the United States in the first two decades of the 1800s. Many were unchurched and without Bibles, and Christians felt challenged to put Bibles into the homes of these newcomers. In response to the need, 130 Bible societies sprang up within the states and other territories. Many provided Bibles in the immigrant languages. The Bibles, however, were acquired largely through the good services of The British and Foreign Bible Society. Observers saw a need for an umbrella society under which the local units in the United States could function. To bring this to pass, delegates from twenty-eight locales gathered in New York, and the Society was born on this day in 1816.

The assembled delegates declared that their purpose was "to encourage the wider circulation of the Holy Scriptures throughout the world" and stipulated that none of the Bibles could contain notes or comments. This provision was necessary because notes and comments acceptable to one denomination often offended another. The May 11 board was comprised largely of Christian laymen, with Elias Boudinot, former first president of the Continental Congress and director of the United States Mint, as chairman. The board was eventually developed into the American Bible Society. The Society did not seek to replace regional societies but to assist them. By year's end, forty-one regionals had joined it. The organization grew steadily. By 1995 it had a staff of over 300. More than eighty Protestant denominations provided it with some level of support.

In spite of its efforts to maintain neutrality, the American Bible Society could not please everyone. In 1837, Spencer H. Cone founded a rival society when many Baptists pulled their support from the American Bible Society. The rift occurred because the Society refused to produce a Bengali New Testament that used the Baptists' preference for the translation of the Greek word *baptizo*.

The Society's initial efforts had been to get Bibles to the American frontier. After a time, however, the frontier disappeared. Although the American Bible Society still maintained concern for the US (issuing its low-vocabulary *Good News for Modern Man*, for example), it turned increasingly to foreign needs, usually producing Bibles in close association with missionaries.

By the mid-1980s, the American Bible Society had printed Scriptures in over 1,000 languages. It sent skilled linguists into the field to check translations and provided inexpensive reproduction for the finished product.

A page from the *Codex Sinaiticus*, one of the valuable Greek manuscripts on which modern translations of th Bible are based. (Courtesy of the Christian History Institute archives.)

Eugene Nida joined the Society in 1943 and became one of its luminaries. He personally visited over 50 nations and worked on more than 100 translation projects. His books educated thousands of would-be translators. He was also closely associated with the Summer Institute of Linguistics, which gave practical linguistic training to missionaries.

The American Bible Society distributes hundreds of millions of pieces of low-cost Christian literature every year. It has promoted cooperation between Catholics and Protestants in the work of translation.

Other Events

330: Constantine the Great dedicated Constantinople as a Christian city, but he also set up an image of the sun-god with his own features and invoked the "genius," or attending spirit, of the city.

1610: Matteo Ricci, a Jesuit, died on this day. He adopted Chinese dress and customs in his zeal to convert the Chinese.

1825: The American Tract Society organized in New York as an amalgamation of several smaller societies.

1881: The Protestant mystic Henri Frederic Amiel died. He left a 1,700-page journal full of psychological and spiritual insights.

1926: J.R.R. Tolkien and C.S. Lewis had their first long spiritual conversation. Soon afterward, Lewis converted to Christ. Tolkien and Lewis were core members of the Inklings, a Christian literary group at Oxford.

Constantine the Great. (Firth, John B. *Constantine the Great: The Reorganisation of the Empire and the Triumph of the Church*. New York/London: G.P. Putnam's Sons, 1905.)

MAY

12

Cardinal Without a Position

Cardinal John Henry Newman. (Courtesy of the Christian History Institute archives.)

"I shall not die; I shall not die, for I have not sinned against the light." In restless, fever-tossed dreams at Leonforte, Sicily, a young English vicar repeated those words again and again. His health improved, and he said, "God still has a work for me to do. I have a work to do in England." Later, while at sea on his return from Italy, the vicar, John Henry Newman, composed the hymn "Lead, Kindly Light."

On Newman's first Sunday back in England, John Keble preached the sermon "National Apostasy." As far as Newman was concerned, that was the beginning of the Oxford Movement in which he played so prominent a part.

Newman preached at Oxford, calling men to repentance. His messages attracted large numbers and appealed for holiness in terms such as these:

> What can this world offer comparable with insight into spiritual things, that keen faith, that heavenly peace, that high sanctity, that everlasting righteousness, that hope of glory, which they have, who in sincerity love and follow our Lord Jesus Christ? Let us beg and pray Him day by day to reveal Himself to our souls more fully, to quicken our senses, to give us sight and hearing, taste and touch of the world to come.

The Church in Ireland had taken some heavy blows from the English government. The government took the stance that it had absolute authority over the Church. Subsequently, the Anglicans felt threatened. This was the case in England as well. Newman's concern led him to join in issuing a series of Tracts for the Times. Through the tracts he hoped to define more clearly the Church of England's doctrine and position so the Church would not be subject to governmental whims.

One of Newman's tracts argued that the Church of England had disassociated itself only from the excesses of the Roman Catholic Church, not its fundamentals. This stirred a cry of outrage. Newman resigned his posts and went to Littlemore with a group of friends to rethink his place in the Anglican Church. After much deliberation and prayer, he decided he must leave it and join the Roman Church. On a visit to Rome, he was ordained.

His secession from the Anglicans threw England into an uproar, not only because of his influential sermons and writings, but also because many of England's leaders were his friends. Many of his friends and family members ostracized him. To them, his choice seemed a betrayal.

Novelist Charles Kingsley accused Newman of teaching that priestly lies are acceptable. Newman (with deep love for the truth) said he had taught no such thing. An exchange developed between the two men. Finally Newman answered Kingsley's accusations with a masterpiece: *Apologia pro Vita Sua* (*Apology for My Life*).

The *Apology* was not the first writing that Newman had done. He had written *The Idea of the University*, another respected work. Poetry also came easily to him: He actually threw away the now-acclaimed poem "The Dream of Gerontius," thinking it was worthless. A friend rescued it and goaded Newman into printing it. Sir Edward Elgar set it to music in the twentieth century.

On this day in 1879, Newman was made cardinal-deacon of the Title of St. George by Leo XIII. The move was extraordinary. Although he was an ordained priest, he held no churchly function of any sort.

"The cloud is lifted from me forever," said Newman. He had faithfully adhered to his deepest principles but had not expected the honor. The Oxford Movement persisted with great strength even after Newman became a Catholic. Oxford later elected him an honorary fellow, restoring his association with them.

William Carey, who more than anyone convinced Protestants that they should engage in world missions. (McLean, Archibald. *Epoch Makers of Modern Missions*. Cincinnati: Fleming H. Revell Co., 1912.)

OTHER EVENTS

1003: Pope Sylvester II, known to science as Gerbert, died on this day. Deeply interested in the sciences and mathematics, he had tutored Otho III who later elevated Sylvester to the papacy, making him the first French pope.

1328: Pope Nicholas V was crowned. He was a lover of literature and the arts and spent much effort on improving Rome. His Concordat with Vienna secured recognition of papal rights to control benefices and sees.

1552: Dominicans created the University of Lima by royal decree.

1622: Philip Neri was canonized. After selling his books to aid the poor, Neri founded the Fathers of the Oratory order.

1792: Englishman William Carey published an eighty-seven-page tract on Christians' obligation to send missionaries to foreign lands. The tract became the manifesto of Protestant missions.

1963: A.W. Tozer, a Christian and Missionary Alliance pastor famed for his devotional books, died on this day. He had preached his last sermon just a week before.

MAY 13

She Wanted to Taste the Full Suffering of Death

The woman's prayer was unusual, to say the least. She began by asking to understand Christ's passion. She also asked to receive a gift of three wounds from God: the wound of true contrition, the wound of genuine compassion and the wound of sincere longing for God. These have been common enough requests throughout Church history, so that was not what set her prayer apart. The unusual part of her request was this: She asked to be allowed to come as close to dying as it was possible to come and yet still live.

What could prompt Julian of Norwich to make such a petition? She wanted to know the full suffering of death, to face the terror of demonic assault, to be so far gone that the last rites would be given her. She wanted no more to live for earthly comforts. By such an experience, she hoped to be wholly cleansed and, after she recovered, to be able to live a life that was more worthy of God and to die a better death in the end. She longed to be with God.

Midway through her thirty-first year, her prayer was answered. Julian became deathly ill. She was prostrate for three days. On the fourth, the last rites were administered to her. She lingered two more days and nights. On the third day, her sight failed, the room became dark around her and her breathing grew short. She said, "I knew for certain I was passing away."

Suddenly, on this day in 1373 (or May 8—there is some confusion in the original manuscripts), her pain lifted and she felt as fit as she ever had. Astonished at the miracle, she asked that she might experience Christ's passion in her own body. At once she saw the God-man with red blood trickling from the crown of thorns:

> And I had a strong, deep, conviction that it was He Himself and none other that showed me this vision. At the same moment the Trinity filled me with heartfelt joy, and I knew that all eternity was like this for those who attain heaven. For the Trinity is God and God the Trinity; the Trinity is our Maker and keeper, our eternal lover, joy and bliss—all through our Lord Jesus Christ.

That night she received fifteen "showings," or visions. As soon as the visions left, she was again in great pain and apparently close to death. When someone asked her how she was doing, she replied that she had raved that day. Immediately she was ashamed, because in her heart she knew the visions were real. She was then attacked by Satan, not as an angel of light but in fiendish form. Soon afterward, she received a sixteenth vision, which confirmed the others. She soon recovered.

Julian took her name when she became an anchoress, a woman who lives in seclusion for religious reasons. However, Julian's seclusion was by no means complete, for she counseled many people who came to her. Furthermore, she had a scribe to whom she dictated the first book to come from the hand of an English woman: *Revelations of Divine Love*, in which she reported the contents of the sixteen visions she said the Lord had given her.

A painting from Norwich Cathedral, located in Julian's town, which depicts the resurrection of Christ. Julian of Norwich claimed she saw the risen and glorified Christ in sixteen visions or "showings." (Quennell, C.H.B. *The Cathedral Church of Norwich*. London: George Bell & Sons, 1900.)

Julian contemplated her visions for twenty years before committing them to parchment. Her teachings were similar to those of other mystics. She shares language similar to contemporary and earlier English works. There are some odd elements that give one pause, such as her emphasis on the motherhood of Christ. She seemed to teach Universalism—that every human soul will be saved. But on the whole, her showings are a passionate testimony to the grace of God, the glorious bliss prepared for those who love Him and an appeal that we turn from sin for the sake of Christ, who suffered so deeply for us.

Other Events

1607: One hundred and five Anglicans landed at Jamestown. With them was Chaplain Robert Hunt, who set up the first Anglican church in America the following day. They met beneath an awning hung between trees. According to Captain John Smith, the group held daily common prayer morning and evening and two sermons each Sunday and partook of communion every three months.

1619: John Barneveld, a seventy-one-year-old Dutch statesman, was executed. He sided with the Remonstrants (Arminians) against the Calvinists.

1817: Philadelphia's local Sunday schools united to form the Sunday and Adult School Union.

1981: Ali Agca, a Turkish gunman, seriously wounded Pope John Paul II in an assassination attempt. Upon his recovery, John Paul visited Agca in prison and forgave him.

1982: A bayonet-brandishing priest approached Pope John Paul II at Fatima.

John of Barneveldt, who was executed for his support of Arminian views and states' rights. (Motley, John Lothrop. *Life and Death of John of Barneveld, Advocate of Holland*. New York: Harper & Brothers, 1874.)

May

14

Union Jack Down, but Israel Survived

Control of Jerusalem, a city holy to three faiths, remains a hot concern. (Armitage, Thomas. *A History of the Baptists: Traced by Their Principles and Practices, From the Time of our Lord and Saviour Jesus Christ to the Present*. New York: Bryan, Taylor and Co., 1893.)

A few turn-of-the-century books on Bible prophecy said it would happen. But most books spiritualized the predictions.

Up to the last moment, the United States urged the Jews to be cautious. Accept a truce and don't declare nationhood, advised General Marshall. War was inevitable if the Jews stuck to their plans. The United States, he said, could not help Israel.

On paper, the odds seemed impossible. The forces arrayed against Israel were enormous, and some of them were British-trained. The Arabs far outnumbered the Jews, whose old weapons were no match for newer Arab equipment. The Arabs had air support; Israel had none. The Arabs controlled half of Jerusalem. Israel's advantages were an intimate knowledge of the terrain, a superb grasp of military tactics, unity of command and control of internal lines. The Jews rated their chances as just barely even. On May 12, the Jewish leadership discussed the problem all night and finally voted to proceed with a declaration of nationhood.

At 8 a.m. on this day in 1948, the British lowered the Union Jack from over Jerusalem. For the Arabs, the lowering of the flag was the signal for war. By mid-afternoon, conflict was raging across Palestine. At 4 p.m. David Ben-Gurion read the Declaration of Israeli Independence. He said that Jewish sufferings and their historic roots in Palestine gave them a moral right to possess the land.

After 1,878 years, Israel had a nation again—if they could keep it. The Israelis offered peace, but the sultry day had already turned into one of raging battles. Arab troops had ridden to battle with cheers ringing in their ears and flowers decorating their vehicles. Now they were deadlocked in a desperate struggle. Israel's general, Moshe Dayan, had only two old field pieces (moveable artillery), but he used them so effectively that Syrian tanks disengaged. Iraqi conscripts had to be chained to their guns.

The fiercest fighting was in the south against Jordanians and Egyptians. Jerusalem's Jews were outgunned, and Arabs held the high ground. Fighting was intense in the historic city, and many died on both sides. British General Glubb threw his troops against the Jews, but skilled Jewish street fighters with homemade mortars inflicted fifty-percent casualties on some of his companies.

In the end, Israel held. Students of the Bible who had insisted, on the basis of prophecy, that Israel would once again become a nation saw in these events the fulfillment of biblical predictions and promises.

Pope John XII. (Peake, Elizabeth. *History of the German Emperors and Their Contemporaries*. Philadelphia: J.B. Lippincott & Co., 1874.)

Other Events

964: Pope John XII, a playboy pope, died on this day. He was the first to change his name on acceding to the papal throne (which he did at the age of eighteen). After first swearing allegiance to Emperor Otho I, he revolted. Otho deposed him and installed a new pope, whom John promptly excommunicated.

1796: English physician Edward Jenner administered his first successful smallpox vaccination made from cowpox to an eight-year-old boy named Phipps. Thanks to Jenner's perseverance, much of the world has been rid of the smallpox virus. Jenner championed vaccination, although it cost him most of his own medical practice and prestige. His careful studies and follow-up tests founded the modern discipline of immunology.

Jenner was a selfless Christian: He was hauling firewood for the poor the day before he died. His writings contain a plea that Christ receive his imperishable soul. He once said, "I do not wonder that men are grateful to me, but I am surprised that they do not feel gratitude to God for making me a medium of good."

1890: Rosa J. Young was born in Rosebud, Alabama. She pioneered education and founded Lutheran churches among Alabama's African-American community.

1901: Althea Brown, an African-American, was commissioned to go to the Congo as a missionary. She performed heroically under uprisings, war conditions, family separations and more. At a time when modern linguistic training was not available to missionaries, she persevered in preparing a grammar of the Bukuba language.

The Thundering Scot Turns the Tables at Blackfriar

May 15

When John Knox first preached, his sermons were rants against Roman Catholic practices. They gave his listeners something to protest against but nothing to replace what they were asked to discard. Knox had sided with Scottish firebrands early in the Reformation. He saw Wishart burned at the stake at the order of Cardinal Beaton. When ruffians who had been George Wishart's supporters assassinated Beaton in turn, Knox became their chaplain. He was later captured by the French soldiers who were aiding the Scottish throne, and Knox was sentenced to a French galley. After two years behind an oar, he had less love than ever for Roman Catholics.

In 1556, after a visit to Geneva, Knox returned to preach a new kind of sermon in his homeland, a sermon that not only tore down the old but also showed his listeners that as God's elect they must build a new kind of Church.

Many nobles came to hear Knox speak of the nation he envisioned, a nation in which the true *Kirk* (Church), with Christ at its head, would triumph. The bishops of the old order resisted Knox's new vision. If Knox were to have his way—and his growing popularity indicated that he might—they would be robbed of their authority and their teachings would be outlawed. They summoned him to appear at the Church of the Blackfriars in Edinburgh to face legal proceedings. Knox appeared before them on this day in 1556.

If the bishops had hoped to humble him, they were disappointed. In fact, he turned the tables on them. Many Scots of high standing, including William Keith, the earl Marischal, came to Blackfriars with him. In the face of their power, the regent, Mary of Guise (mother of Mary, Queen of Scots) saw nothing for it but to dismiss the summons. Knox stepped out to preach to large crowds in Edinburgh. He wrote the regent a letter of thanks and asked for toleration of all Protestants. She treated his appeal with disdain.

Scotland was not yet ready for Knox's brand of reform. The nobles wanted to revive feudalism; the government hired a mercenary army to enforce its will. Once again Knox left for Geneva, where he ministered to fellow exiles. In Geneva he embarrassed Calvin by issuing, over Calvin's objections, a "blast" against women rulers. Knox may later have rued his hastiness when the Protestant Elizabeth came to the throne of England and he had to find a way out of his words because he needed her help.

When Knox returned to Scotland, he thundered loudly for reform. Riots broke out, and his followers smashed Roman Catholic images. Civil war ensued. Several times

John Knox, the "Thundering Scot." (Daniels, W.H. *Illustrated History of Methodism in Great Britain and America, From the Days of the Wesleys to the Present Time*. New York: Phillips & Hunt, 1880.)

the reformer and the queen of Scotland met face-to-face. Each found in the other a powerful opponent. Knox told her solemnly, "I am sent to preach the evangel of Jesus Christ to such as please to hear it; and it hath two parts, repentance and faith." Mary did not accept the gospel according to Knox; she preferred the teaching of her Roman Catholic guides. In the end she abdicated her throne after a personal scandal and the mysterious murder of her husband.

Knox remained preeminent in the life of his nation. When the constitution of the Church of Scotland was formulated, he was a key player.

Knox is remembered as the "Thundering Scot." More than any other major reformer, he legitimized revolution. In his view, Christians have an obligation, under certain circumstances, to revolt against tyranny.

Other Events

719: Wynfrith of England was consecrated bishop under the name Boniface. He carried the gospel across Germany and Prussia.

1213: John, king of England, submitted to the pope, making England and Ireland papal fiefs. The pope had laid the kingdom under interdict because John refused to accept Stephen Langton as archbishop of Canterbury.

1525: The German Peasant Revolt, which included radical Anabaptists, was quelled at Muhlausen, dashing the peasants' hopes of freedom.

1948: Father Edward Flanagan, who organized Boy's Town, believing there is no such thing as a bad boy, died on this day.

1951: Archbishop Grösz of Hungary was arrested for refusing to sign a government peace appeal.

1972: In Wisconsin vs. Yoder, the US Supreme Court said that the Amish couldn't be compelled to send their children to public schools against their religious convictions.

1984: Francis Schaeffer, a Christian apologist, died. With his wife, Edith, he operated L'Abri, an apologetics ministry for intellectuals. He wrote a number of widely read books, including *Escape from Reason, The God Who Is There* and *A Christian Manifesto*.

Peasants involved in the German Peasant Revolt of 1525 were armed with only farm implements and other makeshift weapons. (Bezold, Friedrich von. *Geschichte der Deutschen Reformation*. Berlin: Grote, 1890.)

MAY

16

A Time to Feast

John of Nepomuk is revered in Czechoslovakia. (Baring-Gould, S. *Lives of the Saints*. Edinburgh: John Grant, 1914.)

John of Nepomuk was vicar-general to the archdiocese of Prague. As such he had to carry out the orders of his superior, Archbishop John of Genzenstein, who was in the midst of a quarrel with the king of Bohemia. John's obedience to his superior made him a patron saint of Bohemia.

King Wenceslaus IV, a wicked and cruel man, became enraged after the Church prevented him from confiscating a tract of land. It had been his intention to use the lands to create a new diocese and set up a crony of his as its bishop. So, in March of 1393, Wenceslaus ordered John of Nepomuk and the dean of the cathedral tortured. In his fury, he personally assisted in the cruelties, applying a burning torch to John's side.

Once his anger was sated, Wenceslaus decided to free the victims but stipulated that they must say nothing of what he'd done to them. John, however, was too far gone to be released. Seeing that John was dying, Wenceslaus made up his mind to get rid of the evidence of his brutal handiwork and trussed John up with a gag so he could not cry out. John was tied up and then carried secretly through town and dumped in the River Moldau.

Wenceslaus's attempt to cover up his crime failed: John's body washed ashore the very next day. The people immediately recognized the corpse and buried John in the Cathedral of St. Vitus. The Bohemians considered him both martyr and saint and revered his relics, honoring him in much the same way as Ireland honors Patrick. A metal plaque was affixed to the bridge from which John was thrown.

In 1729, Pope Benedict XIII agreed with the Bohemians that John had been a saint and canonized him. This day, May 16, became his feast day. Roman Catholics, Anglicans, Copts, the Orthodox and some other denominations honor certain days as feast days. Feasts commemorating major events in Christ's life must be observed by all Roman Catholics, and so must some feasts in honor of Mary. There are, however, many feasts that are not obligatory for all Christians, but only within limited regions. St. Patrick's feast day is obligatory in Ireland, for example, but not in the Czech Republic. Every saint is awarded a fixed feast date on which to be commemorated. These are non-obligatory or lesser feasts; otherwise every day of the year would be booked (and sometimes overbooked), because of the many saints who have been canonized.

John of Nepomuk earned his feast due to a petty quarrel. In the popular version of his story, he is made out to be not only a martyr but also a hero. It is said Wenceslaus was so spiteful to him because the priest refused to tell the king what the queen had said in the privacy of confession.

London's Broad Street at about the time that David Nasmith turned his attention toward the city's spiritual needs. (Loftie, W.J. *London City: Its History, Streets, Traffic, Buildings and People*. London: The Leadenhall Press, 1891.)

OTHER EVENTS

1569: Dirk Willem, an Anabaptist, was burned at the stake. He was captured because he turned to save a pursuer who had fallen through the ice. The man whose life he saved promptly arrested him.

1835: A few men met in David Nasmith's little home to found the London City Mission. Nasmith had already founded the first Protestant city mission in Glasgow nine years earlier.

1945: G. Campbell Morgan, one of the great expositors of the Bible, died on this day. He began to preach at thirteen, but his faith faltered in the face of materialism. For years he neglected his Bible. Then a change occurred. He said of this change:

> I bought a new Bible and began to read it with an open mind and a determined will. That Bible found me. . . . Since that time I have lived for one end—to preach the teachings of the Book that found me.

1957: Harold Jackson and Joseph Brown signed an agreement to buy land for New Tribes Mission to create a boot camp in Australia to facilitate efforts to reach Papua for Christ.

MAY 17

In Answer to a Dream for the Outback

If it is true that Jesus is God's Son, and that through Him whosoever will may approach the Father Himself, what more honorable calling can a man follow than to realize this fact and act upon it?

With that meditation, John Flynn convinced himself that God meant for him to be a minister.

Flynn was born in 1880 at Moliagul in Victoria, Australia. He imbibed his faith from his father, a lay pastor in a Methodist church. His mother had died when Flynn was three. A year after her death, Flynn's father transferred to a school near Melbourne. The nearest church was Presbyterian, and so Flynn attended a Presbyterian church and became a Presbyterian minister.

Australia's outback intrigued him. Looking across it he saw the same things anyone else saw: dust and deadly isolation, regrettable deaths that could have been prevented and would have been if there had been medical care, souls untaught in the rudiments of faith and minds stunted for lack of schooling. He saw all that.

But he also saw more than that. He saw railroads begging to be laid and radio stations to be built. He saw a network of nursing centers that were close enough to every bush station to give people a real chance of survival after an accident. He saw a group of roving parsons who could reach even the most remote parts of that barren land. Above all, he saw air ambulances that could rush doctors to the side of urgent cases and bear those patients to medical centers. If no one else saw it yet—well, he figured he'd have to make them see it.

Flynn volunteered for mission work with shearers and made an adventurous camel trek across the desert. He learned that bushmen, lacking pastors, did not even have a burial service to say over a dead mate. Few had the training to handle the medical crises that struck often in that rugged land. And so he compiled the *Bushman's Companion*, a handbook of first-aid and spiritual fundamentals. Thousands of copies were distributed for free.

In 1911, Flynn volunteered for a parish that stretched from the Flinder's Range in South Australia to Oodnadatta, deep in the Great Victoria Desert. The Presbyterian Church placed a nurse at Oodnadatta to provide medical assistance to the vast, neglected region. With efforts to fund and build a "hospital" as well as preaching treks to lonely outposts, Flynn's great work began.

He founded a magazine to promote the outback and filled its pages with photographs, maps and big visions. The Presbyterian Church appointed him head of the Australian Inland Mission.

Flynn spoke of his vision for the outback to all who would listen. At his instigation, committees were formed to raise money for the mission. He overcame hurdles as big as the desert itself: uninterested governments, conflicting state interests, medical rivalries, bushmen too proud to accept a "handout." He learned patience.

Piece by piece, Flynn's patience paid off. Rail lines crawled across the outback. Padres patrolled the desert. Nursing stations appeared. Books were supplied.

Flynn was quick to see the potential of the airplane. If doctors could fly to patients, they would provide a mantle of safety to outback homesteads. He appealed for planes and the establishment of flying doctors at seven strategic locations. Again he had an uphill fight, and again his persistence won out: The world's first civilian flying doctor service was born. Doctor K. St. Vincent Welch answered his first call on this day in 1928, flying to a minor emergency. Soon hundreds were helped through the vision of a man who considered no project too big for Christ.

John Flynn dreamed big visions for Australia's outback and through Christ saw them fulfilled. (Courtesy of the Australian Religious Film Society.)

OTHER EVENTS

1637: The Puritan lawyer John Winthrop was elected the first governor of the Massachusetts Bay colony. His term of office was one year, and he was reelected several times.

1763: The extraordinary man of letters, Samuel Johnson, who set the tone for his age, met James Boswell. Boswell left us a vivid portrait of Johnson's peculiarities. Johnson's practical faith once caused him to carry home a prostitute who had collapsed in the snow. He supported several elderly people in his home. He also wrote prayers.

1972: Tutsi tribesmen executed Father Michael Kayoya of Burundi (a small nation in eastern Africa). He was one of thousands who were massacred in genocidal murders. About one-half of all Catholic catechists in Berundi were killed by the Tutsi.

Samuel Johnson was unusual in both his habits and influence. (Meakin, Annette M.B. *Hannah More, a Biographical Study*. London: Smith, Elder & Co., 1911.)

May 18

Death of a Hero: Marquette Had Worked Sick

Heroic Jacques Marquette is laid under a shade to die. (Thwaites, Reuben G. *Father Marquette*. New York: D. Appleton, 1902.)

How often the work of Christ has been done by men and women who were not well. Father Jacques Marquette is typical of a host of Christians who labored for Christ even when their health had failed. This roster of fame includes John Wycliffe, Charles Wesley, Mother Teresa and many others.

Born in Laon, France, Marquette was thoughtful and gentle as a child. From an early age he had been determined to become a missionary. At the age of seventeen he became a Jesuit novice. After studying and teaching for many years, he was granted his heart's desire in 1666 when his superiors allowed him to transfer to Quebec. He was twenty-nine years old.

He quickly mastered Algonquian, a language widely understood among the North American Indians. After that he was manager of several posts along the Great Lakes. Threats by the fierce Sioux drove him to found a defensible mission at St. Ignaz on the straits between Lakes Huron and Superior.

In 1672, Louis Joliet was sent to investigate a rumor that there was a great river in the interior of North America. Marquette was authorized to join Joliet, and he jumped at the chance:

> The Father had long premeditated this undertaking, influenced by a most ardent desire to extend the Kingdom of Jesus Christ, and to make Him known and adored by all the peoples of that country. He saw himself, as it were, at the door of these new nations when, as early as the year 1670, he was laboring . . . among the Outaouacs; he even saw occasionally various persons belonging to these new peoples, from whom he obtained all the information that he could. This induced him to make several efforts to commence this undertaking, but ever in vain; and he even lost all hope of succeeding therein, when God brought about for him [this] opportunity.

With a small party of Frenchmen, Marquette and Joliet crossed Wisconsin in 1673 and followed waterways to the mighty Mississippi. Down the wide water-road they traveled, as far as the Arkansas River. By then it was apparent that the Mississippi did not empty into the Pacific but rather into the Gulf of Mexico. Spanish territory lay ahead and therefore the Frenchmen turned back.

On the return trip, Joliet's log was lost in an accident and Marquette's personal journal became the record of the expedition. His journal is of great importance to historians because of its detailed description of their journey.

The exertions of the voyage left Father Marquette seriously ill. Nonetheless, he determined to preach Christ among the peaceable Illinois Indians, whose language he had learned. Allowing himself only a short rest, he embarked for Illinois in October of 1674.

In Illinois, he found himself too sick to work. He recovered enough to preach the Easter sermon in 1675, but when it became clear that he was dying, he asked his companions to take him back to St. Ignaz. His suffering caused the party to put in at the Michigan river that is now named after him. They landed where Ludington stands today. There he died on this day in 1675.

Of all the Jesuit missionaries who labored in America, Marquette's name is among the best-known because of his humble and pure character and his great contribution to opening up the heartland of America. Millions of tourists have visited Mackinac Island where he built his mission station.

A Puritan. (Courtesy of the Christian History Institute archives.)

Other Events

1631: Puritans in Massachusetts said that none but Puritans could be freemen and only freemen might vote.

1737: Catherine of Genoa was canonized. She had opened a number of hospitals and helped the poor.

1808: Jacob Albright, first bishop of what became known as the Evangelical Association, died on this day. He began as a Methodist preaching to Germans in America but gradually developed an independent organization. After his death, the Evangelical Church united with the United Brethren, becoming the Evangelical United Brethren Church.

1843: The Church of Scotland split in protest of lay patronage (the "right" of certain wealthy and powerful laymen to appoint ministers). Thomas Chalmers and his associates formed the Free Church of Scotland, sacrificing the financial support that the government of Scotland gave Presbyterian pastors of the established Church.

1926: Aimee Semple McPherson, a flamboyant Pentecostal evangelist of doubtful morals, disappeared. When she reappeared, she claimed she had been kidnapped, but it was suspected that she had run off for a tryst with a lover.

The Scholar for an Empire Dies

England lost her greatest teacher and western Europe gained a fine scholar when Alcuin of York met Charlemagne in Parma in 781. The noble-born Englishman with an international reputation for scholarship headed the school at York, but Charlemagne urged him to share his talents with an entire empire. When Alcuin agreed, the king bestowed the abbeys of Ferrières and St. Loup on him.

From 782 to 790, Alcuin transplanted Anglo-Saxon learning to the Continent. He was steeped in the teaching tradition of the Venerable Bede and trained the best minds among the Franks. In addition to preparing elementary textbooks in dialog form and brainteasers that called for the shrewd use of geometry and algebra, he reformed laws and advised the emperor. It was Alcuin who urged Charlemagne to delay answering Pope Leo III when the pontiff pleaded for protection from the Lombards. This forced the pope to come to the emperor.

Unfortunately, the emperor did not listen when Alcuin pleaded with him not to force conversion on the heathen Saxons. Enraged by the king's actions, the Saxons unleashed the dreadful "Viking" invasions on Christendom.

Alcuin founded the Carolingian palace library. He developed a script of small characters called "Carolingian Minuscule," which allowed more words than before to be written on a single page of expensive parchment. The script was of great beauty and was later employed by the earliest printers.

In 790 Alcuin returned to England, but he was soon recalled by Charlemagne. The teacher-priest was given the Abbey of St. Martin in Tours. Immediately, it became a mecca for the scholars of Europe, who were eager to learn all they could from the master. One of Alcuin's most notable students was the encyclopedist Rhabanus Maurus.

Alcuin summed up his own contribution, saying:

> [I] dispensed the honey of the Scripture, intoxicated my students with the wine of ancient learning, fed them the apples of grammatical refinement, and adorned them with the knowledge of astronomy.

Actually, Alcuin cared for astronomy only to the extent that it was useful for calculating the all-important Christian date of Easter.

Neither his astronomy nor his other writings were very original. His letters, however, open a window onto the age. Those letters, 312 of which survive, were addressed to recipients by some personal characteristic or by their latinized names. All of them were written in Latin, as were his sermons, poems, theology, epistles and history.

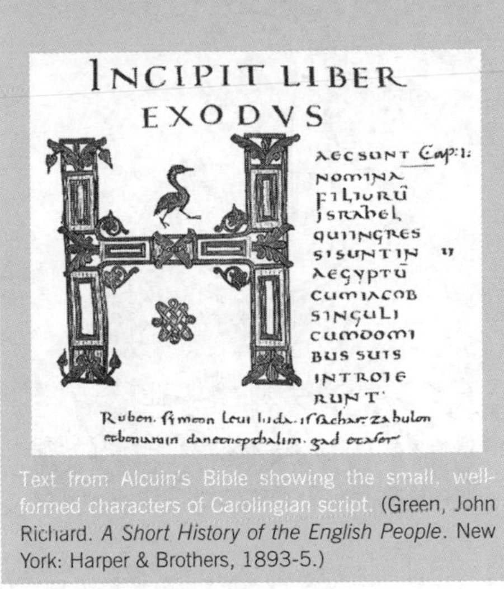

Text from Alcuin's Bible showing the small, well-formed characters of Carolingian script. (Green, John Richard. *A Short History of the English People*. New York: Harper & Brothers, 1893-5.)

Alcuin was strictly Orthodox, a faithful guide to the Church. He raised the level of knowledge of churchmen and stimulated the minds of his contemporaries in an age besieged by barbarian invasions. In doing so, he molded the tenor of Europe's thought and left a legacy of trained minds to keep alive the embers of religion, culture and science in Europe. He died on this day in 804.

Other Events

715: St. Gregory II was consecrated pope. He was a strong supporter of Boniface's mission to the Germans and opposed the use of icons in worship.

988: Archbishop Dunstan of Canterbury died. Driven from court with violence by those who were jealous of his many attainments, he became a monk and sometimes advised—and sometimes reprimanded—kings. Appointed archbishop, he sought to integrate the Danes fully into the life of the Church and the nation.

1662: An act of the English parliament ejected nonconformist ministers from the pulpits of the nation's established Church.

1780: The day was uncommonly dark in New England, and many thought Judgment Day had come. Speculation suggests that a volcanic cloud was the cause.

1845: John Franklin sailed to find the Northwest Passage. Neither he nor any of his men ever returned from the Arctic. Said to be a Christian, he did more than read a prayer book to his sailors; he actually preached to them. His men agreed they'd rather hear him preach than any parson in England.

John Franklin, explorer, sailed to search for the Northwest Passage. (Mossman, Samuel. *Heroes of Discovery*. Edinburgh: Edmonston and Douglas, 1868.)

Although a young man at the time, Athanasius provided deep insights to the Council of Nicea. (Firth, John B. *Constantine the Great: The Reorganisation of the Empire and the Triumph of the Church*. New York/London: G.P. Putnam's Sons, 1905.)

May 20

God or Man? Pivotal Council

Three hundred and twelve bishops were gathered. In the center of the room, on a throne, lay the four Gospels. The emperor himself, dressed in a purple gown and with a silver diadem upon his brow, opened the council. It was he who had called them together, and upon convening the meeting, he said: "I rejoice to see you here, yet I should be more pleased to see unity and affection among you." The council was held in Nicea on this day in 325. The next few days would be devoted primarily to one purpose: finding a theology to describe who Jesus is.

Bishop Arius was preaching that Christ was a creation of God—the first of all his creatures, to be sure, but a creation nonetheless. He was not of the substance or nature of God. "There was a time when the Son was not," Arius and his followers insisted. They even made up songs with catchy tunes to propagandize their ideas among the masses.

Bishop Alexander of Alexandria was horrified. Jesus, the Word, had coexisted eternally with God the Father, he argued. If Christ were not God, then man could not be saved, for only an infinite and holy God can forgive sin. He deposed Arius, but Arius did not go quietly. He gathered followers and continued to teach his troubling doctrine. The factions rioted, and the unity of the empire was shaken. Constantine was alarmed by the strife, so he called a council.

As the council progressed, the bishop of Nicomedia rose to defend Arius's views, attempting to prove logically that Jesus, the Son of God, was a created being. Bishops of opposing opinion snatched his speech from his hand and flung it in shreds to the floor. They had suffered for Christ, some of them greatly, in the persecutions of Diocletian, and they weren't about to stand by and hear their Lord blasphemed. Otherwise, to what purpose had they borne their gouged eyes, scourged backs, hamstrung legs and scorched hands?

The issues of Nicea boiled down to this: If Christ is not God, how can He overcome the infinite gap between God and man? If a created being could do it, there were angels aplenty with the power. Indeed, why could not any good man himself bridge the gap? On the other hand, Jesus had to be truly man, otherwise how could he represent mankind?

At some point the council decided that their best course was to write a creed. This is what they came up with:

> We believe in one God, the Father, Almighty, maker of all things visible and invisible. And in one Lord Jesus Christ, the Son of God, begotten of the Father, only-begotten, that is, from the substance of the Father; God from God, Light from Light, Very God from Very God, begotten not made, of one substance with the Father, and through whom all things were made, both in Heaven and on earth; who for us men and our salvation came down and was incarnate, was made man, suffered, and rose again on the third day, ascending into Heaven, and is coming again to judge the living and the dead; And in the Holy Spirit. And those who say: "There was a time when he was not," and "Before he was begotten he was not," and "He came into being from nothing," or those who pretend that the Son of God is of another substance or "essence" or "created" or "alterable" or "mutable," the catholic and apostolic church places under a curse.

The Creed of Nicea became a document of fundamental importance to the Church. That so many of the bishops who approved it had suffered greatly for Christ only added to its significance.

Ira Sankey provided the music in Dwight L. Moody's evangelistic campaigns. (Thompson, C.L. *Times of Refreshing, Being a History of American Revivals with Their Philosophy and Methods*. Rockford: Golden Censer Co. Publishers, 1878.)

Other Events

1232: Anthony of Padua was canonized. Many miracles were attributed to him.

1277: Pope John XXI died after being crushed in the collapse of his private observatory.

1527: Anabaptist leader Michael Sattler had his tongue cut out, was tortured and was burned as an arch heretic. Once a monk, he was appalled by the corruption he saw in the established Church. After serious Bible study, he joined the Anabaptists.

1861: The chief on the Island of Erromanga (Vanuatu) blamed missionaries because his children were the only two who died from measles. In reprisal, he killed George and Ellen Gordon.

1874: Ira Sankey, who sang in Moody's revival services, found the words to his popular song "The Lost Sheep" set them to music, and sang them the next day for the first time.

1937: Jesse Overholtzer chartered Child Evangelism Fellowship.

1950: Under the Communist regime, the Polish parliament (Sejm) expropriated all religious property.

May 21

Charles Wesley Lacking No More

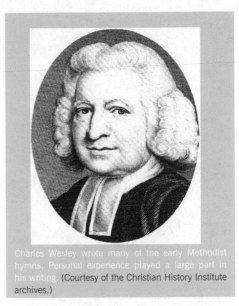

Charles and John Wesley longed for a deeper walk with God. With some other men at Oxford, including George Whitefield, they formed a "Holy Club." Through rigorous spiritual exercises, they sought personal peace with the Almighty.

Charles was ordained in 1735. The brothers then sailed to Georgia, where, after his conversion, John would seek to convert souls while Charles acted as secretary to the colony's governor. Ill health forced Charles to return to England after only a year in the New World.

Charles felt that something was lacking in his life. He did not feel that the work he did was fruitful, and he was unable to escape a sense of emptiness. Inside he felt hollow.

While sick with pleurisy, he lay upon a bed at the home of Thomas Bray, a Christian brazier (bronze worker). Charles felt that what he needed was the witness of the Holy Spirit and began to pray for Him. Charles woke up on this day, Pentecost Sunday, in 1738, hoping it would be the day.

John and some friends came to him and sang a hymn to the Holy Spirit. This increased Charles's hopefulness, and when they had left, he began to pray, reminding Christ of His promise to send a Comforter. He cast himself solely on Christ in reliance of His promise.

As he lay back to rest, Charles heard a voice saying, "In the name of Jesus of Nazareth, arise, and believe, and thou shalt be healed of all thine infirmities." The voice was that of the brazier's wife. Nonetheless, Charles lay still, hardly daring to hope, his heart palpitating, but he murmured, "I believe, I believe." In his journal he credits that as the day he received the witness of the Holy Spirit. His brother John was converted a few days later.

Afterward, John traveled around England, preaching outdoors for the most part, and teaching and organizing renewal groups within the Church of England. During this time, the Wesleys and other field preachers were frequently attacked. It took bravery to sing and preach with objects flying at them.

The groups formed by the Wesleys became known as Methodists. Although still connected with the Church of England, these groups usually met separately, because their worship services differed from those of the Church of England in many respects. In nothing did they differ more than in music. Whereas Anglicans mostly sang or chanted psalms, the Methodists sang hymns, many of which were penned by Charles.

Some of his best-known hymns include "And Can It Be that I Should Gain," "Arise, My Soul, Arise!" "A Charge to Keep I Have," "Hark, the Herald Angels Sing" and "Depth of Mercy! Can There Be." Many others of his verses have also blessed the Church.

Charles Wesley wrote many of the early Methodist hymns. Personal experience played a large part in his writing. (Courtesy of the Christian History Institute archives.)

A year after his conversion, Charles Wesley commemorated the event by writing what is possibly his best-known hymn:

O, for a thousand tongues to sing
My great Redeemer's praise,
The glories of my God and King,
The triumphs of His grace.

1382: Today (or possibly May 19), a synod, meeting at Blackfriars, London, to condemn Wycliffe and his followers was shaken by an earthquake. The terrified clergymen fled.

1535: William Tyndale was arrested after being betrayed by Henry Phillips, whom Tyndale had helped financially.

1536: Geneva joined the Reformation when mass was suspended after William Farel preached.

1690: John Eliot, an early Puritan missionary to the American Indians, died on this day.

1719: Pierre Poiret, a Protestant mystic whose personal life was holy and who developed the first full-fledged system of dispensationalist Bible interpretation, died on this day.

1972: Michelangelo's *Pieta*, one of the most profound masterpieces of religious sculpture, was attacked by a Hungarian madman wielding a hammer. Shouting, "I am Jesus Christ!" Lazlo Toth cracked off the left arm, smashed a hand and damaged the nose and left eye of the sorrowing Madonna, who holds the dead Christ in her lap.

John Wycliffe. (Hendrickson, Ford. *Martyrs and Witnesses*. Detroit: Protestant Missionary Pub. Co., 1917.)

Athanasius, a strong proponent of Christ's deity. (Baring-Gould, S. *Lives of the Saints*. Edinburgh: John Grant, 1914.)

May 22

Semi-Arians Ridiculed for Their "Dated Creed"

One of the greatest wars of all times was fought with pens, speeches, councils, ridicule and exile. It was the battle to define the central doctrine of Christianity: who Christ is in relation to God the Father. The battles raged for most of the fourth century. Bishop Arius claimed that Christ was a created being and that there was a time when Christ was not. This view became known as Arianism. The Council of Nicea rejected it, saying that Christ is of the same substance and essence as God the Father; in other words, Christ *is* God.

Arius had gained a strong following, and although Emperor Constantine had supported the creed of Nicea while he lived, some of his successors did not. They fell under the spell of Arian advisors. Arians appointed their own bishops throughout the empire, and Arianism maintained a strong footing.

However, there were many voices raised for unity. They felt that the empire could tear itself apart over theology. As crazy as it may sound, theologians tried to work out formulas that would satisfy both sides. Logically, Christ either is truly God who took on the form of a man, or He is a created being. If He is "almost God" or some other in-between being, then He is not God but a created being. However, the theologians used their formulas to try to get around this with vague wording.

One attempt at compromise took place on this day in 359 at Sirmium in the eastern empire. A council that did not represent the entire Church, consisting mostly of a number of bishops who leaned toward Arianism, issued a creed. While on the surface it condemned Arianism, it objected to the creed of Nicea for saying that Christ was of the same essence as God the Father. Christ, said this new creed, was begotten of the Father—but how or when we do not know. Jesus is only "like" God, it said.

However, the writers of the new creed made a tactical mistake: In their preface, they stated, "The Catholic [Universal] Faith was published . . . on May 22." This opened them to ridicule since everyone knew that the faith had already been around for three centuries. Those who favored the Nicene Creed, with its clear statement of Christ's divinity, heaped ridicule on the newer creed, nicknaming it the "Dated Creed." That is the name it goes by to this day.

Pressures for unity were great, from the emperor on down, and so churches east and west signed on to the new creed, although some made changes in its wording first. On the whole, the Dated Creed wasn't much different than the Nicene Creed, except for a few lines. However, the Dated Creed did not stand. Athanasius, bishop of Alexandria, and other pro-Nicene theologians refused to accept any compromise that made the Son less than equal to God the Father. Later, Church councils settled the matter once again in favor of the divinity of Christ.

In the end, orthodox logic won: As someone has remarked, God the Father could not be eternally a Father unless God the Son were eternally a Son.

Felix Mendelssohn, whose oratorio *St. Paul* debuted on this day. (Bourne, C.E. *The Great Composers or Stories of the Lives of Eminent Musicians*. London: S. Sonnenschein, Lowery & Co., 1887.)

Other Events

1533: The first Augustinian friars arrived in Mexico to help with its evangelization. Franciscans and Dominicans had been working in Mexico for nine years. The missionaries waded rivers, battled bugs and studied numerous languages in order to reach the Mexican people with the gospel.

1560: The scholar John Fischenham was brought to the Tower of London for refusing to take the oath of supremacy (which would make Queen Elizabeth head of the Church). He spent twenty-four years as a prisoner there.

1653: Malcontents of the ancient Syro-Malabar Church of India chose their own bishop, Mar Thomas I, without approval from Rome.

1690: Johann Schutz, German lawyer, hymn writer and ardent Pietist, died. He spurred the Pietist leader Jacob Spener to begin prayer meetings and wrote the hymn "Sing Praise to God Who Reigns Above."

1836: Felix Mendelssohn's oratorio *St. Paul* premiered at the Lower Rhine Music Festival in Düsseldorf.

1944: The Gospel Mission of South America was incorporated by Rev. William Strong in Conception, Chile. He had founded the work under the name Soldier's Gospel Mission several years earlier.

MAY 23

What a Dirty Way to Begin a War

Too many times in history it has happened: A religious minority is promised rights and then those rights are stolen by religious leaders. In desperation, the minority rises up, peace is shattered and bloodshed follows. The terrible Thirty Years' War, which wasted central Europe from 1618-1648, may have been unavoidable, but its initial spark was one rather small incident.

Greater Bohemia, which consisted of Bohemia, Silesia, Moravia and Lusatia, had been torn between Catholics and Hussites and other Protestants ever since the martyrdom of the reformer Jan Hus. Although the non-Catholics had a majority on paper, they differed so greatly among themselves that no coalition was possible. Political power resided with the Roman Catholics.

Under a Letter of Majesty issued by Emperor Rudolph II, freedom of conscience and worship were granted in Bohemia. However, this freedom was not total. All Protestants were required to form one denomination. They were, however, permitted to build churches in cities that had none. Rudolph died before an interpretation of the act could be made. So, Catholics invented various pretexts to forbid Protestants to build churches.

Rudolph's successor, the weak and elderly Matthias, placed power in the hands of an ardent Catholic who sought to centralize the government. Matthias's heir-apparent was Jesuit-trained and had objections to allowing Protestants the freedom to worship in whatever fashion they preferred. Protestants were fearful of what might be done to their few remaining freedoms.

Matthias left Prague. In his absence, the region was ruled by regents, many of whom had resisted the Letter of Majesty. These regents arrested Protestant delegates who came to complain that they weren't allowed to build churches as promised.

Under Rudolph's letter, Protestants had been given the right to elect "protectors" to settle internal disputes and also to negotiate for them with the Catholics. The protectors gathered in Prague on May 5, 1618, contenting themselves with drawing up a letter to Matthias. They set another meeting for May 21.

The response from Matthias came back so quickly that the protectors were sure their complaint had never been sent to him. They accused the regents of duplicity. The meeting on May 21 quickly turned nasty, and the regents presented the protectors with a letter from Matthias dissolving the assembly. The protectors met again on May 22, no doubt to plot their next move.

"Defenestration" is from the Latin *de* meaning "out of," and *fenestra*, meaning "window." On this day in 1618, the protectors flung two of the offending regents out of a window, intending to kill them. This was the famous Defenestration of Prague, which sparked the terrible Thirty Years' War.

At the Defenestration of Prague Bohemian protectors hurled two of the councilors out the window. (Lord, John. *Beacon Lights of History*. New York: James Clarke, 1886.)

Ironically, the men who were thrown out the window were not seriously hurt; sources say they landed in a soft manure pile. What a dirty way to start a war!

OTHER EVENTS

1381: Cyprian was finally received as metropolitan in Moscow. He had been promised the position at the advent of Alexius's death, but when Alexius died, Cyprian was denied the post because he was Serbian. Eventually, he was declared a saint by the Russian Church.

1498: Florentine reformer Savonarola was burned to death.

1551: Saint Philip Neri was ordained. He founded the Oratorian order.

1891: The Chapel Car idea was conceived. Rev. Boston W. Smith came up with the idea of bringing specially outfitted rail cars, ten feet wide by sixty feet long, into unchurched "Wild West" communities, where they could serve as churches until permanent buildings were established. A dozen of these cars were set on rail sidings. They did more to tame the American West than all the gunmen who dominate Hollywood films.

Florentine reformer Savonarola. (Lord, John. *Beacon Lights of History*. New York: James Clarke, 1886.)

John Wesley. (Hendrickson, Ford. *Martyrs and Witnesses*. Detroit: Protestant Missionary Pub. Co., 1917.)

MAY 24

A Heart Strangely Warmed

John Wesley was in despair. He did not have the faith to justify continuing to preach. He became ill, and when death stared him in the face, he was fearful and found little comfort in the "faith" he did have. To his friend Peter Bohler, a Moravian, Wesley confessed his growing misery and told him that he had decided to give up the ministry. Bohler counseled otherwise, advising Wesley, "Preach faith till you have it. And then because you have it you will preach faith."

Wesley acted on Bohler's advice. He entered a prison and preached faith in Christ alone for the forgiveness of sins and eternal life. One of the prisoners was immediately converted. Wesley was astonished. He had been struggling for years and there in that prison was a man who had been transformed instantly. Wesley made a study of the New Testament and found to his astonishment that the longest recorded delay in salvation was three days—while the Apostle Paul waited for his eyes to open (see Acts 9:1-19).

Other Christians assured him that their personal experiences had also been instantaneous. Wesley found himself crying out, "Lord, help my unbelief!" However, he felt dull within and little motivated even to pray for his own salvation. On this day in 1738, he opened his Bible at about five o'clock in the morning and came across these words: "Whereby are given unto us exceeding great and precious promises: that by these ye might be partakers of the divine nature" (2 Peter 1:4, KJV). He read similar words in other places.

That evening he reluctantly attended a meeting in Aldersgate. Someone read from Martin Luther's *Preface to the Epistle to Romans*. At about 8:45 p.m.,

> [W]hile he was describing the change which God works in the heart through faith in Christ, I felt my heart strangely warmed. I felt I did trust in Christ, Christ alone for salvation; and an assurance was given me that He had taken away my sins, even mine, and saved me from the law of sin and death.

It took Wesley time to learn how to live the life of faith, for he was not always joyful and therefore thought he had fallen from salvation. It took time for him to see that in Christianity it is not Christ and good works that save a man but Christ alone who saves, resulting in good works.

Afterward Wesley was mightily used of the Lord to reform England. His Methodists became a national force. Wesley rode thousands of miles across England (as much as 20,000 a year) preaching as only a man filled with the Holy Spirit can preach, bringing the gospel to all who would listen. He acted "as though he were out of breath in pursuit of souls."

He often faced danger from mobs. At Roughlee he was struck in the face and head, clubs were flourished around him and the mob threatened to murder him. At Hull, stones and clods of earth were thrown at him. At Wednesbury a mob tried to kill him but succeeded only in tearing his clothes to tatters, thanks to the brave defense put up by a woman and three other Methodists who battled the mob around him. The mob's ringleader later became a Christian, saying, "I think that he [Wesley] was a man of God and God was with him, when so many of us could not kill one man."

Wherever Wesley preached, lives were changed and manners and morals altered for the better. It is often conjectured that his preaching helped to spare England the kind of revolution that occurred in France.

Samuel F.B. Morse demonstrated a workable telegraph. (Courtesy of the Christian History Institute archives.)

OTHER EVENTS

1430: Joan of Arc was captured by the English, who soon convicted her as a sorceress and burned her.

1689: The Toleration Act, passed by the British parliament, guaranteed the religious liberties of dissenters to "ease" scrupulous consciences.

1830: John Williams sailed to the Society Islands as a missionary. There he learned native languages and built a sixty-foot boat that enabled him to visit Samoa and the New Hebrides. In the New Hebrides, he was killed by cannibals.

1844: Christian inventor Samuel F.B. Morse demonstrated the first practical telegraph with the message "What hath God wrought?"

1861: Mary Webb died on this day. Although bound to a wheelchair from youth, she founded the first women's missionary society in America and coordinated the work of 200 other missionary societies.

May 25

Common Denominator for Dissimilar Things

What do the musical form called the "oratorio," the Counter-Reformation, the Jesuits, lay ministries, a new Roman Catholic order and John Henry Newman have in common? Philip Neri.

The son of a lawyer and part of a noble family, Philip Neri was a merry lad, nicknamed *Pippo buono*, or "good little Phil." He was notable for his self-discipline and love of learning. At the age of seventeen he was sent to work with an uncle, a wealthy merchant, who offered to bequeath his business to Neri. But trade was repugnant to Neri. At eighteen he renounced the lucrative offer and went to Rome, where he supported himself by tutoring two boys, who rapidly improved in their studies.

Neri studied, fasted and prayed. He especially admired the life and work of Savonarola. To all who knew Neri, he seemed destined for the priesthood. How astonished they were when instead he sold his books, gave the proceeds to the poor and became a lay evangelist in Rome! Corrupt clergymen in the great city had caused many citizens to become cynical toward the things of God. Neri hoped to fill the people of Rome with renewed fervor for the faith of the fathers.

For thirteen years he pursued an individualistic course, steeping himself in piety, meditating on the Gospels, visiting the catacombs and winning friends and acquaintances to Christ through warmth and personal concern. During this time, on the eve of Pentecost in 1544, while earnestly asking the Holy Spirit to bestow His gifts upon him, Neri experienced an extraordinary event: A globe of fire entered his body and dilated his heart. He was filled with waves of divine love and fell to the ground, crying, "Enough, Lord, I can bear no more!"

In 1548 Neri left his solitary path and organized a group of laymen to assist impoverished or sick pilgrims. His spiritual director, Father Rosa, urged Neri to become a priest, arguing that he would be better able to serve the world if he were ordained. Neri consented.

As priest of San Girolamo della Carità, Neri's confessional drew many pilgrims and converts. To further their sanctification, he developed a series of informal afternoon talks and discussions, combined with prayers and hymns. His door was always open to all. His room was called the "home of Christian mirth."

Several of Philip's followers became priests. At the Church of San Giovanni dei Fiorentini, they formed a community but took no vows. They ate, prayed and worked together in an oratory built over the church, and on this day in 1574, they became the nucleus of a new order, the Congregation of the Oratory. Neri adapted the work he had developed at San Girolamo to his new church. Often the talks and Bible readings were accompanied by musical pieces composed by his follower, Palestrina. Thus the oratorio was born.

Philip Neri. (Jameson, Mrs. *Legends of the Monastic Orders*. London: Longmans, Green, and Co., 1872.)

A church building at Rome was given to the Oratorians. In Rome, Philip labored with much success to turn worldly Church leaders back to personal holiness. The spiritual leaders and other great men of the age, including Ignatius of Loyola, the founder of the Jesuits, came to Neri for advice. Next to Loyola, Neri is considered the greatest of the Roman Catholic Counter-Reformation figures. The Catholic converts John Henry Newman and Frederick Faber founded Congregations of Oratorians in England.

The Congregation of the Oratory was approved by Pope Gregory XIII in 1575 for prayer and preaching. About fifty congregations exist today.

Other Events

709: Aldhelm, bishop of Sherbourne, died on this day. He was an effective evangelist in eighth-century England as well as a scholar of high repute.

1261: Pope Alexander IV died. He had been an unwilling pope, but he ruled prudently in spiritual matters. Even so, he lost control of Rome.

1790: The Universalists, who teach that all souls will eventually be saved, formally organized their denomination in Philadelphia.

1803: The Massachusetts Baptist Missionary Society voted to publish a missionary magazine now known as *The American Baptist*, the oldest surviving religious magazine in the United States.

1805: William Paley died on this day. He developed an influential, although not original, apologetic based on natural history. He made the design argument his own by using the analogy of a clockmaker and a watch.

1830: The American Sunday School Union committed itself to establishing Sunday schools everywhere in the Mississippi Valley, a daring vision and dramatic act of faith.

Aldhelm. (Baring-Gould, S. *Lives of the Saints*. Edinburgh: John Grant, 1914.)

Bede. (Armitage, Thomas. *A History of the Baptists: Traced by Their Principles and Practices, From the Time of our Lord and Saviour Jesus Christ to the Present*. New York: Bryan, Taylor and Co., 1893.)

May 26

Bede Not Bitter in Suffering

As he suffered from a serious lung infection, Bede sang, prayed and urged his pupils to learn quickly, for he did not have much time left to live. He warned them that it was a fearful thing to fall unprepared into the hands of the living God. Then he divided his few possessions, including a little precious pepper, among his fellow monks. Far from being bitter at the advent of his death, Bede thanked God, believing his pains were a scourging at the hands of a loving Father. He labored hard to complete a translation of the Gospel of John and to finish some extracts from the works of Isidore of Seville before his life ended.

On this day in 735, his secretary, a lad named Wilbert, said, "Dear master, there is one sentence still unfinished."

"Very well," Bede replied, "write it down." After a short while, the lad said, "Now it is finished."

Bede replied:

> You have spoken truly. It is well finished. Now raise my head in your hands, for it would give me great joy to sit facing the holy place where I used to pray, so that I may sit and call on my Father.

Chanting "Glory be to the Father, and to the Son," Bede died. So passed one of the most noble men ever to live.

Bede is known as "the Venerable," a name applied to no other major figure of history. He is also called the "Father of English History." No student need dig too deeply to appreciate why both names are deserved. Bede's life was filled with piety, and his *Ecclesiastical History of the English Nation* is the best source we have on the early history of the Anglo-Saxons in England. Bede selected his anecdotes with care, crediting his sources when possible. His history has narrative interest and lucidity. Its events are reported without prejudice but with wide learning and in a dignified tone.

In an autobiographical sketch, Bede told of many of his other writings, the bulk of them scriptural interpretations. He said that he was a servant of Christ and a priest at the monastery of Peter and Paul at Wearmouth and Jarrow:

> I was born on the lands of this monastery, and on reaching seven years of age, I was entrusted by my family first to the most reverend Abbot Benedict and later to Abbot Ceolfrid for my education.

There is speculation that his parents died while he was very young. This seems to be supported by Bede's own words:

> I have spent all the remainder of my life in this monastery and devoted myself entirely to the study of the Scriptures. And while I have observed the regular discipline and sung the choir offices daily in church, my chief delight has always been in study, teaching and writing. I was ordained deacon in my nineteenth year, and priest in my thirtieth.

As a young man he survived a plague that wiped out most of the choir. He had cheated death once but would not do so again. The prayer with which he closed his history would aptly fit his death:

> I pray you, noble Jesus, that as you have graciously granted me joyfully to imbibe the words of Your Knowledge, so You will also of Your bounty grant me to come at length to Yourself, the fount of all wisdom, and to dwell in Your presence forever.

Augustine of Canterbury. (Baring-Gould, S. *Lives of the Saints*. Edinburgh: John Grant, 1914.)

Other Events

604: St. Augustine of Canterbury, who brought the gospel to southern England, died.

1328: William of Occam fled from Avignon to join Emperor Louis of Bavaria against Pope John XXII. This extraordinary thinker frequently used Occam's razor, the principle that we should adopt the simplest explanation that covers all the facts.

1839: St. Alphonso Liguori was canonized. He founded the Redemptorist order and conducted missionary work among the Italian peasantry. In 1871 he was declared a doctor of the Catholic Church.

1858: The United Presbyterian Church of North America formed from the Associate Reformed Church of America and the Associate Presbyterian Synod.

MAY

27

Terrible Outbreak of Anti-Semitism

Tension grew early between Jews and Christians. Christianity was at first a Jewish sect. Christ was a Jew, and so were the apostles. The first converts were Jews. But Peter, Paul and other apostles extended the gospel to Gentiles.

The willingness of Christians to accept Gentiles without requiring them to obey the Mosaic laws infuriated some Jews. Early on, the Jews persecuted Christians. Saul, one of the persecutors, became a convert to the new faith and its greatest spokesman under his new name, Paul. His decision to take the gospel to Gentiles was received with bitterness in Jerusalem. He was subsequently often arrested and imprisoned.

The gap between Christian and Jew widened when Christian Jews refused to support Judea's rebellion against Rome. Christians were seen as unpatriotic by Jews. Truly, Christ's words were fulfilled: "I did not come to bring peace, but a sword" (Matthew 10:34), for the division widened. For their part, Christians increasingly saw Jews as hostile and felt they were deliberately rejecting the light of the gospel. Jerusalem fell to the Roman general Titus in AD 70, and the Jewish temple was demolished.

After Christianity became the official religion of the Roman empire in the late fourth century, Jews were discriminated against. Jesus had been a Jew, but Christians seemed to forget that he had said, "Inasmuch as ye have done it unto one of the least of these my brethren, ye have done it unto me" (Matthew 25:40, KJV). Church and state alike deprived the Jewish people of their rights. Their patriarchate was abolished, and they were forbidden to build new synagogues.

Even before Constantine and Theodosius made Christianity the religious power of the empire, Christian thinkers had called Jews "God-killers" and "children of the devil." In the fifth century, Augustine described the Jews as a people to be suppressed but preserved so that they might put their trust in Christ at the Second Coming. Increasingly, as the Middle Ages progressed, Jews were harassed. Anti-Semitism became an open attitude. Jews were accused of murdering Christian children. They were maligned as Christ-killers. Certain of their customs rankled their Christian neighbors. Despite papal bulls that spoke out against anti-Semitism, it erupted again and again.

One of the worst outbreaks occurred at the time of the First Crusade. Godfrey of Bouillon, leader of the crusade, declared that the blood of Christ must be avenged with the blood of Jews. He announced his intention to either convert or wipe out every Jew in Europe. He marched into the Rhine Valley, where Jews were numerous, pious and prosperous, and began butchering them. To save their lives, some Jews consented to conversion; those who refused were executed. The bravest Jewish women killed their children and themselves rather than violate their consciences by embracing a faith they did not follow.

This day in 1096 may have witnessed the single worst day of atrocities against the Jews. Archbishop Ruthard of Mainz took pity on the Jews and hid 1,300 of the descendants of Jacob in his cellars. The mob learned about it, broke in and killed over a thousand of the Jews. The compassionate archbishop saved the rest by protecting them in his cathedral.

Mainz Cathedral hundreds of years after the great Jewish persecution. (Velt, Andreas Ludwig. *Mainzer Domherren: Vom Ende des 16. Bis Zum Ausgang des 18. Jahrhunderts, in Leben, Haus und Habe: Ein Beitrag zur Geschichte der Kultur der Geistlichkeit.* Mainz: Kirchheim, 1924.)

Other Events

1564: John Calvin died on this day. Few theologians have been as influential.

1647: Achash Young was hanged as a witch, the first such execution in Massachusetts.

1661: Archibald Campbell, earl of Argyle, was beheaded. He was accused of treason because of his association with the Scottish Covenanters.

1814: Pope Pius VII returned to Rome. He had crowned Napoleon, but the Frenchman repaid him by seizing papal lands. Pius excommunicated those involved, for which he was imprisoned and prevented from returning to Rome until this date.

John Calvin. (Courtesy of the Christian History Institute archives.)

May

28

The Spanish Armada Sails to Its Doom

The doomed Spanish Armada at Maracaibo. (Avery, Elroy McKendree. *History of the United States and Its People: From Their Earliest Records to the Present Time*. Cleveland, OH: The Burrows Brothers Company, 1904.)

On this day in 1588, Medina Sidonia's flagship, the *San Martin*, led the greatest fleet ever assembled up to that time out of the Lisbon River to sea. They were bound for England. Philip, king of Spain, had had enough of the pesky English, who pretended to be at peace with him while actually waging war against him. Above all, the Spanish loathed Sir Francis Drake, who harried and harassed them at sea and along their coasts in Europe and Latin America.

There were religious reasons for Spain's attempted invasion as well. Spain was Catholic, England Protestant. Nothing would please the Spanish empire more than to force the island nation back into the Roman fold. Its policy had been aimed at this for decades.

Aboard the 130 newly outfitted ships of the Armada were 19,000 soldiers who were ready to invade and conquer England. But from the start, the Spanish fleet experienced difficulties. The Armada met with bad weather. Also, because of the differences between each ship's capabilities, they had difficulty keeping all of the ships in formation. Furthermore, Drake's bold attack on Cadiz in 1587 had delayed the Armada's invasion for a year. More important, Drake had burned vast quantities of wood and hoops that were intended to make barrels, and as a result, and of having eaten its freshest supplies over the winter, the Armada found itself with spoiled rations. Plague began among the men. The ships had to regroup at Finnisterre and deal with the problems, and it cost them a month's delay.

As the Spanish were dealing with their various setbacks, Drake was trying to convince Queen Elizabeth that the English should attack the Spanish in their own waters. Elizabeth said "no." She did not want to commit her nation to war. In preparation for the Armada's arrival, Drake brought his fleet into Portsmouth Harbor, but the wind turned and the entire fleet was almost trapped there. The English captains were able to quickly "warp" out (hauled their ships around on anchors) and thus were able to leave the harbor. Sailing under Philip's inflexible orders, the Spanish missed a golden opportunity to seriously maul the English fleet as it struggled to leave the harbor.

When the two fleets finally did meet in battle, the initial strategy of the English proved flawed. They harassed the Spanish from a distance, but shells from the long-range guns to which they had committed their fleet could not penetrate the Spanish hulls. The Spanish formation, although briefly threatened by storms, remained intact, and the Armada arrived in the Straits of Dover on August 6.

The English launched fireboats against the Spanish, who panicked and broke formation trying to get free. Harassed by English and Dutch boats, the Armada put up a fight, but when its shot ran out, the English sailed in close and began pounding the big ships to pieces. Attempting to stick together, the Armada sailed in the only direction it could: north. The sailors tried to take their ships around Scotland and back down the Atlantic past Ireland and then on to home. At least fifty-one of the ships were destroyed, and thousands of men perished.

The defeat of the Armada helped to preserve the Reformation in England. Philip, when he heard of the magnitude of the disaster, wrote, "I hope that God has not permitted so much evil for everything has been done in His service." But Protestants gloated in letters and pamphlets and on medals. "God breathed and they were scattered," said one of Elizabeth's medals.

John Woolman was an early abolitionist. (Woolman, John. *The Journal and Essays of John Woolman*. New York: Macmillan Company, 1922.)

Other Events

1403: German university masters attacked John Wycliffe's reform-minded doctrines, which had spread to their nation by way of Jan Hus and others.

1663: Joseph Alleine, a nonconformist Puritan preacher in Anglican England, was thrown into prison because he continued to preach after the Act of Uniformity required him to step down. Afraid of losing souls, he worked himself to an early grave. His book *Alleine's Alarm* is a Puritan classic. A characteristic passage from Alleine is this:

> Oh, better were it for you to die in a jail, in a ditch, in a dungeon, than to die in your sins. . . . Your sins will follow you when your friends leave you, and all worldly enjoyments shake hands with you. Your sins will not die with you as a prisoner's other debts will; but they will go to judgment with you there to be your accusers; and they will go to hell with you there to be your tormentors.

1772: John Woolman, an American Quaker and abolitionist, was at sea traveling to England and felt sick according to his journal. Woolman noted that any "departure from the simplicity that there is in Christ becomes as distinguishable as light from darkness to such who are crucified to the world."

1949: A Communist party congress in Czechoslovakia declared its right to educate children in atheistic Leninism regardless of their parent's religious views.

May 29

Worn Down and Taken on the "Last Day of the World"

Around 1420 the Turks besieged Constantinople but failed to take it. The Christian city, all that was left of once-mighty Byzantium, seemed impregnable. Its triple walls had repelled attack time and again throughout its history. Only once had the city fallen and that only by treachery from within. Nearly 100 emperors had held Constantinople's throne since Constantine dedicated the city in 311.

In 1453, Mehmed II, sultan of the Ottomans, cruel and patient, besieged Constantinople. He erected a fortress across the strait from the city and brought up ships and his dreaded Janissaries (captured Christians who had been trained into an effective fighting force). Mehmed also cast a cannon that could hurl 500-pound stones across an astonishing distance of 1 mile. With this and other guns, he lashed Constantinople. He was unaware that the city was down to a mere 7,000 defenders.

Night and day, Mehmed's artillery smashed the city, reducing the outer walls to rubble. The defenders bravely erected makeshift structures, which held the Turks at bay. Since they were still unable to break through, the Turks began to murmur against Mehmed. He decided to try another approach: He attempted to break the chain with which the Christian city kept his boats away. He failed, and so he built a slipway of greased planks 1,400 yards from the Bosporus Strait over steep Galata and dragged 80 small ships over it into the inner waterway of the Golden Horn. From there they attacked the city but were again brought to a stalemate by the defenders.

Despite the Christians' success, their morale was low. The defenders felt that God had deserted them. The infidel armies were overwhelming and it seemed just a matter of time before the 7,000 were worn down as stone worn away by water. Mehmed carefully surveyed the walls. He brought all of his firepower to bear against the most damaged points and arrayed his troops for greatest effectiveness, with the Janissaries facing the most damaged center. Around 1:30 a.m. on this day in 1453, he ordered an assault.

The Christians fought with furious determination. Even the Janissaries could not smash them. The Turks were repulsed. But a gate left open allowed a few to break through. They were killed, but before they died they left flags on the city wall. The outermost of Constantinople's defenders, looking back, saw the Muslim flags and thought the city had been taken. They wavered. Mehmed noticed it and hurled his Janissaries at them. As dawn broke, the Christian line collapsed.

The point at which Constantinople was breached. (Pears, Edwin. *Destruction of the Greek Empire and the Story of the Capture of Constantinople by the Turks*. New York: Haskell House, 1903.)

The Byzantine emperor died fighting as if he were a common soldier. Other defenders fled home to protect their families. The enraged Muslims murdered indiscriminately. Those who died quickly were the lucky ones, for they did not have to witness as churches were looted and the sacramental chalices that had memorialized Christ's shed blood were used to slake Muslim throats. They escaped the sight of their wives, daughters and young sons ravished on the altars.

The land where Paul and Barnabas had preached salvation through Christ's death and resurrection now belonged entirely to Islam. To Byzantium's few survivors, it was the last day of the world.

Other Events

1536: Pope Paul III called a council to begin on May 12, 1538, in response to the Reformation movement on the Continent. Only five bishops appeared in Cenza. After six weeks, Paul deferred the council's opening date. Not until five years later, on November 1, 1542, after three summons, did the council finally meet—at Trent. Even then, few bishops showed up, but Trent became one of the most important Roman Catholic councils.

1546: Bravos set upon and killed Cardinal Beaton of St. Andrews, who had sent George Wishart to the stake.

1934: The Confessing Church in Germany issued the Barmen Declaration, which repudiated claims of the Hitler regime.

1954: Pope Pius X was canonized. His papacy lasted from 1903 to 1914. Of simple peasant origins, he was marked by zeal and piety, remarking, "We have no other program in the Supreme Pontificate but that of restoring all things in Christ."

Pope Paul III. (Bezold, Friedrich von. *Geschichte der Deutschen Reformation*. Berlin: Grote, 1890.)

Ruins at Caesarea, the home of historian Eusebius. (Courtesy of Datafoto.)

MAY 30

Eusebius, First Church Historian, Dies

Suppose you are a survivor of an outlawed organization whose origins go back to around 1700, seventy-six years before America became an independent nation. "Tell the story of your people," you are urged.

The problem is, your people were an illegal group. In fact, the government tried to exterminate them. Your leaders were captured and killed, and many of the group's letters and books were burned. They left no public festivals, no monuments—very little by which historians ordinarily trace history. And to make your task more challenging, your people were scattered over most of the known world. How could you possibly put together their story? That is the kind of task Eusebius of Caesarea tackled.

His people were Christians who had been persecuted for almost 300 years. Then, when Constantine became emperor, a measure of peace came to the believers. At last the story of the Church could be told.

Eusebius was the one for the job. He had already prepared a chronology of the Bible and the early Church, trying to establish the dates of Christ's death and the events that followed. This was a difficult undertaking, because many different calendars were in use at the time and he had to match up events recorded under one system to events recorded under others.

Eusebius's ten-volume history is our best authority on early Christian history. We owe him a special debt because he quotes from many sources that no longer exist. We are blessed that he showed an interest in a broad range of material. He traced the lines of apostolic succession in key cities. Thus we know how the Church progressed in the big towns. The Church has always been nourished with the blood of martyrs. Eusebius told the stories of many who suffered for Christ.

He was also interested in debates over which books should be in the Bible, and he gave us various views of the matter. Because of this we know a good deal about how we got the New Testament as we now know it. Eusebius also traced the threads of heresy. Through him we know of challenges to orthodoxy in the early centuries of the faith. Above all, Eusebius described how God preserved the Church and poured his grace upon it. Eusebius even followed the woeful fate of the Jews and their struggles.

Late in life, Eusebius was invited to become bishop of Antioch. He turned the offer down. His backers appealed to the emperor to compel him to accept. Instead, Constantine praised Eusebius for refusing.

Eusebius died at the age of seventy-four on this day in 339. In addition to all his other writings, he left behind commentaries on Isaiah and the Psalms, a geography of the Bible and a concordance of the Gospels. He wrote books to clear up differences in the Gospels. Finally, he produced an account of the martyrs of Palestine, whom he had personally known. But his history remains his most important contribution to the Church and the one by which his name will always be remembered, for it gave us our past.

OTHER EVENTS

1221: The Fourth General Chapter of the Franciscans opened. St. Francis, an old man by that time, was present. Brother Elias held the office of vicar-general. Two thousand Franciscans attended, among them the man who became famous as St. Anthony of Padua. Francis proposed a mission to Germany, and eighty monks leaped up, volunteering to go. St. Anthony was unnoticed in the throng, recovering from illness.

1416: The Council of Constance burned Jerome of Prague, an associate of Jan Hus. Both had called for true reform.

1650: Hymn writer Joachim Neander died. His most famous hymn is "Praise to the Lord, the Almighty, the King of Creation."

1867: Father Weld accepted Gerard Manley Hopkins into the Jesuits. Best known today as a poet, Hopkins worked as a priest among the poor, leaving his poems unpublished lest they distract him from his priestly work.

1933: Apolo (Kivebulaya), an extraordinary Ugandan evangelist to the Congo, died. After being beaten and imprisoned, he once saw a vision of Jesus shining like the sun. In the vision, Jesus said to Apolo, "Take heart, for I am with you." Apolo enjoyed great success after that. Thirty years after his death there were 25,000 Christians in the Congo.

Francis of Assisi with birds. He was present at the Fourth General Chapter of the Franciscans. (Baring-Gould, S. *Lives of the Saints*. Edinburgh: John Grant, 1914.)

Accidental Discovery of the Catacombs of Rome

May 31

Forbidden to bury their dead in regular burial grounds, the Christians of Rome interred them in underground vaults used by the poor. Called catacombs, the vaults were built outside the city and subjected to severe building codes for fear they might collapse. So many martyrs found their final rest in these sites that Christians began to hold special memorial services in them. Except during the worst of the persecutions, Christians were allowed control of their own catacombs. Widespread use of catacombs for Christian burial seems to have dated from the third century.

The Christians employed skilled workmen to dig the catacombs, which were anywhere from two to five levels deep. Shafts allowed light to shine in and fresh air to enter. Bodies were placed two to a tomb and also interred under floors.

Christianity has transformed whatever it touched, even those gloomy crypts. On the walls Christians painted depictions of events from the Old and New Testaments: Christ and the apostles, Daniel's friends in the furnace, Christ as the Good Shepherd, the discovery of Moses in the bulrushes.

There is also much graffiti in the catacombs. "Oh relentless Fortune, who delights in cruel death, Why is Maximus so early snatched from me?" wrote a pagan. But Christians wrote in a different vein: "Julia in peace with the saints," or "In your prayers, pray for us, for we know that you dwell in Christ."

On this day in 1578, an entrance to one of the catacombs north of Rome on the Via Salaria was accidentally discovered. The import of the find was not recognized at first. In fact, the man who would understand its value was hardly two years old that day.

When he was just eighteen, Antonio Bosio committed himself to the lifelong study of archaeology. It was he who first recognized the significance of the entrance on the Via Salaria. In December 1593, before he was twenty, Bosio began exploring the catacombs. Gradually he found links between them, narrow passageways that had been dug from one to another. Some passages were blocked. Making his own forays and also questioning local peasants, he searched for other entrances and found thirty of them. During one dry period, however, from 1600 to 1618, he found only two. It must have taken great tenacity to keep the search alive for so long.

Twenty-seven years after his first descent into a catacomb, Bosio completed a book on the tombs, naming it *Roma Sotterranea*, which means "subterranean Rome." Beginning with the Vatican cemetery, he worked in a counterclockwise direction around Rome, describing each of the many catacombs he had visited, which was by no means all of them. Like every good archaeologist, Bosio added historical detail to his findings. He wrote, for instance, of the 4,000 Christians martyred by Hadrian on the Via Appia rather than deny the Christ who redeemed them. The book did not see print until five years after he died. Colleagues prepared prints for it.

Jesus and the Samaritan woman, a wall painting from the Catacomb of Calixtus II. (Goodyear, W.H. *Roman and Medieval Art*. Meadville, PA/New York: Flood and Vincent, 1893.)

Unfortunately, not everyone who entered the catacombs had as lofty motives as Bosio. Fortune hunters came to plunder the graves for relics to sell, inventing stories about them to make them more appealing to potential buyers.

To an accidental discovery and Antonio Bosio's quick wit we owe a chapter of Christianity that otherwise might have been lost. Unfortunately, some of the catacombs he explored have since been destroyed.

Other Events

1701: Alexander Cruden was born in Aberdeen, Scotland. He compiled the first complete concordance of the Bible. He developed mental problems after a romantic disappointment and was sometimes violent. He was placed in an asylum but released in 1722. He had made a hobby of tracing words through the Bible, and in 1736 he began to compile his concordance. Eighteen months later, he published the work. He became obsessed with correcting people's sins, especially swearing and Sabbath-breaking, which led to his nickname "Alexander the Corrector." He died suddenly in 1770 while praying. His concordance was so valuable to ministers that Spurgeon claimed that "half-crazy" Cruden had done more for Bible scholarship than any of the scholars to that point.

1792: William Carey preached his famed sermon on missions. A cobbler, he was converted, developed a heart for missions, went hungry to buy himself books and convinced others of the need of missions. He took as his text Isaiah 54:1-2 with its call to enlarge one's tent. "Attempt great things for God! Expect great things from God," he said.

1803: Presbyterians appointed Rev. Gideon Blackburn as their first missionary to the Cherokee nation of the American Indians.

Charles Spurgeon (shown here) praised "half-mad" Alexander Cruden. (Conwell, Russell H. *Life of Charles Haddon Spurgeon, The World's Great Preacher*. Philadelphia: Edgewood Pub. Co., 1892.)

Wrong Faith

A Quaker in the stocks in early New England. (Guizot, M. François. *France: Nations of the World*. New York: P.F. Collier & Son, 1898.)

Did the Massachusetts Puritans rely too heavily on works and not enough on grace? Some early settlers thought so. Salvation was by grace for those who were filled with the Holy Spirit, taught Anne Hutchinson, and Mary Dyer agreed. To the Puritans this seemed antinomian, that is, opposed to law.

Dyer was a "very proper and fair woman" according to Governor John Winthrop. With her husband, William, she came to the New England colony in 1635 and joined a Boston church. At first all went well. But when Anne Hutchinson began to put forth her views, Dyer was convinced by them. Her husband also adopted the ideas and was disenfranchised in 1637, which meant he was denied the right to vote (imagine having to hold the right religious views in order to vote!). When Anne was expelled from an assembly in 1638, Dyer was the only person who stood with her, walking with her from the building.

Dyer had a stillborn child, and the congregation suggested cruelly that it was in punishment from God. Rumor claimed it was a monster:

> This year there was a hideous monster born at Boston, in New England, of one Mrs. Dyer Dyer, a co-partner with the said Mrs. Hutchinson, in the aforesaid heresies; the said monster, as it was related to me, was without head, but horns like a beast, scales or a rough skin like the fish, called the thornback; it had legs and claws like a fowl, and in other respects as a woman child; the Lord declaring his detestation of their monstrous errors, as was then thought by some, by this prodigious birth. (Nathaniel Morton, *New England's Memorial*. Cambridge, 1669.)

The Dyers were expelled from the colony. Soon after, they joined Roger Williams and Anne Hutchinson in founding Providence, Rhode Island.

Dyer Dyer traveled to England in 1650. The views of George Fox, the Quaker, appealed to her and seemed the logical extension of what she already believed, so she became a Quaker. On her return to Rhode Island, she taught her views in Boston and was arrested and jailed but released through her husband's entreaty.

After her release, she made missionary trips into New Haven and Boston. In 1659 she visited Quaker friends who were jailed in Boston and was warned by authorities to get out of town and never return. She did return, however, and was condemned to die in September 1659. Two Quakers who had traveled with her "to look the bloody law in the face," (that is, to challenge the death penalty) were executed. The first, William Robinson, predicted divine wrath on the killers. The second, Marmaduke Stevenson, said, "Be it known unto all this day that we suffer not as evil-doers but for consciences' sake." Dyer was reprieved when the hood was already over her eyes and the noose around her neck.

Once more Dyer put her life on the line. For a fourth time she defied Massachusetts law and preached in the Puritan colony. She was arrested and condemned to death, all pleas by her family falling on deaf ears. The authorities would not agree to let her go unless she swore never to return. This she would not do: "[I]n obedience to the will of the Lord I came, and in His will I abide faithful to the death."

On this day in 1660, Boston authorities hanged her. To them she was simply a hard-headed heretic. But like many of the early Quakers, she was willing to pay the price of her faith.

Dyer left seven children behind. Quakers eventually won civil rights in America. Christianity, despite ugly chapters such as this, has gradually taught us to extend human rights to all people. Dyer Dyer, with her gospel of grace, was an important player in that battle.

Other Events

1096: Bishop Egilbert agreed to save the Jews of Trier (Treves) from rampaging crusaders, but only if they were baptized. Many Jewish women preferred to die, first killing their children and then throwing themselves into the river Moselle.

1671: James Guthrie, a Scottish Covenanter pastor, was executed for saying that Christ, not King Charles of England, was the head of the Church. "Christ being the Head of the Church, it behoves us to see that to Him only we render obedience," he said.

1741: The Presbyterian Church in the North American colonies split into New Sides vs. Old Sides over revival methods. The factions reunited in 1758.

1826: William Lloyd Garrison published "The Exile's Departure," a poem by the American Quaker John Greenleaf Whittier, bringing Whittier to international attention. Both men were against slavery. Whittier is now better known for poems such as "The Eternal Goodness" and "Snowbound."

1887: Samuel Logan Brengle offered himself to William Booth and the Salvation Army. Booth was cool to the suggestion, but Brengle proved to be a zealous general of the army in New England.

1940: Alfred Loisey, a radical modernist student of the Bible, died on this day. The Roman Catholic Church had excommunicated him for his views.

John Greenleaf Whittier used his poetic pen to oppose slavery. (Perry, Bliss. *John Greenleaf Whittier: A Sketch of His Life*. Boston/New York: Houghton, Mifflin and Company, 1907.)

June

2 The Anti-Catholic Gordon Riots

Troops arrive on the scene during the Gordon riots. (Castro, J. Paul de. *The Gordon Riots*. London: H. Milford, Oxford University Press, 1926.)

"No Popes! Down with the Catholic Relief Bill!" On this day in 1780, 50,000 people, shouting and shaking their fists and all wearing blue badges on their hats and carrying blue flags, marched toward the House of Commons in London.

For 200 years, since the time of Queen Elizabeth I, Catholics in Protestant England had lived under restrictions. But after the Revolutionary War broke out in America, King George III's ministers thought it would be wise to pass a law restoring Catholic rights. They feared that otherwise Ireland might grab the chance to revolt while Britain was busy fighting in America. Some officials also thought it was a shame that Catholics had fewer rights than England's other citizens.

But Lord George Gordon, a retired navy lieutenant, hated the Roman Church. He collected thousands of signatures on a petition to overturn the Catholic Relief Act that was passed in 1778. With 50,000 people at his back, he marched to Parliament to present the petition.

The mob turned ugly, as they so often do. Smashing windows and breaking down doors, they looted Catholic homes and set them on fire. For over a week the rampage continued. Unpopular Protestant leaders suffered as well.

Writing a letter to a friend, Ignatius Sancho, the talented composer and writer, said:

> Gracious God! what's the matter now? I was obliged to leave off—the shouts of the mob—the horrid clashing of swords—and the clutter of a multitude in swiftest motion—drew me to the door.

He had already described at least 100,000

> poor, miserable, ragged rabble, from twelve to sixty years of age, with blue cockades in their hats, besides half as many women and children, all parading the streets, the bridge, the park, ready for any and every mischief.

The rioters robbed anyone unfortunate enough to step into their path. They also broke into Catholic chapels and attacked London prisons: King's Bench Fleet and Newgate. Newgate, in fact, was set on fire, and all its prisoners freed. When the mob attacked the Bank of England, John Wilkes, chamberlain of London, ordered his men to shoot. Several rioters fell dead. More people died in a brewery that caught fire. On the evening of June 6, Prime Minister Lord North barely escaped the mob by forcing his coach horses into a gallop. He lost his hat, which the crowd tore up. The pieces were passed around like trophies.

On June 7, the army was finally called in. By then, fires burned everywhere, and there was no way to put them out because the mobs had destroyed the equipment. Soldiers and horsemen began shooting into the crowds or charging into them with swords and bayonets. Close to 500 people were killed or wounded before the riot was stopped.

Later, fifty-two of the ringleaders were convicted, and about twenty-five were executed for their part in the shameful episode. The Catholic Relief Act was not overturned.

Neal Dow advocated prohibition against alcohol. (Dow, Neal. *The Reminiscences of Neal Dow: Recollections of Eighty Years*. Portland, ME: The Evening Express Pub. Co., 1898.)

Other Events

304: Persecutors disemboweled Syrian bishop St. Erasmus during the reign of Diocletian.

553: The Second Council of Constantinople ended. Led by the patriarch Eutychus, it was attended solely by Orientals and Africans. It condemned the controversial Three Chapters and may have deposed Pope Vigilius, who refused to attend.

597: St. Augustine of Canterbury baptized Ethelbert. Ethelbert had insisted on meeting St. Augustine in the open air, believing the missionary's "magic" wouldn't work out of doors.

1537: Pope Paul III said the Indians of the Americas must not be enslaved. Under pressure from the colonists, he soon withdrew the order, which was called *Sublimis Deus*.

1621: One Japanese Christian, Paul Mori, was tied in a sack and drowned at sea, and another, Joachim Kawakubo, was decapitated.

1851: The state of Maine passed a Prohibition law against alcoholism. The law was the brainchild of Quaker Neal Dow.

June 3

William Passavant Tried to Meet Every Need He Saw

Pastor William Passavant had no money with which to care for the many sick people he had taken in. This was a normal state of affairs for the compassionate Lutheran minister. He went out of the house, saying, "The Lord will provide. I am going out to get some money and will be back to dinner." He returned with a man who was shaking with fever. "The Lord has not sent us money," he said, "but He has sent us one of His people to be cared for." Whenever Passavant saw a desperate need, he tried to meet it.

In the nineteenth century, government charity did not exist on the scale it does today. Unless the Church and private organizations met needs, people suffered. And so, without money, Passavant opened Sunday schools, hospitals, orphanages, immigrant stations, libraries and colleges. He did so without fund-raising appeals or financial gimmicks—he believed that all such methods dishonored God. His work went on no matter how the world went. If the stock market plunged or plague left more people sick and orphaned, he took on more tasks despite fewer hands and smaller contributions.

All day he labored and often late into the night as well. Then, while others slept, he knelt praying. "What must we do that we may work the work of God?" he asked. "We must believe the declaration of Christ, 'This is the work of God, that ye believe on him whom he hath sent' " (John 6:29, KJV).

"The Church is not merely a sheepfold, but a workshop," he declared. His conviction led him to say, "How necessary, when death robs the child of its natural protector, that the Church of the Redeemer should stand in his place." And yet people who thought of themselves as Christians harassed Passavant. Some were terrified that they might catch diseases from the people he helped. Others resented him because his godliness brought their spiritual anemia to light.

Through it all, Passavant persevered. God rewarded his bold and loving faith with success time and time again. After he died on this day in 1894, people looked back with amazement at all that he had accomplished. The many institutions that he had opened became foundational to the Lutheran Services Organization, which is the largest Church social program in the nation.

Passavant was born in western Pennsylvania and studied at Jefferson College before training for the ministry at Gettysburg Seminary. Under the influence of Samuel Schmucker, he followed a new, more liberal Lutheranism, but conservative theologian Charles Porterfield Krauth drew him back to more traditional beliefs. As a matter of fact, the *Missionary*, a monthly periodical that Passavant edited, spread Krauth's theology. Passavant helped found the Pittsburgh Synod.

Passavant was a man who took to heart Christ's teachings and commands. In addition to all his other labors, he pastored in Pittsburgh and founded and edited church magazines. Despite his extraordinary faith, his name is almost unknown in the nation to which he contributed so much.

William Passavant, a one-man brigade for social assistance. (Wentz, Abdel Ross. *The Lutheran Church in American History*. Philadelphia: The United Lutheran Publication House, 1923.)

Other Events

1162: Thomas à Becket was consecrated archbishop of Canterbury. He opposed his former friend, King Henry II, so obstinately in so many matters that the exasperated king wished aloud to be rid of him. It is uncertain whether or not Henry's comment actually led to Becket's death, but in December of 1170, four of Henry's knights hacked Becket to death at his altar.

1726: Philip William Otterbein was born in Dillenberg, Germany. In 1752 he emigrated to America. As a reformed minister, he preached and built churches. In 1800, with Martin Boehm, he cofounded the Church of the United Brethren in Christ in America. Otterbein died in 1813.

1879: Hymn writer Francis Ridley Havergal died on this day in a nursing home. She cried out, "Come, Lord Jesus. Come and fetch me. Oh, run! run!"

1886: When thirty-two pages of the Buganda court refused to renounce Christianity, they were burned to death on this day.

1926: Bob Childress was packed and on the road to Buffalo Mountain in Virginia, his original home, where he taught his people to substitute love for revenge.

1936: Theologian H.R. Mackintosh of the Church of Scotland died. Forgiveness of sins was the focus of his message.

Bob Childress returned to his home in the hills with a message of love to replace traditional vengeance. (Courtesy of Diana Severance.)

Fundamental Orders: Four Simple Rules of Government

John Davenport, principle author of The Fundamental Orders of Connecticut. (Wilson, Woodrow. *A History of the American People*. New York/London: Harper & Bros., 1902.)

The settlers of New Haven, Connecticut, believed that God cared how they governed themselves. They paid the Indians for land they used and began building a future. Scripture would rule them, they decided. They agreed to meditate and pray for God's illumination on the best way to organize and govern themselves.

The first log cabin of New Haven went up in the fall of 1637. A few men wintered on the bay that year, and in the spring more arrived. Among them was Rev. John Davenport. On his first Sabbath day in New Haven, Davenport preached to the little company under one of the many elms that would give the city its nickname, "City of Elms."

Before coming to the New World, Davenport had distinguished himself as a pastor in England. Because of his Puritan leanings, fellow churchmen resisted his election to the vicarage of St. Stephens in London. He was allowed to take the post only after denying he was a Puritan. He proved bold and faithful. During the great plague of 1625, he stayed on the job.

Over time, Davenport showed his true colors, becoming closely linked with the Puritans. When Archbishop Laud, who persecuted Puritans, took power in England, Davenport fled to Holland. Eventually he migrated to New England and became a shining light there. He was as bold there as he had been in London. When the king's men came looking for two of the judges who had condemned Charles I to death, Davenport helped to hide them.

On this day in 1639, the New Haven settlers assembled in a barn where Rev. John Davenport preached and led his congregation in earnest prayer. They came to agreement on a covenant to guide them. Called The Fundamental Orders of Connecticut, the covenant was based on the Word of God and commonsense notions drawn from it:

> [W]ell knowing where a people are gathered together, the Word of God requires that to maintain the peace and union of such a people, there should be an orderly and decent Government established according to God, to order and dispose of the affairs of the people at all seasons as occasion shall require; do therefore associate and conjoin ourselves to be as one Public State or Commonwealth; and do for ourselves and our successors . . . enter into Combination and Confederation together, to maintain and preserve the liberty and purity of the Gospel of our Lord Jesus which we now profess, as also, the discipline of the Churches, which according to the truth of the said Gospel is now practiced amongst us; as also in our civil affairs to be guided and governed.

During his sermon that day, Davenport presented four questions designed to draw the colonists together. He asked: (1) Does not Scripture contain the perfect rule for government by men in commonwealth, church and family? (2) Did those present wish to enter such a covenant? (3) Did the planters present wish to enter the Church as soon as God should fit them to do so? (4) Would they establish a civil order to implement these articles and ensure prosperity for themselves and their descendants? The planters voted by raised hands.

The organization they created was theocratic. Only free men could be Church members, and only Church members could vote. Twelve were chosen to rule the colony, and seven of them were also to serve as the seven pillars of the Church. With the help of nine assistants, they organized the Church. They also elected a magistrate and imposed wage and price controls.

Old Swedes Church. (Perry, William Stevens. *The History of the American Episcopal Church: 1587-1883*. Boston: J.R. Osgood, 1885.)

Other Events

1699: Trinity Lutheran Church, "Old Swedes Church," at Wilmington, Delaware, was dedicated. Eric Tobias Bjoerk was pastor.

1843: Protestant mystic Johann Christian Friedrich Hölderlin died on this day. Although sometimes a pastor, he is better known as a poet inspired by Greek forms. He suffered mental illness toward the end of his life.

1946: The Soviet Military Administration of East Germany (SMA) declared that it alone had the right to educate children. The Communists hoped to ensure that the children became atheists.

1948: The first radio station of the Far East Broadcasting company went on the air. Located in the Philippines, it was given an "impossible" deadline to meet. Sloshing through water and broadcasting without a rehearsal, the team met the challenge.

1950: Frank Buchman made a Moral Rearmament speech at Gelsenkirchen in the Ruhr. He was awarded the scarlet ribbon and Cross of Chevalier of the Legion of Honor. Originally an unspiritual Lutheran minister, he later experienced a conversion and began exploring ways of bringing international peace through focus on Christ. Moral Rearmament was but one of his projects. This was also his date of birth in 1878.

June 5

Vladimir Led His Subjects Through Baptism

"O God who created heaven and earth: Look down upon these new people and grant them to know You, the true God." Just months before, the Russian prince who prayed this prayer had been a cruel and lustful playboy. He had even tried to impose a national pagan religion on his people. But a change had come to Prince Vladimir's thinking. If tradition is correct, it was on this day in 988 that Vladimir was baptized with hundreds of the men and women of Kiev.

Although Vladimir ruled in the region of Ukraine, his conversion also marked the rise of Orthodoxy in Russia. Vladimir's grandmother, Princess Olga, had earlier tried to make Christianity the official religion of her country, but without much success. Yet she prayed earnestly for her grandson. Her hopes and prayers were rewarded when Vladimir turned to Christ. It would become the boast of Russia that from that day forward (at least until the Communists took over) the country was never without a recognized saint somewhere within its borders.

Before his conversion, say the legends, Vladimir examined the great faiths of his age. He immediately rejected Judaism, saying that if the Jews had so offended God that He would not allow them to return to their land, they were unfit to teach anyone about faith. Islamic teachings on sex appealed to his playboy nature, but their restrictions on wine and swine disgusted him. Vladimir did not care for the Germans who represented the Church of Rome. But an Orthodox teacher, who pointed out fulfilled Scripture, charmed him. Vladimir sent diplomats to observe the various faiths. When his agents returned from Constantinople, they claimed that they had been almost transported to heaven during an Orthodox service that was held in Hagia Sophia ("Holy Wisdom"), the most splendid church of the age. Vladimir opted for Orthodoxy.

Whether these stories are true or not, there were good reasons for Vladimir to adopt the faith practiced by his immediate neighbors in Byzantium and eastern Europe. The eastern European languages were related to the Russian language, and their lands were close to one another. The rich culture of Eastern Christianity also appealed to Russian tastes. Once adopted, Orthodoxy placed its stamp on the character of all the Russian people. By it their land was transformed from pagan barbarism to become known as "Holy Russia." Several times in Russian history, the Church became the throbbing heart of the nation as it struggled against foreign invasion or occupation.

An old coin bearing the image of Vladimir. (Howe, Sonia E. *Some Russian Heroes, Saints, and Sinners: Legendary and Historical*. Philadelphia: J.B. Lippincott, 1917.)

Vladimir was also remade by the new faith. He took a genuine interest in Christianity and gave evidence that his heart had changed. Not only did he turn away from his former sexual pleasures, but he also lost much of the careless cruelty that had marked him before. He even abandoned the death penalty.

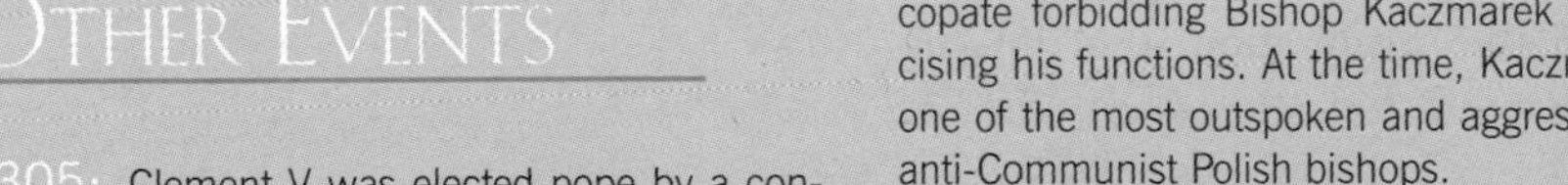

Other Events

1305: Clement V was elected pope by a conclave that had been deadlocked for over a year. Afterward, he moved the papacy from Rome to Avignon. His highest achievement was the completion of the ecclesiastical laws, a task begun over a century earlier.

1568: Spaniards beheaded Counts Egmont and Hoorn at Brussels, rousing the Netherlands to furious resistance. William of Orange decided to become a Calvinist, and he led the resistance against Catholic Spain.

1942: Bandits hacked sixty women and children to death in Burma at a Christian school. Head mistress Daw Pwa Sein died nobly.

1959: The secretary of state for ecclesiastical affairs in Poland wrote a letter to the Polish episcopate forbidding Bishop Kaczmarek from exercising his functions. At the time, Kaczmarek was one of the most outspoken and aggressive of the anti-Communist Polish bishops.

Clement V moved the papacy to Avignon. (Montor, Chevalier Artaud de. *Lives and Times of the Popes*. New York: Catholic Publication Society of America, 1911.)

The YMCA became an international organization and soon came to New York. (Richmond, J.F. *New York and Its Institutions, 1609-1872: A Library of Information, Pertaining to the Great Metropolis, Past and Present*. New York: E.B. Treat, 1872.)

6 Associating Young Men for Christ

Over the years, Christian associations may have done the world more real good than all government agencies put together. One such association was the Young Men's Christian Association (YMCA).

The YMCA's first report expressed why it was formed:

> Until recently the young men engaged in pursuits of business were totally neglected. They were treated as though deprived of mind, as though formed only to labor and sleep . . . without a moment for spiritual or mental culture, without the disposition or even the strength for the performance of those devotional exercises which are necessary to the maintenance of a spiritual life.

Country boys like George Williams were shocked at the degradation of working men in London. Williams, who was strongly influenced by a rather unusual combination of religious forces—the Quakers and American evangelist Charles Finney—began a work among his fellow employees. Soon he had won many to Christ. A go-getter in business too, he rapidly advanced to partnership in the drapery firm where he worked and used his own income to support evangelical causes.

The era was one of evangelical advance. Associations to deal with the dreadful social and moral consequences of the industrial revolution were springing up everywhere in Protestant countries. Williams and other like-minded young men recognized the need for social reform and so on this day in 1844, twelve men, all but one of them associates of Williams' firm, met and decided to create the Young Men's Christian Association. Its original intent was merely to work with employees of other drapery houses.

The YMCA rented a hall and assumed the task of reclaiming men through lectures, exercise and innocent amusement. Prominent men threw their weight behind the work. Lord Shaftesbury, who had been president of The British and Foreign Bible Society, was YMCA president for a time. Thomas Binney, the English nonconformist, and other evangelical leaders also gave their support.

In 1855 the organization went international. At that time its leaders declared:

> The Young Men's Christian Association seeks to unite those young men who, regarding Jesus Christ as their God and Savior according to the Holy Scriptures, desire to be His disciples in their faith and in their life, and to associate their efforts for the extension of His Kingdom amongst young men.

The YMCA was so badly needed that it caught on like wildfire. Long before Williams' death in 1905, it had reached a membership of 150,000 in Britain and nearly half a million in America. Hundreds of thousands of young men were turned away from vice to lives of wholesome usefulness.

For his service to the well-being of the nation, Queen Victoria knighted Williams. Today the YMCA does not have the evangelical impulse it once did. Nonetheless, it continues to assist in producing physical and intellectual well-being in men and women throughout the world. Although now largely forgotten, its early non-denominational Christian ideals gave rise to an organization that improved the lives of millions.

Titus Coan's church in Hawaii had the largest congregation in the world. (Johnston, Julia H. *Fifty Missionary Heroes Every Boy and Girl Should Know*. New York/Chicago: Fleming H. Revell Company, 1913.)

Other Events

1835: Missionary Titus Coan arrived in Honolulu. At one time, his church had more members than any other in the world.

1882: George Matheson, a blind clergyman, penned the hymn "O Love That Will Not Let Me Go."

1925: Harold Wildish boarded the *Amakura* for South America. He had given his life to Christ but had no clear-cut vision of what he should do about it. Then he received word to fill the place of a missionary who was ill. He had only one pound in his wallet. He went upstairs and spread the letter out before the Lord, saying, "You know what I need." In the mail the next morning, he received a check for £25. "But I must have thirty-five," he prayed. (That was equivalent to about US$175 at the time.) The next day he received another letter from the same businessman. "I could not sleep last night thinking of you. I believe you must need the enclosed ten pounds."

1933: Indian evangelist Bakht Singh arrived in Bombay, starving, but selling Bibles and witnessing at all costs. He urged men to learn the secrets of developing a life of Christ in the soul.

Seeing Jerusalem: McCheyne's Big Day

What was the most special day of your life? Was it a visit with a favorite person? Your wedding? A trip to someplace you'd always wanted to visit? For Robert Murray McCheyne, one of the most special events in his life happened on this day in 1839. That is when he entered Jerusalem, the city where Jesus Christ had walked the earth, died on a cross and appeared after He rose from the dead. Here is how McCheyne described the day:

> One of the most privileged days of our life. . . . We entered a defile of the most romantic character; wild rocks and verdant hills; wildflowers of every color and fragrance scented our path. Sometimes we came upon a clump of beautiful olive trees, then wild again. . . .
>
> Our camels carried us up this pass for four hours; and our turbaned Bedouins added by their strange figures to the scene. The terracing of all the hills is the most remarkable feature of Judean scenery. Every foot of the rockiest mountains may in this way be covered with vines. We thought of Isaiah wandering here, and David and Solomon. Still all was wilderness. The hand of man had been actively employed upon every mountain, but where were these laborers now? . . .
>
> We came down upon Garieh, a village embosomed in figs and pomegranates. Ascending again, we came down into the valley of Elah, where David slew Goliath. Another long and steep ascent of a most rugged hill brought us into a strange scene—a desert of sunburnt rocks. I . . . knew that Jerusalem was near. I left my camel and went before, hurrying over the burning rocks. In about half an hour Jerusalem came in sight.

The view saddened him, and he quoted Scripture verses about Jerusalem's desolation:

> "How doth the city sit solitary, that was full of people!" [Lamentations 1:1, KJV]. It is, indeed, very desolate. Read the two first chapters of Lamentations, and you have a vivid picture of our first sight of Jerusalem. . . . I think I had better not attempt to tell you about Jerusalem. There is so much to describe, and I know not where to begin. . . . The plague is still in Jerusalem, so that we must keep ourselves in quarantine.

Jerusalem was precious to McCheyne because of Christ, who was indeed the main theme of his sermons:

> Now, brethren, could I lift you away to that time when God was alone from all eternity; could I have shown you the glory of Jesus then, how He dwelt in the bosom of the Father, and was daily His delight; and could I have told you, "That is the glorious Being who is to undertake the cause of poor lost sinners, that is He who is going to put himself in their room to suffer all they should suffer, and obey all they should obey—consider Jesus, look long and earnestly, weigh every consideration in the balance of the soundest judgment, consider His rank, His nearness, His dearness to God, the Father, consider His power, His glory, His equality to God the Father in everything; consider, and say do you think you would entrust your case to Him? Do you think He would be a sufficient Savior? Oh, brethren, would not every soul cry out, 'He is enough—I want no other Savior?'"

Robert Murray McCheyne, a soul in love with Christ. (Bonar, Andrew A. *Memoir and Remains of the Rev. Robert Murray M'Cheyne: Minister of St. Peter's Church, Dundee*. Edinburg: W. Oliphant, 1880.)

Ill health had forced the beloved minister to give up his pulpit for a time. He made the trip to Israel at the request of the Scottish Church in order to bring back a report on the condition of the Jews. Everyone hoped that travel and relief from the demands of the ministry would act as a cure. Indeed, his health improved a little, and he was able to work for four more years, but he died in 1843, when he was just thirty, and was widely mourned by the many he had brought to know Christ.

Other Events

553: Pope Vigilius died in Syracuse on his way back to Rome from Constantinople. The Fifth Ecumenical Council was held while he was there, but he refused to attend because he disagreed with its aim. Emperor Justinian would only allow Vigilius to return to Rome after he had joined the council in condemning the Three Chapters (writings suspected of Nestorian leanings). The move angered many in the western half of the Church because the condemned works were popular there.

1834: Samuel and Marie Gobat left Marie's home in Beuggen, Germany, bound for missionary work in Ethiopia where they endured great sorrow.

1891: Charles H. Spurgeon preached his last sermon at London's Metropolitan Tabernacle. An influential Baptist, he preached to congregations numbering in the thousands.

1913: According to his own account, George Bennard introduced a new hymn, "The Old Rugged Cross," during a revival he was conducting at Pokagon, Michigan. It became one of the most popular hymns in America.

Vigilius, in an artist's conception. (Montor, Chevalier Artaud de. *Lives and Times of the Popes*. New York: Catholic Publication Society of America, 1911.)

June 8

Vikings Loot Lindisfarne

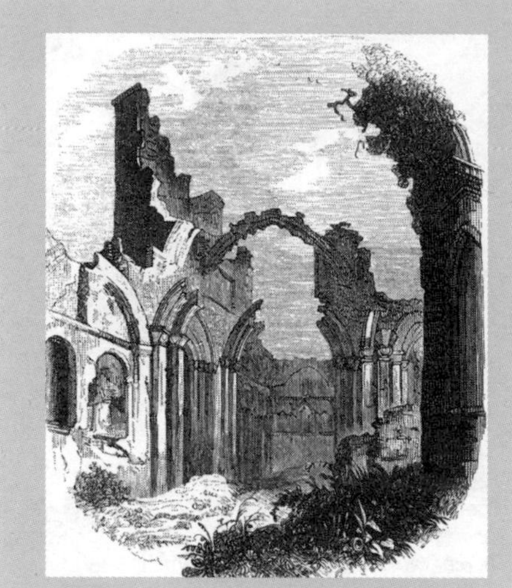

Ruins at Lindisfarne. (Craik, George L., Charles MacFarlane, et al. *The Pictorial History of England: Being a History of the People, as Well as a History of the Kingdom*. New York: Harper & Brothers, 1846-8.)

A monk shouted to get everyone's attention, pointing frantically out to sea. His fellow monks quickly turned from what they were doing and soon saw what their comrade was pointing at: ships!

The monks, living on the little island of Lindisfarne, off the coast of Northumbria, England, must have felt apprehension as the ships came closer. As armed men leaped from their ships, there could be no doubt: The island was being raided.

Omens of disaster had trembled in the air all that year. Although Christian in name, Northumbria's understanding of the true gospel was clouded by its pagan past, and the people still believed in omens. And that year, there had been many such signs that "miserably frightened the people," according to the *Anglo-Saxon Chronicle*:

> There were immense flashes of lightening, and fiery dragons were seen flying in the air. A great famine immediately followed these signs; and a little after that.

A little after that, on this day in 793, Vikings attacked the church on Lindisfarne Island. The raiders hacked the monks to death or dragged them into the sea and drowned them. The Vikings were after the unguarded treasures of Lindisfarne's rich and beautiful sanctuaries.

Many people had given silver and gold to the monastery, some of them believing their souls could find eternal peace through such gifts and the prayers that were offered because of those gifts. On the island were golden crucifixes, coiled shepherd's staves, silver plates for the bread and wine of mass and ivory chests in which reposed the relics of saints. The chapel walls hung with shimmering tapestries, and in the writing room one could find some of the most beautiful illuminated manuscripts ever made.

When the Vikings left, all of the treasures were either destroyed or bagged in the bottom of their boats. The monks lay dead around their altars.

This was the first major Viking attack recorded in England. Few had even contemplated such a raid from the sea. That the first blow fell where it did shocked a people who had thought of the dead saints as powerful intercessors. Alcuin, the greatest scholar of the day, was an Englishman living in the court of Charlemagne. He wrote, "What assurance is there for the churches of Britain, if St. Cuthbert, with so great a number of saints, defends not its own?"

The Vikings had only begun. Over the course of the next two years, they were back for more easy pickings, attacking other wealthy religious houses. Their invasions were repeated for over a century. Eventually, when the nation had been bled of its wealth, the Vikings began to settle the land.

Other Events

597: Columba, Irish evangelist to Scotland, transcribed a psalm this evening, wrote a note in its margin and died early the next morning.

1290: Beatrice, the woman Dante had worshiped from afar, died on this day. Her death caused Dante to begin philosophic studies that would influence the eventual production of his great Christian epic *The Divine Comedy*.

1621: John Yukinoura Jirocmon, a Christian, was executed on a remote Japanese island. He died saying, "From here it is not far to Paradise."

1727: Auguste Hermann Francke, a Pietist Lutheran pastor, educator and philanthropist, died on this day.

1837: Alexander Merensky was born in Panten, Germany. A revival in Germany brought him to Christ, and he became a missionary in South Africa, where he founded a mission station known as Botshabelo. All sorts of practical skills were taught there. Merensky built a fort on the station's land to protect the Christian converts who were there. The fort became a museum in the twentieth century.

1978: Russian novelist and Orthodox believer Alexander Solzhenitsyn gave an impressive speech at Harvard, in which he pointed out some trends that he said were undermining consensus in the West. He called for a return to faith.

Dante gazes on the heavenly Beatrice. (Courtesy of the Christian History Institute archives.)

A Charter for Georgia

It would hardly seem that a charter, bristling with legal terms, would have much to do with Christian history, but the charter signed by King George II of England on this day in 1732, did: It created the colony of Georgia.

Religious reasons for creating the colony did not top the charter. The government's main concern was to get debtors off its hands and to show an English presence between the Carolinas and Florida. But religious considerations were high in the mind of the man who did more than anyone else to promote the plan to colonize Georgia. James Oglethorpe wrote:

> In America there are fertile lands sufficient to support all the useless poor in England, and distressed Protestants in Europe; yet thousands starve for want of mere sustenance.
>
> Christianity will be extended by carrying out this design since the good discipline established by the society will reform the manners of those miserable people, who shall be helped by it; and the example of a whole colony, which shall behave in a just, moral, and religious manner, will contribute greatly toward the conversion of the Indians, and remove the prejudices received from the wicked lives of such who have scarce any thing of Christianity but the name.*

In writing this, Oglethorpe had William Penn's noble experiment, Pennsylvania, in mind.

And so Georgia began as a charitable venture. Realizing that poor people had no way to pay their passage from England to America, the company agreed to pay their fares for them. What is more, it provided them with tools and food until the colony could get on its feet.

Were the goals of the charter met? Not one of the first settlers was from debtors' prison. Farmers and traders were sent instead. Debtors came later. In its first ten years of existence, the company shipped over 1,800 people to Georgia, more than a third of whom were displaced Europeans.

Georgia's military objectives were more successful. Its forts helped tame the region and also presented a strong military front between the Carolinas and Spanish Florida. Oglethorpe proved to be a wise military leader and later defeated a Floridian Spanish force double the size of his own.

Unlike some colonies, Georgia did not established a religion. Any Protestant settler could worship as he or she pleased. King George spelled that out in the charter:

> All such persons except Papists [Catholics] shall have a free exercise of their religion so [long as] they be contented with the quiet and peaceable enjoyment of the same not giving offence or scandal to the government.

Oglethorpe wanted to see Georgia set up as a Christian state. (Northrop, Henry Davenport. *New Century History of Our Country and Its Island Possessions*. Chicago: American Educational League, 1900.)

Oglethorpe was concerned with morals as well as religious freedom. He fought hard to make slavery illegal and to keep rum out of the colony. The settlers fought just as hard to allow both. The result was that Oglethorpe was recalled to England and the settlers got their way. In England, Oglethorpe remained interested in America as long as he lived.

*The quotations in this article have been translated into modern English for ease of comprehension.

Other Events

1717: Madame Guyon, a mystic and inspiration to French archbishop François Fenelon, died.

1790: Robert Robinson, the author of the beloved hymn "Come Thou Fount of Every Blessing," died. He had been converted after he heard evangelist George Whitefield preach. He had gone to heckle Whitefield but fell under deep conviction instead, which made him miserable for three years until he yielded to Christ.

1834: William Carey, the Baptist "Father of Modern Protestant Missions," died on this day.

1846: Pope Gregory XVI died. He was an autocrat who opposed democratic changes and strained the papal treasury with war projects. He was a strong sponsor of world missions.

1885: Emily Tubman died in Augusta, Georgia. A member of the Disciples of Christ, she used her large fortune to further the gospel. Twenty years before the Emancipation Proclamation, she freed her slaves. During the Civil War, she imported America's first ice machine to ease the suffering of wounded soldiers.

Pope Gregory XVI opposed democratic changes but was a strong advocate of world missions. (Montor, Chevalier Artaud de. *Lives and Times of the Popes*. New York: Catholic Publication Society of America, 1911.)

François Fenelon wrote spiritual classics that are beloved to this day. (Upham, Thomas C. *The Life and Religious Experiences of Madame de la Mothe Guyon*. New York, 1877.)

June 10

Awarded Second Place: Prince and Bishop

Imagine running a race and coming in first, but being awarded only second place. That's essentially what happened to François Fenelon. On this day in 1695, he was consecrated archbishop of Cambrai, one of the richest and most important sees in France. However, because of his purity, spiritual depth, wisdom and skill with people, many of his contemporaries thought he should have been made archbishop of the more influential Paris instead. In their minds, as well as in Fenelon's, Cambrai was second place.

Fenelon was proposed for the see by Louis XIV and consecrated by Bishop Bossuet, both of whom would later turn on him. At the time of his consecration, however, Cambrai was the king's reward to Fenelon for taming the king's grandson, the duke of Burgundy, a sickly child who was prone to temper tantrums.

The king had selected Fenelon to train the duke because Fenelon had a reputation as an educational innovator. In mastering the duke of Burgundy, Fenelon showed great love and patience. He wrote dozens of texts and fables for his passionate pupil, every one of them steeped in Christian ideas. He taught the lad that love would hold a kingdom together better than pomp or force. He made the boy see that he disgraced himself when he lost his temper. A characteristic Fenelon technique was to forbid the entire household to speak a single syllable to the lad when he was in one of his rages. Only when the boy spoke calmly and politely did he receive attention.

On one occasion, the boy rejected Fenelon's discipline. "No, no, sir," he said to his teacher, pulling rank on him. "I remember who I am and who you are." Fenelon remained silent all that day, for it was his maxim that one should never punish while angry. The next morning, however, he woke the lad, reminded him of his rebellious words, showed him Fenelon's authority from the king and said he was requesting an end to the arrangement under which he tutored the boy. The boy had so much pride he could not bear that it become known he had outworn Fenelon's notable patience. He apologized in tears.

Fenelon's support of Quietism and its chief French proponent, Madame Guyon, brought him into trouble with Bossuet. Fenelon was deeply impressed by Jeanne Guyon. As a young widow, she rejected all marriage proposals and formal systems of faith and sought to meet Christ in her innermost being. When she refused to renounce her beliefs, Bossuet jailed her for eight years.

Bishop Bossuet was sometimes called the "Pope of France." He wrote a critique against Quietist mysticism and asked Fenelon to read it. Fenelon disagreed so completely with Bossuet's critique that he wrote a book of his own called *Maxims of the Saints*, showing that the great saints of the Church had held a view closer to Guyon's. The angry Bossuet sought the king's support to have the *Maxims* suppressed.

The king was only too happy to oblige. Fenelon was in hot water with him because he had written an instructional book called *Telemachus, Son of Odyssus* for training the duke. The fictional work amounted to a quiet rebuke of King Louis's often unchristian policies and practices. The king prohibited the duke from seeing Fenelon and pressured the pope to condemn the archbishop's *Maxims*. After delaying as long as he could, the pope issued a mild censure. Fenelon accepted the restrictions meekly.

He remained archbishop of Cambrai and put many of France's bishops to shame by his faithful fulfillment of his duties. His works remain in print today and provide continual inspiration to many Christians.

Pius VII, who tangled with Napoleon. (Courtesy of the University of Texas collection of public domain portraits on the Web.)

Other Events

1194: The people of Chartres ran from their homes in despair when they saw their cathedral in flames. It wasn't their church's first fire, but this time a miracle happened. Monks trapped inside the structure emerged unscathed from a vault with the cathedral's relics. Reenergized, the town built the church anew.

1381: English mobs, demanding improved conditions, sacked the palace of Archbishop Sudbury in Canterbury. They saw him as a government toady. Sudbury was away in London, where the crowds captured and killed him a few days later.

1555: Thomas Hawkes was martyred in England for refusing to baptize a baby. He said he took the Bible for his final authority and infant baptism wasn't taught there. The Catholic bishops burned him alive as an example of what happened to those who questioned the Church's practices.

1809: Pope Pius VII excommunicated Napoleon, who had seized papal lands.

1925: The inaugural service of the United Church of Canada was held on this day.

1950: Seventy-three electors were to meet in the Cathedral of Belgrade to elect a new patriarch, but the Communist regime only allowed twenty-seven to attend. They arrested Joseph of Skopje, who was expected to become the next patriarch of Hungary, and sent him to an isolated monastery. The electors chose a government man in his place.

From Slave Boy to Bishop of West Africa

Adjai was a hard worker from an early age. At the age of eight he undertook heavy chores. Over the next four years, he showed sturdy enterprise, raising his own chickens and yams and selling them. He amassed quite a string of the cowrie shells that the Africans used for money. When a group of forty boys was put to work on a farm eight miles from town, Adjai was put in charge of them.

Adjai was born around 1809 into a pagan family at Oshogun in the land that is now known as Nigeria. His name was given to him by a pagan priest, who indicated that the boy was to have a significant future. Adjai was dedicated to Olorun, the supreme god of his people.

The priest's words proved true, but when Adjai was twelve it must have seemed otherwise. A mixed force of Foulah tribesmen, ex-slaves and Muslims attacked Oshogun. The men of the town defended their families valiantly, but the enemy numbers were too great for them. Their wall was smashed, and the foe entered Oshogun. Adjai never saw his father again because, with his sister, brother, mother and grandmother, he was marched off as a slave with a rope around his neck.

Adjai was sold to an African in that region, and he determined to work hard so that he would not be sent to the coast for resale overseas. He hoped that, although they had been sold to different people, he would be able to remain somewhere near his family. His strategy seemed to work, because those slaves who were lazy and complained were sold swiftly, but Adjai remained where he was for quite a while. However, he was eventually sold to a woman of Toko, who in turn sold him to the coast. On the cruel march to the sea, many Africans died of fever. Others were whipped to keep them on their feet. Adjai's stamina allowed him to escape both fates.

Portuguese traders bought Adjai in 1821 and packed him like a sardine into the stuffy hold of their ship with dozens of other slaves. He was destined for Brazil. Britain had outlawed slavery a few years earlier and was enforcing the law upon all nations. British warships spotted the Portuguese slaver and boarded it, freeing the slaves. Adjai made himself useful aboard the warship, winning favor with the sailors.

The British warship released Adjai at Freeport in Liberia. There he was introduced to the gospel by a group from the Anglican Church Missionary Society. He learned to read, became a Christian and was baptized in the Anglican faith on December 11, 1825. At his baptism, the sixteen year-old boy took the name Samuel Adjai Crowther, after a member of the mission society.

Crowther's hard work brought him the favor of the missionaries. The Daveys, a missionary couple, asked him to accompany them on a trip to London. The young man leaped at the chance to gain firsthand knowledge of the outside world. Back in Africa the following year, he entered the newly opened Fourah Bay College at Freetown to study for the ministry.

Crowther took holy orders in the Anglican Church on this day in 1843. Through hard work and determined study, he continued to advance. He married a fellow student, Asano (Susan Thompson), and began a family of his own. Trusted completely by the mission staff, Crowther became a missionary to Nigeria and earned the trust of Africans too, winning thousands to Christ on his grueling treks.

Geographers honored him for his exploratory notes. He prepared a dictionary of Yoruba, his native language, and translated church works into his native tongue. The former slave was made the first African bishop of the Anglican Church. His diocese encompassed all of West Africa.

Adjai is captured. (Page, Jesse. *Samuel Crowther: The Slave Boy Who Became Bishop of the Niger*. New York: Fleming H. Revell Co., 1889.)

Other Events

1292 (probable date): Roger Bacon, a Franciscan monk and original thinker, died. He predicted the invention of aircraft, submarines, engines, suspension bridges and more.

1799: The man who would become the first African-American Methodist bishop in the US, Richard Allen, was ordained as a deacon in the Methodist Episcopal Church.

1923: The Chinese Trio left Hwo Chow to set out for Central Asia, uncertain where and to what the Lord was sending them. They preached the gospel to hundreds of cities and villages in the Gobi Desert.

1936: J. Gresham Machen and associates founded the Presbyterian Church of North America in Philadelphia. They believed that the United Presbyterian Church had become too liberal.

Roger Bacon. (Redgrove, H. Stanley. *Roger Bacon, Father of Experimental Science, etc.* London: William Rider, 1920.)

James Gilmour, Apostle to Mongolia

James Gilmour equipped to tramp in Mongolia. (Lovett, Richard. *James Gilmour of Mongolia*. Chicago: Student Missionary Campaign Library, n.d.)

James Gilmour was discouraged. Working alone in Mongolia, he poured out his heart in his diary:

> [P]reached to 24,000 people, treated 7,500 patients, distributed 10,000 books and tracts . . . and out of all this there are only two men who have openly confessed Christ.

Actually, two converts in eight months was double the fruit that he had seen in his first fourteen years on the mission field, during which time he had won only one convert.

James Gilmour led an unusual—some would say eccentric—life. Born in Cathkin, Scotland, on this day in 1843, he learned to trust Christ from his godly parents and grandparents. His mother read him stories of missionaries. As a boy, Gilmour loved nature and wandered alone among the hills and glens of his homeland, much as he would later wander alone in Mongolia.

Because of his parents' prosperity, he was able to afford an education. He worked hard to master his subjects at Glasgow University and became an outstanding student. Yet to him, Christianity was not a mere classroom exercise. In the evenings, he went alone to speak with workers as they walked home, reminding them of their eternal souls. His efforts to save others did not stop at speech. One time, when he found a friend drinking, he opened the window and poured the liquor onto the ground, remarking that it was better for it to be there than in a man who was made in God's image.

In 1870, he sailed for China, planning to work in Mongolia. Soon after his arrival, twenty-two Roman Catholic priests were massacred. Gilmour was willing to die, if it advanced God's work, but fortunately calm prevailed. In August 1870, he set out for Mongolia.

He learned Mongolian and engaged in years of seemingly fruitless evangelism. The common folk accepted him because he came with all his goods in a backpack, just as their own holy men did. His expenses averaged just six cents a day. But his voluntary poverty barred him from inns. Eventually he had to rent a mule just to raise his caste enough to be accepted as a guest. He healed the sick with simple remedies, and medicine soon became his main tool for touching lives.

Gilmour began to pray for a helper. He saw a portrait of a young woman and became convinced that God meant her for him. He wrote a letter asking her to marry him. No other correspondence had passed between them, and they had never met. Miss Emily Prankard prayed for guidance and was convinced that God meant for the marriage to happen. She accepted Gilmour's proposal, sight unseen. Is it eccentric to accept God's advice? They were happy. She braved Mongolia's dust storms and tiresome mutton with him and quickly learned the language. Gilmour considered her a better missionary than himself.

Eleven years and two sons later, Emily died. Gilmour sent the boys back to Scotland to be reared by their grandparents. Worn out with travels and lack of necessities, he died in North China at the age of forty-seven from a severe and sudden case of typhus.

Slaves under guard at Jamestown. It was to end such practices that the World Anti-Slavery Conference was held. (Wilson, Woodrow. *A History of the American People*. New York/London: Harper & Bros., 1902.)

Other Events

1744: David Brainerd was ordained in New Jersey. His life would be short but well spent in efforts to evangelize American Indians. The journal he wrote influenced many Christians to give up their own lives for the work of Christ's kingdom.

1804: David Abeel was born in New Brunswick, New Jersey. As a missionary to the Far East, he inspired women through his appeals to evangelize Asia.

1840: The World Anti-Slavery Conference erupted into shouting because it was a male-only event but American women demanded admission.

1842: Thomas Arnold died, one day before his forty-seventh birthday. He was a prominent Christian educator, immortalized in Thomas Hughes's novel *Tom Brown's School Days*.

1914: A day of demonstration was held for Harriet Tubman, the escaped slave who rescued over 300 fellow slaves, bringing them out on the Underground Railroad. A woman of deep and simple faith, she credited her success to the Lord.

June 13

The Boxer Uprising Spells Terror

During much of the nineteenth century, Europe and Japan had humiliated the ancient nation of China. Britain, France and Japan defeated it in wars. In one of the most serious policy blunders of history, Britain forced the Chinese to buy opium, blighting thousands of lives with addiction.

Christian missionaries to China were hated because their words were so different from the teachings of the Chinese sages. Widespread rumors accused the missionaries of all sorts of bizarre and cruel behavior. At the same time, Western powers demanded protection for missionaries and insisted on special trade favors.

A "secret" society emerged, dedicated to kicking the hated foreigners out of China. Like America's Ku Klux Klan, which terrorized blacks, Catholics and Jews, this group terrorized Chinese Christians, whom they considered traitors who had adopted Western ideas. Newspapers called the secret society "Boxers," because their Chinese name meant "righteous harmony fists." The Boxers led an uprising that began in 1898 and lasted into 1900.

Hundreds of missionaries and thousands of Chinese Christians lost their lives during that time. Many tried to escape to Peking, thinking they would be safe there. The Chou family, stationed forty miles northeast of Peking, abandoned everything and fled toward the city. But they found themselves in an even more difficult position, for on this day in 1900, violence erupted in Peking itself.

Hungry and thirsty, the Chous found no one willing to take them in. Villagers were afraid of reprisals from the Boxers if they assisted the hated traitors. Mr. Chou was captured. Mrs. Chou pleaded for his life. The village elders swore that even if he was their own relative they would hand him over to the Boxers to be killed. Mr. Chou said, "Never mind. Let them do as they wish." He went with joy to his execution.

Left to fend for her five children, Mrs. Chou became so weak from hunger and exhaustion that she could no longer carry her baby, who was only a month old. She had to make a terrible choice: either save him or the older children. Crying to passersby, "Someone, please take my baby," Mrs. Chou laid him by the side of a busy path and staggered on with her four eldest children.

Hot pursuit forced them to huddle in a hole in a ruined building while Boxers searched just feet away for them. The Lord preserved Mrs. Chou and the four remaining children. Her heart was filled with deep sadness for her husband and baby.

Mrs. Chou and her four surviving children. (Headland, Isaac T. *Chinese Heroes*. New York: Eaton & Mains; Cincinnati: Jennings & Pye, 1902.)

Other Events

1236: St. Anthony, the "Wonder Worker of Padua," died on this day.

1525: Martin Luther became engaged to Katherina von Bora, a nun whom he had helped escaped from her convent by hiding her in an empty fish barrel.

1663: Samuel Willard was ordained. The clergyman was driven from his frontier church in Massachusetts when Indians destroyed the village where it was located. He then became a pastor in Boston and vice president of Harvard. He opposed the witch trials of his day.

1795: Thomas Arnold was born in East Cowles, England. He changed the face of English public education by his reforms at Rugby, which included increased trust in students.

1861: Karl Harrington was born. A well-known classical scholar and author of books on medieval Latin and Roman poets, he was also a Methodist choir leader and composer. His best-known hymn tune is the music to the Christmas carol "There's a Song in the Air!"

Thomas Arnold, master of Rugby, reformed English public education. (Hubbard, Elbert. *Little Journeys to the Homes of the Great*. 13 volumes. New York: W.H. Wise & Co., 1916.)

Gregory of Nyssa. (Baring-Gould, S. *Lives of the Saints*. Edinburgh: John Grant, 1914.)

June

14 Gregory of Nyssa, Early Scholar

In front of Gregory's eyes were the remains of forty brave men who had died rather than betray Jesus. Throughout Cappadocia (a region now in central Turkey), their story was well-known. But to see their actual bones transformed the story into reality.

The forty had defied their emperor's order to pour out a drink offering (libation) to a heathen god and were whipped, imprisoned and finally exposed naked all night on ice to die. As he stood looking at the remains of those brave men, Gregory, who considered himself a Christian, suddenly realized that God had the right to demand his whole life.

At once, he determined to live his life completely for Christ. But what did the Lord want of him? To become a priest? Gregory thought about it but decided it wasn't for him. Instead, he became a professional orator (more or less a lawyer) like his father. He married and settled down but served the Church as an active layman.

Gregory's brother, known to us as Basil the Great, liked to put people in slots of his own choosing. He needed bishops who would support him against the Arian heresy (which denied the full divinity of Christ). He urged Gregory to reconsider becoming a priest, and Gregory finally conceded. (This did not alter his marriage because at that time priests were allowed to be married.)

Soon Basil made Gregory the bishop of Nyssa, a small town near Caesarea. But his appointment was a disaster. Gregory was not made for administration. He was naïve and did not get along with the Church and its Arians. His opponents accused him of mismanagement and embezzling Church funds. The latter accusation was false.

He was arrested but escaped. In his absence, a local council deposed him. For two years he wandered the region until a change in politics changed his status. A new emperor came to the throne and issued an edict of tolerance concerning the religious conflict. Gregory returned to Nyssa, where he was warmly welcomed.

Basil died soon afterward, and Gregory took on a more important role in the defense of orthodox belief. He was a leader in two councils and defended the Trinity.

He also wrote many books, the best of which are considered to be beautifully written. His book on Moses urged people to a deeper spiritual life. He taught that it is not so much our sins that keep us out of heaven as our unwillingness to accept God's freely offered forgiveness. For example, when the Israelites came out of Egypt, they grumbled, worshipped an idol and engaged in a sexual orgy. In spite of all this, God led them toward the Promised Land. What kept them out was their refusal to believe the report of Joshua and Caleb. Instead, they accepted the report of the ten frightened spies. Gregory taught that just as the Israelites should have believed Joshua and Caleb so they could enter the Promised Land, we must believe Christ if we are to enter heaven.

The Lutheran Church commemorates Gregory of Nyssa on this day.

G.K. Chesterton, witty defender of the Christian faith. (Courtesy of the University of Texas collection of public domain portraits on the Web.)

Other Events

1715: Rev. Robert Norden took an oath of allegiance at Prince George County Court in Virginia on this day. This cleared the way for him to become the first pastor of a Baptist church in Virginia.

1936: G.K. Chesterton, an influential Roman Catholic apologist and wit noted for his use of paradox, died on this day.

1948: Cardinal Mindszenty ordered church bells tolled throughout Hungary in protest of the nation's secularization law.

1949: Archbishop Beran of Czechoslovakia tried to preach his Corpus Christi sermon in the Cathedral of St. Vitus, but Communist agitators broke it up with catcalls.

1966: The Vatican abolished the *Index of Prohibited Books*, which had been established in 1557. Among the many books that made the list over the years was Victor Hugo's novel *Les Miserables* and the writings of Galileo.

Reluctant Signature Gives England Her Great Charter

In the English-speaking world no document has been more important for getting civil rights started than the Magna Carta. It was forced on King John by angry noblemen with the help of a churchman.

John was a cruel tyrant whose nobles were ready to revolt. He had his problems with the Church too. When Stephen Langton was appointed archbishop of Canterbury, the highest religious post in England, John refused him his seat. Although Archbishop Langton was a man so holy that it was said he put all Rome to shame, John drove him and his friends and family out of England. An interdict by Pope Innocent III finally compelled John to give in. When Langton took his seat in Canterbury, he had little liking for the king and sympathized with the rebellious noblemen. By throwing his influence behind John's rebel barons, Langton increased their chance of winning concessions from the king.

The archbishop brought to their attention an old charter granted by Henry I, the youngest son of William the Conqueror. The barons built a new charter on the principles embodied in the old and presented it to King John at the field of Runnymead on this day in 1215. John grudgingly pressed his seal to it.

Runnymead was not the end of the story, however. John was not going to limit his power without a fight. He appealed to the pope, and the pope overruled the Magna Carta. But the barons prepared a new version.

The charter was supposed to prevent war between the king and his nobles. It actually almost started one because John wouldn't stick to the agreement. With the pope taking John's side, the nobles were in such despair that they invited Louis, the dauphin of France, to take the English crown. John died before that could become a reality.

After John died, King Henry III accepted the Magna Carta and reissued it, making it law. Since then, English kings have sometimes been made to swear to uphold the provisions of the charter before they are allowed to take the crown.

Scholars have grumbled that the Magna Carta placed too much emphasis on concerns of the Church and knights. It is true that the charter dealt with religious issues. The very first "chapter" says:

> In the first place [we] have granted to God and by this our present Charter have confirmed, for us and our heirs in perpetuity, that the English Church shall be free, and shall have its rights undiminished and liberties unimpaired.

John, king of England, gave reluctant consent to the Magna Carta but quickly moved to have the pope nullify it. (Besant, Sir Walter. *Medieval London: Ecclesiastical*. London: A. & C. Black, 1906.)

However, the Magna Carta's two most lasting provisions have benefited much of the world. These are the right to a trial by a jury of one's peers and a prohibition against new taxes without permission of national representatives. Also in the charter is the idea that barons may check a king. This might be seen as the seed of the modern English parliament. At any rate, the monarchy was not absolute.

The meeting at Runnymead was an important historical event. The rights secured by the Magna Carta, or similar rights, have been widely accepted in Christian nations. In fact, the whole notion of the rights of man seems to be a particularly Judeo-Christian concept, which originally gained its strength from the biblical teachings that every man is made in the image of God and is a repository of the Holy Spirit and a brother to Christ.

Other Events

313: Emperor Licinius rode in triumph into Nicomedia (a city about fifty miles from modern Istanbul, Turkey), where he proclaimed toleration for Christians. After a falling out with co-emperor Constantine, Licinius returned to persecuting believers.

1520: Pope Leo X issued the bull *Exsurge Domine*, declaring Martin Luther a heretic.

1649: The first witchcraft trial in Massachusetts resulted in the hanging of Margaret Jones. This was not one of the Salem trials.

1818: Samuel John Mills, one of the founders of the American missionary movement, died at sea either on this day or on June 16 while returning from Liberia. He was one of four Andover students who, forced to take refuge in the shelter of a haystack during a rainstorm, prayed together and resolved to appeal for the creation of an American missionary endeavor. Mills was also instrumental in founding the American Bible Society.

1941: Evelyn Underhill, theologian and mystic, died. She wrote many books on mysticism and taught that the life of contemplation and prayer is for any Christian. She gave her mornings to writing and her afternoons to visiting the poor and to the direction of souls.

Bulla contra Errores Martini Lutheri et sequatium.

A bull against Martin Luther. He burned it. (Bezold, Friedrich von. *Geschichte der Deutschen Reformation*. Berlin: Grote, 1890.)

Joseph Butler, one of the best-known apologists of all time. (Butler, Joseph. *Analogy of Religion*. London: H.G. Bohn, 1856.)

June

16

Bishop Joseph Butler Dies at Bath

Joseph Butler was in Bath, hoping that the natural hot springs there would do him good, for he was not feeling well at all. Just in case the remedy should prove unsuccessful and he succumbed to his illness, he gave orders that his speculative, unfinished manuscripts be burned.

A bishop of the Church of England, Butler had written the most famous apologetic of his age, *Analogy of Religion, Natural and Revealed, to the Constitution and Course of Nature*. A religious philosophy known as Deism argued that God had made the world but had never used prophets, visions, angels or revelations to teach men about Himself. Deists attacked the Bible, saying it had imperfections that proved it wasn't from the hand of God. Butler's book was written to answer the Deists.

In his *Analogy*, Butler used an argument that had been written by the Greek theologian Origen centuries earlier:

> Those who believe the author of nature to be also the author of Scripture must expect to find in Scripture the same sorts of difficulties that they find in nature.

For example, a Deist might complain that Scripture says God visits the iniquities of the fathers upon the children to the third and fourth generation. How could that be fair? Butler replied that nature does the same thing. To give a modern example, a pregnant woman takes LSD. Her daughter is born with deformities, and in turn she gives birth to another defective child either because of carrying LSD-mutated genes or because of labor difficulties owing to her own malformation. It was unreasonable to accept nature as coming from God but to deny God's revelation when it affirms the very principles that we see in nature. The point is, our decisions do affect other people and so we should endeavor to make decisions that take into account the interests of others.

This is just what the Scripture teaches, although it adds grace to the equation—God often breaks the cycle of nature and sets things right. The natural equivalent of grace would be for the daughter or grandchild in the above example to receive medical attention that corrects the problems.

Butler also argued that nature itself suggests that man is immortal, saying that some things make sense only if this life is a probationary period. The existence of conscience is a strong support for the Christian claim that there is a moral law, he said. The *Analogy* was a cool and reasoned piece of writing, so much so that Butler scarcely discussed sin or hell.

Did Butler get infected with the disease he was trying to cure? After he met John Wesley, he condemned "the pretending to extraordinary revelations and gifts of the Holy Spirit" as "a horrid thing—a very horrid thing." He also described revelation as a "horrid thing," which seems a peculiar statement for a defender of divine revelation to make! But by acknowledging that the great doctrines of Christianity cannot be proven by philosophy, Butler showed that Christianity has enough probability to make acceptance of it a reasonable response.

Butler died, after all, while at Bath, on this day in 1752. Just as he had requested, his manuscripts were burned.

Catherine Mumford Booth, "Mother of the Salvation Army." (Booth-Tucker, Frederick de Lautour. *The Life of Catherine Booth: The Mother of the Salvation Army*. New York: Fleming H. Revell Co., 1892.)

Other Events

1410: Archbishop Zybnek of Czechoslovakia ordered the burning of the reformer John Wycliffe's works. Jan Hus, declared a heretic by the Council of Constance, had assimilated Wycliffe's teachings.

1701: The Society for the Propagation of the Gospel in Foreign Parts was chartered in England.

1855: William Booth and Catherine Mumford married. They became one of the greatest husband-wife evangelical teams known to history and founded the Salvation Army.

1923: The Soviets published Patriarch Tikhon's "self-criticism" after he yielded to them under extreme pressure.

1948: The Ortutay program in Hungary was adopted by the Hungarian parliament. Its principal measure called for nationalization of religious schools, which was promptly implemented over strenuous objections by Christians.

June 17

On Watch for the Lord

Imagine that you have a big house and plenty of land. A refugee shows up at your door, asking if he might camp out in your backyard. Moved by compassion, you say "yes." A little later he asks if some of his relatives, who are also homeless, might come and live on your property as well. You are a Christian. They are Christians. How can you turn them away? Again you say "yes." More refugees hear of your generosity and come to live on your land. And then more and more arrive. Soon there are hundreds. What have you gotten yourself into?

This actually happened to a twenty-two-year-old German nobleman in 1722. His name was Count Nikolaus Ludwig von Zinzendorf, and he was the heir of a leading European family. His estate was in East Germany. As you might expect, the neighbors were not pleased when he gave asylum to "riff-raff," but there was no stopping the influx. On this day in 1722, Moravians first asked Zinzendorf if they might settle on his land. He gave them permission and that December, ten of them planted themselves there. By May of 1725 there were ninety. And by 1727 there were over 300. The place became known as "Herrnhut," meaning "The Lord's Watch."

Zinzendorf was born on May 26, 1700, in Dresden, Germany, and was reared under strong Christian influence. Even as a child he showed a deep spiritual awareness. When invading Swedish soldiers broke into the castle where he lived, they were astounded to observe the six-year-old at his prayers. Zinzendorf later trained at Halle under the pictist August Francke.

At twenty, the nobleman was overcome while observing a painting of Christ crowned with thorns. An inscription below the painting read: "I have done this for you; what have you done for Me?" Zinzendorf responded, "I have loved Him for a long time, but I have never actually done anything for Him. From now on I will do whatever He leads me to do."

The Moravians living on Zinzendorf's property rapidly organized into an efficient and productive society. But several other Christian denominations were also represented among them, and soon jealous discord threatened to undermine them. Yet, looking at them, Zinzendorf realized that instead of being burdened, he was blessed with a historic opportunity to break down religious differences. He organized everyone into "bands," small-group ministries, who met together regularly to discuss their spiritual growth, to study Scripture, pray together, reprove and encourage each other.

They repented of their divisions and on August 13, 1727, experienced a powerful outpouring of the Holy Spirit. Then followed fervent prayer as they sought the purpose for which God had brought them together. A twenty-four-hour-a-day prayer vigil was organized. At least two people were at prayer every hour of the day for over 100 years! From a shaky start emerged one of the most powerful mission movements the world has ever known.

Count Nikolaus von Zinzendorf opened his lands to refugees. (Hyde, A.B. *Story of Methodism*. Greenfield, MA: Willey and Co., 1887.)

William Carey is popularly hailed as the "Father of Modern Protestant Missions." In Carey's classic *Enquiry Regarding the Obligation of Christians,* he used the Moravian experience as his model.

Other Events

362: Emperor Julian the Apostate ordered that all schoolmasters and professors must obtain a license before teaching, thus excluding Christians from educating youth.

1535: Henry VIII had the staunch Roman Catholic bishop John Fisher arraigned; five days later Fisher was beheaded at the Tower of London on trumped-up charges. His real "crime" was refusing to sign a document that declared King Henry VIII's unwelcome marriage to Catherine of Aragon unlawful.

1773: The Orthodox Church in Russia published Catherine's edict of religious freedom.

1791: Selina Hastings, Lady Huntingdon of Wales, died on this day. She was a supporter of Howel Harris, George Whitefield and other open-air preachers and Methodists.

1963: The US Supreme Court ruled that reading the Lord's Prayer or Bible verses aloud in public schools was unconstitutional.

Selina Hastings, countess of Huntington, used her influence to support the Methodists. (Daniels, W.H. *Illustrated History of Methodism in Great Britain and America, From the Days of the Wesleys to the Present Time*. New York: Phillips & Hunt, 1880.)

Ephrem the Syrian. (Baring-Gould, S. *Lives of the Saints*. Edinburgh: John Grant, 1914.)

June 18 Hymnist and Only Syrian Father

St. Ephrem the Syrian was so afraid of being made a bishop that on one occasion he pretended to be insane to escape induction into the Church. He was never made a bishop, but he did become recognized as a doctor of the Church.

He was born around 306 at Nisibis in Mesopotamia. When the Persians forced Emperor Jovianus to give up the territory of Nisibis, Ephrem and many other Christians migrated to Edessa (in modern Turkey).

During his years at Edessa, Ephrem lived in a cave and ate only barley bread and vegetables. Bald, short, without a beard and shriveled in his skin, he was a true ascetic. Nonetheless he took an active part in the affairs of the city, where his dirty, patched robe must have made him something to behold.

Ephrem was already famous as a teacher. He seemed to have had no trouble landing a job. In Edessa he was involved with a school of biblical interpretation. This school took a halfway position between Antioch (which took the Bible very literally) and Alexandria (which saw almost everything as a "type" of something else). Ephrem was the school's most famous representative.

The Roman Catholic Church finds support for much of its teaching in Ephrem's work. Centuries before the doctrine of the Immaculate Conception became official dogma, Ephrem taught it. This teaching says that Mary was spared the taint of original sin at the time she was conceived in her mother's womb. Ephrem also believed that Christ really is in the loaf and the wine during the Eucharist. He taught that the bishops who followed Peter in Rome were the leaders of the Church. He agreed with the idea of purgatory and also said that dead saints could intercede for people.

St. Ephrem wrote many hymns. He put so much emphasis on their place in formal worship that the use of hymns spread from Edessa to the whole Christian world. He saw hymns as a means of Christian education. Therefore, many of his songs take faith as their theme. Others were written to counter the heresies of Marcion, Manes (founder of Manicheism) and Bardesanes. Some are about the Crucifixion, paradise, the Church, death and even virginity. These were widely sung and "lent luster to the Christian assemblies," according to one early Church historian. The Syrians called him "the Harp of the Holy Ghost."

Here are words that Ephrem imagined a soul saying as it left its body in death:

> As my provision for my journey,
> I have taken you O, you Son of God!
> And when I am hungry I will eat of You,
> You Savior of the world!
> The fire will keep far off from my members,
> seeing in me the savor of Your body and blood.
> Baptism shall become to me a ship which cannot sink,
> And I shall see you there, O Lord,
> In the day of resurrection.

He produced commentaries on virtually the whole Bible. Of Christ he wrote this beautiful tribute: "He alone sufficeth for all, yet none for him sufficeth. Altar He is and lamb, victim and sacrificer, priest as well as food." His work was highly influential and was reproduced in the Georgian, Slavic, Coptic, Arabic, Greek and Latin languages. Jerome, famed as the translator who gave the Church the Vulgate Bible, said of Ephrem that "his writings are publicly read in some churches after the Sacred Scriptures."

Ephrem's last public act was to distribute grain to Edessa's starving poor during a famine. No one else was trusted for the task. He is believed to have died old and withered on this day (his feast day) in the year 373. In 1920 he became the only Syrian father honored as a doctor of the universal Church.

Anne Askew burns for refusing to accept the full Roman Catholic teaching on the Eucharist. (Besant, Sir Walter. *London in the Time of the Tudors*. London: A. & C. Black, 1904.)

Other Events

1376: Catherine of Siena set out from her hometown to coax the pope, residing in Avignon, France, to return the papacy to Rome.

1415: The final formulation of charges against reformer Jan Hus of Bohemia was presented to him by the Council of Constance.

1546: Anne Askew, an English Protestant, was condemned. Racked and tortured for refusing to say that priests could make bread into the body of Christ, she was burned at Smithfield a month later.

1849: William B. Tappan, who wrote the hymn "'Tis Midnight and on Olive's Brow," died on this day.

1945: The Committee of Initiative for the Transfer of Greek Catholics to the Orthodox Church was given sole authority to force Greek Orthodox believers in Poland to unite with the Russian Orthodox Church for easier management by the Communists.

1956: Dawson Trotman, who founded the discipleship ministry called the Navigators, drowned while attempting to rescue a drowning girl. Billy Graham preached at Trotman's funeral service.

For Father: The First Father's Day

Many of our national anniversaries have Christian roots. You know that Christmas, Easter and Thanksgiving are Christian holidays. You may even know that Halloween was once a Christian day, closely tied to All Souls' Day. But did you know that Father's Day has Christian roots as well?

The first widely promoted Father's Day celebration was held in Spokane, Washington, on this day in 1910. Louise Dodd envisioned the event as being focused on special religious services and involving small gifts as well as loving greetings from children to their fathers. She brought up the suggestion to her pastor and he communicated it to the local pastors' association. The mayor of the city and the governor of the state endorsed her concept and issued proclamations in its support. The famed politician William Jennings Bryan even weighed in with words of approval. The third Sunday in June was established as the date of the celebration.

Dodd dearly loved her own father, who had raised her in the absence of a mother. His wife died in childbirth, leaving him with six children. Somehow he overcame all the difficulties of rearing them while at the same time operating his farm. His devotion to his children sparked Dodd's inspiration.

Father's day was slow to catch on. Despite the governor's proclamation, what Dodd had done was not well-known even in her own state. And so the idea of honoring fathers with a special day was actually reinvented independently in several other places. Each local group thought it was starting something new. Coincidentally, circumstances led other founders to independently choose the month of June for their celebration, and that was the month that stuck. By 1916 President Woodrow Wilson had endorsed the idea of a fathers' day, and in 1924 Calvin Coolidge recommended that the whole nation observe it "to impress upon fathers the full measure of their obligation" and to strengthen intimate ties between fathers and children.

Hymns were written about fathers and fatherhood. Ralph Waldo Emerson, a transcendentalist philosopher from New England, authored one that begins:

> We love the venerable home
> Our fathers built to God;
> In heav'n are kept their grateful vows,
> Their dust endears the sod.

The ideals of fatherhood are strong in the Bible. Unlike the gods of other religions, the Judeo-Christian God is portrayed as a loving Father. A psalmist told us that God pities us as a father pities his children (see Psalm 103:13, KJV), and Moses said that God carried the Israelites through the wilderness as a father (see Deuteronomy 1:31, KJV). Jesus gave the world the story of the Prodigal Son, a boy who demands his inheritance, squanders it, returns repentant and is embraced by his loving father (see Luke 15:11-32). Christ declared that God was His own intimate Father and claimed to express the Father in human terms (see John 15:5-14).

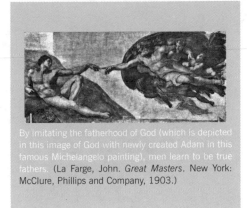

By imitating the fatherhood of God (which is depicted in this image of God with newly created Adam in this famous Michelangelo painting), men learn to be true fathers. (La Farge, John. *Great Masters*. New York: McClure, Phillips and Company, 1903.)

The Bible also says that God so loved the children He created that He gave His beloved Son for the salvation of others (see John 3:16). In addition, the tender appeals of the apostles John and Paul to their "children" helped foster the attitude of responsible fatherhood. In light of such teachings, it is little wonder that wherever the Christian ideal has prospered, fatherhood has taken on a deeper and more lyrical meaning than in the world at large.

Louise Dodd's father exhibited the kind of self-sacrificing love that is talked about in the Bible. Thanks to Dodd's appreciation for her father's love, we now have a national day of recognition for all fathers.

Other Events

325: Tradition says the Council of Nicea opened on May 20 and Bishop Hosius announced the Nicene Creed on this day a month later. The creed was formulated in response to the Arian heresy that denied Christ's divinity. It declared that Jesus was "God from very God."

1535: Henry VIII ordered Carthusian monks butchered at Tyburn. They were among those who rejected Henry's claim to headship of the English Church. Their bishop was butchered three days later.

1623: Blaise Pascal was born at Clermont-Ferrand, France. He became a notable mathematician and scientist as well as an apologist for Christianity and for Jansenism.

1977: Blessed John Neumann, the first American-born male to be declared a saint, was canonized by the Roman Catholic Church. He founded the parochial school system.

Blaise Pascal, a genius in several fields, wrote the *Pensees*, a famous defense of Christianity. (Pascal, Blaise. *Pensees*, Harvard Classics series. New York: P.F. Collier & Son, 1910.)

Indian converts in jail. (Taylor, William. *The Story of My Life: An Account of What I Have Thought and Said and Done in My Ministry of More Than Fifty-Three Years in Christian Lands and Among the Heathen.* New York: Hunt & Eaton, 1895.)

June

20

Irregular Synod: Clash of East and West

The origins of Christianity in India are lost in legend and the obscurity of centuries. It is certain, however, that the gospel reached India early on.

When Europeans arrived in India in the fifteenth century, they found churches already in existence, with thousands of Christians attached to them. Christians even had their own caste. The Christianity that existed, however, was strongly colored by Nestorianism, the most prominent sect in the East.

Shortly after Vasco da Gama rounded Cape Hope on his triumphant voyage of discovery, the Portugese sent a few missionaries to India. Trinitarians, Franciscans, Dominicans and Jesuits found their way to the Asian subcontinent and sought to win converts to Christ. For the most part they were successful only with pariahs (outcasts) and low castes, or with those who already had a Christian tradition. The famous Roman Catholic missionary to India, Francis Xavier, had his greatest success among a group of fishermen who were already Christian in name, although not in practice. He learned enough of their language to translate a few key texts: the Lord's Prayer, the Ten Commandments, a catechism and the Apostles' Creed. With this smattering of the gospel, the Indian Christians remained vital for generations.

For the most part, the villainy of the Portugese explorers and conquerors led upper-class Indians to despise the faith the explorers brought to India because it seemed so at odds with their behavior. Furthermore, the fact that most Christians were in the lower castes caused the higher Indian castes to shy away from the religion. To counter this, one Catholic missionary, Madura Nobili, adopted the dress and lifestyle of an upper-class Hindu priest, ate like a native, complied with every Hindu custom that was not absolutely contrary to the Bible and taught the people in their own languages. Despite his admirable efforts to "become all things to all men" (1 Corinthians 9:22) that he might win some to Christ, he still had little success with the upper castes.

Other early missionaries concentrated on winning a group of existing Christians into the Roman Catholic Church. These Christians were concentrated along the Malabar coast and were known as the Church of St. Thomas, from whom they claimed their origin. According to legend, Thomas was martyred in India, and bones that were said to be his were preserved in an Indian church.

When Alexis de Menzez was appointed archbishop of Goa, he determined to correct the lapses and errors of the Indian Christians. Unknown to him, the offspring of Thomas's mission were under the Catholic patriarch of Chaldea. Menzez held a synod at Diamper on this day in 1599. His methods were arbitrary and high-handed, revealing a typical colonial mind-set. He even went so far as to singlehandedly override and change articles that the council adopted.

The Menzez articles were accepted by the 660 Indian lay Christians and 130 of their Christian brethren who were gathered at the synod. According to observers, the Indians did not understand what they were signing. Later, when they realized that Menzez had made changes that they had been unaware of, India's Christians repudiated the Diamper agreement. The Indians had to be wooed back by the Roman Church, which did not accept the validity of the local synod.

Abigail Adams, who trusted that God would support the fledgling United States. (Courtesy of the University of Texas collection of public domain portraits on the Web.)

Other Events

1776: Does God take sides? Evidently Abigail Adams thought so. She wrote to her husband, John, future President of the US:

> I feel no anxiety at the large armament designed against us. The remarkable interpositions of heaven in our favor cannot be too gratefully acknowledged. He who fed the Israelites in the wilderness, who clothes the lilies of the field and feeds the young ravens when they cry, will not forsake a people engaged in so right a cause, if we remember His loving kindness.

1885: Moravians landed in Alaska and founded the Bethel Mission.

1907: Reuben A. Torrey received his doctor of divinity degree from Wheaton. A prominent evangelist, Torrey wrote the popular study aid *What the Bible Teaches*.

1946: Bishop Jiosofat Kocylowskyj was ordered on May 14 to "voluntarily" leave Poland for Russia. He refused, so on this day he was hauled out of his house, beaten severely and sent to Russia. Other bishops received similar treatment.

1965: The bodies of missionaries Tim Van Dyke and Steve Welsh, martyred the day before in Colombia, South America, were found and transferred to the US for burial.

First Stone but No Fanfare

The foundation stone of one of the most famous churches in the Christian world, St. Paul's Cathedral in London, was laid without special ceremony or fanfare on this day in 1675. Many reasons have been given for the lack of fanfare. One such reason was that the king may have feared for his safety. He had recently implemented financial measures that were unpopular in the city and caused great distress. There was also ill-will between the king and Archbishop Seldon. Furthermore, there had been a good deal of controversy over the plans for the cathedral. At any rate, only a few onlookers observed as the first stone was lowered deep into the ground and set in place by Thomas Strong, a master mason.

Old St. Paul's had burned down in the great London fire of 1666. It had already been in bad repair, so various sin taxes had been applied to its restoration under architect Inigo Jones. After the fire, King Charles II appointed Christopher Wren chief architect to rebuild the cathedral. Although he had no formal training as an architect, Wren was a genius who contributed to many sciences and built several public works. Wren's simple and elegant proposals were fiercely contested by a design committee because each member wanted a pet feature included. Their plan has been described as a monstrosity.

Christopher Wren, a practical man, agreed to the committee's plan—with the stipulation that he be allowed to make such modifications as would prove necessary during the actual construction. He modified so continuously that the finished work more closely resembled his own original design than the committee's hybrid. This miffed the committee so much that they got Wren sacked.

An extraordinary coincidence occurred during the rebuilding. When Wren began to lay out the shape of his proposed dome, he called a workman to bring him a bit of stone. The workman grabbed the first piece that came to hand. Inscribed on it in Latin was the word *Resurgam*: "May I rise again." St. Paul's rose swiftly. Few cathedrals are built in a single lifetime, but Wren completed the project in just thirty-five years. To Wren, a staunch Protestant, the preaching of the gospel was the primary function of a church, and he designed the interior so that the pulpit would be the center of attention. He forbade his workmen to curse while working on the project on pain of dismissal, reminding them that they were engaged in holy work. After his death, Wren was entombed within the cathedral. On his commemoration stone is written: "*Si monumentum requiris, circumspice*"—"If you would see his monument, look around."

St. Paul's Cathedral, landmark of London. (Milman, Lena. *Sir Christopher Wren*. London: Duckworth and Co.; New York: C. Scribner's Sons, 1908.)

As an interesting historical sidelight, German efforts to destroy the cathedral by bombing in World War II never succeeded. It became a symbol of faith for the nation.

Other Events

1639: Increase Mather was born in Dorchester, Massachusetts. Ordained in 1657, he became the pastor of North Church in Boston in 1664 and remained there until his death in 1723. He wrote nearly 100 books and also served as president of Harvard.

1691: Rev. John Flavel preached his last sermon, taking as his text First Corinthians 10:12, which reads, "Wherefore let him that thinketh he standeth take heed lest he fall" (KJV). Flavel urged that those who were careless about their Christian profession show a deeper concern for their souls.

Flavel was representative of the best of England's seventeenth-century nonconformists. Given a choice between prosperity in London and poverty in Dartmouth, he chose poverty. He was known for his passionate prayers. For instance, learning that a sea battle was in progress and knowing that many Dartmouth boys were in the navy, he led his people in prayer and fasting. Not one of Dartmouth's many sailors died in that battle. Flavel died unexpectedly of a stroke a few days after his last sermon.

1897: Clara H. Scott, who wrote the hymn "Open My Eyes that I May See," died on this day. She was killed when thrown from a buggy by a runaway horse.

1963: Pope Paul VI was elected. Before his rise to the papacy, he stood strong in the face of Communism. In his coronation address, he remarked, "We will continue to offer untiringly to today's world the remedy for its ills, the answer to its appeals: Christ and his unfathomable riches."

Increase Mather. (Murdock, Kenneth Ballard. *Increase Mather, The Foremost American Puritan*. Cambridge, MA: Harvard University Press, 1925.)

Galileo Galilei. Despite the belief of the Inquisition, his theory proved to be sound. (Lord, John. *Beacon Lights of History*. New York: James Clarke, 1886.)

June

22 Galileo Renounces His Views Before the Inquisition

Galileo was frustrated because a web of deceit and hatred had closed around him. As the sixty-nine-year-old man faced the Inquisition on this day in 1633, he hoped to get at least two changes in the statement his judges insisted he sign. He pleaded:

> Do not make me say I have not been a good Catholic for I have been one and will remain one no matter what my enemies say. And I will not say that I intended to deceive anyone, especially with the publication of my book. I submitted it in good faith to the church censors and printed it only after legally obtaining a license.

The judges agreed. The words were rewritten—as they should have been. For, as Galileo knew, most of the men who were sentencing him held his same opinions—that the earth spun on its axis and orbited the sun.

With the new injunction before him, Galileo knelt and repeated the words demanded of him. He was strongly "suspected of heresy." He had "held and believed that the Sun is the center of the world and immovable and that the Earth is not the center and moves."

Galileo then signed another statement:

> I, the said Galileo Galilei, have abjured [renounced], sworn, promised and bound myself as above; and in witness of the truth thereof I have with my own hand subscribed the present document of my abjuration and recited it word for word at Rome, in the convent of the Minerva, this twenty-second day of June, 1633.*

This is one of the most famous trials in history. The Church often takes all the blame for the fiasco of justice that took place that day in Rome. It had the unfortunate effect of branding the Roman Catholic Church as anti-science, when in fact famous Catholics of the Middle Ages—Robert Grosseteste, Thomas of Bradwardine, Nikolaus Oresme and others—had done much to advance and promote science. Galileo himself was a staunch Catholic.

There is no doubt the Church was most in the wrong. A commission formed by Pope John Paul II in the 1980s admitted as much. But was it fully responsible? No, for there were, in fact, two other parties at fault as well.

One was Galileo himself. His vanity, sarcastic words, contempt for lesser minds and half-truths had earned him fierce enemies among the intellectuals of Europe—especially among the Jesuits. Galileo even fudged at least one experiment.

The second culprit was naturalism, the science of the day. Advocates of the pagan philosopher Aristotle resisted Galileo's findings because they did not agree with Aristotle's claims. The pope and cardinals would not have acted as they did if dozens of these "scientists" had not said Galileo was wrong. Some hated Galileo, who had hurt their feelings. Others felt that Aristotle and the Bible should not be overturned without solid evidence. It did not matter that both Johann Kepler and Galileo had shown that the Bible could be interpreted to agree with the new science. Their own eyes showed them that the sun, not the earth, moved. Galileo could not provide hard evidence to the contrary. Solid proof for the earth's rotation on its axis was 200 years away, when Léon Foucault proved it with pendulums and gyroscopes.

* Quoted from Giorgio de Santillana's thorough study, *The Crime of Galileo*.

Kateri Tekakwitha kept herself pure amid scenes of debauchery. (Campbell, Thomas J. *Pioneer Priests of North America, 1642-1710*. New York: America Press, 1913.)

Other Events

Annual: Paulinus's day is celebrated. Born to wealth in Gaul (France) Paulinus became a lawyer but gave up the high life to adopt a simple, caring lifestyle with his wife. It is said he introduced bells into Christian worship.

431: The First Council of Ephesus met in St. Mary's Church, lasting through July 17. It excommunicated Nestorius and deposed Cyril until Western bishops arrived and reestablished him. It confirmed the pope's decrees against Pelagianism.

1276: Pope Innocent V died. He wrote Bible commentaries.

1606: The Peace of Vienna granted toleration to Protestants within the Hapsburg Empire.

1750: Jonathan Edwards was driven from his pulpit at Northampton, Massachusetts, because he called for holiness.

1981: Kateri Tekakwitha, an American Indian woman who was born about 1656, was beatified by Pope John Paul II. She lived a life of Christian purity amidst scenes of grossest debauchery.

Whose Life? Blasphemy in Poetic Garb

It was heresy, plain and simple. In his *Vie de Jésus* (*Life of Christ*), published on this day in 1863, J.E. Renan claimed that Jesus was a magnetic teacher with a vivid personality and "merely an incomparable man." He also said that none of the supernatural elements in Christ's scriptural biographies were true. The book raised an immediate storm between various factions: Atheists said it did not go far enough in stripping veneration from the person of Christ; Christian believers deplored its blasphemous denial of Christ's divinity.

However, the book did appeal to a wide audience of people who wanted the emotion of religion without the substance. They readily fell in with Renan's sentimental view of Christ. *Vie de Jésus* was read because it fit the mood of the day: Deism reigned, and the skepticism of the French philosophers had undermined the faith of many. In Germany, theologians such as David Friedrich Strauss had already denied the supernatural element of the gospel on "scientific," textual and archaeological grounds. It is ironic to note that, since then, superior scientific methods and new findings of archaeology, such as the Dead Sea Scrolls, have repudiated much of the "advanced" thinking of the nineteenth century and broadened our understanding of the world Christ entered. Despite this, however, the anti-Christian theologians have not reversed their claims.

In addition to appealing to the Deistic tendencies of general society, Renan's *Vie de Jésus* also gained recognition because of his fame as an orientalist. He had been able to study in the Holy Lands because of a boon from Napoleon III, and his first work, a history of Semitic languages, won him a prize.

Vie de Jésus was also read because it was a work of stylistic beauty. In the French, its lure was heightened by poetic passages. Even in translation its force is not completely lost:

> The idea of being all-powerful by suffering and resignation, and of triumphing over force by purity of heart, is indeed an idea peculiar to Jesus.

Yet despite its clever phrasing and beautiful language, Renan's *Vie de Jésus* is still just heresy, for his Jesus is not the gospel's. Renan denied a transcendent God.

Here is how Renan described the disciples' reaction to Jesus's teaching against riches:

> An admirable idea governed Jesus in all this, as well as the band of joyous children [the disciples] who accompanied him and made him for eternity the true creator of the peace of the soul, the great consoler of life.

This, of course, is pure sentimentality and has nothing to do with the terrible resistance Christ met—resistance that cut Him to His soul. Rather than joyous children, the disciples are better described as impulsive, quarrelsome men who constantly had to be corrected by their Master.

And the Resurrection? Renan turned it into piffle:

Renan depicted in the study where he wrote *Vie de Jésus*, which denied Christ's divinity. (Mott, Lewis Freeman. *Ernest Renan*. New York/London: D. Appleton and Co., 1921.)

> The strong imagination of Mary Magdalene played an important part in this circumstance. Divine power of love! Sacred moments in which the passion of one possessed gave to the world a resuscitated God!

Renan removed the divine from Christ, rendering Him down until little was left but a decent role model.

Other Events

1530: Melanchthon was hard at work preparing the Augsburg Confession, which was to be presented to Emperor Charles V two days later. The document became one of the fundamental statements of the Lutheran faith.

1738: Samuel Medley was born in Chestnut, England. As a youth he served in the Royal Navy and was severely wounded off Port Lagos in 1759. Converted after reading a sermon by Isaac Watts, he joined the Eagle Street Baptist Church (now Kingsgate Church) in London. He became a pastor first in Watford and then in Liverpool. His ministry in Liverpool was immensely successful, and the congregation became so large that they erected a new edifice in 1790. He wrote a large number of hymns. Among the best-known were "O Could I Speak the Matchless Worth" and "Awake, My Soul, to Joyful Lays."

1941: Father Walter J. Ciszek was arrested in Russia. His book, *He Leadeth Me*, recounts his experiences and sufferings. He had entered Russia to bring the gospel in spite of Communist barriers against doing so.

Philip Melanchthon. (Sixteenth-century Cranach portrait. Courtesy of the Christian History Institute archives.)

June 24

King Gustaf of Sweden Rages at the Diet of Vesteras

Gustaf Vasa stormed until he got what he wanted. (Bezold, Friedrich von. *Geschichte der Deutschen Reformation*. Berlin: Grote, 1890.)

"Our unbearable political and economic situation is the fault of the bishops and their huge wealth," Gustaf Vasa said to the Diet of Sweden. At his command it had assembled in Vesteras on this day in 1527. The gist of his speech is summed up in those few words. The Roman Church in Sweden would have to give up most of its riches.

To put more pressure on the Catholics, Vasa offered to arrange a debate between them and the Lutherans. This was a hint that the established Church could be replaced. Hans Brask, the Catholic bishop from Linkoping, spoke for his party. The Catholic Church would not discuss religious matters with the heretics, he said.

Vasa reacted with rage. He renounced all claim to the throne. Under the circumstances, he stormed, how could he govern Sweden? He would step down!

Immediately the Diet panicked. Vasa was all that stood between them and civil war. Who else had the authority to lead the nation? Just a few years earlier, Christian II of Denmark had been their king. Christian was so cruel that his own people had booted him out of Denmark.

Sweden had suffered under King Christian too. With the help of Archbishop Trolle, the king lured eighty nationalistic nobles and two Catholic bishops into his grasp and butchered them. The event was known as the Bloodbath of Stockholm.

Vasa was a young nobleman who escaped King Christian's net and hid in the countryside. When he heard that his father had been murdered in the bloodbath, he launched a furious revolt against the Danes. After three years of struggle, he made Sweden an independent country.

Gustaf supported the Lutheran reformation. In fact, his speech to the Diet was written by Lutheran sympathizers. (However, he harassed the Lutherans too when it suited him.)

Hans Brask saw that the Catholics would have to cut a deal with the king. They agreed to support him politically and financially if only he would leave the Catholic faith and its liturgy alone. Vasa agreed. At that time, most Swedes still favored the Catholic Church. However, the Church was forced to give huge amounts of land and money to Vasa and the noblemen. This is what Vasa had aimed at all along. It meant he now had the funds to run his government.

Gradually Vasa pushed the Catholic Church into a corner. Although Catholics appealed to Rome, the popes could do little to help. Italy was just too far away.

After the reformers published the Bible and other books in Swedish, the Swedes came to prefer Reformation doctrines and practices. Step by step their Diet changed the religious rules until the country was Protestant. But the first step was taken in Vesteras this day.

Other Events

1579: The first English religious service was held in the Americas. Rev. Francis Fletcher, sailing with Sir Francis Drake, read from the *Book of Common Prayer* in California. The pilgrimage spot is marked with a granite cross, and the day is observed by many Episcopalians.

1615: Mass was celebrated for the first time in Quebec (near today's Montreal).

1687: John Albert Bengal was born in Winnenden, Germany. He studied at the University of Tubingen. To answer doubts that he developed while handling different Bible texts, he compared many manuscripts, trying to determine the principles on which one version should be accepted over another when they disagreed. From this study he developed techniques of analysis that made him the first Protestant textual critic. He printed a revised Greek New Testament based on his findings.

1892: Kamil Abdul Messiah died, believed martyred; he was a Syrian who did much to help Samuel Zwemer's mission work among Muslims.

1934: Women of the Westphalian Auxiliary in Germany boldly proclaimed their allegiance to the Barmen Confession, which rejected Nazi racial claims.

First Mass in Quebec, near Montreal. (Parkman, Francis. *The Jesuits in North America in the Seventeenth Century*. Boston: Little, Brown, and Company, 1897.)

June 25

Clairvaux Founded

When Bernard joined a monastery, it was not one of the old, well-established and rich abbeys, but Citeaux, a monastery newly founded by the reform-minded Cistercians. With characteristic zeal, he brought thirty other recruits with him. Not surprisingly, three years later he was appointed abbot of his own monastery.

On this day in 1115, in an isolated valley in Champagne, France, he founded the famed monastery of Clairvaux. The monastery had existed only in the minds of himself and twelve followers who set out to build it. Once built, the monastery grew so rapidly that it soon founded sister monasteries. Bernard founded seventy monasteries in all. These in turn founded others. Thanks to his zeal, the Cistercian order was the fastest growing of the day.

Like other Cistercians, Bernard wanted a thorough return to the strict rule of St. Benedict. He ruined his health with fasts and hard work. His followers had to appeal to him to relax his stern regimen, because it was too hard for them. And yet, despite the hardships, the monastery continued to grow.

Bernard's stirring sermons grabbed listeners. For example, in a sermon for Epiphany, he painted the difference between spiritual and worldly kingdoms:

> What are you doing? Hey, magi! What are you doing? Are you worshipping a baby in the lap of his mother? In a stable? An infant in diapers? Is this supposed to be God? The Scriptures tell us that God dwells in his temple, the Lord has his throne in the heavens and you, you look for him in a dirty stable!

Bernard was spiritually minded. His teachings focused on love and holiness. They were saturated with allusions to Scripture and, indeed, the Cistercians gave a high place to God's Word. Bernard argued vehemently against those philosophers, such as Peter Abelard, who introduced a spirit of doubt into theology. He wanted God to be known and adored.

At the same time, Bernard was a practical and active man. Not only did he cause monasteries to spring up where none had been before, but he also took part in the affairs of his day. He preached in support of the Second Crusade. It failed. He threw all his influence behind Innocent II against the antipope Anacletus II. Thanks in large part to Bernard, Innocent II was acknowledged as the true pope. Bernard wrote the rule for the new order of the Knights Templars, who were sworn to defend the Holy Land. He sent hundreds of influential letters to the leaders of his era and made peace between a French king and his subjects.

St. Bernard has a vision. (Jameson, Mrs. *Legends of the Monastic Orders*. London: Longmans, Green, and Co., 1872.)

And what became of Clairvaux? Sadly, after the start of the French Revolution, its cells ceased to house monks and were used to house prisoners instead.

Other Events

1493: The papal bull *Piis Fidelium* empowered Friar Bernard Boyl (the first priest in America) with broad powers that conflicted with those given to Columbus.

1530: The Lutherans' Augsburg Confession was presented to Emperor Charles V and signed by German princes. This summary of Lutheran faith was written by Melanchthon.

1580: The Lutherans published the *Book of Concord*, which contained all the official confessions and catechisms of their Church.

1630: Five hundred souls in Scotland were saved through a John Livingstone sermon. Feeling as if he was useless, he had gathered with friends to pray fervently before he preached.

1957: Delegates created the United Church of Christ in Cleveland, Ohio, on the stage of a music hall.

1962: The US Supreme Court banned prayers in public schools on a case brought from New York. Federal statistics show that schools worsened on dozens of measurable problems after that: Grades went down, teen pregnancy increased and so forth.

Emperor Charles V received the Augsburg Confession on this day. (Bezold, Friedrich von. *Geschichte der Deutschen Reformation*. Berlin: Grote, 1890.)

Noble Alexander. (Courtesy of Voice of the Martyrs. Used by permission.)

June

26

Noble Alexander Stepped Off the Plane

On this day in 1984, a black man stepped off an airplane in Washington, DC. It happens every day. But this was not an incident to shrug at. The man recognized it as the power of God at work.

Twenty-two years before, on March 20, 1962, that man, Noble Alexander, had gone to prison in Castro's Cuba. He had preached a sermon about sin, and Castro's agents had interpreted his mention of Lucifer's struggle with God as a veiled reference to the Castro regime. A lawyer whom Alexander had never met entered a guilty plea on his behalf for supposedly having attempted to kill Castro.

From his cell, Alexander continued to win souls. He established churches in some of the most brutal prisons of the world, including the Isle of Pines. Tom White, American director of the Voice of the Martyrs who spent seventeen months in Cuba's prisons for dropping Christian leaflets from an airplane, described Alexander as his prison pastor: "a short, muscular black man with a smile like sunshine."

Alexander's sunshine smile was a smile of deep joy, the joy that came from suffering for Christ and for His name. Alexander's back was scarred from beatings and from shrapnel fired into him as he worshipped. There were emotional scars, too, from months spent in isolation. Yet despite the hardships he endured, he kept smiling, for he knew that his cause was a just and holy one. During the long years of his imprisonment, he insisted over and over, "I will die free!" That phrase became the name of a book he wrote.

One day Alexander was caught with a page of the Bible smuggled to him in a bar of soap. When he refused to say where it came from (Tom White), he was beaten and sent to isolation for three months. He also suffered for refusing to work on the Sabbath. As a Seventh Day Adventist, he considered it a violation of God's law.

During his stay in prison, Alexander's wife divorced him and married a Communist leader. It did not erase the smile of faith from his face or the spirit of love from his sermons. He managed to be secretly ordained by visiting churchmen. He also led Protestant worship services in the prisons. The Protestant prisoners gathered and sang with homemade songbooks, which had been lovingly copied by hand.

Christian groups worked to win Alexander's release. Rev. Jesse Jackson even visited Cuba on Noble's behalf. After he was freed and he returned to the States, Alexander continued to preach, speaking in the United States, Canada and the Netherlands. He pastored for fifteen years and then died in July of 2002.

The Beatitudes from William Tyndale's Bible. (Courtesy of the Christian History Institute archives.)

Other Events

684: St. Benedict II was consecrated pope. A humble, charitable man, he was successful in freeing the papal elections from the requirement of imperial confirmation.

1097: Armies of the First Crusade gained control of Nicea (now Iznik, Turkey).

1515: After receiving his master of arts degree on this day, William Tyndale went on to make an English translation of the Bible from which the Authorized (King James) Version borrowed heavily.

1932: Edith Seville and Francis Schaeffer both rose to refute a Unitarian speaker. The two outspoken apologists later ended up marrying. They became evangelists to intellectuals. Francis later teamed up with Dr. C. Everett Koop to produce the film series Whatever Happened to the Human Race?

1934: The Reformed Church in the United States and the Evangelical Synod of North America merged as the Evangelical and Reformed Church. The two bodies had Swiss and German roots.

First of Many Enthusiastic Sermons

George Whitefield made it his business to find salvation for his soul. He joined a group of likeminded men, the Holy Club, to which John and Charles Wesley also belonged, and exceeded the other members in zeal and good works. He was a familiar visitor of prisoners. For long hours he studied religious works. He fasted until his health broke. He prayed on his knees under a hedge in the cold. But, for all his hard work, his soul was still unsatisfied.

He would have despaired, except he felt that the Lord had promised him he would be saved. The Wesleys sailed to Georgia on a futile mission. They too would find peace later only when their hearts were warmed by the Holy Spirit. This did not come about until each recognized that salvation was by grace, a free gift through Jesus Christ rather than by works. They realized that to live a life of faith was to be born again; it was to be "in" Christ and to have Christ in oneself. When Whitefield grasped this, peace flooded his heart.

He returned to school, pouring out the newly found truth to others. As his health recovered, he trained toward being ordained so that he could enter full-time ministry. His efforts at private evangelism continued, but what had been labor before had become a work of joy. Yet as his ordination neared, he trembled. In May he was publicly examined by men who wanted to trip him up and embarrass him. He feared the same thing would happen at his ordination. And despite having studied the Scriptures line-by-line on his knees, he felt unprepared. As the day for ordination approached, he tried to find relief in prayer.

Kindly Bishop Benson believed Whitefield was the kind of man the Church needed. To ease the young man's mind, he promised there would be no public examination at his ordination.

June 20, 1736, came. Whitefield later wrote, "I attempted to behave with unaffected devotion, suitable to the greatness of the office I was to undertake." He read over Paul's advice to Timothy and determined to let no one despise him for his youth. The ordination went well.

A week later, on this day in 1736, Whitefield preached his first sermon. He took as his topic the need for Christians to help one another. At first he was awkward and overly aware that his mother, brothers, sisters and many others who had known him as a youngster were in the audience. As he proceeded with his sermon, however, the Spirit filled him. Those who had come to listen were so moved by the authority of his words that many responded with outbreaks of emotion. However, stiff parishioners, apparently untouched by the power of Whitefield's words, complained to the bishop that some hearers had gone "mad." This didn't do anything to improve Whitefield's stature in their eyes.

Despite the opinions of those few opposing individuals, Whitefield continued to preach. In fact, he went on to preach almost nonstop for the rest of his life. On this day in 1739, he wrote:

> Preached in the morning to about a thousand people in my brother's field. Went to public prayer at the Cathedral. . . . Visited some sick persons in the afternoon who sent for me. Preached at night to upward of three thousand. Great numbers were melted into tears; and most, I believe, went convicted away. Thanks be to God Who thus giveth us the victory through our Lord Jesus Christ.

He became a force in the Great Awakening, which brought fresh life to America's churches.

Whitefield's last sermon was preached in 1770 when he was desperately ill. Mounting a barrel, he urged his listeners to examine themselves to determine whether they were in the faith. He pointed out that to be saved, they must be born again. The following morning he died.

The young George Whitefield. (Daniels, W.H. *Illustrated History of Methodism in Great Britain and America, From the Days of the Wesleys to the Present Time*. New York: Phillips & Hunt, 1880.)

Other Events

363 (probable date): Julian the Apostate died. Alarmed at the success of Christians, he urged pagans to institute charities like those the Christians offered.

444: Cyril, patriarch of Alexandria, died on this day. He was an intractable foe of Nestorius, who refused to call the Virgin Mary "Mother of God."

1556: Thirteen Protestant believers died at the stake during the reign of Queen Mary of England. It was the largest number of people martyred in a single execution during her rule.

1865: Hudson Taylor established the China Inland Mission, one of the most successful mission ventures in history. It is now known as the Oriental Mission Society (OMS).

Julian the Apostate. (Courtesy of the Christian History Institute archives.)

John, spiritual grandfather of Irenaeus. (Bell, Mrs. Arthur. *Saints in Christian Art*. London: George Bell, 1901-4.)

June

28

Remembering Irenaeus, Bishop of Lyons

Irenaeus's heart was full. He wished his friend Marcianus could be with him so that they could talk about Christ, but that was impossible. So he picked up his pen. They might be separated by distance, but a letter could capture his feelings. He dipped the quill in ink and began to write:

> Knowing, my beloved Marcianus, your desire to walk in godliness, which alone leads man to life eternal, I rejoice with you and make my prayer that you may preserve your faith entire and so be pleasing to God who made you.

Irenaeus wrote many things, not only to Marcianus, but to others. His writings are of the utmost importance, for they show the state of Christianity in the second century.

Heresy had gained destructive power. In another lengthy writing, Irenaeus made a list of the current heresies and found Christian answers to the false claims they made. One of his arguments was that only the universal Church possessed the truth—which it had passed from bishop to bishop. Irenaeus was in a strong position when making this claim: He had personally known Polycarp, the martyred bishop from Asia Minor, who in turn had known St. John and other apostles.

One heresy of the day that Irenaeus took the trouble to answer was Gnosticism, which claimed that one needed a special, hidden knowledge if one's soul was to be saved. Irenaeus must have had this in mind when he wrote to Marcianus, saying:

> This then is the order of the rule of our faith, and the foundation of the building, and the stability of our conversation: God, the Father, not made, not material, invisible; one God, the creator of all things: this is the first point of our faith. The second point is: The Word of God, Son of God, Christ Jesus our Lord. . . . And the third point is: The Holy Spirit, through whom the prophets prophesied, and the fathers learned the things of God, and the righteous were led forth into the way of righteousness; and who in the end of the times was poured out in a new way upon mankind in all the earth, renewing man unto God.
>
> And for this reason the baptism of our regeneration proceeds through these three points: God the Father bestowing on us regeneration through His Son by the Holy Spirit. For as many as carry [in them] the Spirit of God are led to the Word, that is to the Son; and the Son brings them to the Father; and the Father causes them to possess incorruption.

Irenaeus became a leader in the Church in Lyons, France. In 177, the Lyons leadership sent him to Rome with a message. While he was away, his bishop and many other Christians died as martyrs in the arena in a savage spectacle. These included Blandina, one of history's best-known female martyrs.

Irenaeus declared that the true Church had the truth because it had Scripture on its side, as well as the memories of those who had known the apostles. It also had the authority of the bishop of Rome, sound reason and the guidance of the Holy Spirit.

Irenaeus's feast is on this day.

Innocent IV, who convened the Council of Lyons in 1245. (Barry, William. *Story of the Nations: Papal Monarchy*. Whitefish, MT: Kessinger Publishing, 1911.)

Other Events

767: Pope St. Paul I died. He turned to Pépin of France to assist him in disputes with the Lombards and the Byzantine emperor.

1245: Innocent IV convened the Council of Lyons to deal with the five wounds of the Church: bad clergy lives, schism with Greeks, onslaught of Saracens, invasion of Hungary by Tartars and rupture of the Church with Emperor Frederick II. Frederick was solemnly deposed because of his quarrel with Pope Innocent IV, who had been banished from Rome.

1851: Eliza Edmunds Hewitt was born in Philadelphia. A public school teacher, she suffered serious spinal trouble that curtailed her career and often confined her to bed. While abed, she wrote Sunday school material and several well-loved hymns, including "Sunshine in My Soul," "When We All Get to Heaven" and "More About Jesus Would I Know."

1890: Samuel Zwemer sailed from his homeland in the United States on a Dutch liner called the *Obdam*. He was bound for the Middle East, where he would spend his life converting Muslims to Christianity and educating Christians about Muslim culture.

1959: When they came to worship, the Christians of Krasnik, Poland, found that the Communists had barricaded their church and removed its decorations. Thousands marched in protest to city hall. Riots developed. The rioters wrecked the Communist party offices, and the state militia had to take refuge from the fury of the common folk.

The First Keswick Convention

The town of Keswick lies below Skiddaw Mountain in the beautiful Lake District of northwestern England. At times, some of England's most famous Romantic era poets lived and wrote there: Samuel Coleridge, Percy Shelley, Robert Southey and William Wordsworth. The area, rich with historical associations, is often visited by students of literature, hikers and lovers of natural beauty.

Keswick is also a renowned name in Christian circles, a name associated with the strongest holiness movement of the late nineteenth and early twentieth centuries. Just as famous poets are linked to Keswick, so are many of the greatest names in faith: Hudson Taylor, Evan Hopkins, Andrew Murray, F.B. Meyer and more.

Rev. T.D. Hartford-Battersby, a well-educated canon in the Church of England, hungered for something deeper in his heart. He attended holiness conferences at Oxford and Brighton, England, and came away with a changed heart:

> We were taken out of ourselves; we were led step by step, after deep and close searching of heart, to such a consecration of ourselves to God, as in the ordinary times of a religious life, hardly seemed possible . . . to the enjoyment of a peace in trusting Christ for present and future sanctification which exceeded our utmost hopes.

Battersby's reaction to these conferences was not the result of intense emotion and excitement, but of a deep stirring of his soul.

Battersby and a Quaker friend, Robert Wilson, found themselves so inspired and transformed that they wanted to share their joyful experience with others. They chose a date just three weeks after the Brighton meeting and selected Keswick (where Battersby worked) as the site. They issued invitations to "Union Meetings for the Promotion of Practical Holiness."

The conference almost crashed. Amid rumors of personal wrongdoing, Pearsall Smith, its key speaker, canceled out just days before the opening. Other speakers withdrew.

Nevertheless, the conference opened as scheduled on this day in 1875. About 800 people from all over the United Kingdom attended the meeting, which was held in a tent. Said Battersby:

> The Lord has been showing us, in a wonderful way, that if He chooses to lay aside one instrument, He can and will find others to testify of His truth, and to carry on His work.

"Hole in the Sky," in the beautiful Lake District near where Keswick first gathered. (Courtesy of Norman Johnsen.)

Following Pearsall's withdrawal, the movement came in for harsh criticism. But after much prayer, Battersby and Wilson again determined to hold a meeting the following year. Keswick grew, attracting thousands who longed for a deeper walk with God. Branches formed in many other nations.

What began as a spur-of-the-moment holiness convention held in a tent became a worldwide movement for godliness. Keswick continues to promote Christian discipleship to this day.

Other Events

440 (probable date): Pope Leo the Great announced that Saints Peter and Paul had replaced Romulus and Remus as the patrons of Rome. As a result, Saints Peter and Paul are celebrated on this day.

1555: The first provincial council of Mexico convened in a desperate attempt by the Church to protect the Indians from the rapacity of the conquistadors.

1629: Samuel Skelton and Francis Higginson arrived in Massachusetts on the ship *Talbot*. They were the first Presbyterian pastors in the American colonies.

1810: At the urging of college students, the American Board of Commissioners for Foreign Missions, a Congregationalist body, was formed. It was America's first foreign mission society.

1948: A pastoral letter signed by the Rumanian Uniate Church's Episcopacy on the Feast of Saints Peter and Paul explained why this group remained attached to Rome. The signers were sent to prison; some of them died there.

1959: Abuna Basilios became the first patriarch of Ethiopia not controlled by the Egyptian Copts.

Leo the Great, who declared Peter and Paul the saints of Rome. (Montor, Chevalier Artaud de. *Lives and Times of the Popes*. New York: Catholic Publication Society of America, 1911.)

Thomas Huxley, who defended evolution. (Mitchell, Chalmers. *Thomas Henry Huxley: A Sketch of His Life and Work*. New York: G.P. Putnam's Sons, 1900.)

With the publication of *The Origin of Species by Means of Natural Selection* in 1859, Englishman Charles Darwin unloosed a storm of controversy that to this day has not subsided. Religion and science clashed head-on over the theory. Believers resented what they perceived as Darwin's attempt to rule God out of creation. On the other hand, a certain group of scientists resented inaccurate and closed-minded reactions from the religious community (although the strongest objections came from the scientific community itself). Darwin had amassed an enormous quantity of detail, which he reckoned proved that evolution across kinds had taken place.

Pandita Ramabai prayed earnestly for an outpouring of the Holy Spirit. Her community experienced that outpouring on this day in 1905. (Ramabai, Pandita. *Testimony of Our Inexhaustible Treasure*. Kedgaon, India: Pandita Ramabia Mukti Mission, 1907.)

June 30

Evolution Controversies: Soapy Sam Bested?

On this day in 1860, six months after the publication of *The Origin of Species*, evolution was the topic of a meeting of the British Association. Seven hundred people showed up. An American, Dr. Draper, was to speak on the "Intellectual Development of Europe Considered with Reference to the Views of Mr. Darwin." He spoke for an hour, and then other speakers took off on the theme. A number of churchmen were on the platform, among them Bishop "Soapy Sam" Wilberforce.

The crowd called for popular Soapy Sam to speak. Wilberforce, after attempting to defer to another speaker, finally rose to speak. The great anatomist Sir Richard Owen had coached him in what to say. However, Wilberforce was not deeply grounded in the sciences, so instead of addressing the theory on scientific grounds, he castigated it with good humor and made it appear absurd. The crowd loved his approach.

The agnostic Thomas Huxley had been coaxed into attending the meeting. Carried away with the applause, Wilberforce turned to Huxley with a mocking question: Was it through his grandfather or grandmother that he claimed descent from a monkey?

Huxley slapped his knee and whispered a very un-agnostic comment: "The Lord has delivered him into mine hands." Wilberforce sat down with the audience still applauding his speech. They then called on Huxley, who rose with defiance to speak. He explained Darwin's key ideas and exposed what he claimed was Wilberforce's ignorance and error. He would not be ashamed of a monkey in his ancestry, he said, but he would be ashamed to be "connected with a man who used great gifts to obscure the truth." The crowd applauded. Wilberforce was humiliated.

That was over a century ago, yet the debate still rages on. And, sadly, Christians have often tried to oppose evolution without a full grasp of the scientific arguments that they must address and answer. But in recent years, as the irreducible complexity of life and complete absence of a mechanism to drive evolution becomes ever more apparent, the scientific community itself has sometimes turned to desperate hypotheses such as claiming that life was seeded from outer space. The evolution debate is far from over.

And what of Huxley? Dr. Douglas Adams reported that the great agnostic asked a Christian friend to stay home from church one Sunday morning and share with him all that Christ had done for him. Having listened, Huxley said with tears in his eyes, " I would give my right hand if I could believe that!"

Other Events

1073: Gregory VII (Hildebrand) was consecrated. His reign was marred by continual skirmishes with Emperor Henry II.

1315: Mystic and missionary Raymond Lull is thought to have died on this date. He was persuaded by a vision to seek the conversion of Muslims. He founded a school to train men for the task, studied Islamic culture and may have been stoned in Bougie, North Africa. His memorial is on this day.

1905: An outpouring of the Holy Spirit descended upon Pandita Ramabai's community in India.

The Chief Purpose of Man Debated

"What is the chief end of man? The chief end of man is to glorify God and enjoy Him forever." Those are the astonishing first words of the Westminster Shorter Catechism. We might have expected this instruction book of Christian doctrine to begin with discussions of God, or Creation, or Jesus, or salvation, but it doesn't. You won't find any mention in it of family, jobs, ethics or right doctrine either. Instead, it begins with us and why we are on earth. There is no beating around the bush; it goes right to the deepest, most gnawing question of our entire existence. We are pointed to sheer perpetual pleasure as the underlying reason for our existence and are told that it is readily available if we find it in the One who put us here for His own reasons.

On this day in 1643, the 151 men who gave us that statement met together for the first session of the Westminster Assembly. The assembly was comprised of 10 men from the English House of Lords, 20 from the House of Commons and 121 who were "excellent divines."

The assembly came about because of unhappiness with Church of England doctrine as it stood. In that day, the state ran the only really legal Church in England. However, many Englishmen did not like its forms or the thirty-nine articles that governed it. They appealed on several occasions to the parliament and the reigning king for changes. The people of Scotland even took up arms over the issue. Parliament, which was heavily weighted with Puritans and Presbyterians, was willing to call an assembly of theologians to advise them on the situation, but King Charles I was against it. But, Parliament had reached the point of frequently ignoring King Charles's wishes, so they did so again and issued an order for the assembly to gather.

Can you imagine praying and preaching for eight hours straight? That is what the "excellent divines" did in their first meeting. Dr. Twisse, the chairman of the assembly, opened with a short prayer, then Mr. Marshall followed with two hours of confession for the sins of the members. He was followed by Mr. Arrowsmith, who preached for an hour. And on it went, with more prayers and sermons, a psalm, a short pep talk on the confessed heart, another prayer and a blessing. Robert Baillie, who took notes, said, "This day was the sweetest that I have seen in England."

Sweet though the time may have been, the long sessions that followed still must have been tough to endure. The assembly had to pass rules warning members not to skip prayer, not to whisper to each other during debates, not to change seats and not to bring books and papers to read while the debates were going on.

At first the assembly tried to merely "clean up" the thirty-nine articles of the Church of England. After years of little progress, however, Parliament became impatient. And so the Westminster Assembly changed tack and wrote the Longer and Shorter Catechisms, which are still used all over the world today.

The Westminster Assembly. (Courtesy of the Christian History Institute archives.)

The work was carefully done and backed up by Scripture. The clergy often prepared statements in advance. When two or three rose to speak at once, the assembly shouted the name of the person they wanted to hear. The members voted "yes" and "no" on issues. Usually this was by voice vote, but when the vote was close they stood to be counted.

The assembly also wrote a confession of faith, a book of psalms and a directory for worship and laid out a form for Presbyterian Church government.

Other Events

1555: Queen Mary Tudor's Catholic government burned Protestant John Bradford to death in England. In the Tower of London, he had ministered to criminals. As he was led to his death, crowds lined the way, weeping and praying for the sweet and gentle man.

John Bradford and an apprentice prepare to burn. (Besant, Sir Walter. *London in the Time of the Tudors*. London: A. & C. Black, 1904.)

1750: Jonathan Edwards preached his last sermon at Northhampton, where he had been voted out of the pulpit. He said:

> How often have I spoken to you, instructed, counseled, warned, directed and fed you, and administered ordinances among you, as the people which were committed to my care, and whose precious souls I had the charge of? But in all probability, this will never be again.

1835: Robert Murray McCheyne was licensed to preach at the Presbytery of Annam, where he became a famous pastor. At one time he wrote: "It seems to be making Christ a Minister of Sin to go straight from the swine trough to the best robe." He came to see, however, that "the weight of my sin should act like the weight of a clock; the heavier it is, the faster it makes it go!"

1899: The Christian Commercial Men's Association (now known as the Gideons) was founded by John Nicholson, Samuel Hill and William J. Knights for the purpose of Christian fellowship and evangelistic effort among traveling businessmen.

1903: The Indian warrior Geronimo was baptized on this day in a Methodist church.

The first meeting of the Salvation Army in its ragged tent. (Booth-Tucker, Frederick de Lautour. *The Life of Catherine Booth: The Mother of the Salvation Army*. New York: Fleming H. Revell Co., 1892.)

July 2

The Salvation Army Is Founded

The tent was tattered. Patches sewn onto it merely ripped the rotted canvas further. The ground on which it was pitched was an unused Quaker graveyard. But despite the less-than-auspicious surroundings, the man who preached on this day in 1865 was confident in what he had to say. Using the "scientific" revival methods pioneered by Charles Finney, he pointed to sinners and called them to repentance. When William Booth preached the first of nine sermons in that tattered tent, he did so under the name of the East London Christian Mission. Thirteen years later, that mission became the Salvation Army.

The Salvation Army: Every major city in the United States and Britain has a post, and there are many in other countries as well. Near Christmastime, Salvation Army workers ring bells for donations. Their work helps the poor and suffering wherever they are found.

From his teenage years, Booth had worked in "missions" to save souls. In fact, he had a running skirmish with his Wesleyan Methodist denomination because of his impatience to preach without proper credentials and his eagerness to bring to church the kind of people who left lice on the pews. A comfortable middle-class segment of Methodists tried to restrain him from preaching and at one point took away his membership (class ticket) because he was suspected of being a "reformer," a group they had expelled for calling for evangelization of the poor and outcast.

Later Booth joined the Reformed Methodists and preached around the English countryside. At about the same time, he met the woman who would become his wife, Catherine Mumford, who was deeply moved by the first sermon she heard him preach. She had to go home sick from the meeting, and he escorted her. That was the start of their courtship. They married in 1855. Seldom have a man and wife labored together to do so much good.

Standing in that much-patched tent, the misery of London's millions struck home to Booth. Himself a child of poverty and often at his wit's end as to how to feed his own family, he understood only too well the desperate needs of the poor.

Catherine understood the needs of the poor too. Although she was of higher social standing and better education than her husband, she nonetheless sympathized with the urban poor. She even worked among London's prostitutes, attempting to help them get to the point where they would no longer have to sell themselves for money. She was a strong advocate of female ministry and preached as often as her husband—and just as well, if not better. Often her speaking engagements were the main support for the pair's growing family. Thanks to her insistence on allowing women to preach, the Salvation Army had a majority of women ministers from the start.

The Booths realized that they had to meet more than spiritual needs, for the physical needs of the common people were crushing. And so the Booths attempted, through the Salvation Army, to reach those physical needs. Their approach met furious opposition in its early days, especially from tavern keepers who saw their trade drop off when their clients were converted. Among the Army's most implacable foes were pastors who detested its "brash" methods. Booth was repeatedly attacked and had objects thrown at him. Worse, some of his workers were killed by those who opposed the work they were doing.

Despite such opposition the Salvation Army became a force for good in England, America and many other lands.

James Garfield, Christian President. (Northrop, Henry Davenport. *New Century History of Our Country and Its Island Possessions*. Chicago: American Educational League, 1900.)

Other Events

862: St. Swithan died. This beloved English saint asked to be buried where "passersby might tread on his grave and where the rain from the eaves might fall upon it." When his body was moved to Winchester Cathedral ninety-nine years after his death, it rained for many days, leading to a legend that if it rains on St. Swithan's day, there will be forty days of rain.

1515: William Tyndale was licensed with his master of arts degree. He placed the Bible above philosophy and made a superb English translation of God's Word, which became the basis for several succeeding versions, including the King James (Authorized) Version.

1881: James Abram Garfield, President of the United States and a convert and preacher of the Disciples of Christ, was shot by a disappointed office-seeker. Garfield, not yet fifty, had been in office for only four months. He lingered in great misery for two months before he died.

1946: The Religion Analysis Service began to inform believers about cults and "isms."

1950: Martinez Quintana, an evangelical Christian in Colombia, was shot dead by a Catholic mob.

The Apostle Saint Thomas

Thomas putting his hand on Christ's side. (Bell, Mrs. Arthur. *Saints in Christian Art*. London: George Bell, 1901-4.)

The Brahmin priests were furious. A man named Thomas had come to India from the West, preaching a new religion, and thousands of people were going over to his strange new teaching. And a foolish cult it was too that had as its hero a crucified criminal, whom Thomas claimed was raised to life. But people will believe anything! The priests' control over the minds of the Indian people was in danger, which meant danger to their incomes too. They decided that Thomas must be gotten out of the way.

On this day, July 3, some churches celebrate the Feast of St. Thomas. Thomas was one of Christ's twelve apostles. His name is mentioned by all four Gospel writers, some of whom call him "the twin," but John is the only one who tells us anything about what Thomas said or did.

In Scripture, the first time Thomas is recorded as speaking was when Jesus had just learned of the death of Lazarus. Jesus declared that He would go to visit Mary and Martha, but the other disciples protested because the Jewish leaders in Jerusalem had just tried to kill Him. But Thomas took his master's side. Heroically, he said, "Let us also go, that we may die with him" (John 11:16). If the legends and accounts of his life are true, he proved his bravery again and again in his subsequent career.

Thomas next spoke up at the Last Supper. When Jesus said He must go to the Father, Thomas admitted his ignorance. He said, "I don't know where you are going or the way there" (see John 14:5). In reply, Jesus uttered one of the greatest statements in the Bible:

> I am the way and the truth and the life. No one comes to the Father except through me. If you really knew me, you would know my Father as well. From now on, you do know him and have seen him. (John 14:6-7)

Finally, after Christ rose from the dead, He showed Himself to the disciples. Thomas alone missed that meeting. When the other disciples reported that Jesus had appeared to them, Thomas said he would not believe unless he saw the nail prints in Christ's hands and touched His wounded side. Later, Jesus did appear to Thomas and showed him those wounds.

Thomas immediately understood the implications of what he had been shown. God the Father, by raising Christ from the dead, proved that Christ was all He claimed to be. Thomas fell before Jesus, declaring Him "my Lord and my God!" (John 20:28). This is one of the most triumphant testimonies of faith in the Bible.

After the Holy Spirit came upon the apostles, Thomas carried the gospel eastward. Strong traditions link his name with Iran and India. All accounts agree that he was martyred.

Thomas probably died in India, at Mylapore near Chennai (now known as Madras). According to the best record we have, an angry pagan priest drove a spear through Thomas's body while he knelt in prayer. Unfortunately, Portuguese adventurers who thought that the Christians of Malabar were heretics destroyed precious documents that might have shed light on Thomas's history. And so the writings of Christians who have an ancient church named for Thomas and who can point to a tomb where he was buried are lost forever.

Other Events

529: The dedication of a new church at Orange (modern-day Arausio, France) became the occasion for thirteen bishops to issue a document that clarified the roles of grace and free will in salvation. Pope Boniface II approved the statement when it was submitted to him. The council is known as the Synod of Orange and was responding to theological teachings known as Semi-Pelagianism.

1448: Jean de Lastic, Grand Master of Rhodes, wrote from Ethiopia to Charles VII, king of France, telling about Zār'a Ya'iqob's victories over the Saracens. His letter refers to Prester John, a legendary Christian king who had originally been thought to rule in Asia but was later assumed to rule in Africa.

1907: Pope St. Pius X, in his encyclical *Lamentabili*, formally condemned the "modernist" intellectual movement as it exhibited itself in the Catholic Church.

1973: The Securities and Exchange Commission filed charges against Jerry Falwell's Thomas Road Baptist Church, claiming financial hanky-panky. The church argued that the attack was politically motivated because of Falwell's conservative views. The church eventually won substantial exoneration in court.

Pope St. Pius X, who condemned modernism. (Courtesy of the University of Texas collection of public domain portraits on the Web.)

Anne Boleyn was a friend of Protestants like Frith. (Pollard, Albert Frederick. *Thomas Cranmer and the English Reformation, 1489-1556*. Hamden, CT: Archon Books, 1905.)

July 4

John Frith Burns for His Beliefs

"I understand the Church of God in a wide sense," said John Frith. "It contains all those whom we regard as members of Christ. It is a net thrown into the sea."

Frith was a man of peace in an age when people fought and killed over religious ideas. He believed that any person who lived a godly life for the sake of Christ belonged to Him, whether or not that person held Frith's views. He said:

> The opinions for which men go to war aren't worth the terrible tragedies that they make. Let there be no longer any question among us of Zwinglians or Lutherans, for neither Zwingle nor Luther died for us, and we must be one in Christ Jesus.*

Ironically, on this day in 1533, John Frith, a man of peace and purity, was burned to death at the stake because of his religious views. Frith had quoted Scripture verses to argue that the bread and the wine served at the Eucharist do not actually turn into Jesus's flesh and blood. He had also denied that there is a purgatory after death.

Frith did not seek martyrdom, but he was willing to face it. After joining with Church reformers during his years at university, he was thrown into prison. When freed, he joined William Tyndale in Germany and helped him with his Bible translation. But when Frith remembered the people in England who did not understand how to turn to God, he felt he had to go back, however much danger there was to him.

In England, Frith was arrested as a vagabond. He dared not give his name lest he be executed; he saved himself by quoting elegant Greek and Latin lines to a local scholar. After his release, he secretly went from place to place preaching. Sir Thomas More, who was chancellor to the king for the rest of that year, ordered Frith arrested. He offered a great reward to anyone who would deliver Frith over to the authorities. More's agents hunted everywhere for Frith, just as they hunted everywhere for Tyndale. Frith planned to escape back to Germany, but he was betrayed as he tried to get aboard his ship and he was sent to prison. While in prison, he prayed to be able to convert at least one of his enemies to the truth. His prayer was answered when Sir Thomas More's son-in-law switched to Protestant views.

Frith was killed because of a favor he had done for one of his Protestant hearers while he had still been free. The man had pleaded with Frith to write down his teachings on the Eucharist. Frith hadn't wanted to, but finally agreed. "We must eat and drink the body and blood of Christ, not with the teeth, but with [our] hearing and through faith," he wrote. His views on the Lord's Supper were important because he was the first Englishman to state the essential position that was later adopted by the Church of England as its doctrine.

Unfortunately, Frith's writing fell into the hands of a spy. Frith's enemies had intended for him to pay for his heresy with his life, but when Anne Boleyn became queen, she favored the Protestants, and conditions for captives like Frith were eased. Frith was even allowed out of prison on day passes. But then his writing landed in Sir Thomas More's hands. That sealed Frith's fate. He was convicted and taken to Smithfield to be burned. A young man named Andrew Hewitt was chained with him. Frith encouraged Hewitt to trust his soul to God. It took the men two hours to die, because the wind blew the fire away from their bodies.

*Some of these quotes have been adapted into modern English for ease of understanding.

Pulcheria Augusta, regent of the East, as imagined by an artist. (Brooks, Elbridge Streeter. *Historic Girls: Stories of Girls Who Have Influenced the History of Their Times*. New York: Putnam, 1915.)

Other Events

371: Martin of Tours was consecrated against his will. To escape the press of the world, he founded the first monastery in France.

414: Pulcheria was proclaimed Augusta of the Roman Empire. She convoked the Council of Chalcedon.

965: Pope Benedict V died on this day. Emperor Otho I wanted a different man made pope. So, enraged at Benedict's appointment, Otho held Benedict captive until his death on this day.

993: The first official Roman Catholic saint, Ulrich of Augsburg, was named. Before this, saints were declared rather haphazardly. To formalize the system, the Church established rules of canonization.

1187: Crusader knights were wiped out by Saladin at Jerusalem, negating the gains of the First Crusade.

1648: Antoine Daniel, a Jesuit among the Hurons, was martyred by the Iroquois Indians.

1848: Viscount Rene de Chateaubriand died. Originally a skeptical French historian, he converted to Christianity at his mother's death and wrote *The Genius of Christianity*, showing the superiority of Christianity to other religions. His views did not expunge his vices, however.

July 5

Joking Just Before His Utopian Head Rolled

On this day in 1535, Sir Thomas More, an English genius of letters, wrote his last note using a piece of charcoal. Days earlier he had been sentenced to be hung and disemboweled, but Henry VIII had changed the sentence to beheading. The letter More wrote was to his beloved daughter, Margaret. Because the next day was the Eve of St. Thomas, his namesake, he wrote, "Therefore tomorrow long I to go to God: it were a day very meet and convenient for me."

As a young man, More showed the kind of brilliance that could only lead to eminence. He became a lawyer and also wrote memorable works such as a biography of Richard III and his most famous work, the book *Utopia*, in which he called for reason to master human affairs. From 1518 onward, Henry VIII employed More in his service. For twelve years the humanist rose steadily through the political ranks. He was made undersecretary of the treasury, speaker of Parliament and high steward of both Oxford and Cambridge. He even became lord chancellor. A loyal Catholic, More wrote against the reformers, especially William Tyndale. He opposed Tyndale's attempts to put the Bible into the English language. As lord chancellor, he applied force against "heretics," reportedly even torturing them with his own hands in his home's dungeon. His loyalty to the Church was bound to bring him afoul of Henry when the king proclaimed himself head of the English Church. Other clergy submitted to Henry completely, but More resigned his post, pleading sickness.

Sir Thomas More, so well-known abroad, had to submit to Henry or the king could not rest easy. Every effort was made to trap the wary and scrupulous lawyer, but More could not be bribed and kept close control of his tongue. However, despite his efforts to fade into obscurity on the issue, More was brought before a council called together by Henry and asked why he did not support the king's antipapal action. More explained that he had on numerous previous occasions explained to the king himself why he did not agree with the king's actions. In view of More's extraordinary popularity, it was deemed wise by the council to discontinue their pursuit of him on the issue.

In March of 1534, an Act of Succession was passed that required anyone who was asked to take an oath acknowledging the children of King Henry and Anne Boleyn as legitimate heirs to the throne. More was among those asked to take the oath, and when he refused on April 17, 1534, he was consigned to the Tower of London. At first he was allowed books and visits, but later even those few luxuries were withdrawn.

Meanwhile, More refused to express his opinion on the issues he knew could condemn him. In response, his opponents condemned him for refusing to speak. Sir Richard Rich, the solicitor-general, held a conversation with More and later played the Judas, perjuring himself at More's trial and claiming that More had spoken out against Parliament's authority to confer ecclesiastical supremacy on Henry. On July 1, More was convicted of treason. With nothing left to lose, he declared his opposition to the king's course of action. Afterward he wrote a prayer for the salvation of his enemies and pled for courage:

> Good Lord, give me the grace, in all my fear and agony, to have recourse to that great fear and wonderful agony that Thou, my sweet Savior, hadst at the Mount of Olivet.

Other Events

649: Pope St. Martin I was consecrated. He was known for his fight against Monothelitism, the heresy that said that although Christ had two wills, the human and the divine, the divine was so dominant that it deprived His human aspect of any ability to act.

1809: Pope Pius VII was arrested by Napoleon. Pius had excommunicated the Corsican dictator for grabbing the Papal States.

1985: Ambushers murdered Bob Chappel of Wycliffe Bible Translators, opening fire on his van near Lea, Papua.

Sir Thomas More as chancellor. (Bezold, Friedrich von. *Geschichte der Deutschen Reformation*. Berlin: Grote, 1890.)

Along with the letter in charcoal, More sent his daughter Margaret his hair shirt. He was granted his wish to die the next day. On the morning of July 6, 1535, he was told to make ready.

More joked with the executioner and proclaimed himself the king's good servant, "but God's first." At 9 a.m. he was beheaded. After his bloody death, his head was exhibited on London Bridge. In 1886 Leo XIII beatified More, and in 1935 Pius XI canonized him as an English martyr.

Pope St. Martin I in an artist's rendering. (Montor, Chevalier Artaud de. *Lives and Times of the Popes*. New York: Catholic Publication Society of America, 1911.)

Pope St. Leo as imagined by an artist. (Montor, Chevalier Artaud de. *Lives and Times of the Popes*. New York: Catholic Publication Society of America, 1911.)

July 6

Eastern Schism: Anathema On You Too!

It was inevitable that the division of the Roman Empire into two separate entities would eventually be echoed in the Church. The break came when Michael Cerularius was patriarch of Constantinople and St. Leo was pope in Rome. In 1053, Cerularius circulated a treatise criticizing the practices of the Western Church in strong terms. He said that the Catholic policy that did not allow their clergy to marry was contrary to Scripture and tradition. He also charged that the Catholic practice of using unleavened bread in the Eucharist was wrong. But the most serious of his concerns was that the Latin Church had added the word *filoque* to the Nicene Creed, which meant that the Holy Spirit proceeded from both Father and Son.

Jan Hus. (Bezold, Friedrich von. *Geschichte der Deutschen Reformation*. Berlin: Grote, 1890.)

Cerularius excommunicated all bishops of Constantinople who used the Western ritual and closed down their churches. This incensed Leo. He demanded that Cerularius submit to the pope and stated that any church that refused to recognize the pontiff as supreme was an assembly of heretics, a synagogue of Satan. The Eastern patriarch wasn't about to accept that characterization.

The five patriarchs—of Antioch, Jerusalem, Alexandria, Constantinople and Rome—were equals. The bishop of Rome, as patriarch of the West, was given the courtesy title of "first among equals," and in a tie vote he could make the final determination according to tradition up to that point. However, his power was not to go beyond that. Therefore, Leo's growing claims to authority were deemed unacceptable by his fellow patriarchs, who believed (and who still believe) that Christ alone is the head of the Church.

Leo sent legates, headed by Cardinal Humbert, an unyielding man, to discuss the issues. Before the legates could complete their mission, Leo died. Humbert was so rude to Cerularius that Cerularius refused to speak with him. Aggravated by this treatment, the legates marched into St. Sophia on this day in 1054 and placed a bull on the altar, excommunicating Cerularius. After this act, Humbert made a grand exit, shaking the dust off his feet and calling on God to judge Cerularius.

Cerularius convoked a council and once more blasted Western practices. The Easterners anathematized Humbert and condemned all who had drawn up the bull against them.

There was no chance of reconciliation between the factions. The once-united Church was now divided into two: Eastern Orthodox and Roman Catholic. Later, a number of Orthodox churches submitted to Rome while maintaining their own rites and traditions. These became the Byzantine rite or Uniate churches, which still exist in countries as distant in time and place as the United States.

The rift was inevitable—traditions and doctrine had been diverging for hundreds of years. By the time of the crusades and the subsequent cruelties inflicted by their participants, East and West would be even farther apart. Many of the crusaders' violent acts were against fellow believers of the East whom they did not recognize as Christians. The unity of love that Christ had said should mark His followers was broken.

Other Events

1415: Jan Hus was burned at the stake as a heretic. The Bohemian leader taught against many practices of the Roman Catholic Church.

1813: Granville Sharp died on this day. Sharp had been a member of the "Clapham Sect," of which William Wilberforce was the most prominent voice. Sharp contested slavery, winning an important court ruling that no person could remain a slave upon English soil. He was also a Bible scholar.

1861: James Stewart sailed from Southhampton, England, to South Africa on the *Celt*. In South Africa he founded Lovedale, a training center for African Christians.

JULY 7

Tindley's Faith Set Him Singing

On this day, probably in 1851, Charles Albert Tindley was born in Maryland, a slave state, to a slave father and a free mother. He was sent to work with other slaves, although he had been born free. Despite his difficult circumstances, he taught himself to read and took Bible classes at night.

After the Civil War and emancipation changed the future of America's black people forever, Tindley married and moved north to Philadelphia. To support his wife and himself, the determined man worked as a hod carrier, toting building supplies at the Bainbridge Street Methodist Episcopal Church. He continued his education, studying at a local Bible institution, preparing for the ministry and taking correspondence courses from Boston Theological Seminary.

When Tindley took his examination to become a Methodist minister, he was working as a sexton (essentially a church janitor) at the Bainbridge church. After becoming a minister, Tindley went on to earn his doctorate and teach himself Greek and Hebrew through correspondence courses.

What motivated him was faith. It was the kind of faith that could face a bare table with confidence. At one point there was nothing to eat in the Tindley household. He told his wife to set the table. "Why?" she asked, knowing full well that the cupboards were bare. Tindley insisted, saying that God would provide. Shortly afterward, there was a knock on the door. A man had brought them dinner, saying that his family had cooked too much.

God proved that Tindley's faith was not misplaced and gave him success as a minister. Tindley's booming voice and talent for songs made him an outstanding music leader. He is often credited as the "Father of Gospel Music." In the course of time, he became pastor of the same Bainbridge church at which he had worked as a common laborer. It had 130 members when he took over. Under Charles's leadership, the mixed-race congregation grew to about 10,000 members and had to build a bigger meeting place.

Tindley wrote some of the most original and beloved songs in our hymnbooks, songs such as "Nothing Between My Soul and the Savior" and "We'll Understand It By and By."

Although his church was big, it was poor. Finances were always a problem. Was it from personal experience that Tindley penned stanza two of "We'll Understand It By and By"?

Charles Tindley, the true "Father of Gospel Music." (Courtesy of cyberhymnal.org. Available online at: <http://www.cyberhymnal.org/bio/t/i/tindley_ca.htm>.

We are often destitute of the things
that life demands,
Want of food and want of shelter,
thirsty hills and barren lands;
We are trusting in the Lord,
and according to God's Word,
We will understand it better by and by.

Tindley injured his foot and died shortly after, when gangrene spread from the wound. The victorious pastor was sixty-nine.

Other Events

303 (probable date): Procopius, a valiant young man who stood against pagan worship in Caesaria, was executed on this day. His story was recounted by the contemporary Church historian Eusebius of Caesaria.

1220: Thomas à Becket's shrine was dedicated in Canterbury and became a popular pilgrim attraction. He had been murdered by knights of the English king, Henry II.

1585: On this day, the Edict of Nemours banned all Protestantism and expelled the Huguenots from France.

1878: Francis Grimké, son of a slave, was ordained in the Presbyterian Church in the United States. Abolitionist Angelina Weld had aided him in attending Princeton Theological Seminary. Grimké helped organize the American Negro Academy in 1897.

1944: George Washington Truett died on this day. He pastored the First Baptist Church of Dallas, which grew to 7,800 members. Thousands of people pressed in to hear him preach, and many tried to imitate his example.

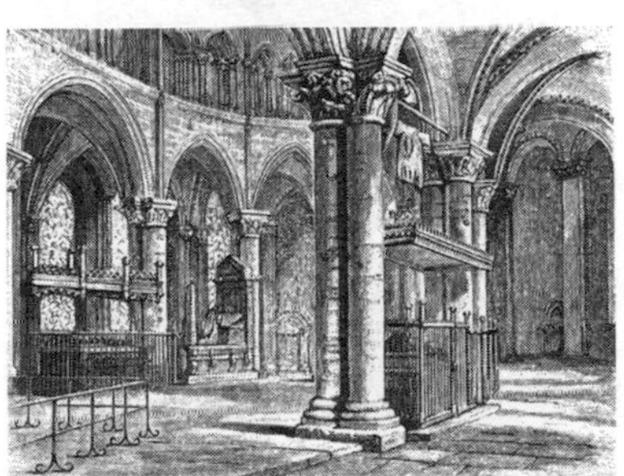

Becket's shrine. (Hare, Augustus J.C. *Biographical Sketches*. London: George Allen, 1895.)

Jonathan Edwards. (Lossing, Benson J. *Eminent Americans*. New York: Hovendon Company, 1890.)

JULY

8

Not His Usual Style

> All you that never passed under a great change of heart by the mighty power of the Spirit of God upon your souls; all that were never born again, and made new creatures, and raised from being dead in sin . . . you are thus in the hands of an angry God; 'tis nothing but his mere pleasure that keeps you from being this moment swallowed up in everlasting destruction.

These words are from one of the most famous sermons in American history, which was preached on this day in 1741.

Jonathan Edwards was ordained into Christian ministry in a Congregationalist church in Northhampton, Massachusetts, in 1727. Having given "all that I am and have to God, so that I am not in any respect my own," he directed his whole intellect to working out the implications of faith and supporting true piety.

Although best remembered for his hellfire sermon, "Sinners in the Hands of an Angry God," Edwards was no hell-fire preacher. He carefully prepared his sermons with detailed logic and read his messages to the congregation. They were all the more powerful for their calm and well-reasoned exposition of Scripture. Salvation is not by works, he taught, but by the grace of God acting in a person's heart. He said that salvation depended upon faith in God's work in Christ on the cross rather than on a person's own works. He also examined and explained the implications of the thoughts of Sir Isaac Newton and John Locke, showing that their discoveries pointed to God, not away from Him.

Edwards was well-equipped to make such arguments. Born in the Puritan town of East Windsor, Connecticut, he was educated at home by his parents. Before he was thirteen he entered Yale College, where his bright and logical mind relished the new sciences. He gained proficiency in Hebrew, Greek and Latin. His youthful scientific essays show acute powers of observation. He also wrote works that were seminal to the field of psychology and, while still a teenager, he worked out an idealism similar to George Berkeley's.

Toward the end of his college days, however, Edwards felt distress in his soul. One day he was reading First Timothy 1:17: "Now to the King eternal, immortal, invisible, the only God, be honor and glory for ever and ever. Amen." Edwards later wrote, "There came into my soul, and was as it were through it, a sense of the glory of the Divine Being; a new sense, quite different from anything I had ever experienced before. . . ." Enraptured by God's majesty and worth, Edwards' heart panted:

> to lie low before God, as in the dust; that I might be nothing, and that God might be all, that I might become as a little child . . . from about that time I began to have a new kind of apprehension and ideas of Christ, and the work of redemption, and the glorious way of salvation by Him.

If Edwards sometimes preached of hell, he also displayed before his listeners the glories of heaven and of the God who had made the universe. He appealed to them to seek holiness. Under his teaching, waves of revival swept through his community and spread outward in what became known as the Great Awakening. With keen insight, he dissected religious experience and distinguished between true and false religious phenomena. But his uncompromising rebukes against sin and his refusal to permit the unconverted to partake of the Lord's Supper led him into difficulties with his congregation. Unwilling to walk all the way with him, they dismissed him in his twenty-third year with them.

In the face of this blow, Edwards trusted God without fear. He had been ordained to preach the gospel, and preach he did, to the Housatonic Indians and a small white congregation. Later he accepted the headship of the College of New Jersey (now Princeton) but died within a month of his appointment. He who had preached, "Therefore let everyone that is out of Christ now awake and fly from the wrath to come," died in good conscience.

One of his last works was his *Dissertation Concerning the End for Which God Created the World*. In it he showed that God's ultimate purpose in creation is not the salvation of man and the redemption of the world but the revelation of His own glory.

Blessed Pope Eugene III. (Montor, Chevalier Artaud de. *Lives and Times of the Popes*. New York: Catholic Publication Society of America, 1911.)

Other Events

1153: Blessed Pope Eugene III died. He had fled to France because of disturbances in Rome. There he held several synods and promoted intellectual revival in the Church.

1868: Russian evangelical Stundists made their first defense before the high authorities of their nation. The Stundists aroused anger by opposing the use of icons in churches. Later they merged with the Baptists.

1884: Isaac A. Dorner died on this day. He was a Lutheran theologian who remained Christ-centered even while incorporating the insights of Immanuel Kant, Georg Hegel and Friedrich Schleiermacher into his writings.

July 9

Nineteen Die Defending the Catholic Faith

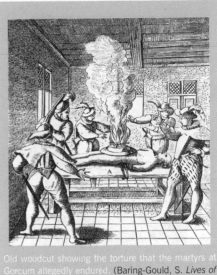

"You may all go free if only you will admit that the pope is in no way head of the Church."

The pressure was on, but the nineteen Catholic prisoners refused to repeat the required words. They had already refused to renounce the doctrine of transubstantiation, the teaching that the bread and the wine of the Eucharist actually become the body and the blood of Christ.

During the religious wars that followed the Reformation, hideous atrocities were perpetrated on both sides. Another such perpetration was about to take place. Catholic Spain had ruled the lowlands of northwestern Europe with an iron hand. In defiance of Spanish rule, however, much of the region became Protestant. Later, Catholics and Protestants alike united in rebellion against Spain, but their unity soon broke down over religious differences. Catholic Spain tortured Protestants; Protestant mobs smashed Catholic images and looted their churches. Eventually, after the little states won freedom from Spain, the Catholics formed the nation we know as Belgium, while Protestants formed the Netherlands. But meanwhile, there were pockets of Catholics within Protestant areas.

One such pocket was in the small coastal town of Gorcum. It had two Catholic parishes and a Franciscan friary. Much of the Protestant resistance was carried on from the sea by fighters known as Sea Beggars. The Sea Beggars seized Gorcum on June 26, 1572. They captured the Franciscans and some other Catholic leaders.

After their capture, the men were held in prison for several days. Then, early in July, they were brought by boat to Briel. There they were paraded around the town square and forced to sing the Litany of the Saints while their Calvinist captors jeered. Compelled to debate with Calvinist preachers, they clung to their Catholic beliefs.

Meanwhile, the farmers and fishermen of Gorcum demanded their religious leaders back. Even Protestants called for mercy on the men. William of Orange, leader of the resistance, sent an order commanding that priests and other religious leaders be left alone.

But Lumey, the admiral of the Sea Beggars, had other ideas. He ordered the men hanged. On this day in 1572, under the supervision of an ex-Catholic priest, they were strung up in a turf shed outside Briel and mutilated. Among the nineteen who died that day was Joannes van Hoornaer, a brave Dominican, who when he had heard that the Franciscans were in captivity, hurried to administer the sacraments to them. He died along with those to whom he had ministered. Another priest also voluntarily joined them. This man was notorious for his womanizing. When this was pointed out to him, he said, "Fornicator I always was; heretic I never was."

Old woodcut showing the torture that the martyrs at Gorcum allegedly endured. (Baring-Gould, S. *Lives of the Saints*. Edinburgh: John Grant, 1914.)

Other Events

381: A general church council began at Constantinople. It reaffirmed the Nicene Creed, but its statement has not survived.

1584: William of Orange, leader of the Protestant revolt in the Netherlands against Catholic Spain, was stabbed to death. His last words were "My God, have mercy on my soul and on these poor people."

1609: A royal charter issued by King Rudolf II allowed freedom of conscience to Bohemians.

1926: Sister Alphonsa, Rose Hawthorne Lathrop, died on this day. She was the daughter of the Unitarian novelist Nathaniel Hawthorne but became a Catholic convert and the foundress of hospices to help cancer victims.

1949: When the Roman Catholic Internuncio to Czechoslavakia (now the Czech Republic) returned to Rome, the Communist government of Czechoslovakia did not allow his successor into the country.

Rose Hawthorne Lathrop founded a cancer hospice. (Courtesy of the Dominican Sisters of Hawthorne archives. Used by permission.)

Japanese Original

Toyohiko Kagawa. (Kagawa, Toyohiko. *Love, The Law of Life*. Philadelphia: The John C. Winston Co., 1929.)

Japan has never been very receptive to the gospel. Missions begun on the small island nation have received little response. While the work of such men as Francis Xavier and Nikolai Kasatkin, was exceptional in bringing thousands to a Christian confession, the work of others generally produced only handfuls of converts. This is true not only of foreign missionaries but also of Japan's foremost homegrown missionary, Toyohiko Kagawa.

Kagawa was born on this day in 1888. Both of his parents died while he was very young. As a teenager, he became a Christian under the influence of Presbyterian missionaries and was baptized. He received theological training at Kobe and at Princeton University.

After almost losing his life to an illness, he vowed to help the poor. At that time, Japan was going through great upheavals due to its transition to capitalism. Common laborers suffered much during this time. Kagawa moved into a slum in order to be able to witness about Christ to the people living there. "I am a socialist because I am a Christian," he said. He slept in hovels the size of a jail cell and shared what little he had with all who were in need. More than that, he organized Japan's first labor and peasant unions. With the coming of Communism, he increased his emphasis on the kingdom of God. His activism convinced the government to rebuild the slums.

Kagawa is recognized as a successful author as well as a missionary. He wrote a best-selling autobiographical novel entitled *Across the Death Line* and another called *Before the Dawn*. His other writings include several pamphlets and various meditations. He used the revenue from his books for relief for the poor, while he and his family subsisted on a small monthly salary.

For Kagawa, the cross symbolized the power of the love of Christ and the power of suffering for the sake of righteousness. That is why he chose Japan's worst slums as his field of labor and lived among those whom he sought to help.

Despite the good work that he did among the poor of Japan, Kagawa was not highly regarded in Japanese theological circles. His own explanation of this was:

> There are theologians, preachers and religious leaders, not a few, who think that the essential thing about Christianity is to clothe Christ with forms and formulas. They look with disdain upon those who actually follow Christ and toil and moil, motivated by brotherly love and passion to serve. . . . They conceive pulpit religion to be much more refined than movements for the actual realizations of brotherly love among men. . . . The religion Jesus taught was diametrically the opposite of this. He set up no definitions about God, but taught the actual practical practice of love.

The emperor of Japan posthumously awarded Kagawa Japan's highest honor, the Order of the Sacred Treasure. One year after Kagawa's death, a two-volume work entitled *Biography of Kagawa by 103 People* was issued. Doctors, professors, patients, workers, writers, teachers and others each contributed an essay to the book in testimony to the work that Kagawa had done.

William Jennings Bryan. (Courtesy of the University of Texas collection of public domain portraits on the Web.)

Other Events

Annual: The feast of Antony of the Caves, founder of Russian monasticism, is celebrated on this day. Antony died in May of 1073.

1922: The chief medical officer of the Nigerian government trekked for two days to Egbe, deep in the nation, to inspect the new maternity center that had been constructed by pioneer missionary Tommy Titcomb. When he arrived, he looked around and asked where the hospital was. The missionary pointed to a group of rude thatched huts and explained that they were the hospital. Seeing that the chief medical officer was ready to turn around and begin his return journey, the missionary convinced the officer to enter the buildings. As they walked over and around mothers and babies everywhere, the medical officer said, "I don't understand this at all. We have a beautiful hospital in Ilorin, and yet we've never been able to get the mothers to come. Here your building is full."

"Doctor," Titcomb answered, "we can explain that. This little place is built on love and the Word of God. . . . In all our work we have but one purpose—to tell these people about God's love for them in Jesus Christ." The inspector filed a favorable report.

1925: The Scopes Monkey Trial began on this day. The state of Tennessee had forbidden the teaching of evolution in its public schools. William Jennings Bryan, a fundamentalist lawyer, argued the prosecution case and won, but since then, popular culture has assigned the victory to Clarence Darrow.

First Quakers to Reach Boston Are Arrested

July 11

The authorities in Boston, Massachusetts, were dismayed. Aboard the *Swallow*, which had just sailed into harbor on this day in 1656, were two Quaker women, the first Quakers to reach the colony. At that time, Massachusetts was a Puritan commonwealth. Its leaders believed that a Christian state had an obligation to regulate religious belief and behavior. They felt that admitting believers from other denominations would eventually unbalance the arrangement between government and Church. They thought this was especially true of Quakers, who were notorious for their acts of civil disobedience whenever their personal convictions conflicted with government policy. To most denominations of the day, the Quakers, with their rejection of traditional theology, could be defined with one word: *heretics*.

Deputy Governor Richard Bellingham acted quickly. He confined Ann Austin and Mary Fisher to the ship they had arrived on and ordered the public executioner to burn all of the literature the women had brought with them. He knew that the power of print could go where evangelists could not and was determined to keep the Quaker "propaganda" away from the people of Massachusetts.

On second thought, it seemed better to Bellingham to place the women where the state, not a shipmaster, had control of them. So he brought them ashore: Austin, an old woman and the mother of five children; Fisher, a thirty-three-year-old former serving maid. Earlier that year Fisher had been whipped in England for saying that it was wrong to make a vocation out of preaching.

In Boston, the two underwent a severe ordeal. They were examined by the magistrates and

> found not only to be transgressors of the former laws, but to hold very dangerous, heretical, and blasphemous opinions; and they do also acknowledge that they came here purposely to propagate their said errors and heresies, bringing with them and spreading here sundry books, wherein are contained most corrupt, heretical, and blasphemous doctrines contrary to the truth of the gospel here professed amongst us.

Bellingham refused them food. He cut off their light by boarding up the prison window and refused them candles and writing materials. Both were stripped and searched for signs of witchcraft. Bellingham would have been pleased to have hanged them had anything been found. To ensure that no one caught their radical ideas, the men in power declared that anyone attempting to speak with the women would be fined five pounds— a hefty amount in those days.

The Quaker women had come by way of Barbados to publish the truth as they saw it. Now hunger gnawed at their bellies, but they continued to pray. It seems God heard them, for an innkeeper bribed the jailer five shillings a week to smuggle food to the hungry women.

A Quaker prisoner. (Perry, William Stevens. *The History of the American Episcopal Church: 1587-1883*. Boston: J.R. Osgood, 1885.)

At the end of five weeks, the Massachusetts government brought the women out and sent them home on the ship that had brought them. The ship's captain was made to deposit £100 as a guarantee that he'd return them to England. No doubt the Puritans hoped to make the transportation of Quakers a money-losing proposition for ship owners.

Eventually, sterner measures were used against Quakers. Some were whipped, some were abandoned in forests, some had their ears cut off and some were hung. But Quakers kept coming and their persistence eventually helped win America's civil rights.

Other Events

1533: After wavering on the decision, Pope Clement VII excommunicated King Henry VIII of England and annulled his divorce and remarriage.

1742: Benedict XIV issued the bull *Ex Qu Singulari*, which removed the "permissions" that had allowed Chinese Christians to vary from Roman practice, especially in the matter of ancestor veneration. The new restrictions outraged the Chinese emperor, who subsequently expelled most Catholic missionaries from China.

1870: When it became known that an evangelical group called the Stundists (similar to Baptists) were returning icons to their priests, saying that they no longer needed them, Orthodox Russians were outraged. Persecution and exile followed for many Stundists, and in 1894 Stundism was outlawed by the state as a "particularly dangerous sect" for this and other reasons.

1953: Tanganyikan bishops issued a pastoral letter titled "Africans and the Christian Way of Life." They addressed the politics, education and economics of Tanganyika.

Pope Clement VII, who excommunicated King Henry VIII. (Pollard, Albert Frederick. *Thomas Cranmer and the English Reformation, 1489-1556*. Hamden, CT: Archon Books, 1905.)

An artist's rendering of David Brainerd riding away from an Indian camp. (The teepees are inaccurate.) (Courtesy of the Christian History Institute archives, Glimpses #79.)

JULY 12

Sterling Conversion, Unspeakable Glory

David Brainerd lived for only twenty-nine years, but what he did with those few years inspired many to follow Christ. Some, such as William Carey and Henry Martyn, followed his footsteps onto the mission field.

At the age of seven Brainerd began to seek the Lord. His journal shows that he struggled greatly in coming to Christ. To replace self-righteous works with faith seemed to him a very difficult thing to do. He found himself struggling to prefer God's glory over his own salvation. His physical health might well have aggravated his spiritual struggles. But despite his struggles, Brainerd found peace at last. It began with an utter sense of lostness:

> One morning while I was walking in a solitary place (as usual) and came near a thick bunch of hazels, I felt at once unusually lost and at the greatest stand and felt that all my contrivances and projections respecting my deliverance and salvation were brought to a final issue.

From Friday morning through Sunday evening he was in the greatest agony of spirit, eventually feeling that the Spirit of God had quite left him. In his own account of his subsequent conversion on this day in 1739, he said:

> By this time the sun was scarce half an hour high, as I remember, as I was walking in a dark thick grove, "unspeakable glory" seemed to open to the view and apprehension of my soul. By the glory I saw I don't mean any external brightness, for I saw no such thing, nor do I intend any imagination of a body of light or splendor somewhere away in the third heaven, or anything of that nature. But it was a new inward apprehension or view that I had of God; such as I never had before, nor anything that I had the least remembrance of it. I stood still and wondered and admired.

He came to want to exalt God above all things, as had Christ, and remained in great joy for about a week.

After his conversion, Brainerd enrolled for his ministerial degree at Yale. He was not allowed to receive the degree he had earned, however, because he was accused of commenting that one teacher had no more grace than a chair. Although Brainerd swore he had no recollection of making the remark, he offered to apologize. His offer was refused. Three professors who took his side resigned and were later instrumental in founding Princeton.

Brainerd, despite his problems at Yale, was commissioned by the Scotland Society for the Propagation of Christian Knowledge as a missionary to the Indians. He labored for about three years among several races until ill health forced him to leave. Engaged to marry one of Jonathan Edwards' daughters, he was nursed in that preacher's home, where he died on October 9, 1747. Edwards preached Brainerd's funeral service and edited his journal, adding comments of his own. It was published under the title *The Life of David Brainerd*.

King Henry II of England does penance for urging the murder of Archbishop Becket. (Jameson, Mrs. *Legends of the Monastic Orders*. London: Longmans, Green, and Co., 1872.)

Other Events

1174: King Henry II of England did public penance after Thomas á Becket's assassination, which his hasty words had instigated.

1536: The convocation (the lower house of English Parliament) accepted ten articles, the first confession of faith of the newly formed Church of England.

1536: Erasmus, the popular scholar whose writings fostered the Reformation, died on this day.

1555: Four Protestants—John Bland, John Frankesh, Nichols Sheterden and Humphrey Middleton—were burned at the stake in England under Queen Mary's Catholic government for having refused to deny their faith.

1612: John Cotton took the pulpit at St. Botolph's in Boston, England. He would move on to Boston, New England, where he won fame as an American founding father. He said many pithy things, such as:

> God did not love us for our goodness, neither will he cast us off for our wickedness. Yet this is no encouragement to licentiousness, for God knows how to put us to anguishes and straits and crosses, and yet to reserve everlasting life for us.

1691: François Fenelon received a mild censure from the pope for some of his writings. King Louis XIV of France had pressed hard for condemnation of Fenelon's writings. Upon receiving the censure, Fenelon immediately preached the virtue of obedience to superiors.

July 13

A Miserable, Dirty Town for the Judsons

Adoniram Judson is often singled out as the first American foreign missionary. This is only partly true. When he sailed for India in 1812, he was but one of four men traveling as Congregationalist missionaries to the Orient. His wife, Ann, was with him as well. The credit of evangelizing Burma is as much hers as his, if only because she saved his life so that he could carry on the work. Her ability to learn the language greatly assisted his efforts. Her letters home made their adventures so vivid in the minds of Americans that "Judson" became a household name.

Although the Judsons sailed as Congregationalists under the mission board that Judson had helped to form, in a curious twist he did not remain Congregationalist. On the ship on the way to India, he became convinced that his Church's doctrine of baptism was incorrect. Once they reached Calcutta, the Judsons were baptized by immersion. They immediately broke their connection with the board that had sent them out and appealed to Baptist churches of the United States to form a new mission to support them. This became a reality, and now there were two missions rather than one, both instigated by Judson.

The Judsons were expelled from India by the British East India Company, so they sailed to Burma and began a work there. On this day in 1813, the two first laid eyes on Rangoon, the city where they began their Burmese work. It was "a miserable, dirty town." The houses were made of thatch and there was virtually no sewage system—filth flowed into the creeks and was carried off at high tide.

The Judsons soon discovered that spiritual fruit would be slow in coming. Christianity was not favored by the king, and so brutal was the despotism of the overlords that the common people dared not embrace the new faith. It took five years before the Judsons baptized their first convert.

In the meantime, Judson preached in a building he built in the city. He and Ann mastered the Burmese language, and while he labored to translate the Bible, she produced a catechism. To find words to convey religious meaning, they often had to turn to a related language because Burmese lacked the necessary vocabulary.

In 1824, when England and Burma went to war, Judson was imprisoned as a spy. Ann worked night and day for his release. Both suffered greatly. Judson was hung in torturous positions. Ann lost her health because of a difficult labor, a tropical fever and her exertions to free her husband. Their sickly child did not survive long. Ann died shortly after Judson's twenty-one-month captivity ended. After his release and Ann's death, Judson suffered despair and depression.

Thirty years after Ann and he first left the United States, Judson returned to his native country for a short visit, after which he went back to Burma. He died soon after his return. He left behind 7,000 converts. Today the Burmese Church has grown to over 2 million.

Judson displays his newly completed Siamese Bible. (Armitage, Thomas. *A History of the Baptists: Traced by Their Principles and Practices, From the Time of our Lord and Saviour Jesus Christ to the Present*. New York: Bryan, Taylor and Co., 1893.)

Other Events

574: Pope John III died on this day. During his lifetime, the Lombards repeatedly ravaged Italy.

1787: The Northwest Ordinance was adopted by the Congress of the United States. It included wording showing that religious instruction was an important consideration of the government.

1825: Henry Blodget was born on this day. An American, he became a missionary to China for the Congregational Church. During his forty years of service, he helped translate the Bible into a Mandarin dialect.

1960: Joy Lewis, wife of apologist C.S. Lewis, died on this day. He later wrote *A Grief Observed*, detailing the spiritual comfort that had finally eased his anguish over Joy's death.

1968: Henry F. Blood of Wycliffe Bible Translators died of pneumonia and malnutrition while in Vietnamese hands. Captured in the Tet Offensive six months earlier, his character impressed fellow captive Mike Benge, who became a Christian.

Henry Blodget, missionary to China. (Beach, Harlan P. *Dawn on the Hills of T'ang or Missions in China*. New York: Student Volunteer Movement, 1905.)

JULY

14

Keble and Company

John Keble, who preached the sermon that set the Oxford Movement going. (Lock, Walter. *John Keble, A Biography*. London: Methuen, 1894.)

Sunday, July 14, Mr. Keble preached the Assize Sermon in the University Pulpit. It was published under the title of "National Apostasy." I have ever considered and kept the day, as the start of the religious movement of 1833.

So wrote John Henry Newman as the closing words of Part III of *Apologia Pro Vita Sua*. The religious movement of which he spoke was the Oxford Movement, a stirring toward reformation by the high church adherents of the Church of England. ("High church" refers to those elements of ritual and doctrine which hark back to Roman Catholic roots.) The movement's immediate cause was the attempted suppression by the British government of ten bishoprics in Ireland, but the reform leaders were also disturbed by a general decay and loss of moral fiber in the Church. At issue also were the words of the creed, "I believe in one holy catholic and apostolic church," which the rapid fission of Protestantism into sects seemed to set at naught.

Keble declared that England had been acknowledged as a Christian nation for centuries. Logically this meant that the nation was bound by the laws of Christ's Church. If public opinion was calling for action in defiance of those laws, the nation was apostate. Oxford men of the highest caliber gathered around Keble and tried to form a plan of action. Among these were the notable scholars John Henry Newman and Richard Hurrell Froude.

In order to bolster its position, the Oxford Movement sought a basis for authority in the past of the Church. They looked to creeds and apostolic succession as outward manifestations of ancient authority. Some of the intellectuals who joined the movement also took an interest in reviving the architectural styles and arts that had long been associated with the faith. Newman and others sought a new level of spiritual life for the Church. Newman promoted these ideals by preaching a sermon titled "Holiness Necessary for Future Blessedness."

The Oxford Movement began as an effort to reform the Church of England. It reached a crisis in 1841 when Newman issued Tract 90 in his continuing series. The tract claimed that the thirty-nine articles of the Church of England could be interpreted in a Catholic way. In the furor that resulted, he was forbidden to publish more such tracts as a Church of England clergyman. He resigned his positions and, like Henry Manning and William Ward, became a Roman Catholic. Keble, Edward Pusey and Charles Marriott remained in the Church of England and took leadership of the Oxford Movement. The overall effect of the movement was to restore a higher level of spirituality among the English clergy. It also forced a reexamination of the doctrinal and authoritative bases of the Church.

Bonaventure, who was highly regarded as a spiritual writer and leader. (Endres, Jos Ant. *Die Zeit de Hochscholastik: Thomas von Aquin*. Mainz: Kircheim & Co., 1910.)

OTHER EVENTS

1274 (or July 15): St. Bonaventure, a Franciscan philosopher, theologian and mystic, died on this day. Bonaventure became the leader of the Franciscans, in which capacity he had to settle many disputes. Pope Sixtus IV canonized him in 1482.

1773: The first American Conference of Methodist Preachers commenced this day, headed by Thomas Coke and the zealous general superintendent, Francis Asbury.

1850: J. Neander died. Born a Jew named David Mendel, he changed his name to Neander ("New Man") at his conversion and became an influential historian of the Church. He authored the hymn "Praise to the Lord, the Almighty, the King of Creation."

1857: Baptism of Ting Ang, the first Methodist convert in China.

JULY 15

Scientists and Christians

When Charles II chartered the Royal Society on this day in 1662, it was the first scientific society in history. Not surprisingly, active Christians, with their interest in God's creation, brought it into existence. In fact, its original membership was overwhelmingly Puritan in makeup. It grew out of the meetings of the so-called "invisibles" who gathered at the home of Robert Boyle's favorite sister, Katherine. She supported the parliamentarians (and Puritans) in the revolt against Charles I. She had a deep intelligence and welcomed the group into her house so that she might share their new findings.

Since they were not bound by tradition, Puritan schools fostered the study of science. Theodore Haak, a professor at the largely Puritan Gresham College, initiated the meetings of the "invisibles." Other Protestant schools revolutionized medicine at about the same time, and it was a Protestant school that trained John Dalton, the author of modern atomic theory. Chief architect and secretary of the Royal Society after the Restoration was John Wilkins, whose religious inclinations later led him to become a bishop and to prepare arguments in defense of Scripture.

John Willis also helped inaugurate the Royal Society. Considered one of the best doctors of his generation, he was so strong in his attachment to the Church of England that he was cold-shouldered at the royal court, which was inclined toward Romanism. Among his charities, he funded a clergyman to conduct worship services at hours when average working men could attend.

Robert Boyle's faith is well-known, not only because of the apologetics he wrote but because he endowed a lecture series to defend Christianity. He assisted persecuted Welsh clergymen. In addition, he subsidized Scripture translation and did research into Bible languages. An innovative chemist, he gave us Boyle's Law of Gases and wrote a book that exploded alchemy. He is often called the "Father of Modern Chemistry."

Christopher Wren, perhaps the most accomplished man of his day, was also a founding member of the society. Best known for rebuilding St. Paul's Cathedral, he was an anatomist who prepared the drawings for Willis's *Cerebri Anatome*. He was also a geometer (Newton classed him among the best), a physicist who did crater impact studies, a meteorologist and a surveyor. He attempted some of the first blood transfusions and made microscopic studies of insects. He was also a man of solid faith.

The motto adopted by the organization was "Nothing by mere authority." Almost every famous scientist of Britain has been a member since then, including Sir Isaac Newton.

Sir Christopher Wren, one of the early members of the Royal Society. (Milman, Lena. *Sir Christopher Wren*. London: Duckworth and Co.; New York: C. Scribner's Sons, 1908.)

The Christian roots of modern, self-replicating science run deep. Those who think faith must blind us to fact should look again at the history of the formation of the Royal Society.

OTHER EVENTS

1099: Jerusalem fell to the First Crusade. The "Christians" butchered and looted indiscriminately.

1549: Led by Francis Xavier, Spanish Jesuits became the first Christian missionaries to enter Japan.

1801: A concordat between Napoleon and the Vatican reestablished the Catholic religion in France, where it had been suppressed in the French Revolution.

1846: President Lincoln noted he had "never denied the truth of the Scriptures; and I have never spoken with intentional disrespect of religion in general or of any denomination of Christians in particular." Rumors had it that he had mocked Christianity in prior years.

1851: Anne-Marie "Nanette" Javouhey an extraordinary peasant girl who took the gospel to French territories in Africa and South America, died on this day.

Napoleon made a deal to reestablish the Roman Catholic Church in France. (Lester, Charles Edwards. *The Napoleon Dynasty, or The History of the Bonaparte Family. An Entirely New Work*. New York: Cornish, Lamport & Co., 1852.)

Edmund Campion. (Taunton, Ethelred. *The History of the Jesuits in England, 1580-1773*. London: Methuen, 1901.)

July 16

A Diamond of England Surrounded and Taken

Edmund Campion was a brilliant lad. At thirteen years old, the schoolboy was called on to recite a Latin greeting for Queen Mary when she entered London in 1553. As a student at Oxford he shone. Elevated by Elizabeth when she came to the throne, Campion's future looked rosy. Lord Cecil called him a "diamond of England." After he fled England, Campion wrote highly praised dramas.

Campion left England because of his faith. As a Roman Catholic, he was unwilling to renounce pope for queen and therefore was forced to leave or stay and face persecution. He escaped England and took vows as a Jesuit. Posted at first to Prague, he later was recalled to Rome. There he was ordered to infiltrate England and minister to English Catholics. As Christopher Buckley and James MacGuire portray it in a stage play, Campion replied with horror, "I'm to return to England." A priest with him said, "Edmund, you've got to do something. It's a death warrant."

Although knowing this quite probably to be true, Campion nonetheless remained faithful to his Jesuit vows and obediently returned to England. In preparation for his inevitable capture and death, he wrote his "Challenge to the Privy Council," otherwise known as "Campion's Brag." In it he insisted that his reasons for returning to his homeland were not political:

> My charge is of free cost to preach the Gospel, to minister the sacraments, to instruct the simple, to reform sinners, to confute errors; in brief, to cry alarm spiritual against foul vice and proud ignorance, wherewith many [of] my dear countrymen are abused.

Campion's courage and brilliance (combined with genuine holiness) restored heart to the Catholics to whom he ministered. For a year he eluded his captors, moving from home to home. In the end, however, he was betrayed. A government agent, pretending to be a devout Catholic, obtained entrance into a house through a past friendship with the household cook. Campion was saying mass there and the agent got word to the local authorities. A sheriff and his men surrounded the house on this day in 1581, and the next afternoon, after many hours of searching,

> David Jenkins, by God's great goodness, espied a certain secret place, which he quickly found to be hollow; and with a pin of iron which he had in his hand . . . he forthwith did break a hole into the said place: where then presently he perceived the said priests lying close together upon a bed . . . where they had meat and drink sufficient to have relieved them three or four days together.

Campion was racked, offered bribes and tortured. Because he refused to recant, he was hung, drawn and quartered at Tyburn. At his sentencing, he said, "In condemning us you condemn all your own ancestors—all the ancient priests, bishops, and kings—all that was once the glory of England. . . ." He might have added, "and of Europe." The brilliant "diamond of England" suffered a brave martyrdom for his faith.

Statue commemorating Junipero Serra. (James, George Wharton. *Palou's Life of Junipero Serra*. Pasadena, CA: G.W. James, 1913.)

Other Events

1338: German princes declared at Rense that an emperor's authority comes directly from God and is awarded by the electors' votes without need of papal approval.

1769: Father Junipero Serra founded the San Diego Mission. The Franciscan settlement was the first permanent Spanish site in California.

1773: Pressured by those who feared the growing power of the Jesuits, Pope Clement XIV dissolved the order. It was restored forty-one years later by Pope Pius VIII.

1805: Johann Christoph Blumhart was born in Stuttgart, Germany. Reared a Pietist, Blumhart became a pastor but grew sick of his powerless Christianity. "I wish all this religious warmth and comfort would die," he said, and he set out to deal with the sick, mentally ill and demon-possessed, for whom he founded a spa at Bad Boll. In another memorable remark, he declared, "People don't need Christianity. They need Christ."

1972: Moiseyev was martyred by the Soviets. The young soldier lived a life of such faith that many of his comrades were converted. Soviet authorities claimed his death was an accidental drowning.

July
17

First Sermon from the "Joy to the World!" Man

In the annals of hymn writing, Isaac Watts shines as a leading luminary. In other Reformation countries, hymns were employed in worship, but they were seldom used in the English Church before Watts was born. Anglicans sang the Psalms. Psalm singing, which at first had been a welcome innovation, had deteriorated into a kind of chant. Each line was first read out by a clerk and then sung back by the congregation. Through Isaac Watts' influence, that began to change.

Watts was born in Southampton, England, on this day in 1674. He fell under conviction for his sins in 1688 and learned to trust Christ to erase them about a year later. His father was twice imprisoned for refusing to bend to the Church of England's beliefs. Some of that pluck carried over to Watts, who refused to take an all-expenses-paid education at the personal cost of conforming himself to the Church of England. After attaining his education under more difficult circumstances, Watts became a preacher. He gave his first sermon on this day in 1798 at Mark Lane in London. His qualities were such that the church soon named him its assistant pastor. Shortly afterward, he became seriously ill and suffered such poor health for the remainder of his life that he was often unable to carry out his church duties.

A kindly friend, Sir Thomas Abney, took Watts under his roof, and there Watts lived for thirty years. The church also showed much wisdom and charity in continuing to support him despite his fevers and neuralgia. A lady who fell in love with him from reading his hymns rejected an offer of marriage to him when she saw how small and ugly he was. Despite her rejection of him, however, they continued to write to each other.

Watts may have lacked physical beauty, but the beauty of his words found their mark. Scarcely a hymnbook today in the English-speaking nations is without one or more of his hymns. Psalm singing had fallen into a sad state, and Church leaders were seriously questioning what to do. Watts boldly called for a new kind of psalm, rewritten in light of the New Testament gospel: "We preach the gospel and pray in Christ's name, and then check [stifle] the aroused devotions of Christians by giving out a song of the old dispensation."

Acting on his own word, he published a collection of Christianized psalms in 1719. Even before this, in 1707, he published his *Hymns and Spiritual Songs*. Among them is the renowned carol "Joy to the World!" These songs, not his sermons, are his true gift to the Church, and they inspired Charles Wesley's even more successful endeavors.

Isaac Watts, who revived church singing with modernized Psalms. (Daniels, W.H. *Illustrated History of Methodism in Great Britain and America, From the Days of the Wesleys to the Present Time*. New York: Phillips & Hunt, 1880.)

Watts faced fierce opposition. Many church leaders were opposed to his efforts and some called his hymns "Watts' Whims." The common people, however, delighted in them. Eventually the Church of England revised its stand and began adding hymns to its worship. Some of Watts' most famous songs present the gospel, as found in "When I Survey the Wondrous Cross":

When I survey the wondrous cross
  On which the Prince of glory died,
My richest gain I count but loss,
  And pour contempt on all my pride.

Other Events

180: Twelve simple Christians were condemned and died bravely in Carthage.

431: The Council of Ephesus I ended. Presided over by Cyril, bishop of Alexandria, it deposed Nestorius.

885: Pope St. Leo IV died. He built up the defenses of Rome and crowned Louis II emperor.

1274: The Council of Lyons II ended. An attempt was made to reunite the Eastern and Western Churches, but although accord seemed to be reached, nothing came of it.

1917: Charles Fuller was converted under the preaching of Paul Rader, a former boxer and wrestler. Unable to muster enough courage to go forward in front of all the people at the meeting, Fuller drove to a nearby park and turned his life over to Christ under the shade of an eucalyptus tree. He went on to become a minister and a widely heard preacher on the *Old Fashioned Bible Hour*. He was also a cofounder of Fuller Theological Seminary.

Cyril, bishop of Alexandria. (Baring-Gould, S. *Lives of the Saints*. Edinburgh: John Grant, 1914.)

First Female Doctor

Teresa of Avila. The Holy Spirit as a dove speaks to her. (Colvill, Helen Hester. *St. Theresa of Spain*. New York: Dutton, 1909.)

The town of Avila sits almost exactly in the heart of Spain. Teresa, who was born in 1515 in Avila, was molded by the throb of passion in Spain, that most fiercely Catholic of European nations. Spain's romances, saints, conquistadors and knights appealed to the headstrong girl.

At the time of Teresa's youth, the Moors still held bastions of power within Spain. As a child, perhaps only five years old, she talked her older brother into sneaking out of town with her so they could enter Moorish territory and become martyrs for Christ. An uncle found them and brought them back. Later, she ran away to a nunnery. After reading the writings of St. Jerome, she longed for a deeper, stricter life. But as she herself admitted, she went to the nunnery less for love of Christ than for hope of a quick entrance into heaven.

Statue of St. Thomas Aquinas, the great Dominican scholar. (Endres, Jos Ant. *Die Zeit de Hochscholastik: Thomas von Aquin*. Mainz: Kircheim & Co., 1910.)

While still young and new to the nunnery, Teresa became seriously ill. No remedy worked to cure her. After several years of worsening health, she fell into a coma and was thought by the sisters to be dead. They would have buried her had not her father forbidden it, swearing that life still remained in her. After four days of lying unconscious, Teresa woke to severe pain and paralysis. Only after three years of suffering did she regain the full use of her legs.

Teresa began to feel that she was wasting her life in the convent. While teaching others to pray, she found that she herself could not commune with the Lord for a long time because she felt herself to be a hypocrite, living a life displeasing to the Lord. Aware of the frivolity of her course and its baneful effect on her prayer life, she groped to be closer to Christ. Then she began to see visions. Some attributed them to demons; others encouraged her to trust them. During this time, she mentored the ecstatic mystic St. John of the Cross. Together they became the founders of the Discalced (shoeless) Carmelites.

Teresa was no idle visionary. Practical at heart, she became a leader of reform in the Carmelites and founded many nunneries dedicated to a deeper walk with Christ. No one was to enter those houses except women devoted to spiritual living. Let other nunneries be places to deposit women who had no other home. Hers would be no such thing.

Heavy managerial duties fell on Teresa. It was a struggle to find enough for her nuns to eat; their living conditions were sometimes deplorable. Teresa did her best to overcome these limitations.

In addition to her work among the Carmelites, she also wrote religious and meditative books. One of her superiors commanded her to write an autobiography, which she did. She also wrote *Way of Perfection* and *Meditations on the Canticle*. In her writing she transcended the ideas of love she had imbibed from romances as a child:

> [R]eal love of God does not consist in tear-shedding nor in that sweetness and tenderness for which we usually long . . . but in serving God in justice, fortitude of the soul and humility.

Her mystical writings won her enduring fame. On this day in 1970, Pope Paul VI named Teresa of Avila the first ever female doctor of the Church. She took her place beside such great names as St. Augustine and St. Jerome.

Other Events

1323: Thomas Aquinas, one of the greatest of the scholastics, was canonized by Pope John XXII. Thomas wrote *Summa Theologica* and the *Summa Contra Gentiles*. He synthesized Aristotelian thought with Christian.

1870: The dogma of papal infallibility in faith and morals was enunciated on this day. Catholics opposed to the dogma of papal infallibility adopted the name "Old Catholics." Inspired by Professor Dollinger of Munich, they held a tradition similar to that of the Anglicans.

First Women's Rights Convention

"It is high time we publicize the wrongs done to women," said Elizabeth Cady Stanton. It was July of 1848. Of the five women gathered in Martha Wright's home in Waterloo, New York, all of them except Stanton were Quakers. One of them, Lucretia Mott, was a preacher of some note. Most had been active in the movements against alcohol and slavery and had attended numerous conventions.

"You're right," they said. What women needed was a convention to air their views. It still galled them that at the World Anti-Slavery Convention held in London in 1840, Mott and Stanton had been refused participation even though they were official American delegates. In fact, they had been forced to sit behind a screen during the convention. It was time to end this bias, they said. Action must be taken!

And so action was taken. An ad in the *Seneca County Courier* on July 14 read:

> A Convention to discuss the social, civil and religious condition and rights of women will be held in the Wesleyan Chapel, at Seneca Falls, N.Y., on Wednesday and Thursday, the 19th and 20th of July, current; commencing at 10 o'clock, A.M.

Elizabeth Cady Stanton was delegated to draw up a document representing the sentiments of the women. Modeling her manifesto on the American Declaration of Independence, she stated eighteen wrongs perpetrated against women and emphasized strong religious reasons for women's rights: "All men and women are endowed by their Creator with inalienable rights."

Stanton also pointed out that a woman must be allowed to act as her conscience dictates:

> [B]eing invested by the Creator with the same capabilities and same consciousness of responsibility for their exercise, it is demonstrably the right and duty of woman, equally with man, to promote every righteous cause by every righteous means; and especially in regard to the great subjects of morals and religion.

Christ Jesus treated women with respect. Not surprisingly, Christianity has elevated women more than any other world religion. And so it was that Christian women in a Christian church acting on a largely Christian agenda initiated the women's rights movement on this day in 1848.

About 300 people gathered for the convention, most of them women. All of Stanton's resolves passed unanimously, except the demand for the right to vote. "Why, Lizzie, thee will make us ridiculous," Mott protested. But ex-slave Frederick Douglass encouraged the women to go for it. As Stanton later said, "[T]he power to make the laws was the right through which all other rights could be secured."

The Seneca Falls meeting was booed across America, but it did succeed in drawing attention to gender discrimination. Despite this hopeful beginning, however, it was seventy years before women obtained the right to vote. When that day came, only one of the women who had attended the Seneca Falls convention was still alive to cast a ballot.

Quaker Lucretia Mott was at the center of the first women's rights conference. (Foster, Warren Dunham, ed. *Heroines of Modern Religion*. New York: Sturgis & Walton Co., 1913.)

Other Events

64: Rome burned on this day. Emperor Nero blamed its destruction on Christians, who were then persecuted.

1099: Three years after setting out, the soldiers of the First Crusade defeated the Saracens (Muslims) at the Battle of Ascalon, a Palestinian city. Christians controlled the Holy Land for a century after that.

1759: St. Seraphim of Sarov was born at Kursk, Russia. He was the original and most famous Staret, which literally means "spiritual teacher." He entered the monastery of Sarov when he was nineteen years of age. For forty-five years he led the life of a contemplative, first in the monastery and then later in an isolated hut.

1838: Christmas Evans, considered one of the greatest Welsh preachers, died on this day.

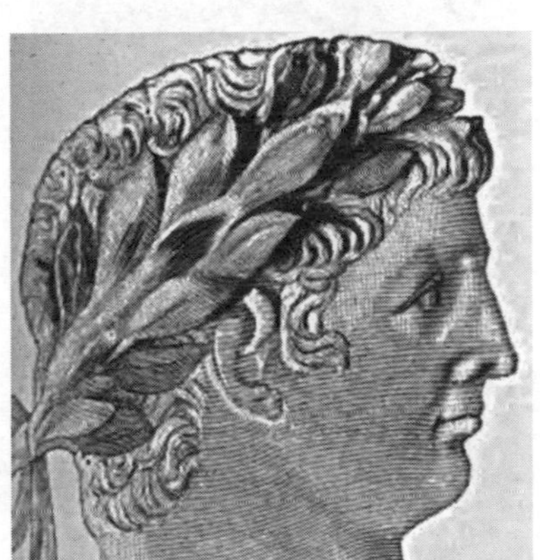

Nero, who used Christians as scapegoats. (Courtesy of the University of Texas collection of public domain portraits on the Web.)

Believe it or not, Peter Lombard was more popular throughout the Middle Ages than Thomas Aquinas (who is shown here). (Endres, Jos Ant. *Die Zeit de Hochscholastik: Thomas von Aquin*. Mainz: Kircheim & Co., 1910.)

JULY

20

Author of the Famous *Sentences* Dies

As Peter Lombard sharpened his goose quill, his mind groped for an illustration. The Trinity was truth, but a truth no less difficult to explain in the twelfth century than it is today. He wrote:

> No sufficient knowledge of the Trinity can be had. Nor could it be had . . . without the relation of doctrine or of inward inspiration.*

That did not mean that nothing could be said on the subject, he hastened to add. Things that we can see help us understand invisible things:

> Memory, understanding, and will are one: one mind, one essence. . . . In those three, a kind of trinity appears. So the rational mind considering these three and that one essence in which they appear, extends itself to contemplation of the Creator and sees unity in trinity and trinity in unity. For it understands that there is one God, one essence, one principle.

The Trinity was just one issue that Lombard dealt with. Medieval scholarship relied heavily on authority, so to make the task of students and professors easier, the well-read teacher gathered crucial quotes from the main authorities on a subject into one work. Lombard's compilation of the quotes of religious authorities became known as the *Four Books of Sentences*.

Lombard arranged quotes from the Bible and from the Church fathers by topics into divisions called books. He subdivided all this material under questions. Since the authorities often did not agree on the answers to those questions, he analyzed their language and gave his own resolution between them. But when it suited him, he made no attempt to resolve their differences. On the whole, little in the work was original to him—which was as he intended.

In spite of this, *Sentences* became the foremost theology textbook of the thirteenth century, admired for its superb organization. Long after Lombard died, which is sometimes said to have occurred on this day in 1164,** his work was the standard text in universities. In fact, it held a prominent place until the sixteenth century. It was more popular than Thomas Aquinas's writings.

One reason for the popularity of *Sentences* was that Lombard left many questions open, giving later scholars an opportunity to suggest their own answers. Scholars who wanted to make a name for themselves wrote commentaries on Lombard's *Sentences*. Among those who did so were such famous scholars as Thomas Aquinas, St. Bonaventure, John Duns Scotus and William of Ockham.

As is often the case, popularity brought Lombard's work under attack. One complaint against him was that he stressed the divinity of Christ over His humanity. But the Fourth Lateran council (1215) upheld this orthodoxy.

Because of his influence as the author of *Sentences*, Lombard also influenced church doctrine. He wrote that a sacrament is both a symbol of grace and a means to grace. He decided that seven Church functions fulfilled his conditions: Baptism, Confirmation, Eucharist (Protestants call it Communion), Penance (confessing a sin and receiving a discipline for it), Extreme Unction (anointing with oil as a symbol of repentance and healing, usually when a person is at death's door), Holy Orders and Matrimony. The Council of Trent adopted Lombard's position as the official doctrine of the Roman Church. For the most part, Protestants limit the sacraments to Baptism and the Lord's Supper.

*The quotes from Lombard's writings on the Trinity are adapted into modern English from Runes' *Treasury of Philosophy*.

**The 1956 edition of *Encyclopedia Americana* gives this day as the date of his death.

Isaac Backus, influential Baptist leader in New England. (Armitage, Thomas. *A History of the Baptists: Traced by Their Principles and Practices, From the Time of our Lord and Saviour Jesus Christ to the Present*. New York: Bryan, Taylor and Co., 1893.)

Other Events

1054: Earlier in the year, the Roman Catholic Church had slapped an excommunication on the rail of the Hagia Sophia. In retaliation, the Orthodox Church issued an excommunication against the Roman Catholic Church.

1751: On this day, Isaac Backus decided to resolve the issue of baptism to his own satisfaction once and for all. As a result he became an influential Baptist minister.

1903: Pope Leo XIII died. A most noble-minded man, poet, scholar and peacemaker, he defended the divine nature of Christ in all its phases, from Virgin Birth through Resurrection and Ascension, and answered Renan's skeptical *Life of Christ*. He issued encyclicals against Socialism and for Thomism (the philosophy of St. Thomas Aquinas). His relations with the Church in the United States were close.

1962: Pope John XXIII invited churches that were separated from the Roman Church to send observers to the upcoming Vatican II ecumenical council.

July 21

Abolished but Still Controversial

The Society of Jesus (Jesuits) was founded during the Reformation era in 1534. St. Ignatius of Loyola became the society's first general when Pope Paul III approved it in 1540. Famed missionary St. Francis Xavier was one of the original seven Jesuits. A deep love of Christ animated those first Jesuits and many more after them.

The Jesuits were a driving force in the Counter-Reformation. Their energy and drive carried Catholicism beyond its pre-Reformation bounds and gained territory equivalent to that which had been lost to Protestants. By emphasizing missions and education, the Jesuits exerted an influence beyond their numbers. Not that their numbers remained small—even before Ignatius's death the society had almost a thousand members. In time, it became the largest of the Roman Catholic orders. Jesuits became known as the schoolmasters of Europe and were prominent as confessors to kings and emperors.

Their influence was resented. This was partly their own fault. The Jesuits developed a system of logic and morality called casuistry, which seemed to offer loopholes for all sorts of wrongdoing. In France, Blaise Pascal wrote his blistering *Provincial Letters* to expose alleged Jesuitical abuses. Elsewhere, Jesuitical controversies over rites, their theological disputes and their close adherence to Rome earned them many foes.

Because Jesuits took their orders from no local authority but only the popes and their own generals, they were viewed with suspicion as foreign agents. Such was the case with Edmund Campion and Robert Southwell, who were Jesuit missionaries to England. Both were executed, although there was no evidence that either had committed treason. They had merely administered the Catholic rites to congregations that had been driven underground.

Cries against the Jesuits rose louder and louder until, on this day in 1773, Pope Clement XIV dissolved the order completely. (It had already been abolished in France and Spain.) Clement refused to condemn the society but merely noted he was making an administrative move for the peace of the Church. The effect of the order's suppression was hurtful for the Roman Church, for it shut down much mission work and many schools.

Some Jesuits were allowed to remain in existence, and in 1814 the society was restored. Today's Jesuits are sometimes almost as controversial as their forebears. In South America some are closely identified with "liberation theology," which many Catholics consider heretical because of its emphasis on worldly aims and a materialistic interpretation of doctrine.

Jesuits boarding coaches to leave Paris. (Ridpath, John C. *Cyclopedia of Universal History*. Cincinnati: Jones Brothers Publishing, 1890.)

Other Events

1495: Savonarola was summoned to Rome to answer charges about his role in reforming Florence. Convinced that his life was in danger, he refused to go.

1829: Priscilla Jane Owens, who became a teacher in Baltimore's schools and at the Union Square Methodist Episcopal Church, was born. For her Sunday school kids she wrote the delightfully upbeat hymns "We Have an Anchor" and "We Have Heard the Joyful Sound." She died in 1907.

1900: Albert Schweitzer received his licentiate in theology. He became famed as a musicologist, theologian, doctor and missionary. Although liberal in his thinking, he clung tenaciously to the doctrine of Christ's resurrection.

1936: Bill McChesney, an American who became a missionary to the Congo (then Zaire), was born. While in the Congo, he was murdered by Simba rebels on November 25, 1964.

1958: A state prosecutor raided the Monastery of the Black Mother of God in Poland, outraging Polish Roman Catholics who venerate the site.

Savonarola medal. (Villari, Pasquale. *Life and Times of Girolamo Savonarola*. New York: C. Scribner's Sons, 1888.)

Cameron lifts a prayer at Ayrsmoss. (Dryerre, J. Meldrum. *Heroes and Heroines of the Scottish Covenanters*. London: S.W. Partridge, 1897.)

July

22

Lion of the Covenant

On this day in 1680, a company of English dragoons (heavily armed mounted troops) surprised and surrounded a Scottish preacher and his small band of armed men. Deciding to fight to the death rather than be taken against his will, the leader of the Scottish group, Richard Cameron, prayed, "Lord, spare the green and take the ripe." The skirmish took place at Ayrsmoss and sprang out of the complicated web of religion and politics that composed English and Scottish relations at the time.

King Charles II had imposed Church of England forms of worship on parts of Scotland. Cameron was born in one such region and grew up accepting the English forms. But in many places, Scots did not accept the imposition of English rule on their religious beliefs and practices. They swore to a covenant to uphold their Presbyterian tradition. After hearing Presbyterian outdoor preachers, Cameron converted to their beliefs. Because he had a natural gift of oratory, Covenant leaders felt Cameron was called to preach the gospel. And so he became an outdoor preacher, embracing the sternest position of the Scottish reformers, which held that anyone who had accepted an indulgence to return to the Anglican worship should be shunned. Cameron had been tutoring the children of Sir Walter Scott (not the famed novelist), but Scott dismissed Cameron, saying his views were too radical.

No doubt Scottish resentment against the English played a part in forming Cameron's position. Nonetheless, he had the gospel at heart. Thousands hung on the words of his sermons, weeping when his eloquent appeals for repentance and submission to Christ touched their hearts. After receiving ordination in the Netherlands (no one in Scotland dared do it), Cameron returned home to preach.

During Cameron's absence from Scotland, Charles II had offered another indulgence and Cameron attacked it savagely. With other religious leaders he drew up the revolutionary Sanquhar Declaration, which disowned Charles II's authority and went so far as to boldly declare war on him. Cameron prophesied the overthrow of the Stuart line for, among other things, "usurping the royal prerogatives of King Jesus." Cameron was nicknamed the "Lion of the Covenant" for his fierce advocation of Presbyterian ideals.

Needless to say, Cameron's life was in danger. A reward of 5,000 marks was placed on his head. A small band of guards accompanied him when he traveled, but their swords proved insufficient when they were charged by English dragoons. The Scots put up a fierce resistance, but in the end, the dragoons hacked the Scots to death and Richard Cameron died. His head and hands were cut off and displayed on an Edinburgh gate.

"They that take the sword shall perish with the sword," said Jesus (Matthew 26:52, KJV). That Cameron took up the sword in defense of his beliefs was hardly surprising. John Knox, the man who more than any other brought the Reformation to Scotland, taught that a people's elected leaders may overthrow tyrants who resist God's law.

The English partly fulfilled Cameron's prophecy regarding the Stuart line. In a bloodless revolution, Parliament drove James II into exile and summoned William III of Orange to the throne. However, William and Mary ruled by right of Mary's Stuart blood.

The attack on Beziers. (Courtesy of the Christian History Institute archives.)

Other Events

259: Dionysius was elected bishop of Rome. His commentaries won many to the faith, and his labors helped restore a Church decimated by severe persecution.

1209: Beziers, France, was captured and sacked during the Albigensian "Crusade." Many in the town were Catholic. The papal legate was reported to have said, "Kill them all; God will know His own."

1660: Nonconformist pastor Richard Baxter preached a sermon on "The Life of Faith" to King Charles II of England. It is doubtful that the sensual king profited much from the lesson.

1680: Madame Guyon of France claimed to have achieved union with Christ on this day. Her mysticism inspired Bishop François Fenelon to seek a deeper spirituality. Guyon's writings breathed passion for Christ, but she was imprisoned by the Catholic Church.

Jenny Hurled a Stool

Charles I, king of Great Britain, wished to enforce his will upon the Church of England. For this and other mistakes, a largely Puritan Parliament separated his head from his shoulders. Long before that fateful day, however, Charles made one of his most grievous mistakes. He elevated a tyrannical bishop to become archbishop of Canterbury, the highest position in the Church of England.

This was none other than William Laud, a stickler for minute forms and details in worship. Like Charles, Laud wanted to return as nearly to Catholic forms as the break with Rome would permit. In fact, many Scots thought that Charles wanted to make Britain Catholic again. They saw Laud's changes and rules as a prelude to that step.

Laud persecuted Puritans and Presbyterians fiercely. The Puritans were those who wished to purify the English Church of those elements carried over from Catholicism that they considered to be superstitious or erroneous. The Puritans had suffered grievously at Laud's hands. Some, like Alexander Leighton and William Prynne, had been mutilated and jailed.

One of Laud's "innovations," bent on restoring the Church to its former practice and power, was the introduction of a new service book. Laud was big on having people bow at the name of Christ and follow all the rules of the *Book of Common Prayer* with exactitude.

The effort to enforce the new service book was met with outrage. Most congregations caused such a stir that their bishops wisely did not even try to implement Laud's orders. In Edinburgh, however, in a church attended largely by the king's local dignitaries and supporters, the clergy determined to follow the archbishop's order. They proceeded to do so on this day in 1637.

Unfortunately for the dean who began to perform the revised ritual, common folk also attended the church. They were immediately in an uproar over the change and called the dean the devil's spawn. At that time the women had no pews—they sat on stools they themselves brought to church. One, identified as Jenny Geddes, picked up her stool and hurled it at the dean. Dozens of other outraged churchgoers threw objects at the clergy, and, when the bishop remonstrated them, someone threw a stool at him too.

The crowd had to be cleared by force because they refused to listen to their magistrates. Laud's experiment in restoring the high church services had failed. Laud himself was imprisoned in 1640 and brought to trial a few years later on charges of high treason. William Prynne, whom he had mutilated, was set as judge over him and returned a guilty verdict with relish. Laud was beheaded.

The stool that Jenny Geddes threw at a church dean who was trying to implement the revised rituals proposed by William Laud. (Maxwell, David. *Bygone Scotland*. London: William Andrews & Co., The Hull Press, 1894.)

Other Events

1184: Fontevrault Abbey, France, received a papal bull of privileges. Women were permitted a good deal of autonomy without supervision by men.

1431: The Council of Basel opened and continued despite orders from the pope to disband. It claimed to have authority over popes, so it is not accepted by Rome as a legitimate council. Pope Eugene, however, ratified some of its pronouncements.

1583: London printer John Day, whose press fed the Reformation of England, died on this day. Among the works he printed was *Actes and Monuments* (now known as *Foxe's Book of Martyrs*). A period of exile on the continent during the reign of Queen Mary enabled Day to acquire the latest advances in printing technology, which he put to use when Queen Elizabeth ascended the throne.

1742: Susannah Wesley, mother of the evangelists Charles and John Wesley, died. She overcame poverty and ill health to leave a lasting impression on the world through her children.

1764: Gilbert Tennent died on this day. He was a strong supporter of George Whitefield's evangelistic ministry, so much so that the Presbyterian Church divided over revival methods. Later, he helped reunify the factions.

Susannah Wesley, mother of Charles and John Wesley. (Courtesy of the Christian History Institute archives.)

Thomas à Kempis: Did he author *The Imitation of Christ*? (Herbermann, Charles G., et al, eds. *Catholic Encyclopedia*. New York: Robert Appleton, 1908-14.)

July

24

Thomas à Kempis: Priest, Monk and Writer

By the fifteenth century, the Church in Europe was filthy with corruption. Popes, cardinals and bishops lived in gross sin. But among many common people and certain leaders, there was a hunger for decency and a longing for closeness to God.

This desire manifested itself in many ways. Reform movements sprang up and were often subsequently crushed by the leaders of a corrupt Church. Mystics gained multitudes of followers. And the Brethren of the Common Life, founded by a wealthy Dutchman named Gerard Groot, came into being. After living for many years in the luxury of the corrupt Church, Groot's heart changed, and he began to preach repentance. After a time, he was forbidden to preach. Then he became a teacher, and youth flocked to him. He spent his entire inheritance promoting his vision of a simple life enriched with mysticism and ordinary work. The chief concern of the Brethren was to imitate the life of Christ.

Groot died young of the plague, but his work lived on. Soon there were several communes of the Brethren in the Netherlands. To one of these communities, young Thomas Hammerken ("Little Hammer") came from the German town of Kempen, following in the footsteps of an older brother who had already joined the Brethren. Hammerken received a warm welcome and ended up spending seventy years with the Brethren, holding various positions and earning his keep by copying manuscripts.

Hammerken, better known as Thomas á Kempis, became a priest and preached sermons, some of which still survive today in written form. Among his other writings was a chronicle of his community, Mount St Agnes. His most famous writing was a devotional classic called *The Imitation of Christ*. Since he published it anonymously, it has been credited to many other individuals. Some scholars still dispute his authorship, but its use of unusual words is similar to that of his other manuscripts. Also, copies exist with his name on them, and people who survived him spoke of him as the author. Today, most scholars agree that at the very least he compiled the book.

The Imitation of Christ encouraged mystical devotion to our Savior and distrusted the human intellect. Here is a little of what á Kempis had to say about the Eucharist:

> What means this most gracious honor and this friendly invitation? How shall I dare to come, I who am conscious of no good on which to presume? How shall I lead You into my house, I who have so often offended in Your most kindly sight? Angels and archangels revere You, the holy and the just fear You, and You say: "Come to Me: all of you!" If You, Lord, had not said it, who would have believed it to be true? And if You had not commanded, who would dare approach?

Thomas à Kempis died on this day in 1471. Although contemporaries considered him a saint, he was not named one by the Catholic Church. However, the Episcopal Church honors him on this day.

Other Events

1216: Cencio Savelli was consecrated pope, taking the name Honorius III. He is especially notable for confirming two major religious orders: the Dominicans and the Franciscans.

1534: Christian explorer Jacques Cartier, who claimed Canada for France, made the European discovery of the St. Laurence River.

1816: Charles Bowles, an African-American, preached his first sermon. He was a Freewill Baptist who spoke with such authority that racists who had come prepared to throw him into a pond repented and asked to be baptized in it instead.

1921: C.I. Scofield, who edited the influential Scofield Reference Bible, died on this day. Its notes have influenced many Christians. He also pastored churches and founded a mission to Latin America.

1934: The Rhineland Women's Auxiliary in Nazi Germany joined the Westphalian Auxiliary in backing the Barmen Declaration of the Confessing Church, which resisted the Nazis.

Jacques Cartier at Hochelaga in 1535. (Leacock, Stephen. *The Mariner of St. Malo: A Chronicle of the Voyages of Jacques Cartier*. Toronto: Glasgow, Brook & Company, 1915.)

July 25

Henry IV Rejects His Childhood Faith

Henry IV, "the Great," remains the most popular of the French kings. However, there was a time when it was doubtful that he could take the throne. The chief difficulty lay in the fact that he had been reared a Protestant (French Huguenot) in a nation whose majority was Roman Catholic.

By renouncing Protestantism, Henry escaped the St. Bartholomew's Day Massacre in which Catholics butchered several thousand Protestants. He was held captive by the French royal family, but he escaped and rejoined the Protestants and led them to successful victories. Meanwhile, the deaths of key members of the royal line made him the legal heir to the French throne.

However, the pope had excommunicated Henry for his religious views. French Catholics might have appreciated his flair, but were unwilling to see a "heretic" on the throne. The Catholic league had even gotten a law passed that barred Henry from the throne.

Moderate Catholics, however, recognizing that Henry was the only person with a real hope of governing the war-torn country, urged him to renounce his childhood faith and become a Catholic. Henry replied that one's religion was not as easily changed as one's shirt. Nonetheless, he talked with his advisors, and they assured him that one could be saved as truly in the Roman Church as under Calvinism.

Four-and-a-half years passed between the day when the throne became vacant and Henry's announcement that he would convert to Catholicism. In July of 1593, he made his way to Saint-Denis to speak with a score of Catholic bishops and theologians, who helped him resolve his remaining questions. His last objections removed, Henry abjured Protestantism on this day in 1593.

Dressed in white satin, the heir to the throne marched through the hot streets of Saint-Denis accompanied by trumpeters, a Swiss guard and many nobles. The crowds shouted "*Vive le roi!*" ("Long live the king!") as he passed. At the Basilica of Saint-Denis, an archbishop met Henry and heard him ask to be received into the communion of the Catholic, apostolic Roman Church.

"Do you truly desire it?" asked the archbishop.

"Yes, I wish and desire it," said Henry. Popular legend also has him say at some point, "Paris is worth a mass." This is probably fiction.

Still, Henry's problems were not over. The pope wanted to make an example of him and refused to remove his excommunication without forcing humiliating penances on Henry. However, political dangers and King Henry VIII of England's break with the Catholic Church brought the pope to a more reasonable attitude.

When Henry became king, he issued the Edict of Nantes, protecting the rights of his former Protestant allies. He adopted policies which, for the most part, brought peace and prosperity to France. The chief blot on his character was his passion for mistresses. He was assassinated by a dagger-wielding fanatic seventeen years after his famous abjuration.

Henry IV, who allegedly said, "Paris is worth a mass." (Courtesy of the University of Texas collection of public domain portraits on the Web.)

Other Events

408: St. Olympias, a deaconess and the friend of the notable preacher and martyr John Chrysostom, died. She sent Chrysostom money when he was exiled. She also showed courage in refusing to marry a man whom the emperor picked for her.

1587: Japanese general Hideyoshi banished the Jesuits from Japan. He had tolerated them for many years for economic reasons, although their presence in the nation was technically illegal.

1795: William Romaine, an evangelical preacher, spoke his last words, "Holy, Holy, Holy Blessed Jesus! To thee be endless praise," and died around midnight.

1817: John Fawcett, who wrote the hymn "Blest Be the Tie That Binds," died on this day.

1823: Benjamin T. Roberts was born. He was converted at age twenty and was admitted to the Genesee Methodist Conference. In 1857 he wrote an article criticizing the Methodists for departing from foundational truths. Kicked out of the ministry for this, he became a key player in founding the Free Methodists. Seventeen years after his death, the Methodists acknowledged they had wronged him.

Benjamin T. Roberts founded the Free Methodists. (Roberts, Benson Howard. *Benjamin Titus Roberts, Late General Superintendent of the Free Methodist Church*. North Chili, NY: The Earnest Christian Office, 1900.)

William Wilberforce, friend of the slaves. (Meakin, Annette M.B. *Hannah More, A Biographical Study*. London: Smith, Elder & Co., 1911.)

July

26

Liberation at Last—As He Lay Dying

No man fought as hard to abolish slavery as William Wilberforce did. A member of Parliament, he introduced anti-slavery measures year after year for forty years until he retired in 1825. On this day in 1833, as he lay dying, word was brought to him that the bill to outlaw slavery everywhere in the British empire had passed in Parliament. The dream for which he had struggled for decades was within sight of fulfillment!

Wilberforce had not always been a serious opponent of slavery. When he was younger, he was a witty, somewhat dissipated man-about-town who misspent his time at Cambridge. He was invited to every party in town.

A friend of William Pitt (who became prime minister) and a member of Parliament, Wilberforce seemed assured of a bright political future. And then in 1784, after winning his election in Yorkshire, he accompanied his sister, who was going to the Riviera for her health. Isaac Milner, a tutor at Queen's College Cambridge and an acquaintance of Wilberforce's from his college days, was asked along, and he agreed to go.

Milner had become a deep and evangelical Christian. He began to persuade Wilberforce to commit his life to Christ. Wilberforce had always thought himself a Christian, but his talks with Milner shed light on the fact that he needed to make a total commitment to Christ. He struggled in anguish for several months. For part of that time he read Philip Doddridge's *The Rise and Progress of Religion in the Soul* and witnessed in it a faith far deeper than anything he had known. Gradually he yielded.

At once he began to wonder if it was proper for him to hold a seat in government. He confided in Pitt, who, wanting Wilberforce as an ally, urged him to remain for the good he could do. Still unsettled in his conscience, Wilberforce conferred with John Newton. Newton, remembered today as the author of the hymn "Amazing Grace," had been converted while a blasphemous sailor and slaver. He counseled Wilberforce to remain in politics and to champion good causes.

Pitt and other of Wilberforce's friends suggested that he take up the slavery issue. After many doubts, Wilberforce decided it was what God wanted. He also felt he must tackle causes that would raise the standard of life and morals in England. The friends who gathered around him and supported him in his work became known as the Clapham Sect because most of them lived in the village of Clapham.

Rarely in history have so many owed so much to so few. These dozen or so Clapham men and women not only fought against slavery but also against every sort of vice. Many of the sect members were wealthy, and they employed their worldly goods on behalf of godly causes. Education of the masses, support of Bible societies, private charity, protection of chimney sweeps, creation of Sunday schools and orphanages—these and dozens of other causes received their attention. But it is the abolition of slavery that remains their greatest achievement.

Thomas Babingdon Macaulay, whose influential speech became the evangelical position on India. (Trevelyan, G. Otto. *The Life and Letters of Lord Macaulay*. New York: Harper & Brothers, 1876.)

Other Events

1581: The northern provinces of the Netherlands declared independence from Spain, which persecuted their Protestant faith.

1622: Japanese Christians John Mat Suzuki and Paul Tsukamoto were decapitated for their faith.

1804: Hieromonk Gedeon began a preaching tour among the Kodiak of Alaska, which led them to become Orthodox Christians.

1833: Thomas Babingdon Macaulay made a speech on the question regarding India's governance, outlining the positions he felt Britain should take. Influenced by Christian ideals, he urged that India be given self-rule. His speech became the evangelical position on India.

1837: Phoebe Palmer, an American Methodist, received sanctifying grace. Her experience challenged many others and gave impetus to the Methodist holiness movement.

1869: By obtaining royal assent to a bill to disestablish the Anglican Church as the state Church of Ireland, British Prime Minister Gladstone hoped to improve English relations with Ireland.

1987: Peter Dyneka, evangelist to East Europeans, died on this day. Russian-born, he was converted after migrating to the United States. For his energetic efforts to spread the gospel he was known as "Peter Dynamite."

July 27

Clement of Ohrid Is Laid in the Earth

The grief at St. Pantaleimonth's Monastery was deep. On this day in 916, the founder of their monastery was to be laid to rest. Everyone recognized that a mighty man had passed from among them.

Clement of Ohrid (a town located in what is now Bulgaria) had died just a few days earlier. With his passing went a link to the heroic age of Cyril and Methodius, apostles to the Slavs. Clement was one of the five faithful disciples whom Cyril and Methodius had entrusted with carrying on their mission after they died. The others were Nahum, Gorazd, Angelarius and Sava, all "of equal learning and maturity as apostles."

Equal they may have been, but if so, Clement was the first among equals. This was because of his immense learning. Clement wrote over fifty books. In fact, he is considered to be the first Slavic writer. Much of his work consisted of translations of psalms, chants, moral writings and church material. But Clement also wrote the biographies of his teachers Cyril and Methodius, about the lives of other saints and church poems. He translated portions of Scripture. Much of the Slavonic liturgy (church service) was based on his work.

In the tenth century, Ohrid was considered a backwater of Bulgaria. Because of a disagreement with Prince Simeon of Bulgaria, Clement was not appointed as a royal advisor in 893. Instead, the prince showed that he was unhappy with Clement by sending him to Ohrid.

The reason for the falling out was that Clement opposed revising the alphabet along Greek lines (that is, adopting a "Hellenic" form). He wanted to stick with the alphabet developed by Cyril and Methodius. The majority of Simeon's advisors voted with Clement. Prince Simeon, however, was afraid there would be a backlash from the powerful Byzantine Empire that ruled the East if his country persisted in developing along nationalistic lines. He ordered Clement to make some changes in the Glagolitic script (an ancient Bulgarian script), but Clement was unwilling to do so. As a result, Clement suffered attacks from the Greek party.

Great men, Clement among them, do not let defeat sideline them completely. He opened a school in Ohrid in which St. Nahum also taught. This attracted large numbers of students and grew into the first Slavonic university. Clement and Nahum employed the Glagolitic script. Ancient traditions say the two friends trained over 3,000 students, many of whom became priests, thus forever stamping the Balkans with their personal imprint.

Near the end of his life, Clement, exhausted from a life of hard labors and Greek opposition, stopped working. Perhaps he was not unhappy to lay down his work when he died on July 17, 916. Shortly after his death, he was named a saint. He is still one of the most revered figures in Bulgarian history.

Clement of Ohrid from a fifteenth-century fresco. (Source unknown.)

Other Events

Annual: At his transfiguration, Christ's glory was revealed to three disciples. The feast of Christ's transfiguration is observed in some churches on this day.

432: Pope St. Celestine I died. His pontificate had to resist numerous heresies. He supported St. Augustine of Hippo and may have sent St. Patrick to evangelize Ireland.

1099: Pope Urban II, who urged the First Crusade, died on this day.

1649: Inspired by the mission work of John Eliot among the American Indians, the British House of Commons ordered an Act for Promoting and Propagating the Gospel in New England. Edward Winslow was a leader in forming the society. It was the world's first Protestant foreign mission society.

1681: Five Scottish Presbyterians had their heads hacked off by the British government for their principled opposition to its religious policies. Among them was Donald Cargill, whose preaching "came from the heart and went to the heart." As the hood was placed over his eyes, he asked all who loved God to sing a hymn of praise for what God had done in his soul.

1901: Brooke Foss Westcott, Bible scholar, died. He and J.F.A. Hort revised the Greek text of the New Testament. As bishop of Durham, he averted labor problems through his sympathy for coal miners.

The feast of Christ's transfiguration is observed in some churches on this day. (Bell, Mrs. Arthur. *Saints in Christian Art*. London: George Bell, 1901-4.)

July 28

Religion as an Insurance Policy

Andreas Feuerbach, whose bad relationship with his father may have had something to do with his hatred of God. (Jodl, Friedrich. *Ludwig Feuerbach*. Stuttgart: Fr. Frommans Verlag, 1921.)

On this day in 1804, Ludwig Andreas Feuerbach was born. His father was a well-known jurist who exerted tremendous influence in the field of German law. He was also a petty, moralizing tyrant at home, betraying Feuerbach's mother for another man's wife.

It has been remarked that the ranks of atheists are most often joined by men who hate their fathers. Feuerbach, who had much reason to dislike his father, attacked Christianity mercilessly. Like his follower, Karl Marx, he adopted materialist presuppositions and therefore considered his critique of the faith scientific.

As a youth, Feuerbach became deeply interested in religion and pored over Hebrew texts. He studied theology at Heidelberg and then won permission to transfer to Berlin. Because of his involvement in a student club, he came under the suspicion of the police and was held up from becoming a professor. He was able to show he was not involved in any secret organization, and on this day in 1824, his twentieth birthday, he was admitted to the theology faculty. He had, however, already become a follower of Georg Hegel, the noted German idealist. He would never teach theology.

His first move was to transfer to the philosophy department. Financial difficulties led him to relocate to Erlanger, where he lectured on philosophy for many years as a private lecturer. His first lecture attacked Christianity. By 1830 he had anonymously issued a book titled *Thoughts on Death and Immortality*. He wrote mockingly that religion was "merely a kind of insurance company." His authorship of the book became known and barred him from advancement. Feuerbach's father was appalled. Believe such things privately, but do not ruin your career by openly flaunting public opinion, he urged.

Feuerbach's response was to issue *The Essence of Christianity*. In this and his other works, he declared religion a fantasy—an attempt at wish fulfillment: "The more empty life is, the more concrete is God. . . . Only the poor man has a rich God." He went on to say that man wants to be a god with godlike powers; because he cannot have these powers, he dreams up a god who does. Practical men, however, turn to science and technology, which can satisfy real needs.

What would Feuerbach have thought of the life of his fellow German George Müller, who proved the practicality of faith by scientifically recording every prayer and its answer? Feuerbach saw religion emerging from the feeling of dependence. Müller learned to come to God in Christ's name for every need.

Feuerbach's idea prospered for a decade. *The Essence of Christianity* went through eleven printings. It eventually faded into virtual oblivion, though not without influencing Wagner and Nietzsche. George Eliot translated Feuerbach's work into English. Ernest Renan, who himself tried to "de-mythologize" the life of Christ, nonetheless was shocked enough to describe Feuerbach as anti-Christ.

Pope Victor II, zealous opposer of the practice of selling religious offices. (Montor, Chevalier Artaud de. *Lives and Times of the Popes*. New York: Catholic Publication Society of America, 1911.)

Other Events

1057: Pope Victor II died. He was zealous in his opposition of the practice of selling religious offices. During his pontificate, the Eastern and Western Churches separated, although he was not the one who instigated the anathema that led to the rupture.

1410: Jan Hus defended Wycliffe's *De Trinitate* in a disputation. Archbishop Stynko of Prague ordered 200 of Wycliffe's books burned. The following year, Hus was excommunicated for refusing to appear before Pope John XXIII, who was himself soon forced to resign for immoral behavior.

1750: Johann Sebastian Bach died on this day. He was considered by some to be the greatest composer who lived because of his remarkable originality and the innovations by which he incorporated Reformation thinking into music.

1880: Francis Pfanner landed at Port Elizabeth, South Africa, where he founded Marienhill Mission.

1940: The Christian and Missionary Alliance began work in the Andes mountains of Colombia. Four years later, missionaries baptized eighteen converts in a cold mountain stream. Fifty years later there were 17 churches and 2,000 converts.

One Step to Heaven from a Filthy Prison Camp

In 1938, when friends urged Robert A. Jaffray to stay in his Canadian homeland, he refused. He sensed that war was imminent in the Pacific, but he meant to die in Asia, in the East Indies, because that was where his heart was.

Jaffray was the heir of the owner of the *Toronto Globe*, and he was a successful insurance salesman. After he became a Christian at age sixteen, he began to feel God's call to foreign missions. He spoke to his father, who demanded that Jaffray give up the impractical idea. Jaffray had heart problems and diabetes: How could he possibly consider going overseas? The older Jaffray was willing to allow his son to become a leader in the Canadian Presbyterian Church, but when Jaffray insisted on enrolling in A.B. Simpson's New York mission school, his father flatly declared that Jaffray would not have a penny of help.

So, Jaffray worked his way through school. Then he went to China. For fifty years, he served as a missionary in Southeast Asia, studying maps, praying constantly and working nonstop to extend God's kingdom into regions where the gospel had never been heard. In order to take the strain off his weak heart, he had a desk made that he could pull over his bed rather like a hospital tray. He usually rose at four o'clock in the morning to begin work, though.

Wherever Jaffray and his coworkers won souls, he insisted that a church be formed to hold the new converts together. He also insisted that those churches be given self-responsibility and be organized to run themselves. The results were similar to those churches described in the Bible in the Acts of the Apostles—great growth and much persecution. As soon as possible, Jaffray planted Bible schools to train the new Christians and printed material to support their Christian endeavor.

Jaffray's work was hard and dangerous. Once he and other missionaries were captured by Chinese bandits. The bandits demanded money to let them pass. Made bold by Christ, Jaffray turned the tables, demanding that their captors support them instead. Christian missionaries were funded by others to carry God's word, he explained. The bandits respected Jaffray for his courage but still forced the missionaries to march into the hills. Jaffray wondered if his heart would endure the strain, which left even the rugged bandits exhausted, but his health actually improved. He spoke many times to the robbers about Christ, and the hardened men and women wept. Finally, they sent him to fetch a ransom.

Later, Jaffray and his associates were used by God to open a major work in Indochina, where they witnessed thousands of conversions and powerful miracles. Late in Jaffray's life, God impressed upon him that he must open a mission field in the West Indies. He did so, and the mission flourished despite the Great Depression. Because Western workers were scarce, Jaffray used Chinese missionaries to spread the gospel there.

The Japanese captured Jaffray and his family while he was in the Indies. For a year they housed him in a camp with his wife and daughter but then moved him to a men's camp whose buildings once housed pigs. The men suffered dysentery. Shortly before his death, Jaffray was transferred to an even worse camp. He died on this day in 1945. The missionary who had lived beside him said later, "One of the great blessings of my life was the privilege I had of being interned with Dr. Jaffray on the island Celebes. I learned to love him as a great man of vision and faith."

Other Events

1685: Quaker theologian Robert Barclay petitioned that prisoners of conscience be allowed to go overseas rather than remain sequestered in prison.

1791: James Manning, a Baptist, died. He was president of Rhode Island College (now Brown University) and was noted for his firm stand against state oppression of Baptists in Massachusetts and Connecticut.

1833: William Wilberforce, the parliamentarian who did so much to end slavery throughout the British empire, died on this day.

Robert A. Jaffray, missionary to Asia. (Courtesy of The Christian and Missionary Alliance archives. Used by permission.)

James Manning, notable New England Baptist. (Armitage, Thomas. *A History of the Baptists: Traced by Their Principles and Practices, From the Time of our Lord and Saviour Jesus Christ to the Present*. New York: Bryan, Taylor and Co., 1893.)

July 30

A Big Man Makes a Confession

G.K. Chesterton, well-known for his Father Brown detective stories. (Courtesy of the University of Texas collection of public domain portraits on the Web.)

G.K. Chesterton wielded one of the great pens of his day. His Father Brown detective stories are as delightful to nibble as a piece of your favorite dessert. Renowned in literature, Chesterton was also a passionate and humorous apologist for the Christian Church, particularly the Catholic Church. As a young man he showed considerable literary talent and began to edit a little paper. In time it became his life's work. He wrote a lot of criticism, for he had an uncanny knack of seeing what was crucial in any author's work and had the clarity to smell the real worth or the real flaw of any argument.

Paradox was his forte. Paradox, said Chesterton, "is truth standing on her head to attract attention." As used by Chesterton, paradox is either a statement that at first glance seems false but actually is true or a "commonsense" view exposed as false. He used it so frequently it could become tiresome in his longer works, but in his short essays it is scintillating and refreshing. Here is an example on the topic of history from *The Everlasting Man*, his paean to Christ which shows that the spiritual is more real than those things we consider tangible reality:

> So long as we neglect [the] subjective side of history, which may more simply be called the inside of history, there will always be a certain limitation on that science which can be better transcended by art. So long as the historian cannot do that, fiction will be truer than fact.

Chesterton could be absentminded. Once, he dropped a garter and while down on the floor groping for it, he found a book and began to read it, the garter, completely forgotten. He would stand in the middle of traffic, lost to his surroundings, deep in thought. Still, he had tremendous concentration for writing and was ever fixed on the eternal truths that make the wisdom of this world foolish. Thus he could say succinctly of the agnostic George Bernard Shaw:

> He started from points of view which no one else was clever enough to discover and he is at last discovering points of view which no one else was ever stupid enough to forget.

On this day in 1922, Chesterton took a walk with Father O'Connor. Chesterton's 400 pounds were to be baptized into the Church that he had defended all his life. Looking for his prayer book, he accidentally pulled out a three-penny thriller instead. At last he found the appropriate text and made his first confession. Asked why he joined the Catholic Church, Chesterton replied, "To get rid of my sins."

Artist's conception of Pope St. Vitalin. (Montor, Chevalier Artaud de. *Lives and Times of the Popes*. New York: Catholic Publication Society of America, 1911.)

Other Events

579: Pope Benedict I died during a siege of Rome. He had resigned the papacy, unable to cope with invasions and famine.

657: Pope St. Vitalian was enthroned. He received the Roman emperor with marks of respect, but the emperor plundered Rome anyway. Vitalian is said to have introduced the organ into church use.

1233: Conrad of Marburg, an overzealous inquisitor, was murdered for his cruelties.

1540: Without a public hearing or knowing the charges of heresy against him, John Barnes was burned at Smithfield, England.

1547: John Knox was captured by the French, having become chaplain to the killers of Cardinal Beaton of St. Andrews. Knox was sentenced to the galleys. Eventually he escaped to become the leader of the Scottish Reformation.

1820: Johannes Gossner, a German evangelical, preached his first Russian sermon. Many Russians were converted through his influence.

1860: Lutheran theologian August F.C. Vilmar died. He migrated from liberalism to conservatism, stressing the objective facts of salvation.

JULY 31

Advocate of the Oppressed

When Bartolomé de Las Casas, who was later known as the "Father to the Indians," first traveled to the Spanish conquests in America, he was twenty-four years old and no priest. To the contrary, he was following in conquistador footsteps. Like many Spanish youth, he settled on a plantation, where he enjoyed the benefits of the forced labor of native conscripts.

One day in 1509, a Dominican monk, Father Montesinos, spoke from the pulpit, berating the Spanish colonists for their cruel treatment of the natives. He asked, How could men call themselves Christians and perpetrate the barbarities these butchers daily unleashed against their helpless charges?

Las Casas' conscience was cut to the quick. While others screamed threats and abuse at the preacher, he went out and freed his slaves. Then he returned to Montesinos for advice as to what he should do next. Montesinos trained Las Casas to be a priest, and Las Casas became the first Spaniard ordained in the new world.

Thereafter, Las Casas labored for the Indians as few men have before or since. His whole life was devoted to that single cause. He wrote books documenting the cruelty done to them. He argued with those who ruled the colonies. Five times he crossed the ocean to plead with the king of Spain on behalf of the Indians, reminding the king that the pope granted Spain its possessions in the New World on the ground that Spain would evangelize the Indians. The king agreed, and laws were passed ordering better treatment of the Indians. In the New World those laws were ignored by men who knew the king was powerless to enforce them. But the Indians knew Las Casas as their benefactor and revered his name.

As a last resort, Las Casas prevailed upon Church authorities to refuse confession to men who continued their barbarities and did not return stolen loot and free their slaves. Priests who courageously carried out this directive were threatened and had to flee, while other wicked priests continued to offer absolution to the brutal men under their charge.

When Las Casas was old, the king offered him the richest ecclesiastical see in gold-rich Peru. Las Casas refused it. He begged to be sent to the poorest place, someplace where many natives remained unconverted so he would have much work to do for the Lord. He was given a place in impoverished Mexico.

He worked there for three years and then was forced to return to Spain to answer charges his enemies had trumped up against him. He went home fighting. Once again he proved that it was cruelty that had led to the revolts that the colonists tried to blame on his teaching. All the same, he was not allowed to return to his beloved Indians. On this day in 1566, he died. When the news reached the people whom he had done so much for, they lamented in their villages and lit bonfires in honor of his passing.

Bartolomé de Las Casas, "Father to the Indians." (MacNutt, Francis. *Augustus Bartholomew de Las Casas: His Life, His Apostolate, and His Writings*. New York: Putnam, 1909.)

OTHER EVENTS

1367: Giovanni Colombini, a Roman Catholic religious leader, died on this day. He had devoted himself to serving the sick and needy and founded a religious order to carry on the work. Three hundred years later, Pope Clement IX dissolved the order.

1556: On this day, Loyola, founder of the Jesuits, died of an acute gallbladder attack. He spent the day before his death in prayer.

1703: Daniel Defoe, famed as the author of the novel *Robinson Crusoe*, spent the day in the pillory for writing a satire called "The Shortest Way with the Dissenters." A dissenter himself, his pamphlet solemnly recommended a policy of killing all those believers who would not conform to the Church of England. He then wrote a poem title "Ode to the Pillory," which won him such favor that while he was in the instrument of punishment he had flowers thrown at him rather than the usual refuse.

1889: Horatius Bonar, the writer of such hymns as "I Heard the Voice of Jesus Say," died. He was also an influential scholar of the Scottish Free Church.

1970: The complete New American Standard Bible was published.

Horatius Bonar, famed hymn writer. (Brown, Theron and Hezekiah Butterworth. *The Story of the Hymns and Tunes*. New York: American Tract Society, 1906.)

Lyons Crowd Roars for Blood

Ruins of the theatre of Lyons, where Christian blood was shed. (Courtesy of Tony Lane.)

The mob in the amphitheater roared. This day in 177* was a holiday to celebrate the greatness of Rome. For entertainment, the people of Lyons (then called Lugdunum) were enjoying the torture of members of a vile sect called Christianity. The governor of Gaul (now France) had been expected to show his patriotism by sponsoring entertainment for the whole city. It was expensive to hire gladiators, boxers and wrestlers. He realized it would be a lot cheaper to torture Christians for holiday entertainment.

Christianity had arrived in Lyons about twenty-five years earlier when Polycarp of Smyrna (in modern Turkey) sent Pothinus as a missionary to Gaul. Through diligent work, Pothinus established church groups in Lyons and nearby Viennes. As the groups grew, spiritual resistance mounted, and persecution of Christians began. They were shut out of businesses and houses. Mobs beat, stoned and robbed them. But in spite of the fate they faced, when believers were arrested by city authorities they boldly confessed their allegiance to Christ.

In 177, some Christians were imprisoned to await the arrival of the governor to the region. Their unbelieving servants were also seized. Under threat, the servants invented lies about the Christians, saying they practiced cannibalism and incest. These accusations enraged the authorities and gave them an excuse to punish the Christians.

They confined the Christians to the darkest and nastiest part of the prison, where many of them suffocated. Pothinus, the ninety-two-year-old bishop of Lyons, died in his cell after being tortured. His cell was about the size of a modern electric dishwasher.

Some Christians were placed in stocks; others were seated on a red-hot iron grill. After torture, some of the Christians were taken to the amphitheater for wild beasts to devour as the crowd watched. Among that group was the slave girl Blandina, who had already endured every imaginable torture and cruelty. She was suspended on a stake and exposed to the wild beasts. Because she appeared to be hanging on a cross, she inspired the other Christians. When they looked at her, they were reminded of Christ on the cross and His eternal glory.

In the midst of her pain and suffering, Blandina cried out, "I am a Christian and there is nothing vile done by us." Although the crowd detested the Christians, they had to admit that they had never seen a woman so stoutly endure so many terrible tortures. She died comparing her death to marriage, since she was going to be with Christ, her bridegroom.

Sanctus, a deacon from Viennes, also stood firm in his faith, even when red-hot plates were fastened to the most tender parts of his body. He showed that "nothing is fearful where the love of the Father is, and nothing is painful where there is the glory of Christ." With such hope, the Christians exhorted and encouraged each other to the end.

Their bodies were exposed for six days, then burned to ashes and thrown into the Rhone River. The bodies of those who suffocated were thrown to the dogs, and guards were stationed to prevent other Christians from burying them. By doing this, the pagans hoped to destroy the Christians' hope of resurrection.

*This date is far from certain, but there is ancient documentation of the events that seems to support it.

Other Events

314: The Council of Arles, called to deal with the Donatist question, only made the Donatists more determined to stick with their principles. They had broken away from the North African Church, which they felt was too lax on those who broke under persecution.

1546: Jesuit Jacques Lefevre died on this day. One of the original six Jesuits gathered by Ignatius Loyola, he founded the Jesuit University at Cologne.

1787: St. Alphonsus Liguori died. He took the gospel to Italian peasants and founded the Congregation of the Most Holy Redeemer, which spread rapidly through Europe.

1834: Robert Morrison, the first Protestant missionary to China, died on this day. He was fifty-two and had translated the Bible into Chinese.

1883: Missionary Harold Schofield died. He expired praying that England's universities would see revival, an event that was fulfilled in the work of the Cambridge Seven.

1950: Czechoslovakia issued a law that said that any priest consecrated without permission of the state was to go to prison for three years.

Robert Morrison, first Protestant missionary to China. (Dennis, James S. *Christian Missions and Social Progress*. New York: Fleming H. Revell Co., 1897-1906.)

A statue of Isaac Jogues, missionary to the Iroquois, at Dunwoodie College. (Courtesy of the Christian History Institute archives.)

August 2

Tortured for Duty, He Would Not Desert

Isaac Jogues wept before the Lord in long hours of prayer, asking God to accept his life if only the Indians of North America might be won to Christ. One night he heard what he took to be a word from the Lord, saying: "Your prayers are granted. It will happen as you have asked. Take heart! Be courageous!"

Born in France and trained as a Jesuit, Jogues begged for an opportunity to win souls in Canada and was given it. His master prophesied that he would die nowhere else. Jogues quickly showed he could endure much for Christ and for the sake of the gospel. Contempt, daily threat of death, filthy food, exposure to the elements—these were commonplace as he worked among the Huron tribes. After several years, when a volunteer was sought for a dangerous mission, he stepped forward.

On this day in 1643, the party of Hurons and Frenchmen with whom Jogues was traveling was ambushed by the Iroquois. Jogues, hidden in tall grass, could have escaped. With his own eyes he had previously witnessed Indian tortures. No one would have blamed him if he had stayed hidden. But "the idea of flight appalled me. Could I . . . desert my Frenchmen and my poor savages without giving them the aid which the Church of my God had entrusted to me?" He decided that it was his responsibility to join them and fulfill his responsibility as their spiritual guide, no matter what tortures he personally endured.

Jogues stepped from the tall grass and was seized with the rest. Terrible tortures followed. The men were forced to run the gauntlet again and again at different villages. Their fingernails were pulled out by the roots and the tender tips bitten repeatedly. Fire was applied to their bodies. Through it all Jogues maintained his Christian witness. When he urged one young Frenchman to escape, the lad refused, saying, "Your fate will be mine," and he swore to join the Society of Jesus (the Jesuits) if he lived.

Jogues survived the repeated tortures and was eventually "adopted" by an elderly native woman. The Iroquois came to respect him. At one point, when he escaped to a Dutch ship, the Indians threatened to kill every Hollander in America if Jogues was not returned. Jogues voluntarily gave himself up rather than risk others' lives. After several months, he was ransomed by the Dutch.

The pope gave Jogues special dispensation as to the manner of serving the Eucharist with his lacerated hands. Jogues himself asked to be allowed to return and preach to the Iroquois who had tormented him. Permission was granted. Peace seemed at hand with the Iroquois, but it failed. Although admiring his bravery, the Iroquois seized Jogues, and one of their braves used his tomahawk to kill Jogues. Later the murderer was captured and tried by the French. Before the brave was hung, he converted and took the name "Isaac Jogues" at his baptism.

Pope Stephen X, who undertook the reform of the Western Church. (Montor, Chevalier Artaud de. *Lives and Times of the Popes*. New York: Catholic Publication Society of America, 1911.)

Other Events

1057: Pope Stephen X was consecrated. During his papacy, he undertook the reform of the Western Church. The split, which had already begun between East and West, became final.

1555: James Abbes was martyred at Bury, England. The bishop of Norwich gave him money to recant his Protestant convictions. Abbes returned later and threw down the money, saying he had been wrong to accept it. The bishop then tried to reason with Abbes, but when that did not change his mind, the bishop had him burned.

1640: The Iroquois butchered Joseph Chiwatenhwa, a faithful Huron Christian who was carrying a message to the Jesuits.

1814: Pope Pius VII reestablished the Jesuits after forty years of suppression.

1844: Isaac Hecker made his confession and was received into the Church. He founded the Paulists in an effort to win Americans to Catholic Christianity.

1908: Frederick Franson, who founded The Evangelical Alliance Mission of Chicago, died on this day.

Jeremy Taylor Comes Down with Fever

Jeremy Taylor did not know which of his two books to consult. A week earlier, the author of the spiritual classics *On Holy Living* and *On Holy Dying* had visited a church member who was dying of fever. Then, on this day in 1667, Taylor took to bed, having fallen sick himself.

On Holy Living and *On Holy Dying* were guidebooks to actions, thoughts and prayers suitable to Christians. They became popular in Taylor's day and have remained in print ever since. For the most part they were instructions for careful living, but once in a while Taylor broke into a prayer like this:

> And now, Lord, who hast done so much for me, be pleased only to make it effectual in me. . . . Teach me to live wholly for my Savior Jesus, and to be ready to die for Jesus, and to be conformable to His life and sufferings, and to be united to Him by inseparable unions. . . . O sweetest Savior, clothe my soul with Thy holy robe; hide my sins in Thy wounds, and bury them in Thy grave.

When Taylor took to bed, he was in Ireland. Although it was a reward for his loyalty to the crown during the English Civil War, he did not want to be there. Plead as he would, however, he could not persuade King Charles II to find him a position in England.

Taylor had been a clergyman since he was twenty years old. His sermons attracted the attention of William Laud, a powerful bishop and the violent persecutor of many who did not accept the king's religious views. Laud became Taylor's patron and cleared a path for the young preacher.

Taylor was accused of wanting to return to Roman Catholicism. Since this was not true, he eagerly seized an opportunity to preach a message against the accusations. Taylor's sermon argued that recusancy (a refusal to obey established authority) was a sin. He said that England's Roman Catholics should attend Church of England services as per the king's wishes. For Taylor, obedience meant standing by the king, and consequently, he became a Royalist.

Captured at the battle of Cardigan Castle, Taylor went to prison for his faithfulness to the monarchy. On two occasions, rebels imprisoned him at Chepstow. But when the monarchy was restored, Charles II appointed Taylor to the position in the Irish Church.

Taylor did not do well in Ireland. He had a knack for antagonizing the ministers under him who rejected the Church of England forms that Charles insisted upon. At times Taylor feared for his life, which is why he pleaded with Charles to be allowed to return to England.

In the end it was a moot point. If the ups and downs of Taylor's life were tied to the fortunes of the crown, his death was tied to his performance of duty, not to martyrdom. Having caught the fever from his church member, he died ten days later. He was fifty-four years old.

Jeremy Taylor, author of classic devotional books.
(Evelyn, John. *Diary and Correspondence of John Evelyn*. London: Henry G. Bohn, 1859.)

Other Events

1476: Pope Sixtus IV extended the supposed benefit of indulgences to ameliorate the condition of those in purgatory.

1492: Christopher Columbus sailed on the voyage that would lead him to discover the New World.

1528: Martin and Katie Luther suffered the sorrow of losing their infant daughter, Elisabeth.

1770: Christopher Dock's *Schulordnung*, the first American teacher's manual, was published on this day. Dock wanted his pupils to "be well instructed in the knowledge of godliness" and emphasized methods of kindness over force.

1872: Anthony Ashley Cooper, seventh earl of Shaftesbury, laid the foundation stone of a large housing complex named after him at Battersea, England. Cooper was a Christian lord who worked hard to improve the conditions of workers. Over 100,000 paid their respects to him when he died in 1885.

1874: Henry Harmon Spalding, a missionary to the Nez Percé Indians, died. He reduced their language to writing and translated Scripture into it. When Idaho became a state, the majority of its Presbyterians were Indians, the fruit of Spalding's labor.

Pope Sixtus IV, who extended indulgences.
(Montor, Chevalier Artaud de. *Lives and Times of the Popes*. New York: Catholic Publication Society of America, 1911.)

Women march on Versailles in the French Revolution. (Robinson, James Harvey. *Medieval and Modern Times*. Boston: Ginn and Co., 1919.)

August

4 Under Revolutionary "Freedom"

On the whole, the French Revolution was hostile to Christianity and to that which the Church had built over the centuries. The revolutionists pursued an erratic policy toward Church and faith. At times they attempted to sway the priests to their side. Very early in the revolution, before King Louis XVI was executed, the Catholic Church was declared the only Church of the nation. But, more often than not the revolutionists acted contrary to the interests of the Church.

As early as August of 1789, a mere month after Parisians stormed the Bastille, various Church fees were abolished. When the Declaration of the Rights of Man and Citizen was issued, it merely tolerated religion, with the words: "No one is to be molested for his opinions, even his religious opinions. . . ." A decree in November 1789 declared that all Church property was at the disposal of the nation. A month later a vast amount of Church property was sold. Early the next year religious vows were forbidden. Yet the National Assembly agreed to pay the priests' stipends. When the pope condemned the Declaration of the Rights of Man and Citizen, half of the priests swore to uphold the new constitution, whereas the rest refused. Those who refused were considered anti-revolutionists (called "non-jurors").

Non-jurors were forbidden to preach in their churches. They could only hold mass. Many non-jurors therefore renounced state pay and embraced poverty. Increasingly they came under restriction and attack.

Historically, churchmen were not without blame for these developments. Bishops had been largely drawn from the old ruling classes. There are many cases on record of their brutality and intolerance. The cruelties of the Inquisition in France were notorious. Christ's love all too often had not been shown.

Also, churchmen had helped perpetuate many superstitions, which particularly rankled the Philosophés, who used these facts as a rationale to reject the Church and embrace Deism, agnosticism or atheism. Many who occupied high positions within the Revolution thought as the Philosophés did.

It must have pleased them greatly to close all religious houses on this day in 1792. Cluny, an abbey hoary with tradition, was destroyed. Other abbeys became prisons. Later that month, an oath of liberty and equality was devised which all clergy were told they must accept. On August 26, with passions running high, a decree ordered all non-juring clergy out of the nation within two weeks. Only the sick and aged were excused from the order. The penalty for disobeying the order was exportation to Guiana.

Before the revolution was over, French priests were hunted, harassed and executed. Robespierre, a powerful member of the Committee of Public Safety, proclaimed a Deist god and at last the "Goddess Reason" was made the official deity of a France whose zigzags in policy were quite often unreasonable. Some venerable Catholic buildings became the scenes of mocking rites.

Wilfred Grenfell transformed Newfoundland. (Grenfell, Wilfred Thomason. *A Labrador Doctor: The Autobiography of Wilfred Thomason Grenfell*. Boston: Houghton Mifflin Company, 1919.)

Other Events

1821: Rev. William C. Blair, the first Sunday school missionary of the United States, began his work. He traveled 2,500 miles, mostly on horseback, visited 6 states, founded 61 Sunday schools, inspected 35 others and established 4 adult schools and 6 tract societies in his first year. He thought he had done too little and regretted that illness had hindered him. But the Sunday and Adult School Union was so pleased with his performance they hired more missionaries.

1874: Methodist minister John H. Vincent and manufacturer Lewis Miller established the Chautauqua Assembly, a two-week summer retreat to train Sunday school teachers and church workers, combining serious study with summer recreation.

1879: Leo XIII urged the study of true philosophy, especially Thomism, in his bull *Aeterni Patris*. He said that there was no conflict between science and truth.

1892: Medical missionary Wilfred Grenfell sailed into Labrador's waters to begin his ministry. He brought hope and taught self-help to the destitute fisher folk of the province.

An Odd Path to Sainthood

In most ages, the life of a king was often troubled and short. When Oswald's father, king of Northumbria, was killed by enemies, eleven-year-old Oswald fled to Scotland. There he took refuge with St. Columba's monks on the isle of Iona. During his stay there, the monks led him to Christ.

In 633 King Edwin of Northumbria perished in battle against Penda and Cadwallon. Oswald, his nephew (or possibly his younger brother—sources are uncertain about their familial relationship), succeeded him to the throne. Cadwallon ravaged Northumbria, so Oswald marched against him. Few of the men in Oswald's tiny force knew Christ or wanted to. But, on the eve of battle, Oswald boldly set up a cross, holding it upright while dirt was packed into the hole that had been dug for it. He then cried out:

> Let us now kneel down and together pray to the almighty and only true God that He will mercifully defend us from our enemy; for He knows that we fight in defense of our lives and country.

According to old reports, that night, while Oswald rested, St. Columba of Iona appeared to him in a vision, assuring him that he would have victory. Although the enemy's numbers were far greater than his own, Oswald did win the battle. As a result, his people became willing to follow Christ. Oswald restored order throughout Northumbria and brought missionaries from Scotland to teach his people. Chief among these was St. Aiden. Oswald himself offered to be Aiden's translator so that his people might hear and understand the gospel. Thousands became Christians. The isle of Lindisfarne was given to Aiden for a bishop's seat, and a famous monastery was founded there. Churches sprang up all across Northumbria.

The king won a reputation of prayerfulness. So often did he praise God and lift petitions to Him that even at meals he kept his hands in an attitude of prayer. In the few short years that he reigned, Oswald's kingdom gained such preeminence that all the other kings of England became subject to him. Oswald journeyed through his lands establishing his people in faith and freeing slaves, many of whom he made monks.

He was also known for his charity. Once he gave a silver dish with its contents of meat to the poor who clamored at his gate. St. Aiden blessed his hand for the deed, exclaiming, "May this hand never perish." Oddly that hand was indeed preserved after Oswald's death and was seen in good condition 500 years later. The cross he had erected before his battle with Cadwallon was said to heal many who soaked little pieces of it in water and then swallowed them.

King Oswald (seated) speaks with the missionary Aiden. (Courtesy of the Christian History Institute archives.)

Oswald's death came in battle. The pagan ruler Penda of Mercia, who had defeated Edwin, raised an army and on this day in 642, he met Oswald with overwhelming force. Surrounded by enemies, Oswald prayed one last prayer for God's mercy on the souls of his soldiers. He is considered a martyr because he died at the hand of a pagan while defending a Christian nation and was consequently named a saint.

Other Events

1540: Joseph Scaliger was born in Agen, France. He became the most brilliant Protestant scholar of his era, a master of many fields, and he is often compared to Aristotle.

1751: Rev. John Cuthbertson arrived in America from Scotland. He was the first Scottish Covenanter preacher sent to the New World. He kept a valuable diary of family names, marriages and baptisms, which is a treasure trove for genealogists today.

1900: James Healy, the first African-American Roman Catholic bishop, died. He was an indefatigable worker who crisscrossed Maine constantly as he established sixty new churches, sixty-eight missions, eighteen convents and eighteen schools. African Americans criticized him, saying that the light-skinned ex-slave did not identify with their interests.

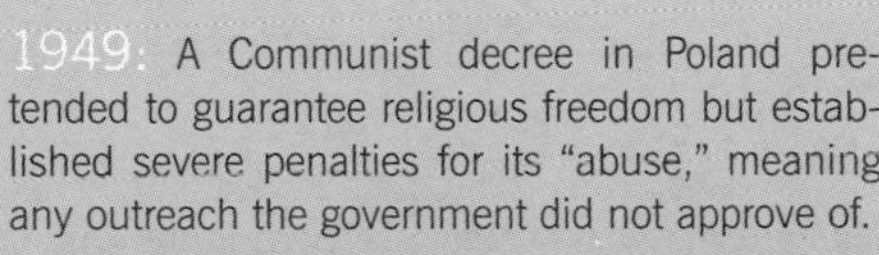

1949: A Communist decree in Poland pretended to guarantee religious freedom but established severe penalties for its "abuse," meaning any outreach the government did not approve of.

Joseph Scaliger was likened to Aristotle. (Robinson, George W., tr. *Autobiography of Joseph Scaliger with Autobiographical Selections from His Letters, His Testament and the Funeral Orations by Daniel Heinsius and Dominicus Baudius*. Cambridge, MA: Harvard University Press, 1927.)

A camp meeting. (Courtesy of the Christian History Institute archives.)

August 6

Getting the Jerks and Other Strange Behaviors

"Lord, make it like Cane Ridge." This was the prayer of revivalists across America. Cane Ridge had become the most famous of the frontier revivals during the Second Great Awakening.

Revival has often emerged after intense prayer and confession, and Cane Ridge was no exception. Recognizing that many people on the western frontier were indifferent to faith or actively opposed to it, pastors and Christians began to set aside time to pray that revival might come. Convinced that sin impedes revival, many churches tried to clean up their own ranks by removing from fellowship those who had drifted into overt sin.

Revival began in 1800 in Kentucky. Under the exhortations of a fiery preacher, James McGready, in Logan County, a woman who had been seeking the assurance of salvation for a long time suddenly broke into songs and shouts of joy. People began to weep and wanted similar assurance. News of their newfound hope spread like wildfire through Kentucky, and people in nearby regions began to attend the services, thirsting to partake of salvation. Several small revivals spread out from that center. But the "main attraction" was still to come.

In those days, Christians used to gather for special services in which three or more days of worship would be capped by the sharing of the Lord's Supper. So charged was the atmosphere in Kentucky that everyone expected great things when the Presbyterian minister Barton W. Stone scheduled a Communion for the first week of August. Instead of the usual hundreds, thousands of people thronged toward Cane Ridge, hungering for a taste of God. Cane Ridge (a small town a day's ride from Lexington in those times of primitive transportation) was inundated with humanity. Many came prepared to camp out, which is where such services received the name "camp meeting."

Those who arrived by Friday night may have been disappointed, because nothing visible happened, although some spent the entire night in prayer. But on Saturday evening a powerful enthusiasm swept the crowd. Men, women and children shrieked and fainted. Preachers shouted to the crowd and urged repentance. Some of the penitents became hysterical. Light-headedness was common. Individuals began to jerk. Scoffers stood by and mocked.

Sunday morning began calmly with Communion. But soon, under the preaching and hymns of a Methodist minister, the crowds grew emotional. Many fell to their knees, crying for forgiveness. People counseled one another on spiritual matters. They sang, shouted, danced, groaned or wept uncontrollably. Some fell into coma-like states.

Instead of breaking up on Sunday, the services continued through the night and into the following week, lasting until this day in 1801, with as many as 25,000 attending. Thousands confessed the Lord. A year later, the excited talk in the area was still of religion.

Dominic, founder of the Dominican order, in meditation. (Endres, Jos Ant. *Die Zeit de Hochscholastik: Thomas von Aquin*. Mainz: Kircheim & Co., 1910.)

Other Events

258: Bishop of Rome (pope) St. Sixtus II, who was captured while holding services in the catacombs, was martyred. He was executed on his bishop's chair.

655: Pope St. Martin I died. He was imprisoned and then banished by Emperor Constans II, who rejected the Orthodox doctrine that Christ had two wills, human and divine.

1221: Dominic, founder of the Dominican order, died on this day. His love of people was proven to be genuine. In fact, he once offered himself as a slave to a Moor in exchange for the son of a widow.

1942: Missionary Vivian Redlich was martyred by the Japanese in Papua. He had refused to leave his converts and flee while he still had the opportunity, even though he knew he was in danger.

1950: Debilius of Germany demanded that people be allowed to live by their convictions. Although a Lutheran, he was standing up for Jehovah's Witnesses.

AUGUST 7

Stepping Forward for America

Around 1760, fifteen-year-old Francis Asbury was converted in his father's barn. Reared in a Christian home, he had been brought up in the Church of England, but the Methodist revival took hold of him as it did so many others during that time. From the instant that he was converted, Asbury saw the marks of salvation in himself. He was, "happy, free from guilt and fear, had power over sin, and felt great inward joy." His conversion also led him to read the Scriptures, pray and reach out to others. He began meetings with other young men and taught them about God.

At the time of his conversion, Asbury was working as a saddler. His family was very poor, and he had even had to take work at the age of eleven to help support his family. After his conversion, he was not content merely to exercise his hands, however skillfully, but walked a considerable distance to exercise his soul at an evangelical church where revivalists spoke. He became a Methodist helper and exhorted when he could, despite persecution. At seventeen he was licensed by the Methodists as a local preacher. As soon as he turned twenty-one, he gave up his saddler's work and devoted himself completely to preaching.

Like John Wesley, Asbury worked out a system to make the best use of his time and to develop steady habits. He learned to be methodical, and this blessed his work in later years. Through self-directed study, he filled the holes in his education. At four o'clock each morning he rose to read and study. He set himself a goal to read 100 pages a day and often spent 10 hours or more in doing so. At one point, he gave an hour each day to studying the Old Testament in Hebrew, a language he taught himself.

One August, the young man, then twenty-six years old, attended a Methodist conference in Bristol. For months he had felt strongly the pull of the American need for the gospel. On this day in 1771, when Wesley said, "Our brethren in America call aloud for help. Who are willing to go over and help them?" Asbury offered himself. Several other candidates also stepped forward, but Wesley sensed that Asbury was the man to send.

No one could have labored harder than Asbury did. When he arrived in America and set out to reach the people, he found that they had settled in small, widely scattered congregations. To meet their needs, he rode incessantly—5,000 miles a year. He preached 17,000 sermons, ordained 3,000 preachers, founded 5 schools and distributed thousands of pieces of literature. With his organizational skills he divided America into circuits, and he recruited other preachers to help him cover the whole country. His circuit riders learned the hard life from him. Many, such as Peter Cartwright, became famous in their own turn. So hard did Asbury work that his health often suffered.

Francis Asbury. (Daniels, W.H. *Illustrated History of Methodism in Great Britain and America, From the Days of the Wesleys to the Present Time*. New York: Phillips & Hunt, 1880.)

At the time of Asbury's death, the Methodist Episcopal Church was the largest denomination in the United States. In him Christ showed what could be done with a single dedicated life

OTHER EVENTS

Annual: John Mason Neale is remembered in the Church of England and the Episcopal Church on this day. He translated old Latin hymns into English, including "All Glory, Laud and Honor" and "O Come, O Come, Emmanuel." He also wrote the Christmas carol "Good King Wenceslas." Because it was thought that he wanted to return England to Roman Church forms, he was harassed and even mauled by opponents.

1587: William Allen was made a cardinal. He had left England when Protestant Queen Elizabeth came to power. He urged Catholics to rebel against the queen, founded the college of Douai to train English priests and oversaw the Douai translation of the Bible that was used by English-speaking Catholics for many years.

1903: At the instigation of bush parson C.H.S. Matthews, the foundation stone of the Brotherhood House was laid in Dubba, Australia.

1955: Wang Ming-Dao, evangelical pastor, preached his last sermon knowing that he might be arrested the next day. Its title was "The Son of Man Is Betrayed into the Hands of Sinners." Soon after midnight he was arrested by Chinese Communists.

The Brotherhood House. (Matthews, Ch. H.S. *A Parson in the Australian Bush*. London: E. Arnold, 1908.)

Dürer's later *Jerome in His Study*. (La Farge, John. *Great Masters*. New York: McClure, Phillips and Company, 1903.)

August 8

Oh, the Promise of Youth!

The year that is known for Columbus's first voyage to America also witnessed the publication of St. Jerome's *Letters* at Bâle, Germany, on this day in 1492. The book itself was not as significant as its title page, which boasted a woodcut of Jerome by a rising young artist. Within a few years men would say that Germany had just two artists: Hans Holbein and Albrecht Dürer. Few would achieve Dürer's skill with engravings.

Dürer placed his *St. Jerome* in a homey, European building. The lines of the picture were simple, and yet the cloth of Jerome's robe was full of folds and encased all but the great scholar's face. The face seemed somewhat anxious, not particularly scholarly or spiritual. Books stood on a shelf behind Jerome, and there was some illusion of depth as the young artist worked with the new Renaissance techniques of perspective and shadow. The lion at Jerome's feet, however, was almost a caricature.

In 1512 Dürer did another *St. Jerome*. By then his mastery was complete. Using the technique of dry point, he placed Jerome out of doors beneath a tree. Jerome looked every inch the prophet. His muscular arms were bare, and his hands were couched in prayer. He sat amidst rocky crags. The lion rested its head upon great padded feet. Halftones abounded in the image, adding a feeling of incredible depth. The second *St. Jerome* is considered one of the greatest works ever done, full of proportion and inner life. Dürer did another *Jerome* in 1514, which placed the great scholar in an elongated room and showed perspective at its best.

Dürer's works often served to further Christian education. At that time, few people could read, so pictures were used to instruct the illiterate. Dürer did some of the best of these teaching images. Imbued with a Renaissance zest for knowledge and a mastery of self and the world, and with a Reformation hunger for a new relationship with God, Dürer drew an incredible range of subject material—allegories, animals, Bible stories, buildings, fantasy, figure studies, plants, portraits, self-portraits, utensils, etc.—into his largely religious works and did it all well.

As soon as Martin Luther took his famous stand at Wittenberg, Dürer became his admirer. When Luther was kidnapped, Dürer exclaimed in his diary, "O God, if Luther is dead, who will henceforth explain to us the gospel?"

Dürer's art reflected his understanding of faith. In his *Malencolia*, the dreadful apparition of a comet (representing God's wrath) is buried in a rainbow (representing His mercy). In the end Dürer probably never left the Catholic faith of his pious parents, although one friend claimed he had. He died too young to see the outcome of the Reformation, yet his work is an example of the vital role of Christian faith in the arts of the Western world.

The cruel Duke of Alva. (Young, Alexander. *History of the Netherlands (Holland and Belgium)*. Boston: Estes and Lauriat, 1884.)

Other Events

449: The "Robber" Council of Ephesus met. This was presided over by Dioscoros, who admitted only documents favorable to his Monophysite position.

701: Pope St. Sergius died. When he opposed some rulings of the Eastern Church, Emperor Justinian II ordered him arrested, but the Exarch of Ravenna protected Sergius.

1567: The Spanish Duke of Alva, after a heroic four-month march over the Alps, arrived in the Netherlands to put down a Protestant revolt, which he did with singular ferocity.

1694: Antoine Arnoauld, the Jansenist leader who fought to keep Jansen's ideas from condemnation by the Catholic Church, died on this day.

1852: Swedish-born Gustaf Palmquist baptized three converts in the Mississippi River at Rock Island, Illinois, initiating the organization that was later known as the Baptist General Conference. A century-and-a-half later, this denomination had grown to over 800,000 members.

1941: The Serbian Orthodox Church presented a memorandum to General Dankelman, commander in chief of the armed forces of Serbia, protesting atrocities committed against the Serbs.

August 9

Karl F.A. Gutzlaff Died in Disgrace

On this day in 1851, Karl Gutzlaff died in disgrace. In large measure, he had himself to blame, which was a pity, because he had used genuinely original ideas and methods to try to bring the gospel to the people of China.

Gutzlaff was a true mission pioneer. He was one of the first Protestant missionaries to adopt the Chinese manner of dress so that he could relate better to the Chinese people. Under the Netherlands Missionary Society, he had worked for three years among Chinese who were living in Indonesia and Singapore. Then he became the first Protestant missionary to reach Thailand, which he did in 1828 at the age of twenty-five.

In Thailand, his first effort was to begin translation of the New Testament into Siamese. In 1829, he married Miss Newell, a self-supporting missionary, and the two completed the project together. In the second year of their marriage, his wife and baby daughter died. After their deaths, Gutzlaff wandered up the coast of China, handing out Chinese language tracts prepared by Robert Morrison.

At that time, China only allowed Westerners into certain port cities. Although Christianity had been introduced into China as early as AD 60 and had been reintroduced in the seventh century, and again by Jesuits in the sixteenth century, almost no Chinese were Christians. Gutzlaff looked at the huge land with longing, wondering how he could get the gospel to its people.

He worked a secular job by day, and in his spare time he conceived a solution to the restriction on where Westerners could do evangelization: He would send native Chinese to convert others. Among other activities, they would sell and distribute Chinese New Testaments. In 1844, he founded an institute to train Chinese Christian workers. It was a great idea, and if Gutzlaff had found some way of checking up on the 300 Chinese he "converted" and sent out as missionaries, it might have succeeded.

The evangelists returned glowing reports and wonderful statistics. Sometime in the late 1840s Gutzlaff enthusiastically reported 2,781 converts and 1,000 New Testaments distributed. His success made traditional missionaries look bad. But as he was touring Europe in 1848, Gutzlaff had a guilty secret. It seems he already knew that he was being hoaxed by many of his "converts." He was afraid of losing funding, however, so he kept quiet. But missionaries in Hong Kong did not—they investigated and sent a report to Europe.

Although some of Gutzlaff's missionaries were genuine converts, the majority proved to be opium addicts who never traveled anywhere near the towns they claimed to visit. Delighted for a chance at easy money, they made up their reports and sold the Testaments back to the printer, who in turn resold them to Gutzlaff. Some even used their mission employment as a cover for opium sales. These problems, in addition to Gutzlaff's support of the Opium Wars and of the treaty that forced China to give up Hong Kong, made his name hated in China.

Shattered by the exposure of his failure, Gutzlaff returned to China, where he died shortly afterward in 1851. However, the Chinese Evangelization Society that he formed lived on to send out Hudson Taylor, who founded the successful China Inland Mission. Taylor called Gutzlaff the grandfather of the China Inland Mission.

A national Chinese evangelist. (Northrop, Henry Davenport. *The Flowery Kingdom and the Land of the Mikado, or, China, Japan and Corea*. Toronto: Winston, Phillips, 1894.)

Other Events

1253: The pope approved St. Clare of Assisi's rule for the religious order the Poor Clares, which was modeled on the Franciscan rule.

1378: French bishops declared Pope Urban II's election invalid, a declaration that began the Great Schism in which two and even three rival popes ruled at once. After his election, Urban had become overbearing, alienating the men who chose him.

1921: Florence Matheny was born in Marion, Iowa. About the time that she chose to attend Seattle Pacific College, she read about Jacob DeShazer, a former Doolittle raider (World War II flyers) who had spent forty months in a Japanese prisoner-of-war camp and who planned to train so he could bring the gospel to Japan. "What a coincidence it would be if he should choose the same college I have chosen," she thought. "I might even get to shake his hand!" They met at college, and she did more than shake his hand: She became his wife. They shared a long and productive ministry together.

1942: Edith Stein, Jewish-Catholic philosopher, and her sister Rosa died in a gas chamber at Auschwitz.

1951: Jesuit bishop Tsiang Beda of Shanghai was arrested. When he was asked to head China's "reform" Church, he refused, was arrested and died in prison.

Edith Stein, famous Jewish-Catholic philosopher. (Courtesy of Institute of Carmelite Studies from Neyer, Maria Amata. *Edith Stein: Her Life in Photos and Documents*. Washington, DC: ICS Publications, 1998-9. Used by express written permission of Josephine Koeppel, OCD.)

AUGUST 10

St. Lawrence Grilled by Greedy Official

Lawrence brought before Decius. (Bell, Mrs. Arthur. *Saints in Christian Art*. London: George Bell, 1901-4.)

"Will you go to heaven and leave me behind?" asked Lawrence, one of the seven deacons of Rome. He was genuinely upset. Was there some fault in him that God would send the rest of the Church leaders to death but spare him?

Sixtus II, bishop of Rome (pope) in the year 258, comforted Lawrence, telling him that God was keeping Lawrence back to undergo an even greater ordeal. "Be comforted, you will follow me in three days," he is supposed to have predicted.

Roman Emperor Valerian had ordered the deaths of all of Rome's bishops, priests and deacons. However, the prefect (Roman magistrate) who carried out the order knew that, as deacon, Lawrence had charge of the Church's money. "I'll let you go free," he promised, "if you will turn the money over to me."

According to the oldest traditions we have, Lawrence agreed to bring the Church's treasures to the prefect. "But it will take me a few days," he said. "The Church is very rich." Released to carry out his promise, Lawrence distributed the Church's goods among the poor. He then gathered the city's lame, its blind and its beggars. On the third day, he appeared before the prefect. "Come out and see the wondrous riches of God," he said.

Following Lawrence outside, the prefect raged, "What is the meaning of this?" when he saw the people gathered there. Lawrence explained that the poor people would some day have new bodies and live forever in heaven. The treasure of the Holy Spirit was hidden in them as if in jars of clay (see 2 Corinthians 4:7).

Thwarted from getting his gold and believing that he would be the laughingstock of Rome, the prefect ordered a slow death for Lawrence. On this day in 258, Lawrence was tortured by having his arms dislocated and then was laid upon a grill and slowly roasted to death. During his ordeal, he is said to have suggested that his killers turn him over, remarking that he was "done" on the one side. He was so calm that the pagans who looked on were greatly impressed.

That is how the legends tell the story, but the facts are not easy to establish. What is certain is that Lawrence was martyred on this day. A hundred years later his story was so well-known that the famous Bishop Ambrose of Milan wrote about him, and so did others. By then, Emperor Constantine had long since built a chapel in Lawrence's memory. Later popes built other memorials, and these became Rome's Church of San Lorenzo.

Ferdinand Magellan, who brought Christianity to the Philippines. (Avery, Elroy McKendree. *History of the United States and Its People: From Their Earliest Records to the Present Time*. Cleveland, OH: The Burrows Brothers Company, 1904.)

OTHER EVENTS

1519: Magellan left Spain to circle the world. On the way, he introduced Christianity to the Philippine Islands.

1622: Japanese Kirishitan Augustin Ota (Christians) were put to the sword on Iki.

1886: Joseph M. Scriven died by drowning in circumstances that suggested suicide. In Ireland his fiancée died shortly before he was to marry her. He moved to Canada and again became engaged, but the second woman also died before the wedding could take place. The two deaths left him deeply depressed. He wrote the hymn "What a Friend We Have in Jesus."

America's First Methodist Clergyman

Barbara Heck's eyes blazed as she stood in Philip Embury's living room. "Philip, you must preach to us, or we shall all go to hell together and God will require our blood at your hands!" It wasn't the first time that Heck had confronted Embury about this. In fact, she'd become a nag on the subject. But Embury could not remember seeing her so upset before.

Heck, a Methodist from Ireland, believed that it was a sin to waste time. When she returned home from an errand one day to find a game of cards in progress in her home, it was too much. Her family well knew that she thought cards frivolous and sinful, a worldly amusement. She reprimanded the players, flung the pack of cards into the fireplace and fell on her knees in prayer. Then she told Embury that he must preach.

Heck was Embury's cousin. Both of their families had emigrated from Ireland, although Heck came over a year later than Embury. In the old world, Embury had been a Methodist preacher. Although on this day in 1760, his first full day in America, he had the distinction of being the only Methodist preacher to have settled in Britain's American colonies, he was too busy scraping out a living in New York to take up church work. He held family devotions and attended Lutheran services, but the little group of Methodists whom he lived amongst had lost their thirst for divine things and had grown spiritually lukewarm. Heck saw the danger and urged Embury to do something about it. But Embury took some convincing. He said, "I cannot preach, for I have neither a house nor congregation."

"Preach in your own house first, and to our own company," said Heck.

Embury finally gave in and preached his first sermon in his own rented house to five people. This is thought to be the first Methodist sermon preached in America. After that, Embury held services every Thursday evening and twice on Sunday.

The congregation of five people increased. Soon they had to rent a large room in order to accommodate their growing numbers. Rumors about the Methodists helped the church grow, because some of the people who came to investigate them were impressed and joined. Captain Webb, a Methodist military man who had been converted in Bristol, England, under John Wesley, joined Embury. Webb was a bold evangelist and began to speak to his neighbors as well as at the soldiers' barracks and in the rum shops near the Methodists' rented hall.

Philip Embury, America's first Methodist pastor. (Daniels, W.H. *Illustrated History of Methodism in Great Britain and America, From the Days of the Wesleys to the Present Time*. New York: Phillips & Hunt, 1880.)

Standing in his scarlet uniform, Webb proclaimed that all their "knowledge and religion were not worth a rush, unless their sins were forgiven, and they had the witness of God's Spirit with theirs that they were the children of God."

The little Methodist society began to grow. Eventually it built a church. One of the members wrote a letter to John Wesley, describing the situation and asking for legal advice on how to deed the land. He added, "We want an able and experienced preacher; one who has both gifts and grace necessary for the work." This prompted Wesley to send the first Methodist missionaries to America.

OTHER EVENTS

1253: St. Clare, founder of the Order of the Poor Clares, died.

1264: Urban IV approved the Corpus Christi celebration for "all Christians."

1464: Nicholas of Cusa died on this day. He was a Church diplomat and council member and was also the first to say that space is curved, declaring this on theological grounds: Only if space is curved, he said, can God be equally at the center of every point.

1880: Bud Robinson was converted at a Methodist camp meeting. He became a well-known and colorful Nazarene evangelist.

1884: The government of Japan disestablished its national religion with promises of toleration to other faiths.

1949: All birth registers of Poland's parishes were confiscated by the Communist government.

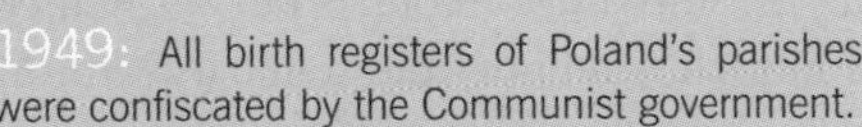

St. Clare of Assisi, founder of the Order of the Poor Clares. (Baring-Gould, S. *Lives of the Saints*. Edinburgh: John Grant, 1914.)

Nassau Hall at Princeton. (Mills, W. Jay. *Glimpses of Colonial Society and the Life at Princeton College, 1766-1773*. Philadelphia: J.B. Lippincott Company, 1903.)

August 12

Archibald Alexander Assumes New Princeton Post

> Who is He that speaks? It is the voice of "Immanuel, God with us." What man or angel could invite a guilty world to come to him? Neither Moses nor Elijah, nor Paul, nor John, presumed to call men to look to them for rest. Only He in whom "dwelt all the fulness of the Godhead bodily," could give rest to every troubled soul.

The man who preached this as part of his sermon was Archibald Alexander. He had memorized the catechism at the age of seven and begun his Latin studies even earlier. At the age of seventeen he made a public profession of faith in Christ. He preached his first sermon shortly afterward, without any preparation, because he was asked to fill in at the last moment. He spoke so clearly and confidently that the Presbyterian Church licensed him to preach when he was just nineteen. The move was justified: Alexander soon led a revival in North Carolina.

After 1812, the lecture halls of Princeton Seminary were also stirred by his passion for Christ. Alexander had urged the creation of the seminary. For centuries, a single individual could master in a lifetime all that was taught at a university, but knowledge had increased so much after the scientific revolution that by the nineteenth century no one man could know it all. Educational leaders found it necessary to create separate medical schools, law schools and seminaries. Seminaries were also needed to provide pastors for the growing population of the United States.

Princeton Theological Seminary opened in response to these developments. Its purpose was

> to unite in those who shall sustain the ministerial office, religion and literature; that piety of the heart, which is the fruit only of the renewing and sanctifying grace of God, with solid learning; believing that religion without learning, or learning without religion, in the ministers of the gospel, must ultimately prove injurious to the church.

On this day in 1812, the denomination chose Alexander to be its professor. He not only organized all the courses but taught them all himself, stamping the seminary with his own unique blend of deep scholarship and Christian fervor. Alexander combined the learning and faith that the school hoped to impart to its students. For example, because zealots claimed that the Bible forbids drinking, he deliberately sipped a little wine in company just to show that it taught otherwise.

His appeals were not just intellectual but to the heart as well, as these words from his sermon show:

> Do not for a moment suppose that you must make yourself better, or prepare your heart for a worthy reception of Christ, but come at once—come as you are. He saves none because their sins are comparatively few and unnoticed by their fellow-men; He rejects none because their sins are many and great. . . . The promise is that He will give you rest.

Please note: The sermon passages are quoted from "Christ's Gracious Invitation," University of North Carolina at Chapel Hill, from a text which may be used freely by individuals for research, teaching and personal use as long as this statement of availability is included.

Joseph Lister, who discovered antiseptic medicine. (Courtesy of the Christian History Institute archives.)

Other Events

1859: Ashbel Green Simenton landed in Rio de Janeiro, Brazil, where he founded the first Presbyterian church. He said, "The work is so perfectly hopeless by mere human agency that they who undertake it must either find support by resting upon the power of God, or else despair."

1865: Antiseptic medicine was first used in surgery by its discoverer, Quaker-bred Joseph Lister. He had taken up medicine because most professions in Britain were closed to him under laws that discriminated against his faith.

1947: Missionaries of the New Tribes Mission set up camp on the border between Bolivia and Brazil, at the railroad town of Ipias, near a jungle trail on which Ayorè Indians traveled each year to get salt. The men wanted to win the fierce tribe to Christianity. Instead, five of the missionaries were killed in November. However, New Tribes persisted in efforts to share the gospel, and in the end, many Ayorè were converted.

August 13

Remains of Pope's Opponent Returned to Rome

Under persecution, many early Christians had been killed at various times. These martyrs were called "witnesses." The bodies of two witnesses who died in exile were returned to Rome on this day in 236.*

When Maximinus Thrax was Roman emperor, he exiled Pontianus and Hippolytus to the island of Sardinia, where they probably slaved in the mines. They died there, but their remains had been brought back to Rome for a decent burial. Pontianus, who had been bishop of Rome until his exile, was laid in the tomb of Callistus, an earlier bishop of Rome (they would come to be called popes from the word *papa*, meaning "father"). Hippolytus, who had also been a bishop in or near Rome, was buried somewhere along the Tiburtine Road.

In the sixteenth century, workmen digging near an ancient church on the Tiburtine Road uncovered a marble statue of a bishop seated in a chair, wearing a pallium (a cloth that symbolizes full Episcopal authority). Pope Pius IV declared it to be Saint Hippolytus.

Next to nothing is known about Pontianus, but quite a bit is known about Hippolytus. He was the most important theologian of the Roman Church up to that time—although his work was little known in the Middle Ages because he wrote in Greek. He wrote against heresy in one of his books. In it he explained what the Gnostics (who believed they were saved by secret knowledge) and other groups taught, and he showed where they went wrong.

This would be enough to make Hippolytus worth remembering. But beyond that, his case is often cited in arguments regarding the authority of the Roman Church and its claim that popes are infallible when speaking *ex cathedra*.

To begin with, Hippolytus was a "great-grandson" of St. John the Apostle. That is, his line of apostolic succession can be traced directly to John. He was commissioned by St. Irenaeus, who was commissioned by Polycarp, who was commissioned by St. John himself. So there can be no question about Hippolytus's legitimacy as a bishop. What is more, from the fourth century on, the Roman Church venerated Hippolytus as a saint. Even popes acknowledged him as a saint.

It must be remembered, however, that he was also the first "antipope" (a pope elected illegally at the same time as another pope). He spoke out strongly against the wrongdoing, cruelty and doctrinal errors of the bishops of Rome. This struck a responsive chord with the Roman population, and a segment elected him bishop of Rome in opposition to Callistus. Hippolytus continued in opposition to the bishops of Rome until he went into exile.

Emperor Maximinus Thrax. He exiled Hippolytus. (Rostovtzeff, M. *The Social and Economic History of the Roman Empire*. Oxford: Clarendon, 1926.)

Hippolytus was an expert on heresy, and he insisted that some of the popes of his day were heretics. Scholars use this information to build a strong case against papal infallibility in matters of morals and faith.

*The year is open to question.

Other Events

587: Radegunda, queen of the Franks, died on this day. She was instrumental in evangelizing the Franks and founded a convent.

662: St. Maximus the Confessor died. He had been a vigorous opponent of the heresy known as Monothelitism, for which he was dreadfully persecuted and tortured. He had his tongue cut out and his right hand chopped off, was exposed to hunger and cold, was spat upon, was imprisoned with common criminals and was exhibited on street corners. The result was that his ideas won.

1553: Michael Servetus was arrested in Geneva, where he was soon burned to death for rejecting the Trinity.

1878: Elizabeth Prentiss, the school teacher who wrote the hymn "More Love to Thee, O Christ," died.

1908: Ira D. Sankey, who collaborated with Dwight L. Moody in evangelistic services and wrote such familiar hymns as "Faith Is the Victory" and "Simply Trusting Every Day," died on this day. Sankey met Moody at a YMCA convention in Indianapolis and six months later became his song evangelist. His melodious voice was soothing and comforting but carried deep conviction. He believed that souls could be saved with each note he sang and so gave the ministry his best effort. Sankey wrote new songs as they were needed. Among the best-loved are the "Ninety and Nine" and "For You I Am Praying." After Moody's death, Sankey's health broke, and he became blind. He spent his last years at his home in Brooklyn.

Radegunda, queen of Franks, who was instrumental in evangelizing the Franks. (Fleury, Edouard de. *Histoire de Sainte Radegonde, Reine de France*. À Poitiers: Chez H. Oudin; À Paris: Chez Th. Le Clerc Jeune, 1843.)

Muslims praying. Raymond Lull saw the need for missions to the followers of Mohammed. (Barrows, John Henry, ed. *The World's Parliament of Religions*. Chicago: Parliament Pub. Co., 1893.)

AUGUST
14
Raymond Lull, Troubadour for God

Based on the way he spent his youth, Raymond Lull seemed an unlikely person to remind the Church of its missionary vision. Until he was about thirty years old, Lull spent his time as a court gallant—that is, a fashionable ladies' man—and poet. He squandered his life in frivolity, romantic stories, love poems and seduction.

> But Jesus Christ, of his great clemency,
> Five times upon the cross appeared to me,
> That I might think upon him lovingly,
> And cause his name proclaimed abroad to be.

It is reported that Lull's conversion was precipitated by a shock. He tried to lure a beautiful woman into bed with him. With quiet dignity, the woman opened her dress and revealed a cancer-eaten breast. In a flash, Lull saw the futility of his lusts, and he later transferred his love to the eternal Christ.

Born in Majorca, Spain, Lull lapped up Jewish and Islamic lore. He was the first Christian philosopher to study the Jewish *Kabbala* (a book filled with mystical and occult knowledge) and one of the first to read the writings of the Islamic mystics known as *Sufis*. He developed a passion to win Muslims to Christ and took up the challenge of the grand mufti of Bugia: "If you hold that the law of Christ is true and that of Mohammed false, you must prove it by necessary reasons," that is, by airtight logic.

Convinced that true reason could produce no results contradictory to true faith, Lull poured his intelligence into philosophy. The result was a philosophy of "combination" by which he thought all knowledge could be derived by combining every idea with every other idea. Although admired for centuries because it was clever, his *Ars Magna* was actually a dead end. But Lull went beyond mere philosophy. His passion was too deep to stop with scholarly games.

The first crusades, the intent of which had been to convert the Middle East, had failed. Recognizing this, Lull crisscrossed Europe urging kings, popes and cardinals to develop mission schools and to evangelize the Islamic people. He said:

> Missionaries will convert the world by preaching, but also through the shedding of tears and blood and with great labor, and through a bitter death.

His three-point plan was simple. First, missionaries must obtain a comprehensive knowledge of Arabic and other Middle Eastern languages. Then, they must study Islamic literature until they could refute any Muslim argument. Finally, they must give their lives in witness to Christ. He convinced the pope to allow Christian universities to teach the Jewish and Islamic languages and literature.

Lull followed this plan himself. He established a missionary school and personally studied Islamic lore. Three times he sailed to Islamic countries to reason with Islamic scholars. The first time he was exported just when several imams (Moslem religious leaders) had requested baptism. The second time he was imprisoned for six months. On this day in 1314, when he was in his eighties, he sailed a third time for Islamic North Africa. For a year he preached Christ and the Trinity openly but then was brutally stoned. Christian merchants carried the broken man back to Spain aboard their ship. It is likely that he died in sight of Majorca.

A young William Penn, whose case aided in winning Englishmen the right to the freedom of religious expression. (Wilson, Woodrow. *A History of the American People*. New York/London: Harper & Bros., 1902.)

OTHER EVENTS

1457: *The Book of Psalms*, printed by Fust and Schoeffer, was one of the earliest products of the first presses.

1670: William Penn and his associates were arrested for preaching in the streets. Their defense became the case that won Englishmen the right to the freedom of religious expression and made it illegal for judges to tamper with juries.

1785: John Fletcher, a noble-minded and zealous Methodist pastor who briefly succeeded Wesley as head of the Methodists, died on this day.

1848: Sarah F. Adams died. She was a Unitarian, and she wrote a catechism for children that included the hymn "Nearer, My God, to Thee."

1941: Maximilian Kolbe was martyred. After a prisoner escaped from a Nazi camp, the Nazis picked ten men at random to die so that the remaining prisoners would be hesitant to let others escape. Maximilian took the place of one of the ten and led hymns and prayers until he starved to death.

August 15

Diabolical Death of Agnes Prest

The city of Exeter in southwestern England existed before the Roman conquest. It was the chief settlement of the Dumnonii tribe. What is now Exeter fell to the Anglo-Saxons in the tenth century and to William the Conqueror in the eleventh. Situated in the county of Devon, one of its main tourist attractions is a beautiful cathedral. Another site worth visiting, which few tourists know about, is an obelisk that was erected in 1909 as a memorial to Thomas Benet, who died on January 10, 1531, and Agnes Prest, who died on this day in 1557. They are known as the Exeter Martyrs.

Prest was originally from Cornwall, but she lived for a while in Exeter as a servant. Later she returned to Cornwall and married a man who lived in Launceston. They made their living spinning wool. Prest was cheerful, patient, sober and never idle. She was uneducated but knew the Bible almost by heart. The chief sadness in her life was the difference in religion between herself and her husband. He was a Roman Catholic and she a Protestant, and they tried hard to convert each other. Their children were brought up Catholic.

At last, Prest left home and stayed with friends, trying to support herself by spinning. However, she missed her family and returned home. There she was greeted with hostility by her husband and friends. They led her to the parish priest and accused her of heresy. She was arrested and spent a quarter of a year in the Launceston jail.

Prest was interrogated by Bishop Touberville. The chief point of contention was her reluctance to accept transubstantiation. Despite this issue, the bishop gave her a month's parole, and she went to work as a servant in the home of the keeper of the bishop's prison. Although she had the freedom to walk about on her own, she was continually approached by clergymen trying to get her to change her mind. But she stood firm in her Protestant beliefs. One day, after she was overheard expressing criticism of statues used in Catholic worship, she was returned to the prison.

Prest was tried at the guildhall before John Petre, mayor of Exeter, in the presence of the bishop. She could not be moved from her profession of faith, so a sentence of death was issued.

No one knows the exact spot where Prest was burned, but it is said she was led outside the city walls to Southernhay by the sheriff and city officials. Her last words on this day in 1557 were, "I am the Resurrection and the Life, saith Christ. He that believeth in Me, though he were dead, yet shall he live, and he that believeth in Me shall never die" (see John 11:25-26, KJV).

The Spinners by Velazquez. Agnes Prest tried to make her living by spinning. (La Farge, John. *Great Masters*. New York: McClure, Phillips and Company, 1903.)

Other Events

347: The proconsul of Africa proclaimed the unity of the African Church under Gratus after years of conflict between the Catholic Church and the Donatists. Donatus withdrew into exile.

1070: William the Conqueror, having deposed the archbishop of Canterbury, replaced him with his own man, Lanfranc. Lanfranc patterned the English Church along French lines.

1514: Bartolomé de Las Casas renounced his *encomieda* (colonial lands), believing they were an offense to God because of the mistreatment of Indians on such lands.

1790: Father John Carroll was consecrated bishop of Baltimore, thus separating US Catholics from English oversight.

1964: Rebels took over the compound in Africa where the Christian doctor Helen Roseveare was staying. She wrote of the terrifying and humiliating experiences that followed in books that have encouraged many other Christians.

Lanfranc became archbishop of Canterbury by William the Conqueror's hand. (Courtesy of the Christian History Institute archives.)

The room where John Woolman, an austere Quaker who greatly affected abolition, died. (Woolman, John. *The Journal and Essays of John Woolman*. New York: Macmillan Company, 1922.)

August 16

Sixteenth of Eighth Month

Like many of the Society of Friends (Quakers), John Woolman resisted the use of heathen names for the months and days. Throughout his famous journal, the dates are noted in the cumbersome style "sixteenth of eighth month" and the like.

This day, the sixteenth of the eighth month of 1772, was a Sunday. Two months earlier Woolman had arrived in England to visit fellow Quakers. He made the arduous, six-week trip in steerage, feeling that the ornaments carved on the main cabin were ostentatious and unnecessary for the simplicity to which Christians are called. He had endured rough seas and one fierce tempest that drove him belowdecks for seventeen hours for his health's sake. His decision to travel in steerage was blessed by the Lord, however, for it granted him an opportunity to witness the hard lives of the sailors, to observe the depravity of their conduct and its influence on their young apprentices and to converse with them regarding eternity and salvation.

Scruples such as his objection to the ship's cabin ornaments were common to John Woolman. In England he refused to use the stage coaches even to send or receive his post because the coaches recklessly endangered lives and were brutal to animals. His entry for this day in 1772 notes:

> I have heard Friends [Quakers] say in several places that it is common for horses to be killed with hard driving, and that many others are driven till they grow blind. Post-boys pursue their business, each one to his stage, all night through the winter. Some boys who ride long stages suffer greatly in winter nights, and at several places I have heard of their being frozen to death. So great is the hurry in the spirit of this world, that in aiming to do business quickly, and to gain wealth, the creation at this day doth loudly groan.

As his journal shows, Woolman devoutly sought to follow the Lord. At times he suffered grievously over things that to most people would seem trifles, such as whether he should wear a dyed cap or a plain one. If he felt that anything was displeasing to the Lord, he acted on the knowledge. Thus he spent no more time on his own trade than was necessary to maintain himself and his family in austere simplicity. The rest of his hours were spent in travel and meetings at which he urged Quakers to resist the slave trade and other abuses such as the cruel labor practices that were forced on children.

His influence on abolition was great. Two decades after his death, the Quakers of America banned slave holding among their members.

The sixteenth day of the eighth month was almost the last entry in Woolman's journal. Two months later he died at the age of fifty-two. His journal, which modestly does not describe his own influence, is recognized as a masterpiece of American literature and unaffected simplicity of style.

John the Constant from a Lucas Cranach painting. (Courtesy of the Christian History Institute archives.)

Other Events

Annual: The feast of St. Stephen of Hungary is celebrated. With the help of soldiers from the Holy Roman Empire, Stephen united Hungary and became its first king. He was named a saint for Christianizing the region by bringing in Benedictine preachers, building churches and compelling pagans to convert by force.

1532: John the Constant, coruler of a German state, died. He was a loyal friend of the Reformation.

1642: John Campanius sailed for the New World as a Swedish chaplain. In America, he built the first Lutheran church, learned the Lanape Lanni language and kept the earliest regular weather records in the colonies.

1661: Thomas Fuller, a popular and witty Royalist preacher of seventeenth-century England, died. He was one of the first Englishmen to make a living by writing. His fame rests chiefly on two books: *A Church History of Britain* and *Worthies of England*.

1990: Baptist missionary Clark Alan Jacobsen was arrested and killed by government troops in Liberia.

August 17

Scottish Parliament Ratifies Protestant Confession

There could be no mistaking the Scottish reformers' feelings about the leadership of the old tradition (language modernized):

> Not one of Scotland's Catholic priests is legally a minister—not if we go by God's Word, the practice of the apostles, and their own ancient laws. They are all thieves and murderers. Yes, they are even rebels and traitors to the legal authority of empires, kings, and princes. We stand here ready to prove it ourselves. They shouldn't be allowed in any reformed commonwealth. (John Knox. *John Knox's History of the Reformation in Scotland*.)

The Protestants in Scotland were insisting that their nation's parliament take action to reform the nation's faith. The sixteenth-century Reformation had spread to Scotland, and after serious suffering, the Protestants, led by John Knox, had gained the upper hand. Now they wanted to capitalize on their gains.

On August 13, 1560, Parliament agreed. The legislators instructed the Protestants to prepare a plain account of the doctrines with which they wanted to replace the old Catholic teachings. Once they had done so, Parliament would establish the revisions as the only wholesome and true doctrines "necessary to be believed and received" within Scotland.

Knox, Scotland's leading reformer, and five other ministers—John Winram, John Spottiswoode, John Willock, John Douglas and John Row—went to work. In just four days they had the Scots Confession ready.

On this day in 1560, Knox and his associates presented the Scots Confession to Parliament. The entire document was read aloud twice through for the sake of the legislators. It consisted of twenty-five short chapters, each of which was backed by Scripture references. Topics covered in the document included the doctrine of God the Father, the Son and the Holy Spirit; mankind's origin and sin; the role of the Church; good works; the relation of Church and state; the law; the future life; and more. Of all the topics covered, the nature and work of Christ received the most attention. The following is the short chapter on Christ's resurrection (with spelling and language modernized):

> We believe without doubt that, since it was impossible that the sorrows of death should keep in bondage the Author of life, that our Lord Jesus Christ crucified, dead, and buried, who descended into hell, did rise again for our justification; and destroying him who was the author of death, brought life again to us that were subject to death and to its bondage. We know that his resurrection was confirmed by the testimony of his very enemies [and] by the resurrection of the dead, whose tombs did open, and they did arise and appear to many within the city of Jerusalem. It was also confirmed by the testimony of angels, and by the senses and judgments of his apostles, and of others, who had conversation, and did eat and drink with him after his resurrection.

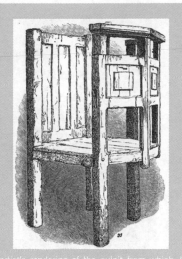

An artist's rendering of the pulpit from which John Knox revolutionized Scotland. (Maxwell, David. *Bygone Scotland*. London: William Andrews & Co., The Hull Press, 1894.)

During the parliamentary readings, the six Johns stood by, ready to answer any questions that might arise. According to Knox, the Catholic bishops who were present did not raise any objections. Perhaps they recognized that public opinion was against them.

By an overwhelming margin, Parliament ratified and approved the document, declaring it to be sound doctrine grounded upon the infallible truth of God. The few who voted against it gave as their reason, "We will believe as our fathers believed."

Other Events

1635: Richard Mather, the founder of the Mather dynasty in New England, arrived in Boston.

1662: Expelled from their pulpits by law, 2,000 non-conformist preachers preached farewell sermons to their congregations in England.

1809: Thomas Campbell and his followers formed the Christian Association of Washington. The association sprang out of the Presbyterian Church and became known first as Campbellites and then as Disciples of Christ.

1927: Theodore Epp was converted at a Bible conference at which Norman B. Harrison preached from the first chapter of Ephesians. Epp went on to found the Back to the Bible ministry.

1992: Bautista Silva died on this day. A Spanish-speaking Venezuelan Indian and the son of a chief, he helped Kathy Earle and Mary Lou Yount translate the Bible for the Pioroa tribe. He was converted to Christ and traveled from village to village telling others about Him. At the time of Silva's death, there were over fifty churches in the tribe.

Richard Mather, founder of the New England Mather dynasty. (Murdock, Kenneth Ballard. *Increase Mather, The Foremost American Puritan*. Cambridge, MA: Harvard University Press, 1925.)

August 18

Not a Coward

Cameron Townsend in 1917 at the age of twenty. (Courtesy of W.C. Townsend archives. Used by permission of Cal Hibbard.)

Cameron Townsend had to rethink matters. "You are all cowards," Stella Zimmerman had barked. "There are a million men going off to war, yet you two are leaving us women to do the Lord's work alone!" The young man was aware that God was calling him to spread the gospel to those who had never heard it. He had even signed up to be a Bible colporteur in Guatamala. But then the United States had declared war against Germany, and it seemed as though his plans must change.

It looked as if he would be drafted, since he was in the National Guard. As a patriot he was eager to go, but Zimmerman's words checked him, and he decided to ask for a deferment. "Go," said his captain. "You'll do a lot more good selling Bibles in Central America than you would shooting Germans in France."

And so, on this day in 1917, Townsend and a spiritually minded friend said good-bye to friends and family at the Los Angeles train station and headed for San Francisco. From there they would go by ship to Central America. However, in San Francisco they encountered delays in finding a ship. They seized the opportunity to make a little more money to support themselves in their wilderness adventure. A month later, the two sailed for the mission field. Townsend found the work difficult, and at times he almost despaired. He was revolted by the food, was unable to communicate, felt homesick and was made sick by the heat. Despite all of those things, however, he trusted the Lord and persisted.

He soon realized how desperately the Indians needed the gospel in their own languages. In 1918 he made up his mind to translate the Scriptures into the very difficult Cakchiquel language. He began the work with few tools, but, overcoming great obstacles, he learned the language, wrote it down and translated the gospel into it.

He developed a vision to see each Indian language translated. Remembering his early difficulties, he founded two organizations to help new missionaries over the initial rough spots of their work. The first was Summer Institute of Linguistics. As missionaries began to multiply, the other was Wycliffe Bible Translators, which grew into the world's largest mission.

One old chief asked Townsend, "Why haven't you come sooner? . . . We have been wondering what sin we committed against God that kept Him from sending you to us." Said Townsend, "The fault is not theirs. God has sent but we have refused to go." Thanks to Townsend and others, the Bible was translated into more languages in the last 100 years than in all the centuries before.

St. Helena, looking much too young, bears the true cross. (Bell, Mrs. Arthur. *Saints in Christian Art*. London: George Bell, 1901-4.)

Other Events

328: St. Helena, the mother of Constantine, died on this day. She visited Jerusalem at eighty years of age, supervised excavations and purportedly found the true cross. She identified several of the places associated with Christ. She was buried in the Church of the Holy Apostles in Constantinople.

1276: Pope Hadrian V died about fifty days after taking office. When elected, he said, "Would to God you were congratulating a healthy cardinal instead of a dying pope."

1732: A farewell hymn-sing for Leonard Dober and David Nitschmann, who were leaving Herrnhut to become missionaries, was held on this day.

1792: Former monks and nuns were forbidden to teach in France; Nuns were told to nurse instead.

1944: John Sung, a brilliant Chinese evangelist, died. He went to the United States to study and took degrees in the sciences, but the Scripture verse "For what is a man profited, if he shall gain the whole word, and lose his own soul?" (Matthew 16:26, KJV) kept running through his head. So he entered Union Theological Seminary. There he was taught modern biblical criticism and told that God was dead. On the verge of losing his faith, he prayed earnestly and studied the Bible one night. Suddenly his soul was transformed; he wept and shouted for joy and raced to tell other students what God had done for him. School authorities thought he had gone insane and committed him to an asylum, where he was held for 193 days. Upon his release, he sailed back to China, throwing his awards and diplomas, which he considered worthless, into the ocean. He dedicated the rest of his life to spreading the gospel in his homeland.

A Gentle Man Died Cruelly

The deaths of some martyrs are understandable: By their bravery and dissent from established authority, their persecution became inevitable. Not so the death of Thomas Bilney. Bilney was a meek, scrupulous and tender-minded man who posed no threat to anyone. His doctrines differed hardly a whit from those of the authorities who put him to death. In fact, two years after his death, his doctrines were adopted in the England that had executed him.

Bilney was ordained as a priest in 1519. Like many others, he sought to win God's approval by fasts, penances, masses and vigils, but he found that they were powerless to relieve his conscience. Then, after reading what Erasmus wrote about St. Paul's epistles, he felt "a marvelous comfort and quietness, insomuch as my bruised bones leapt for joy." His Bible shows that he saturated himself in Scripture thereafter, marking it up with notes and underlining it. He came to realize that salvation was through Christ alone. Rites, rituals, works—he declared all of them mere emptiness unless done in Christ. His sweetness of character and devotion to Scripture soon won Hugh Latimer, John Lambert, Matthew Parker and Robert Barnes to Christ.

Freed from the need to work to attain salvation, Bilney worked even harder. He seldom slept, ate little, prayed much and obtained a license to preach throughout the countryside. Latimer and he became almost inseparable, visiting the lepers and prisoners of Cambridge. Latimer called him "a simple, good soul not fit for this world."

What got Bilney into trouble was his denunciation of the worship of relics and saints. He said that pilgrimages to Canterbury could do nothing for the soul and that the idolatry of Christendom had kept the Jews from Christ. Cardinal Wolsey became alarmed and had Bilney arrested. Confronted by the weight of the Church and dreading the fire, Bilney recanted. He did not differ from the Church over the Eucharist, confession, the mass or any substantial doctrine, only on specific emphases and on the matter of relics and pilgrimages. After a year in prison, Bilney was freed.

He was, however, so scrupulous that he could scarcely bear to open the Scripture, feeling that the whole Bible condemned his betrayal of his principles. He repeated again that salvation is by faith, not works, and that relics are helpless to save. After two years of deep despondency, he began to preach again, gathering boldness.

He was once again seized and tried. As a lapsed "heretic" he could be burned, and it was so ordered. To prepare his mind for the ordeal, he burnt his finger in a fire. He readily allowed himself to be confessed and accepted one last mass, since he had never challenged those things. Cheerfully he went to his death. After urging a large crowd to live godly lives and admitting error in preaching against fasts (which he had always practiced), the fire was lit beneath him. He died cruelly on this day in 1531, crying "Jesus!" and "I believe!" as the flames consumed his body.

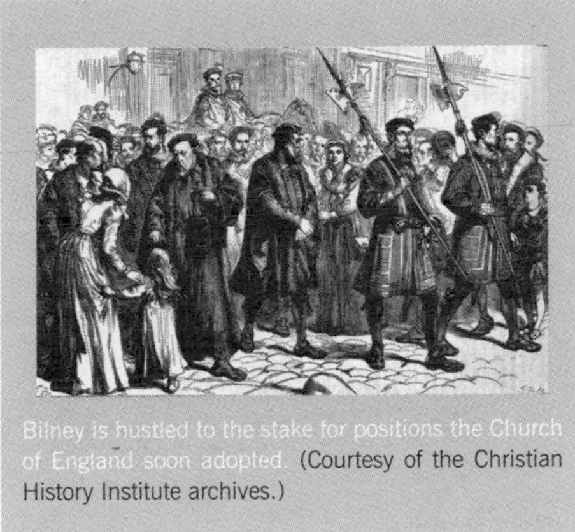
Bilney is hustled to the stake for positions the Church of England soon adopted. (Courtesy of the Christian History Institute archives.)

Other Events

302 (probable date): Andrew the Martyr was cornered and killed near the straits of Taurus. Earlier he had won 1,000 soldiers to Christ after selecting them rather like Gideon selected his 300 to fight a much larger force.

440: Pope St. Sixtus III died. He approved the acts of the Council of Ephesus of 431.

1559: John Craig, scheduled to die as a heretic the next day, was miraculously released from an Italian prison. Men were sent to track him down, but the captain who caught up with him recognized him as the one who had tended the captain when he was wounded years before. In gratitude, he helped Craig escape.

1561: Mary Stuart, a Catholic, landed in Scotland, where she faced continual conflict with John Knox, the Protestant reformer.

1835: German-born William Nast, founder of German Methodism, was appointed a missionary to Germans in Ohio. He organized hundreds of German converts into churches.

1949: In Czechoslovakia, Lozik and Probozny were made bishops without government approval. The government had blocked roads to keep people from attending the ceremony, but 100 priests, 10 bishops and 12,000 people showed up anyway.

Mary Stuart, Catholic opponent of Protestant reformer John Knox. (Lang, Andrew. *John Knox and the Reformation*. London/New York/Bombay: Longmans, Green and Co., 1905.)

August 20

Death by Association

"Bring out your dead!" Medieval people raised heavy smoke in the streets and marked infected houses in an effort to stop the plague. (Courtesy of the Christian History Institute archives.)

When he died on this day in 1384, Gerard Groot left behind him a band of followers who were dedicated to reforming the Church, spreading the gospel in all Christendom and putting the Scriptures into the hands and minds of the common people. He died as he lived, devoted to the Body of Christ: Despite personal risk, he visited a beloved follower who was infected by the plague. As a result, Groot caught the disease himself and died at the age of forty-four. He had labored for only ten years for Christ.

Groot was born in 1340 and was not converted until 1374. His parents were well-to-do, and until the time of his conversion he had lived a life of luxury. Immediately upon his conversion, he dedicated his life to Christ and gave up almost everything he owned. He decided he would be poor like Christ. Indeed, his entire mission would be Christ-centered and aim at taking men deeper into their knowledge of Jesus. After two years as a guest in a Carthusian monastery, Groot became a deacon and obtained permission to preach.

As a traveling preacher, he worked his way through the lowlands—Flanders, Guelders and Holland—speaking against the abuses that were so common in the Church. So severe were Groot's attacks on these errors that the Church stripped him of his authorization to preach. His life was in danger, but the plague carried him off before action could take place.

Groot had gathered men around him to copy Scripture and religious texts. From the revenues they earned by doing this, they supported themselves and helped the poor. The band became known as the Brethren of Common Life. Eighteen houses of these Brethren formed before Groot died. Groot also gathered a group of women called the Sisters of Common Life. These groups did not take monastic vows nor were they required to remain celibate. Anyone could leave the group at any time. Their aim was to live the life of Christ while engaged in everyday work. This way of life became known as *Devotio Moderna* (the modern way of serving God). The Brethren became deeply interested in education and in larger cities used their residences as schools. They produced some famous pupils.

Among those trained by or connected with the Brethren of Common Life were men whose names live on to this day. Nicholas Cusa wrote works of considerable influence among the scientists and churchmen of his day and rose to a cardinalate. Thomas á Kempis wrote (or collated—scholars can't agree on this) the devotional classic *The Imitation of Christ*. Another pupil of the Brethren of Common Life, Erasmus, became the greatest scholar of his age and an agent of reform.

It is obvious that even after his death, Groot's influence did not die.

Kenneth Pike, cofounder of Summer Institute of Linguistics. (Pike, Eunice V. *Ken Pike: Scholar and Christian*. Dallas, TX: Summer Institute of Linguistics, 1981. Used by permission.)

Other Events

984: Pope John XIV, held in prison by the antipope Boniface, died on this day.

1153: Bernard of Clairvaux died on this day at the hour of Tierce (the third hour). His spiritual depth is admired by Protestants and Catholics alike.

1527: Anabaptists held their "Martyr Synod" at Augsburg. It was called this because most of the Anabaptist leaders who attended were martyred within five years. At the meeting, the Anabaptists divided up Europe for missionary enterprise. Among those who attended were Hans Denck, Hans Hut, Jörg von Passau, Ludwig Hetzer, Jakob Gross, Jakob Dachser, Sigmund Salminger, Eitelhans Langenmantel, Leonhard Dorfbrunner and Gall Fischer. Only three of these men lived to see the fifth year of the movement, the rest falling easy prey to their enemies because they had no bases, little support and poor lines of communication.

1902: Althea Brown, an African-American woman, sailed for Africa as a missionary. She would die young there of malaria and sleeping sickness.

1935: Kenneth Pike crossed into Mexico for the first time with Cameron Townsend. Later he became a trailblazing linguist and a founder of Summer Institute of Linguistics.

AUGUST 21

Turning from the Bible to Aristotle and Lombard

A decisive moment in medieval scholasticism came when Alexander of Hales substituted Peter Lombard's *Sentences* in place of the Bible as his basic text for his classes. Like many who came after him, he also wrote a commentary on Lombard's work.

Alexander was born in Hales, Shropshire, England. He studied and taught in Paris and became a brilliant scholar. In his own day he was called the "unanswerable doctor" and "king of theology." Although his method looked back to ancient authority, he was an innovator within the scholastic system.

In addition to making Lombard's *Sentences* his basic text, Alexander was the first scholastic philosopher to build a summary of Christian theology using the newly discovered writings of Aristotle as its key authority. Because he became a Franciscan friar at the height of his career, Aristotle's teachings exerted a strong influence on Franciscan theology. Alexander didn't stop with Aristotle, but also included Arabic ideas, as well as the more standard ideas of the neo-Platonists and Augustine of Hippo.

Christian summaries were not a new idea. Many people had already written them. They were arranged under "questions." But because Alexander (and the others who worked on the *Summa Universae Theologiae*) quoted Aristotle as a reference to almost every question, using newly recovered books on logic, metaphysics, physics and ethics, he paved the way for scholars like Albert the Great and St. Thomas Aquinas, who reconciled much of Aristotle's thinking with Christian theology. In fact, Aquinas considered Alexander his favorite scholar and closely followed the outline of the *Summa Universae Theologiae* when he wrote his own, more famous *Summa Theologica*. He probably never actually studied with Alexander, though.

Alexander is regarded as a founder of the Franciscan school of theology. In large measure, he followed the path of Bonaventure, the first really great Franciscan theologian.

Some of the little we know about Alexander comes from the writings of Roger Bacon, who was critical of him. Bacon thought Alexander got too much praise while real contributors to knowledge remained unknown.

Shortly after attending the Council of Lyons in Paris, Alexander died on this day in 1245, probably during an epidemic.

One of the charges leveled by the reformer was that priests were better-educated in philosophy than in the Bible. Alexander helped bring about that state of affairs. Today we remember the works of those who learned from him more than we do his own work. However, he continues to be studied by scholars interested in that time period.

Aristotle. In the thirteenth century, rediscovery of Aristotle's works changed Christian theology through scholars such as Alexander of Hales. (Singer, Charles. *Studies in the History and Method of Science*. Oxford: Clarendon Press, 1921.)

OTHER EVENTS

1874: Theodore Tilton sued the popular Congregational clergyman Henry Ward Beecher for alienating the affections of Mrs. Tilton. A jury found Beecher not guilty of the alleged adultery by a vote of nine to three.

1940: Leon Trotsky was murdered in Mexico City. As a young Jewish man, he and his friend Abraham Silverstein had an opportunity to hear the gospel of Christ. Silverstein was converted and became a missionary to Jews. Trotsky rejected the gospel and died an atheist at the hands of his former Bolshevik comrades.

1978: Robert T. Ketcham died on this day. He was one of the founders of the General Association of Regular Baptists and a notable preacher and soul winner. Over 5,000 people professed Christ under his preaching. He personally baptized 3,093 individuals. His books and pamphlets were widely distributed.

Mrs. Elizabeth Tilton, focus of the scandal surrounding Henry Ward Beecher. (Doyle, J.E.P. *Plymouth Church and Its Pastor, or Henry Ward Beecher and His Accusers*. New York: Park Publishing Company, 1874.)

Gottfrief Wilhelm Leibnitz was not only a coinventor of calculus but was also one of many who have tried to reunify the Church over the centuries. (Hart, Ivor B. *Makers of Science*. London: Oxford University, 1923.)

AUGUST

22

World War II Intervened

The Church is the Body of Christ—one body. As Nicea's authoritative creed puts it, "We believe in . . . one holy catholic and apostolic church." While it is true that the true Church is invisible and that Christ alone knows who belongs to Him, many Christians are unhappy that the visible Church should appear so fragmented, particularly when those fragments attack one another.

Since the Reformation, with its breakup of the Western Church, men have striven to restore unity to the Church—some by the sword, some through reason and goodwill. In the latter category were individuals such as Martin Bucer, who worked to iron out divisions within Protestantism; Gottfried Wilhelm Leibnitz, who tried to gather an international conference to discuss reunification of Lutherans and Catholics; and Hugo Grotius, who cried like a voice in the wilderness not only for international law but for reconciliation. Count Nikolaus von Zinzendorf founded a successful experiment at Herrnhut that welded together a diverse group of refugees into a group known as the Moravians. Many more could be named.

In more recent times, John R. Mott organized the 1910 International Missionary Conference, which was held in Edinburgh. Well-attended, the conference fostered other movements. Out of it sprang the International Missionary Council in 1921. Bishop Charles Brent of the United States returned from Edinburgh fired up to create the World Conference of Faith and Order, which came into being in 1927 at Lausanne. Brent wanted to confront doctrinal issues head on. With a vision of Christendom united for the rebuilding of a world ravaged by World War I, Archbishop Nathan Söderblom of Uppsala spearheaded a drive to bring Christians to Stockholm in 1925 for a Life and Work Conference.

The World Conference of Faith and Order proposed creating a World Council of Churches. A 1937 meeting of Life and Faith agreed to explore joining this movement. At Utrecht in 1938 the two movements united and set up a preliminary headquarters in Geneva. Roman Catholics and Russian Orthodox refused to get involved. The Russians said, "Orthodox Christians must regard the Holy Orthodox Catholic Church as the true Church of Christ, one and unique." For Orthodox or Catholics to join was to suggest that all "Churches" were equal. Some regional Orthodox, however, did send delegates and observers to the various meetings. The World Council of Churches planned to hold its first conference shortly after its formation, but World War II intervened.

Not until this day in 1948 was the conference's plan fulfilled. Then the World Council of Churches (WCC) was born in Amsterdam. The International Missionary Council merged with the WCC a few years later. Later the Roman Catholic Church changed its stance and sent observers to WCC meetings and also held its own ecumenical council. Third-world nations became increasingly involved in the council.

Other Events

565: Columba, a missionary from Ireland, reportedly confronted a monster at Loch Ness, setting off a long train of sightings. The story appears in a book filled with the saint's alleged miracles.

1241: Pope Gregory IX, who persecuted the French heretic sect of Albigensians, died.

1751: Isaac Backus was re-baptized and became a prominent Baptist.

1885: William Paton Mackay, who wrote the hymn "Revive Us Again," died on this day. He was a Scottish Presbyterian who had been a medical doctor before he entered the pulpit.

1952: Lewis Sperry Chafer, an American Presbyterian theologian, author and educator, died. Once a traveling evangelist, he founded Dallas Theological Seminary.

1968: Pope Paul VI became the first reigning pope to visit Latin America.

Loch Ness, the site of Columba's alleged monster sighting. (Hill, George Birkbeck Norman. *Footsteps of Dr. Johnson (Scotland)*. London: S. Low, Marson, Searle & Rivington [limited], 1890.)

August 23

Not Peace, but a Sword

In France after the Reformation, Calvinists known as Huguenots sprang up in large numbers. The Roman Catholic Church persecuted them. Sometimes manipulated by unscrupulous leaders, the Huguenots rose to defend their rights. Soon war ravaged France. Although far fewer in number than their foes, the Huguenots fought so fiercely that they forced concessions from the French majority—concessions that allowed them to build churches and manage affairs in cities where they had majorities. The bloodshed that issued out of the conflict imprinted animosity between the Protestants and the Catholics. Out of that smoldering hatred flared up one of the most despicable events of Church history.

In Paris on August 22, 1572, an attempt was made to assassinate the Huguenot leader Admiral de Coligny, a French patriot. He was wounded in the attack and went home to recover. Accounts disagree as to what happened next and who was responsible. However, it is clear that on this day in 1572, the government finalized a plot to kill all Huguenots in Paris.

Late this night or early the next morning, armed men led by the Guises, a powerful political faction, broke into Coligny's apartment, overcame his guards and killed him. Coligny's death was the signal for a general butchery of the Huguenots. They were slaughtered in cold blood well into the morning of August 24 in Paris and for several days afterward in outlying regions. This atrocity is known as the St. Bartholomew's Day Massacre because it lasted into that saint's day, August 24. As many as 70,000 perished during the massacre. The rest fled to fortified cities and fought back.

Their movement became known as *La Cause* (The Cause) and pitted them against the Catholic Holy League (*La Sainte Ligue*). Brutal fighting raged across France. Charles IX publicly claimed he had ordered the massacre, but many historians think the plot was the work of Catherine de Medici, who felt that her power was threatened. Possibly Charles, by taking credit, was trying to reap a political benefit from the gruesome event. If so, he won few plaudits outside of Catholic regions. Pope Gregory XIII struck a special medallion to commemorate the "holy" act, but most other Europeans reacted with horror.

The St. Bartholomew's Day Massacre was not the end of the matter. When Protestant Henry of Navarre converted to Catholicism and became King Henry IV, he granted his Huguenot compatriots a number of rights under the Edict of Nantes. The rights were gradually eroded, more Huguenot revolts occurred and eventually hundreds of thousands of them fled the country.

The St. Bartholomew's Day Massacre. (Courtesy of the Christian History Institute archives.)

Other Events

1744: Rowland Hill was born in Shropshire, England. He became a minister and worked among the poorest and sickest in England, to the scandal of his elite family. Because he preached out-of-doors and worked with outcasts, he was denied admission to the Church of England priesthood. He wrote Village Dialogs in which he made remarks like:

> Every man who goes to heaven must have the name of new-man. We must not expect to enter there unless we are created anew in Christ Jesus unto good works, which God hath before ordained that we should walk in them.

Rowland was also in on the formation of The British and Foreign Bible Society, The London Missionary Society and The Religious Tract Society.

1838: The first of Mt. Holyoke College's classes graduated. The school was founded by Christian teacher Mary Lyon as the first American college for women.

1926: Methodist holiness clergyman Russel K. Carter died. He wrote the hymn favorite "Standing on the Promises."

1936: The Confessing Church of Germany read its full declaration, including appeals to save the Jews.

1952: Frederick Kenyon, biblical archaeologist and author of *Our Bible and the Ancient Manuscripts*, died on this day. He had a knack for making his findings intelligible to lay people.

Mount Holyoke. (Dunning, Albert E. *Congregationalists in America: A Popular History of Their Origin, Belief, Polity, Growth and Work*. New York: J.A. Hill, 1894.)

August 24

The City Taken That Took the World

Alaric enters Rome. (Lord, John. *Beacon Lights of History*. New York: James Clarke, 1886.)

On this day in 410, the city of Rome, once master of the Mediterranean, fell to Alaric and his Visigoth armies. Apparently someone opened the city gate from within. The medieval historian Procopius said it may have been done by slaves whom Alaric had treacherously given as a token of friendship to the Senators, or it may have been by the servants of an aristocratic woman who felt the city had suffered long enough.

Afterward, refugees from Rome showed up all around the Mediterranean world. In Palestine, Bible translator Jerome described once-haughty women reduced to working for a crust of bread. He wrote letters lamenting the fall of the imperial city. Like everyone else, he could not avoid the symbolism of the event: "My voice sticks in my throat; and, as I dictate, sobs choke my utterance. The City which had taken the whole world was itself taken."

Gaspard de Coligny, who was murdered on this day. (Baird, Henry Martyn. *Theodore Beza: The Councilor of the French Reformation*. New York: G.P. Putnam's Sons, 1899.)

In the sack of Rome, Christians died alongside pagans. Some Christian women suffered rape, even though the Visigoths claimed to be Christians. Some of these women, following the historical example of the famous pagan girl Lucretia, killed themselves for shame. Others fled to North Africa as refugees, where they were taunted by pagans who asked them why their God had not protected them. Some were also accused of cowardice for not killing themselves.

Why had Christians suffered in the sack of Rome? According to the Bible, God would have spared Sodom if there had been just ten righteous souls in it (see Genesis 18:16-33). Rome was a city with thousands of Christians—and a major Church center as well—and yet God had allowed it to be ravaged.

Various people put this question to the greatest living Christian thinker of the day: Augustine of Hippo. He responded by writing a masterpiece entitled *The City of God and the City of Man*. It was the world's first "modern" history in the sense that it offered an account of world history with a teleological explanation—that is, an explanation showing that events have "purpose," or destination.

Augustine took a different approach in his work than Jerome did in his letters. Instead of merely lamenting the fall of the city, he sought an explanation in Christian theology. He pointed out that although the God of Christianity had not stopped the event from happening, Christianity had indeed made a difference in the outcome. Augustine reminded his readers that the barbarian invaders had spared most of the churches and that even pagans had taken refuge in the sacred buildings. Christians, said Augustine, have always suffered and will always suffer in this world. To phrase it as a modern cliché, God never promised Christians a rose garden here on earth.

To Augustine's way of thinking, the fall of Rome was less important than it seemed to most of his contemporaries. What was really going on was a far deeper warfare—the war between God's kingdom and man's. He pointed out that if God's kingdom was not clearly distinguishable in this world, it was because not everyone who said he was a Christian really was. To the heathen who blamed Christianity for the downfall of the Roman Empire, Augustine showed that pagan practices actually were at fault for the weakness of the empire. In book 2, chapter 4 of *The City of God and the City of Man*, Augustine asked:

> Why were the gods so negligent as to allow the morals of their worshippers to sink to so low a depth? . . . Why did not those gods . . . lay down moral precepts that would help their devotees to lead a decent life?

In chapter 21 of the same book, he notes:

> However great and good your natural gifts may be, it takes true piety to make them pure and perfect; with impurity they merely end in loss and pain.

Augustine's long and loosely argued book was finished many years after the fall of Rome. *The City of God* colored all later European historical writing. That much good, at least, came out of Alaric's sack of Rome.

Other Events

1519: Gaspard de Coligny was murdered early in the morning in Paris. Highly favored at the French court, he nonetheless came out on the side of the Huguenots, becoming their hero during the religious strife of the 1560s. His assassination by the court precipitated the St. Bartholomew's Day Massacre.

1779: St. Cosmas Aitolos was martyred. He carried the gospel into Albania, but when he preached against the cruel practices of the reigning classes, he was murdered.

Parting Blessings

In 1731 Count Nikolaus von Zinzendorf returned to Herrnhut from Copenhagen with an appeal that would greatly affect the Moravians' impact on the world. He had met two Eskimos from Hans Egede's Greenland mission who told him that it seemed as if the Greenland mission was about to fail. Zinzendorf's response was to ask, "Shouldn't Herrnhut then send someone to take Egede's place?" The Moravians agreed. In a meeting held on August 21, 1732, Christian David, a carpenter, and some other laymen were designated to go. They arrived in Greenland in May of 1733.

In Copenhagen, the count had also met a former slave, Anthony Ulrich of St. Thomas Island. Anthony described the terrible brutality of slavery on the island: Slaves were utterly without Christ and were whipped if they even went near a church. The account, relayed through Zinzendorf to the brethren at Herrnhut, greatly shocked them. Two close friends, Leonard Dober and Tobias Leupold, were unable to sleep because of it. They thought that surely Christ would want them to go to St. Thomas, even if they had to become slaves themselves in order to witness to the Negroes.

They asked permission to go but were refused. Everyone in the community saw only obstacles. The young men persisted and finally asked that the lot be drawn to determine if the Lord would allow them to go. Dober was selected; Leupold was not. David Nitschmann, a man of experience and honor, offered to accompany Dober for a few months and help him get established on the island.

The community of Herrnhut blessed the two men and sent them to Copenhagen to find a ship bound for St. Thomas. Many brethren were still opposed to the experiment, but Dober was determined to lay his life down, if need be, to bring the gospel to the slaves. Zinzendorf rode partway with them—to Bautzen, Germany—giving his final blessing to Dober on this day in 1732.

While on their 300-mile trip to Copenhagen, Dober and Nitschmann met much skepticism. Virtually everyone told them it was folly to go to St. Thomas. They said that to preach to slaves was absurd and that fever would undoubtedly kill the missionaries. Even Anthony, the former slave, changed his mind about the wisdom of sending missionaries to the island, but he nonetheless wrote Dober and Nitschmann a letter of introduction to his sister, who was still on the island.

In Copenhagen, help came from an unexpected quarter: Princess Charlotte Amelia learned of the mission and was moved to give funds and a Bible. A Dutch ship was found to take the two men to St. Thomas, and they sailed in October. During the voyage the sailors continually scoffed at the mission, which they said must fail. They tried to frighten the two men with stories of plague on the island.

After much labor and years of fruitless suffering, Dober won his first convert—a boy. Anthony's sister was also brought to Christ. From these humble beginnings, the Moravians later extended their work to the whole world, effecting change and repentance in many places.

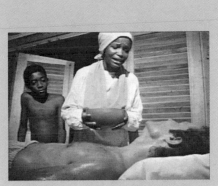

Slaves treat the feverish Dober. (Courtesy of Gateway Films/Vision Video.)

Other Events

303: Genesius, acting in a play mocking Christians, remembered his own Christian roots and publicly called aloud for salvation. Emperor Diocletian was infuriated and had Genesius tortured and beheaded.

1410: Cardinal Odo de Colonna decided in favor of Archbishop Zybnek against reform in Bohemia.

1936: The Chinese government ordered all foreigners to leave Suchow, compelling the Chinese Trio to leave too.

1940: Japanese Christian socialist Toyohiko Kagawa was arrested as a traitor as he left a church service. He often spoke out against evil government policies.

1945: Missionary John Birch was martyred in China. The US government, which knew the details of his death, tried to cover them up. The conservative John Birch Society, which attempts to expose such cover-ups, took its name from this incident.

A coin with an image of Emporer Diocletian's head on it. Diocletian had the actor Genesius tortured and beheaded for calling out for salvation during a performance. (Rostovtzeff, Mikhail. *The Social and Economic History of the Roman Empire*. Oxford/New York: Oxford University Press, 1926.)

Henry Melchior Muhlenberg, who founded the Lutheran Synod of Pennsylvania. (Wolf, Edmund Jacob. *The Lutherans in America: A Story of Struggle, Progress, Influence and Marvelous Growth*. New York: J.A. Hill, 1889.)

August 26

First Lutheran Synod in the Colonies

Although there had been Lutherans in the American colonies since at least 1643, it was not until 1748 that the first Lutheran synod was established.

Lutherans lived on Manhattan Island at least as early as 1643. The Swedish Lutherans were not treated kindly by the other Protestants of the area, who were strict Calvinists in the tradition of the Synod of Dort. The Calvinists compelled Lutheran children to be baptized by Calvinist preachers and to accept the doctrines of the Synod of Dort. Peter Stuyvesant, the famous governor of New Amsterdam (now New York), was especially harsh on them. He fined and imprisoned Lutherans for holding even informal services.

The Lutherans complained to the directors of the Dutch West India Company in Holland and applied to the Lutheran consistory in Amsterdam for a Lutheran pastor. In 1669 Rev. Joseph Fabricius was sent to them, but things did not go well, and he was replaced by Bernhard Anton Arsenius, who was there from 1671 to 1691.

The Lutheran Church continued to struggle forward, but with no central organization to hold it together, factionalism became a real threat. Then in 1741, Rev. Henry Melchior Muhlenberg accepted a call to go to Pennsylvania. He reached Philadelphia on November 15, 1742, and preached his first sermon there on December 5. Two new churches were built during Muhlenberg's time there, including one in Trappe, Pennsylvania, near whose walls Muhlenberg was later buried.

But the most important work undertaken by Muhlenberg was the founding of the Lutheran Synod of Pennsylvania, which was officially established on this day in 1748. Although rather informal—it had no constitution in the beginning—the synod gave form and focus to the Lutheran communities in the state. It was a significant moment in the long and illustrious history of Lutheranism in America.

From 1754 to 1760, no regular meetings of the synod were held, but in 1760, primarily through the influence of Muhlenberg's friend, Provost Karl Magnus Wrangel, the synod meetings were revived. Muhlenberg wrote the constitution for the mother congregation at St. Michaels in Philadelphia, and the Lutherans adopted it in 1762. It became the basis for plans of local church government in American Lutheran churches today.

Maud Booth, who, with her husband, founded Volunteers of America, worked with prisoners. (Foster, Warren Dunham, ed. *Heroines of Modern Religion*. New York: Sturgis & Walton Co., 1913.)

Other Events

1708: Ebenezer Erskine, moved by the preface of the Ten Commandments, "I am the Lord thy God" (Exodus 20:2, KJV), wrote out a covenant:

> I offer myself up, soul and body, unto God the Father, Son and Holy Ghost. I flee for shelter to the blood of Jesus. I will live to Him; I will die to Him. I take heaven and earth to witness that all I am and all I have are His.

He preached in Scotland, suffering persecution and dying a worn-out man. He founded the Scottish Secessionist Church.

1832: Adam Clarke, English Methodist clergyman and author of a popular Bible commentary, died on this day.

1846: On this day Felix Mendelssohn's oratorio *Elijah* was first performed.

1948: Maud Ballington Booth died. She and her husband disagreed with the methods of the Salvation Army and formed the Volunteers of America. Booth devoted herself to the poor and to the Volunteer Prison League.

1956: One-and-a-half million Polish pilgrims to Czestochowa's shrine of the Black Madonna made this vow: "I promise to do everything in my power so that Poland may become the true kingdom of thy son."

August 27

Ordered Out of France

Pierre Viret was the most sought-after preacher of sixteenth century France. Among the cities that invited him to preach were Paris, Orléans, Avignon, Montauban and Montpellier. He was stationed at Nimes at the time, but Viret accepted Montpellier's offer, believing Christ wanted him there. Once there, he converted almost the entire faculty of the city's medical college to Reformation Christianity. But unlike John Calvin, John Knox and other well-known reformers, Pierre Viret's name gets little recognition today.

Curiously enough, Viret was not even a Frenchman. He was born in the little Swiss town of Orbe in 1511. His parents were poor, but Viret took advantage of a free education to begin his life of scholarship. Eventually he attended the University of Paris. There, as in Switzerland, some of his teachers were Lutheran sympathizers, and through their influence he became a convert to Reformation faith.

William Farel, the same man who later convinced John Calvin to become a preacher, convinced Viret too. From then on, Viret's whole life was dedicated to godliness and spreading the gospel. He was very effective in his work—so effective, in fact, that he was severely wounded by Catholic enemies who tried to close his mouth by stabbing him to death. Later, Catholics poisoned his spinach. He survived, but he suffered stomach problems ever after.

An admirable thing about Viret was that the ugly attacks and the riots that accompanied his sermons did not warp his spirit. To the contrary, he preached just as lovingly to his enemies as ever. Although he was staunchly Protestant, he labored to bring about reconciliation between Catholics and Protestants.

He worked for many years in Lausanne and Geneva before beginning his work in France. Thousands attended his sermons, and whole regions came to Christ under his teaching. Although the Huguenots are often described as French Calvinists, many were actually converts to Viret's teachings, which were slightly different than Calvin's. (For instance, he viewed the Lord's Supper as more symbolic than Calvin did.) When Viret was at Lyons in southern France, Catholics regained control of that region. On this day in 1565, Viret received a notice telling him to get out, so he went to Navarre, which was ruled by the Protestant queen, Jeanne d'Albret.

A few years later, Viret and eleven other ministers were captured by the Catholics. Seven of them were executed. Viret, however, was freed because the commander had heard so much good about him from other Catholics.

Pierre Viret, who preached the Reformation in France. (Baird, Henry Martyn. *Theodore Beza: The Councilor of the French Reformation*. New York: G.P. Putnam's Sons, 1899.)

Viret suffered many things in his life. His first wife and his children by her died of the plague. His second wife and two children also died of the plague. These griefs made him a sympathetic figure to those who had suffered similarly. Despite ill health, Viret preached countless sermons and wrote almost fifty books. He died at the age of sixty, worn out with hard work and suffering.

Other Events

Unknown: St. Monica's day is celebrated. Her determination helped bring her son, Augustine, to Christ.

1640: An agreement allowing religious freedom made Rhode Island the first colony to grant full religious tolerance.

1660: The works of John Milton, who supported Parliament in the strife with the king, were burned by royal decree when the monarchy was restored. Milton was imprisoned for a short while but continued work on his epic, *Paradise Lost*. The charge against him was that he supported an elder-run church (the Presbyterian form), not bishop-run churches (the Episcopal form) and attacked the English monarchy.

1727: This is the day that the famous 100-year prayer meeting began in Herrnhut, Germany. Count Nikolaus von Zinzendorf's Moravian community began an around-the-clock "prayer chain" with twenty-four men and twenty-four women covenanted to each take an hour of the day for prayer.

St. Monica with her son, Augustine. (Lord, John. *Beacon Lights of History*. New York: James Clarke, 1886.)

A statue of Hugo Grotius, whose work was recognized as the basis of international law. (Courtesy of Datafoto.)

AUGUST 28

He Died Thinking He Had Failed

Some men are not able to judge the value of their own work. Hugo Grotius was one such person. On his deathbed he lamented the worthlessness of all he had done. He died on this day in 1645, convinced that he was a failure.

He had been given the name Huig de Groot at his birth, but he later Latinized his name. He proved to be a precocious lad. At the age of ten he won accolades for his grasp of the Latin language. When he was eleven he was called a second Erasmus. At fourteen he completely revised Martianus Capella's encyclopedia after having read all the ancient authorities for himself. He followed this with translations of Simon Stevin, the eminent scientist and mathematician, and of Aratus, the Greek statesman. At the age of fifteen he held public disputations and was made attaché to the great John van Barneveld on a crucial peace mission. By seventeen he had argued his first legal case and at twenty-two had written a book (not published), which embodied his best ideas.

Grotius's first venture into international law was his book *Mare Liberum*, which argued for freedom of the seas. He took his stand firmly on the rights of man. Although he cited massive numbers of sources, he also exhibited a great deal of originality and common sense and wrote in a readable style.

The Netherlands entered a period of severe theological disputation. Arminians and Calvinists were at odds. The states general issued an Edict of Pacification to cool tempers on both sides, which failed. Barneveld, Grotius and others saw Prince Maurice of Orange becoming a dictator. They supported the states general in negotiating a twelve-year truce with Spain. This infuriated Maurice. When Barneveld and Grotius suggested a peace formula, Maurice maneuvered to get Barneveld executed and Grotius imprisoned for life.

With the help of his faithful wife, Grotius escaped after first committing himself to the Lord and then hiding in a book box. He was honored in other European countries for his work.

While in exile, he wrote his most famous book, *The Law of War and Peace*. The book was badly needed, for Christian Europe was in a tragic turmoil. Wars of great cruelty ravaged the land. No mercy was shown anyone except by a few enlightened leaders such as Adolphus Gustavus, who admired Grotius's work.

Although a Christian, Grotius relied far less on biblical arguments than was common for the time. Instead, he showed from Christian and heathen history how good men of all ages had been merciful and kept faith in international affairs. In 1648, three years after Grotius's death, the Peace of Westphalia embodied many of the principles he had set forth. Two hundred years later, his work was recognized as the basis of international law.

Augustine, who stamped the Church with his personality and ideas. (Courtesy of the University of Texas collection of public domain portraits on the Web.)

OTHER EVENTS

430: St. Augustine of Hippo, who, more than any other man since the apostles, stamped the Church with his personality and ideas, died on this day.

1645: King Ladislas IV of Poland convened a conference at Torun (Thorn) to try to resolve differences between the Catholic Church and Protestant factions. Less than a month later, the conferees gave up, having failed in their objective.

1858: Eleazar Williams, an adventurer and missionary to Iroquois Indians, died. Although part Mohawk, he claimed to be the "lost" dauphin of France.

1866: Gerard Manley Hopkins, an English poet, wrote to John Henry Newman, asking for an audience so that he could convert to Roman Catholicism. Hopkins became a Jesuit priest and wrote many Christian poems of the highest caliber:

> Glory be to God for dappled things—
> For skies of couple-color as a brinded cow.

1953: Bill Bright incorporated Campus Crusade for Christ in Los Angeles. It became one of the leading evangelistic organizations of the twentieth century.

August 29

Old and "Ready to Be Gone"

Right from his arrival in the Massachusetts colony in 1631, John Eliot was active in its affairs. In addition to raising a large family, he pastored, taught, wrote many books, took part in various public events (such as the trial of Anne Hutchinson) and reached out to the Indians whom everyone said should be evangelized but whom no one else did much about. For his work with them he is called the "Apostle to the Indians."

He was tired: "I am old, ready to be gone, and desire to leave as many books as I can," wrote Eliot on this day in 1686 to his English sponsor, Robert Boyle. Eliot had learned the Indian language, created an alphabet for it and translated the Bible for them.

Now he was old and the Bibles were tattered—the Indians so loved the Old Testament that they had worn out all their copies. Eliot wanted to edit and reprint the Testament, which had been the loving labor of his life.

But, the Society for the Propagation of the Gospel in New England said "no." They told him to just reprint the New Testament and the Psalms—any more was too expensive. Let the natives learn English, they said. Eliot pleaded against this decision and when that brought no result, he took decisive action. After receiving an unexpected gift from an English supporter (it was far less than the amount needed for the Old Testament, but he trusted that the rest would come from somewhere) Eliot took the whole sum to the printer and ordered the work to begin. Later his conscience smote him, and he wondered what right he had to defy the society that had supported him for so long.

He spoke to the commissioners of Boston, and, greatly to his surprise, the men decided he had been right in trying to get the Old Testament reprinted for the Indians. They told him that if the society did not defray the cost, they'd see that the printer got paid. The commissioners wrote to England for him and obtained consensus to continue the work. Eliot was grateful. He had labored for nine years on the revision, pleading all the while for a new edition. Now he felt his life had not been wasted.

Still he had much to do. He was getting ready to print his *Practice of Piety* and to redo an Indian-language catechism and primer. He did not have much time left, for his strength was failing. He died three-and-a-half years after writing his letter to Boyle.

Eliot did not succeed in converting a large portion of the Algonquins, despite translating the Bible for them. Those few who did come to believe formed Christian villages. Regrettably, most of them were wiped out during King Philip's War because they were between the two sides. The other Algonquins butchered them as traitors, and the whites, who did not see them as brothers in Christ, massacred them in their hatred of the Indians who were warring on them.

John Eliot, "Apostle to the Indians," preaching. (Byington, Ezra Hoyt. *The Puritan as Colonist and Reformer*. Boston: Little, Brown, 1899.)

Other Events

29: This is the traditional date for the beheading of John the Baptist. A forerunner to Christ, John said:

> I indeed baptize you with water; but one mightier than I cometh, the latchet of whose shoes I am not worthy to unloose: he shall baptize you with the Holy Ghost and with fire." (Luke 3:16, KJV)

Upon seeing Jesus some time later, John remarked:

> Behold the Lamb of God, which taketh away the sin of the world. This is he of whom I said, After me cometh a man which is preferred before me: for he was before me. (John 1:29-30, KJV)

1683: John Dick, a fugitive Scotsman who stood up for Presbyterianism when Charles II was demanding that the Church of Scotland accept Church of England forms, was captured and brought before the Committee of Public Affairs. Although Dick escaped, he was recaptured a few months later and hanged.

1928: W.A. Criswell was ordained at San Jacinto Baptist in Amarillo, Texas. He became the popular minister of First Baptist Church in Dallas, which was one of the largest Southern Baptist churches of the time.

John the Baptist beheaded. (Baring-Gould, S. *Lives of the Saints*. Edinburgh: John Grant, 1914.)

Samson Occom. He didn't get the salary or the credit for the missionary work he did among his fellow Indians. (Ninde, Edward S. *The Story of the American Hymn*. New York: Abingdon, 1921.)

August 30

American Indian Missionary

There was a great stir of religion in these parts of the world both amongst the Indians as well as the English, and about this time I began to think about the Christian religion, and was under great trouble of mind for some time.

That is how Samson Occom, direct descendant of the great Mohegan chief Uncas, described the effect of the Great Awakening on himself when he was sixteen years old. As a consequence of that "great stir of religion," he put his faith in Jesus Christ.

Following his conversion, Occom shared the gospel with other Indians. Then in 1743, when he was twenty, he went to study with Rev. Eleazar Wheelock, who ran a school. By attending Wheelock's school, Occom hoped to learn to read so that he could study the Bible for himself. In this, he was successful. Despite poor eyesight, he became the first American Indian to publish works in the English language, including sermons, hymns and a short autobiography.

Word of Occom's work among the Indians impressed American religious leaders. Wheelock himself recognized that if more Indians could be trained as Occom had been, they could carry the gospel to their own people, so he threw open his school to Indians.

Meanwhile, Presbyterian leaders in Long Island took notice of Occom's work as well. He had not been able to go to college and get his theological training because of his poor eyesight; nonetheless, they ordained him on this day in 1759 to go as a missionary among his own people. To its shame, the Church never paid Occom what it paid its white preachers. But, despite his total poverty and continual bad health, Occom worked tirelessly to convert Indians and to pass on to them the things he had learned in school.

Rev. Wheelock found that few Indians attended his school. He realized that it was because the school was far from centers frequented by the Native Americans. He looked about for a new location and settled on the Connecticut Valley of New Hampshire, where an Indian trail led across the area. He solicited funds to build an Indian school there, but among settlers who had had their fill of Indian wars the scheme met with a cool reception and did not raise enough money. Wheelock realized he'd have to find funds overseas.

That is how it came about that Samson Occom sailed to England in 1765. Preaching from church to church with his traveling companion, Rev. Daniel Whitaker, Occom became a sensation and drew large crowds. He raised the enormous sum of 12,000 pounds. Thus, it is largely owing to Occom that the institution we know as Dartmouth University was created. The money was banked and its interest drawn to build the new school. Unfortunately, Rev. Wheelock did not abide by his original intent. Instead of using the money primarily for Indian education, he diverted it to the education of "English" youth.

Occom felt betrayed and believed he had been used. It seemed to him that Wheelock saw him not as a brother, equal in Christ, but as an exhibit or a performing monkey. In spite of his pain at this abuse, or because of it, Occom clung even more tightly to Christ. To the end of his life, he preached among the Indian tribes and pleaded for their rights and privileges.

Occom's wife found him dead on July 14, 1792. Evidently he had just completed writing an article and had collapsed while walking back to his house. Hundreds of Indians attended his funeral.

Anne Hutchinson, who attracted more followers than many male ministers. (Hubbard, Elbert. *Little Journeys to the Homes of the Great*. 13 volumes. New York: W.H. Wise & Co., 1916.)

Other Events

303: Felix, a town pastor in North Africa who had refused to give up copies of Scripture passages, died a prisoner in the hold of a ship on his way to Rome.

1637: A synod was called in Cambridge, Massachusetts, to deal with Anne Hutchinson. Jealousy was involved, because she attracted more followers than the male ministers. Also, she taught grace over works, which conflicted with the views of the Puritans, many of whom had become works-oriented.

1856: African Americans of the Methodist Episcopal Church established Wilberforce College, the second black college in America.

1894: Bob Jones, Sr., was converted at eleven years of age. By age fifteen he was licensed to preach as a Methodist. He went on to preach thousands of fundamentalist sermons and to found Bob Jones College in Tennessee. It is now a university and has been relocated to South Carolina.

Preaching to the Pope

Next to St. Francis of Assisi, St. Bonaventure was the most eminent of the Franciscan friars. He was not only governor general of his order, but the man who gave them their definitive doctrine and the sixth person ever to be named a primary doctor of the Church. At that time he was given the name "Doctor Seraphicus."

His theology teaches that God cannot be known rationally but must be apprehended mystically. To be pure of heart is a truer way to God than to have a razor-sharp mind. Love, he said (following St. Paul), supersedes knowledge. Bonaventure's teachings were strongly Christ-centered, even his biography of St. Francis, who taught men "to conform their lives to the life of Christ."

Bonaventure was no arid scholar. To learn the needs of the Franciscan order, he went out and visited his friars, winning such love from them that there was much weeping at his death. Then too his theology was not dry, but mystical. He did not load his work down with tedious digressions into subtle points but made every effort to teach plainly. And his biography of St. Francis is an example of good investigative reporting, for he interviewed many brothers who were still living and had known the great saint.

He was zealous for souls and preached much. An extensive collection of his sermons remains in existence. Bonaventure taught that man needs grace in order to stand straight—only through Jesus Christ can he be put right with God. Christ as the Word incarnate was an important theme in Bonaventure's preaching. He said that the grace of the sacraments healed the soul of the accumulated effects of sin, both deliberate and inherited.

On this day in 1264, Bonaventure preached a sermon on the "Blessed Sacrament" before Pope Urban IV and his council. In the sermon he pointed out that we are made complete by partaking of the Eucharist with appropriate contemplation. By contemplation he meant a generous, prayerful and even mystical mindset that results in losing oneself in the adoration of God.

In his apology for varieties of religious orders, Bonaventure notes that no one order can capture the fullness of Christ, although each tries to capture something of His perfection. Hence, there are many ways of serving Christ and approaching His perfection. Vows are merely aids to living a life that imitates Christ.

Because of the warmth of his religious feeling, Bonaventure is highly regarded as a theologian. He managed to avoid the pitfalls of pagan philosophy, and it is because of him that Franciscan thought is largely Augustinian in orientation.

St. Bonaventure by Michelangelo. (Potter, Mary Knight. *Art of the Vatican: Being a Brief History of the Palace, and an Account of the Principal Art Treasures Within Its Walls*. Boston: L.C. Page & Co., 1903.)

Other Events

Annual: George Scholarios is remembered by the Orthodox Church on this day for his defense against reunion with Rome. He was the first patriarch of Constantinople after it fell to Muslims.

1181: Pope Alexander III, who is considered one of the greatest popes, died on this day. He excommunicated Emperor Frederick I, who had set up an antipope. Frederick capitulated. Under Alexander, a Church council confirmed the exclusive right of papal elections to the College of Cardinals.

1240: Raymond Nonnatus died in Cardona, Spain. He suffered greatly while ransoming Christians from the Moors and was named a cardinal shortly before his death.

1534: Jan of Leyden declared himself "King David" as he led a peasant revolt in Germany.

1688: Sixty-nine-year-old John Bunyan, English Puritan author and preacher, died on this day. One of England's most famous authors, he maintained his pastoral duties until his death, which was caused by a cold caught from riding through the rain while he was trying to reconcile a father and son.

Jan of Leyden, who led a peasant revolt. (Tumbült, Georg. *Die Wiedertäufer: Die Socialen und Religiösen Bewegungen zur Zeit der Reformation*. Bielefeld: Leipzig, Velhagen & Klasing, 1899.)

Carthage Dunking

1

What happens if a Christian is baptized by an unworthy or improperly ordained minister? Is that baptism valid? The Church has faced this question several times during its history. Under the prodding of the dynamic bishop and martyr Cyprian, North African Christians faced the issue in Carthage during the third century.

During the Decian Persecutions, which broke out in the year 250, many Christians poured libations to the emperor rather than suffer torture. Others bribed the authorities to obtain certificates saying they had sacrificed even when they had not. Later, some of these, who were sometimes called *lapsi*, or the "lapsed," felt remorse for their betrayal of Christ, who had suffered so much for them. They asked to be readmitted to the Church.

Schism developed over whether the *lapsi* should be allowed to reenter the Church or not. Led by Novatian, some Christians formed their own congregations, saying no lapsed person should be readmitted. The Novatians ordained their own priests, who baptized new Christians. Later some Novatians wanted to unite with the Catholic Church. Cyprian said this was only possible if they were rebaptized within the Catholic Church by "legitimate" priests. Another group wanted to let the lapsed return on different terms than Cyprian's. They also broke away and elected their own bishop, Cecilianus, who baptized converts.

Believing that Church unity was at stake, Cyprian took a tough stand against accepting baptism by schismatics, arguing that no sacrament administered outside the universal Church had validity. Since there can be only one Church, he considered the breakaway groups to be without the Holy Spirit. He summoned councils that met in Carthage in 251, 252, 253, 255 and 256 to address the issues raised by the *lapsi* and Novatians. On this day in 256, the North African synod voted unanimously with Cyprian. Baptized "heretics" who entered the Catholic fold must be baptized again.

However, this vote did not stand. Stephen, bishop of Rome, ordered Cyprian to accept the lapsed into the Church without a second baptism. Cyprian refused, asking, "[H]ow can he who lacks the spirit confer the spirit?" For a long time he resisted, but, under threat of excommunication, he eventually yielded. Today, Rome uses this concession by Cyprian to prove that at that early time the bishops of the Roman world had international authority.

Cyprian died a martyr. He had been accused of cowardice for hiding during the Decian Persecutions. In 258 he vindicated himself, boldly testifying to his faith as he went to his beheading. Stephen too was martyred—a year before Cyprian. The Council of Arles in 314 upheld Stephen's decision. They said that as long as a person was baptized in the name of the Father, the Son and the Holy Spirit, he or she was truly baptized, regardless of who conferred the rite.

Cyprian, who vindicated himself of any cowardice during the Decian Persecutions by boldly testifying to his faith on his way to being beheaded. (Courtesy of the Christian History Institute archives.)

Other Events

1159: Pope Adrian IV, the only English pope, died on this day. He was a firm but kindly man who suffered under the rulers Arnold of Brescia and Frederick of Barbarossa.

1646: The Congregational churches of Massachusetts met in the Cambridge Synod to hammer out the Church/state relationship. When all was said and done, they adopted the Westminster Confession of Faith, agreed to a congregational form of government and issued the Cambridge Platform.

1784: John Wesley designated Francis Asbury and Thomas Coke to lead the United States Methodists.

1836: Missionaries Marcus Whitman, H.H. Spalding and their families reached Walla Walla, Washington. Narcissa Whitman was the first white woman to cross the continent. Eleven years later, Whitman, his wife and twelve associates were killed by Native Americans, prompting Congress to organize the Oregon Territory.

1894: Miss Annie M. Reynolds became the first general secretary of the Young Women's Christian Association (YWCA).

1901: Isabella Thoburn died of Asiatic cholera. The missionary-educator had traveled to India with Clara Swain.

Isabella Thoburn, a missionary-educator to India. (Johnston, Julia H. *Fifty Missionary Heroes Every Boy and Girl Should Know*. New York/Chicago: Fleming H. Revell Company, 1913.)

SEPTEMBER

2

Bohemian Revolt

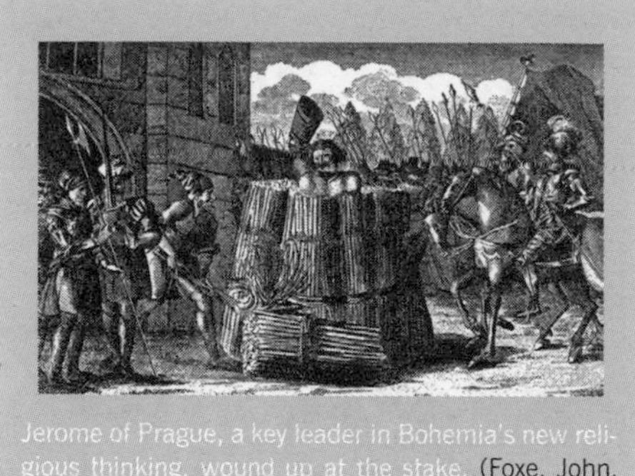

Jerome of Prague, a key leader in Bohemia's new religious thinking, wound up at the stake. (Foxe, John, et al. *Foxe's Christian Martyrs of the World*. Chicago: Moody Press, n.d.)

A full century before the Reformation that started with Martin Luther—the Reformation that made Germany a Protestant nation—an almost identical movement swept through Bohemia. The country's noblest luminary, Jan Hus, was not around to guide the reformation and check its most strident voices, for he was burned at the stake after an unjust trial before the Council of Constance. Hus's followers, representing conflicting interests, were unable to sustain unity and disintegrated in a welter of internal squabbles.

The reformation began when Jerome of Prague visited Oxford. He returned to Bohemia with Wycliffe's teachings under his belt. Hus, a popular and competent teacher, assimilated Wycliffe's gospel and began to spread it throughout Bohemia. It was a Bible-centered teaching that set forth the simple doctrines of Scripture.

The serfs of Bohemia responded with joy; the Bible seemed to promise a new order of liberation and equality, symbolized by their participation in not just the bread of communion but of the wine as well. Persecuted Christians, such as the Waldenses, embraced Hus's doctrine, for it was Bible-centered, and that was what Peter Waldo had urged them to pursue.

The Bohemian nobles saw the ensuing Church reform as one means to shake off the grip of the Roman Catholic German invaders who ruled Bohemia. The nobles responded with fury to Hus's death in a pyre of flame. On this day in 1415, an assemblage of Bohemian and Moravian notables sent the Council of Constance a document underscored with the signatures of 500 prominent men, declaring they would fight to the last drop of their blood to defend the true doctrines of Christ.

And fight they did. A Bohemian revolution had begun. They butchered the anti-Hussites that King Wenceslas packed onto Prague's New Town Council. When Pope Martin V launched a crusade against the "heretics," Bohemian men swarmed into national armies so they could help defend their homeland. Under the brilliant military leadership of the blind general Jan Zizka they defeated several large forces. Victorious on the field of battle, the revolutionaries proceeded to slaughter monks and Germans alike and to impose their religious views by force of arms. Most of Bohemia fell under their control.

Their reign lasted for about twenty years, but then it began to disintegrate. Conflicting ambitions, unfulfilled promises and lawlessness fragmented the allies and drove the upper classes back into the Roman Church. Nonetheless, a faithful non-Catholic Church, the Unity of the Brethren (Moravians), survived the chaos, and, despite fierce persecution, refused to be stamped out. It was two centuries before Catholics had complete control of Bohemia again.

Simeon Stylites, who lived atop a pillar for thirty-six years. (Baring-Gould, S. *Lives of the Saints*. Edinburgh: John Grant, 1914.)

OTHER EVENTS

459: Simeon Stylites, who spent thirty-six years atop a pillar praying, fasting and preaching, died on this day. His last pillar was more than fifty feet tall.

909: A French duke, William the Pious, offered Berno of Blaume the land for a monastery at Cluny. Cluny became a center of reform for three centuries.

1636: John Brebeuf, a Jesuit missionary in North America, baptized the first Iroquois to become a Christian. The man, a Seneca chief, was later tortured to death.

1857: François Coillard sailed for Cape Town in the ship *Trafalger*. He was a man of sweet disposition who gave up scholarly pursuits to win Africans to Christ and once braved a hail of bullets to plead for the lives of black Christians.

1973: J.R.R. Tolkien died at the age of eighty-one. He was a linguist and a novelist who created the fantasy favorites *The Hobbit* and The Lord of the Rings trilogy. He was also a devout Catholic. Fans of famous author C.S. Lewis know that Tolkien helped lead the great apologist to Christ.

SEPTEMBER 3

Denmark's First Day Without Grundtvig

Herr Nikolai Frederik Severin Grundtvig was dead. On this day in 1872, Danes realized that the man who had become a national institution had passed from them. The controversial bishop had died the day before in Copenhagen. Whether they personally liked his positions or not, Danes had to admit that Grundtvig had permanently changed their lives.

For many years Grundtvig struggled with his faith. Danish Lutheranism had become rationalistic, and there was little life in most churches. These factors made Grundtvig doubt what was in his heart. Then, when he was twenty-eight, he finally resolved his spiritual conflict and began to assist his ailing father with church work. He also planned to become a minister.

His first sermon created an uproar. In it he asked, "Why has the Lord's Word disappeared from His House?" The state Church censured him. Grundtvig reconsidered his decision to enter the ministry but decided to go ahead and was ordained the next year.

With the censure hanging over him, he did not find it easy to locate a pastorate, but eventually he did. Then, beginning in 1815, he headed a school that sought to free the Church from state control. He became a leader in educational reform in Denmark, promoting the concept of folk schools in which young adults would educate themselves. He was especially concerned with making the study of the Danish language more important than Latin in his nation's schools. His writing had a powerful influence on the thought of his day, and his schools are credited with keeping Denmark's nineteenth-century Lutheran revival alive.

In 1826, Grundtvig had to resign his pulpit after he made a blistering attack on the rationalism of H.N. Clausen. By this time, Grundtvig was already well-known for a study of Northern mythology in which he argued that poetry speaks better to mankind than prose and is the best medium for conveying spiritual truth to the soul. Although he attacked Schelling and other philosophers for the false ideas of Romanticism, he himself was thoroughly Romantic and translated and introduced Anglo-Saxon and Norse literature into Denmark. This included *Beowulf* and the sagas of Iceland. He also wrote religious poems, sermons that called for a return to the spirit of Luther and fervent Christian hymns such as:

> We are God's house of living stones,
> Builded for His habitation;
> He through baptismal grace us owns,
> Heirs of His wondrous salvation.

Nikolai F.S. Grundtvig in 1843. (From an 1843 oil painting by C.A. Jensen.)

The established Church wasn't sure what to do with Grundtvig. He was too well-known to ignore but too controversial to assign to a pulpit. In 1839, the Church made him pastor of a hospital chapel, where he stayed for the rest of his life. Eventually the state Church gave him the rank of bishop but not the duties.

Meanwhile, Grundtvig helped to peacefully bring parliamentary government to Denmark. His religious renewal movement, known as Grundtvigism, was carried to other nations. In America, Danish immigrants who favored his views were called "Happy Danes" and formed the American Evangelical Lutheran Church.

Other Events

590: Pope St. Gregory I, "the Great," was consecrated. He exerted a powerful influence on the Middle Ages through his writings and reform of Church music.

1905 (probable date): Sundar Singh, formerly an enemy of Christ who had converted after Jesus appeared to him in a dramatic vision, was baptized on this day.

1924: Isobel Kuhn enrolled in Moody Bible Institute. She became known for her mission work in Southeast Asia and her inspirational books such as *In the Arena*.

1943: Stalin held a conference with Metropolitans Sergius and Nicholas and announced that Sergius was to be patriarch of Moscow and all Russia.

1958: Bentley Deforest Ackley, who had been a total alcoholic before his conversion, died on this day. He wrote 3,600 hymns and became evangelist Billy Sunday's organist and secretary. His most popular work was the music to the hymn "With Thy Spirit Fill Me."

Gregory I, "the Great." (Baring-Gould, S. *Lives of the Saints*. Edinburgh: John Grant, 1914.)

Junks (small boats) in Fuchau Harbor. (Hyde, A.B. *Story of Methodism*. Greenfield, MA: Willey and Co., 1887.)

SEPTEMBER

4 Timeless Power of Individual Acts

American Methodist missions to China were created largely through the influence and prompting of one extraordinary woman, Phoebe Palmer. She is best known in our day as the writer of revival hymns such as this one on Christ's blood:

> The cleansing stream I see, I see!
> I plunge, and oh, it cleanseth me;
> Oh, praise the Lord, it cleanseth me,
> yes, cleanseth me.

As a Methodist layperson, she worked tirelessly for social change and improvement and was a key influence in nineteenth-century Methodist revival. She was also the driving force behind the funding of the first Methodist missionaries to China. She had considered going to China herself, but decided she was needed more where she was. But she and her husband pledged the first $1,000 and stimulated others to raise similar amounts.

Supported by the direct efforts of Phoebe Palmer and her husband, the first American Methodist missionaries to China—Moses White, Robert Maclay and Henry Hickok—reached Fuchau in the land of Confucius on this day in 1847. The Methodists were not the first denomination to send missionaries to China. Many other missions had preceded them, including the China Inland Mission, which was founded by Hudson Taylor.

Fuchau was a city of over 600,000 souls. The people were friendly enough, but the missionaries' efforts seemed fruitless. Seven years later they had seen no evidence that a single soul had been converted. In all, ten years passed before they baptized their first convert, Ting Ang, on July 7, 1857.

By 1867 only a tiny fraction of Fuchau's population, a mere 450 people, had become Christians—enough to fill a single church. That may seem like an insignificant number, particularly in light of the vast number of people residing in Fuchau. However, the seemingly insignificant work of the Methodists in Fuchau was one of many streams that contributed to today's resilient and faithful Chinese Church.

Such tiny beginnings suggest the timeless power of individual acts of goodness. Phoebe Palmer was a prominent face in that concourse of Christian effort.

John Cotton, who was influential in New England. (Avery, Elroy McKendree. *History of the United States and Its People: From Their Earliest Records to the Present Time*. Cleveland, OH: The Burrows Brothers Company, 1904.)

Other Events

422: Pope St. Boniface I died on this day. He had been awarded the pontificate by the emperor over his rival Eulalius, who had been consecrated on the same day. Boniface supported Augustine of Hippo on the issue of Pelagianism.

1633: Ministers John Cotton and Thomas Hooker arrived at Boston, Massachusetts, from England, where they became notable leaders of New England communities.

1939: Evangelist and Bible scholar W.E. Biederwolf died. The night before his demise, he told his wife, "I am soon going to exchange my cross for a crown." He wrote many Christian books. One of the best-known was the Millennium Bible (now known as The Second Coming Bible).

1965: German medical missionary Albert Schweitzer, who was also a scholar, musician and philosopher, died on this day.

1984: Joseph Cardinal Ratzinger, cardinal prefect of the Congregation for the Doctrine of the Faith in Rome, denounced aspects of liberation theology, a popular movement in Latin America that combined Marxist sociology with Catholic thought.

Their Very Name Means "Egypt"

The Copts have a long and ancient Christian heritage. They are a people of Egyptian heritage whose very name is from an Arabic word derived from a Greek word meaning "Egyptian." They became Christians in the time of the apostles. Tradition credits Mark as the one who first brought the Christian faith to Egypt. During the fifth century, the Copts rejected the ruling of the Council of Chalcedon on the two natures of Christ and adopted a belief that has long been referred to as Monophysitism but should be called Miaphysitism.* Monophysitism is the belief that Christ has only one nature, a merging of the human and divine. By choosing to follow an interpretation seemingly contrary to Chalcedon, the Copts distanced themselves from the rest of the Church.

After the Islamic conquest of Egypt, the Copts clung stubbornly to their faith. With a long tradition of martyrdom behind them already, they were not about to yield in spiritual matters to Islam. In the twentieth century their faith cost the Copts a great deal. When Egypt threw off British rule under Nasser, Copts were persecuted by Islamic fundamentalists. They were publicly humiliated and discriminated against when they sought jobs. Their brave role in winning independence was written out of the textbooks.

Anwar Sadat tried to soften Islamic antipathy toward the Copts. As late as 1977 he participated in a Coptic wedding. This only raised fundamentalist ire against the Copts and Sadat. Throughout the 1970s, Coptic churches were often broken into or set on fire. When Coptic priests protested, they were jailed. The property of many Coptic Christians was vandalized and looted.

In 1976 the Copts formed an organization to protest against persecution. Pope (meaning "Father") Shenouda III, the Coptic patriarch, was an active member of the organization. The Islamic majority saw this as subversive, thinking wrongly that the Copts were discussing ways to form their own nation. As a result of this misinterpretation of their purpose, the families of some of the Coptic priests were murdered. A Coptic seminary was bombed. But when Copts advertised their plight in American newspapers, an infuriated Sadat vowed to punish Shenouda. The Egyptian media began to attribute all Egypt's problems to the Christians.

The crisis came when Muslims seized a Copt's land to build a mosque. The Copt fired his rifle in self-defense, and a three-day war between local Copts and Muslims resulted. The Muslims said that the fact that Copts had guns proved they intended to revolt. Muslims retaliated by burning Christians to death in their homes and flinging babies out of upper-story windows.

The interior of a Coptic church. (Tyndale, Walter. *Below the Cataracts*. Philadelphia: J.B. Lippincott Co., 1907.)

Sadat jailed a few of the Muslim ringleaders but soon released them. Shenouda protested their release. In retaliation, on this day in 1981, Sadat exiled Shenouda to a monastery in western Egypt. Sadat's act did not appease the Islamic fundamentalists, who were also furious at his peace talks with Israel. On October 6 they assassinated him.

*Copts prefer that their position be known as Miaphysitism. "Monophysite" suggests that Christ has only one nature: the divine. "Miaphysites" state that His nature, while one, is a composite of both the human and divine.

Other Events

1234: Pope Gregory IX issued *Liber Rex Pacificus*, compiling and editing into one collection what had previously been scattered in several books.

1516: On this day, Glarean, an influential teacher of the early Reformation era, wrote in a letter to Erasmus, "You taught me to know Christ."

1536: Pope Paul III created the diocese of Cuzco, Peru. Latin America remains predominantly Roman Catholic to this day.

1538: King Henry VIII ordered Bibles placed in English churches. This was an answer to Bible translator William Tyndale's lifelong longing and dying prayer. At the stake he had said, "Lord, open the king of England's eyes."

1538: Valverde and twenty Dominicans arrived to take charge of the diocese of Cuzco.

1826: Samuel Simon Schmucker delivered the inaugural address of the new Theological Seminary of the General Synod of Lutherans at Gettysburg, located on Seminary Ridge at which the Battle of Gettysburg would be fought.

1860: Three Catholic colleges were founded on the same day in the United States: Loyola in Chicago, St. John's in New York City and Canisius in Buffalo, New York.

Henry VIII, who ordered Bibles to be placed in English churches. (Pollard, Albert Frederick. *Thomas Cranmer and the English Reformation, 1489-1556*. Hamden, CT: Archon Books, 1905.)

September

6

Oberlin Recognizes Women's Equality

The founders of Oberlin College were inspired by the work of this man, John F. Oberlin. (Beard, Augustus Field. *The Story of John Frederic Oberlin*. Boston/New York: The Pilgrim Press, 1909.)

On this day in 1837, Oberlin Collegiate Institute in Ohio granted equal status to men and women. It was the first American college to do so. This milestone in the cause for women's equality was a direct result of Christian ideals.

As with so many of America's early schools, Oberlin came into existence at the hands of Christians. In this case, it was Rev. John J. Shipherd and Philo P. Steward, who dreamed of a school of higher education for Ohio. Their motive was "to train teachers and other Christian leaders for the boundless, most-desolate fields in the West." At that time, Ohio was on the western frontier of the young nation.

Alvah Hovey, Baptist educator. (Armitage, Thomas. *A History of the Baptists: Traced by Their Principles and Practices, From the Time of our Lord and Saviour Jesus Christ to the Present.* New York: Bryan, Taylor and Co., 1893.)

They drew their inspiration from the work of John Frederick Oberlin, a pastor who had achieved wonders in educating peasants in the Alsatian region of Europe (in France). The new school was named after him.

Steward wrote that the institute intended to seek

> the elevation of the female character, bringing within the reach of the misjudged and neglected sex all the instructive privileges which hitherto have unreasonably distinguished the leading sex from theirs.

Jesus taught women alongside men. Paul informed his readers that "there is neither male nor female: for ye are all one in Christ Jesus" (Galatians 3:28, KJV). Oberlin's founders took these biblical examples to heart. They also had a practical reason for educating women: Mothers and sisters often provided whatever rudiments of learning boys acquired on the frontier. Therefore, the better trained the women were, the better trained the men would be. From the day it opened its doors in 1833, Oberlin was coeducational, although for its first four years women were expected to follow a separate educational track from the men.

In 1835 the school had shocked the American people by declaring that it would admit black students alongside white. Similarly, the school's experiment with educating men and women together shocked many contemporaries. They feared a breakdown in sexual morals. At that point, Oberlin Collegiate Institute might have gone under had it not already gained the support of America's leading evangelist, Charles Finney. Finney was a famous revival leader, and his endorsement gave the school a great boost.

Asa Mahan, a well-known holiness leader, was Oberlin's first president. Under his direction, the school taught that Christian conversion should be linked with a commitment to a changed society. Holiness should be the mark of every Christian, and this holy character should result in personal actions to reform society. Oberlin Collegiate Institute was to be God's college for converting and reforming society. As a result of this theological agenda, Oberlin became a center of abolitionism. It even became a station on the Underground Railroad, helping runaway slaves escape to freedom.

Oberlin Collegiate Institute was chartered by the state of Ohio as Oberlin College in 1850. In 1862, the college combined two strands of its social vision when it granted the first degree in the world to be issued to a black woman named Mary Jane Paterson. She went on to become a teacher in Philadelphia and Washington.

Other Events

972: Pope John XIII died. During his troubled reign, he was driven from his see by the Roman nobles and had to be restored by Emperor Otho I. The Poles and Hungarians were converted to Catholicism in these years.

1529: The Anabaptist leader George Blaurock was burned for his faith. He had established congregations in the Austrian Tyrol.

1849: E.R. Baierlein, who labored among the Chippewa Indians of Michigan, was ordained on this day. He treated the Chippewa as beloved brothers who could freely come in and out of his home.

1903: American Alvah Hovey, a Baptist clergyman and president of Newton Theological Seminary, died.

1941: Jews in Germany were made to wear a star, a Nazi residue of long-lasting "Christian" anti-Semitism.

She Knew Everyone

Hannah More is often remembered more for her influence and associations than for her particular accomplishments—a womanly Samuel Johnson, if you will. As a matter of fact, Johnson was one of her friends, as were William Wilberforce, the Macaulays and John Newton.

In her early years, More enjoyed the high life. She kept up a lively correspondence and was part of every festivity. To the end of her days she was on easy terms with "infidels" such as the politician Horace Walpole. During those years she wrote a number of plays, many of which were successful. In fact, the famous actor, David Garrick, patronized them. Without her contact with John Newton and William Wilberforce, More may have taken a significantly different track in life. However, her association with those two men channeled her mind and energies toward moral issues, and she became deeply religious.

In later life, More felt a nagging guilt for writing plays and so wrote only educational and religious tracts. Education became her forte. As a girl she'd learned the techniques of pedagogy while helping her sisters operate girls' schools. As an adult, moved by the need for Christian action, she flung her energies into the business of establishing Sunday schools in the brutal coal-mining district of Mendip Hills in England, where atrocities had turned the people living there nearly into animals. These schools didn't teach just Bible lessons, as do modern Sunday schools, but rather reading, gardening, cooking, personal hygiene, sewing and civic virtue. Bible lessons and moral conclusions were taught as well.

There was terrific opposition to More's schools from clergy and mine owners. They feared that men who could read the Bible could also read propaganda. They were right, but the good done by exposing the masses to Scripture far outweighed any problems that arose from their education. Many developed Christ-centered lives as a result of attending More's schools.

The miners desperately needed knowledge in order to improve their lives. They were so ill-educated that they did not even know how to properly use the little money they earned. Most did not know how to grow vegetables to supplement their meals or how to cook so as to make the most of the food they had. More's homemaking classes taught such practicalities.

In addition to schooling the lower classes, More fought for justice in such everyday matters as obtaining honest bread weights. She succeeded in getting bread laws in place in forty parishes.

Lovely Hannah More wrote for the stage and for Christ. (Meakin, Annette M.B. *Hannah More, A Biographical Study*. London: Smith, Elder & Co., 1911.)

Toward the end of her life, More, whose days had been a whirlwind of activity, became weak and had to limit visits to two days a week. But her vivacity, wit and charity evoked love from the rising generation. When she died peacefully on this day in 1833, she had spent much of her life improving the condition of her fellow men. The effect of her individual efforts cannot be measured.

Other Events

1303: The French broke into the papal palace at Anagni and tried to force Pope Boniface to repeal *Unam Sanctam*, which made strong claims for the papacy, saying that the salvation of every soul required obedience to the pope. Boniface would not take it back.

1605: The Seminario de San Bartolome was founded, the first Jesuit college in the nation of Colombia in South America.

1785: Britain's first Sunday school conference took place at Prescott Street Baptist Church of London. It was organized by a layman, William Fox.

1823: Samuel Marsden was shipwrecked off the coast of New Zealand, where he was taking the gospel to the Maori people.

1897: Scotswoman Jane Borthwick, who translated German hymns, including the well-known "Be Still, My Soul," into English, died on this day.

1950: The Hungarian Communist government's Decree #14 dissolved all religious orders.

Samuel Marsden, "Apostle to the Maori." (Saunders, Alfred. *History of New Zealand, 1642-1861*. Christchurch, New Zealand: Whitcombe & Tombs, 1896-9.)

September

8 Prominent Shanghai Church Leaders Arrested

A Chinese house church in Orange, California. (Courtesy of Open Doors.)

Bishop Ignatius Kung Min Pei of Shanghai spoke to the priests assembled at a retreat:

> You must not have any more illusions about our situation. . . . You have to face prison and death head-on. This is your destiny. It was prepared for you because Almighty God loves you. What is there to be afraid of?

It was early in the 1950s, and Communism's dark clouds hung over the Chinese Church. Were Kung's words mere bravado? He would soon be put to the test.

Because of its atheistic philosophy, the Chinese Communist government has always hated Christianity. If the Church must exist, China's leaders want it under Communist control. Because of this, there has been cruel persecution of the Church in China. Every effort is made to force independent leaders into the state-operated Church or to break those who will not yield.

Bishop Kung was one of those who would not yield. In the face of Communist pressure, he continued to carry out his Catholic ministry. In 1953, despite government attempts to keep the men away by blockading the streets, he openly led Shanghai's young Catholic men in a special evening of devotion to the Sacred Heart of Jesus.

On this day in 1955, the Communists arrested Bishop Kung and about 320 other Roman Catholics. Many of those arrested suffered long years in prison, known no longer by their names but by numbers. For five years, Kung was held in prison without a trial. Finally, he was convicted of treason and sentenced to life. In order to go free, all he had to do was renounce the pope and accept the Communist puppet Church. He refused to do either.

And so, for thirty years he had to live the Christian life by relying directly on the Spirit of Jesus, because he was denied letters, books or the Bible. Much of those thirty years was spent in such strict isolation that no one, including the guards, was permitted to speak to him. He was not even allowed eye contact with another human being.

He was denied visitors, including representatives of human rights groups. But at least the world knew he was still alive—another bishop was held in such secrecy that he was thought to be dead. Another captive, Jesuit Francis Xavier Ts'ai, was forbidden to even move his lips in prayer. He used to silently repeat "My good Jesus, glorify Yourself, and the rest counts for little."

While in prison, Bishop Kung was named a cardinal of the Church. The Communists finally released him after three decades of captivity and placed him under house arrest. In 1987 he was allowed to attend a banquet with a Filipino cardinal but was seated at the opposite end of the table and forbidden to speak with him. At the end of the banquet, Cardinal Kung lifted his voice to sing a Latin hymn. Its words conveyed a message to the Filipino cardinal, who relayed the message to the world: Cardinal Kung had not faltered in his love for Christ or his allegiance to the Church.

In 1988, Cardinal Kung was permitted to leave China and take up residence in the United States.

Other Events

1499: Peter Martyr Vermigli was born in Florence. One of the greatest scholars of the age, he adopted Reformation ideas and helped a nun named Catherine escape from her cloister one night so that he could marry her. His theological views, always more liberal than those of the majority wherever he went, upset people so much that throughout his adult life he was always on the run, never living anywhere longer than eight years.

1565: The first North American Roman Catholic parish was founded at St. Augustine, Florida.

1654: Peter Clavigero, a Jesuit priest who collected an immense amount of information on the Indians of Mexico and California, died on this day.

1907: In the encyclical *Pascendi Dominici Gregis*, Pope Pius X denounced the heresy of modernism.

1928: Pius XI's *Rerum Orientalium* directed the Western Church to study the Eastern Church.

1947: Prominent Christian author and apologist C.S. Lewis appeared on the cover of *Time* magazine.

1957: Pius XII wisely urged the Church to watch modern communications for use by the Church.

Old Gate at St. Augustine, Florida. (Wilson, Woodrow. *A History of the American People*. New York/London: Harper & Bros., 1902.)

Alexander Men Axed on His Way to Church

On this day in 1990, Father Alexander Men left home as usual at 6:30 a.m., walking to the station to catch the train that would take him to church. He had a heavy schedule ahead of him that day, including baptisms and funeral services. But, as it turned out, others would have to complete his duties for him.

Did a snapping twig or the heavy breathing of his assailant alert Men to danger? We will never know. An enemy felled Alexander Men with a blow to the back of his head with an axe, the traditional Russian weapon of revenge. Men managed to drag himself back up the path to the gate outside his house, but he died before help could arrive.

Who would want to kill the churchman whose personal ministry had brought thousands to Christ? A writer whose apologetics led him to be called the Russian C.S. Lewis? The majority of Russians immediately suspected the KGB—the dreaded Russian secret police. But the KGB said Men was probably killed by anti-Semitic monks in the Orthodox Church. Later they revised their opinion and said it was likely a relative or someone from his parish who had committed the crime, although they named no suspects.

All of those groups had motives. The KGB had reason to hate and fear Men because he was so successful in turning men and women to Christ. In fact, he was called a "one-man antidote to decades of Marxist propaganda." The KGB had him under constant scrutiny and brought him in for frequent interrogation.

Anti-Semites had reason to hate him, because Men was a Christian Jew. Conservatives in the Russian Orthodox Church rejected Men because he encouraged a more open-minded attitude toward other Christians. He said, "The walls we erect between ourselves are not high enough to reach up to God." And finally, Jews might have felt that his Christianity was a rejection of Judaism.

Men was unique. He was born in 1935, during the "catacomb years"—the period when Stalin was trying with all his might to stamp out Christianity. The Church was forced to go "underground"—that is, to meet secretly. Men's Jewish mother converted to Christianity and had her son secretly baptized. From an early age, Men was determined to become a Christian priest. It was inevitable that he would become an apologist for the Church, for he had a powerful intellect—at the age of thirteen, he had been poring over Immanuel Kant's difficult philosophy.

The Church accepted Men for the priesthood despite his Jewish descent because during those difficult days there were fewer ministry candidates than usual. Men became a nationally known religious figure. His writings were circulated and copied by hand or on typewriters in the underground press. By advancing arguments that satisfied intelligent minds, Men encouraged several notable figures, Alexander Solzhenitsyn among them, to return to the Church.

The night before he died, Men spoke to a gathering of 600 people. He pointed out that it was absurd to say the world had no meaning. To say something had no meaning, one must recognize and judge it by meaning. He showed the new meaning Christ has given the commandment to love our neighbor as ourselves:

> Christ gave it a completely new sound with the words "as I have loved you," because he remained with us in this filthy, bloody and sinful world out of self-giving love. For this reason he said that the one who would follow him must deny himself (not his personality—for that is holy—but his ego of false self-affirmation), give himself up, take up his cross, which is to say his service in suffering and joy, then follow him.

Alexander Men (left) was often compared to C.S. Lewis. (Courtesy of the Amen Page. Available online at: <http://home.earthlink.net/~amenpage/> Used by permission of Alan Carmack.)

Other Events

1411: Pope Gregory XII issued a bull of indulgences, which Jan Hus of Bohemia denounced.

1519: Melanchthon presented his thesis for the Baccalaureate of Theology. It stressed the authority of Scripture.

1561: The Poissy Conference met in France to discuss differences between Catholics and Protestants. Theodore Beza was the chief debater for the Protestants, and Ippolito d'Este, papal legate, for Rome. Catherine de Medici attended.

1948: The Communist government of Hungary, in its ongoing persecution of the Church, announced the arrest of top Lutherans on charges of illegal manipulation of funds.

1964: Roman Catholic missionary Pierre Laval died on this day, which is observed as a Mauritian National Holiday. Laval was a French doctor who gave up his practice to work with the people of Mauritius island, converting thousands to godly living. He encouraged hundreds who were in irregular liaisons to marry and generally changed the spiritual climate of the African island.

The Poissy Conference. (Baird, Henry Martyn. *Theodore Beza: The Councilor of the French Reformation*. New York: G.P. Putnam's Sons, 1899.)

August Gottlieb Spangenberg, who led the Moravians in America. (Townsend, W.J., H.B. Workman and George Eayrs, eds. *A New History of Methodism*. Vol. 1. London: Hodder and Stoughton, 1909.)

September 10

Searching for a New Home in North Carolina

Today it takes only a few hours to drive from east to west across North Carolina. In the 1750s, however, the same route was a grueling, multi-day trek. On this day in 1752,* an expedition of Moravian men under the leadership of August Gottlieb Spangenberg set off from Edenton, North Carolina. They headed west at the invitation of John Carteret, the earl of Granville, proprietor to much of the colony.

Spangenberg was a good choice as leader. Born in Prussia, he came under the influence of Count Nikolaus von Zinzendorf, the dedicated leader of the Moravians. Spangenberg joined the Moravians when he was dismissed from the theological faculty at the University of Halle because of his religious views. Zinzendorf sent him to America where he negotiated land in Georgia for Moravians who expected to be expelled from Germany. Spangenberg founded several other Moravian settlements and eventually became their American bishop.

The Moravian reputation for sober hard work was well-known to Carteret. He felt that if he could point to a flourishing community of the godly folk on his land, he could attract more settlers. Although the first English settlement in the New World had been at Roanoke, North Carolina, the state lagged behind others in development because of hostile Indians, mismanagement, high taxes and the economic rivalry of neighboring Virginia. John Carteret's offer to the Moravians was aimed at improving matters.

The Moravians agreed to Carteret's offer and headed out for western North Carolina. However, they became lost in the mountains in December. Eventually, they recovered their bearings and selected the best land they could find. They bought 99,000 acres in what is now Forsyth County. Spangenberg named the area Wachau after a valley in Austria.

After staking out their land, the Moravians settled it the next year, sending a team of fifteen unmarried men to the region. The men chosen were evidence of one of the Moravians' secrets to success: practicality. Among the men chosen to settle the land were represented all of the essential professions and skills of the day: minister, surgeon, shoemaker, cooper (barrel maker), sieve maker, business manager, carpenter and so forth.

The little band created their first settlement at a place they named Bethabara. They cut two-and-a-half miles of road, cleared land, planted crops, made furniture, imported livestock, constructed an oven for baking, built homes and even opened a mill. Within six years, there were seventy Moravians living at Bethabara. The little town's palisade served as a fort during the French and Indian War. After the war ended in 1760, the Moravians planted the cities of Bethania and Salem.

The American Moravians under Spangenberg were deeply concerned with mission work among the Indians. In fact, Spangenberg even wrote a lengthy pamphlet on missions. His philosophy of missions could be summed up in a few excerpts from that pamphlet:

> In our labor among the heathen, we will particularly endeavor that they become converted to Christ Jesus with all their heart.
>
> To comprise the whole briefly together, the labors of the brethren among the heathen aim at this, that they might be enabled to say of a truth: "Whether we live, we live unto the Lord; and whether we die, we die unto the Lord: whether we live, therefore, or die, we are the Lord's."

***Note:** Under American reckoning, the date would still have been August 30. On September 2, 1752, the Gregorian calendar was adopted and September 14 followed September 2 in North Carolina. However, Protestant Germans had adopted the Gregorian calendar fifty-two years earlier.

Celestine I, who convoked the Council of Ephesus. (Montor, Chevalier Artaud de. *Lives and Times of the Popes*. New York: Catholic Publication Society of America, 1911.)

Other Events

422: Celestine was elected pope. During his tenure, he convoked the Council of Ephesus to combat the Nestorian heresy (the belief that Christ had two natures and two persons) and may have sent Patrick to Ireland as a missionary.

1224: The Franciscans first arrived in England, where their austerity and love had a great influence on many, including Bishop Robert Grosseteste, who undertook reform in light of their thinking.

1622: Spinola, an Italian Jesuit, was roasted alive at Nagasaki.

1718: The Collegiate School at New Haven, Connecticut, founded in 1701 by Congregationalists who feared Harvard was straying from its Calvinist roots, changed its name to Yale. Elihu Yale, a retired merchant, was honored by the name change after he made a substantial contribution to the college.

1958: Anna-Greta Stjarne, just thirty-one years old, was martyred in Ethiopia. She was attacked by bandits as she walked down a road.

1958: Kornelius Isaak, a Mennonite missionary, was wounded in Paraguay by a Morro Indian arrow and died the next day.

Columbian Parliament Pretends the Unequal Are Equal

When you encounter Buddhists in airport terminals and Eastern mysticism of all types within the New Age movement, you can thank (or blame) the World's Columbian Exposition. The event was held in Chicago in honor of the 400th year of Christopher Columbus's voyage to the New World. It was not just a big trade fair: In addition to art exhibitions and technical, engineering, transportation, architectural and other displays, it called together a conference of world religious leaders.

This Parliament of World Religions opened on this day in 1893. Its inspiration lay in the suggestion of Charles C. Bonney, a Swedenborgian (Swedenborgians denied the Trinity but said that there are three essential principles in one divine being, Jesus Christ). John Henry Barrows, one of Chicago's most liberal clergymen, promoted the event. He claimed later that he had hoped leaders of world religions would be convinced of the superiority of Christianity.

Many Christians, such as D.L. Moody, refused to participate. Most Protestant evangelicals agreed that to participate was to presuppose the equality of religions. Salvation is in Christ alone, they protested. However, the Roman Catholic Church sent delegates, as did some liberal Protestant denominations. Other representation included a dozen Buddhists, eight Hindus, two Shintoists, a Jain, a Taoist and a couple of Muslims, Confucians and Zoroastrians. The results produced by the parliament were just about what evangelicals anticipated: The speeches were largely anti-Christian and denounced Christian missions.

To many Americans, Christianity began to seem like just one among many equal traditions. Some began to think of Asian faiths as legitimate alternatives to Christianity. Great interest was generated in Buddhism and Hinduism. Swami Vivekananda of the Hindu tradition and Anagarika Dharmapala of the Buddhists toured the United States. The outcome was the establishment of Vedanta and Buddhist societies in the United States. D.T. Suzuki, a Buddhist who was dispatched to the United States by another attendee of the conference, translated Buddhist works into English and established a Zen presence, including the founding of America's first Zen monasteries.

Many other Eastern gurus, seeing ripe fields, have since set up shop in the United States. Americans have increasingly turned from traditional Christianity to homemade cults, many of which include motifs from Eastern religions. As a consequence of this new exposure, Americans have become more devoted to the idea of religious pluralism. And since the Columbian Exposition, Eastern religions and their symbols have increasingly infiltrated American thought.

This, of course, presents a foundational challenge to the basic Judeo-Christian heritage of America, with implications for the future identity and destiny of the nation.

John Henry Barrows, who was the main promoter of the Parliament of Religions. (Barrows, John Henry, ed. *The World's Parliament of Religions*. Chicago: Parliament Pub. Co., 1893.)

Other Events

506: The Council of Agde in southern France dealt with many issues, including drunkenness among the clergy.

1570: Reformer Johann Brenz died. He was a strong advocate of Martin Luther's teachings, and he served Duke Christoph at Stuttgart, Germany, in organizing the Reformation at Wuerttember. He stood out because he was one of the few who urged tolerance in that intolerant age, even opposing the persecution of the Anabaptists.

1649: There was a massacre in Drogheada, Ireland, on this day, possibly on the orders of Oliver Cromwell.

1672: Solomon Stoddard was ordained. He would later allow individuals who were uncertain of their state of grace to partake of the Lord's Supper.

1857: Angered by President Buchanan's order to remove Brigham Young from the governorship of Utah Territory and resentful of years of persecution against them, Mormons massacred a wagon train of 135 emigrants, most of whom were from Arkansas and Missouri. The massacre at Mountain Meadow, Utah, was first painted as the work of Indians, but the truth eventually leaked out.

1949: The Communist government of Poland secularized all religious hospitals.

Oliver Cromwell, who is blamed for the massacre in Drogheada, Ireland. (Evelyn, John. *Diary and Correspondence of John Evelyn*. London: Henry G. Bohn, 1859.)

September
12

Birth of an Enthusiast

John Fletcher, who spoke of the peace, joy, love and holiness that comes with new birth in Jesus Christ. (Hyde, A.B. *Story of Methodism*. Greenfield, MA: Willey and Co., 1887.)

"I went to see a man that had one foot in the grave; but I found a man that had one foot in heaven!" So wrote one of John Fletcher's visitors after meeting the godly preacher. Fletcher had become gravely ill because of his strenuous efforts for the kingdom of Christ.

Fletcher was born in Switzerland on this day in 1729. He was educated at Nyon, and as a young man he intended to enter the army, but a series of circumstances foiled his plans. Then, while visiting England in 1752, he fell under the influence of Methodism and determined immediately to become a pastor. Five years later he was ordained. After assisting John Wesley and preaching to French-speaking Swiss expatriates, he threw himself into assisting the vicar of Madeley in England.

Madeley was a hard town. Fletcher had to literally chase down sinners so he could share the gospel with them. No matter what the excuse they gave for not attending church, he tried to rob them of it. He even walked through the streets ringing a bell loudly at five o'clock in the morning to deny anyone the excuse that they could not waken themselves on Sunday morning.

No weather could keep him indoors. He was always available wherever and whenever he was needed. He gave of himself so greatly to help the poor that his health broke, and he developed a condition that was aggravated by his constant exposure to the elements.

Fletcher was strong in his insistence on regeneration, stating that only with a new birth, a new creation, did one belong to Christ. This was a constant theme of his sermons and writings. In a sketch telling of his conversion, he said he was a religious enthusiast at the age of eighteen, but did not apprehend Christ from his heart. A nightmare in which he found himself rejected with the damned woke him to a real need for Christ. He saw that all the good works he'd done had been from pride or from fear of hell, not for love of God. Nonetheless, he felt that the fear he went through was an essential part of becoming a Christian:

> The state of the true Christian is a state of peace, joy, love and holiness; but before a man attains it, he must go through a course of fear, anxiety and repentance, whether long or short; for no one was ever cured in soul by the great physician, Jesus Christ, till he felt himself sin-sick, and was loaded in his conscience with the burden of his iniquities; especially that of a hard impenitent heart, which he could not himself break and soften.

Fletcher wrote and wrote. And although born and reared in Switzerland, he thoroughly adopted the English language as his own and left many fine works written in it. He is considered one of the great early Methodist theologians.

Henry Longfellow. His poem, "The Village Blacksmith," referred to John Alden, who was one of the Pilgrim fathers of Massachusetts. (Courtesy of the University of Texas collection of public domain portraits on the Web.)

Other Events

1687: John Alden, one of the pilgrim fathers of Massachusetts, died. He is remembered from lines in Henry Longfellow's poem "The Village Blacksmith."

1707: Samuel Willard, an influential pastor in Massachusetts who was opposed to the witch trials, died on this day.

1805: Reformed theologian Johann Jakob Herzog was born, probably in Basel, Switzerland. A staunch opponent of theologies that portrayed Christ as less than divine, Herzog is best remembered as the coauthor of the *Schaff-Herzog Encyclopedia of Religious Knowledge*.

1818: George Duffield, Jr., was born in Carlisle, Pennsylvania. Ordained a Presbyterian minister in 1840, he dedicated himself to building up small congregations in New York, New Jersey, Pennsylvania, Illinois and Michigan. Duffield is most famous for his hymn "Stand Up, Stand Up for Jesus," which he wrote in 1858 after the sudden death of his close friend Dudley A. Ting, an Episcopal minister. In his last moments, the dying Ting had said to his sorrowful father, "Stand up for Jesus, Father, stand up for Jesus. And tell my brethren of the ministry wherever you meet them, to stand up for Jesus!"

1865: A.B. Simpson was ordained to the Presbyterian ministry. When he was forced to leave his church after he took uncompromising stands, he founded The Christian and Missionary Alliance.

September 13

Beginning of Protestant Mission Work in Korea

Robert J. Thomas was haunted by the thought of Korea. He was a Welsh missionary to China and knew that the people of the "Hermit Kingdom," as Korea was sometimes known, needed the gospel. But Korea, observing how Westerners had mistreated China, closed its doors to foreigners. Because of this, Thomas, burning with evangelistic zeal, felt he must do something about the people's ignorance of eternal life.

On this day in 1865, he arrived on the coast of Korea and began to learn what he could about the people and their language. By this action, Thomas became the first Protestant missionary to the ancient land, whose name means "chosen." Roman Catholics had converted many Koreans starting in the late 1700s. They were so successful that in 1863, 8,000 Korean Catholics were slaughtered by a government that feared foreign influence.

Lacking Korean language material, Thomas handed out tracts and New Testaments in Chinese. Then, in 1866 he learned that an American boat, the *General Sherman*, was going to try to establish trade relations between Korea and the United States. He offered to accompany the boat as an interpreter in exchange for a chance to spread the gospel. That August, the *General Sherman* sailed up the Taedong River toward Pyongyang. Thomas tossed gospel tracts onto the riverbank as the ship proceeded.

As the ship made its way up the river, Korean officials spotted it and ordered the Americans to leave at once. The Americans defied the warning. They paid for their arrogance with their lives. Soon after being told to leave, they ran aground and stuck fast in the river's muddy bottom.

The governor of the province, Pak Kyu Su, attacked the ship. When the Koreans tried to board, waving machetes, the Americans opened fire. Over the next two weeks, the Americans held the Koreans off, killing twenty and wounding many more. By September 3, the Koreans were fed up. They launched a burning boat downriver at the *General Sherman* to set it on fire too. The Americans had to escape ashore or burn to death.

As the sailors fled from the boat, the Koreans killed them. Thomas had to flee with the rest. True to his mission, he leaped from the boat carrying a bundle of Bibles and crying, "Jesus, Jesus!" in Korean to the attackers. He tried to offer them the Bibles as he struggled ashore. A Korean whacked his head off with a stroke of a machete.

Korean children. (Northrop, Henry Davenport. *The Flowery Kingdom and the Land of the Mikado, or, China, Japan and Corea*. Toronto: Winston, Phillips, 1894.)

Seemingly, Thomas's efforts had been in vain, but God worked in the heart of the man who had killed him. Convinced by Thomas's beaming face that he had been a good man, the Korean kept one of the Bibles. He wall papered his house with it, and people came from far and near to read its words. A church grew. A nephew of Thomas's killer became a pastor.

Today forty percent of South Koreans and unknown numbers of North Koreans are Christians, and the nation has some of the largest congregations in the world.

Other Events

1541: John Calvin returned to Geneva to an uproarious welcome. He spent the rest of his life trying to establish a godly society there, at the request of the city authorities who had banished him three years earlier.

1635: Massachusetts ordered thirty-two-year-old Roger Williams into exile for his outspoken advocacy of separation of Church and state, among other things. Williams went on to found Rhode Island and the first Baptist church in the American colonies.

1845: The hymn "Sweet Hour of Prayer" was first published, with words by William W. Walford and music by William Bradbury.

1888: Newly arrived missionaries Jonathan Goforth and James Frazer Smith began a tour of Honan Province, China.

1900: Anthony Talamo Rossi, who used his wealth as a successful businessman to found a mission to Sicily, was born on this day.

William Bradbury wrote the tunes to numerous hymns, including "Sweet Hour of Prayer." (Hall, Jacob Henry. *Biography of Gospel Song and Hymn Writers*. New York: Fleming H. Revell, 1914.)

Francis of Assisi receives the stigmata. (Bell, Mrs. Arthur. *Saints in Christian Art*. London: George Bell, 1901-4.)

September 14

His Vision

When Francis of Assisi was in his early forties, he gave up leadership of the Franciscans, the great monastic order he had founded. He did not do so in a fit of pique or bitterness but with a quiet acceptance that events had moved beyond him. His simple and stringent rule was too difficult for many of those who had swarmed into the order because of his fame and the powerful preaching of his followers. They wanted the rule relaxed, and relaxed it would be.

However, if Francis had thought that he could be just one of the brothers, he was mistaken. None had such zeal as he. Of no one else would such legends be told. To no other would such visions come.

Francis decided to spend some days before the Feast of the Assumption at Mt. Alvernia. As he stayed in that wilderness, a flock of birds settled around and upon him, to the astonishment of his few companions and of succeeding generations.

At Mt. Alvernia, Francis decided he needed more solitude. The sense of his own sin was heavy upon him, and he longed for a taste of heaven in order to bear the pain of his past wrongdoing. He found a lonely spot in the forest across a chasm. Only one man was allowed to approach him in his solitude: his spiritual son, Leo. Even Leo had to call out and receive permission before crossing the limb that served as a bridge to Francis's place of isolation.

The brothers feared for Francis, who was gravely ill. One night when Leo approached the chasm and called out, Francis did not answer. Leo called again, thinking that perhaps his master had taken ill. Fearful of disobeying his master's orders, and yet even more fearful that the holy leader might be dying unattended, Leo crossed the limb.

Francis's cell was empty. Leo, with the bright moon allowing him to see, went some way past the cell and heard a voice. It was Francis, praying, "Who are you, my dearest Lord? And who am I, a most vile worm and Your most unprofitable servant?" Leo saw a light shine down upon Francis and knew that words were spoken to him, although Leo himself could not hear them. Francis raised his hands into the light. Then the light disappeared. Leo turned to creep away, but Francis heard him and called out, demanding to know who was there. Leo confessed he had broken the command.

Francis was gentle with Leo, for he knew that the transgression had been made in love. Francis told Leo that he had been commanded to give three gifts, which were as golden balls in his bosom: poverty, chastity and obedience. He had held them up to the Lord. The two men then read and prayed together.

Then, on this day in 1224, the day of the Feast of the Holy Cross, as Francis was communing with the Lord, a seraph appeared to him. The figure of Christ crucified appeared between the seraph's wings. Joy and agony suffused Francis. His prayers for forgiveness, to share Christ's sufferings, to be purified, had been heard. When the angel left, in what is regarded as one of the classic experiences of all Christian history, Francis's hands, feet and sides bore five wounds, the marks of the stigmata. Two years later the saint died.

This was a memorable day for Francis Scott Key and the United States. (Ninde, Edward S. *The Story of the American Hymn*. New York: Abingdon, 1921.)

Other Events

407: Elderly bishop John Chrysostom died at Comana while on a forced march. He had been banished from Constantinople because he spoke out against behavior that touched too close to the empress.

1321: Dante Alighieri, author of *The Divine Comedy*, died on this day.

1741: George Frederick Handel finished composing "The Messiah," which he had begun only twenty-four days earlier.

1814: Francis Scott Key, an Episcopalian and the cofounder of the American Sunday School Union, wrote "The Star-Spangled Banner" during the shelling of Fort McHenry in the War of 1812. The poem became the United States national anthem.

1926: An international conference on Christian missions in Africa debated whether to lift restrictions on black missionaries.

1975: Mother Elizabeth Ann Seton was canonized, the first American-born saint of the Roman Catholic Church.

Beer Garden Becomes Garden Mission

One day, while Sarah Dunn was struggling with putting up an elaborate decoration in her family's New York home, she heard an almost audible voice that asked, "What are you doing to decorate your heavenly home?" That marked the beginning of her passion to convert people to Christianity, although it did not prevent her from marrying worldly businessman Colonel George R. Clarke some years later, after she moved to Chicago.

Later, God spoke to Sarah again and warned her about the time she wasted in social functions. She persuaded her husband, who had become a Christian, to visit the city slums with her. He went but was more interested in making money than in dealing with human wrecks. However, while he was on a business trip 1,000 miles away, he felt the Lord Jesus stab him with sharp conviction that people mattered more than money. He dropped to his knees and consecrated himself to God's service. Immediately he telegraphed his wife of his change of plans.

Upon his return to Chicago, Clarke began to preach to the broken men and women of Chicago's slums. His friends considered him one of the world's worst preachers. And yet through his love and concern, lives were changed.

On this day in 1877, Colonel and Sarah Clarke opened a mission on South Clark Street. In a space that had once housed a tiny store, they set up enough wooden benches to seat forty people. As the Colonel wept and struggled to speak words that would change hearts, Sarah did her best to keep order among the noisy, obscene and drunken people who came in. The two saw it as a work of the Holy Spirit when many lives were changed.

Five years later, the mission moved to a bigger building that had been the Pacific Beer Garden. Dwight L. Moody suggested its new name. "Strike out the 'beer' and add 'mission,'" he said. And so the Pacific Garden Mission got its name. Among those converted in its meetings were Billy Sunday, who became an evangelist; Mel Trotter, who was on his way to commit suicide when he wandered in; and Harry Monroe, who became a powerful leader of the very organization that had inspired him to follow Christ.

Moody considered the Pacific Garden Mission the greatest slum work in the world and often preached there. The mission leaders kept their sermons simple:

> Nobody was ever too bad for Jesus to save. Amen, glory! You aren't saved because you're good; if you were good, you wouldn't need to be saved. But Jesus died for your sins. He paid it all, glory to God! Make him your savior tonight. Come down this aisle for prayer. Come just as you are.*

And men and women did—prostitutes, gangsters, alcoholics, gamblers. They would stand in meetings and tell of how God had delivered them from their sins and given them a new life. Their testimonies to the power of Christ played a big part in winning others to follow Jesus.

Billy Sunday was one man who walked out of the Pacific Garden Mission, founded by Colonel and Sarah Clarke, with new life. (Courtesy of the Christian History Institute archives.)

The Pacific Garden Mission changed its location again after many years and is still going strong to this day. Its stories of people who are "unshackled" air as weekly radio broadcasts and have the power to move hearts. Most observers would say God picked right when he chose Colonel and Sarah Clarke to work for Him.

*Quoted from Harry Saulnier in Carl F.H. Henry's *The Pacific Garden Mission*.

OTHER EVENTS

366: St. Damasus I, who would urge Jerome to make a translation of the Scriptures into Latin, became pope.

1510 (probable date): Catherine of Genoa, who developed hospitals and helped the poor, died on this day.

1622: Father Camillo Constanzo was burned alive at Hirado, Japan, in a heroic martyrdom witnessed by thousands.

1833: Arthur Henry Hallam, Alfred, Lord Tennyson's friend and prospective brother-in-law, died. Tennyson composed one of the most famous elegies in English to him: *In Memoriam A.H.H.*

1920: In his encyclical *Spiritus Paraclitus*, Pope Benedict XV restated the Catholic position on Scripture as "composed by men inspired of the Holy Ghost" with God Himself as its principal author. But he noted that the individual authors were not robots.

Arthur Hallam. His death evoked Tennyson's notable elegy *In Memoriam A.H.H.* (Brookfield, Frances M. *The Cambridge "Apostles"*. New York: C. Scribner's Sons, 1906.)

16 The "Tenth Muse" Silenced

The Bradstreet home. (Bradstreet, Anne, John Harvard Ellis, ed. *The Works of Anne Bradstreet in Prose and Verse*. New York: P. Smith, 1867.)

In 1650, Master Stephen Bowtell, a London publisher and bookseller, published a book of poems titled *The Tenth Muse Lately Sprung up in America, or Severall Poems. . . .* The book is a milestone in English and American literature. For one thing, *The Tenth Muse* contained the first verses by an American that could stand beside English poetry. But *The Tenth Muse* is important for more than its place of origin: It was the first volume of enduring English-language poetry to be produced by a woman. The author was Anne Bradstreet.

Anne Bradstreet was a Puritan, the daughter of Thomas Dudley, who served as a governor of Massachusetts Bay Colony. When just sixteen, Anne wed Simon Bradstreet and sailed with him for the New World. Life was hard, not only because the New World was untamed but because she was ill often, lost her home in a fire, had a daughter die at the age of four and was separated from her beloved husband for extended periods when duty took him to England. These experiences, viewed through the lens of faith, found their way into Anne's finest poems.

Written in spite of bouts of illness, blows of personal tragedy and the tedium of household chores (she reared four sons and four daughters), Bradstreet's poems nonetheless show originality and craftsmanship. Their themes were often religious, the spelling quaint and the meanings plain:

> Lord, be thou Pilott to the ship,
> And send them prosperous gailes;
> In storms and sickness, Lord,
> preserve.
> Thy goodness never failes.

Bradstreet's God was real, and she cried out to Him, "My Father's God, be God of me and mine." In a short autobiography of her religious experiences she wrote:

> Among all my experiences of God's gracious dealings with me, I have constantly observed this—that he has never suffered me long to sit loose from him, but by one affliction or other has made me look home and search what was amiss.

Christ was the center of her devotion:

> [T]here is but one Christ, who is the Sun of Righteousness, in the midst of an innumerable company of saints and angels; those saints have their degrees even in this life, some are stars of the first magnitude, and some of lesser degree; and others (and indeed the most in number), but small and obscure, yet all receive their luster (be it more or less) from that glorious sun that enlightens all in all.

On this day in 1672, the voice of the "Tenth Muse" was silenced by consumption. Her son wrote that she "wasted to skin and bone," was tortured by rheumatism and had a leaking sore that disfigured her arm. Sick and weary, she had looked forward to death, saying:

> Now I can wait, looking every day when my Savior shall call for me. . . . O let me ever see you who are invisible, and I shall not be unwilling to come, though by so rough a messenger.

Anne Bradstreet was no Dante or Milton, yet her poems, rich in biblical allusions, were not mere jingles or ditties. Their images anticipated the Romantic movement of a century later.

John Colet, Catholic reformer, humanist and friend of Erasmus. (Lupton, J.H. *A Life of John Colet, D.D., Dean of St. Paul's and Founder of St. Paul's School. With an Appendix of Some of His English Writings.* London: George Bell and Sons, 1887.)

Other Events

681: The Third Council of Constantinople adjourned, having settled the Monothelite controversy in the Eastern Church. Monothelites, who believed Christ had only "one will," were condemned as heretics by the council, which proclaimed the orthodox belief of two wills in Christ: divine and human.

1406: Metropolitan Cyprian of Moscow died. He was later canonized by the Orthodox Churches of the Balkans and Russia.

1498: Torquemeda, head of the Spanish Inquisition, died. He burned hundreds of victims and tortured thousands more.

1519: John Colet, an English scholar, Catholic reformer and friend of Erasmus, died on this day.

1882: Edward B. Pusey died at Ascot Priory. He was one of the Tractarians of the Oxford Movement, which sought to restore the purity of the English Church, reinterpreting the thirty-nine articles that all Anglicans were required to accept.

1892: Edward V. Neale, a Christian Socialist who founded London's first cooperative stores, died.

Sybil of the Rhine

Contemporaries called Hildegard "Sybil of the Rhine." By any measure she was an extraordinary woman, one of the few who transcended the limitations imposed on women by the Middle Ages to alter the events of her own time and imprint her personality on the future.

At the age of five, Hildegard of Bingen began to see visions; at eight, she joined her Aunt Jutta as a recluse. When she was fourteen, Hildegard became a nun herself. For much of her life she was abbess of a Benedictine convent.

Somehow she acquired an education. Not until she was forty-two did she begin to write the books that made her famous. Once she did begin writing, however, her output was prodigious and varied. She compiled an encyclopedia of natural science and clinical medicine. Her medical works included exorcisms along with much medieval lore. She wrote the first known morality play and a song cycle with these words in it:

> It is very hard to resist what tastes of the apple. Set us upright Savior, Christ. . . . O most beautiful form! O most sweet savor of desirable delight! We ever sigh after you in fearful exile, when will we see you and dwell with you?

Hildegard's hundreds of letters of advice and rebuke went out to kings and commoners alike. She wrote the biographies of two saints. This output, coming from the pen of a woman, was extraordinary in an age when women seldom learned to read. She was considered a prophetess, and St. Bernard of Clairvaux and various popes endorsed her visions. People everywhere listened to her.

Her book of visions, *Scivias*, took her ten years to complete. She incorporated twenty-six drawings of things she had seen in her strange waking visions. Modern medicine suggests that these shimmering lines of light were actually the auras associated with migraines. Her own account, however, suggests more:

> [W]hen I was forty-two years and seven months old, heaven was opened and a fiery light of exceeding brilliance came and permeated my whole brain, and inflamed my whole heart and my whole breast, not like a burning but a warming flame, as the sun warms anything its rays touch.

Immediately after the vision, she understood the meaning of the Scriptures.

At the age of sixty, Hildegard began to make preaching tours. The theme of her sermons was that the Church was corrupt and needed cleansing. She scathed easygoing, fat

The new heavens, earth and ordering of the elements. Drawing from Hildegard of Bingen's *Scivias*. (Singer, Charles Joseph. *From Magic to Science: Essays on the Scientific Twilight*. London: Ernest Benn, 1928.)

clergymen and those who were "lukewarm and sluggish" in serving God's justice and negligent in expounding the depths of Scripture.

Hildegard died at the age of eighty-two on this day in 1179. Although she was largely forgotten for many generations, awareness of her life enjoyed a new surge in the mid-1990s, with television programs, books and music releases devoted to her. And not without cause, for she was one of the most talented and original women ever to live.

Other Events

335: Jerusalem's Church of the Holy Sepulchre was consecrated.

1516: While in Madrid, Bartolomé de Las Casas was named priest "Procurator of the Indies," giving him status as protector of Latin America's much-abused Indians.

1575: Swiss reformer Heinrich Bullinger died. Next to John Calvin, he may have been the most influential second-generation reformer.

1577: The Peace of Bergerac ended the seventh war between Catholics and Huguenots in France.

1717: Presbyterians formed the Synod of Philadelphia, their first in America. There were 19 ministers, 40 churches and 3,000 members involved.

1776: Franciscan friar Francisco Palou presided over the inauguration of a royal fort at San Francisco, an event taken as the founding of the great city.

A later, rebuilt Church of the Holy Sepulcher. (Barrows, John Henry, ed. *The World's Parliament of Religions*. Chicago: Parliament Pub. Co., 1893.)

SEPTEMBER 18

Baptists Are Particularly Dangerous

Oncken, a founder of the Russian Baptist Church. (Armitage, Thomas. *A History of the Baptists: Traced by Their Principles and Practices, From the Time of our Lord and Saviour Jesus Christ to the Present*. New York: Bryan, Taylor and Co., 1893.)

"Baptists are particularly dangerous," noted a Russian newspaper in 1972. "Every Russian Baptist tries to win adherents to his faith." Indeed, there was some truth to this, for Johann Gerhardt Oncken, one of the first German Baptists, taught that "every Baptist is a missionary," and it was through the testimony of German artisans sent by Oncken to Russia that the Baptist faith took hold in that nation. However, the real growth of Baptists in Russia came after World War I.

During the war, Russian prisoners were taught by German missionaries, and once the war ended, they returned home to convert others. By 1950 there were an estimated 2 million Russian Baptists, the largest proportion of whom were in the Ukraine.

The Communists forced all evangelicals into a single union—the All Union Council of Evangelical Christians and Baptists (AUCECB). Under Khrushchev, the Communists launched a major crackdown, accompanied by heavy propaganda, against all churches, especially the Baptists. This lasted from 1959 to 1964. The Communists demanded that baptisms be discouraged, that young people no longer be taught religion and that ministers no longer try to win new converts but merely maintain the congregations they already had. When Metropolitan Nikolai of the Orthodox Church died, leaders of the AUCECB grew frightened and knuckled under. Nikolai had resisted Soviet demands, and his death looked like murder.

The Baptists, however, were unwilling to capitulate. They held to their convictions that faith cannot be compromised and that the gospel must be preached to others. In 1961, Baptist leaders formed a committee that challenged the union leadership. They called for sanctification of the Church and urged local churches to discipline leaders who cooperated with the state. These Reform Baptists were largely descendants of the original Oncken Baptists. Their brave leader, A.F. Prokofiev, soon found himself in prison with 100 other evangelical leaders. Georgi Vins, who had worked beside him, stepped into the breach. A number of women formed a Council of Prisoner's Relatives to make the world aware of the plight of their godly men.

On this day in 1965, the Baptists broke from their forced union with other evangelicals, forming their own organization, the Council of Churches of Evangelical Christian Baptists (CCECB). Georgi Vins was the council's secretary.

Vins had no illusions about what it would cost him to take this stand. His father had been imprisoned and beaten for his religious stance. Vins was forced underground in 1970. When he was captured in 1974, he faced the same treatment as his father. Eventually a letter campaign won his release to the United States.

By their tough stand, Baptists forced concessions from the Soviet government. Much of Khrushchev's legislation was rescinded. Restrictions were lifted from the AUCECB but left on the CCECB as the government tried to force the Baptist churches back into the all-faiths union.

Pope Sixtus V, who approved the acts of the council of Lima. (Potter, Mary Knight. *Art of the Vatican: Being a Brief History of the Palace, and an Account of the Principal Art Treasures Within Its Walls*. Boston: L.C. Page & Co., 1903.)

OTHER EVENTS

1591: Having been approved by Pope Sixtus V in 1588, the acts of the Lima council were published. The most important of the American Provincial Councils, it was convened by Archbishop Totibio of Lima.

1634: Anne Hutchinson arrived from England in Boston, Massachusetts, where she caused quite a ruckus and got herself banished.

1884: Admirers packed the Brooklyn Tabernacle, New York, for the funeral of Jerry McAuley, founder of New York's Water Street Mission, a pioneer among American rescue missions.

1905: Scottish clergyman George MacDonald, who wrote novels to support himself after he left the Church because of theological divergence (he had begun to teach Universalism, the belief that everyone would be saved after death if not in this life), died. His novels have been translated from their original Gaelic into modern English. The best of them, originally titled *Alec Forbes*, has been renamed *The Maiden's Bequest*.

Thomas John Barnardo's Head Felt Heavy

On this day in 1905, sixty-year-old "Dr." Thomas Barnardo complained that his head felt heavy. Asking his wife to allow him to rest it on her for a moment, he slipped out of this life. His funeral was attended by 1,500 boys, along with many poor people and rough men who sobbed openly. Barnardo had been a friend to neglected children. At the time of his death, about 8,000 were living in homes he had founded.

Born in Ireland, Barnardo was a restless boy who bored easily and would not stick to his lessons. He failed his exams and had to leave school at sixteen. He was then apprenticed to a wine merchant. That year he was converted to evangelical Christianity. At once, he began visiting homes to tell others about the gospel and to teach the Bible in "ragged schools" (schools for poor children). He joined the Plymouth Brethren.

Hearing about the work of Hudson Taylor in China, Barnardo was filled with enthusiasm and found the means to attend medical school in London so that he could prepare for the mission field. While living near the hospital, he continued working in the slums, where his message was not always a welcome one. In fact, he once had a couple of ribs broken and at other times he was roughed up in other ways.

But Barnardo was persistent. Once again he became involved in a ragged school. It was after one evening's lesson that he met (according to his own story) a young fellow named Jim Jarvis, who was evidently reluctant to leave. It turned out that Jarvis had no home. "Well, but where did you sleep last night?" asked Barnardo.

"Down in Whitechapel, sir, along the Haymarket in one of them carts as is filled with hay; and I met a chap and he telled me to come here to school, as perhaps you'd let me lie near the fire all night."

Although still attracted toward his goal of becoming a missionary in China, Barnardo was touched by Jarvis's plight and as a result increased the scope of his work among London's neglected youth. In response to an article he wrote, he was offered money to continue his London work. Eventually he gave up the China idea and developed his successful East End Juvenile Mission among neglected young people.

The mission included schools, meal programs, a job agency and homes for boys, for girls and for the feebleminded. An innovative marketer, Barnardo came up with novel ways to raise funds. One was to take before and after photographs of every child who entered his homes. These were printed and sold in packs. Another was to form a league of middle-class youth to raise contributions for his schemes. Generally his ideas outran his funding, but he would not stick to the limits placed on him by his boards. He milked stories like Jarvis's for all they were worth. What is more, he changed the details of his stories as needed for fund-raising.

John Barnardo, who loved beggar children. (Pike, G. Holden. *Children Reclaimed for Life: the Story of Dr. Barnardo's Work in London*. London: Hodder and Stoughton, 1875.)

Not all of Barnardo's methods would stand muster today. For example, he shipped large numbers of children to Canada and Australia, and although he meant well, many of those children suffered severely in the relocation.

Wrapped up in his cause and always in need of more funds to spread the work, Barnardo left himself open to charges of dishonesty. He inflated his figures and altered stories. Accusations were proven against him. This seemed not to faze him, and he struggled for the poor until the day of his death. Thousands owed a better existence to him.

Other Events

690: Theodore of Tarsus died after serving as archbishop for twenty-one years. He came to a divided Church and left a united one. The Venerable Bede considered the days of Theodore's service to be England's happiest religious era.

1630: The poet George Herbert was ordained a priest of the Anglican Church. He wrote mystical poetry that is still found in anthologies of English literature.

1914: Germans bombarded the Cathedral of Reims during World War I and damaged it badly.

1947: The first New Tribes missionaries sailed from San Francisco for Shanghai.

1971: American archaeologist William F. Albright, one of the most renowned excavators of the Middle East, died on this day. He was a Methodist and did much to substantiate the accuracy of the Bible.

George Herbert, who wrote mystical verse. (Hyde, A.G. *George Herbert and His Times*. London: Methuen, 1906.)

September 20

Sunny South Seas Massacre

John Patteson shields his men with the boat's rudder. (Lambert, John C. *The Romance of Missionary Heroism*. London: Seeley, 1907.)

John Coleridge Patteson was deeply distressed. Lawless white sailors were grabbing natives of the Pacific islands as workers for plantations. He wrote:

> The deportation of natives is going on to a very great extent here as in the New Hebrides and Banks Islands. Means of all kinds are employed: sinking canoes and capturing the natives, enticing men on board, and getting them below, and then securing hatches and imprisoning them. Natives are retaliating.

Patteson noted that some islands had few men left. He and other missionaries pleaded to no avail for an end to the dreadful system.

On September 16, 1871, Patteson's ship lay off the Santa Cruz group of islands, a place where every effort to start a mission work had failed. He did not think that he was in much danger, for the islanders remembered him from previous visits, even if they did not understand why he came to them.

Pedro Menendez, who massacred Huguenots in Florida. (Avery, Elroy McKendree. *History of the United States and Its People: From Their Earliest Records to the Present Time*. Cleveland, OH: The Burrows Brothers Company, 1904.)

Patteson was in the Pacific as a missionary. Born in 1827, he was reared by godly parents who used patience, explanation and other forms of discipline to help him overcome his natural laziness and flaring temper. In 1855, he heard Bishop Selwyn speak of the need for workers in the islands of the Pacific Ocean. Patteson made up his mind to become one of those workers, and a year later, he was there.

The young man undertook an enormous amount of work. He toured and preached on the islands many times, mastered twenty-three Polynesian languages and ran the mission college. Selwyn had decided that the way to spread the gospel was to bring young men of the islands to a central location to convert them and teach them the gospel to carry back to their own people. Patteson was a key worker in this plan. Although he worked hard, he was wise enough to realize that results might not appear immediately:

> Our Savior, the first of all Christian missionaries, was thirty years of His life preparing and being prepared for His work. Three years He spake as never man spake, and did not His work at that time look a failure? He made no mistakes either in what He taught or the way of teaching it, and He succeeded, though not to the eyes of men. Should not we be contented with success like His? And with how much less ought we not to be contented! So! The wonder is that by our means any result is accomplished at all.

Patteson worked himself hard—so hard, indeed, under the tropical sun that he became desperately ill. At forty, he spoke of himself as an old man. He was just forty-three when a friend wrote:

> Few have had to be at once head of a college, sole tutor and steward, as well as primary schoolmaster all at once, or afterwards united these charges with those of the bishop, examining chaplain and theological professor, with the interludes of voyages which involved intense anxiety and watchfulness, as well as the hardships of those unrestful nights in native huts, and the exhaustion of the tropical climate. No wonder then that he was already as one whose work was well-nigh done, and to whom rest was near.

After Patteson recuperated from his illness, he sailed back to the islands. Before going ashore on this day in 1871, he preached on the death of Stephen, which is recorded in Acts 7:54-60. The text proved appropriate. Frustrated natives of Nukapu Island clubbed Patteson to death and attached five knots made out of local fiber to his body, indicating that he was killed in retaliation for five men who had recently been stolen by white sailors. Three native mission workers were shot with arrows at the same time.

Patteson's death achieved what his life never had. Public outcry over the massacre on Nukapu Island was so great in England that the practice of forced labor had to stop. The British navy enforced the ban.

Other Events

1565: The Spaniard Pedro Menendez massacred the Protestant Huguenots who had settled in Florida. He gloated in his letters that he had killed heretics, but a stronger motive may have been his desire to keep France from colonizing America.

1884: A young doctor named Horace Newton Allen of Delaware became the first resident Protestant missionary in Korea, arriving at Chemulpo on this day. He was there under the direction of the Presbyterian Board of Foreign Missions. By saving the life of a prince, he won favor with the ruling authorities and became a court physician.

1921: William J. Kirkpatrick, who wrote the music to many well-known hymns including "We Have Heard the Joyful Sound," and "Redeemed, How I Love to Proclaim It," died on this day.

September 21

Biography of a Biographer

Matthew, one of Christ's disciples. (Bell, Mrs. Arthur. *Saints in Christian Art*. London: George Bell, 1901-4.)

Little enough is known of any of the apostles. We have the most detail about Paul, Peter and John. We have the least about those apostles who bring up the tail of the apostolic lists. Matthew falls somewhere in between the two groups.

His name was originally Levi. We know that Matthew and Levi are the same because the gospels of Matthew and Luke record a feast at which Jesus was criticized for association with publicans: Luke attributes this banquet to Levi; Matthew attributes it to Matthew. In his Gospel, Matthew tells that Christ approached him as he collected taxes and said, "Follow me" (9:9). Immediately, Matthew arose and followed.

Since he worked a booth near Capernaum, Matthew must have already heard of Christ. For all we know, Matthew may have been one of the tax collectors converted by John. Although tax collectors were generally hated by the Jews as rapacious instruments of the oppressive Romans, nothing says Matthew was dishonest.

At any rate, Matthew rose immediately and followed Jesus, leaving his past behind. His humility is shown in the fact that he calls himself "Matthew the publican" (10:3, KJV), branding himself with the profession the Jews most hated.

His original name, Levi, suggests that he was a man of the priestly tribe. When he wrote his Gospel, after years of exposure to the teachings of Christ and days of fierce persecution, his was the only one of the four that directly addressed the Jews. Matthew showed deep interest in the priestly and scribal functions of his class. His Gospel, more than any other, focuses on law and the fulfillment of Scriptures, on genealogy and on other details that reflect his Jewish background. Christ's fierce denunciations of the Pharisees and His prophecies of the end of the temple are most fully recorded in the writing of this apostle (see 23-24).

Matthew's interest in money finds expression too. The parable of the talents is found only in his account (see 25:14-30), along with many other beautiful passages of great richness. Herbert Lockyer noted that Matthew used more words for money than any other gospel writer.

Matthew was well-to-do. As soon as he came to Christ, he threw a party and invited others of his unsavory profession (see 9:9-12). He wanted to share Christ with them. No doubt similar concerns motivated him when he wrote his Gospel in an attempt to share Christ with the whole Jewish race.

We have nothing but legend about Matthew's death. His feast in the Roman Catholic calendar is celebrated on this day.

Other Events

1096: Irate Seljuk Turks surrounded the fortress of Xerigordon, near Nicaea, eventually killing most of the thirsty crusaders inside.

1522: Martin Luther's German New Testament was first published.

1558: Worn out with care, Charles V, Holy Roman Emperor, died. He had retired to a monastery some months earlier.

1695: John Glas was born at Auchtermuchty, Scotland. He became convinced that churches were meant to be gatherings of true believers, not state churches for people who happened to live in a parish. Consequently, he formed the Glasite Church, an independent Presbyterian sect. They were often known as Sandemanians after Glas's son-in-law, who took over leadership after Glas died in 1773.

1933: Martin Niemoller sent out a circular asking pastors to join a Pastors' Emergency League to resist Nazi abuses.

1992: Christian and Missionary Alliance radio broadcaster Greg Hapalla was martyred while taping a show in the Philippines.

Charles V, who was worn out with care. (Bezold, Friedrich von. *Geschichte der Deutschen Reformation*. Berlin: Grote, 1890.)

September 22

More Going on Than a Trip to the Zoo

C.S. Lewis, a major twentieth-century apologist and thinker. (Courtesy of the Christian History Institute archives.)

Individuals have surrendered their lives to Christ in all sorts of places. The revivalist Charles G. Finney converted in a woods. John Newton, author of the hymn "Amazing Grace," repented while lashed to a ship's wheel in a storm. Chuck Colson, founder of Prison Ministries, asked God into his life while crying in a car on a roadside.

C.S. Lewis converted while riding to a zoo in his brother's motorcycle sidecar. "When we set out I did not believe that Jesus is the Son of God and when we reached the zoo I did." Jack, as he preferred to be called, had already become a Theist—one who believes there is a God. He was converted on this day in 1931, following a long talk he'd had on September 19 with two Christian friends, J.R.R. Tolkien and Hugo Dyson.

Tolkien, who was soon to create the most imitated fantasy of our century, The Lord of the Rings trilogy, argued that even myths can originate in God, preserving truth, however distorted. He said that one might do God's work by writing myths. Lewis, on the other hand, doubted that myths embodied truth at all. The three argued until 3 a.m., when Tolkien went home. Dyson and Lewis walked and talked some more. Dyson insisted that Christianity works, putting the believer at peace, freeing him of sin and providing outside help to straighten him out.

On Christmas Day of that same year, Lewis joined the Church and took communion. He felt that faith had given him a solid footing. Prior to his conversion he had lacked a sense of direction for his talent, but by the middle of 1932 he had written the first of the many books that made him one of the best-loved twentieth-century Christian apologists: *The Pilgrim's Regress*. He would go on to create Narnia, his own wonderful fantasy world.

Lewis's renown grew, and he was asked to present a series of radio talks. The broadcasts were eventually brought together and published in his book *Mere Christianity*, which includes probably the most famous quotation of all of apologetics:

> A man who was merely a man and said the sort of things Jesus said would not be a great moral teacher. He would either be a lunatic—on the level with a man who says he is a poached egg—or else He would be the devil of hell. You must make your choice. Either He was and is the Son of God: or else a madman or something worse. You can shut Him up for a fool, you can spit at Him and kill Him as a demon; or you can fall at His feet and call Him Lord and God. But let us not come with any patronizing nonsense about His being a great human teacher. He has not left that open to us. He did not intend to.

Like so many other great men who were not converted in a "conventional" way, after his conversion, Lewis went on to have a great impact on literature as well as on Christianity.

Nathan Hale, a great American patriot, was hanged this day. (Johnston, Henry Phelps. *Nathan Hale, 1776: Biography and Memorials*. New Haven, CT: Yale University Press, 1914.)

Other Events

530: Pope Boniface II was consecrated into a divided Church. Sixty out of seventy bishops preferred Dioscorus as pope because they were fearful of Ostrogoth influence over Boniface. Dioscorus's death ended the crisis.

1566: Johann Agricola, German theologian and reformer, died on this day. He had once been a friend of Martin Luther, but their relationship had deteriorated over the issue of the authority of the Law of Moses on modern lives.

1734: Followers of Kaspar von Schwenckenfelder arrived in Philadelphia. Schwenckenfelder had been a prominent Roman Catholic but became an evangelistic preacher. His followers suffered persecution in Europe for over 100 years. In 1733, some looked over the situation in Philadelphia, liked it and sent word home. In gratitude for their deliverance, the newcomers to America set apart this day for thanksgiving.

1776: The American patriot and Christian Nathan Hale was executed as a spy by the British. He urged onlookers to prepare for death and was reported to have said, "I only regret that I have but one life to lose for my country."

Jeremy Lamphier Led Prayer Revival

Jeremy Lamphier had hoped for more, but six people were six people. And did not Scripture say, "For where two or three are gathered together in my name, there am I in the midst of them" (Matthew 18:20, KJV)? So on this day in 1857, at lunchtime, he did not moan about the small number who turned out in response to his advertisement. Instead, he knelt with the others in the rented hall on Fulton Street in New York City and prayed for a spiritual revival in America.

America did indeed need prayer. The nation was in spiritual, political and economic decline. Many people were disillusioned with spiritual things because of preachers who had repeatedly predicted the end of the world in the 1840s. Also, agitation over slavery was breeding political unrest, and civil war seemed near. To top things off, that year financial panic had hit as well. Banks failed, railroads went bankrupt, factories closed and unemployment increased.

In lower Manhattan, a Dutch Reformed church had been steadily losing members, so the board hired Lamphier to reverse the trend by implementing an active visitation program. Despite his visits to their homes, however, church members were listless. So Lamphier rented a hall on Fulton Street and advertised prayer meetings. Then conditions in the United States got worse: The Bank of Philadelphia failed. By the third week of Lamphier's program, forty people were participating in the prayer meetings and they asked Lamphier to hold daily meetings.

On October 10, the stock market crashed. Suddenly people were flocking to the prayer meetings. Within 6 months, 10,000 people were gathering daily for prayer in New York City alone.

Other cities experienced a renewed interest in prayer as well. In Chicago, the Metropolitan Theater was filled every day with 2,000 praying people. In Louisville, several thousand went to the Masonic Temple for prayer each morning. In Cleveland, 2,000 assembled for daily prayer, and St. Louis churches were filled for months at a time. In many places tents were set up for prayer. The newly formed YMCA also played an important role in holding prayer meetings and spreading the revival throughout the country.

In February 1858, Gordon Bennett of the *New York Herald* gave extensive coverage to the prayer revival. Not to be outdone, the *New York Tribune* devoted an entire issue in April 1858 to news of the revival. Word of the revival traveled west by telegraph. It was the first revival that the media played an important role in spreading.

Laypeople, not church leaders, led it with prayer rather than preaching as the focus. The meetings themselves were informal—within a five-minute limit, any person might pray, speak, lead in song or give a word of testimony. In spite of their loose organization, the prayer meetings avoided the emotionalism displayed in earlier revivals.

Thus the small prayer meeting of Jeremy Lamphier on this day led to the Third Great Awakening. It was the first revival to begin in America and spread worldwide. The revival passed to Ireland, Scotland, Wales, England, the better part of Europe, South Africa, India, Australia and the Pacific Islands.

Men and women praying at benches as a revivalist speaks. (Courtesy of the Christian History Institute archives.)

People from each of the social classes became interested in salvation. Backsliders returned to faith, conversions increased and Christians desired deeper instruction in spiritual truths. Families established daily devotions, and entire communities underwent a noticeable change in morals. Preaching, which in many places had become intellectual and lifeless, began to concentrate on the truths of the gospel of Christ and His cross. As James Buchanan of Scotland summarized, it was a time when "new spiritual life was imparted to the dead, and new spiritual health imparted to the living."

Other Events

1122: Henry V of the Holy Roman Empire renounced investiture of ring and crozier at the Concordat of Worms, promising freedom of election of clergy and restoration of Church property.

1571: John Jewel, the English Church reformer who more than any other created a scholarly defense of Anglicanism, died on this day.

1595: Led by Fray Juan de Silva, the Spanish began an intensive missionary campaign in the American southeast. In the following two years, 1,500 Native Americans in the area of Florida, Georgia and South Carolina were converted.

1867: Bishop Samuel Adjai Crowther wrote a letter pleading for help. The Anglican African bishop was being held by chief Obokko for a ransom of 1,000 bags of cowrie shells.

1950: The first of the "Unshackled" broadcasts aired. This program, originating from the Pacific Garden Mission, still tells stories of men who found that Christ alone could free them from sinful obsessions.

Holy Roman Emperor Henry V, who promised freedom of election of clergy and restoration of Church property. (Peake, Elizabeth. *History of the German Emperors and Their Contemporaries*. Philadelphia: J.B. Lippincott & Co., 1874.)

A picturesque view of Utrecht. (Courtesy of Ben Merghart.)

September 24

Old Catholics Issue Declaration of Utrecht

On July 18, 1870, the First Vatican Council declared by an overwhelming majority that

> the Roman Pontiff, when he speaks ex cathedra, that is, when in discharge of the office of pastor and teacher of all Christians, by virtue of his supreme apostolic authority he defines a doctrine regarding faith or morals to be held by the universal Church, is possessed of that infallibility with which the divine Redeemer willed that his church should be endowed.

In other words, the pope was "infallible" under certain carefully defined conditions. The decision was sent to the faithful in a letter entitled *Pastor Aeternus*.

The vote may have made sense to the Vatican Council, but to others it was not so obvious. Protestants worldwide denied its claim, as did a small percentage of Catholics. To political analysts, the doctrine seemed politically motivated. The ideas of the Roman Church were under attack. Italy had confiscated lands long controlled by the popes. The pope had even fled from the Vatican for a time. Some analysts claimed that because the Church could not assert its supremacy in political matters, it was throwing its weight around in the spiritual realm.

One of the Roman Church's most gifted historians, Johann Joseph Ignaz von Dollinger, wrote a long letter in which he said that he could not accept the pope's infallibility "as a Christian, a theologian, a historical student and a citizen." His strong opposition was echoed by several bishops, although all of them backed down when the Church put pressure on them.

Other scholars and about 60,000 Catholic laypeople did not yield to the letter. They withdrew from the Roman Church and called themselves Old Catholics. To them it was a matter of truth. They saw instances when popes, speaking authoritatively, had made mistakes—in fact, a couple of popes even seemed to have supported heresy.

Dollinger never joined the Old Catholics. Neither did he ever return to the Roman Church. He was urged to do so on his deathbed but replied:

> Ought I (in obedience to your suggestion) to appear before the Eternal Judge, my conscience burdened with a double perjury? . . . I think that what I have written so far will suffice to make clear to you that with such convictions one may stand even on the threshold of eternity in a condition of inner peace and spiritual calm.

At the Council of Utrecht on this day in 1889, the Old Catholics laid out the guidelines of their theology. They agreed that the pope was "first among equals," but rejected

> the decrees of the so-called Council of the Vatican, which were promulgated July 18th, 1870, concerning the infallibility and the universal Episcopate of the Bishop of Rome, decrees which are in contradiction with the faith of the ancient Church, and which destroy its ancient canonical constitution [divisions of power in old church laws] by attributing to the pope the plenitude of ecclesiastical powers over all dioceses [areas that bishops control] and over all the faithful.

The Declaration of Utrecht also rejected the decrees of the Council of Trent with regard to discipline and denied the dogma of the Immaculate Conception. It closed with the hope that by professing sound doctrine and laying aside errors that had crept into the Catholic Church "we shall be able to combat efficaciously the great evils of our day, which are unbelief and indifference in matters of religion."

Pope Innocent II had a troubled papacy. (Montor, Chevalier Artaud de. *Lives and Times of the Popes*. New York: Catholic Publication Society of America, 1911.)

Other Events

787: The Second Nicean Council opened with an address read by Empress Irene of the Roman Empire. The council condemned iconoclasm (the destruction and removal of icons). The Roman Catholic Church counts this as the seventh of twenty-one ecumenical councils; the Eastern Orthodox Churches consider this the last of the ecumenical councils.

1143: Pope Innocent II died. During Innocent II's troubled papacy, a rival pope ruled Rome more often than he. Innocent excommunicated Roger of Sicily but was forced to rescind the act.

1757: Rev. Aaron Burr, president of the college at Princeton and the son-in-law of Jonathan Edwards, died. Edwards was appointed in Burr's place at Princeton five days after Burr's death.

1868: Henry Hart Milman, hymn writer and impartial Church historian, died on this day.

1939: Juji Nakada, a Japanese evangelist, died. It was at his invitation that Charles and Lettie Cowman established a Bible institute,the Oriental and Missionary Society (OMS), in Japan.

Colorful Peter Cartwright, Circuit Rider

September 25

When Peter Cartwright died on this day in 1872, the frontier lost a colorful and influential preacher. Cartwright was born in Virginia in 1785, just two years after the Treaty of Paris ended the American Revolution. He was taken west to Kentucky, and there he became a tough guy in rough Logan County, which was known as "Rogue's Harbor" because of its swarms of bad men.

His Methodist mother pleaded and prayed for his salvation. Her prayers won. During a camp meeting, sixteen-year-old Cartwright was convicted of his sinfulness and his need for a Savior. For hours he cried out to God for forgiveness until finally the peace of Christ flooded his soul. At once he joined the Methodist Episcopal Church. Within two years he became a traveling preacher, bringing the gospel to the backwoods of the new nation. His rough past and hardy constitution served him well, for he faced floods, thieves, hunger and disease. He met every challenge head-on.

Once, Cartwright warned General Andrew Jackson (future President of the United States) that Jackson would be damned to hell just as quickly as any other man if he did not repent. Another preacher apologized to the general for Cartwright's bluntness. Jackson retorted that Christ's ministers ought to love everybody and fear no mortal man, adding that he wished he had a few thousand officers like Cartwright.

Rowdies often interrupted Cartwright's meetings. When one thug promised to whip him, Cartwright invited the man to step into the woods with him. The two started for the trees. Leaping over a fence at the edge of the campground, Cartwright landed painfully and clutched his side. The bully shouted that the preacher was going for a dagger and took to his heels.

Crowds flocked to hear Cartwright's sermons. Throughout Kentucky, Tennessee and Illinois, he preached to hosts of men and women for three hours at a stretch, several times a week. Women wept and strong men trembled. Nearly 10,000 people came to Christ in meetings that sometimes ran day and night. Cartwright baptized thousands, adding them to the Church. He urged new converts to build meeting houses. To meet a desperate need for preachers, he championed the creation of Methodist colleges. Wherever he went, he left behind religious books and tracts to convert and strengthen souls. The joy of soul-winning compensated him for all his hardships.

And the hardships were many. Several times Cartwright went for days without food. Once he returned from his circuit with just six borrowed cents in his pocket. His father had to outfit him with clothes, a saddle and a horse before he could ride again.

Traveling preachers were paid a measly $30 to 50 a year. Nonetheless, Cartwright married. His family experienced tragedy when, forced to camp in the open one night, they were startled awake when a tree snapped in two; Cartwright flung up his arms to deflect

Peter Cartwright's *Autobiography* is mined by historians for details on life on the frontier. (Daniels, W.H. *Illustrated History of Methodism in Great Britain and America, From the Days of the Wesleys to the Present Time*. New York: Phillips & Hunt, 1880.)

the falling timber, but it crushed his youngest daughter to death.

In 1823 Cartwright sold his Kentucky farm because he feared his daughters would marry slave owners. Slavery, he felt, sapped independence of spirit. His family readily agreed to the change, and his bishop appointed him to a circuit in Illinois.

In Illinois, Cartwright braved floods. Once he had to chase his saddlebags which were swept downstream. Yet in every circumstance, the Lord brought him to safety.

While in Illinois Cartwright ran in a political race against Abraham Lincoln, beating him for a seat in the Illinois legislature. But later Lincoln beat him in a race for the US Congress.

Cartwright died at the age of eighty-seven, leaving behind an autobiography that has become a classic as much for the exploits it recounts as for the pictures it paints of frontier life.

Other Events

1493: Under the orders of Benedictine Bernardo Buil to formally introduce Christianity into the New World, twelve missionaries sailed from Spain with Christopher Columbus's second expedition.

1794: The Russian Orthodox Church established a mission among the Aleutians. This was at the request of Grigorii Ivanovich Shelekov, who founded a hunting settlement among the Kodiaks and appealed to the Russian government to plant Orthodox churches among them as well. He had promised to pay all expenses and provide transportation. Eight monks and two priests baptized 7,000 Aleuts in eight months.

1835: William White, George Washington Doane and several other bishops consecrated Jackson Kemper for his work on the American frontier. He rested little as he shared the gospel and founded several colleges for the Episcopal Church.

1897: In an effort to assist alcoholics on their way to recovery, William Raws established America's first branch of Keswick on 600 acres in New Jersey.

1953: Poland's Communists arrested outspoken Cardinal Wyszynski and restricted him to a monastery.

Bishop Jackson Kemper, who was consecrated for his work on the American frontier. (Perry, William Stevens. *The Episcopate in America*. New York: Christian Literature, 1895.)

September

26

Mr. Lincoln's Fast

"Honest Abe." (Courtesy of the Christian History Institute archives.)

It is uncertain whether or not Abraham Lincoln, one of America's best-known presidents, ever became a committed Christian. As a youth, he mocked the Scriptures. After the death of his favorite son, Willie, he groped for some hope that could give him solace. His wife, Mary, and he attended séances but eventually renounced them as fraudulent.

It is known, however, that the cares and trials of the Civil War drove Lincoln increasingly to his Bible. His lifelong friend, Joshua Speed, remembered finding Lincoln sitting near a window reading his Bible. Speed said to Lincoln, "If you have recovered from your skepticism [about the veracity of the Bible] I am sorry to say that I have not!" With an earnest look on his face, Lincoln replied: "You are wrong, Speed; take all of this book upon reason that you can, and the balance on faith, and you will live and die a happier and better man."

Many of Lincoln's communications alluded to God. In his personal correspondence to Mrs. Gurney, a Quakeress, he wrote, "We hoped for a happy termination of this terrible war before this; but God knows best and has ruled otherwise." Increasingly he saw himself as an instrument of the Lord's will, inscrutable though that might be.

He wrestled to understand why the North continued to lose even though its cause, the abolition of slavery and the preservation of the Union, seemed the more justifiable side. In the end, in a note not written for public consumption, Lincoln is said to have concluded that "the will of God prevails. . . . Both [sides] may be wrong. . . . In the present civil war it is quite possible God's purpose is something quite different from the purpose of either party."

Lincoln realized that there was as much sin to evoke God's wrath upon the Union as there was on the slave-owning Confederacy. So, on August 12, 1861, he issued a proclamation in the northern states for a day of public humiliation, prayer and fasting

> to be observed by the people of the United States with religious solemnities. . . . It is peculiarly fit for us to recognize the hand of God in this terrible visitation, and in sorrowful remembrance of our own faults and crimes as a nation and as individuals to humble ourselves before Him, and to pray for His mercy.

The fast was observed on this day in 1861, the last Thursday of the month. Despite Lincoln's attempts to bring the war to an end, the fighting ground along for another three years, chewing up the lives and limbs of men in prodigious numbers.

Lincoln's assassination in April of 1865 deprived his nation of a great leader. He left a legacy of great and often profoundly moral words.

Condé, whose actions precipitated the second Huguenot war. (Baird, Henry Martyn. *Theodore Beza: The Councilor of the French Reformation*. New York: G.P. Putnam's Sons, 1899.)

Other Events

611: Irish abbot Colman Eloto, to whom legend ascribes a pet fly that used to mark his place in his book, died on this day. He founded a monastery at Lynally.

1460: Pope Pius II assembled European leaders, then delivered a three-hour sermon to inspire them to launch a new crusade against the Turks. The speech swayed the listeners, but then Cardinal Bessarion added a three-hour harangue of his own. After six hours of preaching, the European princes lost interest and never mounted the crusade.

1567: Huguenot leader Condé tried to seize the young king of France. This action gave Catholics a cause to launch what became the second Huguenot war.

1626: Lancelot Andrewes died on this day. He exerted a good deal of influence on the development of Anglican theology and authored the spiritual classic *Private Devotions*. He also helped make the King James translation of the Bible.

September 27

Modern Ecumenical Church

The pages of this book could quite easily be filled with records of Church divisions and splits. The story of Protestantism has been one of ever-accelerating fission. Sects have risen, shone brightly, grown great and then split over questions of doctrine and purity or dwindled in the face of some newly emergent faith. Hundreds of Protestant denominations have come into being, each holding stubbornly to a few articles of difference that separate them from others that exhibit equal evidence of faith.

It wouldn't be nearly as easy to fill a book with stories of Churches overcoming divisions and finding reconciliation and healing. Reversals of the divisive trend in Churches have been all too rare. And yet for the Christians of South India, a remarkable reversal occurred at the start of this century.

Christians are a very small minority in India, and their groups were often at odds with each other. In 1855, the groups acknowledged this fact and began talks in an effort to bring about the unification of South Indian Protestant Churches. Despite a number of seemingly futile meetings and continued divisiveness between the Churches, a spirit of persistence and patience endured. More than half a century after the talks began, results were finally achieved: In 1908 Presbyterians and Congregationalists fused into one new body.

The talks continued and moved on to include the Anglicans. As early as 1888, Anglican leaders, taking to heart the Apostles' Creed, which speaks of one holy, catholic (i.e., universal) church, began to contemplate seriously what must take place if they were to unite with other Churches. Unification was possible, they concluded, but only if certain essential beliefs were kept. The Lambeth Conference of 1888 (so named because Anglicans from all over the world gathered under the auspices of the archbishop of Canterbury, usually at the Lambeth Palace) issued a list of four fundamentals that must be accepted by any church that would merge with the Anglicans. The list was called the Lambeth Quadrilateral.

The Lambeth Quadrilateral declared that the Holy Scriptures of the Old and New Testaments contain all of the things necessary for salvation and are the rule and ultimate standard of faith. It also said that the Apostles' Creed is the symbol for baptism and the Nicene Creed is the sufficient statement of faith. Baptism and the Lord's Supper are the two essential sacraments, instituted by the Lord Jesus Christ Himself. The two sacraments must be observed with the words and elements He Himself ordained. The Church must have a "historic" episcopate, that is, a succession of ordination traceable (in theory, at least) back to the apostles.

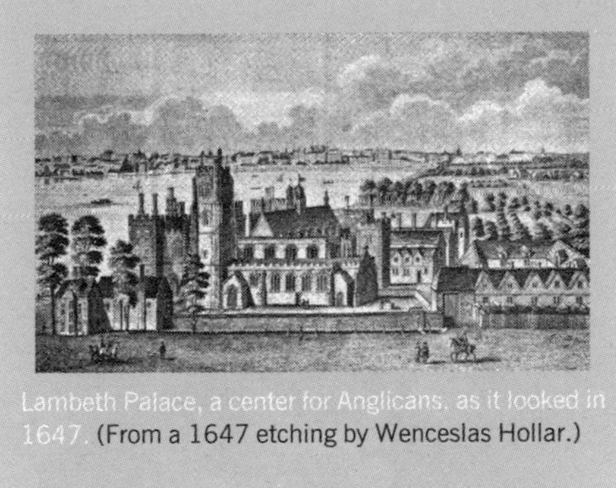

Lambeth Palace, a center for Anglicans, as it looked in 1647. (From a 1647 etching by Wenceslas Hollar.)

On this day in 1947, after twenty-eight years of talks, the Anglicans of all Southern India, Ceylon and Burma united into the Church of India, joining those Congregationalists and Presbyterians who had already merged together. Almost half a million Anglicans were involved. The merger was inaugurated at Madras. Three Anglican bishops consecrated nine new bishops. It was the biggest ecumenical merger to that time, and it immediately prompted other regions of India to begin similar negotiations for reunification.

Other Events

1370: Urban V, having returned the papacy to Rome, abandoned it again and returned to France against the warnings of Catherine of Siena. He also founded the universities of Cracow and Viennes.

1540: Pope Paul III officially approved the Society of Jesus (Jesuits). Loyola was the order's first general.

1660: St. Vincent de Paul died. After giving his life to serving the poor, he founded the first Confraternity of Charity in 1617, the Congregation of the Mission in 1625 and the Daughters of Charity in 1633 (the first non-monastic women's order completely given to the care of the sick and the poor). Canonized in 1737, St. Vincent was named patron saint of all charitable works in 1885.

1829: Dr. J.J. Parrot climbed Mt. Ararat in Turkey, the first modern ascent of the mountain that is widely believed to hold the remains of Noah's ark.

1997: Dr. Allan R. MacRae, one of the founders of the Biblical Theological Seminary in Philadelphia, died on this day. He emphasized the reliability of Scripture in his years as president of the school.

Vincent de Paul gave his name to a line of charity stores in the United States. (Bell, Mrs. Arthur. *Saints in Christian Art*. London: George Bell, 1901-4.)

SEPTEMBER

28

Good King Wenceslas Attacked by Greedy Brother

Pope Benedict XIV (shown here) did not want Wenceslas included in the Roman Missal as a martyr. (Montor, Chevalier Artaud de. *Lives and Times of the Popes*. New York: Catholic Publication Society of America, 1911.)

The choir sang with gusto because the carol had a cheerful tune and was well loved:

Good King Wenceslas looked out
On the feast of Stephen,
When the snow lay round about,
Deep and crisp and even.

However, few of those singing or listening had heard the true story behind the song. Few knew that there really was a Wenceslas, a tenth-century Christian duke who ruled for about seven years in Bohemia (which is now part of Czech Republic).

Wenceslas was brought up by his Christian grandmother, Ludmila. She taught him that faith had to be put into action or it was a sham. Because of her teaching and example, Wenceslas learned true concern for the poor and suffering. That is the spirit John Mason Neale captured when he wrote his carol. In the song, the prince goes out on a cold night to feed a poor man who is gathering winter fuel. When a page complains of the cold and difficulty, Wenceslas urges the page to follow in Wenceslas's tracks—a mirror of the way we are to follow in Christ's footsteps:

Mark my footsteps, my good page,
Tread thou in them boldly:
Thou shalt find the winter's rage
Freeze thy blood less coldly.

Wenceslas was just thirteen when his father died in the year 921. Ludmila acted as regent for the young man, but Wenceslas's mother, Drahomira, wanted the throne for herself. She killed Ludmila and assumed control of the country.

Wenceslas did not wait to come of age before seizing the throne from his murderous mother and banishing her to a neighboring country. During his short reign, Wenceslas encouraged German missionaries to preach in Bohemia. He urged his people to convert to Christianity, even going so far as to punish those who held out. At the same time, he reformed his country's judicial system and courted peace with neighboring nations, especially Germany. He was known for his charity to the poor.

Wenceslas had a younger brother, Boleslaw, who was made in the same mold as Drahomira. Some Bohemian nobles resented the fact that Wenceslas submitted to neighboring Germany, so they urged Boleslaw to take action.

Boleslaw plotted. When Wenceslas went to mass on this day in 929, his brother followed him to the church door. Recognizing that trouble was afoot, Wenceslas said, "Brother, you were a good subject to me yesterday."

"And now I intend to be a better one!" shouted Boleslaw and struck his brother in the head with his sword.

Wenceslas had strength enough to fling his brother to the ground, whereupon one of Boleslaw's men stabbed Wenceslas in the hand. Wenceslas sought refuge in the church, but two other assassins struck him down at the door.

Bohemians look at Wenceslas as a martyr and their foremost saint. His picture appeared on their coins, and his crown was a symbol of Czech independence. Despite opposition from Pope Benedict XIV, Wenceslas was included in the Roman Missal. And an English hymn writer immortalized him in a carol.

Jeanne d'Albret, who was called by the pope to answer for heresy. (Baird, Henry Martyn. *Theodore Beza: The Councilor of the French Reformation*. New York: G.P. Putnam's Sons, 1899.)

Other Events

1066: William the Conqueror changed the English Church by invading England on this day and afterward appointing his own men, who had been involved in Norman Church reforms, to key positions.

1230: Gregory IX reinterpreted the Franciscan rule of poverty, removing some of its stricter provisions. When he offered to do the same for the Poor Clares, Clare stoutly resisted.

1563: The pope commanded Jeanne D'Albret, Huguenot queen of Navarre, to appear for examination of heresy on pain of losing her lands. Since her lands were French territories, the French government, which had no more liking for Protestants than the pope, took her side.

1808: Andover Theological Seminary in Massachusetts opened to train orthodox Congregational Church ministers. It is the oldest theological school in New England.

1951: The Peace Committee, a Communist front for Catholic clergy, was founded by the Czechoslovakian Communists to enlist clergy into socialist work under minister Plojhar.

1978: Pope John Paul I died in bed of a heart attack while reading *The Imitation of Christ*. He had been pope for only thirty-three days. Rumors said he was poisoned.

Oastler's Letter Shocked Engand

Richard Oastler was outraged. Having been born into a Wesleyan Methodist family and educated by Moravians, he was a man of conscience who believed words should be matched with deeds. That is why he took up his pen to write a letter blasting "Yorkshire Slavery." The letter was published on this day in 1830 in the Leeds *Mercury*.

"It is the pride of Britain that a slave cannot exist on her soil," he began. Oastler declared himself to be in complete sympathy with efforts to end slavery. Slavery was not limited to the colonies, he said:

> Let truth speak out, appalling as the statement may appear. The fact is true. Thousands of our fellow-creatures and fellow-subjects, both male and female, the miserable inhabitants of a Yorkshire town [Yorkshire now represented in Parliament by the giant of anti-slavery principles], are this very moment existing in a state of slavery, more horrid than are the victims of that hellish system "colonial" slavery.

Their slavery took a different form, to be sure, but slavery it was, all the same:

> Thousands of little children, both male and female, but principally female, from seven to fourteen years of age, are daily compelled to labor from six o'clock in the morning to seven in the evening, with only—Britons, blush while you read it!—with only thirty minutes allowed for eating and recreation.

Action was needed, Oastler asserted:

> Vow one by one, vow altogether, vow with heart and voice, eternal enmity against oppression by your brethren's hands; Till man nor woman under Britain's laws, nor son nor daughter born within her empire, shall buy, or sell, or HIRE, or BE A SLAVE!

From that day forward, Oastler was as good as his word. He labored without ceasing to get conditions improved for workers. That very September, one of the factory owners, John Wood, approached Oastler, saying:

> I have had no sleep tonight. I have been reading the Bible and in every page I have read my own condemnation. I cannot allow you to leave me without a pledge that you will use all your influence in trying to remove from our factory system the cruelties which are practiced in our mills.

Oastler promised to do what he could. "I felt that we were each of us in the presence of the Highest and I knew that that vow was recorded in Heaven," he said.

His letter was read by John Hobhouse, a radical member of Parliament. Hobhouse immediately introduced a bill that prohibited children under nine from working, eliminated night work for children, and limited their hours of employment to ten a day. A modified bill without teeth in it soon passed, but Oastler had to fight for a stronger act that would be enforced by penalties.

In another letter written four years later, Oastler said:

Young boys working the midnight shift in a glass factory. (Spargo, John. *The Bitter Cry of the Children*. New York: Macmillan, 1906.)

> The mill-owners obtained their wealth by overworking and by defrauding the factory children. They were praying people, but took care their work people should neither have time nor strength to pray. These hypocrites pretended it was necessary to keep these poor infant slaves at this excruciating labor just to preserve them from "bad company" and to prevent them learning "bad habits."

Oastler helped form Short Time Committees in major industrial cities to improve hours of work. He advocated sabotage of machinery in cases where employers were especially cruel.

The next time that you have to work no more than an eight-hour day, remember Richard Oastler and his "Yorkshire Slavery" letter, which fired the shot that changed your world.

Other Events

440: Pope Leo I "the Great" was consecrated. He strengthened the authority of the Church, suppressed the Manichean heresy and wrote important letters:

> The effect of our communion in the body and blood of Christ is that we are transformed into what we consume, and that he in whom we have died and in whom we have risen from the dead lives and is manifested in every movement of our body and of our spirit.

1642: An angry Indian had Jesuit missionary St. René Goupil tomahawked for making the sign of the cross over one of the Indian's grandchildren.

1770: George Whitefield preached his last sermon, a two-hour exposition that started with the text, "Test yourselves to see if you are in the faith." He died the next day, saying, "I would rather wear out than rust out."

1987: Evangelist Pat Robertson resigned his ministries to run for President of the United States.

George Whitefield, who died the day after he preached his final sermon. (Avery, Elroy McKendree. *History of the United States and Its People: From Their Earliest Records to the Present Time*. Cleveland, OH: The Burrows Brothers Company, 1904.)

30

Fall and Rise

Jerome, the great biblical scholar, on his deathbed. (Bell, Mrs. Arthur. *Saints in Christian Art*. London: George Bell, 1901-4.)

When the Vandals sacked Rome in 410, the great biblical scholar Jerome was not there to see the fall of the grand city. Like Abraham avoiding Sodom, Jerome had avoided Rome for most of his life. Years before, protesting the moral laxity of his generation, he fled into the desert with friends and lived on so little that he came close to killing himself. Two of his friends did die, broken by fasting and cruel weather. Jerome survived and returned to Rome to become secretary to Pope Damasus. Although he lived in the city, he kept apart from it, living the life of an ascetic in the midst of pomp.

Jerome may have hoped to become bishop of Rome himself one day, but his savage pen prevented it. All his life he was quarrelsome and sarcastic. He especially blasted the folly of Rome's women and the greed of its men. People were only too glad to hit back at him. The death of his pupil Blesilla from fasting was blamed on him. That is why Jerome, sponsored by the wealthy widow Paulina, mother of Blesilla, migrated to Bethlehem after Damasus died.

It was perhaps inevitable that Jerome should have become the greatest Christian scholar of his age. Well versed in the classics, he loved the beauty of words. His one luxury was books. While in the desert, he dreamed that he was hauled before Christ in the judgment. When asked his condition, he claimed to be a Christian. The great judge told him he lied. Jerome was a Ciceronian. Dumb before this accusation, he was ordered flogged. When Jerome woke, there were bruises on his back. Never again did pagan wisdom dominate his mind.

When asked by Damasus to correct errors in the Latin Bible translations of the day, Jerome did so. The Bible became his passion. He learned Hebrew and made a complete new translation of the Scriptures into Latin. He chose his words for effect and made the translation a literary treasure much as the Authorized (King James) Version became for the English language. At first, Jerome did not include the apocryphal books. When commanded to do so, he placed them in a separate category. His translation became known as the Vulgate, taken from the word *vulgar* meaning "mob" or "common people," because it was written in the popular tongue of the empire. It was the Bible of the Middle Ages.

In addition to the Vulgate, Jerome also produced Bible commentaries. He was at work on a commentary on Ezekiel on this day in 420 when he died peacefully. His body was by then as thin as a shadow from fasting, and his voice and sight were failing.

Phillip Doddridge sailed for Portugal in an attempt to regain his health. (Daniels, W.H. *Illustrated History of Methodism in Great Britain and America, From the Days of the Wesleys to the Present Time*. New York: Phillips & Hunt, 1880.)

Other Events

653: Honorius, archbishop of Canterbury, died. He consecrated England's first island-born bishops.

1751: Phillip Doddridge, clergyman and author of the influential book *The Rise and Progress of Religion in the Soul,* sailed from Falmouth, England, for the warmer climate of Portugal in the hope of recovering from consumption. He died a month later.

1865: Francis Wayland, a Baptist clergyman, died in Providence, Rhode Island. While president of Brown University, he greatly raised the school's standards.

1943: Pope Pius XII issued the encyclical *Divino Afflante Spiritu*, which urged more use of textual criticism among Roman Catholic scholars.

1970: The New American Bible, a Roman Catholic version of the Book, was published as a direct outcome of the encyclical *Divino Afflante Spiritu*.

No Handshake After the Marburg Colloquy

From the earliest days of the Church, there have been differences over doctrines and how to interpret Scripture. Paul's teaching of salvation apart from the Law of Moses was at first offensive to Jewish Christian leaders in Jerusalem, but after a meeting and discussion together, the two sides reached a decision that allowed Paul to continue work among the Gentiles. This Council of Jerusalem was the first of many to seek to settle differences among fellow Christians.

The Colloquy of Marburg, which began on this day in 1529, was the first council of Protestants. It was an attempt to resolve controversies that had arisen between the two reformers Ulrich Zwingli and Martin Luther.

Zwingli in Switzerland and Luther in Germany had each recognized the errors and corruption of the medieval Church. Both tried to turn the Church back to the profound simplicity of faith in Christ alone for salvation. Both firmly believed that the Scriptures alone were God's word of guidance and direction for the Church. Yet strong disagreement arose over the meaning of Holy Communion. The Roman Catholic Church taught that in the ceremony of the mass, the priest was given special powers so that the bread and the wine were transformed into the literal body and blood of Christ.

Neither Zwingli nor Luther found that view acceptable or supported by Scripture. Christ had ascended into heaven, and His resurrected body was in heaven, not on earth, they argued. Luther maintained that in the sacrament, Christ's body and blood were present "in, with and under" the bread and wine. For Zwingli, Christ was present not physically, but spiritually in the hearts of believers. He argued that when Christ said, "This is my body" (Matthew 26:26; Mark 14:22; Luke 22:19; 1 Corinthians 11:24) or "This is my blood" (Matthew 26:28; Mark 14:24; see Luke 22:20) at the Last Supper, He was not speaking any more literally than when He said, "I am the vine" (John 15:5) or "I am the door" (John 10:9, KJV). Neither Zwingli nor Luther could accept the other's viewpoint, and the debate became harsh.

Philip of Hesse, a German ruler, invited the reformers to come to his territory to resolve their differences. Behind Philip's desire for peace between Zwingli and Luther was his hope that a political alliance of the Protestant states might be formed, thus weakening the Catholic Hapsburgs and the Holy Roman Empire.

Luther went to the Marburg conference reluctantly. Zwingli, however, was eager for peace. At the conference, he prayed:

> Fill us, O Lord and Father of us all, we beseech thee, with thy gentle Spirit, and dispel on both sides all the clouds of misunderstanding and passion. Make an end to the strife of blind fury. . . . Guard us against abusing our powers, and enable us to employ them with all earnestness for the promotion of holiness.

Marburg Castle, site of the meeting at which Luther refused Zwingli a handshake. (McGiffert, Arthur Cushman. *Martin Luther, the Man and His Work*. New York: The Century Co., 1911.)

Peace was not to be had, however. Though the reformers agreed on the doctrines of the Trinity, the person of Christ, His death and resurrection, original sin, justification by faith, the Holy Spirit and the number of sacraments, they could not agree on the details regarding Communion. Zwingli wished to be forbearing with others on such issues. Luther thought Zwingli was not attaching enough significance to his doctrine and would not shake Zwingli's hand as a token of Christian brotherhood. The Lord's Supper, given by Jesus as a sign, among other things, of the unity of His people, became in this case the occasion of division.

Other Events

1061: Alexander II became pope, the first to be elected by the college of cardinals.

1555: Giovanni Peirlugi da Palestrina was appointed choir master to St. John Lateran. His music was some of the best before Bach's.

1883: A.B. Simpson founded the Missionary Training Institute, later known as Nyack College, the first mission school in America.

1885: Lord Shaftesbury, Ashley Cooper, seventh earl of Shaftesbury, who used his wealth to improve the lot of the poor, died on this day.

1946: Rev. Jack McAlister founded the World Literature Crusade in Canada to distribute Bibles and gospel literature. Originally it was called Every Home for Christ.

1948: The Communist government of Rumania announced that 1.5 million people loyal to the Catholic Church were being turned over to Orthodoxy.

1961: Christian Broadcasting Network (CBN) began TV broadcasts. Millions watched its show *The 700 Club*.

Palestrina, who wrote lovely Christian works and became a priest. (Chapin, Anna Alice. *Masters of Music*. New York: Dodd, Mead and Company, 1905.)

The founders of the Baptist Missionary Society in Mrs. Wallis's parlor. (Dennis, James S. *Christian Missions and Social Progress*. New York: Fleming H. Revell Co., 1897-1906.)

2 Expecting Great Things from God

The group of young men who met in Mrs. Beeby Wallis's parlor on this day in 1792 seemed an unlikely bunch to begin a major worldwide mission work. All twelve ministers were from small churches in the district of Kettering, England. Two had churches with congregations of less than twenty-five each. However, the men had become increasingly convinced that their churches should send the gospel message to the far-flung corners of the globe.

Many Christians in the eighteenth century had come to accept the idea that the heathen had rejected the gospel and would be held accountable for their rejection on the coming day of judgment. Some even argued that if God wanted the heathen saved, He would enlighten them without any human help. Young pastor William Carey couldn't accept such views, however. He said the apostles were commanded to teach all nations, and since the promise of the gospel was still true, surely the command to teach the nations was still true as well. Carey wrote out his thoughts on the state of the world in his day, the need for missions and the methods that should be used in carrying out the task. In May 1792 he published the work as *An Enquiry into the Obligation of Christians to Use Means for the Conversion of the Heathens*.

Point by point, Carey answered objections that had been put forward against missionary activity. Were heathen lands too distant? Navigation had improved greatly in the last centuries. Were heathen ways barbarous? Merchants and traders didn't seem to mind the inconvenience of dealing with them. Was there physical danger to missionary activity or difficulties in procuring supplies? Language barriers? If these all could be overcome in the interest of commerce and profit, surely they could be overcome for the kingdom of Christ. Carey encouraged his readers to "expect great things from God; attempt great things for God."

Carey's *Enquiry* and his impassioned address on missions at the semiannual ministers' meeting at Kettering stirred the men to action. When they met on this day in 1792 in Mrs. Wallis's parlor, they formed the Baptist Missionary Society as a means of spreading the gospel among the heathen. Andrew Fuller was appointed secretary, and a small snuff box with a picture of St. Paul's conversion on the lid became the treasury. Each minister wrote down what he thought he could give. It was very little for such a grand purpose, but hadn't the Lord done much with a boy's five loaves and two fishes?

The next year the society sent Carey to India. There he translated the New Testament into Bengali. As he worked, his influence extended throughout much of the East, to Burma, the East Indies and China.

The Baptist Missionary Society was the first foreign missionary society created by the evangelical revival of the last half of the eighteenth century. In short order other missionary societies were also established, and a new era in missions began as the gospel was increasingly spread outside of the West to the regions of Africa and Asia. Carey was right: "Expect great things from God; attempt great things for God."

Urban IV, who died on this day in 1187. (Montor, Chevalier Artaud de. *Lives and Times of the Popes*. New York: Catholic Publication Society of America, 1911.)

Other Events

1187: Muslim general Saladin captured Jerusalem from the crusaders.

1264: Pope Urban IV died. He instituted the feast of Corpus Cristi, expanded the number of French cardinals and excommunicated Manfred, because Manfred held territories that the popes had awarded to Charles I of Anjou.

1528: William Tyndale issued his tract "Obedience of a Christian Man" from the Continent where he was a refugee. In the preface, he replied to objections against translating the Bible into English:

> They say our tongue is too rude. It is not so. Greek and Hebrew go more easily into English than into Latin. Has not God made the English tongue as well as others? They allow you to read in English of Robin Hood, Bevis of Hampton, Hercules, Troilus, and a thousand ribald or filthy tales. It is only the Scripture that is forbidden. It is therefore clearer than the sun that this forbiddal is not for love of your souls, which they care for as the fox doth for the geese.

October 3

Thomas Gallaudet's Silent Treatment

Gallaudet was a missionary with a difference. His work was not in steamy jungles or among primitive tribesmen. He did not sail the seas to reach his work. His souls were not immigrants or gangsters. No, Thomas Gallaudet's subjects were silent people.

Like his father before him, he was concerned with the problems of the deaf. The older Gallaudet had founded a school for deaf mutes and married a deaf mute named Sophia (Gallaudet's mother). In his turn, Gallaudet married a deaf mute too—Elizabeth Budd, one of his college students. This background prepared him for his special ministry.

In 1850, Gallaudet began a deaf class in St. Stephens Church in New York. It quickly outgrew its space. The next year, he was ordained as an Episcopal priest. The death of a deaf student from tuberculosis convinced Gallaudet that more had to be done for the spiritual needs of those who could not hear. With help from his denomination, he set out to improve his outreach by establishing a church for the deaf. On this day, a Sunday, in 1852, he held the world's first church service for the deaf in the little Washington Square chapel of New York University.

Seven years later, his congregation bought a church building and a rectory. The St. Ann's Church for the Deaf was the world's first all-deaf church. At that first service, Gallaudet preached a sermon on Christ's parable of the sower and compared the beginning of the deaf work with seed that had been sown:

> Our Saviour, being the everlasting Word by whom all things were made, could use the imagery of the natural world more strikingly and appropriately than anyone else, to set forth and illustrate the great moral principles which he came to promulgate and enforce. How clearly and powerfully does he teach us, by his reference to the growth of the seed, that the doctrines of the everlasting gospel—the principles of the kingdom of God, of which he was the Head—produce their effects upon the hearts of mankind in a silent, gradual, mysterious, unfathomable manner—that the ripe fruit of Christian character comes at length from the planting in the soul of the germ of the new spiritual life. Our Lord also doubtless intended to teach his apostles that the growth of the spiritual kingdom of the faithful, brought into outward communion by baptism, should start from feeble beginnings and have such a strangely gradual, yet vigorous growth, that they should not know how the work went on. Our Saviour, in his parables upon these subjects, evidently teaches that man must use certain appointed means, believing that, in consequence of the operation of certain great laws of God, he will eventually gather in the bountiful harvest, though he knoweth not how. . . .
>
> Our church was started on the first Sunday of October 1852, in the smaller chapel of the New-York University. . . . Our small grain of mustard seed was planted by a small band of the faithful, hoping that they had commenced an effort for the glory of God and the good of mankind, yet not knowing what the future would bring forth.

Under Gallaudet's leadership, St. Ann's undertook mission work for the deaf. Thomas Gallaudet's deep spirituality can be seen not only in his concern for those who cannot hear, but in this verse from a lovely hymn he wrote:

> Jesus, in sickness and in pain,
> Be near to succor me,
> My sinking spirit still sustain;
> To Thee I turn, to Thee.

Thomas Gallaudet, who cared deeply for the deaf. (Courtesy of Justus.Anglican.org. Used by permission of Marshall.)

Other Events

1226: St. Francis of Assisi, mystic and founder of the Franciscan order, died on this day.

1690: Robert Barclay, the Quaker theologian who systemized Quaker beliefs, died.

1789: United States President George Washington named November 26 as a day of national thanksgiving for the ratification of the Constitution.

1863: United States President Abraham Lincoln designated the last Thursday in November as Thanksgiving Day, nationalizing a Pilgrim tradition.

1877: The Union Church of Christ was organized in Japan.

President George Washington proclaimed a day of thanksgiving. (Northrop, Henry Davenport. *New Century History of Our Country and Its Island Possessions*. Chicago: American Educational League, 1900.)

Thomas Cromwell, shown here, gave Miles Coverdale a leg up. (Pollard, Albert Frederick. *Thomas Cranmer and the English Reformation, 1489-1556*. Hamden, CT: Archon Books, 1905.)

OCTOBER 4

Coverdale Finished the English-Language Bible

Someone has remarked that the Acts of the Apostles is the only book of the Bible left unfinished. It is always up to us to write the latest chapter.

When William Tyndale was arrested in May 1535, the Bible translation that he had begun included only the New Testament, the Pentateuch and a few historical books of the Old Testament. England was still without a complete printed Bible in the English language. Who would finish the work?

That is where Miles Coverdale stepped in. Using Tyndale's work as his starting point, Coverdale filled in the gaps with his own translations based on the Vulgate and Martin Luther's German Bible. He worked quickly to piece together a complete English Bible. The book, produced by Cervicorn and Soter in Colonge, was printed on this day in 1535.

For several years after that heroic effort, Coverdale was busy with other versions of the English-language Bible. He made a fresh translation of the New Testament based on the Vulgate three years later in 1538. In 1539 he helped put out the Great Bible, so called because of its size. It was the Bible that King Henry VIII of England ordered placed in every parish church.

Who was Coverdale? How did he get involved with Tyndale?

Coverdale was born in York around 1488 and began his religious life as an Augustinian friar, becoming a reformer thanks to the influence of his prior, Robert Barnes. When Barnes got into trouble for his religious beliefs, Coverdale helped him with his defense. Barnes got off that time but was later burned to death.

King Henry's chancellor, Thomas Cromwell, urged Coverdale to undertake a course of study. Coverdale did but soon left his convent to preach in Essex against images and the mass. In 1529, Tyndale invited Coverdale to Hamburg to help with the translation of the Old Testament. The two worked together for eight months. Afterward, Coverdale settled in Antwerp for a time, where a Lutheran merchant paid him to make a complete translation of the Bible into English.

Eventually Coverdale returned to England, where he became bishop of Exeter. During Queen Mary's reign he would have been burned to death except that the king of Denmark petitioned for his release. Coverdale fled to the Continent with his family. After the Catholic queen's death, he returned home and was offered his position at Exeter back. He refused because he could not completely agree with the Church of England. He was looked upon as a leader of the Puritan party of the English Church. (The Puritans were those who wanted to "purify" the English Church of old Roman Church practices.)

Parts of Miles Coverdale's work found their way into English church services and are used to this day. When you hear the Westminster Choir sing a traditional psalm, it is to the words of Coverdale's translation. His translations were never the most popular in England, but they advanced the important work of giving English-speaking Christians the full Bible in their own tongue.

Rembrandt, famed painter of Christian subjects. (Courtesy of the University of Texas collection of public domain portraits on the Web.)

Other Events

1669: Dutch painter Rembrandt Harmensz van Rijn, known as the "painter of the soul" for his unsurpassed Christian art, including *The Return of the Prodigal Son*, died on this day. He was buried in the Westerkerk on October 8.

1890: Catherine Booth, the "Mother of the Salvation Army," died of cancer. She persuaded her husband, William, to make women an integral part of the Salvation Army leadership and movement.

1965: Paul VI became the first pope to visit the United States. While there, he addressed the United Nations in a call for peace.

1966: A special day of prayer for peace commemorated the pope's 1965 visit to the United Nations.

1994: Two Egyptian Christians, Ageeb Sami Yacoub and Ameer Sami Yacoub, who refused to pay *itawa* (protection money) to Muslims, were tied up and murdered in cold blood.

OCTOBER 5

John Henry Livingston Heads Dutch Reform Seminary

Which Church should it be? John Henry Livingston believed that God was calling him to leave his law studies and become a minister; but of which denomination? Born in New Netherlands (New York) thirty years before America's Revolutionary War, it seemed to him that he had three options: Anglican, Presbyterian and Dutch Reform. Of the three, the Dutch Church seemed the least likely because he knew less Dutch than English and the Church was tearing itself apart with quarrels.

But the Dutch Reform was the Church of his grandparents, and Livingston had been brought up in it. He longed to do something to heal its wounds:

> It was powerfully impressed upon my mind, that God would render me . . . an instrument in his hand to compromise and heal these dissensions, and raise the reputation, and establish the dignity and usefulness of the Dutch Church in America.

Consequently, twenty-year-old Livingston sailed to Holland to get his theological degree. Hundreds of prayers went with him, for America's Dutch settlers knew the hopes that the sickly boy carried with him of settling divisions between them and the home country. They hoped that he would succeed and make his way back to minister to them.

Livingston did well in his studies. After his graduation, he returned to America in 1769. For the rest of his life, he worked hard for his Church in the New World. In fact, he did so much for them that he became known as the "Father of the Dutch Reformed Church" in America. He negotiated peace between rivals in America and worked out a measure of independence for the American Church, which at that time was still ruled from Holland. (After the Revolutionary War, it became completely independent.)

Livingston pastored in several cities in New York State, always seeking positions that would allow him to be of the most use. During the Revolutionary War, he had to leave New York City because the British occupied it. When he returned in 1783, he was the only Dutch Reform pastor in the city; three other pulpits were vacant. This meant he carried a huge workload by himself.

On top of his already packed schedule, the Dutch Reform appointed him to an additional task. On this day in 1784, Livingston became their professor of theology. For twenty-six years, he carried out the position's duties without any college to back him up. In addition, he wrote hymns, contributed to the Church constitution, prepared its liturgy, backed missionary endeavors and chaplained the United States Congress.

John Henry Livingston became the head of America's first seminary (New Brunswick), in addition to his many other responsibilities. (Lossing, Benson J. *Eminent Americans*. New York: Hovendon Company, 1890.)

By 1814, Livingston had been living for four years in New Jersey. In 1810, the General Synod of the Reformed Church decided to combine its theological training with Queens College (now known as Rutgers) in New Brunswick, New Jersey. They made Dr. Livingston the president of the college. The hardworking Livingston served as its professor and president until he died in 1825.

OTHER EVENTS

313: Donatus, a strict African bishop, was condemned by Miltiades, bishop of Rome, an event cited by the Roman Church to substantiate the early supremacy of the pope.

869: The Fourth Constantinople Council opened. In six sessions, the council condemned iconoclasm and anathematized Constantinople Patriarch Photius. There was strong disagreement over whether the Holy Spirit proceeded from the Son as well as the Father. To this day, Eastern Orthodox Christians don't consider the Fourth Constantinople Council a true ecumenical council.

1690: Solomon Stoddard preached a famed sermon on the Lord's Supper, relaxing rules for participation.

1744: David Brainerd, who had been kicked out of Yale for allegedly criticizing a tutor and attending a forbidden revival meeting, began missionary work with Native Americans along New Jersey's Susquehannah River.

1964: An ecumenical council called by the Roman Catholic Church said it wanted to reunite all Christians.

1969: Harry Emerson Fosdick died at the age of ninety-one. He pastored Riverside Church in New York City from 1926 to 1946 and authored the enduring hymn "God of Grace and God of Glory." Very influential as an outspoken opponent of fundamentalism, he denied core doctrines of Christianity such as the Virgin Birth.

Harry Emerson Fosdick, author of the hymn "God of Grace and God of Glory." (Courtesy of cyberhymnal.org. Available online at: < http://www.cyberhymnal.org/bio/f/o/fosdick_he.htm>.)

October 6

Burned for the Bible

William Tyndale died for translating Scripture. (Pollard, Albert Frederick. *Thomas Cranmer and the English Reformation, 1489-1556*. Hamden, CT: Archon Books, 1905.)

How many Bibles do you have in your house? For most of us, Bibles are easily accessible, and many of us own several. That we have the Bible in English owes much to William Tyndale, who is sometimes called the "Father of the English Bible." Estimates vary, but most authorities agree that well over half of the King James Version of the Bible and of the Revised Standard Version are taken from the translation of the Bible into English made by Tyndale.

Back in the fourteenth century, John Wycliffe made the first English translation of the Bible, but that was before the invention of the printing press, and all copies had to be handwritten. Also, the few copies that were made were illegal because the Church had banned the unauthorized translation of Scripture into English in 1408.

Over 100 years later, however, Tyndale developed a burning desire to make the Bible available to the common people in England. It was a nice dream, but how was Tyndale to accomplish this when such translations were illegal? He went to London to ask Bishop Tunstall to authorize him to make an English translation of the Bible, but the bishop did not approve the request. Tyndale wasn't one to let the disapproval of men stop him from carrying out what seemed so obviously God's will, however. With the encouragement and support of some British merchants, he decided to go to Europe to complete his translation and then have it printed and smuggled back into England.

In 1524 Tyndale sailed for Germany. In Hamburg he worked on the New Testament, and in Cologne he found a printer who would print it. However, opponents of the Reformation caught wind of Tyndale's activity, and they raided the press. Tyndale escaped with the pages that were already printed and made his way to Worms, where the New Testament was soon published. Six thousand copies were smuggled into England. There bishops did everything they could to eradicate the Bibles—Bishop Tunstall burned copies ceremoniously at St. Paul's; the archbishop of Canterbury bought up copies to destroy them. Tyndale used whatever money found its way to him to print improved editions.

King Henry VIII, then in the throes of his divorce from Queen Catherine, offered Tyndale a safe passage to England to serve as his writer and scholar. Tyndale refused, saying he would not return until the Bible could be legally translated into English. Tyndale continued hiding with merchants in Antwerp and began translating the Old Testament into English while the King's agents searched all over Europe for him.

Tyndale was finally found by an Englishman who pretended to be Tyndale's friend and then turned him over to the authorities. After a year-and-a-half in prison, Tyndale was brought to trial for heresy—for believing, among other things, that the mercy offered in the gospel was sufficient for salvation.

In August 1536, Tyndale was condemned. On this day in 1536, he was strangled, and his dead body was burned at the stake. His last prayer was "Lord, open the King of England's eyes." The prayer was answered in part when three years later, in 1539, Henry VIII required every parish church in England to make a copy of the English Bible available to its parishioners.

St. Bruno, one of the founders of the Carthusian order, reads a letter from Rome. (Jameson, Mrs. *Legends of the Monastic Orders*. London: Green and Co., 1872.)

Other Events

961: St. Bruno, who, with companions, founded the Carthusian order, died on this day.

1683: The first Mennonite migrants to America arrived in Philadelphia. These thirteen German families founded a community that they called Germantown. Their pastor, Francis Daniel Pastorious, was probably the most learned man in America at that time.

1818: James Thompson of Scotland entered Buenos Aires with a boatload of Bibles in an enthusiastic effort to teach the masses to read. He trekked with muleloads of Bibles throughout much of Latin America.

1871: Dwight L. Moody prayed to be baptized with the fire of the Holy Spirit. Two days later the great Chicago fire made the idea of fire all too real!

1919: Baron Paul Nicolay, a French nobleman who worked as an evangelist in Russia with students, died. Quiet, frail, introspective, he nonetheless had a true heart for Christ.

1945: George C. Stebbins, who worked closely with Dwight L. Moody and Ira Sankey in song ministry, died. He authored the hymns "Take My Life and Let It Be," and "Have Thine Own Way, Lord."

1967: Curtis Findley of New Tribes Mission and Don Robinson of Missionary Aviation Fellowship died in a plane crash in Venezuela.

Oddball Church Musician Had Plenty of Verve

In the earliest days of the Puritan settlement of Massachusetts, the Church was the center of social as well as spiritual life. It is not surprising, then, that the earliest American composer would primarily be a composer of church music.

William Billings was born on this day in 1746 in Boston, Massachusetts. When he was older he was apprenticed to a tanner. He had no musical training. Though he became one of the best musicians in colonial America, he never was able to earn his living as a musician. He later even served the town of Boston as a hogreve (a person who kept the swine off the streets) and a street cleaner.

Billings was an unlikely candidate to become an influential musician and composer. He had one sightless eye, a withered arm, legs of different lengths, a loud, rasping voice and generally a slovenly appearance. Yet he was an enthusiastic singing master and a popular composer. He came on the scene at a time when Puritan church music in America was in transition. Singing by rote or "lining out" had lost its hold, but all the psalm-tune books were by foreigners. Billings became aware of the monotony and began chalking tunes on the walls of the tannery or on pieces of leather as he worked. In 1770 he published a collection of songs entitled *The New England Psalm Singer*.

Billings later published six other collections of church music, which often included his own original compositions. He especially favored fugues but also included plainsongs and anthems in his collections. Because of his lack of musical training and ignorance of the principles of harmony, many of Billings' compositions were musically crude, but they provided the variety that was needed by the churches of his day.

Billings abandoned his tanning trade and became a singing teacher and a trainer of choirs in some of the most important churches in Boston, including the Brattle Street Church and the Old South Church. He improved the rhythmic singing of his choirs and had them sing a more exact pitch. Instruments were not used in the Puritan churches, and "striking a tune" could be distressing and disastrous. Billings was the first to introduce the pitch-pipe to get the choir all started on the same pitch. He also introduced the violoncello or bass viola to maintain the pitch.

During the American Revolution, Billings was an ardent supporter of the patriots and wrote several popular songs for their cause. His tune "Chester" became the hymn tune of the Revolution and began with the line "Let tyrants shake their iron rod."

One of the musical schools organized by Billings in 1774 was at Stoughton, Massachusetts. In 1786 this was more formally organized into the Stoughton Musical Society, the oldest musical society in the United States.

THE
VVHOLE
BOOKE OF PSALMES
Faithfully
TRANSLATED *into* ENGLISH
Metre.
Whereunto is prefixed a discourse declaring not only the lawfullnes, but also the necessity of the heavenly Ordinance of singing Scripture Psalmes in the Churches of God.
Coll. III.
Let the word of God dwell plenteously in you, in all wisdome, teaching and exhorting one another in Psalmes, Himnes, and spirituall Songs, singing to the Lord with grace in your hearts.
James v.
If any be afflicted, let him pray, and if any be merry let him sing psalmes.
Imprinted
1640

The *Bay Psalm Book* was the first book printed in the British American colonies, which shows the importance the Puritans placed on worship music. (Wilson, Woodrow. *A History of the American People*. New York/London: Harper & Bros., 1902.)

Other Events

336: Pope St. Mark died. He ruled for only a few months at a time when the Church was battling serious problems with Arianism.

1405: Jean de Gerson preached a powerful sermon before the king of France, rebuking mistreatment of the poor. Ten years later, Gerson led in the condemnation of the reformer Jan Hus at Constance.

1772: John Woolman, an American Quaker, journal writer and abolitionist whose simple and unaffected life and writings won great respect, died on this day.

1787: Henry M. Muhlenberg, "Father of American Lutheranism," died. He ministered in the Philadelphia area for many years and organized the Evangelical Lutheran Ministerium in 1748.

1873: Lottie Moon arrived in China. This heroic woman was born into wealth but, when converted, gave her whole life to Christ and said, "If I had a thousand lives, I would give them all for the women of China."

Woolman Memorial Home, founded in honor of John Woolman. (Woolman, John. *The Journal and Essays of John Woolman*. New York: Macmillan Company, 1922.)

OCTOBER 8

Largest of the Seven Early Councils

Pope Leo the Great summarized the Chalcedonian position. (Baring-Gould, S. *Lives of the Saints*. Edinburgh: John Grant, 1914.)

When Jesus asked his disciples, "Who do people say I am?" (Mark 8:27), he received several answers: Some said he was John the Baptist; some said he was Elijah or Jeremiah or another one of the prophets (see 8:28). The disciple Peter came up with the correct answer when he said, "You are the Christ" (8:29).

The early Christians accepted Peter's confession, but they had different ideas of exactly what it meant for Jesus to be the Christ. What was Jesus's real nature and person like? How was He related to God the Father? To what degree was He truly human? There were many debates over these issues in the fourth through the sixth centuries of the Church.

When Constantine became emperor of the Roman Empire and made Christianity a legal religion, he believed that unity of the Church was important to the political strength of the empire. So in 325 he called a council at Nicea to settle disputes over the nature of Christ. The council issued the Nicene Creed, agreeing that Christ was both man and God and that as the Son of God He had the same divine nature as the Father. Once it was accepted that Jesus was both fully God and fully man, debates began to rage over how Christ's deity was related to his humanity.

One group, the Apollinarians, said the divine Word of Christ took the place of Jesus's human mind and will so that His divine nature was always predominant. Others argued back that if Jesus did not have a human mind and will, He could not be fully human. Yet another group argued that at the Incarnation the divine and human were so combined in the person of Christ as to produce a new, unique individual. Others thought that the divine and human natures of Jesus were kept so separate that it was almost like He was two persons.

In July of 450, Emperor Theodosius died from a fall off his horse, and his empire went to his sister, Pulcheria, who took as her husband the capable general Marcian and ruled through him. At her instigation, one of Marcian's first acts was to call a Church council to deal with some of the religious problems. He hoped for religious unity as a support to the political unity of the empire, which was needed to face the growing military threat from the east. On this day in 451, the largest of the seven ecumenical Church councils assembled at Chalcedon, near Constantinople (modern-day Istanbul). After much debate, on October 22 a Chalcedonian creed was adopted that reaffirmed the divine and human natures of Christ that had been recognized at Nicea and further stated that the two natures of Christ were "without confusion, without conversion, without severance, and without division."

Jesus was affirmed as being both fully divine and fully human. His two natures were combined in one person without His becoming less divine or less human. The work Christ did was the work of His whole person, not of one nature or another. On that day Pope Leo stated the Chalcedonian position that in Christ the lowliness of man and the majesty of God perfectly pervade one another. Some of the Egyptian, Turkish and Eastern Christians could not accept the Chalcedon Creed, but it has been accepted by the Roman Catholic, the Eastern Orthodox and the Protestant Churches.

OTHER EVENTS

314: Constantine's armies defeated Licinus at Cibalae, which strengthened Constantine against this rival.

1585: Heinrich Schutz, who was considered the greatest German Protestant composer before Johann Sebastian Bach, was born. Much of what Schutz wrote was religious, and most of it was in German. He is especially appreciated for his lovely settings of the psalms.

1871: Jerry McAuley opened the Water Street Mission in New York City, probably the first rescue mission in the United States. He had recently been released from prison, pardoned by Governor Horatio Seymour of New York state. His "helping hand for men" was located almost directly under the old Brooklyn Bridge. McAuley was determined to give real help of the kind that could put a man back on his feet and disciple him. McAuley would not just preach. Since the days of Water Street, rescue missions and shelters have become commonplace in every large American city.

Jerry McAuley, who opened America's first city rescue mission. (Offord, R.M., ed. *Jerry McAuley, An Apostle to the Lost*. New York: American Tract Society, 1907.)

Banished!

Freedom of religion and separation of Church and state have become fundamental principles in the United States, but in the colonial period these were radically new ideas. When the Puritans came to Massachusetts in the 1630s, for example, they had no intention of establishing a colony with freedom of religion. Rather, they wanted a colony dedicated to their religion and which would be a shining example of Church and government for Europe to follow. As the Law of Moses regulated Israel's society in Old Testament days, so the Church under Scripture's authority would regulate New England society. There was no place for toleration in Puritan America. Those not in accord with the colony's purposes and government could move elsewhere.

In 1631, a likeable twenty-eight-year-old minister named Roger Williams arrived in Massachusetts. He soon upset the Puritan alliance between the Church and the colonial government. Williams was a splendid speaker with a magnetic personality who was personally liked by all of the leaders of the Massachusetts government. They were saddened, however, by the "extreme" positions he took on some of the major issues of the day.

For example, Williams taught that the king of England had no right to issue the Bay Colony a charter in America, because the Indians owned the land. The argument made by John Cotton and others that the earth was the Lord's and the colonists could freely settle in areas not settled by the Indians was unacceptable to Williams.

Williams' ideas also clashed with the Massachusetts idea of a people covenanted together to form a state or society based on religious truths. Williams believed that the state should have no authority over a man's religious beliefs or conscience, saying that the truth was strong enough to stand without the coercion of the state. Williams became the first person in America to express the idea of religious freedom and liberty of conscience, ideas that were in disagreement with the Puritan goal of establishing a Christian commonwealth as an example to Europe. The leaders of Massachusetts wanted a united body of believers in their colony, but Williams wanted to separate Church and state. Williams then attacked not only the very charter of the Massachusetts colony but the colony's very rationale for existence.

In 1635 the Massachusetts court tried Roger Williams and on this day in 1635 sentenced him to banishment. Rather than accept deportation back to England, Williams fled the colony in January of the next year and lived among the Narragansett Indians. In the summer of 1636 he established a settlement that he named Providence in memory of the Lord's protection of him during his weeks in the wilderness.

Friendly Indians assist Roger Williams to land. (Northrop, Henry Davenport. *New Century History of Our Country and Its Island Possessions*. Chicago: American Educational League, 1900.)

He bought the land from the Indians and allowed complete religious tolerance among later settlers. As other settlements in the area were made, the little colony came to be called Rhode Island. Religious freedom and liberty of conscience were preserved in Rhode Island throughout its colonial history, and it became a haven for those seeking the freedom not found in other colonies.

Other Events

1047: Pope Clement II died on this day, possibly from poison.

1253: Robert Grosseteste, an English reform-minded bishop and a strong supporter of the Franciscans, died. He influenced the thinking of John Wycliffe and was the first man to formulate the scientific method.

1664: Benjamin Keach was hauled before a magistrate and accused of scandalous behavior. His crime? Printing a Baptist primer.

1747: David Brainerd, pioneer missionary to Native Americans in New England, died of tuberculosis (brought on by exposure) at the age of twenty-nine. His journal, published by Jonathan Edwards, inspired hundreds of missionaries, including the "Father of Modern Protestant Missions," William Carey.

1800: Mary Webb, although bound to a wheelchair, organized fourteen Baptist and Congregational women into the Boston Female Society for Missionary Purposes.

Benjamin Keach, "scandalous" printer of a Baptist primer, in the pillory. (Armitage, Thomas. *A History of the Baptists: Traced by Their Principles and Practices, From the Time of our Lord and Saviour Jesus Christ to the Present*. New York: Bryan, Taylor and Co., 1893.)

Europe held out against Islam in the Battle of Tours. (Courtesy of North Wind Picture Archives.)

October 10

Europe Teeters in the Balance

In 610 Mohammed received his call. He began to preach and, after many hardships, developed a significant following. Within a hundred years, Islam had grown into a mighty empire. It conquered much of the Middle East, North Africa, Spain and southern Italy. The Mediterranean became an Islamic lake. Because those areas had formerly been Christian, these developments had tremendous implications for Christianity. That Islam did not capture all of Europe and wipe out Christianity was due in part to Charles Martel, the Frankist mayor of the palace, and his sturdy knights.

At one time it seemed unlikely that Martel would ever amount to anything. He was an illegitimate son, not entitled to authority. When his father died, Martel was even put in prison, but he escaped and built a power base in four short years. He solidified his holdings with unceasing effort, battling the Frisians, Saxons, Alamanni, Bavarians and Aquitanians until most of modern France was brought under his control.

On this day in 732, Martel met the Islamic invaders between Poiters and Tours in a battle that lasted either two days (according to Arab sources) or seven (according to French sources). The Muslims were mounted, and their cavalry employed a new invention: the stirrup. The Franks were on foot. Yet the Franks stood like a wall, and the Muslims withdrew, defeated. Their leader, Abd-ar-Rahman was killed. In their rout, the Arabs suffered heavy losses of men. Europe would remain Christian territory.

At that time, Europe was not wholly Christian. The great mission work that brought it into the Christian fold was still in process. The Church appreciated Martel because he supported Christian expansion among the German races, protecting the notable missionaries Boniface and Willibrord. The Church also appreciated his willingness to challenge the Islamic invaders. The Church gladly loaned the Carolingian leader Church lands to help defray the costs of the resistance against the Muslims.

After his victory, however, Martel incurred ecclesiastical wrath. He required his knights to provide themselves with horses, saddles and spurs. In order that they might pay for these costly innovations, Martel presented them with Church lands. Even more exasperating to the Christian leaders, he awarded Church positions to ungodly, untrained laymen. Church discipline declined, as is the recurring pattern when the Church is made no more than a branch of civil service.

After beating the Muslims at Poiters, Martel also conquered Burgundy. His descendants had great influence on European history. Pépin the Short, his son, aided the popes at crucial moments. His grandson was the famous emperor Charlemagne.

Sir Archibald Johnston, who suffered greatly for his religious and political activities. (Smellie, Alexander. *Men of the Covenant*. New York: Revell, 1903.)

Other Events

1660: Because he sided with Parliament in the English Civil War, Sir Archibald Johnston (Lord Warriston) was declared a fugitive on this day. An attempt to poison him and the removal of sixty ounces of his blood left him mentally impaired, but his opponents put him on trial and sentenced him to death anyway.

1821: Charles Finney was converted. The twenty-nine-year-old law student entered the woods near his home to settle the question of salvation. That night, he experienced a dramatic conversion in which "waves of liquid love" coursed through his body. Finney became one of America's great revivalists, credited with 500,000 conversions.

1879: Rees Howells was born in Wales, the sixth child in a family of eleven. He became a master of intercessory prayer, but not without spiritual struggle:

> I thought I would have no fear of going against the world and its opinions and that it was the easiest thing to be dead to it, but it was the greatest error I ever believed. I had to be pulled through inch by inch; it was the process of sanctification when the self nature and all its lusts had to be changed for the divine nature.

1940: Wilfred T. Grenfell, an extraordinary missionary to Newfoundland and Labrador, died. Exceptionally hardy and gregarious, Grenfell was the ideal man to lead such a mission.

October 11

Quartered with Dung

Ulrich Zwingli was born on the first of January in 1481. The world he entered was passing into a spiritual and political ferment in which he would be a prime mover. As a boy, he early distinguished himself at studies and music. He determined to become a priest and was ordained at the age of twenty-three. Zwingli hand-copied and memorized Paul's letters in the original Greek. Impressed by the reform writings of the great humanist Erasmus, he moved toward reformation possibly even before Martin Luther.

The use of Swiss young men as mercenaries especially evoked Zwingli's ire. Having accompanied two expeditions as a chaplain, he spoke vehemently against the practice that squandered their blood. As priest of Einsiedeln, a city whose income came from pilgrimages, he boldly preached against pilgrimages, labeling them a corruption. When an indulgence was sold in Switzerland, he denounced it.

On the first day of 1519, Zwingli came as pastor to Zurich, the city of his life's work. There he continued his battle against indulgences. Zwingli also announced that he would not read the prescribed lessons but preach the Gospel of Matthew instead. He did so, pouring forth objections to the use of images in the Church, to the mass and to other practices of the Church that he considered to be in error. He asserted that Christ alone is sufficient for salvation.

It is one of the interesting characteristics of the Swiss Reformation that local leaders voted on doctrine, making religious decisions for their constituents. This practice in Zurich was followed by other Swiss Protestants and was one of the stages that led toward the creation of modern democracy.

Zurich's town leaders took to heart Zwingli's teaching. It was they, not Zwingli, who ordered that the Holy Scriptures be taught "without human additions." It was they who challenged theologians to convict Zwingli of error if they could. It was they who ordered images removed from churches.

Protestants and Catholics in Switzerland remained at odds. The Protestants established a blockade, threatening Catholics with starvation. In 1531 the Catholic cantons marched against Zurich. Zwingli joined the troops on the battlefield. A force of 1,500 men from Zurich faced 6,000 from the Catholic cantons. Under feeble leadership and on badly chosen ground near Kappel, the Protestants compounded their problems with critical errors. Failing to maul their opponents at an opportune moment, they allowed the Catholics to gain the cover of a beech wood. Then they did not retreat to a safer line while they were still able to do so. Around 4 p.m. on this day in 1531, the Catholics began the assault. Half an hour later, the Protestants were wiped out. Zwingli was among the dead. His body was quartered and mixed with dung.

Ulrich Zwingli's corpse was treated with contempt. (McGiffert, Arthur Cushman. *Martin Luther, the Man and His Work*. New York: The Century Co., 1911.)

Other Events

1424: Bohemian general Jan Zizka, who defeated Roman Catholic armies in Bohemia, died. Although blind, he led his "Warriors of God" using wagons with guns mounted on them in an early conception of the tank.

1521: Leo X conferred the title "Defender of the Faith" on England's Henry VIII for taking a stand against Martin Luther. Thirteen years later, Henry separated the Church of England from Rome, miffed because Pope Clement VII would not dissolve his marriage with Catherine of Aragon.

1863: James Moulton, who became one of the leading Bible scholars of his day, was born. He had a strong knowledge of the languages of the Middle East and was deeply concerned for the conversion of the Parsees in India, adherents to the ancient Zoroastrian religion. Moulton carried the gospel to them. He died from exhaustion, having labored heroically to save lives when his ship was torpedoed in the Mediterranean as he was returning from Asia.

1946: Yugoslavia's archbishop Stepanic was sentenced to sixteen years in prison. Although 243 priests had been killed by the hostile regime, Stepanic had refused to flee and was arrested at his home. He made a bold testimony at his trial, standing up for the oppressed Church and its murdered priests.

Jan Zizka, the brilliant blind general. (Lützow, Francis. *The Hussite Wars*. London: J.M. Dent, 1914.)

October 12

Columbus Sailed the Ocean Blue

Christopher Columbus sights land. (Northrop, Henry Davenport. *New Century History of Our Country and Its Island Possessions*. Chicago: American Educational League, 1900.)

"Tierra! Tierra!" The men had been on the sea for over thirty days without sight of land, but it was now in plain view. Despair and gloom gave way to hope as the three little ships drew closer and closer to the shore. It was on this day in 1492.

Every American school child has heard the little rhyme "In 1492, Columbus sailed the ocean blue," and the story has often been told of Columbus's dream of finding the East or Asia by sailing west. Often Columbus is used as an example of someone who set goals for himself and would not give up when obstacles thwarted his achievement—he waited at the Spanish court for six years before King Ferdinand and Queen Isabella agreed to sponsor his voyage. He persuaded his men to continue their westward voyage even when they threatened mutiny because they had not yet reached the expected islands of the Orient. Certainly Columbus is a model of determination and courage.

Yet the man was much more complex than the well-known stories may reveal. Columbus was a very devout Catholic who observed all the fasts of the Church and prayed regularly. His very name, Christopher, which means "Christ-bearer," he understood as a title of his destiny to carry the message of the gospel to far-off lands. He diligently searched the Scriptures and thought he found assurance for a call to sail to the far reaches of the globe with the Christian message. Zechariah 9:10 said that "he shall speak peace unto the heathen: and his dominion shall be from sea even to sea, and from the river even to the ends of the earth" (KJV). And Psalm 107:23-24 promised that "they that go down to the sea in ships, that do business in great waters; These see the works of the Lord, and his wonders in the deep" (KJV).

Columbus was particularly concerned with the power of the Ottoman Turks, who controlled the eastern Mediterranean and were threatening Europe. If a way could be found of reaching India by sailing west, the Turks could be attacked from behind, and perhaps the Holy Land itself could be rescued from their hands. Yes, Columbus was interested in trade and riches, but Christian concern also lay behind his plans.

When land was sighted on this day in 1492, in recognition of the divine aid in his voyage, Columbus named the land San Salvador, which means Holy Savior, and prayed:

> O Lord, Almighty and everlasting God, by Thy holy Word Thou hast created the heaven, and the earth, and the sea; blessed and glorified be Thy Name, and praised be Thy Majesty, which hath designed to use us, Thy humble servants, that Thy holy Names may be proclaimed in this second part of the earth.

In keeping with the Christian motive underlying his mission, Columbus at first showed great concern for the manner in which the natives, whom he called Indians, were treated. Unfortunately, Columbus's concern for the salvation of these people was coupled with an attitude of superiority, which saw nothing wrong with forcibly capturing the people and making slaves of them. In later voyages, the missionary drive that was prominent during his first voyage became subordinate to his love of wealth and position.

Philip IV of France, "the Fair," had the Knights Templar tortured. (Barry, William. *Story of the Nations: Papal Monarchy*. Whitefish, MT: Kessinger Publishing, 1911.)

Other Events

1310: Philip IV the Fair arrested all the Knights Templars of France and had them tortured. His intent was to get them to incriminate themselves so that he could take their treasures. Two years later, he pressured Pope Clement V into abolishing the Templars.

1762: The Association of Philadelphia Baptists, meeting in a Lutheran church and moderated by the Rev. Morgan Edwards, voted to establish Rhode Island College, which later became Brown University.

1943: In an attempt to increase its control of the Orthodox Church, the Soviet government established a council for its affairs.

1951: Kimbangu died in Lubumbashi, Congo, where he had been held in prison by Belgian authorities for thirty years. He had preached the gospel of the one God, healed the sick and alarmed colonial administrators who thought he might become the focus of a rebellion. Witnesses said he was a humble man.

1971: The rock musical *Jesus Christ Superstar* debuted on Broadway, creating an uproar because of lyrics that declared that Christ was just a man.

1975: Oliver Plunkett, an Irish martyr, was canonized. He had worked energetically to raise moral and educational standards. He was executed on false charges of treason in 1681.

Last of the Great Reformers

When Theodore Beza died on this day in 1605, he had outlived the rest of the great reformers. He was a tired man, and his mind had begun to falter. Little wonder, for his had been a life of much sorrow, hard work and grueling adventure.

Beza was born in Burgundy in 1519, the son of a county bailiff. His father had marked out a course for him, but it seemed God had marked out another. At nine years of age, Beza was sent to study with the famous Greek scholar Melchior Wolmar. Wolmar's sympathy with the Lutherans rubbed off on his pupil. What fruit this would bear was not yet apparent.

Beza's father wanted Beza to become a lawyer, and Beza did the preliminary studies. However, he preferred literary studies and convinced his father to allow him to switch fields. He became honored as a Latin poet and wit.

Through family connections, Beza received church benefices to live on. Meanwhile, like many clergymen of the day, he contracted a secret marriage. His wife was Claudine Denosse. Then Beza fell dangerously ill. As he lay in bed, he realized that he was a hypocrite, taking money from the Roman Church while secretly married and at heart a Protestant. As soon as he had recovered sufficiently to do so, he fled from France with his wife, leaving behind fame and fortune. Claudine was the deepest joy of his life. Their marriage lasted until her death forty years later.

Beza's wit remained with him throughout his life. Appealing to the king of Navarre, he once said:

> Sire, it is in truth the lot of the Church of God, in whose name I am speaking, to endure blows, and not to strike them. But also may it please you to remember that it is an anvil that has worn out many hammers.

Beza became a leading Huguenot theologian and eventually John Calvin's successor as leader of the Swiss Reformation.

During his long life, he risked dangerous journeys again and again into Catholic France, even traveling by night to escape detection. His life was also in constant danger from false friends who might at any moment turn him over to Catholic authorities. Yet despite the ever-present danger of his situation, he argued the Protestant case before great theologians and political leaders. On occasion he accompanied Huguenot armies and preached for them. Using diplomatic skills honed during his upbringing, he visited the Protestant courts of Europe to win support for suffering French Protestants.

Theodore Beza took Calvin's place as the leader of the Swiss Reformation. (Baird, Henry Martyn. *Theodore Beza: The Councilor of the French Reformation*. New York: G.P. Putnam's Sons, 1899.)

Other Events

Annual: The feast day of St. Colman of Stockerau is celebrated. St. Colman was recognized as a saint through the most unusual set of circumstances. Traveling from the British Isles around 1012 to the Holy Land, he was mistaken for a spy in Austria and was tortured and hanged. The Austrians eventually recognized their mistake and, after miracles were purportedly worked at his grave, they declared him the patron saint of Austria.

1247: A vial, purportedly of Christ's blood and stamped with official seals, was brought to England to the great joy of King Henry and the crowds.

1824: Henry Stephen Cutler was born in Boston, Massachusetts. Famed as a church organist, he also composed the music to the hymn "The Son of God Goes Forth to War" and introduced the choir robe to America.

1836: Theodore Fliedner created the first of the Lutheran deaconess training centers.

1908: The Church of the Nazarene was organized in Texas.

Henry III of England prized his vial of "Christ's blood." (Peake, Elizabeth. *History of the German Emperors and Their Contemporaries*. Philadelphia: J.B. Lippincott & Co., 1874.)

A ford on a Kentucky river, much like the one Jacob Bower crossed after promising his father that he would serve God. (Pusey, Allen. *The Wilderness Road to Kentucky, Its Location and Features*. New York: George H. Doran Company, 1921.)

October

14

Jacob Bower's Life-Changing Promise

Twenty-five-year-old Jacob Bower did not realize where a promise to his father would lead him. That promise would eventually lead him to becoming a masterful frontier evangelist.

As a tenderhearted lad living first in Pennsylvania and then in Kentucky, Bower had longed to know that he would go to heaven; he was sure his mother had. However, when his prayers for forgiveness of sins did not work any change in him, he became a Universalist, adopting the view that all people will eventually be saved. This theory made him wild and careless. While in this spiritual state, he got married.

Early in October 1811, he and his wife visited his father. On this day in 1811, when Bower and his wife left to return home, he felt unusually solemn. His father accompanied them for about four miles to a large creek. When the time came to part, Bower put on as cheerful a face as he could, but he was disturbed by his father's holy life. Before Bower crossed the creek to return home, his father elicited a promise from him. He said, "I want you to promise me that you will serve God and keep out of bad company."

"Well, Father, I will," answered Bower.

In the autobiography that his denomination later asked him to write, Bower said:

> I started to go across the creek, which was about thirty yards across, and as my horse stepped out of the water to rise the bank, instantly my promise stared me in the face.

He could not get it out of his mind. That night, Bower could not eat. He paced restlessly, hiding his face in his hands and sighing a lot. The Baptist they stayed with that night soon discovered what was the matter and urged Bower to trust in Jesus, quoting many Scripture verses. It was all dark to Bower.

The next morning, Bower met a number of African Americans who were going to an execution of a murderer. Bower wondered, "How does that man feel, knowing that he must die today?" Suddenly, it was as if someone had turned the tables on him, saying, "You don't know but that you may die before he does." His "crumbly foundation of Universalism" gave way. He said, "I discovered a God, who, I thought, could not save me and remain just. I could see no way of escaping eternal punishment."

Bower wrestled and prayed for months. The great earthquakes that struck the Midwest in 1811 and 1812 heightened his terror. He could not sleep for fear of not waking the next morning. Not until February of 1812 did he realize that because Christ had suffered on the cross for him personally, he could be forgiven. At that moment he was flooded with peace and joy. It was the beginning of his evangelistic career.

Two years later, Bower became a Baptist minister. In his long, hardworking life, he rode over 40,000 miles carrying the gospel to others, organizing churches and ordaining new ministers. Such was the impact of a father's counsel given on this day in 1811.

Phillips Brooks, known for writing the Christmas carol "O Little Town of Bethlehem." (Barrows, John Henry, ed. *The World's Parliament of Religions*. Chicago: Parliament Pub. Co., 1893.)

Other Events

1735: The Wesleys sailed for Georgia, where John intended to be a missionary and Charles the secretary to Governor Oglethorpe. They soon discovered their own need for genuine conversion.

1816: Rev. Thomas Taylor, a Methodist minister, preached a sermon, saying that he hoped that he would die an old soldier of Christ, sword in hand. He died the same night. These circumstances prompted James Montgomery to write the hymn "Servant of God, Well Done."

1876: When Henry "Harry" Allen Ironside was born in Toronto, Canada, on this day, he was set aside as dead. An hour later, a nurse discovered he had a pulse and placed him in warm water. Ironside survived and became a notable evangelist and pastored at Moody Memorial Church as well. He died in New Zealand in 1951 while on an evangelistic tour.

1891: Phillips Brooks was consecrated as the Episcopalian bishop of the Diocese of Massachusetts. In life, he was famed for his sermons. Today we remember him most for his Christmas hymn "O Little Town of Bethlehem."

"God Has a Work for Me"

"What does God desire of me? What is it He has sent me into the world to do?" Again and again twenty-three-year-old Isaac Hecker asked himself this question without getting an immediate answer. That God had something special for him he did not doubt. At the age of three he had been seriously ill with smallpox. When his godly mother explained to him that he was not expected to live, his reply was characteristic: "No, Mother. I shall not die now. God has a work for me to do in the world and I shall live to do it."

Hecker was a capable young man. At twelve he imitated his grandfather, a clockmaker, by producing a timepiece that ran solidly for forty years. At thirteen he helped to publish a Methodist paper. Later, he worked at a brass foundry and after that baked and sold bread with his brothers. He marched with those who tried to improve the conditions of workers. Yet he was empty inside.

In 1842, at the major point of crisis in his life, he met Orestes Brownson. Brownson was a writer and a critic of great intellectual stature. The older man was also going through a spiritual struggle. Deep friendship grew between the two. Brownson found himself looking to the Roman Catholic Church. By 1844 Hecker wrote, "The Catholic church alone seems to satisfy my wants, my faith, life, soul. . . ." But the Church did not seem to fit American institutions. Hecker's struggles helped Brownson to resolve his own questions and enter the Church. He persuaded Hecker to take the final step and become a Catholic as well. When he did so, Hecker found great peace. Because he wanted to share it with others, he became a priest.

On this day in 1846, Hecker took his vows, joining the Redemptorists. Thereafter, his life unfolded as if by divine plan. He tried to study, but his burning zeal for the nation would not let him concentrate. He was ordained without completing the formalities. Then he found himself expelled from the Redemptorists for violating a canon against traveling to Rome. Devastated by this blow, Hecker wrote home that the Lord would yet intervene. He took his case to Pope Pius IX.

To his surprise and joy, the pope urged Hecker to leave the Redemptorists and form a new order adapted to the needs of America and dedicated to winning Americans. Thus the Paulists came into being, with Hecker as their first superior. Funds appeared when needed. He and the other Paulists worked fervently to win souls. Their chief instrument was educational material. The Paulist Press issued millions of books to deepen Catholic life and attract outsiders. Hecker founded the *Catholic World* and *Young Catholic* magazines.

Through Hecker's faith, thousands came to Christ and to a deeper understanding of faith and holiness.

Isaac Hecker, founder of the Paulists. (Elliott, Walter. *The Life of Father Hecker*. New York: Columbus Press, 1898.)

Other Events

Annual: Feast day of St. Thecla, who worked with Boniface in Germany. In her abbey she instructed pagan women on how to live the Christian life.

1784: Thomas Hastings was born in Connecticut. An albino afflicted with extreme nearsightedness, Hastings taught himself the fundamentals of music. He penned more than 600 hymns, composed more than 1,000 hymn tunes and published more than 50 collections of sacred music, including the music for "Rock of Ages" and "Majestic Sweetness Sits Enthroned upon the Savior's Brow."

1880: Work on the Cologne Cathedral, which had begun in 1248, was completed on this day, using original plans that had been rediscovered forty years earlier.

1915: A German squad executed Edith Cavell, a nurse who had helped Allied soldiers escape capture. At the time of her death she said she recognized that she had to go deeper to true love.

1932: Gladys Aylward sailed from Liverpool for Asia in a heroic effort to bring the gospel to China after being told by mission boards that she was unsuitable for the task. Her heroic adventures inspired the film *Inn of the Sixth Happiness*.

1943: John Hornick, who became a missionary to the Mormons, was converted on this day.

Thomas Hastings, a great hymn and song writer. (Ninde, Edward S. *The Story of the American Hymn*. New York: Abingdon, 1921.)

Ridley and Latimer at the stake. (Hendrickson, Ford. *Martyrs and Witnesses*. Detroit: Protestant Missionary Pub. Co., 1917.)

October 16

"Let the Fire Come"

King Henry VIII had separated the Church of England from the Roman Catholic Church but had not reformed its practices or doctrines to any marked extent. Upon Henry's death, his young son, Edward, became king. Edward's advisors moved the English Church in the direction of a more biblical Christianity. Two such advisors were Nicholas Ridley and Hugh Latimer.

The scholar Ridley had been a chaplain to King Henry VIII and was bishop of London under Edward. He was a preacher, beloved of his congregation, whose very life portrayed the truths of the Christian doctrines he taught. Latimer also became an influential preacher during King Edward's reign. He was an earnest student of the Bible, and as bishop of Worcester he encouraged the teaching of Scripture in English by the people.

When "Bloody" Mary became Queen of England, she worked to bring England back to the Roman Catholic Church. One of her first acts was to arrest Bishop Ridley, Bishop Latimer and Archbishop Thomas Cranmer. After serving time in the Tower of London, the three were taken to Oxford in September of 1555 to be examined by the Lord's Commissioner in Oxford's Divinity School.

When Ridley was asked if he believed the pope was heir to the authority of Peter as the foundation of the Church, Ridley replied that the Church was not built on any man but on the truth Peter confessed: that Christ was the Son of God. Ridley said he could not honor the pope in Rome since the papacy was seeking its own glory and not the glory of God. Neither Ridley nor Latimer could accept the Roman Catholic mass as the sacrifice of Christ. Latimer told the commissioners, "Christ made one oblation and sacrifice for the sins of the whole world, and that a perfect sacrifice; neither needeth there to be, nor can there be, any other propitiatory sacrifice."

Both Ridley and Latimer were burned at the stake in Oxford on this day in 1555. Ridley's brother brought some gunpowder for the men to place around their necks so death would come more quickly, but Ridley still suffered greatly. With a loud voice he cried, "Into thy hands, O Lord, I commend my spirit," but the wood was green and burned only Ridley's lower parts without touching his upper body. He was heard to repeatedly call out, "Lord have mercy upon me! I cannot burn. . . . Let the fire come unto me, I cannot burn." One of the bystanders finally brought the flames to the top of the pyre to hasten Ridley's death.

Latimer died much more quickly. As the flames rose, he encouraged Ridley, "Be of good comfort, Mr. Ridley, and play the man! We shall this day light such a candle by God's grace, in England, as I trust never shall be put out." The martyrdoms of Ridley, Latimer and Cranmer are today commemorated by a martyrs' monument in Oxford. The faith they once died for can now be freely practiced in the land.

Marie Antoinette. (Courtesy of the University of Texas collection of public domain portraits on the Web.)

Other Events

1647: The first Lion Sermon was preached at the Church of St. Katherine Cree in London, commemorating adventurer Sir John Gayer's escape from lions. Separated from his caravan one night, he was surrounded by the snarling beasts. He remembered the story of Daniel and prayed to escape the lion's jaws as Daniel had. He left money in his will to have a sermon preached on this day each year.

1701: Congregationalists who thought Harvard had become too liberal founded the Collegiate School (later known as Yale). Yale is just one of many major world universities with Christian origins.

1793: Executioners came for Marie Antionette and, according to a popular account, found the once-frivolous queen on her knees praying.

1812: Henry Martyn, missionary to India, Persia and Turkey, died on this day.

October 17

Ignatius Faces Wild Beasts

You most likely have seen pictures of Christians facing lions in the arena. Ignatius, bishop of Antioch, was one of those martyred by the ferocious beasts.

Emperor Trajan, flushed with his victory over the Sythians and Dacians, wanted to make his domination complete by compelling religious conformity. So, he decreed that Chritians should unite with the pagans in their worship of multiple gods. Death was the penalty for all who would not bow to the pagan deities.

Trajan learned that Ignatius was uncompromising in his refusal to unite the worship of Christ with submission to heathen gods. So, while Trajan was on a visit to Asia Minor, he arrested Ignatius. When the bishop confessed his faith in Christ, the emperor sent Ignatius in chains to Rome to die.

When Ignatius arrived in Rome, the public games were about to close for the day. He was hustled to the arena at once and thrown to two fierce lions who immediately devoured him. According to various traditions, Ignatius died on this day in 107.

At no time did he try to escape his miserable death. On the contrary, while bound for Rome under armed guard, he wrote a letter to the Church in the imperial capital insisting that no one interfere with his "true sacrifice." What explains such an unlikely attitude?

Here is the answer in Ignatius's own words, given in a letter that he wrote to Smyrna while on his death march:

> [N]earness to the sword is nearness to God; to be among the wild beasts is to be in the arms of God; only let it be in the name of Jesus Christ. I endure all things that I may suffer together with him, since he who became perfect man strengthens me.

What an attitude! It was merely the outworking of the faith Ignatius had preached for many years. "We have not only to be called Christians, but to be Christians," he had written. To die for Christ, even if it meant becoming a sport to bloodthirsty spectators, was to inherit eternal glory.

Ignatius is notable because he was a disciple of John the apostle. According to John Chrysostom, Peter himself appointed Ignatius to the see of Antioch, where he was bishop for forty years. Ignatius was the earliest bishop whose writings speak of the Church as "catholic," meaning "universal."

Ignatius devoured by beasts. (Baring-Gould, S. *Lives of the Saints*. Edinburgh: John Grant, 1914.)

Other Events

1009: Al-Hakim, caliph of Egypt, ordered the Church of the Holy Sepulchre in Jerusalem destroyed.

1119: Pope Calixtus II confirmed the election of Petronille as the first abbess of Fontevrault Abbey. The abbey of strict Benedictines spawned an order of dependent houses in France, Spain and England.

1483: The Spanish Inquisition came under joint direction of Church and state, and Torquemada was appointed over three regions.

1532: Pope Clement VII ordered humane treatment for Jews.

1760: John Fletcher was inducted into the Vicarage of Madeley. Fletcher was a Methodist of deep faith and purpose, and Wesley intended for Fletcher to be his successor.

1940: The United Church of Japan in Christ was formed by a resolution.

1971: Maximilian Kolbe, a Franciscan, was beatified this day. He had voluntarily given his life for a young man in the concentration camp of Auschwitz.

Calixtus II, who confirmed the election of Petronille as the first abbess of Fontevrault Abbey. (Montor, Chevalier Artaud de. *Lives and Times of the Popes*. New York: Catholic Publication Society of America, 1911.)

Edward Winslow, third governor of Massachusetts. (Wilson, Woodrow. *A History of the American People*. New York/London: Harper & Bros., 1902.)

October 18

Puritan Governor and Diplomat

Edward Winslow, destined to become the third governor of Massachusetts, was born on this day in 1595. An old parish register from Droitwich, England, confirms his birth with this entry: "October 20. Edward Wynsloe sonne of Edward Wynsloe was Baptized & Born the xviii th of October being Saterday."

In the time of Winslow's youth, Separatist groups who wanted to leave the Church of England emerged. They objected to rituals and customs that they thought were too similar to the Roman tradition. Persecuted in England, some fled to the Netherlands, where they obtained a measure of religious freedom. While traveling in Europe, Winslow joined the group that later sailed to America on the *Mayflower*.

Winslow's future and fame were fixed by his decision to join the Separatists. He sailed to America, made friends with the Indian chief Massasoit, carried on diplomatic missions for the colony in England and eventually became governor of Massachusetts. His marriage to the widow Susannah White was the first marriage recorded among European settlers in New England.

Like the other leaders of the colony, Winslow's whole outlook was set by his faith. Responding to criticism of the Puritans, he wrote several tracts explaining their motives and how God had guided them to the New World. According to him, the people who sailed from the Netherlands were seeking a place where they might enjoy liberty and experience the Lord's blessings. The early colonists also hoped to demonstrate to others in England

> where they might live, and comfortably subsist and enjoy the like liberties with us, being freed from Anti-Christian bondage, keep their names and nation, and not only be a means to enlarge the dominions of our state, but the church of Christ also.

He also said they wanted to accomplish a mission work among the Indians. He urged his readers not to listen to ignorant or malicious reports about the Puritans, "assuring my self that none will ever be losers by following us as far as we follow Christ." He closed this defense with a prayer that

> the Father of our Lord Jesus Christ, and our Father, accept in Christ what is according to him; discover, pardon, and reform what is amiss among us; and guide us and them by the assistance of the holy Ghost for time to come, till time shall be no more; that the Lord our God may still delight to dwell among his plantations and churches there by his gracious presence, and may go on blessing to bless them with heavenly blessings in these earthly places, that so by his blessing they may not only grow up to a nation, but become an example of good to others. And let all that wish well to Zion say Amen.

On one of Winslow's trips to England, Archbishop Laud threw Winslow into prison on the grounds that he had taught in church, even though he was just a layman and had conducted a marriage ceremony in his capacity of magistrate. Winslow was locked up for seventeen weeks. Later, Oliver Cromwell sent Winslow to attempt the capture of the island of Hispaniola. The expedition failed, and Winslow died at sea shortly afterward, saluted by forty-two guns.

Louis XIV revoked the Edict of Nantes, which had protected Huguenots. (Potter, Mary Knight. *Art of the Vatican: Being a Brief History of the Palace, and an Account of the Principal Art Treasures Within Its Walls*. Boston: L.C. Page & Co., 1903.)

Other Events

1534: Pamphlets in Paris denounced the mass and other Roman Catholic practices. Because of their abusive language, Protestants were persecuted in a backlash.

1685: The revocation of the Edict of Nantes by Louis XIV forced Huguenots to migrate, for the modicum of protection offered by the edict had been removed. Many went to America and South Africa.

1868: Daniel March composed the hymn "Hark, the Voice of Jesus Calling."

1949: Stuart Hamblin, the American country singer who wrote, "It is no secret what God can do; what he's done for others, he'll do for you," died.

Fire!

London was astir with talk of the young preacher Charles Haddon Spurgeon. He lacked the flowery, elaborate sentences of most preachers of the time, but his simple directness spoke to the hearts of his audience. His passion for truth was as strong as that of the older Puritans whom he loved and studied, yet there was nothing stale and musty about his preaching.

Almost as soon as the nineteen-year-old began his ministry at New Park Street Chapel on London's south side, the chapel became too small for the congregation. Though the chapel could seat 1,200 people, seats, aisles and even windowsills were overflowing whenever Spurgeon spoke.

A year after he arrived at New Park Street, the chapel was expanded, but the larger 1,500-capacity building was not sufficient for the thousands thronging to hear Spurgeon. For a time, his congregation rented Exeter Hall, which seated 4,500 people, but it soon proved too small as well.

As the crowds expanded, Spurgeon leased the Surrey Music Hall in the Royal Surrey Gardens for services. It was London's largest, most commodious and most beautiful building, erected for public amusements and carnivals. Many criticized Spurgeon for leasing a building designed for worldly amusements, but the hall held 10,000 to 12,000 people, and that was the number that packed the building for the first service on this day in 1856.

It seemed that at least as many people were outside the building as were inside. The service had only gone for a few minutes when there was the frightening cry of "Fire! The galleries are giving away, the place is falling!" In the ensuing panic to flee the building, many people were trampled. Seven died, and others were seriously injured as a result of the false alarm. Spurgeon was tremendously depressed over the event, and his grief was so deep some feared his reason had left him. He spent hours "in tears by day, and dreams of terror by night." Within two weeks, however, Spurgeon had recovered sufficiently to preach again. The crowds were even bigger than before.

In the spring of 1861, the Metropolitan Tabernacle was completed; it was Spurgeon's pulpit for the next thirty-one years. Throughout those years, an average of 5,000 people attended each morning and evening Sunday service. Spurgeon's was the "megachurch" of nineteenth-century London.

Though he constantly preached to a sea of faces, Spurgeon trembled at the multitudes who came to hear him. He was aware of his awesome responsibility to give them the truth and not just tickle their ears. In his last sermon at Surrey Hall before moving into the Metropolitan Tabernacle, he urged his listeners:

> In God's name, I beseech you, flee to Christ for refuge! Shall there be any of you, whom I shall see on my deathbed, who shall charge me with being unfaithful? Shall these eyes be haunted with visions of men whom I have amused, but into whose heart I have never sought to convey the truth? . . . God avert that worst of ills—unfaithfulness from my head! I pray you, in Christ's stead, be ye reconciled to God!

Charles Spurgeon at his preaching rail. He preached to huge audiences without a microphone. (Courtesy of the Christian History Institute archives.)

Other Events

615: Deusdedit was consecrated pope. A saintly man, he was supposed to have healed a leper by kissing him. He is sometimes called the "earthquake pope" because a major tremor struck Rome a few years into his pontificate.

1186: Pope Urban III extended papal protection to St. Mary's in Clerkenwell. This meant that the woman abbess was directly responsible for the abbey under the pope and without local male supervision.

1745: Once the greatest wit of his age, Irish clergyman Jonathan Swift died insane on this day.

1786: Mennonites Jacob Hoeppner and Johann Bartsch left to visit Russia to determine if Mennonites should settle there. Many did.

1902: American hymn writer William O. Cushing died. Among his most popular hymns were "Under His Wings," "When He Cometh" and "Ring the Bells of Heaven."

1921: Bill Bright, founder of Campus Crusade, was born in Coweta, Oklahoma, a small town near Tulsa.

The saintly Deusdedit as imagined by an artist. (Montor, Chevalier Artaud de. *Lives and Times of the Popes*. New York: Catholic Publication Society of America, 1911.)

October 20

All Good Things Must End

Among the best-known of the Inklings was J.R.R. Tolkien. Depicted here is "Argonath on the River," a scene from his fantasy trilogy The Lord of the Rings. (Courtsey of Vedrana Bosnjak.)

"The best of them were as good as anything I shall live to see," said John Wain, speaking of the Thursday night meetings of the Inklings at various sites in Oxford.

C.S. Lewis was not only an intellectual giant but a man with a gift for friendship. In the 1930s, a number of his friends began to meet informally in his rather shabby college rooms to read their writings and argue over every sort of literary and moral topic. The members shared a belief in the supernatural, which Lewis contrasted with naturalism in his book *Miracles*:

> The Naturalist thinks that the privilege of "being on its own" resides in the total mass of things. . . . The Supernaturalist, on the other hand, believes that the one original or self-existent thing is on a different level from, and more important than, all other things.

One of the most famous members of the group was J.R.R. Tolkien, the author of *The Hobbit* and The Lord of the Rings trilogy. He liked the name Inklings because it suggested half-formed ideas and dabbling with ink. Tolkien was a traditional Roman Catholic and Lewis a Protestant who took the Christian story quite literally.

In addition to Lewis and Tolkien, the group's other leading members were also successful authors. Warnie, Lewis's older brother, published a history of the reign of King Louis XIV. Owen Barfield wrote a fascinating study called *History in English Words* (among many other books). Charles Williams produced weird novels and poetry that few can fully comprehend.

The men owed each other a great deal. Hugo Dyson and Tolkien were strong influences in Lewis's conversion to Christianity. On the other hand, Tolkien said of Lewis:

> The unpayable debt that I owe to him was not "influence" as it is ordinarily understood, but sheer encouragement. He was for long my only audience. Only from him did I ever get the idea that my "stuff" could be more than a private hobby.

The "stuff" that Tolkien was referring to was The Lord of the Rings and its background material.

The men (with an occasional woman, such as Dorothy Sayers, or Lewis's wife, Joy, thrown into the mix) met for perhaps sixteen years. They critiqued each other's work and drew inspiration from one another. Arguments and ideas from Barfield, Williams and Tolkien often reappear in Lewis's works. But over the years, stresses changed their relationships. Lewis's marriage to Joy Davidman was especially damaging to the Inklings, most of whom disliked her personality and resented Lewis's insistence that she be included in the group.

The last Inklings meeting appears to have been a ham supper on this day in 1949. The next week no one turned up, and no one the week after. The Inklings had dissolved.

Lewis and Tolkien made a tremendous impact on Christian thought in the twentieth century, and there is no doubt that the stimulation of the Inklings' meetings helped form their thought.

Flagellants, followers of a practice initiated by the monk Peter Damien. (Besant, Sir Walter. *Medieval London: Ecclesiastical*. London: A. & C. Black, 1906.)

Other Events

1187: Pope Urban II, who promoted the First Crusade, died.

1349: Self-flagellation was condemned by Pope Clement VI. The practice had arisen 200 years earlier, initiated by the monk Peter Damien as a means to help himself suppress his lusts.

1844: Orestes Brownson was taken into the Roman Catholic Church. He was notable as an American intellectual with persuasive views.

1893: Philip Schaff, American historian of the Church, died.

1913: Mary A. Lathbury, author of the hymn "Break Thou the Bread of Life," died on this day.

1935: The Gospel League of Vepery, Madras, India was formed by Indians determined to spread the gospel among their own people. Among the league's members was the notable evangelist Rajamani.

Martin Bucer: Advice From a Pro

When reformer Martin Bucer (or Butzer) handed his book *The Kingdom of Christ*, to John Cheke on this day in 1550, he was sure that Edward VI would see it. The boy-king was under the supervision of men who were in sympathy with the Reformation, one of whom was Cheke, the royal tutor.

Martin Luther, John Calvin, Philipp Melanchthon and Ulrich Zwingli are names from the Reformation that almost everyone recognizes. Martin Bucer's name is not. And yet he was among the five or six most prominent reformers and was the author of many scriptural commentaries. Calvin was deeply influenced by Bucer's thoughts.

Bucer began his religious career as a Dominican but converted to Protestant views in 1521 after reading works by Luther and Erasmus. Excommunicated by the Roman Church in 1522, he moved to Strasbourg where he became a Protestant leader.

With the success of Protestantism, a new problem arose: Whose Protestantism should be followed? Each leader interpreted the Bible differently. For example, Lutherans and Zwinglians could not agree on the exact nature of the Eucharist. Bucer labored to bring the two sides together, proposing formulas that he thought might be acceptable to everyone. His attempts met with distrust on every side. Luther scornfully said to him, "It is better for you to have your enemies than to set up a fictitious fellowship."

Bucer himself thought that "those who do not make a whole-hearted effort to do the things that are pleasing to the Heavenly Father" should not "declare themselves citizens and members of the kingdom of Christ." In 1548 he refused to sign a faulty peace agreement and had to leave Strasbourg. Thomas Cranmer, the archbishop of Canterbury, invited Bucer to England and made him a professor at Cambridge University.

Bucer's sharp eye quickly saw the needs of his adopted country. Friends urged him to write a practical proposal for reform. He called it *De Regno Christi* (*The Kingdom of Christ*). In the preface, Bucer said, "It would seem fitting to write for Your Majesty a little about the fuller acceptance and reestablishment of the Kingdom of Christ in your realm." He defined the kingdom of Christ as God's total administration by which saints are saved and preserved.

Did the book make any difference? Edward died young and had little influence on England's future. However, when the young king wrote an essay on reforms, it echoed Bucer's ideas, listing the same abuses Bucer had named (including wastefulness and official corruption) and suggesting remedies that could have come out of Bucer's work. For example, Bucer's *The Kingdom of Christ* championed education, and Edward likewise championed schools

Sickly young Edward VI took council from reformer Martin Bucer. (Pollard, Albert Frederick. *Thomas Cranmer and the English Reformation, 1489-1556*. Hamden, CT: Archon Books, 1905.)

Bucer died in 1551, but his story didn't end there. After Edward's death, the Catholic queen Mary Tudor considered even the memory of the reformer so dangerous that she had his bones dug up and burned. His tomb was destroyed. Queen Elizabeth promptly reversed Mary's actions and had Cambridge restore Bucer's honors.

Other Events

1885: James Hannington, missionary to Africa, was set upon by twenty thugs and severely beaten. He lived for eight more days, recording his sufferings in a journal. On October 29, his tormenters speared him to death.

1892: James L. Kelso was born in Duluth, Minnesota. He became a Presbyterian and an archaeologist and taught at Pittsburgh Theological Seminary from 1923 onward. He dug in Palestine at Debir, Bethel, Jericho and Nitla. In *An Archaeologist Looks at the Gospels*, Kelso helped bring the world of Christ alive.

1961: Armando Valladares escaped from a Cuban prison, but rescuers stood him up and he was recaptured. Valladares had been placed in prison at the young age of seventeen for refusing to display a Communist slogan on his desk. Despite dreadful treatment, he became a man of such joy that he had to be isolated from other prisoners so he wouldn't "infect" them with his faith. His case became so well-known that Castro's regime couldn't just kill him. Upon Valladares's release, President Ronald Reagan appointed him to be America's representative to a UN human rights commission.

James Hannington, missionary to Africa, faces African spears. (Dawson, Edwin Collas. *James Hannington, First Bishop of Eastern Equatorial Africa: A History of His Life and Work, 1847-1885*. London: Seeley, 1894.)

William Miller, who thought he had figured out when Christ was going to return. (Sears, Clara Endicott. *Days of Delusion: A Strange Bit of History*. Boston/New York: Houghton Mifflin Company, 1924.)

October 22

No Man Knows—Except William Miller?

When will Jesus return? Christ warned that no man knows the day and hour (see Matthew 24:36). This has not stopped eager theologians from announcing dates, however. All of them have subsequently been disappointed by events.

One of the most prominent prediction-makers was Baptist preacher William Miller. Miller gained a large following with his prediction that Christ would return on this day in 1844. His theories were not farfetched if one accepted the biblical interpretations in vogue through much of Church history. The argument goes something like this: The prophet Daniel's eighth chapter speaks of 2,300 days. Many of the greatest scholars of the Church (Augustine and Bede, for example) took these days to stand for years; 490 years (the 70 "weeks" mentioned in Daniel 9:24) were "cut off" from the 2,300 years, leaving 1,810 years. It was assumed that Christ died early in AD 31 with three-and-a-half years of Daniel's seventieth week still to run. Adding those 3 1/2 years to AD 31, brings us to late AD 34, at which time the 1,810 remaining years supposedly began. The addition of 1,810 to 34 brings us to 1,844. Technical considerations placed the date in October 1844.

Under this interpretation, it seemed possible to match actual historical events with the sequence of events in Daniel 11. Byzantium, the pope, Egypt, Turkey, France and other countries supposedly fulfilled various predictions derived from the Bible. The whole argument was developed at length and convinced thousands of people, although interpreters quarreled over which events fulfilled which prophecies.

As many as 100,000 followers gathered at the predicted time in makeshift temples and on hillsides to "meet the bridegroom." Maxwell Pierson Gaddis attended one of these rallies and reported the result. When midnight came and Christ had not returned, people grew restless. Some walked out. One person said allowance must be made for differences of latitude and longitude between Palestine and the United States. At about one o'clock, one of the leaders rose and said:

> I never did fix upon the precise time myself, and I always told my brethren they would get into trouble if they did; but they would not listen to me, but followed other leaders. . . . I believe the most important thing after all is, to be ready.

Humiliated by what has been called "The Great Disappointment," many Millerites shucked their faith completely. Some said Christ had moved into the Holy of Holies on the designated day and commenced a review of the lives of Christians, which they called His "investigative judgment." Others became Seventh Day Adventists. The majority returned to more traditional churches.

Benedict XI, who was thought to have been poisoned by agents of William of Nogaret. (Montor, Chevalier Artaud de. *Lives and Times of the Popes*. New York: Catholic Publication Society of America, 1911.)

Other Events

1303: Benedict XI was elected as pope. He was a Dominican and was thought to have been poisoned by agents of William of Nogaret, whom he had opposed. He lifted excommunication off of the troublesome King Philip IV of France.

1540: John Calvin was invited by letter to return to Geneva, the town from which he had been expelled three years before.

1808: John Addyman was born in Leeds, Yorkshire County, England. He joined the Methodist New Connection, and in 1836, when the New Connection decided to establish a mission in Canada, they chose Addyman as their missionary. His wedding had been set for May 25, 1837, but he was selected for Canada on May 24 and had to push the ceremony back a day. By fusing together remnants of two faltering Canadian Methodist groups, Addyman and his wife, Hannah, created a sizeable denomination before their return to England in 1845.

1808: Benjamin Randall, who founded the Free Will Baptists in the Northern United States, died on this day.

1987: A Gutenberg Bible sold at auction at Christie's for $5.39 million, one of the largest sums ever paid for a printed book.

October 23

Dating Origins

Scores of attempts have been made to compute the earliest biblical date. The most famous is undoubtedly that made by Bishop James Ussher in the seventeenth century.

Ussher was born in Dublin, Ireland, in 1581 and died in England in 1656. He lived through a time of tremendous political and religious upheaval in his native Ireland and in England. Though he was a Puritan in theology, he was a Royalist in his steadfastness to the king and the principle of the divine right of kings. Invited to participate in the Westminster Assembly, which eventually wrote the Westminster Confession and Catechism, Ussher refused because he thought the assembly itself was illegal.

In his day, Ussher was an eminent scholar known to the foremost scholars and statesmen in England. His collected works totaled seventeen volumes. The most famous of these was his *Annals of the Old and New Testament*, published in the 1650s. The work was a detailed chronology and dating of biblical history. In it Ussher said God created the world on the morning of this day in 4004 BC. He arrived at this date partly by adding the ages of Adam and his descendants found in Genesis 5 and 11. He assumed that the Old Testament genealogies did not omit any names and that the periods of time in the texts were all consecutive. Scholars today question both assumptions.

Nevertheless, Ussher's chronology is the earliest and the most celebrated attempt at biblical chronology in English. Someone—no one seems to know who—incorporated Ussher's chronology into the margins of the Authorized Version of the Bible, and it was printed in many Bibles well into the twentieth century.

Exact dates and chronology for ancient and biblical times are difficult to ascertain because dates of particular events are often given relative to other events with unknown dates. For dates to be converted to our modern calendar, they must relate to a fixed event. Years are reckoned by eras, which start at a fixed point in history. The years preceding or following that point are numbered from that point. For example, the ancient Romans numbered their years from the founding of the city of Rome. Five hundred years after Christ, a monk in Rome named Denys le Petit proposed that the birth of Christ be the fixed point or reference for the Christian era. According to his careful research, le Petit felt that Christ was born in the Roman year 753. It was not until three or four centuries later that le Petit's suggestion came into general use in the West.

Bishop James Ussher, acknowledged as the first to attempt creating a biblical chronology in English. (Wills, James. *Lives of Illustrious and Distinguished Irishmen*. Dublin: McGregor, 1840.)

Today the Christian era of reckoning is used throughout the world, though the secular world prefers to call this the "common era" rather than the "Christian era." Interestingly enough, modern historians studying the time of Christ's birth more closely and relating it to the supposed time of King Herod's death usually conclude that Jesus was born around 6 BC. Sounds strange, doesn't it, that Jesus would be born six years "before Christ"?

Other Events

524: Boethius was executed by an Arian king. A Christian philosopher best known for *The Consolation of Philosophy* that was written while he was on death row, Boethius also wrote a defense of the Orthodox doctrine of the Trinity. His work was influential until the Reformation.

787: The second Council of Nicea ended. This council legitimized the veneration of icons.

1641: Ulster Catholics massacred 40,000 Protestants in Ireland.

1684: Massachusetts ended its church membership requirements for voting.

1685: Judge Jeffries had the Baptist Elizabeth Guant burned at the stake for harboring a refugee—who turned around and betrayed her for the sake of a pardon.

1819: Hiram Bingham, Asa Thurston and other missionaries sailed to the Sandwich Islands (Hawaii).

1941: American Baptist scholar Shailer Mathews died. Among his achievements was the *Dictionary of Religion and Ethics*.

Cruel Judge Jeffries sentenced Elizabeth Guant to burn for helping one of her enemies. (Green, John Richard. *A Short History of the English People*. New York: Harper & Brothers, 1893-5.)

October 24 Paton Prevails on Terrible Tanna

John Paton being threatened by the people of Tanna. (Lambert, John C. *The Romance of Missionary Heroism*. London: Seeley, 1907.)

"You will be eaten by cannibals!" Mr. Dickson thought John Paton was foolish to go as a missionary to the New Hebrides. About twenty years earlier, John Williams and James Harris had been killed and eaten in those islands.

But Paton could not to be turned from his purpose:

> Mr. Dickson, you are advanced in years now, and your own prospect is soon to be laid in the grave, there to be eaten by worms; I confess to you, that if I can but live and die serving and honoring the Lord Jesus, it will make no difference to me whether I am eaten by cannibals or by worms; and in the Great Day my resurrection body will rise as fair as yours in the likeness of our risen Redeemer.

Paton did not step straight from school into foreign missions. As a young man, he served as an evangelistic worker in Glasgow, visiting home after home with the gospel in spite of threats and abuse. (He even had the contents of chamber pots dumped on him.) Under those conditions, he learned the steadiness and determination that carried him through his later adventures. The people of Glasgow came to love him so much that they begged him not to leave.

With his wife, Mary, Paton sailed from Scotland in December 1857. On November 5, 1858, they landed on the island of Tanna in the New Hebrides, an island chain northeast of Australia. With them was another young missionary, Joseph Copeland.

The people were as fierce as Paton had been told. Cannibal celebrations took place in sight of the Patons' home, and human blood fouled their drinking water. The natives frightened Copeland so much that he lost his mind and died; they continually threatened Paton. Time and again they lifted their guns to shoot him or raised their axes to bash him in the head, but always they held back as if restrained by a greater power.

Early the next year, Mary bore a son. Both took fever and soon died. With a breaking heart, Paton dug a grave for them and laid them in it. Later he said, "But for Jesus, and the fellowship He vouchsafed me there, I must have gone mad and died beside that lonely grave!"

Paton remained on Tanna. He went from village to village telling of the love of Christ and translating Scripture into the Tannese language. But finally, when all his supplies were stolen and starvation stared him in the face, he made his way across the island to the settlement of a second missionary. The Tannese surrounded the home and set an adjacent building on fire. It appeared that the missionaries would burn to death. But a tornado whipped across the compound, dousing the fire. The savages fled in terror. The next day a sail appeared on the horizon and the missionaries escaped on the boat.

After leaving Tanna, Paton remarried and worked on the smaller island of Aniwa (now Aneityum). He had the joy of seeing the people there come to Christ in a way the people of Tanna never had. On this day in 1869, John Paton observed the Lord's Supper with his first converts on New Hebrides. Eventually all of the Aniwa islanders converted to Christianity.

Other Events

711: Pope Constantine returned safely from Constantinople. He had feared that Emperor Justinian would kill him.

1260: Chartres Cathedral in France, a fine example of Gothic architecture, was consecrated.

1648: The Peace of Westphalia ended central Europe's Thirty Years' War. Extending equal political rights to Catholics and Protestants (including religious minorities), the peace treaties also marked the first use of the term *secularization* in discussing Church property that was to be distributed among the warring parties.

1788: Sarah Josepha Hale was born. She lobbied for the United States' Thanksgiving Day until she got it.

1826: Ann Hasseltine Judson, wife of Burma missionary Adoniram Judson, died. The thirty-seven-year-old woman, a new mother, had worn herself out tending to her captive husband's needs and attempting to deliver him from prison. Her last words were, "It is the will of God; I am not afraid of death."

1956: After receiving her divinity degree from Union Theological Seminary, Margaret Ellen Towner was ordained in her home church in Syracuse, New York, becoming the first woman ordained in the Presbyterian Church.

1964: Pope Paul VI declared Benedict of Nursia the patron saint of Europe. Benedict had founded the influential Benedictine Order centuries earlier.

Ann Hasseltine Judson. (Lossing, Benson J. *Eminent Americans*. New York: Hovendon Company, 1890.)

October 25

Diamond-Dust Socialite Opens Door of Hope

Money, servants, dinners, parties, social balls—Emma Whittemore had it all. Her wealth allowed her to admire herself in dresses that glittered with diamond dust. She and her businessman husband, Sidney Whittemore, moved among the elite of New York, unaware of anything lacking in themselves.

One afternoon, Whittemore's friend, Miss Kelly, persuaded Whittemore to hear an evangelist. Completely on his own, her husband went too. Neither had the slightest idea that the other would be there. Both were stirred by the message and went down to the mourner's bench. Miss Kelly urged Whittemore to visit Water Street, where Jerry McAuley, an ex-convict and reformed drunkard, had opened a mission. Whittemore's husband agreed to allow her to go just once, but only if he escorted her through the rough area of New York City.

"Never can that night be erased from my memory," wrote Whittemore. "From the time we got off the car at Roosevelt Street, each step opened up some new horror." She heard curses and witnessed quarreling, fighting, police abuse and women being dragged off to the police station.

As the meeting progressed, God got such possession of the Whittemores that both of them sat in painful silence as they were convicted of their useless lives. "We arose with a holy determination, born of God Himself, to henceforth live for His glory and praise."

One evening Whittemore spent some time "alone with God, earnestly inquiring of Him" what she was to do. "Suddenly the girls on the street came to my mind." But the thought of working with those wayward women horrified her. "Oh, anything but that!" she pleaded. A deep hush of shame came upon her heart, and she yielded to what the Lord was asking.

But she often found the work unbearable. "Oh, Lord, I cannot, I cannot see these fearful sights again! It simply breaks my heart." In response to her prayer, she always received more love with which she could go on.

If girls were to be rescued, homes were needed to house them. On this day in 1890, "Mother" Whittemore's first Door of Hope ministry was opened. Within 4 years, Door of Hope had helped 325 girls. Eventually Door of Hope went international. By Emma's death in 1931, there were ninety-seven homes in seven countries—the United States, Canada, Great Britain, Germany, Africa, Japan and China.

Emma Whittemore, a socialite, faced a tough test among the destitute of New York City. (Burger, Delores T. *Women Who Changed the Heart of the City: The Untold Story of the City Rescue Mission Movement*. Grand Rapids, MI: Kregel Publications, 1997. Used by permission of Janyre Tromp.)

Other Events

1147: Because of bickering and ineffective leadership, the German armies of the Second Crusade (1147-9) were destroyed by the Saracens at Dorylaeum (in modern Turkey).

1400: English poet Geoffrey Chaucer died in London. He had abruptly stopped writing his famous *Canterbury Tales* some time before. The end of his tales includes a "retraction," where Chaucer himself takes the stage and, nearing the end of his life, apologizes for his "translations and [writings] of worldly vanities." Chaucer was buried in Westminster Abbey, a high honor for a commoner, and became the first of those entombed in what is now called Poets' Corner. He admired reformer John Wycliffe.

1885: Horace Newton Allen, first resident Protestant missionary to Korea, accepted the rank of Chamoan (Mandarin) because only men of that rank could be presented to the king of Korea, and he wanted to seek royal favor for the Church.

1941: Jack Wyrtzen began his radio ministry from Times Square in New York. He had been told by the manager, "No religion on my station," but through a miscommunication, an underling signed Wyrtzen up. He went on to found the Word of Life organization.

Geoffrey Chaucer, shown here, admired reformer John Wycliffe. (Pollard, Alfred W. *Chaucer*. London/New York: Macmillan and Co., 1893.)

Death of a Puritan

Philip Doddridge, who wrote over 400 hymns. (Brown, Theron and Hezekiah Butterworth. *The Story of the Hymns and Tunes*. New York: American Tract Society, 1906.)

Eighteenth-century England produced many excellent hymn writers whose hymns are still sung today—Isaac Watts, Charles Wesley and the Puritan Philip Doddridge, who died on this day in 1751.

Doddridge was born in London, England, on June 26, 1702, the youngest of twenty children. His health was so poor when he was born that he was not expected to live. He continued to be plagued by ill health all of his life. His parents died when he was a boy, but he was cared for by friends of the family.

Recognizing Doddridge's intellectual abilities, a benefactress offered to pay for his studies at Cambridge. Doddridge rejected the offer, however, because he could not accept all that the Church of England taught. He went to a nonconformist seminary instead and became an evangelical, independent church leader. At twenty-seven Doddridge began to pastor the Castle Hill congregational chapel in Northampton, England; he continued there for the next twenty-two years.

While in Northampton, Doddridge prepared young men for ministry in independent churches. Over the years he taught about 200 men, conducting classes in Hebrew, Greek, math, philosophy, Bible and theology. Because of his many accomplishments, the University of Aberdeen conferred a doctor of divinity degree upon him in 1736.

He was a prolific writer. His *The Rise and Progress of Religion in the Soul* was translated into seven languages and continues to edify readers today. Besides a New Testament commentary and other theological works, Doddridge also wrote over 400 hymns. Most of the hymns were written as summaries of his sermons and were to help the congregation express their response to the truths that were taught. None of the hymns were published in Doddridge's own lifetime, though they did circulate in manuscript copies.

At fifty-eight, at the height of his ministry, Doddridge contracted tuberculosis. Friends collected money to send him to Lisbon, Portugal, for a cure; but it was too late. Doddridge died on this day in 1751. He is buried in the English cemetery in Lisbon.

After his death, a friend collected many of Doddridge's hymns and had them published. Several can still be found in today's hymnals, including "Grace! Tis a Charming Sound" and "O Happy Day."

The latter is probably Doddridge's most famous hymn. Based on Second Chronicles 15:15, the hymn expressed the joy of a personal relationship with God. Doddridge himself titled the hymn "Rejoicing in our Covenant Engagement to God." Baptists and Methodists often use the hymn at dedication services for Christian baptism, while the British royalty have used it at confirmation services for court children.

Alfred the Great, whose defeat of the Danes ensured Christianity's survival in England. (Courtesy of the University of Texas collection of public domain portraits on the Web.)

Other Events

366: Supporters of Pope Damasus massacred 137 supporters of Pope Ursinius in their basilica after rival popes were elected.

899 (probable date): Alfred the Great, ruler of Wessex, England, from 871, died. His defeat of the Danes ensured Christianity's survival in England, but he was also known for his ecclesiastical reforms and his desire to revive learning in his country.

1928: Reuben A. Torrey died on this day. An Independent Congregationalist educator and evangelist, pastor of Chicago's Moody Avenue (now Memorial) Church and first superintendent of both the Moody Bible Institute and the Bible Institute of Los Angeles (Biola), Torrey was also one of the editors of *The Fundamentals*, which welded Fundamentalists into a cohesive movement.

1944: William Temple, Anglican Church leader, theologian and philosopher, died. He actively promoted ecumenism.

1966: The first World Congress on Evangelism opened in West Berlin, attracting approximately 600 delegates from about 100 countries.

OCTOBER 27

Bishop Frumentius, Apostle to Ethiopia

"For all you have done, I reward you with your liberty." In Axuma, Ethiopia (then Abyssinia), the old king was dying. Before him stood two young men from Tyre (a region of modern Lebanon) who had been his slaves for several years. One had served as his cupbearer, the other as his secretary. Their names were Edesius and Frumentius.

A curious train of events had brought them to this moment early in the fourth century. As youths, they studied under their Uncle Meropius, a Christian philosopher. Meropius developed an urge to visit Arabia and offered to take the boys, who eagerly embraced the opportunity to see a piece of the world. The outward voyage and their visit went well. As the ship began its homeward journey, it landed at Adulis to take on fresh supplies. One of the sailors got into a fight with the locals, who killed everyone on the ship, including Meropius.

Edesius and Frumentius escaped with their lives because they were studying under a tree at some distance from the brawl. The Ethiopians sent them to their king. He was impressed with their bearing and understanding and made them his personal slaves.

Ethiopia had a long association with Judaism, going back to the days of Solomon, so Frumentius was sent to live with Anbaram, a Jewish priest with Christian sympathies.

When the king died, neither of his sons was old enough to rule. The queen pleaded with Edesius and Frumentius to help her govern the country and educate her sons. The two agreed. They attempted to spread the gospel; among the steps they took was to encourage Christian merchants to worship openly.

When the new king came of age, the two young men left Ethiopia despite his plea that they stay. They followed the Nile to Alexandria. Filled with concern for the salvation of the people who had once held him as a slave, Frumentius appealed to Bishop Athanasius to appoint a bishop to the Ethiopians. Athanasius recognized the value of this step. And who would be better suited to the task than Frumentius himself? Athanasius trained Frumentius, ordained him and sent him back.

Frumentius converted Anbaram and ordained him. He led King Ezana and his brother Sheazana to embrace Christianity and baptized them as well. Frumentius and his coworkers organized Ethiopian Christianity and carried on a mission work in Nubia and Yemen.

Meanwhile, Edesius became a priest too and returned to Tyre. There he met Church historian Rufinus, who included Edesius and Frumentius's story in his works.

The Roman emperor Constantius who favored the Arians (they denied the full divinity of Christ), he wrote a letter to the king of Ethiopia, urging him to expel Frumentius and replace him with an Arian. The Ethiopian monarch refused—Frumentius was still beloved. After his death he became known as "Our Father" and "Father of Peace"—titles that the heads of the Ethiopian Church still assume today.

Axuma Church in Ethiopia, a direct result of Frumentius's work in that African nation. (Bent, J. Theodore. *The Sacred City of the Ethiopians*. London/New York: Longmans, Green, and Co., 1893.)

The impact of Frumentius is proven by inscriptions on coins minted during the second half of King Ezana's reign. The old pagan inscriptions disappeared and Christian ones took their place. Roman Catholics commemorate Frumentius on this day, October 27, but the Orthodox Church holds his celebration in November and the Copts hold it in December.

OTHER EVENTS

Annual: Pilate's Wife's Day is celebrated. In parts of the Eastern Church, Pilate's wife is considered a saint. Tradition gives her the name Claudia, and she is known from John's Gospel to have tried to save Jesus's life after having a dream about His innocence.

625: Honorius I began his reign as pope. His belief in Monothelitism (that Christ had only one will, not two), was later condemned as heresy by the Roman Church. This has long been a point of conflict in discussion of papal infallibility.

1614: This day was the deadline for all missionary material to be handed over to Japanese authorities in a crackdown on Christianity.

1771: Francis Asbury debarked in Philadelphia, having arrived from England to oversee America's few hundred Methodists. During his forty-five-year ministry in America, he traveled on horseback or in carriage an estimated 300,000 miles and delivered 16,500 sermons. By his death, there were 200,000 Methodists in America.

1956: Premier Gomulka of Poland announced the release of Archbishop Wyszynski, whom the nation's Communist government had been holding.

1978: The complete New International Version (NIV) of the Bible was first published by Zondervan of Grand Rapids, Michigan.

Honorius I, who believed in Monothelitism. (Montor, Chevalier Artaud de. *Lives and Times of the Popes*. New York: Catholic Publication Society of America, 1911.)

Constantine's vision and subsequent triumph changed history. (Baring-Gould, S. *Lives of the Saints*. Edinburgh: John Grant, 1914.)

OCTOBER

28 Constantine Triumphs Under the Sign of the Cross

The world experiences at times red-letter days that no historian dare ignore. One of them occurred on this day in 312 when a thirty-two-year-old claimant to the Roman Empire defeated his chief rival to the throne.

Constantine's father had been one of the rulers of the sprawling empire. After his death, his troops named Constantine "Augustus." However, others wanted a piece of the action. One of them, Maxentius, was determined to hold Italy and Africa for himself. Constantine would have to defeat him in order to make good his claim to the throne. Constantine's trusted friend and Church historian Eusebius tells what happened as the "Augustus" prepared for one of the most decisive battles of history:

> Constantine was praying to his father's god, beseeching him to tell him who he was and imploring him to stretch out his right hand to help him in his present difficulties. While he was fervently praying, an incredible sign appeared to him from heaven. (It would be hard to believe his account if it had been told by anyone else. But the victorious emperor long afterwards declared it to the writer of this history—when I was honored to meet and talk with him and he even confirmed his statement by an oath. Thus, who could doubt him, especially since time has established its truth?) He said that about noon, when the day was already beginning to decline, he saw with his own eyes the trophy of a cross of light in the heavens, above the sun, and an inscription that said "Conquer by This" attached to it. Seeing this, he and his army, which followed him on an expedition and witnessed the miracle, were struck with amazement.
>
> He said that he doubted within himself what importance the vision might hold. He continued to ponder its meaning through until he fell asleep. While sleeping, the Christ of God appeared to him with the same sign he had seen earlier in the heavens. God commanded him to make a likeness of that sign which he had seen in the heavens and to use it as a safeguard in all encounters with his enemies.

The upshot was that Constantine defeated Maxentius at the Milvian Bridge in Rome. Constantine honored Christian bishops and meddled in their affairs for the rest of his life. He was baptized on his deathbed, the first Roman emperor to embrace Christianity.

Michael Faraday, a man of Christian character and inventor of the first electric dynamo, holding a magnetic bar. (Courtesy of the Christian History Institute archives.)

Other Events

1646: Missionary John Eliot, at Nonantum, Massachusetts, preached the first worship service for Native Americans in their native language—in a wigwam.

1831: Michael Faraday demonstrated the first electric dynamo. He also exhibited a genuinely Christian character and was a member of the Presbyterian group known as Sandemanians.

1958: Angelo Giuseppe Roncalli was unexpectedly elected pope. He took the name John XXIII. Expected to be a caretaker, he fooled everyone by convening the Second Vatican Council in 1962.

1965: Pope Paul VI proclaimed that Jews are not collectively guilty for Christ's crucifixion.

1972: Pathet Lao Communists tied the hands of Evelyn Anderson and Beatrice Kosin behind them, set their house on fire and moved on. The terrorists also took two male mission workers captive and burned sixty houses.

October 29

Birthday Bash for Abraham Kuyper

On this day in 1907, the Netherlands celebrated the seventieth birthday of Abraham Kuyper. A national proclamation noted that the history of the Netherlands—its Church, government, society, press, schools and sciences—for the previous forty years could not be written without mention of Kuyper's name on almost every page. That was because during that period the biography of Dr. Kuyper was to a considerable extent the history of the Netherlands.

Who was this man who had such a deep impact on his nation? Kuyper was born on October 29, 1837. At first his teachers thought he was dull, but he accelerated in his studies before he became a teen and eventually graduated with highest honors from Leyden University. He went on to receive his doctorate in sacred theology and was a minister at Breesd and Utrecht before going to Amsterdam in 1870.

In Kuyper's early years, the religious life of his nation was nearly dead, its Church cold and formal. The Bible was not taught in schools and had little influence on national life. Kuyper did much to change this by his involvement in the Anti-Revolutionary Party, which derived its name from its opposition to the ideas of the French Revolution and was strongly Protestant in makeup.

In 1872 Kuyper became editor-in-chief of *The Standard*, a daily newspaper that was the official voice of the party. Soon after taking the helm of *The Standard*, Kuyper also became editor of *De Heraut*, a weekly Christian newspaper. He continued as editor of both newspapers for much of his life.

In 1874 Kuyper was elected to the lower house of Parliament and served there until 1877. Three years later he founded the Free University of Amsterdam, which took the Bible as the foundation for every area of knowledge.

As the leader of the Anti-Revolutionary Party, Kuyper was summoned by Queen Wilhelmena to form a cabinet, and thus he became prime minister of the Netherlands. He headed the country for three years, until 1905. Some party members were dissatisfied with Kuyper because he would not keep his Church and political activities separate. To him, they were identical interests since he believed that Christ is king in every department of human life.

Kuyper was a man of tremendous versatility. He was a noted linguist, theologian, university professor, politician, statesman, philosopher, scientist and philanthropist. He was also a man of the people and tried to find time to relate to them.

In 1897, at the twenty-fifth anniversary of his editorship of *The Standard*, Kuyper described the ruling passion of his life:

> That in spite of all worldly opposition, God's holy ordinances shall be established again in the home, in the school, and in the State for the good of the people; to carve as it were into the conscience of the nation the ordinances of the Lord, to which Bible and Creation bear witness, until the nation pays homage again to God.

Christian thinker and statesman Abraham Kuyper. (Courtesy of the Christian History Institute archives.)

Kuyper had the rare combination of being both a great theologian and a great, warm Christian. Every week he wrote a devotional meditation, producing over 2,000 of them in his lifetime. Some of these were collected into his book *To Be Near Unto God*. In it he wrote:

> The fellowship of being near unto God must become reality, in the full and vigorous prosecution of our life. It must permeate and give color to our feeling, our perception, our sensations, our thinking, our imagining, our willing, our acting, our speaking. It must not stand as a foreign factor in our life, but it must be the passion that breathes throughout our whole existence."

Other Events

312: Emperor Constantine restored religious rights in the Roman Empire by edict.

1884: Hundreds of clergy offered their support to James Blaine in his US presidential bid against the "Rum, Romanism and Rebellion" of Grover Cleveland's Democrats. Blaine, who was no angel himself, lost anyhow.

1889: A.B. Simpson incorporated The Christian and Missionary Alliance, an ardent mission movement.

1900: Swiss theologian Frederic L. Godot, best known in America for his *Commentary on John*, died.

1919: A.B. Simpson, founder of The Christian and Missionary Alliance and Nyack College, died on this day.

1966: Pope Paul VI reaffirmed the Roman Catholic stance against artificial birth control.

Emperor Constantine, who restored religious rights in the Roman Empire. (Rostovtzeff, Mikhail. *The Social and Economic History of the Roman Empire*. Oxford/New York: Oxford University Press, 1926.)

George Müller practiced faith, particularly in relying on God for the provision of his physical needs. (Harding, William Henry. *The Life of George Müller*. London: Morgan and Scott, 1914.)

October 30

George Müller Vows No Salary

George Müller lived a wild life in Prussia (part of today's Germany) before his conversion in 1825. Once he came to know the Lord, however, he left behind his old life and became totally devoted to serving the Lord. He went to England to work as a missionary to Jewish people, but once in England the Lord directed him to become pastor of a Brethren congregation.

Müller tried to pattern every practice in his life according to the Word of God, regardless of the customs and traditions that might prevail. Soon he came to believe that as a minister he could not consent to receiving a fixed salary. He gave several reasons for adopting this position: First, a stated salary requires a fixed revenue or income, which cannot be guaranteed to the church unless the people are taxed through pew rentals or some other means. This is contrary to James 2:1-6, which forbids favoring the rich over the poor. Second, circumstances change for individuals—what a person might cheerfully be able to give at one time might be a burden at another time. Third, a fixed income can become a hindrance to the servant of Christ, for he will be tempted to modify his message to please those who are supporting him.

On this day in 1830, Müller explained to his congregation that he would no longer accept a fixed salary from them. He put up a box inside the chapel, to which people could contribute as they desired before the Lord, without any man having to know the giver or the amount. Together, Müller and his wife lived a life of voluntary poverty, following Luke 12:32 and Christ's call in Matthew 6:19 to lay up no treasures on earth. They looked daily to the Lord for His provision, rather than to the "arm of man."

At the end of 1833, Müller recorded in his journal that he had lacked for nothing during the four years he had trusted the Lord alone for his temporal supplies. He also noticed that at each year's close he had very little, if any, in excess. The supply always fit the need, never greater or less. Often the money came from unusual sources, from great distances or from people he had never seen.

Müller made it a point never to ask for money or even to let his needs be expressed as if he were appealing for funds. His appeals were always to his heavenly Father, who in turn would direct His people to care for His own. The gifts Müller received were many and varied—a bride and bridegroom gave money to the Lord's work rather than buy an engagement ring; a lady sold all of her jewelry and gave the proceeds to the Lord; one man sent in a gold watch and chain, saying that a less expensive watch would be a better reminder to him of how swiftly time flies.

Müller's ministry was worldwide and included service to ten churches in the Bristol area and orphanages that cared for 8,000 orphans, as well as a vast ministry of printing and distributing biblical literature. In all of his ministry, Müller looked to the Lord alone for his supply. As Müller himself said, "I have joyfully dedicated my whole life to the object of exemplifying how much may be accomplished by prayer and faith."

John VI, who ruled in favor of the archbishop of Canterbury, as imagined by an artist. (Montor, Chevalier Artaud de. *Lives and Times of the Popes*. New York: Catholic Publication Society of America, 1911.)

Other Events

335: Athanasius, bishop of Alexandria, met Constantine outside Constantinople. Constantine flew into a rage when someone accused Athanasius of holding up grain shipments from Egypt as leverage in his battle against Arianism.

701: Pope John VI was consecrated. One of his acts was to rule in favor of the archbishop of Canterbury, who had ordered the controversial Wilfrid to resign from York and retire to Ripon.

1536: Lutheranism became the official religion of Denmark after reformers had carried the message to that land, converting many to the new interpretation of the old faith.

1768: Philip Embury preached the dedication service of the Methodist chapel he built with his own hands, the first Methodist church house in the New World.

1984: The body of Rev. Jerzy Popieluszko, who was taken by the Polish secret police, was found. He had been abducted eleven days earlier; his corpse showed marks of torture.

OCTOBER 31

Ninety-Five Theses

On this day in 1517, in the little town of Wittenberg, Germany, no one seemed to notice the priest nailing his challenge to debate on the church door; but within the week, copies of his theses were being discussed throughout the surrounding regions. Within a decade, Europe itself was shaken by this simple act. Later generations would mark Martin Luther's nailing of the ninety-five theses on the church door as the beginning of the Protestant Reformation, but what did Luther think he was doing at the time? To answer this question, we need to understand a little about Luther's own spiritual journey.

As a young man in Germany at the beginning of the sixteenth century, Luther was studying law at the university. One day he was caught in a storm and was almost killed by lightening. In a flash, he promised God he would become a monk. In 1505, Luther entered the Augustinian monastery, and in 1507 he became a priest. His monastic leaders sent him to Rome in 1510, but Luther was disenchanted with the ritual and the dead faith he found in the papal city. There was nothing in Rome to mend his despairing spirit or settle his restless soul. He seemed cut off from God, and nowhere could he find a cure for his malady.

Luther was bright, and his superiors had him teach theology in the university. In 1515 he began explaining Paul's epistle to the Romans. Slowly, Paul's words in Romans began to break through the gloom of Luther's soul. Luther wrote:

> My situation was that, although an impeccable monk, I stood before God as a sinner troubled in conscience, and I had no confidence that my merit would assuage him. Night and day I pondered until I saw the connection between the justice of God and the statement "the just shall live by faith." Then I grasped that the justice of God is that righteousness by which through grace and sheer mercy God justifies us through faith. Thereupon I felt myself to be reborn and to have gone through open doors into paradise.

The more Luther's eyes were opened by his study of Romans, the more he saw the corruption of the Church in his day. The glorious truth of justification by faith alone had become buried under a mound of greed, corruption and false teaching. Most galling was the sale of indulgences—the certificates the Church provided, for a fee, to shorten one's stay in purgatory but which were being hawked as pardons for sin. The pope encouraged the sale of indulgences because he needed the money to help pay for rebuilding St. Peter's Basilica in Rome.

Once Luther realized the sufficiency of Christ's sacrifice alone for our sins, he found such practices revolting. The more he studied the Scriptures, the more he saw the need to show the Church how it had strayed from the truth.

So, on this day in 1517, he posted a list of ninety-five propositions on the church door in Wittenberg. In his day, this was the means of inviting scholars to debate important issues. No one took up Luther's challenge to debate, but once news of his proposals became known, many began to discuss the issues Luther had raised.

Luther apparently expected the pope to agree with his position, since it was based on Scripture; but in 1520, the pope issued a decree condemning Luther's views. Luther publicly burned the papal decree. With that act, he also burned his bridges behind him.

Martin Luther in 1520. His ninety-five theses became the launching point of the Protestant Reformation. (McGiffert, Arthur Cushman. *Martin Luther, the Man and His Work*. New York: The Century Co., 1911.)

OTHER EVENTS

1816: Robert Moffat sailed for South Africa, where he established a mission work and translated the Bible. Mission leaders had been reluctant to send him, believing he was unqualified.

1909: The first baptismal service of the Sudan Interior Mission was held. Ninety years later, Sudanese Christians made up about one-third of the country's population despite terrible oppression by the Muslim majority.

1992: Pope John Paul II formally admitted that the Roman Catholic Church was wrong in condemning Galileo Galilei in 1633 for believing that the sun, not the earth, was the center of the solar system.

Robert Moffat proved wrong everyone who thought he wasn't up to the job. (Johnston, Julia H. *Fifty Missionary Heroes Every Boy and Girl Should Know*. New York/Chicago: Fleming H. Revell Company, 1913.)

Unfinished Sistine Chapel Ceiling Unveiled

All of Rome waited in expectation. For months, Michelangelo Buonarroti had worked in secret. Curiosity was aflame. What had he accomplished? Had he succeeded in transferring his skill as a sculptor to work with fresco?

Pope Julius II, as impatient as ever, demanded that Michelangelo unveil the ceiling of the Sistine Chapel although it was far from done. High on the scaffolding, his face just inches from the ceiling, paint dripping into his eyes, Michelangelo had completed only the central vault.

Julius prevailed. Down came the scaffolding, which had been erected with such labor. On this day in 1509, the public surged into the chapel to see what Michelangelo had wrought.

Painters could only gape in astonishment. Michelangelo, who had earlier revolutionized sculpture, had done the same with painting. His nine groups of stories from Genesis stole the breath of his contemporaries. He made his figures appear in perspective and distributed them across the vault in an astonishing inner rhythm that told the stories of Creation, the fall of man and sacred history. (Years later, he added the last judgment to the wall behind the altar.) His rivals immediately began to ape his techniques.

Michelangelo infused much of his art with Christian feeling. He was an admirer of the reformer Savonarola, and his sonnets show that he genuinely desired to know God and considered himself unworthy of Him:

> O my dear God, matched with the much I owe
> All that I am were no real recompense:
> Paying a debt is not munificence.

He had flaws of temper and was accused by enemies of being homosexual, but Michelangelo's art and life reveal an individual concerned for God's glory. A contemporary wrote, "Buonarroti, having lived for ninety years, there was never found through all that time anyone who could with right and justice impute to him a stain or any ugliness of manners."

However, Michelangelo found dealing with Pope Julius a strain. Once when Michelangelo threatened to leave Rome, Julius, in a fury, said he would have Michelangelo flung from his scaffold. Michelangelo immediately took the scaffolding down and refused to add the gold leaf and touch-ups that Julius wanted.

Michelangelo amazed his contemporaries with the Sistine Chapel ceiling. His *Last Judgment* is also from the Sistine Chapel. (La Farge, John. *Great Masters*. New York: McClure, Phillips and Company, 1903.)

Other Events

451: The Council of Chalcedon ended. It was the fourth and largest of the early general councils and repudiated the claim that Christ had only one nature, not two—the human and the divine.

1755: A powerful earthquake killed more than 50,000 people in Lisbon, Portugal. The catastrophe became the subject of many sermons, some of the messages proclaiming it to be a sign that Christ would soon return.

1770: Alexander Cruden, who compiled the famous concordance that bears his name, died. He was found kneeling by his bed with his Bible open in front of him. Cruden compiled his groundbreaking work in just eighteen months despite mental illness.

1776: Spanish Franciscan missionaries founded the San Juan Capistrano Mission in California.

1926: Russian evangelists Prokhanov and Deyneka met in New York. The two went on to work closely to win Eastern Europeans for Christ.

1950: Pope Pius XII released his encyclical *Munificentissimus Deus*, proclaiming the Assumption of the Blessed Virgin Mary. The doctrine teaches that Mary was taken body and soul into heaven at the end of her life, a belief proposed by Gregory of Tours 1400 years earlier.

The assumption of Mary became dogma in 1950. (Bell, Mrs. Arthur. *Saints in Christian Art*. London: George Bell, 1901-4.)

John Calvin. (Munro, Dana Carleton and Merrick Whitcomb. *The Middle Ages and Modern Europe*. New York: D. Appleton and Company, 1912.)

November 2

John Calvin Flees Paris

When the Apostle Paul escaped Damascus by being lowered over the wall in a basket, it was not the last time a Christian evangelist would dramatically flee from persecution. On this day in 1533, John Calvin made a thrilling escape from Paris.

It is not that Calvin was the adventuresome kind. On the contrary, he was frail of health, serious and scholarly. He wanted most of all to be left to quietly pursue his studies. But that is not the way life would turn out for him.

As a young man and a devout Catholic, Calvin studied law at the universities of Orleans and Paris. He was a brilliant student, and with the Protestant Reformation in the air, he began reading Martin Luther. Calvin became a leader of the Reformation in France at the risk of arrest, imprisonment and even death. In 1532, he wrote that "only one . . . salvation is left open for our souls, and that is the mercy of God in Christ. We are saved by grace . . . not by our works." Calvin became the leader of the evangelical party in Paris, often encouraging his followers with the words of Paul: "If God is for us, who can be against us?" (Romans 8:31).

In 1533 the newly elected head of Paris University, Nicholas Cop, asked Calvin to help write his inauguration address. The speech called for reform of the Church by following the New Testament. Calvin attacked the doctrines that had grown out of Scholasticism by pointing out where they fell short in their teaching about faith, God's love or God's grace. "I beg you" he said, "not to tolerate any longer these heresies and abuses." The king and Church authorities were furious. With the police hot on their heels, Cop and Calvin had to flee for their lives.

Calvin lowered himself from a window on bedsheets that were tied together and escaped Paris dressed as a farmer with a hoe on his shoulder. For three years he wandered as a fugitive evangelist under assumed names. He finally settled in Geneva, where the Lord placed him as one of the pivotal leaders of the Reformation and one of its most influential theologians.

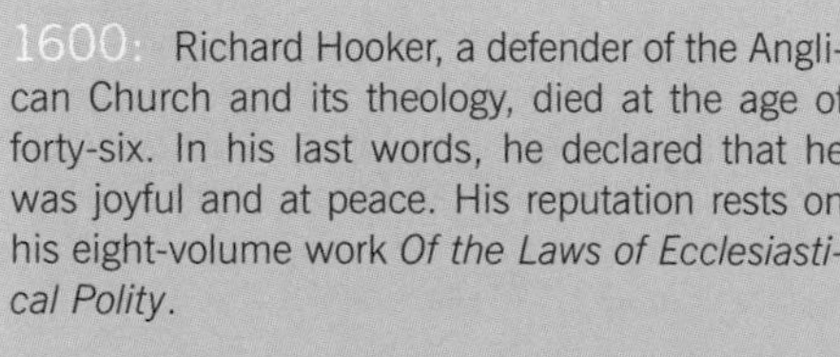

Other Events

1600: Richard Hooker, a defender of the Anglican Church and its theology, died at the age of forty-six. In his last words, he declared that he was joyful and at peace. His reputation rests on his eight-volume work *Of the Laws of Ecclesiastical Polity*.

1789: Revolutionary leaders in France confiscated clergy property.

1815: George Boole, the mathematician who invented Boolean algebra, was born. His mathematics had a direct influence on modern symbolic logic, but he also confessed Christ within the Anglican Communion.

1874: Methodist leader Phoebe Palmer died on this day. She was instrumental in founding Methodist foreign missions and promoting revival.

1917: Arthur Balfour, foreign secretary of England, declared his support for a Palestinian state for Jews.

1927: Poet T.S. Eliot became a British subject. He was confirmed in the Anglican Church this same year. Among his Christian poems is "The Journey of the Magi."

1942: Bud Robinson, a well-known, humorous Nazarene evangelist, died.

Phoebe Palmer, Methodist holiness revival leader, died this day. (Courtesy of the Christian History Institute archives.)

Thomas Coke Lands with Secret Orders

Thomas Coke was pleased. After a "very agreeable voyage" of almost seven weeks, he stood once again on firm soil. On this day in 1784, he landed in New York with secret orders from John Wesley that few Methodists, even in England, knew about.

Just two months earlier, Wesley had quietly ordained Coke as superintendent of the Methodist Church in the American colonies with power to ordain other superintendents in the New World. For several years Wesley had tried to persuade the Church of England to ordain Methodist bishops, but his requests met with rejection. Events in America forced Wesley's hand. The Anglican Church had virtually collapsed in Virginia after the Revolutionary War, and the Methodists, who received the sacraments from Church of England ministers, had nowhere to go. Searching Scripture and historical precedent, Wesley concluded that presbyters like himself had authority to ordain bishops. With the aid of Rev. James Creighton and two newly ordained elders, he did just that.

Within a few days, Thomas Coke sailed. Shortly after arriving in New York, he headed to Philadelphia. On November 14, he preached at Barrett's Chapel, a few miles from Dover, Delaware. After the sermon, a plain, robust man came up to the pulpit and kissed him. It was Francis Asbury, the man who had ridden across America for thirteen years, pouring his energy into the creation and supervision of the Methodist Church.

When Wesley ordained Coke, it was with the understanding that Coke would ordain Asbury to be a superintendent of the American Church. Coke confided his mission to Asbury and a few others, and they all agreed that this should be done in conference. They set a date in December to meet in Baltimore. Messengers rode out to advise all Methodist preachers. Meanwhile, Asbury encouraged Coke to make a 1,000-mile circuit on horseback so that he might learn firsthand the condition of the United States.

During that time, Coke baptized hundreds of converts who had never enjoyed the rite because no bishop had been available. He admired the Virginia countryside, which reminded him of his native Wales.

Sixty Methodist ministers showed up for the Baltimore conference. Asbury refused appointment as superintendent unless the Methodist pastors voted for him—he knew how Americans thought. Coke and he were elected as cobishops and shared power in America. Most of the work rested with Asbury, however, because Coke crossed and recrossed the Atlantic eighteen times in connection with missionary endeavors and became leader of the British Methodists after Wesley died.

Coke achieved the purpose for which he had come to the United States: to establish a legitimate authority to head the American Church. He was still working for Christ when he died years later, a smile on his lips, during a voyage to India, where he hoped to set up a mission.

Thomas Coke sailed to America with secret orders. (Daniels, W.H. *Illustrated History of Methodism in Great Britain and America, From the Days of the Wesleys to the Present Time*. New York: Phillips & Hunt, 1880.)

Other Events

753: Pirminius, the first abbot of Reichenau, Germany, who recorded early evidence for the present Apostles' Creed, died.

1534: The British parliament passed the Supremacy Act, putting the English throne at the head of the nation's Reform Church.

1783: Robert Raikes published a letter in the *Gloucester Journal* about his innovative Sunday schools. They were widely imitated and improved upon by others.

1857: Andrew Murray founded Stellenbosch Theological Seminary in South Africa.

1953: Archbishop Mecislovas Reinys of Vilnius, Lithuania, died in a Communist prison.

1960: Lutheran bishops prepared *The Christian in the DNR* to teach Lutherans how to live under Communism with obedience but without violating their consciences.

Robert Raikes, prime promoter of the Sunday school. (McFarland, John Thomas, et al. *The Encyclopedia of Sunday Schools and Religious Education: Giving a World-Wide View of the History and Progress of Sunday School and the Development of Religious Education*. New York: Thomas Nelson, 1915.)

November 4

Tozer Began His Long-Lasting Chicago Ministry

A.W. Tozer, pastor and influential writer. (Courtesy of The Christian and Missionary Alliance archives. Used by permission.)

A.W. Tozer tossed the letter into the trash. A church on the south side of Chicago wanted him as their pastor, but he was not interested. Nothing in his spirit said to leave Indianapolis, where he was a happy and successful pastor. He threw away more letters from Chicago, but the people wrote again. And again.

Finally, Tozer agreed to preach one Sunday for this persistent congregation. His topic was "God's Westminster Abbey," the faith chapter, Hebrews 11. After the service, people whispered to the church's leaders, "Don't let him get away!"

The leaders were of the same mind. Tozer was a man who had obviously spent time in God's presence. They asked him yet again to pastor them, but he replied, "I do not choose to run."

That evening, he preached on the resurrection of the dead. More than ever, the congregation wanted Tozer as their pastor. Despite his firm rejection, they continued to ask him.

Tozer visited them again. This time, he was a little more open to their advances. Finally, the persistence of Chicago's Southside Gospel Tabernacle paid off. Still uncertain about the move he was making, Tozer accepted their invitation. Elated church leaders announced his decision. On this day in 1928, A.W. Tozer became pastor of Chicago's Southside Gospel Tabernacle.

Born in rural Pennsylvania, with little formal education, Tozer nonetheless became a notable writer. His pithy sayings found their way with increasing frequency into denominational publications. Tozer remained at the South Chicago church for thirty-one years, becoming one of the best-known pastors of The Christian and Missionary Alliance.

The location of the church was ideal—Chicago was booming. Professors and students from the city's Christian colleges found that Tozer challenged not just the heart but also the mind. His ideal was to have a church in which the Spirit of God was noticeable when one merely stepped through the door. He seemed to have achieved his goal.

Tozer put more than prayer and study into his sermons: He kept a supply of balloons to blow up so that he could strengthen his lungs because his speaking voice was not strong.

Tozer preached on all of the major doctrines and through entire books of the Bible. For instance, he spent three years on the Gospel of John. Eventually, he was asked to give sermons on the radio.

He read great literature, and his own writing became as good as what he had read. During his life, he wrote nine books and compiled a tenth. After writing two biographies, he drafted *The Pursuit of God* one night on a train while his heart was bursting to overflowing with the need of men to find "personal heart religion." After his death, other books were gleaned from his editorials and taped sermons. In all, there are over fifty titles, teeming with profound Christian conviction and pithy truths, such as:

> Apart from God, nothing matters. We think that health matters, or knowledge, or art or civilization. And, but for one insistent word, they would matter indeed. That word is eternity.

Hymn writer Augustus Toplady. (Brown, Theron and Hezekiah Butterworth. *The Story of the Hymns and Tunes*. New York: American Tract Society, 1906.)

Other Events

1679: Quaker theologian Robert Barclay was caught in the last English arrest of Quakers. He was the earliest to produce a systematic defense of Quaker beliefs, *Apology for the Quakers*. Although respected by King James II, he was persecuted.

1740: Augustus M. Toplady was born on this day. A highly respected evangelical leader in the Church of England, Toplady wrote the hymn "Rock of Ages."

1794: Anglican, Presbyterian and Independent Church leaders gathered in London to discuss the mission aims of the London Missionary Society. However, the organization did not officially come into being until the following September.

1884: C.T. Studd, one of the Cambridge Seven, met Hudson Taylor, who accepted Studd for service in the China Inland Mission.

1958: Angelo Roncalli became Pope John XXIII. He convened the Second Vatican Council and changed the Church's attitudes toward non-Catholics.

Gunpowder Plot Discovered

5

Religion and politics were inseparable in Reformation-era England. When Pope Pius V excommunicated Queen Elizabeth in 1570, English Catholics did not like obeying a queen whom their pope had banned from the Church. Some even plotted to assassinate her. During Elizabeth's reign, her "secret service" uncovered three Catholic plots to remove her from the throne.

After her death in 1603, small groups of Catholics believed the "disease" of Protestantism in England called for a violent remedy. They made plans to blow up the English House of Lords on the day Parliament was to meet. Many of the country's leaders would be killed—King James I, his royal family, the House of Lords and many from the House of Commons. With all of those leaders dead, the plotters hoped to see England returned to Catholicism.

Working for more than a year, the conspirators in the British plot rented a vault under the House of Lords. They filled it with thirty-six barrels of gunpowder, which they hid under some firewood, and then waited to light the match when Parliament opened. Learning of the plot, the king's men searched the House of Lords on this day in 1605, capturing Guy Fawkes as he stood guard over the gunpowder.

After repeated tortures in the Tower of London, Fawkes revealed the whole plot and named his accomplices. Parliament then passed stricter laws against Catholics, who were then worse off than ever.

The country concluded that the discovery of Fawkes and his plot was God's providence protecting England. The British still ceremoniously search the cellars before opening each session of Parliament, and on Guy Fawkes Day, which is a national holiday, a dummy of Guy Fawkes is hanged in effigy. Thus, the British word *guy* has come to mean a stuffed dummy.

An old woodcut shows the powder plot conspirators. (Courtesy of the Christian History Institute archives.)

OTHER EVENTS

307: A Roman official named Urbanus, who was governing Palestine, handed out a number of cruel sentences to Christians. One Christian named Domninus was burned; others were made to fight as gladiators. A priest was fed to wild beasts. The bishop of Gaza and some of his companions were sentenced to hard labor in copper mines. Some boys were castrated, and three Christian girls were sent to work in brothels. Bishop Pamphilius was imprisoned.

1677: Solomon Stoddard, an influential Congregational minister in New England, allowed all men to partake of the Lord's Supper, even those who were not sure they were saved.

1758: Hans Egede, pioneer missionary to the Eskimos of Greenland, died.

1879: The Christian physicist James Clerk Maxwell, one of the major thinkers on whose mathematics and physics Einstein built his theory of relativity, died on this day. Maxwell's father had hesitated to allow his son to attend university in England lest he lapse from his Presbyterian faith, but it turned out that he need not have feared.

1882: University students mocked Dwight L. Moody in England. Later their ringleader apologized and became a bishop in China.

James Clerk Maxwell. (Hart, Ivor B. *Makers of Science: Mathematics, Physics, Astronomy*. London: Oxford University Press, 1923.)

Sickly Melville Cox sailed to Liberia. (Taylor, S. *Earl Price of Africa*. Cincinnati: The Jennings & Pye Co., 1902.)

6 Sickly Melville Cox Accepted Liberia's Challenge

For seven years, the money to send a missionary to Liberia lay unused because the mission committee could not find anyone willing to take the risk. That is, until Melville Cox stepped forward.

Deathly ill with tuberculosis, he could speak only with pain. In 1830 his wife, baby and several close family members had died within a short span, devastating him but releasing him from ties that might have held him back from the mission field. Now his heart burned with the desire to carry the gospel to people who had never before heard it.

"If you go to Africa, you'll die there," warned a student at Connecticut's Wesleyan University.

"If I die in Africa, you must come and write my epitaph," retorted Cox. He felt that it would be no loss to die far from home—as long as Christ were with him—but hoped that his death would spur forward the cause of mission work. Even his epitaph should reflect that spirit.

"What shall it be?" asked the student.

Cox's reply became a blazing torch to kindle Methodist enthusiasm for missions: "Let a thousand die before Africa be given up!" he exclaimed.

He sailed for Liberia aboard the *Jupiter* on this day in 1832—the first missionary sent to a foreign field by America's Methodists. While sailing, he made plans but recognized that their accomplishment was not up to him:

> In making up my mind and in searching for a passage to go out, I have followed the best light I could obtain. I now leave it all with God.

The following March, he thanked God that he had finally arrived in Liberia.

Cox immediately visited the area's few Christians, gathered them into an assembly, started a church and began writing *Sketches of West Africa*. He opened a school and taught seventy students. But, as had been predicted, his health could not hold up under the strain, and he contracted malaria. He could have returned home on the ship *Hilarity* after his first attack of the deadly tropical disease, but he chose to remain in Africa.

His last journal entry, written June 26, 1833, noted that it had been four days since he had seen a doctor. "This morning I feel as feeble as mortality can well. To God I commit all." In his weak state, he survived almost another month, dying on July 21, 1833, four-and-a-half months after his arrival in Liberia.

During one of his fevers, he had sung a spiritual: "I am happy! I am happy! . . . My days are immortal." Cox's triumphant spirit made his story a powerful tool for recruiting further missionaries.

John Carroll, the first Roman Catholic bishop in the United States. (Lossing, Benson J. *Eminent Americans*. New York: Hovendon Company, 1890.)

Other Events

1525: A Protestant disputation at Zurich, Switzerland, on Church reformation began this day and lasted through November 8.

1789: Pope Pius VI confirmed the election of the Rt. Rev. John Carroll as the first Roman Catholic bishop in the United States. He was appointed to the Diocese of Baltimore.

1857: François Coillard reached South Africa, where he became a notable evangelist and proved to be a profound teacher.

1879: Canada observed its first Thanksgiving Day on the first Thursday in November. Later, Parliament set it for the second Monday of October.

1949: Poland's Communists issued decrees of abolition, which stripped churches of their orphan asylums, spiritual retreats and some real estate.

1977: A dam across Toccoa Creek broke, damaging a Christian and Missionary Alliance college and killing forty individuals who were associated with the school.

Willobrord, Apostle to the Frisians

Willobrord wanted his life to count for more than it did. Twenty years old, he was the son of a prayerful man named Wilgils and a mother who had vowed to give Willobrord to Christian work. Gifted with intelligence, he studied hard at Ripon, where he sat at the feet of Wilfrid, the zealous bishop of York. But, according to Alcuin, the leading scholar of Charlemagne's court, Willobrord "felt an urge to pursue a more rigorous mode of life and was stirred with a desire to travel abroad." He heard of the holy lives of certain Irish saints and made up his mind to learn from them. He studied in Ireland for twelve years.

Then at the age of thirty-three, Willobrord felt the time had come for him to share the gospel with others. Alcuin wrote:

> He had heard that in the northern regions of the world the harvest was great but the laborers few. . . . So he embarked on a ship, taking with him eleven others who shared his enthusiasm for the faith. Some of these afterwards gained the martyr's crown through their constancy in preaching the Gospel, others were later to become bishops and, after their labors in the holy work of preaching, have since gone to their rest in peace.

Willobrord is called the "Apostle of the Frisians." They are no longer a distinct people because during the Middle Ages they were absorbed into the nations that are now Germany and Holland. But around AD 700, their numbers were great and they were widely distributed across Northern Europe.

Their king, Radbod, was no friend of the Church. In fact, he later attacked and destroyed much that the Christians had built. Nonetheless, Willobrord

> had the boldness to present himself at the court of Radbod. Wherever he traveled he proclaimed the Word of God without fear; but though the Frisian king received the man of God in a kind and humble spirit, his heart was hardened against the Word of Life. So when the man of God saw that his efforts were of no avail he turned his missionary course towards the fierce tribes of the Danes.

Willobrord's work was successful. Not only did he convert and train many Christians, but he also advised the Frankish kings, with whom he was closely associated. On one of his two trips to Rome, he was named bishop of Utrecht and was endowed with the pallium (a symbol of papal power). He also founded an abbey at Echternach in Luxemburg. He often retreated there when he found himself in need of spiritual refreshment.

It was at Echternach that Willobrord died; and according to tradition, his death was on this day in 739 (although Alcuin places it a day earlier).

> This holy man, who progressed every day of his life in the work of God, who was pleasing to God and friendly to all the people, was laid to his fathers in the time of the elder Charles, the valiant ruler of the Franks. He was then an old man coming to the end of his days and was about to receive from God a generous reward for his labors. He forsook this world to take possession of heaven and to behold Christ for ever in eternal glory, in whose love he had never ceased to labor as long as he lived in our midst.

Pope Sergius I, depicted here, consecrated Willobrord. (Montor, Chevalier Artaud de. *Lives and Times of the Popes*. New York: Catholic Publication Society of America, 1911.)

OTHER EVENTS

680: The sixth ecumenical Church council was held at Constantinople while St. Agatho was pope.

1837: A pro-slavery mob attacked and killed Rev. Elijah P. Lovejoy, who was attempting to defend his new printing press. This was his third press—the other two had been destroyed by mobs as well.

A mob burns the warehouse where Lovejoy's press was stored. (Tanner, Henry. *The Martyrdom of Lovejoy: An Account of the Life, Trials and Perils of Rev. Elijah P. Lovejoy*. Chicago: Fergus Printing Co., 1881.)

November 8

Patrick Arrives in Ireland

The purported grave of St. Patrick in Down, Ireland. (D'Alton, E.A. *History of Ireland from the Earliest Times to the Present Day*. London: Gresham Publishing, 1910.)

Although there is little concrete information available on the life of St. Patrick, he is still celebrated as an important figure in Christian history. But what do we know about Patrick?

He may have been born in the Christian town of Bonavern, near present-day Glasgow. No one knows for sure. Like almost every "fact" of his life, Patrick's birthplace is a matter of dispute. However, some of his writings are still in existence and provide us with a small glimpse into his life.

Although his mother taught him the Christian faith, Patrick preferred to pursue pleasure. One day while he was playing by the sea, Irish pirates captured him.

> I was sixteen years old and knew not the true God and was carried away captive; but in that strange land [Ireland] the Lord opened my unbelieving eyes, and although late I called my sins to mind, and was converted with my whole heart to the Lord my God, who regarded my low estate, had pity on my youth and ignorance, and consoled me as a father consoles his children. . . .
>
> Well, every day I used to look after sheep and I used to pray often during the day, the love of God and fear of him increased more and more in me and my faith began to grow and my spirit stirred up, so that in one day I would pray as many as a hundred times and nearly as many at night. Even when I was staying out in the woods or on the mountain, I used to rise before dawn for prayer, in snow and frost and rain, and I felt no ill effect and there was no slackness in me. As I now realize, it was because the Spirit was glowing in me.

Patrick escaped and returned to his family in Britain. But even as he rejoiced at being reunited with his loved ones, his heart increasingly longed to go back and share the gospel of Jesus Christ with his former captors. According to one tradition, Patrick and twenty-five companions landed at the mouth of a river to begin their ministry on this day in 432. However, there is no way to confirm this particular date, and many scholars would suggest that even the year is wrong.

After landing in Ireland, Patrick went to preach the gospel of Christ in the region where he had been a slave, speaking in the Irish language he had learned all those years ago. Many accepted Jesus as Redeemer, and soon heathen songs were replaced with hymns praising Jesus Christ as Lord. Patrick once wrote that God's grace had so blessed his efforts that thousands were "born again to God" through his ministry.

Killen, a Presbyterian historian of Ireland wrote:

> [T]here can be no reasonable doubt that Patrick preached the gospel . . . that he was a most zealous and efficient evangelist, and that he is . . . entitled to [be called] "the Apostle of Ireland."

Patrick ministered to the Irish for more than fifty years until he died around AD 493. It is claimed that he reached and baptized in excess of 100,000 people.

Other Events

1308: John Duns Scotus, a Scottish-born philosopher who tangled with the great thinkers of his day and advocated the doctrine of the Immaculate Conception of Mary, died on this day. He was called the "Subtle Doctor."

1674: English poet John Milton, who gave us one of the world's greatest epics, *Paradise Lost*, died on this day.

1845: English archaeologist Austen Henry Layard began digging at Tigris, where he would find the palace of Assurnsirpal II. He later excavated Nineveh, shedding light on disputed biblical accounts.

1920: The influential Dutch theologian Abraham Kuyper, who not only wrote orthodox Calvinist theology, emphasizing grace, but also was elected to his nation's parliament and even served as prime minister of the Netherlands, died.

John Duns Scotus, the "Subtle Doctor." (Endres, Jos Ant. *Die Zeit de Hochscholastik: Thomas von Aquin*. Mainz: Kircheim & Co., 1910.)

Praying Hyde, Intercessor Extraordinaire

"Give me Souls, O God, or I die!" That became the plea of John Hyde, who was born on this day in 1865 in Carrollton, Illinois. Hyde's family were a praying people. Consequently, as a young man, he learned to pray and to expect results.

Hyde's brother Edmund went as a student missionary to Montana, where he contracted a fever and died. Hyde wondered if he should take his brother's place as a missionary. During his senior year at McCormick Theological Seminary, he came to the room of his friend Mr. Konkle near midnight, saying he wanted to hear all of Konkle's arguments in favor of going to the foreign mission field. Konkle said:

> I told him that he knew as much about the foreign field as I did; that I didn't believe it was argument that he needed, and that I thought the way for him to settle it was to lay it before our Father and stay until He decided for him: We sat in silence a while longer, and, saying he believed I was right, he rose and bade me good night.

The next morning Konkle felt a hand on his arm. Looking around, he saw Hyde's face radiant with a new vision. "It's settled, Konkle," he said.

Hyde left for India. Aboard ship, he opened a letter from a friend who wrote that he would pray until Hyde was filled with the Holy Spirit. Angrily Hyde crumpled the letter and hurled it aside. He had yielded his heart to the Lord, gotten his degree, studied Indian languages and was obediently on his way to a life work. How dare his friend suggest he lacked the Spirit? But when he cooled down, Hyde realized that his friend was right. He then pleaded for the power of the Holy Spirit.

The result was that Hyde became a notable intercessor, often paying for his concern with sleepless nights as he brought a multitude of pleas and petitions before the Lord. As a result, he was nicknamed "Praying Hyde."

Revival began when he came late to a meeting:

> I have been having a great controversy with God. I feel that he has wanted me to come here and testify to you concerning some things that he has done for me, and I have been arguing with him that I should not do this. Only this evening . . . have I got peace concerning the matter and have I agreed to obey him, and now I have come to tell you just some things that he has done for me.

Dürer's famous *Hands of an Apostle*, better known as *Praying Hands*. (Courtesy of the Christian History Institute archives.)

He then told those at the meeting how God had freed him from certain sins. Soon his listeners were weeping and confessing their own transgressions.

In 1908, anguished by the sight of sin and souls doomed to hell, Hyde asked the Lord to bring a soul a day into the kingdom of God. Soon he upped that to two souls, and then four. God answered his prayers.

In March of 1911, Hyde had to say goodbye to India. His heart had shifted in his chest and required medical attention. In the United States it was found that he had a malignant brain tumor. Surgery was necessary. On February 17, 1912, he died. His last words were "Shout the victory of Jesus Christ!"

Other Events

1522: Martin Chemnitz, sometimes called the "Second Martin" for the role his writings placed in preserving Lutheran theology, was born. He also coauthored the *Formula of Concord*, which united Lutheran factions.

1541: Calvin's ordinances were placed for vote before the Council of Geneva, where they were accepted. The ordinances completely directed the civil and religious affairs of Geneva.

1620: The *Mayflower*, with its Pilgrim passengers, sighted land and dropped anchor off the coast of the New World.

1729: Quaker evangelist Samuel Neale was born. He was strongly influenced by the female evangelist Mary Peisley, whom he married in 1757. Neale went on to preach in Holland, Germany and America.

1731: Benjamin Banneker, mathematician and surveyor, was born on this day. An African-American Christian, he used biblical arguments to make the case for black emancipation.

1799: Asa Mahan, who became a Congregational clergyman and the first president of Oberlin College, was born on this day.

Asa Mahan, president of Oberlin College. (Fairchild, John. *Oberlin: The Colony and the College, 1833-1883*. Oberlin, OH: E.J. Goodrich, 1883.)

"Dr. Livingstone, I presume?" (Courtesy of the Christian History Institute archives.)

November 10

"Dr. Livingstone, I Presume?"

For years, no one had heard from the Scottish missionary-explorer David Livingstone. In 1866, he had disappeared into the East African interior, searching for the source of the Nile River. Livingstone's reports of his earlier explorations in Africa had fascinated multitudes of readers at home. Once asked why he decided to be a missionary, Livingstone replied, "I was compelled by the love of Christ." Carefully documented biographies have shown, however, that he was usually more concerned to be the first to get somewhere or to accomplish a feat he could boast about.

His *Missionary Travels and Researches in South Africa*, published in 1857, told of his walks totaling more than 20,000 miles back and forth across the African continent. Those explorations helped later missions by providing valuable information about the people and geography of Africa's interior. Unfortunately, it also resulted in the deaths of some who trusted it and found it inaccurate.

Livingstone also awakened the world to the horror of the Arab slave trade, which he called a "monster of iniquity brooding over Africa." By publicizing the evil of slavery, Livingstone worked effectively to see it abolished. For every 20,000 slaves captured and exported, he estimated that 100,000 Africans would be killed, wounded or die of disease. He wrote, "The many skeletons we have seen along the paths of the wilderness attest the awful sacrifice of human life that must be attributed to this trade in hell."

In 1871, concerned that for five years no one had heard from Livingstone, the *New York Herald* sent journalist Henry Stanley to find him. Landing in Zanzibar, Stanley traced Livingstone's steps into the interior. At last, after many narrow escapes, on this day in 1871, Stanley saw a white man by the shores of Lake Tanganyika. Knowing this could be only one person, Stanley greeted the man with his now-famous comment: "Dr. Livingstone, I presume?"

Unable to persuade Livingstone to leave Africa, Stanley returned to England. Greatly impressed with Livingstone's Christianity, Stanley wrote, "It is not of the theoretical kind, but it is a constant, earnest, sincere practice . . . and it is always at work."

Celestine IV. (Montor, Chevalier Artaud de. *Lives and Times of the Popes*. New York: Catholic Publication Society of America, 1911.)

Other Events

461: Pope Leo I, considered the founder of the medieval papacy, died. He used his position and diplomatic skills to negotiate peace with invaders of Italy and led efforts to rebuild Rome when it was laid in ruins by Vandals.

1241: Pope Celestine IV died on this day. The old man was a compromise candidate chosen by just seven cardinals. He died only seventeen days after his election. Since Emperor Henry was holding several cardinals in prison and the rest did not want to go back into a long, drawn-out conclave, it was over a year before the next pope was elected. Sources disagree on the date of Celestine's death.

1793: The French National Assembly abolished Christianity and decreed the worship of the "Goddess Reason."

1886: The first temperance movement in Japan was organized at Yokohama in the Kaigan Church.

1910: The Gideons placed the first of their many Bibles in a hotel.

Compact for the Glory of God

There are more than 160 independent nations in the world. Whether led by a dictatorship or a democracy, most have a written constitution. That of the United States is the oldest. We may take the Constitution for granted, but it marked a turning point in the way nations govern themselves.

How do you suppose that the founding fathers came up with the idea of a written constitution? The idea of a written contract between the people and their government came from a tiny band of fifty Christians called Pilgrims who sailed to America on the *Mayflower* in 1620. The Pilgrims believed that many of the Church of England's traditions were not biblical. Since the state persecuted Church critics as criminals, the Pilgrims became Separatists and fled first to Holland and then to the New World.

On September 6, 1620, leaving behind a sister ship, the *Speedwell*, the *Mayflower* sailed from Plymouth for the New World. Aboard were 101 passengers, some of them unfriendly to the Pilgrim cause. By today's standards, the ship was little bigger than a yacht. Ninety feet long and twenty-six feet wide, it hardly seemed the vessel to alter world history.

The Pilgrims planned to land in Virginia, where they had a charter from King James to govern them, but storms on the Atlantic carried them far north to Cape Cod. Since their charter was not valid in that region, they needed a new government. Some of their party felt that it was wrong for them to settle anywhere but the place the king had designated. It was to keep that dissatisfied element in line that a new legal agreement was needed.

And so on this day in 1620, the Pilgrims drew up and signed the Mayflower Compact:

> In the name of God, Amen! We whose names are underwritten, the loyal subjects of our dread sovereign Lord, King James, by the grace of God, of Great Britain, France and Ireland, King, Defender of the Faith, etc., have undertaken for the glory of God and the advancement of the Christian faith, and honor of our King and Country, a voyage to plant the first colony in the northern parts of Virginia; do by these presents, solemnly and mutually, in the presence of God and of one another covenant and combine ourselves together into a civil body politic for our better ordering and preservation, and furthermore of the ends aforesaid; and by virtue hereof to enact, constitute and frame just and equal laws, ordinances, acts, constitution, and offices from time to time, as shall be thought most mete and convenient for the general good of the colony; unto which we promise all due submission and obedience. In witness whereof we have hereunto subscribed our names, at Cape Cod, the 11th of November.

The compact was modeled on a Church covenant that the Pilgrims had drafted and signed in 1607 when they separated from the English Church and fled to Holland. It not only made them a completely religious entity but broke political ground too in that it placed them under their own governance, although they still paid formal respect to the king of England. The compact probably staved off a mutiny, for tensions were high. For the next fifty years, the Mayflower Compact served the Pilgrims well and became an important precedent for a written American constitution at the convention of 1787.

The *Mayflower* sights land and anchors. (Courtesy of the Christian History Institute archives.)

Other Events

397: Martin of Tours, founder of France's first monastery near Poiters, died. He was notable for his kindness and miracles.

1215: The Fourth Lateran Council was convoked. It promulgated the doctrine of transubstantiation, which said that the bread and the wine of the mass becomes the literal body and blood of Christ.

1921: English theologian and educator Peter Taylor Forsyth died. He wrote *The Person and Place of Jesus Christ*, stressing man's need for atonement and Christ's voluntary provision of it. Nothing would budge Forsyth from the centrality of Christ.

1951: Jesuit Bishop Tsiang Beda of Shanghai died in a Communist prison. He had refused to head the Chinese "Reform" Church.

Martin of Tours, known for his kindness and miracles, divides his cloak with a beggar. (Jameson, Mrs. *Sacred and Legendary Art*, vol 2. London: Longmans, Green, and Co., 1870.)

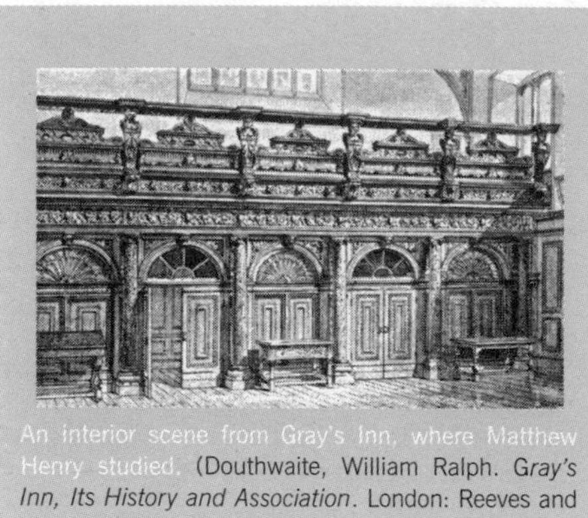

An interior scene from Gray's Inn, where Matthew Henry studied. (Douthwaite, William Ralph. *Gray's Inn, Its History and Association*. London: Reeves and Turner, 1886.)

November 12

The Beginning of an Overwhelming Project

Just because you don't seem to be on the road to accomplishing something big by the time you turn forty does not mean that you won't. Matthew Henry was forty-two on this day in 1704 when he began his famous commentary on the Scriptures. His father Philip's life had looked even less fruitful—but that just proves how deceitful appearances can be.

Philip Henry loved the Bible and made it the centerpiece of family devotions. The nonconformist minister explained a daily passage to his children, following a set of principles for interpretation. Young Henry listened and learned from his father. He had read the Bible himself by age three, and he made his public profession of faith at age nine. His diary showed that as a young teen, he was already filled with piety and recognized the mercies of God. And yet it was his father's training that "made" him and his commentary.

After attending the academy of a noted Puritan teacher, Phil Doolittle of Islington, Henry went to London to study law at Gray's Inn. He was just twenty-two, but his father's influence was working in him. While he was still in law school, he began to preach on the side. While visiting Chester on business, he preached in private homes. Some of the men who listened liked what they heard and asked Henry to become their minister. Henry agreed. The next year he was ordained by six ministers and began his work as a Presbyterian clergyman in Chester. He would spend twenty-four years there before moving on to London.

In 1702, when he was thirty-nine, Henry began to write. That year he prepared a catechism and a book of family hymns. Two years later, remembering the Bible study method that his father had taught him, he began his commentary on the Bible. He must have worked at an incredible pace. On June 22, 1714, just ten years later, he was dead.

Colleagues and friends put his notes into final form and published the work that we know as *Matthew Henry's Commentary*. It has never been out of print since its first publication. Part of the explanation for this is that Henry's commentary was devotional rather than critical. It was aimed at inspiring listeners and teaching them practical living.

Take as an example his commentary on Isaiah 53:1, which says, "Who hath believed our report? And to whom is the arm of the Lord revealed?" (KJV). Matthew Henry saw this as fulfilled in Christ and wrote:

> Of the many that hear the report of the gospel, there are few, very few, that believe it. . . . To this day, of the many that profess to believe the report, there are few that cordially embrace it and submit to the power of it. Therefore people believe not the report of the gospel because the arm of the Lord is not revealed to them . . . the arm of the Lord was made bare in the miracles that were wrought to confirm Christ's doctrine, in the wonderful success of it, and its energy upon the conscience. Though it is a still voice, it is a strong one; but they do not perceive this, nor do they experience in themselves that working of the Spirit which makes the word effectual.

Henry, by fulfilling the labors of his father, showed through his life that God builds on what we do in ways we cannot predict. It proves that we don't have to have done our greatest work before middle age to leave a lasting mark for good on the world.

Canute scolds flatterers. (Craik, George L., Charles MacFarlane, et al. *The Pictorial History of England: Being a History of the People, as Well as a History of the Kingdom*. New York: Harper & Brothers, 1846-8.)

Other Events

1035: Canute the Great of Denmark died. The ruthless king restored churches and monasteries in his kingdom and built several new ones.

1660: John Bunyan was arrested for unlicensed preaching and sentenced to prison. While incarcerated, he penned *Pilgrim's Progress* and *Grace Abounding to the Chief of Sinners*, Puritan classics of the highest worth.

1815: Christian King Pomare II won a great victory over pagan rebels, finally bringing peace to Tahiti. During the battle, Christians shielded pagan allies with their own bodies so that none would be killed before they could convert to Christianity.

1818: Ray Palmer was born. He is principally remembered as the author of the hymn "My Faith Looks Up to Thee, Thou Lamb of Calvary."

1836: Charles Simeon, a famous Anglican evangelical clergyman, died.

November 13

Synod of Dort

James (Jacob) Arminius was uneasy with some of the teachings that had come to be identified with Calvinism. Did God really choose some men to be damned before He created them? Was Christ's death only intended for those who would finally be saved? Does God exercise His sovereignty so fully that man has no choice in his own salvation? Does regeneration come first and then repentance?

As the professor of theology at Leyden, Arminius had promised to teach only those things that conformed to the confessions of faith of the state Church of the Netherlands, which were Calvinist. In his public teaching, Arminius kept his word, but he laid out Scripture readings in such a way as to cast doubt on Calvin's theology (which was heavily indebted to Augustine of Hippo).

In private, Arminius offered a different interpretation of Scripture to interested students. While not varying from a single doctrine of the early Church creeds and accepting much that Calvin taught, Arminius modified the theology to say that man, through ordinary grace, can respond to the gospel and has real choice in his ultimate destiny. Strict Calvinists, such as Dr. Franciscus Gomarus, objected strongly. However, a number of pastors of state Churches adopted Arminian views. Arminius himself downplayed differences for the sake of peace and because of his promises, although he tried to amend the Heidelberg Catechism and a Dutch confession.

After his death, his followers issued a document called a "remonstrance." In it they set out five points in which they differed from Calvin. Inevitably the issue got mixed up with complex politics. The Remonstrants (as Arminians were called) were on the side of those who wanted decentralized government or "states' rights." The Calvinists were on the same side as Maurice, prince of Orange, who was attempting to reduce "states' rights" and create a stronger central government.

The central government called a synod to weigh the issues. On this day in 1618, the Synod of Dort convened. It was controlled by Calvinists who invited other Calvinists from neighboring countries to participate. The assembly existed for one purpose only. to condemn the Remonstrants. The Remonstrants considered this unfair.

And the proceedings were biased. The Calvinists met alone until December 6. Meanwhile, Remonstrants around the country were thrown out of their pulpits. Those Remonstrants who were summoned to the assembly found their movements restricted. They were not allowed to have their strongest speakers represent them. Many other injustices occurred as well.

Franciscus Gomarus, leading opponent of Arminianism. (Young, Alexander. *History of the Netherlands (Holland and Belgium)*. Boston: Estes and Lauriat, 1884.)

Needless to say, with matters so stacked against the Remonstrants, their cause was condemned. One of their supporters, the statesman John Oldenbarneveld, was invited to a meeting with Maurice, where he was arrested. Falsely charged with treason, Oldenbarneveld was beheaded. Another supporter, Hugo Grotius (who became the father of international law), was sentenced to life in prison but managed to escape.

Arminian ideas are found among Wesleyans, Methodists, Nazarenes, Free Will Baptists and in similar traditions, while variations of Calvinism can be detected in the theologies of Reformed, Presbyterian, Calvinist Methodist and some Baptist groups.

Other Events

867: Pope Nicholas I the Great died. A capable administrator, he strengthened the Church in the era after the death of Charlemagne when the Holy Roman Empire broke into warring factions. He deposed Photius in the struggles at Constantinople, aggravating resentment between the Eastern and Western Churches and was a strong advocate for Roman primacy in the Church.

1564: Pope Pius IV ordered all holders of ecclesiastical office to agree to the Council of Trent's Tridentine Profession of Faith as the new, final definition of the Catholic faith.

1644: Massachusetts banished Baptists.

1907: Francis Thompson, the English poet, died. He wrote the "Hound of Heaven" on his deathbed, showing God's grace as a hound pursuing him. After training for the priesthood, Thompson wrecked his life with opium addiction. He said:

> Power is the reward of sadness. It was after Christ had wept over Jerusalem that he uttered some of his most august words; it was when his soul had been sorrowful even unto death that his enemies fell prostrate before his voice. Who suffers, conquers.

1938: Francis Xavier Cabrini, founder of the Missionary Sisters of the Sacred Heart, was the first US citizen to be named a saint by the Roman Catholic Church.

Francis Thompson, who wrote the famous poem "Hound of Heaven." Sketch by Everard Meynell. (Meynell, Everard. *The Life of Francis Thompson*. New York: C. Scribner's Sons, 1916.)

14 Russia's Fighting Saint Alexander

Alexander Nevsky prays before battle. (Howe, Sonia E. *Some Russian Heroes, Saints, and Sinners: Legendary and Historical*. Philadelphia: J.B. Lippincott, 1917.)

Metropolitan Cyril, leader of the Russian Orthodox Church, was serving the Divine Liturgy in the city of Vladimir on this day in 1263. Suddenly he saw a picture in his mind that caused him to vary from the traditional ceremony. According to Russian tradition, he said, "Brethren, know that the sun of the Russian Land has now set." He had just witnessed Alexander Nevsky's soul being carried into heaven.

Nevsky, exhausted as he returned from a laborious trip east to visit his overlord, the great khan of the Mongols, had rested at a monastery in Gorodetz. There he died on this day in 1263, dressed in a monk's clothes.

Gottfried Wilhelm Leibniz, coinventor of calculus. (Leibniz, Gottfried Wilhelm. *Sämtliche Schriften und Briefe: Hrsg. Von der Preussischen Akademie der Wissenschaften*. Darmstadt: O. Reichl, 1923.)

He was only forty-three years old, but in that short life he had become one of the greatest Christian and military leaders that Russia ever produced. Even the atheistic Soviet regime honored him.

Born into a princely family in northeastern Russia, Nevsky was thrust as a teenager into difficult leadership roles. He had to try to hold together many quarrelsome and independent rulers. That he was able to do so most of the time was due to his personal charm and deep spirituality. His devout parents had raised him in the Orthodox faith, teaching him to honor God. As a boy, he spent much time reading the Bible.

The name Nevsky was given to him for a youthful exploit. The Catholic Swedes invaded Orthodox Russia, with whom they had military and religious disputes. Nevsky foresaw the invasion and planted sentries at strategic spots. Warned by these agents when the invasion came, he did not dither, but marched his troops rapidly to the Neva River, where the Swedes were disembarking. To get there, he had to overcome the marshes that spread out between the two armies. But Nevsky was inspired to heroics because he feared that defeat at the hands of Sweden would mean the end of Russian Orthodoxy, which he saw as the soul of his nation. On paper, his army did not stand a chance, for the Mongol invasions had weakened Russia. Yet Nevsky told his men, "God is not on the side of force, but of the just case, the truth."

The Swedes were so confident of victory that they were in no hurry to unload their troops. Their commander lolled in a golden tent. Marching through mist, twenty-year-old Nevsky caught them by surprise, and the Swedes were routed. He was given the name "Nevsky" because of that battle at the Neva River.

The young hero went on to defeat Europe's Teutonic Knights in the famous "Battle on the Ice." He also overcame the Lithuanians. However, he saw that he could not beat the Mongols. He consulted with Metropolitan Cyril to learn God's will. The religious leader advised Nevsky to yield in everything except faith. Nevsky submitted. Since the Mongols required conquered rulers to bow before the Mongol idols and perform pagan rites, Nevsky prepared to die. In their camp, he boldly proclaimed his Christianity and swore he would bow to no handmade image. Impressed by his military exploits and personal boldness, Khan Batu waived the required obeisance.

Nevsky survived three trips to the distant Mongol court. He often had to appease the fierce Asian rulers because of the hot-headed actions of his followers. After Nevsky's early death, the Russians quickly recognized him as a saint.

Other Events

565: Roman Emperor Justinian, who reunited the Eastern and Western empires politically and religiously, erected several basilicas and created an influential law code, died.

1716: The Lutheran philosopher Gottfried Wilhelm Leibniz, who coinvented calculus but also turned down lucrative positions that would have required him to change faiths, died. All the same, he worked hard to reunite Protestants and Catholics.

1890: C.I. Scofield founded the Central American Mission.

Baptism Comes to Ramabai's Widows

In the 1800s, women in India ranked low in society. Some Hindu authorities declared they were lower than pigs. Widows ranked even lower. They might be burned alive on their husbands' funeral pyres or enslaved. Many were sent to temples as prostitutes to make money for the priests. The woman who did more than anyone to change that was Pandita Ramabai.

Ramabai was blessed in her parents. Her father, Anant Dongre, a wealthy Hindu guru, believed women had minds. He fled with his wife to the Gungamul forest of southern India, built a hut and taught her Sanskrit. Under the forest leaves, Ramabai was born in 1858. When she was eight, her mother began teaching her Sanskrit. The girl applied herself diligently. By the time she was twenty, she could recite 18,000 verses of the *Puranas*, a Hindu holy book. She learned several languages: Marathi, Bengali, Hindustani, Kanarese and English.

Although regarded as wise and holy, Dongre had no peace. He led his family on pilgrimages and spent all his money trying to win favor with the gods. Famine came and his health failed.

Dongre died and was followed to the grave by Ramabai's mother and sister. Ramabai and a brother wandered 4,000 miles more, hoping to find favor with the gods. In their quest for truth they suffered cold, hunger and thirst. The promises of their faith proved to be unreliable. Finally, the two gave up their search for salvation and settled in Calcutta.

Ramabai's immense knowledge impressed Calcutta's Hindu scholars. They called her "Pandita," which means "learned." She was the first woman ever awarded this title. Leaders asked her to lecture their wives on the duties of high-born Hindu women. Studying Hindu scriptures that had been denied to her, Ramabai found that the books disagreed on almost everything—except that women are worse than demons. She could not believe this, because her father had taught her otherwise.

In Calcutta, Ramabai first heard about Christ. She discovered that salvation is a free gift from God, not a reward earned by pilgrimages and payments. But Ramabai thought that if she became a Christian she would have to adopt European customs, so she instead joined a cult that combined Christian and Hindu ideas. She left the cult only after a missionary explained that Christianity allows great freedom and that she could eat and dress in the Hindu tradition. Meanwhile, her brother died. Ramabai married, but her husband died of cholera. She was left with a baby daughter, whom she named Manoramabai, "heart's joy."

She pioneered an organization to reform the treatment of women, but felt that God was nudging her to go to England. Although she had no money, she set out. Once there, Church of England sisters took her in, taught her about Christ and had her baptized.

Pandita Ramabai (in white) with some of the widows she aided. (Dennis, James S. *Christian Missions and Social Progress*. New York: Fleming H. Revell Co., 1897-1906.)

Ramabai returned to India and opened a small school. When students converted to Christianity, Hindus complained that Ramabai was betraying her own culture. Ramabai embraced Christianity even more tightly. She created a refuge called *Mukti*, which means "salvation" in many Indian languages. Many women came to her—girl brides so abused they were terrified of a touch, older women who snarled like animals as a result of years of cruelty. She taught them to tend orchards and carry out other tasks that would support them. Many became Christians and evangelists. This day in 1897 was a day of triumph, when a number of widows who had converted under Pandita Ramabai's ministry were baptized by a local missionary at Khedgaon, India.

Other Events

1280: Dominican philospher Albertus Magnus, teacher of St. Thomas Aquinas, died on this day. Known as "Dr. Universalis" for his great learning, Magnus wrote many books, especially on the sciences.

1630: Johann Kepler, discoverer of the laws of planetary motion, died. His arguments for the unity of religion and science were printed with Galileo's work.

1794: John Witherspoon, a Scottish-born pastor-educator who signed the Declaration of Independence, died on this day.

1838: At a city meeting, a committee in Oxford, England, determined to erect a Gothic Cross in memory of the martyrs Thomas Cranmer, Nicholas Ridley and Hugh Latimer.

1885: Mwanga, ruler of Buganda (now part of Uganda), beheaded Anglican convert Joseph Mukasa, a member of the Bugandan royal family.

1917: Oswald Chambers died while serving as a chaplain to British troops in Egypt during World War I. His widow, Gertrude, compiled his notes into books, including the popular *My Utmost for His Highest*.

Albert the Great was known as the "universal doctor" for his great learning. (Endres, Jos Ant. *Die Zeit de Hochscholastik: Thomas von Aquin*. Mainz: Kircheim & Co., 1910.)

November

16

A Key Victory, a Terrible Loss

Gustavus Adolphus on a horse surveys the battlefield of Lutzen where he was shortly to perish himself. (Ruoff, Henry W. *Masters of Achievement: The World's Greatest Leaders in Literature, Art, Religion, Philosophy, Science, Politics and Industry*. Buffalo, NY: The Frontier Press Company, 1910.)

The Battle of Lutzen, one of the most crucial in the Thirty Years' War, was fought on this day in 1632. The horror of the Thirty Years' War in the seventeenth century can hardly be imagined. Out of a German population of 16 million people, only 4 million survived. Before the war, the town of Augsburg had 80,000 people; only 18,000 were left at the war's end. Thirty thousand villages were destroyed. Peaceful peasants were hunted down for sport. Crime was rampant.

The war started in Bohemia. Emperor Ferdinand II, a staunch Roman Catholic, strongly opposed all Protestants. He forbade them to hold meetings, abolished their civil privileges, tore down their churches and schools and publicly hanged them in every village.

A Protestant revolt in Prague soon spread across the Austrian empire. Help came to the Protestants from King Gustavus Adolphus of Sweden. A devout Lutheran, Gustavus believed that God had called him to win religious and political liberty for Europe. As king, he brought Sweden prosperity, new schools, hospitals, libraries and just laws. But Gustavus's greatest strength came from his humility and love of God and men. He was one of the first to take to heart Hugo Grotius's appeals for humane treatment of enemies in war.

King Gustavus landed on German soil in 1630 and at once went into battle with the Catholic Austrian army. He won victories in Pomerania, Saxony, the Rhine and Bavaria. Victory also came at Lutzen on November 16, 1632, but Gustavus was surrounded by enemy soldiers. Before taking his life, they demanded his name. Gustavus is supposed to have replied, "I am the King of Sweden! And this day I seal with my blood the liberties and religion of the German nation."

Other Events

1200: St. Hugh of Avalon died. He was a noble-minded bishop of Lincoln who was beloved by the people because of his kindness to them and his fearless rebuke of wicked authorities. His tomb became a pilgrim shrine.

1845: Protestant hymn writer Frederick Faber announced that he was leaving the Church of England for the Church of Rome. As a Catholic, he founded the Order of the Brothers of God.

1855: Scottish missionary-explorer David Livingstone first saw Victoria Falls, which he named. He once remarked, "God had an only Son, and he was a missionary and physician."

1997: The International Day of Prayer for the Suffering Church began.

Hugh of Lincoln, also known as Hugh of Avalon. (Baring-Gould, S. *Lives of the Saints*. Edinburgh: John Grant, 1914.)

The Real First Christmas?

When was Jesus born in Bethlehem? The Bible tells us with certainty the fact of Jesus's birth and the place, but not the date. Although many Christians celebrate Christ's birthday on December 25, it has not always been so. In fact, one of the early Church fathers, Clement of Alexandria, speculated that Christ was born on this day in 3 *BC*.

In the early Church there was no celebration of Jesus's birth. Each Sunday was a celebration of Christ's resurrection. The Jewish festivals of Passover and Pentecost continued to be celebrated by Jewish converts in the Church for a time since they were closely associated with Christ's death and resurrection. In the third century, some churches in the East began to celebrate January 6 as the Epiphany, the time that Christ revealed himself to the people as the Messiah. Jesus's incarnation—when God became man—was also commemorated at this time. Many speculated that since shepherds were in the field the night Christ was born, it must have been in spring or summer. Some said May 20; others fixed the date on April 19 or 20. Still others thought March 25 most likely. No one really knew then, and no one really knows now.

In 354, the bishop of Rome started to observe December 25 as the date of Christ's birth. Four major Roman festivals were held in December, including Saturnalia, which celebrated the returning sun god. It was easy to adapt this to the Christian celebration of the coming of the Son of God.

As Christianity expanded in Europe, Jesus's birth continued to be celebrated on December 25, and as each nationality converted to Christianity, its own customs were added to the celebration. But if Clement of Alexandria were still alive today, he probably would be wishing us a "Merry Christmas" on this November day.

> For the sake of each of us he laid down his life—worth no less than the universe. He demands of us in return our lives for the sake of each other.
>
> —Clement

Manger scene. (Bell, Mrs. Arthur. *Saints in Christian Art*. London: George Bell, 1901-04.)

Other Events

270: Gregory Thaumaturgus, the "Wonder Worker," a well-loved bishop in Pontus and author of the first Christian biography (on Origen), died on this day. It was said that when he came to NeoCesarea (now in modern Turkey), there were only seventeen Christians. When he died, there were only seventeen non-Christians.

594: Gregory of Tours, historian of the Franks and bishop, died.

1417: The election of Martin V ended the Papal Schism when European nations agreed to support him as pope. Two other claimants to the papacy stepped down or were pushed aside when Martin was elected.

1668: Thirty-four-year-old Joseph Alleine, an English Puritan who burned himself out preaching, died on this day. He wrote *Alleine's Alarm*.

1898: Presbyterians, Methodists and Baptists met in New York to plan the evangelization of the Philippines, which had been opened by the US victory over Spain.

1949: Bishops told the Czech clergy to prepare to renounce their state stipends rather than play Judas by doing the state's will.

1961: Charles H. Mason, founder of the Church of God in Christ, died.

Martin V ended the Papal Schism. (Montor, Chevalier Artaud de. *Lives and Times of the Popes*. New York: Catholic Publication Society of America, 1911.)

NOVEMBER 18

Most Influential Woman in Seventh-Century England

Hild of Whitby kneels. (Courtesy of the Christian History Institute archives.)

Hild was a noblewoman closely related to the kings of Northumbria. Not much is known about her early years beyond the fact that she was baptized at the age of thirteen on April 11, 627. It was part of a mass baptism, which was common to the Middle Ages. Up to that time, King Edwin and the court of Northumbria had been pagans. Following the king's conversion, Paulinus baptized the king and most of his court, including the girl Hild. Hild became a nun twenty years later at the age of thirty-three and spent a year in France with a sister who also had donned the religious habit.

St. Aiden, an apostle to Northumbria, urged Hild to return to her native land, and he put her in charge of a small community of men and women at Hartlepool. She ruled it with such vigor and common sense that she was awarded with a more important double monastery. This was at Streanaeshalch (which the Danes renamed Whitby 200 years later; hence she is known as Hild of Whitby).

Anglo-Saxon historian Bede wrote:

> [S]he obliged those who were under her direction to attend so much to reading of the Holy Scriptures, and to exercise themselves so much in works of justice, that many might be there found fit for ecclesiastical duties and to serve at the altar.
>
> In short, we afterwards saw five bishops taken out of that monastery, and all of them men of singular merit and sanctity, whose names were Bosa, Hedda, Oftfor, John, and Wilfrid.

Hild became renowned for her wise advice. Kings and commoners alike called on her. In fact, she was the most influential woman of her era in Britain. Little wonder, then, that king Oswiu asked her to make arrangements for the most significant council in English history.

The king ruled a divided Church. Some of his subjects wanted to follow the Roman rite, others the old Celtic forms in which they had grown up. Wilfred was the champion of the Roman cause. On the Celtic side stood Bishop Finan and many others. King Oswiu decided to call a synod to decide whether his nation would follow the Roman or the Celtic tradition. He left all of the arrangements in the hands of the capable abbess, Hild.

Hild herself preferred the Celtic forms and argued for them with Bishop Colman at the synod. But Oswiu decided in favor of Wilfred and the Roman Church. A loyal team player, Hild accepted the decision and probably encouraged others to do the same.

Enthusiastic about learning, Hild encouraged the poet Caedmon to sing his religious compositions, which retold the Bible stories in the Anglo-Saxon tongue. He is considered the first vernacular English poet.

After her death on November 17, 680, Hild was recognized as a saint. Her feast is marked on this day in the *American Book of Common Prayer*.

OTHER EVENTS

1210: Pope Innocent III, most powerful of the medieval popes, excommunicated Emperor Otto IV because the emperor displeased the pope with claims of sovereignty in Italy.

1302: Pope Boniface VIII published *Unam Sanctam*, declaring there is "One Holy Catholic and Apostolic Church" outside of which there is "neither salvation nor remission of sins." Emphasizing the pope's position as supreme head of the Church, it demanded that civil powers subjugate themselves to the spiritual. Boniface claimed the title "Vicar of Christ," but died a few weeks later. *Unam Sanctam* roused considerable opposition and brought the Church into temporary decline. Today its teaching has been interpreted almost out of existence.

1626: Pope Urban VIII consecrated St. Peter's Basilica in Rome, which became Christianity's largest church.

1874: The Women's Christian Temperance Union was founded in Cleveland. Prior to the founding of the union, Protestant women across the nation, claiming the power of the Holy Spirit, marched into saloons and demanded they close. Because of the only temporary success of this approach, the women decided to unite as a nationally organized union.

1899: The St. Petersburg Student Christian Movement was founded. Originally intended to work with the foreign population, it soon led to revival in the city as a whole.

Boniface VIII satirized. (Barry, William. *Story of the Nations: Papal Monarchy*. Whitefish, MT: Kessinger Publishing, 1911.)

NOVEMBER 19

She Entered a Castle Finer Than Any of Her Five

To look at her, you would not have guessed that Elizabeth was the daughter of a king and the wife of a prince. In place of gold-cloth dresses, she wore a plain gray robe. Rather than be waited on by scores of servants, she washed lepers with her own hands. Instead of pastries, she ate bread with a little honey. She worked wool like any peasant girl. A Magyar knight who saw her sitting by her cottage, exclaimed in amazement, "Whoever has seen a king's daughter spinning before?"

Elizabeth von Thuringia was born in 1207 in the royal castle of Pozsony (Bratislava, Slovakia). Her mother, Gertrude, was a committed Christian who imparted her faith to her daughter. At the age of four Elizabeth was sent to Wartburg Castle to live with her prospective in-laws to be raised according to their customs. Gertrude was assassinated when Elizabeth was seven. The grieving daughter knelt in the Wartburg chapel, praying for the murderers.

Shortly afterward, Elizabeth's fiancé died. Her in-laws wanted to send her away, complaining she was too holy. However, Ludwig, brother of her deceased fiancé, said he would like to marry Elizabeth. So when Elizabeth was just fourteen, they were wed in a ceremony held in St. George's Church in Eisenach. Elizabeth had brought great wealth to the marriage and now possessed more. She was called "Elizabeth of Many Castles" because she had the choice of five to live in. But wealth did not impress her.

St. Francis of Assisi was calling people to repent, cast aside the chains of wealth and show kindness to the poor. Moved by his message, Elizabeth opened eastern Europe's first orphanage and tended lepers. She even laid a leper in Ludwig's bed. Her angry mother-in-law said to Ludwig, "Come, my son, you shall see one of the wonders your Elizabeth works that I cannot prevent. . . ." But when she flung back the covers, Ludwig claimed it was Jesus he saw lying on the bed.

In 1226, famine raged in Thuringia. The desperate people were forced to eat the bark of trees in order to survive. With Ludwig away, Elizabeth emptied his reserves to feed the hungry. She set up soup kitchens, threw churches open to the homeless and distributed firewood to the weak. Accused by her enemies of bankrupting the treasury, Elizabeth told Ludwig, "I gave God what was His and God has kept for us what was yours and mine."

Ludwig went on crusade, leaving his lands in charge of his brother, Henry. When Elizabeth heard that Ludwig had died, she cried, "The world is dead to me and all that was pleasant in the world."

According to most accounts, Henry threw Elizabeth out of the castle and cut off her allowance. Separated from her children, she walked to Eisenach on a midwinter evening. Despite her misery, she sang and prayed. Reflecting that Jesus too had been an outcast, Elizabeth asked Him to be with her. Jesus showed Himself to her in a vision and said, "If you desire to be with me, I desire to be with you."

Eventually Elizabeth's rights were restored. She tried living in one of her castles but Henry's ill-will was so great that she finally built a simple cottage near Marburg to separate herself from his influence. There she became a lay Franciscan—the first in the German empire. She built a hospital, attended the sick and spun wool. For extra income, she fished.

She died of exhaustion on November 17, 1231. At cock-crow of her last day, she said, "It is now the time when [Christ] rose from the grave and broke the doors of hell, and He will release me." The blind, the lame, demonics and lepers came to her funeral. Four years later, the Church declared her a saint. Convinced that Elizabeth had entered a castle far grander than any she had owned while alive on earth, 200,000 people gathered for the occasion,. For centuries her feast was celebrated on this day.

Elizabeth von Thuringia of Hungary dressed simply. She was a favorite subject of artists for a long time. (Jameson, Mrs. *Legends of the Monastic Orders*. London. Longmans, Green, and Co., 1872.)

Other Events

461: Pope St. Hilary was consecrated. An energetic leader, he consolidated the Church in outlying provinces and built the St. John Lateran Basilica.

1672: Richard Baxter, considered the greatest preacher of his day, preached illegally in his own home after a ten-year silence. "I preached as never sure to preach again, and as a dying man to dying men," he said.

Richard Baxter, preacher and pamphleteer. (Baxter, Richard. *The Autobiography of Richard Baxter*. New York: E.P. Dutton, 1925.)

NOVEMBER

20

Arundel Boards the *Swift* and Changes History

Skulls on a slave trail demonstrate the horror of the trade. (Lambert, John C. *The Romance of Missionary Heroism*. London: Seeley, 1907.)

On this day in 1759, the royal navy ship *Arundel* spotted unidentified sails. Captain Charles Middleton cleared the deck and ran out his guns. But rather than fight, the unidentified ship hove to and allowed herself to be boarded. She was the *Swift* of Bristol. Soon Middleton asked his surgeon, James Ramsay, to go aboard. Ramsay would never forget the horrors he experienced.

A foul stench greeted his nostrils. The *Swift* was a slaver. African men and women were packed like sardines in its hold. Ramsay could barely force himself to climb below, where naked slaves wallowed in blood, feces and vomit, gasping for air. Plague had broken out. Ramsay did what he could to ease their suffering while he inwardly vowed that he would do something to end the dreadful practice of slavery.

But what could he, a lowly surgeon, do? As he reboarded the *Arundel*, he slipped and broke his thigh. When his leg healed, he was so lame that he realized that he could no longer serve on a ship. Every step he took on the rolling deck endangered his life.

Unknown to Ramsay, friends back in England had arranged a lucrative partnership for him. He turned it down because he had in mind to fulfill a childhood dream and become a minister. After study and ordination, he sailed as a pastor to St. Kitts in the West Indies.

His congregation appreciated Ramsay's medical skills but soon were on the outs with him because he opened the church to slaves and prayed for their conversion. As a result of his "offenses," Ramsay endured twenty years of threats and humiliations. He was denounced in his own church. Enemies said that he was unfit to preach to Caucasians; they should send him to Africans. He replied that the souls of the poorest Africans were priceless and he would gladly preach to them. Worn down at last, he admitted defeat and retreated to England.

In his homeland, Ramsay found no personal peace. The shocking sights of the slave trade remained with him. He told friends he'd seen slaves whose hands were chopped off with axes when they were unfortunate enough to tangle them in the gears of sugar presses. Others were burned to death by angry masters. His friends pleaded with him to document these facts. Ramsay hesitated, knowing that the planters would stop at nothing to close his mouth. In the end, however, he agreed to do it. Dipping his quill in ink, he produced *An Essay on the Treatment and Conversion of Slaves in the British Sugar Colonies*. Considered the opening salvo in the British campaign to abolish slavery, it was a best-seller from the moment of its publication.

As Ramsay expected, slave owners attacked him in press and Parliament. He had to defend himself against false charge after false charge. When he published *An Address to the Publick, on the Proposed Bill for the Abolition of the Slave Trade*, a new attack was made on his character in the House of Commons. Ramsay could bear the pressure no longer; he sickened and died. An enemy gloated, "Ramsay is dead—I have killed him."

OTHER EVENTS

869: King Edmund was martyred by the Danes when he refused to submit to them because he believed it was not right for a Christian ruler to submit to a pagan. The Danes tied him to a tree and shot his extremities full of arrows.

1542: At the urging of Bartolomé de Las Casas, Spain passed laws to protect American Indians from rapacious colonists.

1850: Francis "Fanny" Crosby experienced a dramatic conversion that "planted a star in her heart" that no cloud ever eclipsed.

1870: Amanda Smith, feeling dull, saw a vision saying, "Go preach." She did so and became a well-known, worldwide black evangelist.

King Edmund, who was martyred by Danes. (Baring-Gould, S. *Lives of the Saints*. Edinburgh: John Grant, 1914.)

From English to Xhosa

You may have heard complaints about the low skills of some teachers in US classrooms. Tiyo Soga's skills were far lower than that when he began to teach South African children.

Years before, a Scottish missionary named James Stewart founded a mission station called Lovedale, which was dedicated to teaching Africans practical skills. Lovedale offered a competitive exam. Whichever *kafir* (*kafir* is from an Arabic word meaning "infidel") proved best qualified was admitted free of charge. Soga's teacher, Rev. Chalmers, decided to enter the young man in the competition.

When given a simple subtraction problem, Soga stared in dismay at the figures on the chalkboard. The examiner felt sympathy for the young man. "Take away the lower line from the upper," he suggested. Soga brightened. This he understood! He wetted his thumb and erased the bottom line.

William Chalmers was a wise man who saw below the surface. Convinced that Soga was above average in moral and spiritual qualities, he spoke to the head of Lovedale and convinced him to admit Soga despite his dismal performance.

Soga vindicated Chalmers' trust. By hard, steady application, he rose to second in each of his classes—except arithmetic. He was able to recite half of the Shorter Catechism in English, proofs and all, without a single mistake. In due time, he studied in Scotland, where his spiritual life and academics were far above expectation.

Back in Africa, Soga labored to the point of breaking his health, teaching, preaching and raising money for church buildings. He spent days on the trail, walking from *kraal* (village) to *kraal* with the gospel, confronting the godless chiefs. Under the strain of work and poor living conditions, he contracted tuberculosis. Despite failing health, he took on new tasks for the sake of the souls of his people. For love of his people, he even left a station that he himself had built at great cost so that he could move further inland.

All that time, he worked on a translation of *Pilgrim's Progress* into Xhosa, adapting the story to fit his people's daily experiences. He believed that the book, with its vivid imagery, would do more to win souls than any other he could prepare. On this day in 1866, he completed it. *Pilgrim's Progress* had the impact he hoped, and it remains a treasure of the South African Church.

Soga also aided in the revision of the Kafir Bible. At his death from tuberculosis in 1871, its four Gospels were complete. He died at only forty-two, having spent his life recklessly for Christ. His life proved that early failure can be a stepping stone to final success.

Tiyo Soga's shaky educational start did not deter him from becoming a great African missionary. (Cousins, H.T. *From Kaffir Kraal to Pulpit: The Story of Tiyo Soga*. London: S.W. Partridge, 1899.)

Other Events

496: Pope Gelasius, who established the Roman Catholic canon of Scripture, regulated the mass and clashed with Emperor Anastasius of Constantinople by claiming authority over him, died on this day.

1638: A general assembly at Glasgow, Scotland, abolished the Episcopal form of Church government and put the Presbyterian form in its place.

1706: The American clergyman John Williams, having been redeemed from Indian captivity, arrived back in Boston with fifty-seven other captives, including two of his children. He resumed his pastorate and wrote the book *The Redeemed Captive Returning to Zion*.

1852: Union Institute was chartered by the Methodists in North Carolina. Later it was renamed Trinity College, and in 1924 it became Duke University.

Indians restore captives. (Avery, Elroy McKendree. *History of the United States and Its People: From Their Earliest Records to the Present Time*. Cleveland, OH: The Burrows Brothers Company, 1904.)

John Donne, who has been declared the greatest of the metaphysical poets. (Gosse, Edmund. *The Life and Letters of John Donne*. New York: Dodd, Mead and Company, 1899.)

November 22

Leading Metaphysical Poet Becomes Dean

"Death be not proud, though some have called thee mighty and dreadful," wrote John Donne in one of the many memorable lines that he gave us. He wrote such things in the days of his gray hair. In the recklessness of youth he had lived and written in a different strain.

After frittering his small patrimony, gaining a reputation as a man about town and a poet of naughty lines, he sailed in the company of many another bold gallant with Lord Essex on the Cadiz expedition. The expedition did not go well, and Donne returned home no richer than when he had sailed. Lacking money, he eloped with his employer's niece. Perhaps he had hoped for an allowance. Instead, he was dismissed into poverty. All doors to advancement closed before him. Forced onto the charity of friends and to such hackwork as his pen could find, he summed up his sorry state of affairs in a famous epigram: "John Donne—Anne Donne—Undone."

Donne contemplated suicide, but when King James I assumed the English throne, Donne's hope returned. He sought preferment. The king agreed—and offered Donne a position in the Church. Donne resisted. He had been reared Catholic. His brother had even died as a consequence of persecution, and Donne was unsure of his own motives and convictions. Because of Donne's hesitation, James gave the place to another man.

After several years, Donne made a serious study of theology and accepted the reformed doctrine. James subsequently employed Donne as his private chaplain. Two years later, on this day in 1621, Donne became dean of St. Paul's. From that pulpit, his immense wit and intelligence touched the highest level of society. The church was crowded to overflowing when he spoke. Of the depth of his spiritual conviction no one who has examined his religious poetry and the moving "Hymn to God the Father," with its pun on his own name, can doubt:

I have a sin of fear, that when I've spun
My last thread, I shall perish on the
 shore;
But swear by Thyself that at my death
 Thy Son
Shall shine as He shines now and here
 tofore:
And having done that, Thou hast done;
 I fear no more.

Donne loved his wife, Anne, deeply and was left permanently saddened when she died in her thirties. He was convinced that he had caused her death by dragging her from a life of ease to poverty. Gloom entered his work, and he became increasingly morbid. At the end, he was so obsessed with death that he even had his portrait painted in shroud. His lines of poetry that were written against death were probably mere bravado.

If all men are diminished by the death of others, so were others diminished by the death of Donne. It was he who wrote the eloquent line "[N]ever send to know for whom the bell tolls. It tolls for thee." With lines like that to his credit, posterity declares him the greatest of the metaphysical poets.

Symmachus as imagined by an artist. (Montor, Chevalier Artaud de. *Lives and Times of the Popes*. New York: Catholic Publication Society of America, 1911.)

Other Events

498: St. Symmachus was elected pope. His election was disputed by the antipope Laurentius and had to be upheld by emperor Theodoric, involving the state in the decision of who would be pontiff.

1786: Cyrus Kingsbury was born in New Hampshire. He became a Presbyterian missionary, working with several American Indian tribes, especially the Choctaw nation in Oklahoma.

1840: Daniel Webster Whittle was born in Chicopee Falls, Massachusetts. Whittle lost his right arm fighting for the Union in the Battle of Vicksburg and was captured. While in prison, he read the New Testament and was converted to Christianity. After the war he became an evangelist and hymn writer. Among his best-known hymns (written under a pseudonym) are "Showers of Blessing" and "I Know Whom I Have Believed."

1873: Horatio Spafford's four daughters died in a shipping accident. He penned the hymn "It Is Well with My Soul" as he sailed to meet his wife, who had survived the collision.

1950: Paul William Fleming and several other mssionaries died in a plane crash in the Rocky Mountains. They were touring the United States on behalf of New Tribes Mission, which Fleming had cofounded.

November 23

Clement Executed Under Emperor Domitian

Imagine being tied to an anchor and cast into the sea! According to legend, that was the fate that befell Clement of Rome under Emperor Domitian. The legend may well be wrong, because Domitian died in 96 and Church historian Eusebius of Caesarea tells us Clement was martyred on this day in 101.

Clement was only the fourth bishop of Rome, the first possibly being Peter. Did he know Peter and Paul? It is completely possible that those two Spirit-filled men taught Clement. Clement even wrote a letter to the Corinthian Church that echoed the teachings of the apostles. We know next to nothing about the two bishops who came between Peter and Clement. But Clement's letter made him stand tall among the early leaders of the Roman Church.

The Roman Church claims that Clement's letter proves that the popes (although they weren't called by that name for many centuries to come) were already seen as the heads of the whole Christian Church. Protestant and Orthodox scholars disagree, saying it was natural for Corinth to turn to one of the largest and most prestigious churches of the day for advice and arbitration.

However that may be, the sixty-five short chapters of Clement's letter to Corinth were even considered Scripture by some Christians up until the fifth century. Corinth was still having the same kinds of trouble with sexual immorality and infighting that Paul had dealt with in letters written years before. Clement's letter was written because a number of Corinthians had banded together against their church leaders and thrown them out of office. Clement reproved this behavior and suggested a better way:

> God wanted all his beloved ones to have the opportunity to repent and he confirmed this desire by his own almighty will. That is why we should obey his sovereign and glorious will and prayerfully entreat his mercy and kindness. We should be suppliant before him and turn to his compassion, rejecting empty works and quarreling and jealousy which only lead to death.

Clement may have written a sermon that bears his name, and he was said to have gathered together a large collection of Church law called the *Apostolic Constitutions*. Scholars aren't able to verify either claim.

We don't know why Domitian executed Clement. Many of the early bishops of Rome suffered death at the hands of the secular authorities, however, so it is a good guess that Clement stood up for truth in the corrupt capitol of the empire and paid for it with his life.

Apostles Peter and Paul. It is likely that Clement knew both. (Baring-Gould, S. *Lives of the Saints*. Edinburgh: John Grant, 1914.)

Other Events

615: The Irish scholar and missionary Columbanus died in Bobbio, Italy, which was then but a monastery that he had founded. He founded or inspired many monasteries in Europe, where faith had burned low.

1654: Blaise Pascal, a brilliant French mathematician, writer and inventor, was converted when his horses bolted and almost rushed with him off of a bridge. Afterward, he wrote his famous apologetic *Pensees*.

1872: John Bowering, who wrote the hymn "In the Cross of Christ I Glory," died on this day.

1899: Robert Lowry died in Plainfield, New Jersey. The Baptist minister wanted to be known as a great preacher, but it is as a hymn writer that he is remembered today. He wrote the words and music for "Shall We Gather at the River?" "Christ Arose" and "Nothing but the Blood of Jesus." In addition to those popular hymns, he wrote music for several others that are loved by the Church. Three of the best-known are "All the Way My Savior Leads Me," "We're Marching to Zion" and "I Need Thee Every Hour."

1906: William Wrede, a Lutheran New Testament scholar, died. He had taught at major German universities where he applied historical criticism to the New Testament. In his view, the Gospels were the theology of the primitive Church rather than a true biography of Jesus. He thought that the Apostle Paul was the real founder of first-century Christianity.

Robert Lowry. (Ninde, Edward S. *The Story of the American Hymn*. New York: Abingdon, 1921.)

November

24 The House Light Is Extinguished

Oecolampadius, the "house light." (Courtesy of the Christian History Institute archives.)

Today most Protestant churches, at least in the Western world, take for granted that those who attend a church should have some say in how it is run. That hasn't always been so. Even when the Protestant Reformation began in the sixteenth century, Martin Luther and other reformers thought that the Church ought to be directed by the clergy.

One of the first moderns to suggest otherwise was the little-known reformer called Oecolampadius. (His real name was Hussgen, but in those days it was popular to change one's name into Latin. "Hussgen" sounds like the German for "house-shine," so he became "house light" in Latin.) Oecolampadius's suggestion that laymen be allowed a say in Church affairs was shot down when he proposed it to the town council of Basle, Switzerland. However, other reformers, such as John Calvin and John Knox, agreed with him, and so an important element of religious freedom was brought into the Church.

Oecolampadius was a top-notch student of languages. He studied with both Reuchlin and Erasmus, the ground-breaking linguists of the day. He even helped Erasmus edit and publish the same New Testament in Greek that had such a profound influence on the rise of the Reformation.

One way a scholar could earn a little extra money in those days was to translate Greek books for the recently invented printing press. Oecolampadius translated writings of the Greek fathers.

After the Reformation got rolling, he sided with the reformers. Despite weak health, he labored hard for reform in Switzerland.

In 1516, a year before Luther posted his famous theses, Ulrich Zwingli spearheaded a reformation movement in Zurich. He was still a Roman Catholic but insisted on teaching through the Bible. Around 1523, Oecolampadius began a friendship with Zwingli and drifted away from the more conservative Erasmus.

His relationship with Zwingli is often compared to the relationship of Melanchthon with Luther. A peaceful man, Oecolampadius was tolerant of differences in the Protestant beliefs about the Lord's Supper. He also rebuked harsher reformers for their abrasive behavior. He wrote to William Farel, "Your mission is to evangelize, not to curse. Prove yourself to be an evangelist, not a tyrannical legislator. Men want to be led, not driven." Reformation should be orderly, said Oecolampadius.

He worked so hard in spite of his bad health that when he died on this day in 1531, he was only forty-nine. A little-known light of the Reformation was extinguished.

Other Events

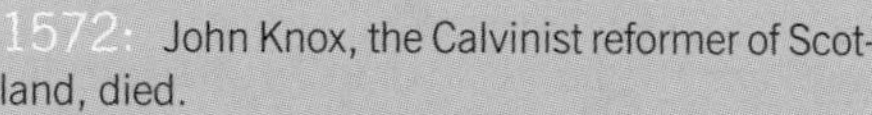

1572: John Knox, the Calvinist reformer of Scotland, died.

1703: At a service held in Philadelphia, Justus Falckner became the first Lutheran pastor ordained in the American colonies.

1838: François Blanchet and Modeste Demer arrived at Vancouver. Their mission was to spread the Catholic faith among the Indians and white settlers of the Oregon Territory, an area of almost 400,000 square miles. It extended from northern California to Alaska and from the Rocky Mountains to the Pacific Ocean. The zeal with which they undertook their duties earned them lasting fame.

1860: Irish clergyman George Croly died. He is remembered as the author of the hymn "Spirit of God, Descend Upon My Heart" but was also a literary figure of some standing. He wrote a biography of King George IV, novels, satires, poems, a play, sermons and theological works. He contributed to many magazines of the day and sometimes employed his pen on behalf of the Tory party, whom he hoped would reward him with a church. This did not happen until he was fifty-five years old, but the church, St. Stephen's in Walbrook, was not considered a prize because it was in a poorer district of London.

1865: Arthur Samuel Peake was born in Leek, England. He was a Methodist Bible commentator and taught at various English colleges and universities. He became the first Rylands professor of biblical criticism and exegesis at Manchester University. His best-known work was a one-volume commentary on the Bible published in 1919, which, in revised form, is still used.

The Falckner coat of arms. Justus Falckner was the first Lutheran pastor to be ordained in the colonies. (Sachse, Julius Friedrich. *Justus Falckner, Mystic and Scholar*. Philadelphia: Printed for the Author, 1903.)

November 25

Arabian Christians Massacred

In the sixth century, the nation of Abyssinia (modern-day Ethiopia) dominated the kingdoms of Himyar and Yemen, located on the southern Arabian peninsula. There were flourishing Christian churches in those areas that looked to Christian Abyssinia for protection.

Yusuf As'ar, a Himyarite Jew better known by nicknames referring to his braids or ponytail—Dhu Nuwas, Dzu Nuwas, Dounaas, or Masruq—seized the throne from his king and revolted against Abyssinia. He sought to expel the Abyssinians from his country. He captured an Abyssinian garrison at Zafar and burned the church there. He burned churches in other areas as well.

The strongest Christian presence was located in the northern Yemen city called Najran (sometimes spelled Nagran or Nadjran). Recognizing this fact, Dhu Nuwas attacked the city. The Christians held the area with desperate valor, and Dhu Nuwas found he could not capture it. So he resorted to treachery, swearing that he would grant the Christians of Najran full amnesty if they would surrender. The Christians, knowing they could not hold out forever, yielded, going against the advice of their leader Arethas (Aretas or Harith).

What happened next was so appalling that some found it hard to believe. In an effort to verify the story, Bishop Simeon of Beth Arsham (a Syrian) traveled to the site, and interviewed eyewitnesses and wrote a report. In it he wrote:

> The Jews amassed all the martyrs' bones and brought them into the church where they heaped them up. They then brought in the priests, deacons, subdeacons, readers, and sons and daughters of the covenant . . . they filled the church from wall to wall, some 2,000 persons according to the men who came from Najran; then they piled wood all round the outside of the church and set light to it, thus burning the church with everyone inside it.

In the ensuing week, hundreds more Christians were martyred, among them many godly women who were killed by the most horrible tortures when they refused to renounce Christ. Some were told, "Deny Christ and the cross and become Jewish like us; then you shall live."

Sources differ as to the date, but one says that it was on this day in 523 that Dhu Nuwas took his vengeance on Arethas and 340 Christian followers, killing them. These men were quickly included in martyr lists in the Greek, Latin and Russian Churches. A song was even written about them by one Johannes Psaltes, although it reports only about 200 deaths.

Other accounts written within a century of the event add that deep pits were dug, filled

An Arabian scene. (Hilprecht, H.V. *Explorations in Bible Lands During the 19th Century*. Philadelphia: A.J. Holman, 1903.)

with combustible material, and set afire. Christians who refused to change faiths were hurled into the flame. Thousands died in this painful martyrdom. Some think that this is the event that the Koran refers to when it says, "Cursed be the diggers of the trench, who lighted the consuming fire and sat around it to watch the faithful being put to the torture!" Muslim commentators deny this.

When word of the atrocities reached Constantinople, the Roman emperor encouraged the Abyssinian king Ellesbaas (Ella Atsbeha or Kaleb) to intervene, as did the patriarch of Alexandra. Ellesbaas was only too willing to do so, since his garrisons had been massacred and his fellow Christians killed. He destroyed Dhu Nuwas and established a Christian kingdom. An Ethiopian-Jewish writing known as the *Kebra Nagast* regarded the downfall of Dhu Nuwas to be the final catastrophe for the kingdom of Judah.

Other Events

311: Peter of Alexandria was beheaded. A man of immense Bible knowledge, he resisted some of Origen's ideas and excommunicated Bishop Miletus as a schismatic. Peter advocated lenient treatment of *lapsi*, Christians who caved in to threats during persecution. He was killed for his stand against the heretical Arian teaching.

1527: The Anabaptist Leonhard Schiemer was arrested in Rattenberg, Austria, and executed early the next year. While on death row, he wrote a letter to his congregation on three kinds of grace: Christ the Light, the cross that we must take up and the oil of the Holy Spirit.

1748: Isaac Watts, who began a movement in the Anglican Church away from chants and psalms to modern hymns, died on this day.

1766: Clement XIII issued a bull against publishing anything out of line with Catholic teaching.

1854: English compiler John Kitto, who set a new, high standard for Bible encyclopedias, died. A fall had left him deaf at age twelve.

1899: Robert Lowry died on this day. He was an American Baptist clergyman who wrote many beloved hymn tunes, including the music to "All the Way My Savior Leads Me," "I Need Thee Every Hour," "Nothing but the Blood of Jesus" and "Marching to Zion."

Clement XIII. (Montor, Chevalier Artaud de. *Lives and Times of the Popes*. New York: Catholic Publication Society of America, 1911.)

John Jewel preached an historic sermon. (Courtesy of the Christian History Institute archives.)

November

26

John Jewel Preached His Historic Sermon

When John Jewel stepped onto the platform of St. Paul's Cross on this day in 1559, he did not know that the sermon he was about to preach would be pointed to by historians as having helped establish the theology of the Church of England.

Jewel was a graduate of Oxford University and became a public orator for the school. Impressed by Peter Martyr's teaching, he joined the reformers. When Catholic Queen Mary came to the throne, his position required him to compose a congratulatory letter to her, which he did. However, his Reformation principles were not firmly fixed yet. After helping Thomas Cranmer and Nicholas Ridley with their defenses, he buckled and signed Catholic articles. Despite this, he was under suspicion and stripped of his position

He fled to the Continent. There he apologized publicly for signing the confession that he did not believe in. Mary died in 1559 and Jewel returned to England. He urged Queen Elizabeth I to adopt a Low Church position (that is, to take a more Puritan and evangelical approach to the Church's services, rather than to keep the Roman Catholic look and feel). She did not. Jewel accommodated his views to the new monarch. The queen appointed him to St. Paul's Cross, where, on this day, he challenged anyone to prove the Roman Church's position from the Bible and the writings of early Church fathers.

He repeated the challenge again the following year. Various Catholics took it up. To defend his position, Jewel wrote (in Latin) *An Apology in Defense of the Church of England*.

This *Apology* was "the first methodical statement of the position of the Church of England against the Church of Rome, and forms the groundwork of all subsequent controversy." In the reign of King James I, Archbishop Bancroft endorsed Jewel's theology and ordered copies placed in all Anglican churches.

Chafing under the charge of heresy, Jewel said he would prove his case from Scripture, arguing:

> But seeing [the Roman Church] can produce nothing out of the Scriptures against us, it is very injurious and cruel to call us Hereticks, who have not revolted from Christ, nor from the Apostles, nor from the Prophets.

John died in 1571 at just forty-nine years old. A man of personal piety, he was also kind to the poor. One of the boys whom he helped was Richard Hooker, who wrote about Jewel with admiration and who also became a notable apologist for the Church of England.

Sojourner Truth, charismatic abolitionist and suffragist. (Courtesy of the University of Texas collection of public domain portraits on the Web.)

Other Events

Annual: The feast of John Berchmans, who died of a violent fever in 1618, is celebrated. He was notable for holiness at a young age. He declared, "If I do not become a saint when I am young, I shall never become one." He was right about that, because he died at just twenty-two years of age.

1646: The Westminster Confession was finished and would be presented to the English parliament on December 4.

1883: Evangelist and abolitionist Sojourner Truth died in Battle Creek, Michigan. Born a slave, Truth experienced visions and voices, which she attributed to God, but she was also involved in a cult group. She was one of the most charismatic abolitionists and suffragists of her day.

1892: Cardinal Charles Lavigerie, a Catholic missionary to Muslims and archbishop of Carthage and Algiers, died. He was a staunch opponent of the slave trade.

1901: American scholar Joseph Henry Thayer, best remembered for his Greek-English Lexicon of the New Testament, died on this day.

November 27

"God Wills It!" Shouted the People

In 1095, Pope Urban II summoned a council to meet at Clermont, France. The Church had fallen on hard times following the lifelong clash between Pope Hildebrand and Emperor Henry IV. Urban II was a vigorous leader and was trying to set things right. At the council, he promoted the concept of a "Truce of God," which would restrain violence at home; and he called for the First Crusade.

On this day in 1095, a great crowd of laymen and clergy gathered in an open field to hear the pope speak. Exactly what he said we do not know. We have five accounts, but each is different from the others. Yet we can follow the gist of the speech.

Urban recounted the sad plight of the Middle East, which at that time was controlled by Muslims. Its churches had been converted to mosques and stables. The streets where Jesus walked were trampled by heathen feet. Christians were persecuted and tortured, and their women were raped. The power of formerly Christian kingdoms had been broken; they could no longer defend the holy places or Christians. Pilgrimages had become virtually impossible.

> To whom therefore has the labor of avenging these wrongs and of recovering the territory fallen, if not upon you? You, upon whom above other nations God has conferred remarkable glory in arms, great courage, bodily activity, and strength to humble the hairy scalp of those who resist you.

The Franks should put aside their squabbles and direct their energies to this task for the sake of Christendom, said Urban. Quoting Scriptures, he admonished his listeners that anyone who held back for love of family was not worthy of Christ, whereas anyone who forsook this world's goods to crusade in the Holy Land would inherit eternal life. He promised remission of sins to anyone who would undertake the expedition to "liberate" the East.

> [A]dvance boldly, as knights of Christ, and rush as quickly as you can to the defense of the Eastern Church. For she it is from whom the joys of your whole salvation have come forth, who poured into your mouths the milk of divine wisdom, who set before you the holy teachings of the gospel.

Moved by the pope's appeal, the crowd shouted with one voice, "It is the will of God! It is the will of God!" Urban said "yes," it *was* the will of God. God had proven it by uniting them in their cry. Since God Himself had placed this cry in their hearts, they were to use it as their battle cry. He also instructed them to embroider the sign of the cross on their clothes. The pope followed up his speech with a letter to the crusaders, confirming what he had said and recapping his promise of remission of sins.

Urban II preached the First Crusade. (Montor, Chevalier Artaud de. *Lives and Times of the Popes*. New York: Catholic Publication Society of America, 1911.)

Other Events

399: St. Anastasius I was elected pope. He condemned the heresies of Donatus and Origen. Charitable and orthodox, he was remembered as a holy man.

1826: Jedidiah Smith entered California's San Bernardino Valley. The hardy explorer, who chalked up a number of firsts, was known for his Christian commitment. He went west to earn the funds to support his aging parents.

1945: After five years of separation from his flock in Borneo by World War II, Earnest Presswood returned to find the church strong. Converts called him "Tuan Change" (Sir Change) because of the miraculous transformations that took place in the lives of those who were converted under his preaching.

1947: E.L. Sukenik of the Hebrew University of Jerusalem saw four pieces of Dead Sea Scroll. He was the first Westerner to recognize their value.

1970: Pope Paul VI was attacked in the Philippines by a dagger-wielding Bolivian disguised as a priest. The pope suffered a wound in the chest.

Jedidiah Smith, mountain man and Christian. (Courtesy of the Christian History Institute archives.)

John of the Cross. (Colvill, Helen Hester. *St. Theresa of Spain*. New York: Dutton, 1909.)

November 28

A Hovel as a Step to Heaven

Christian mystics seek communion with God through their spirits. One of the most famous of all mystics was a sixteenth-century Spaniard, St. John of the Cross. Like many others before and after him, he wrote his finest works while in prison.

Things were not easy for John's family. His father came from well-to-do stock, but because he married Catalina, a woman his family considered beneath their rank, they disinherited him. After that, the couple made their way as poor weavers. John was born in 1542. His father died soon afterward, and Catalina was hard pressed to feed her boys. John attended a school for poor children and learned his letters. At seventeen he studied at a Jesuit school, dividing his time between classes and his duties at a hospital.

John felt that the Lord wanted him to become a friar. He thought that by embracing poverty and going without food, he would grow closer to God. In 1563, he joined the Carmelite order, which had begun as a strict order, taking Elijah as their example and giving special devotion to the Virgin Mary.

John soon decided that the Carmelites were not strict enough. He was about to transfer to another order when he met Teresa of Avila. Teresa was urging Carmelites to return to the original strict poverty of their order. John fell in with Teresa's plan. With two other men, he undertook reform on this day in 1568. The three moved into a farmhouse that was in such bad shape that even Teresa did not think anyone could live in it. John renamed himself St. John of the Cross and became the spiritual leader of the new movement.

A few years later, John found himself in prison for resisting commands from a superior. In prison, he was scourged. But after nine months, he managed to escape and soon reappeared as a leader in another community.

While in prison, John began a commentary on a poem he had written called "Dark Night of the Soul," which was about God's workings in the human heart:

> On a dark night, Kindled in love with
> yearnings—oh, happy chance!—
> I went forth without being observed,
> My house being now at rest.
> In darkness and secure. . . .
> Without light or guide, save that which
> burned in my heart.
> This light guided me More surely than
> the light of noonday. . . .
> Oh, night that guided me, Oh, night
> more lovely than the dawn.

The "Dark Night of the Soul" refers to the time in each soul's life when God brings severe trials to purge it of all wickedness and to enable it to see His glory. Many Christians have described such a state, but few as well as this Spanish poet.

Despite little education, Joseph Parker grew huge congregations and preached through the Bible. (Adamson, William. *The Life of Joseph Parker, Pastor of City Temple*. London: Revell, 1902.)

Other Events

1863: The first annual national Thanksgiving Day was celebrated in the United States. A month earlier, President Lincoln had proclaimed the fourth Thursday of each November a day of national thanks.

1902: Joseph Parker, an English Congregational pastor who preached through the Bible, died on this day. His sermons were printed in twenty-five volumes entitled *The Parker People's Bible*. Surprisingly, his formal education only lasted until he was sixteen.

1904: Jeremiah Eames Rankin, who wrote the hymns "God Be with You 'Til We Meet Again" and "Tell It to Jesus," died.

1971: In Hong Kong, Bishop Gilbert ordained Jane Hwang and Joyce Bennett to the Anglican priesthood—the first two women admitted as priests in the Episcopal Church.

Saturninus Dragged to Death

"This is the one who preaches everywhere that our temples must be torn down and who dares to call our gods devils. It is his presence that imposes silence on our oracles." A man in the crowd outside the pagan temple pointed to Saturninus as he spoke.

Saturninus was in Toulouse as a missionary-bishop by command of Bishop Fabian of Rome. To get from his home to his small church, he had to pass by the Capitol, the chief pagan temple in the town.

Through preaching and miracles, Saturninus converted a number of idolaters. Later accounts, which may be legendary, say that Saturninus restored health to a woman with an advanced case of leprosy by praying for her. When he made the sign of the cross over large numbers of the sick, they also were healed.

No doubt it was loss of trade that stung the pagan priests most. The best evidence we have suggests that it was on this day in 257 that as Saturninus passed by the Capitol, temple leaders seized him and chained him. They gave him an ultimatum: either worship their gods or pay with his blood.

Without hesitation, Saturninus replied:

> I adore one only God, and to him I am ready to offer a sacrifice of praise. Your gods are devils, and are more delighted with the sacrifice of your souls than with those of your bullocks. . . . How can I fear them who, as you acknowledge, tremble before a Christian?

Outraged by this reply, the pagans began to whip the bishop. When they had vented their spite upon him in all sorts of humiliating and cruel acts, they looked for a way to kill him. A bull had been brought in for sacrifice, and they tied Saturninus to the animal and set it loose. The maddened creature dashed through town, dragging the faithful bishop to his death. It continued to gallop about until the ropes holding the bishop broke.

Two faithful women rescued what was left of the bishop's battered body and hid it in a deep ditch so that the pagans could not vent their spite on it. Later, Christians gave his body an honorable burial.

Within two centuries, Christians of Toulouse built a church at the very spot where the ropes had broken and allowed Saturninus's corpse to come to rest. A church stands there to this day and is called the Church of the Taur—"The Church of the Bull." This day is the feast day of Saint Saturninus.

A statue of a bull's head. Saturninus was dragged to his death behind a bull. (Courtesy of Kádár Viktor.)

Other Events

1530: Cardinal Thomas Wolsey died. He was born into a poor family and had vowed to rise in the world, and he did. He became known as the "boy bachelor" when he took his degree at Oxford at the age of fifteen. Brilliant and skillful, Wolsey climbed in status in both Church and state, serving as King Henry VIII's chancellor and as archbishop of York. He became a cardinal, amassed a personal fortune and fathered illegitimate children. When Henry demanded that Wolsey procure Henry a divorce from Catherine, Wolsey would not oblige. The king dismissed him and then ordered him arrested and brought to London for trial. On the way to London, Wolsey fell ill and died. Some said he deliberately overdosed himself on medication to avoid facing public humiliation. Near his end, Wolsey lamented, "If I had served God as diligently as I have done the king, He would not have given me over in my grey hairs."

1847: American Indians massacred missionary Marcus Whitman, his wife and twelve others at Walla Walla, Washington. Whitman had recently returned from a successful 3,000-mile journey to convince the American Board of Commissioners for Foreign Missions not to close down one of his three mission stations. Indian fury came to a head when many died of measles, some because Whitman unwittingly gave them faulty vaccinations.

1950: The National Council of the Churches of Christ in the United States was founded in Cleveland, Ohio, by Protestant and Eastern Orthodox denominations.

Marcus Whitman. (Dennis, James S. *Christian Missions and Social Progress*. New York: Fleming H. Revell Co., 1897-1906.)

Vila, New Hebrides. (Jacomb, Edward. *France and England in the New Hebrides*. Melbourne, Australia: G. Robertson & Co., 1919.)

NOVEMBER

30

John Geddie Sailed for Polynesia

> In accord with the Redeemer's command and assured of His presence, we are going forth to those lands where Satan has established his dark domain. I know that suffering awaits me. But to bear the Redeemer's yoke is an honor to one who has felt the Redeemer's love.

Those words were from John Geddie's parting message to the Canadians who were sending him to the mission field. With his wife, Charlotte, and his children, he sailed from Halifax, Nova Scotia, on this day in 1846, bound for Polynesia. "Wee John," as he was called, was the first Presbyterian sent from Canada to do missionary work. Born in Scotland, he was raised in Nova Scotia and became a minister. He showed such zeal for soul-winning as a pastor on beautiful Prince Edward Island that he became an obvious candidate for mission work abroad.

Eleven months after sailing, the little party landed in Samoa. After exploring the Pacific Islands, they settled on Aneiteum, a small island at the tip of the New Hebrides (Vanuatu) chain near Australia. Conditions on the island were appalling, but perhaps not so bad as on some other islands. Traders exploited and abused the inhabitants and brought them deadly diseases. The natives lived in squalor and ignorance, as they had for centuries. They ate one another and killed a man's wives when he died.

Geddie buckled down to the task of learning the new language so that he could explain Christianity in words the people understood. As he prepared literacy material from which the natives could learn to read the Bible when its translation was complete, he wrote:

> Those are privileged indeed, whom God permits to prepare the key which shall unlock the hidden treasures of divine truth, which makes the soul rich to all eternity.

It did not seem that the natives were interested. For three years Geddie labored and taught, but although his school grew to 120 pupils, wicked practices flourished. When he traveled the forests, the natives hurled stones, clubs and spears at him. Several times he was hurt. He grew discouraged.

Without warning, things changed in 1851. Several chiefs decided to convert to Christianity. Suddenly the churches were overflowing. Little Aneiteum sent missionaries to other islands! Geddie had always insisted that every convert was responsible to tell others. The people of another island, hearing of the transformation the gospel had made, even sent over a pig with which to buy a Christian teacher!

Sixteen years after going to Aneiteum, Geddie and his family returned to Canada for a "rest." They toured the nation telling of their work. While home, Geddie translated the psalms into the Aneiteum language. Demand for the Scripture was so great that the islanders chipped in the equivalent of several hundred dollars to help print the book. This was a great sacrifice for them, because their incomes were so tiny.

Geddie died in 1872. A tablet placed in his memory said, "When he landed in 1848, there were no Christians here, and when he left in 1872 there were no heathen."

John Williams. (Dennis, James S. *Christian Missions and Social Progress*. New York: Fleming H. Revell Co., 1897-1906.)

OTHER EVENTS

Annual: St. Andrew's Day is celebrated. Andrew was the first man recorded as following Jesus. He immediately brought his brother, Peter, to meet Christ. He is mentioned in connection with only three other events in the New Testament. It was he who brought the boy with the loaves and fishes to Jesus when the bread was multiplied (see John 6:8-9), and he carried a message from some Greeks who wanted to see the Master (see John 12:20-22). Andrew was also among the four who asked Jesus about end-time events, eliciting the Olivet Discourse from Jesus (see Mark 13). According to tradition, Andrew died in the region of Bulgaria, crucified on an X-shaped cross.

722: Boniface was consecrated bishop for the task of evangelizing the Germanic tribes. He was highly successful. According to tradition, he originated the custom of having a Christmas tree.

1554: Cardinal Pole announced England's reconciliation with the pope, restoring Catholicism as the official religion of England. The nation had broken with Rome in 1534 when Parliament passed the Act of Supremacy, which made King Henry VIII head of its Church.

1839: Missionary John Williams and his associates were clubbed to death on the island of Erromanga in the New Hebrides.

1888: R.G. LeTourneau was born in Richford, Vermont. He invented huge earth-moving machines but was also notable for his Christian witness and philanthropy.

Remembrance of Nicholas Ferrar

Nicholas Ferrar lived for only forty-five years, but they were some of the most unselfish years any man has ever given the world. His wealthy parents were deeply committed to the Church of England and reared their children in faith. They required each to memorize large portions of Scripture. Every day, they read to the children from *Foxe's Book of Martyrs*. From his birth in 1592 until his premature death, these influences remained strong in Ferrar's life. At six he had a profound religious experience in which he gave his heart to God.

Ferrar learned quickly and studied hard, never wasting an opportunity. In his early teens, he went up to Cambridge, where he continued to pour himself into study. So brilliant was he that his tutor prayed Ferrar wouldn't become a heretic, because he had such power as a thinker and a writer that Orthodox churchmen would have been hard-pressed to answer him.

Ferrar didn't turn from the faith. Forced by ill-health to travel abroad, he continued his studies. Everywhere he went, he studied the arts, methods of manufacture and languages. Everyone thought he was planning some great career for himself. A princess with whom he traveled asked Ferrar to become her secretary. He turned down the offer.

It is a wonder that Ferrar survived to show the world what was in him. Crossing German mountains, he was almost killed when a donkey ran down a slope carrying a large piece of timber that almost struck Ferrar. In the nick of time the donkey slipped so that the wood barely tapped Nicholas, who would otherwise have been hurled over a precipice. In Padua and later in Marseilles, he fell ill of such severe fevers that doctors despaired of saving his life. Sailing to Spain, his ship was approached by Turkish pirates, who would probably have captured them if a better prize hadn't come into view. As he was crossing Spain, he barely escaped bandits.

From Spain Ferrar was summoned home. His family had fallen on hard times and needed him. Ferrar played a prominent part in saving the Virginia company whose affairs he mastered. For instance, King Charles I's council, looking for an excuse to destroy the company, demanded a report on such short notice that they thought no reply could be given. Ferrar parceled out the work between several people, and by working them for several days on two hours of sleep, the huge report was created in time.

By similar hard work, he restored his family's finances and won a seat in Parliament. But Ferrar was tired of the world. When he had set out on his travels, he had promised God he would devote his life to Him if he returned safely. Now Ferrar set out to keep that promise. He desired to form a Protestant community and had Archbishop Laud ordain him as a deacon so that he could lead worship services. This move was seen as a great renunciation by all who knew his capabilities.

About thirty friends and family joined Ferrar in the new community. They lived strictly, eating little and praying and singing at set hours. They offered schooling and medical services to the local people. Ferrar wrote and translated books, which the community bound.

Ferrar died in 1637, declaring, "I have been at a great feast, the Great King's feast." Ten years later, the Puritans drove away the community he had established, burning the church organ and destroying Ferrar's writings. Ferrar is remembered by the Anglican Church on this day, December 1.

Nicholas Ferrar, a man of extraordinary ability. (Hyde, A.G. *George Herbert and His Times*. London: Methuen, 1906.)

Other Events

1145: Pope Eugene III proclaimed the Second Crusade in a bull sent to King Louis VII of France. Intended to recover Edessa from Muslims, the crusade was unsuccessful. Eugene had been made pope although he was not a cardinal.

1589: Edmund Spenser's poem "Fairie Queen" was "entered," a prepublication step necessary in the days of government censorship. The English poet held Christian beliefs.

1955: Martin Luther King, Jr., a Baptist minister, led a Montgomery, Alabama, boycott of the bus system to win Civil Rights for African-Americans after Rosa Parks made the transportation system an issue by refusing to give up her bus seat to a white man.

1989: Pope John Paul II met Soviet leader Mikhail Gorbachev at the Vatican, and the two reestablished diplomatic ties. Gorbachev renounced seventy years of religious oppression in the Soviet Union.

Edmund Spenser, who wrote the poem "Fairie Queen." (Lee, Sidney. *Great Englishmen of the Sixteenth Century*. New York: C. Scribner's Sons, 1904.)

December

2

The Importance of Complete Surrender

Frances Havergal in a pensive mood. (Foster, Warren Dunham, ed. *Heroines of Modern Religion*. New York: Sturgis & Walton Co., 1913.)

After years of spiritual struggle, on this day in 1873 Frances Havergal, a hymn writer and Christian singer, saw the importance of complete Christian surrender. It came over her "as a flash of electric light," and she yielded fully to Christ.

It was not that she wasn't already a Christian. On the contrary, she was one of the most dedicated women of the nineteenth century. The youngest child of a Church of England minister, Havergal had begun reading and memorizing the Bible at the age of four. She eventually memorized the Psalms, Isaiah and most of the New Testament. At seven she was writing poems and would later contribute many to the religious magazines of the day. Several became hymns. In addition to "Take My Life," she wrote such favorites as "I Gave My Life for Thee," "Like a River Glorious" and "Who Is on the Lord's Side?" Havergal also learned several modern languages as well as Greek and Hebrew. Though she was always in frail health, she led an active life, encouraging many people to turn to Jesus and others to seek a deeper spiritual walk.

Because of her lovely voice, Havergal was also sought after as a concert soloist. She was a brilliant pianist too. Havergal maintained a simple faith and confidence in her Lord. She never wrote a line of poetry without praying over it.

Nonetheless, she found a whole new life when she went deeper with Christ. The following year, the Holy Spirit used her to start a little revival. Of the experience, she wrote:

> I went for a little visit of five days. There were ten people in the house; some were unconverted and long prayed for, some converted but not rejoicing Christians. [God] gave me a prayer, "Lord, give me all in this house." And He just did. Before I left the house, everyone got a blessing.

Too happy to sleep, she wrote the hymn "Take My Life and Let It Be, Consecrated."

And Frances practiced what she sang. Two of the lines say, "Take my silver, and my gold./ Not a mite would I withhold." In 1878, four years after writing the hymn, she wrote a friend, saying:

> The Lord has shown me another little step, and, of course, I have taken it with extreme delight. "Take my silver and my gold" now means shipping off all my ornaments to the Church Missionary House, including a jewel cabinet that is really fit for a countess, where all will be accepted and disposed of for me. . . . Nearly fifty articles are being packed up. I don't think I ever packed a box with such pleasure.

John Brown. (Webb, Richard D. *The Life and Letters of John Brown*. London: Smith, Elder & Co., 1861.)

Other Events

1381: Jan Van Ruysbroek, "the Ecstatic Doctor," died. He was so called because of his mysticism, which melded personal experience with metaphysical commentary on Scripture. His life and writings influenced the rise of German mysticism.

1577: John of the Cross, a Spanish mystic and Carmelite, was seized by men who were angry at his reforms.

1859: Robert E. Lee hanged abolitionist John Brown at Charlestown, (West) Virginia. Convinced that only force could end slavery and emboldened by his interpretation of Scripture, Brown had seized a government arsenal at Harper's Ferry. His action increased tension between the Southern and Northern states, helping to precipitate the Civil War.

1929: William Henry Parker, an English Baptist businessman and a Sunday school advocate, died on this day. He wrote the hymn "Tell Me the Story of Jesus."

1948: A government decree transferred all of Rumania's Uniate Church property to the Rumanian State without compensation.

1980: Death squads in El Salvador raped and killed three American nuns and a lay woman. The victims were just four among the 70,000 Salvadorans who died at the hands of terrorists in the 1980s civil war, many of them Catholic clergy.

December

George Smith Discovered a New Flood Story

3

George Smith engraved bank notes by day. At night he studied newly discovered cuneiform tablets—clay writings dug up in the Middle East. After publishing several keen observations about these items, Smith was appointed an assistant at the British Museum.

That is how he stumbled across one of the most fascinating finds from the past. In a paper that was read before the Society of Biblical Archaeology in London on this day in 1872, Smith announced the discovery of a flood story similar to, but differing in details from, the Noah story of the Bible (see Genesis 6-8). This account was part of an early piece of poetry known as the *Gilgamesh Epic*.

London society was electrified. The only problem was, the story broke off at the crucial point. How did it end? The *Times* offered a large reward for anyone who could produce the missing tablets.

Smith jumped at the chance. He thought he knew approximately where in Nineveh the original pieces had been found, and that is where he started to dig. Incredibly, among the thousands of tablets strewn in the ruins, he found the missing pieces within a short time! He also found a long list of ancient kings.

The flood story was only one piece of the *Gilgamesh Epic*. Gilgamesh was a tough Middle-Eastern king. His dissatisfied subjects sent a strong man after him. Gilgamesh and his enemy fought to a draw, after which they became close friends. But when the friend died of a horrible disease, Gilgamesh set out to look for the secret of immortality.

In his journey, he met Utnapishtim—the Noah of the *Gilgamesh Epic*. The elderly Utnapishtim told Gilgamesh the story of the flood. Warned by a god, Utnapishtim had made an ark and sealed it with pitch. Then he made his family go in and he shut the door.

Utnapishtim's story says it rained for six days; the Bible says forty. In the biblical account, the water covered the high mountains. In Utnapishtim's account, it came only to the roofs of the houses. After the waters receded, the Utnapishtim story described him releasing a dove, a sparrow and a crow. The Bible has Noah releasing a dove and a raven.

Immediately, the opponents of the Bible jumped on the story as proof that the Bible was wrong. Their reasoning had serious flaws in it, however. Far from disproving the flood, the epic was independent confirmation of a major inundation. (Today over 200 flood accounts are known from around the entire world.) The evidence suggests that Moses wrote the Genesis flood account based on ancient history; Gilgamesh was merely a tradition derived from the same events. Indeed, several different Gilgamesh epics have been found, differing in detail.

In quality, the two accounts could hardly be more different. Gilgamesh is the story of a boastful man exalting himself, battling even with the gods after a goddess falls in love with him. Genesis, by contrast, tells the story of a man chosen by God because he humbled himself before the Almighty.

Smith died of hunger and disease just four years after making his exciting discovery. He was only thirty-six years old.

This sample of cuneiform describes Sennacharib's conquest of the Israelite city Lachish. (Layard, Austin Henry. *Discoveries Among the Ruins of Nineveh*. New York: G.P. Putnam, 1853.)

Other Events

1154: Pope Anastasius IV died. He restored the Pantheon and extended privileges to the Knights Templars.

1352: Pope Clement VI was struck and killed by lightning. During his papacy, he acquired Avignon in France. He also defended the Franciscans against their enemies, preached a failed crusade, treated the Jews with kindness, raised taxes to support a luxurious papal court and exhibited great personal courage during the Black Death.

1552: The Jesuit missionary Francis Xavier died in China, where he contracted a fever while waiting for permission to preach.

1557: Under the leadership of John Knox, Protestants of Scotland signed their "First Covenant" at Edinburgh, uniting Presbyterians under the name "Congregation of the Lord."

1834: Daniel Lindley left Boston for South Africa, where he became a notable missionary.

1926: Paul White was converted. Throwing himself immediately into Christian evangelization, he eventually became a medical missionary to Tanganyika (Tanzania), Africa. He created the Jungle Doctor series.

Paul White, creator of the Jungle Doctor series. (Used by permission of Mrs. White.)

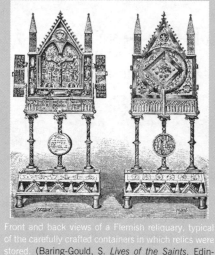

Front and back views of a Flemish reliquary, typical of the carefully crafted containers in which relics were stored. (Baring-Gould, S. *Lives of the Saints*. Edinburgh: John Grant, 1914.)

December 4

Mysterious Relic or a Forgery?

The Shroud of Turin, a cloth bearing the image of a crucified man that is said to have covered Christ at his burial, may be the most famous relic in the world—or it may be the greatest religious hoax ever perpetrated. Reasonable people can be found on either side of the issue, and there are strong arguments on both sides.

When the shroud first appeared in Europe in the twelfth century, its authenticity was immediately questioned. Antipope Clement VII prepared papers declaring it a fraud. Allegedly, the artist who painted the shroud had acknowledged it as a forgery. According to contemporary documents, men for hire pretended that the "relic" cured them to establish its reputation so the forger could make money off of it. At about that same time, Bishop Pierre D'Arcis excommunicated those who showed the shroud, but they were raking in so much money that they found ways to get around his decision.

The Dukes of Savoy guarded the valuable object. In 1502 they requested and obtained papal permission to build a chapel to exhibit the "holy relic." The Sainte Chapelle of the Holy Shroud was officially completed on June 11, 1502. With great fanfare the shroud was exhibited and then locked away. Pope Julius II established a feast and a mass for the shroud. Countless pilgrims visited the site.

The shroud was reputed to have marvelous powers for protecting people. It could not, however, protect itself, when on this day in 1532, its chapel caught fire. Brave individuals rushed in to rescue the cloth. Because the shroud was protected by four locks, Canon Philibert Lambert and two Franciscans had to summon the help of a blacksmith to pry open the grille. By the time they succeeded, the silver casket in which the shroud rested had melted beyond repair, and a drop of molten silver had burned a hole through the shroud's folded layers.

When the Dukes of Savoy transferred their headquarters to Turin, the shroud went with them, and it is as the Shroud of Turin that it is best known.

The shroud was first photographed by Secondo Pia in 1898. The question of its authenticity was suddenly forced open. This time science would have something to say. Pia himself nearly dropped the negative in astonishment. The image on the shroud looks remarkably like a negative itself. Apparently on the principle that the negative of a negative is a positive, Pia's photograph reversed the negative image of the shroud and made it look lifelike! This led to claims that the image must be an authentic negative. Speculation suggested that Christ's radiance at his resurrection had impressed the image on the cloth. Up until then, believers thought the image was formed when embalming spices leached into the cloth.

More than one scientific committee studied the relic. Bishop D'Arcis's warnings and Pope Clement's declaration appear to have been vindicated by modern technology. The scientific conclusion—which is by no means unanimous—is that the shroud is indeed a forgery, painted in tempera. The technique has been reproduced by modern artists who restricted themselves to material that would have been available in the fourteenth century. Carbon dating tests placed the shroud's earliest possible date at AD 1,000, with most tests giving dates that fall between 1260 and 1390—the time period in which the shroud emerged into view in the West.

But the issue remains hotly contested. Recently it has been argued that the carbon dating is inaccurate because of the accumulation of later debris on the cloth. Some claim to have traced references to the relic in Byzantine records. Others argue that pollen spores on the shroud are evidence that it originated in Palestine, but critics say the microscopic resolution used in the testing was insufficient to prove any such thing.

A missionary grave in Africa. (Taylor, S. *Earl Price of Africa*. Cincinnati: The Jennings & Pye Co., 1902.)

Other Events

1093: St. Anselm was consecrated archbishop of Canterbury. Deeply spiritual, he fashioned the ontological argument for God's existence and became the "Father of Scholasticism."

1674: French Jesuit missionary Jacques Marquette erected a log cabin at the future site of Chicago, having grasped its strategic location for mission work. It is believed to be the first building in what became a great city.

1893: Rowland Bingham, Walter Gowans and Thomas Kent arrived in Lagos, Nigeria. They were the first missionaries of the newly formed Sudan Interior Mission.

1896: Peter Cameron Scott died at the age of twenty-nine in Kenya from Blackwater Fever. He was the founder of the African Inland Mission.

1963: The Council of Vatican II issued its Constitution of the Sacred Liturgy, which authorized the limited use of vernacular languages in the mass and sacraments.

1964: Dr. Paul Carlson appeared on the cover of *Time* magazine. He was a medical missionary who became a symbol for events in the Congo when he was seized by Simba rebels and executed.

1972: President Idi Amin ousted fifty missionaries from Uganda, charging that they had ties with Israel or South Africa.

In the Hands of the Communists

"A million a month pass into Christless graves over there [China]," wrote John Stam to his brother. The Chinese need for Christ gnawed at Stam. He believed that God could use him only if he was broken and obedient to the Lord's will, so he studied at Moody Bible Institute and prepared for mission work.

Determined to learn practical faith, Stam relied wholly on the Lord for his needs, convinced that "my God shall supply all your need according to his riches in glory by Christ Jesus" (Philippians 4:19, KJV). Every weekend he traveled 200 miles to minister in a small church. He also trudged the streets of the town, reaching out to the lost. Back in Chicago, he attended a weekly China prayer meeting as he prepared to offer himself to work in the toughest areas of that great, ancient land.

At one of the weekly China prayer meetings, he met Betty Scott. She too was preparing for China. In fact, she had grown up in China, for her parents were missionaries there. The two fell in love. Painfully, they recognized that marriage was not possible because at that time the China Inland Mission was looking for single men to work in sections that were not open to women.

China was in the throes of a civil war that pitted Nationalists against Communists. Many innocent people had died. The Communists were rapidly gaining strength, and missions were under attack, so Stam had reason to be concerned for the future of his missionary endeavors.

He committed the matter to the Lord, whose work, he felt, must come before any human affection. Betty would be leaving for China before him. As a matter of fact, Stam had not yet even been accepted by the China Inland Mission, whereas she had. They parted after a long, tender day of sharing their faith, picnicking, talking and praying.

Stam continued his studies. That summer he went to Philadelphia, home of the China Inland Mission. On July 1, 1932, he was accepted for service in China. Now he could at least head toward the same continent as Betty. He turned down a luxury cruise that was offered him and crossed the ocean in third class on the *Empress of Japan*. Much to his surprise when he arrived in Shanghai, John found that Betty had been transferred there for health reasons.

Violence in the interior of China caused mission authorities to detain Stam in Shanghai. With nothing left to stop them, John and Betty were married. That year, the newlyweds concentrated on learning Chinese. In September of 1934 their daughter, Helen Priscilla, was born.

The Stams were assigned to Tsingteh where the local magistrate assured them they were in no danger from Communists. However, this day in 1934 was their last day of freedom, for bandits attacked early in the morning of December 6 and took John, Betty and Helen captive. The Communists discussed aloud whether to kill the baby and rid themselves of

Typical Chinese beheading, similar to the manner in which John and Betty Stam were killed. (Northrop, Henry Davenport. *The Flowery Kingdom and the Land of the Mikado, or, China, Japan and Corea*. Toronto: Winston, Phillips, 1894.)

the nuisance. An old farmer pleaded for her life. "It's your life for hers, then," said the Communists, and they killed the farmer on the spot.

From Tsingteh, Stam wrote to the China Inland Mission expressing courage in the face of mortal danger, saying, "May God be glorified whether by life or by death." The next day the Stams were force-marched to another town and publicly ridiculed. The following morning they were taken out for execution. After pleading for the life of a Chinese Christian, Stam was beheaded. He died with an expression of joy on his face. Betty quivered once and submitted to the same fate.

Thirty hours later, Helen Stam was found in a house that had been abandoned by the Communists. In the baby's clothes Betty had pinned five dollars, money that enabled Chinese Christians Mr. and Mrs. Lo to hire men to carry Helen to safety.

Other Events

532: St. Sabas, a hermit who became the leader of an early monastic movement and traveled widely preaching against heresy, died on this day.

633: Isidore of Seville (famed as an encyclopedist) presided over a Church council that opened in Toledo. It forbade the compulsory conversion of Jews, said baptism must plunge the person three times and approved hymn singing in the Church.

1484: Pope Innocent VIII issued the bull *Summis Desiderantes* against witchcraft and sorcery in Germany. Implemented by fanatical Dominicans, it led to the persecution and cruel deaths of many suspected witches.

1875: The belated rescue of survivors of the German ship *Deutschland* nearly led to war. The ship had run aground a short distance off the English coast in a terrific storm, and Germany felt the English had been negligent in dealing with them. Among the dead were several nuns whom Gerard Manley Hopkins memorialized in a poem.

1907: Priscilla Jane Owens, an American Methodist school teacher and hymn writer, died. Her best known songs were "Jesus Saves" and "We Have an Anchor."

Pope Innocent VIII's bull led to the persecution of accused witches. (Montor, Chevalier Artaud de. *Lives and Times of the Popes*. New York: Catholic Publication Society of America, 1911.)

December 6

Thomas Experienced a Vision

Thomas Aquinas teaching from a book. (Endres, Jos Ant. *Die Zeit de Hochscholastik: Thomas von Aquin*. Mainz: Kircheim & Co., 1910.)

If you've ever been told you are stupid, you know how seemingly slow-witted Thomas Aquinas felt. He was a large boy whose quick-witted classmates had a name that exactly fitted his case: "Dumb Ox," they jeered, wrapping his stupidity and his large size into a single taunt.

Aquinas ignored them. He knew what he wanted out of life: He wanted to be a godly friar and a scholar. St. Dominic had founded an order of friars who used their brains for God's glory, and Aquinas saw their path as his path.

His rich family was annoyed. It would have been OK for him to become abbot of some great monastery—there was prestige in that! But a begging friar? They determined that Aquinas must change his mind. They locked him up in a tower in their high castle and told him he'd stay there until he caved in to their demands. But Aquinas was as stubborn as they were. When they saw he wasn't changing his mind, his brothers pushed a beautiful courtesan into the room to tempt him. That was the last straw. Bellowing like an ox, he grabbed a blazing stick of wood from the fire and drove the screaming prostitute out.

After two years in the tower, Aquinas got his way. He was allowed to rejoin the Dominicans. The "Dumb Ox" proved to be anything but dumb. Studying the logic and teachings of Aristotle, he adapted them to the use of the Church. He wrote an immense summary of theology and a defense of Christian thought against the "Gentiles."

Aquinas, or St. Thomas Aquinas, as he became known, was the greatest of the medieval theologians. His commonsense philosophy, known as Thomism, undergirds much Catholic thought. He is considered one of the doctors of the Roman Church. Yet he did not consider his knowledge something to brag about. As he pointed out, there are things about God we can take only on faith because God has revealed them to us. While not opposed to reason, they are beyond reason:

> If the only way open to use for the knowledge of God were solely that of reason, the human race would remain in the blackest shadows of ignorance.

Aquinas was called to defend the unity of man's mind. Siger of Brabant taught that a statement could be true in theology although false in philosophy, and Aquinas fought against that idea. He won the battle.

He could have become proud of all of his accomplishments. Instead, he stopped writing. What happened, as best we can make out, was this: While saying mass on this day in 1273, the noble-minded philosopher experienced a heavenly vision. When he was later urged to take up his pen again, Aquinas replied, "Such things have been revealed to me that all that I have written seems to me as so much straw. Now I await the end of my life."

In the twentieth century, his philosophy was revised in light of modern findings. You may meet it under the name "neo-Thomism."

St. Nicholas of Myra. (Jameson, Mrs. *Sacred and Legendary Art*, vol 2. London: Longmans, Green, and Co., 1870.)

Other Events

341 (probable date): St. Nicholas of Myra died. His generosity became legendary and grew into a Christmas tradition.

1648: Thomas Pride of the Parliamentary army blocked about 140 members of Parliament, mostly Presbyterians, from entering and arrested 40 of them. This occurred because Oliver Cromwell had wanted to execute King Charles I, but the Presbyterians balked. The balance of power in Parliament had to be tipped, so Pride carried out a purge, called Pride's Purge, which removed all members of Parliament who were not supporters of Cromwell. What was left of Parliament (about sixty members—the Rump Parliament) abolished the monarchy, and declared themselves the supreme authority in the land and executed Charles.

1787: Cokesbury College, America's first Methodist institution of higher learning, opened in Abingdon, Maryland.

1812: Czar Alexander I signed a decree allowing a Bible society in St. Petersburg, Russia.

Rioters Demanded Ambrose for Milan

Let us say you belong to a big church in an important city like Chicago or London. Your pastor has just died. He taught a heretical doctrine—that Jesus wasn't really divine. Would your church riot over whom to select as its next leader? Would it choose as its compromise candidate a lawyer who had never even been baptized?

That is what happened in Milan, Italy, in 374. The bishop of Milan had supported the Arian heresy, which denied that Christ was fully God. When he died, the Milanese rioted. Some wanted an Arian bishop; others wanted an Orthodox teacher.

Ambrose was a thirty-five-year-old lawyer in town, the son of a nobleman and so skilled in oratory that the governor of northern Italy had designated Ambrose as his successor. This intelligent young man pushed his way through the seething crowd and pleaded with them to maintain the peace. His arguments must have been persuasive: Someone shouted, "Ambrose for bishop!" and soon everyone had picked up the chant.

Ambrose protested. This was the furthest thing from his mind. Why, he hadn't even been baptized! But his protests were of no use. The people wanted him. When Emperor Valentinian approved the selection of Ambrose and threatened severe penalties against anyone who helped hide the lawyer, Ambrose gave in and was baptized.

Eight days later, on this day in 374, Ambrose was consecrated bishop of Milan. He took his new responsibilities seriously. He gave all his possessions to the poor and boned up on theology. Using his legal skills and Greek learning, he defended the Church and its people.

The oratorical skills of the lawyer did not desert him when he took the pulpit. He spoke ad lib, not writing out his sermons. These were so good that the great Augustine of Hippo was influenced toward Christ through listening to Ambrose. Ambrose was a defender of Orthodoxy against Arianism. He kept up a frequent correspondence with Basil the Great, a famed bishop of the Middle East. Because of the quality of Ambrose's writings, he is classed with Jerome, Augustine and Gregory the Great as one of the four Latin Church fathers.

Bold where the Church was concerned, Ambrose even barred Emperor Theodosius from entering the sanctuary until the ruler publicly repented of a massacre he had perpetrated in Thessalonica. One stipulation Ambrose placed on the emperor was that he must allow thirty days to elapse between ordering any death sentence and carrying it out, so that he would have time to cool down and change his mind if necessary.

Ambrose counseled gentleness rather than harshness with those who had betrayed the faith under torture:

> Therefore the Lord Jesus had compassion upon us in order to call us to Himself, not frighten us away. He came in meekness, He came in humility, and so He said: "Come unto Me, all ye that labor and are heavy laden, and I will refresh you." So, then, the Lord Jesus refreshes, and does not shut out nor cast off, and fitly chose such disciples as should be interpreters of the Lord's will, as should gather together and not drive away the people of God.

Ambrose, shown enthroned here, resisted becoming bishop of Milan. (Bell, Mrs. Arthur. *Saints in Christian Art*. London: George Bell, 1901-4.)

Ambrose died on Good Friday in 397. As he lay dying, he extended his arms like Christ on the cross. Christ appeared to him in his last agony. His death made such an impression on the public that five bishops could hardly cope with all the people who requested to be baptized the next day.

Other Events

1254: Pope Innocent IV died. His most notorious act was to issue a bull allowing the torture of people who were denounced to the Inquisition in order to force confessions from them; the same bull unjustly permitted confiscation of victims' property and allowed accusers to remain anonymous.

1542: Emperor Charles V placed a reward of 100 gold guilders on Menno Simon's head. Simon had the audacity to be an Anabaptist.

1678: Father Louis Hennepin, visiting Niagara Falls, drew the first known sketch of the awe-inspiring landmark.

1965: The Greek Orthodox and Roman Catholic Churches removed the mutual excommunications that they had laid on each other over a millennium earlier.

Innocent IV employed torture on people who were denounced to the Inquisition. (Barry, William. *Story of the Nations: Papal Monarchy*. Whitefish, MT: Kessinger Publishing, 1911.)

December 8

Popular Christian Literature

Richard Baxter wrote popular Christian literature. (Powicke, Frederick J. *A Life of the Rev. Richard Baxter, 1615-1691*. Boston: Houghton Mifflin, 1924.)

In today's Christian bookstores you can find literally hundreds of books that seek to uplift you spiritually. Did you ever wonder who first came up with the idea of writing such popular Christian literature for the layperson? It seems to have begun with Richard Baxter, a Puritan minister who suffered his share of trials for conscience's sake in the seventeenth century.

Although his family was loyal to the Church of England, Baxter was greatly influenced by the Puritans. He admired the sharp contrast between their blameless lives and many of the clergy of the established Church—the Church of England. As a young man, Baxter taught school and studied theology. In 1641 he became pastor in the church at Kidderminster, and his powerful preaching of God's Word soon transformed the town. Visiting travelers reported that instead of widespread immorality, they began to hear praise and prayer coming from every house.

With the outbreak of England's civil war between the king and Parliament, Baxter served for a time as chaplain to the parliamentary forces. Suffering from failing health and seemingly at the point of death, Baxter wrote *The Saint's Everlasting Rest*. It shows how hope of eternal life in heaven should be the driving force that controls the Christian's conduct. The English people were just emerging from the civil war when the book appeared in print, and it became standard reading in Puritan households. Baxter's timeless advice was to keep "heaven in your eye at all times."

Another of Baxter's books, *Call to the Unconverted*, exhorted the reader to turn away from sin unto a holy life. It was so successful that he wrote a whole series of similar conversion books with personal appeals to readers, each one designed to bring people to repent. No one had written such a series before. Baxter constantly stressed the importance of sanctification—the lifelong journey in which Christians, with God's help, set themselves apart to become more and more like Christ.

A third book by Baxter, *The Reformed Pastor*, taught other pastors how they could succeed in their towns as he had in Kidderminster. Altogether, he wrote 128 books and an amazing number of sermons. His full works came to 35,000 pages.

On this day in 1691, Richard Baxter died. Although he was considered the greatest preacher of his day and sold many books, because he stood against the state Church he lived next door to poverty.

John Pecham's tomb. (Green, John Richard. *A Short History of the English People*. New York: Harper & Brothers, 1893-5.)

Other Events

1292: The Englishman John Pecham died on this day. He was archbishop of Canterbury and a popularizer of science.

1811: Elihu Burritt was born in New Britain, Connecticut, the youngest of ten children. His family could not afford to send him to school, so Burritt was apprenticed to a blacksmith. He developed a longing to read the Scriptures in their original languages and taught himself to do so while working the forge. By the age of thirty he had learned fifty languages. Because of his wide reading, he was known as the "Learned Blacksmith." He became editor of a Christian magazine and a champion of peace in the home as well as between nations. Typical of his though was this admonition: "Be ever gentle with the children God has given you. Watch over them constantly; reprove them earnestly, but not in anger." He taught that all war is inconsistent with Christianity. President Abraham Lincoln made Burritt consul to Birmingham, England. Burritt died in 1879.

1854: Pope Pius IX, in his letter *Ineffabilis Deus*, declared that Mary was freed from original sin at the "first instant of conception." This is known as the dogma of the Immaculate Conception.

1900: Rose Lathrop and Alice Huber made their vows as Dominican tertiaries. They became Sister Alphonsa and Sister Rose and founded the Servants of Relief for Incurable Cancer.

December 9

Layman Robert Cushman's Famous Sermon

The Pilgrims at Plymouth colony felt a chill of fear. An Indian had just reported a white sail off the coast of Cape Cod. Was this a French raider from Canada? Miles Standish armed the men, and they prepared to meet any assault. Great was their relief when the ship turned out to be the *Fortune*, an English vessel bringing more colonists. While many of the newcomers were not Pilgrims, one of the men who disembarked from the boat had been a Puritan leader in Leyden, the Dutch city where the Puritans had previously lived in exile. This was the deacon Robert Cushman.

Cushman had come to straighten out affairs in the colony. The men who had financed the settlement were angry that the *Mayflower* had been held so long by the Pilgrims—and then sent home empty. The colonists might have at least loaded it with timber! The company wanted a return on their investments. And they wanted some amended articles to be signed too.

At Plymouth, settlers were sick of the company policy of share and share alike. Some demanded that the land be parceled out in private chunks. Cushman warned them strongly against this kind of talk and said that their backers were in no mood to be trifled with. If the colonists hoped for future supplies, they must agree to company terms.

Oddly enough for such a religious group, there was no ordained minister among their number. Cushman, a deacon, was the nearest thing. To settle the jealousies and animosities among the settlers, he preached a sermon on this day in 1621. It was the first Protestant sermon on American soil to be printed there.

It was titled "A Sermon Preached at Plimmoth in New England, December 9, 1621 in an Assemblie of his Majesties faithful Subjects, there inhabiting. Wherein is shewed the danger of selfe love, and the sweetnesse of true Friendship. Together with a Preface, shewing the state of the Country, and Condition of the Savages."

Cushman quoted Paul's words to the quarreling Corinthians as an example for the disgruntled settlers: "Let no man seek his own, but every man another's wealth (1 Corinthians 10:24, KJV).

> The occasion of these words of the Apostle Paul, was because of the abuses which were in the Church of Corinth. Which abuses arose chiefly through swelling pride, self-love and conceitedness.
>
> [I]t is lawful sometimes for men to gather wealth, and grow rich, even as there was a time for Joseph to store up corn, but a godly and sincere Christian will see when this time is, and will not hoard up when he seeth others of his brethren and associates to want, but then is a time, if he have anything to fetch out and disperse it. . . . [Y]ou must seek still the wealth of one another.

He pointed out that it was in their self-interest to do so, for, "Even as we deal with others, ourselves and others shall be dealt withal . . . for it is the merciful that shall obtain mercy."

Miles Standish (shown here) prepared to repel invaders, but the ship was English. Aboard was Robert Cushman. (Wilson, Woodrow. *A History of the American People*. New York/London: Harper & Bros., 1902.)

The settlers listened to Cushman. Not only did they sign the despised articles, but they also filled the *Fortune* with wood and furs. Cushman sailed for England. Unfortunately, the ship was seized by French privateers, who stripped it of everything of value. Cushman was freed, but once again the colony was a money-losing proposition.

Other Events

Annual: The feast day of the Seven Martyrs of Samosata—Hipparchus, Philothea, James, Paragrus, Habebus, Romanus and Lollianus—who were crucified for refusing to join in a pagan celebration, is celebrated on this day.

1835: George Müller of Bristol publicly presented his plan for an orphanage. It opened the following year. Before his death, he housed over 10,000 orphans in a faith-based ministry.

1896: William Henry Sheppard, an African-American missionary to Africa, wrote a letter to supporters at home, promising to prove that he merited the trust they had placed in him.

1968: The influential theologian Karl Barth died. He was well-known for his commentary on Paul's letter to the Romans, his *Dogmatics* and his part in drafting the Barmen Declaration, which opposed Nazi dogma.

1978: The Sorbonne, one of the most prestigious universities in France, awarded Kenneth Pike an honorary degree for linguistic work which had enabled virtual amateurs to crack unwritten languages all around the world and translate the Bible into them.

Kenneth Pike receives a well-deserved honorary degree. (Pike, Eunice V. *Ken Pike: Scholar and Christian*. Dallas, TX: Summer Institute of Linguistics, 1981. Used by permission.)

Kaspar Schwenckfeld. (Courtesy of the Christian History Institute archives.)

December 10

Kaspar Who?

Two-and-a-quarter centuries after Kaspar Schwenkfeld's death on this day in 1561, small groups of his followers in Pennsylvania continue to follow his teachings. Who was this man whose influence, though restricted and largely unknown, has nevertheless crossed continents and centuries?

Kaspar Schwenkfeld was born into the Silesian nobility in 1489, three years before Christopher Columbus's famous voyage. Silesia was a small province in central Europe. Schwenkfeld was deeply affected by the writings of Martin Luther and began a serious study of the Scriptures. In 1519, he experienced what he called a "visitation of God."

The more he studied the Scriptures, the more Schwenkfeld discovered areas of Luther's theology with which he disagreed. He especially had problems with Lutheran teachings on justification by faith alone, the freedom of man's will and the futility of human works. Schwenkfeld also developed a unique understanding of the Lord's Supper that was distinct from that of Luther and the other reformers. Schwenkfeld believed that the Christian at the Lord's Supper ate the spiritual body of Christ, which would grow as a planted seed and transform the individual into the image of God and the person of Christ.

In 1541 Schwenkfeld published his *Great Confession on the Glory of Christ*. Many considered the work heretical. Schwenkfeld taught that Christ had two natures, divine and human, but His human nature was a kind of "celestial flesh." Jesus's flesh was increasingly made more divine while He was on earth, so He was eventually transfigured, resurrected and taken up to heaven. It was this flesh Schwenkfeld thought believers partook of at the Lord's Supper. Because of this view, Schwenkfeld's followers were often called "Confessors of the Glory of Christ."

The number of Schwenkfeld's followers diminished greatly after the Thirty Years' War in 1648. By 1700 there were only about 1,500 remaining in lower Silesia. When the Austrian emperor established a Jesuit mission to bring them back into the Catholic Church, many fled Silesia, leaving their property and possessions behind. Some found refuge on the lands of Count Nikolaus von Zinzendorf before going to Pennsylvania in the 1530s. Five congregations of Schwenkfelders remain in Pennsylvania today.

Papal bull against Luther. (Bezold, Friedrich von. *Geschichte der Deutschen Reformation*. Berlin: Grote, 1890.)

Other Events

536: Count Belisarius of Byzantium, reputedly a Christian, entered Rome, where he made a magnificent defense of the ancient city. Later the jealous emperor is said to have put out the heroic general's eyes with red-hot wires.

1520: German reformer Martin Luther publicly burned Pope Leo X's bull *Exsurge Domine*, which demanded that Luther recant his "heresies," including that of justification by faith alone.

1735: George Oglethorpe, governor of the Georgia colony in America, met John and Charles Wesley. Impressed by their zeal, he asked them to undertake a mission to his colony.

1871: Edward, prince of Wales, lay gravely ill. His wife, Alexandria, picked up her Bible and read these words: "Call upon me in the day of trouble: I will deliver thee" (Psalm 50:15, KJV). She believed them and asked both nation and Church to pray. Four days later, Edward took a turn for the better. Although he lived a playboy life, thirty years later at his coronation, he remembered the words and had them included in the ceremony: "I called to you in the day of trouble and you heard me."

1968: Thomas Merton, a Trappist monk who was deeply involved in peace causes, died. He was well-known for his best-selling autobiography, *The Seven Story Mountain*.

December 11

Song of an Illegitimate Child

Students of history remember that in 1792 King Louis XVI of France went on trial for treason before the Revolutionary Convention that had replaced the French National Assembly. His head would roll by the following January. But on this day in 1792, a few days before Christmas—the same day, in fact, that the French king faced his cruel judges—a virtually unnoticed event took place: Joseph Mohr was born in Salzburg. His name will forever be associated with the Christmas season.

At the time of his birth, it appeared that his name would be associated with nothing but disgrace. He was an illegitimate child—his mother's third. His father was a soldier who boarded with the family. When Franz Joseph Mohr learned he'd gotten Ann Schoiber pregnant, he fled the home and deserted the army, leaving Schoiber to face the penalties, which included a steep fine, alone. She was a knitter who earned little. It would have taken her a full year's wages to pay the penalty.

The town's brutal executioner stepped into the picture. He would pay the fine and become the child's godfather. He hoped by doing this to improve his own reputation. But young Mohr's life now bore another stigma: godson of the feared and hated executioner. He was banned from attending school or learning a trade or even from holding a job.

Mohr loved to sing. While playing on steps leading up to a Capuchin monastery, he was overheard singing by Johann Nepomuk Hiernle, a Benedictine monk and cathedral choirmaster. Hiernle thought the boy's voice so good he could not bear to see it wasted. He found Schoiber and arranged for Mohr to study with his elite students.

Hiernle's kindness was not wasted. Mohr proved to be an outstanding student and mastered the organ, violin and guitar by the time he was twelve. He always placed in the top quarter of the class. His training continued, and he was ordained a priest in 1815.

Over the course of his life, he was assigned duties in many towns, but it was while he was yet a young assistant in Oberndorf that he ensured his lasting fame. He wrote the words to a new Christmas carol and asked the church organist, Franz Gruber, to set them to music. On Christmas Eve in 1818, the two first sang what has since become the most popular Christmas carol of all time: "Silent Night, Holy Night." The carol captures the awesome humility of a God who stooped not just to the level of mankind, but to the lowest level, to be born among animals and announced to common shepherds.

In his last post, at Wagrain, Mohr opened a school that took in poor children. He gave virtually his entire income to the project and died as poor as he was born. He left us the riches of "Silent Night," which has been translated into close to 200 languages. Millions who have never heard of Louis XVI sing Mohr's words every Christmas.

Nativity scene. (Bell, Mrs. Arthur. *Saints in Christian Art*. London: George Bell, 1901-4.)

Other Events

1187: Pope Gregory VIII died. During his pontificate the Muslims recaptured the Holy Land. He absolved England's King Henry II of the murder of Archbishop Thomas á Becket after Henry's public penance.

1189: King Richard I "the Lionheart" left England on the Third Crusade to retake Jerusalem, which had fallen to Muslim General Saladin. He negotiated a treaty allowing Christians access to the holy places.

1640: Puritans introduced a petition into the English Parliament, asking for the abolition of the Church episcopacy, "with all its dependencies, roots and branches." Although the House of Commons accepted the "Roots and Branch Petition," the House of Lords (which had many Anglican bishops) rejected it, and the Church of England episcopacy remained.

1825: Samuel Adjai Crowther was baptized at the age of sixteen. Formerly a slave, he became the first Anglican bishop of West Africa.

1910: Lars Skrefsrud, cofounder of the Santal mission in India, died. Formerly a convict, he had been unwanted by the Norwegian Mission Society but left 20,000 Christian converts behind him.

1983: Pope John Paul II visited a Lutheran church in Rome as a first move toward reconciling the Protestant Church to Rome.

Samuel Adjai Crowther as bishop of West Africa. (Page, Jesse. *Samuel Crowther: The Slave Boy Who Became Bishop of the Niger*. New York: Fleming H. Revell Co., 1889.)

Russian Orthodoxy developed a distinctive Church architecture. This is the famous St. Basil's Cathedral in Moscow. (Meakin, Annette M.B. *Russia: Travels and Studies*. Philadelphia: J.B. Lipincott Co., 1906.)

DECEMBER

12

Deposing Autocratic Patriarch Nikon

Jesus Christ came in meekness and humility, renouncing the emblems of power and status. He did not impose his ways on anyone or force a form of worship. When his disciples jockeyed for position, he urged them to serve one another. His followers through the ages did not always grasp the implications of this teaching or follow it.

A case in point occurred in the events that led a council to depose Nikon, patriarch of Moscow, on this day in 1667. Greek and Russian prelates joined in making the decision, which Tsar Alexis Romanov demanded. The tsar was easily able to attain his objective because the high-handed Nikon was most unpopular.

Mistakes, mistranslations and simple differences had crept into the Russian liturgy. For instance, the Russians signed the cross with two fingers rather than three, as the Greeks did. Nikon insisted on reform. But many Christians who grew up with the traditional Russian forms protested the change back to the Greek. If the Greeks were so correct, why had God placed most of Orthodoxy under Turkish rule? Nikon responded in autocratic fashion and, with state cooperation, attempted to crush anyone who refused to accept his new service book.

It is not clear why Romanov stepped in; probably he did so because Nikon tried to shake off state control of the Church. Under pressure from the tsar, Nikon resigned but was reluctant to let go of his power. He continued to agitate for restoration of his authority. In fact, he even returned to Moscow and tried to take up his duties as if nothing had happened. The tsar wanted to replace Nikon, but, to avoid charges that there were two patriarchs, he requested that Nikon be formally deposed.

The synod agreed. Anger, hurt feelings and retaliation were apparent in its decision:

> Whereas we have now learned that Nikon lived tyrannically, and not meekly as befits a prelate, and that he was given to iniquity, rapacity, and tyranny, we debar him, in accordance with the divine and sacred canons of the evangelizing apostles and of the ecumenical and local Orthodox councils, from every sacerdotal function, so that henceforth he shall have no power to perform any episcopal act . . . and we decree with the entire local church council that henceforth he be known as a common monk called Nikon, and not as patriarch of Moscow; he will be assigned a place to dwell to the very end of his days, and may it be some old and suitable monastery, where he can lament his sins in great silence.

Though he was banished to a monastery on the White Sea, Nikon's reforms were kept. The persecution of Old Believers that he had instigated persisted. Later, the dying Romanov implored the forgiveness of the former patriarch. After fourteen years of imprisonment (which was sometimes very harsh) Nikon was invited back to Moscow by a new tsar, but he died on the way. He was buried with full honors.

Peter Martyr Vermigli. (Baird, Henry Martyn. *Theodore Beza: The Councilor of the French Reformation*. New York: G.P. Putnam's Sons, 1899.)

Other Events

1531: An apparition calling itself the Blessed Virgin Mary, mother of Jesus, appeared to Indian convert Juan Diego, instructing him to tell his bishop to build a chapel on a site, which, until the Spanish conquest, had supported a pagan temple to Tonantzin, goddess of the earth and growing corn. The bishop did not believe Juan. The entity reappeared and reputedly poured Castilian roses (not found in the New World at that time) into Juan's homespun blanket. When the roses were poured out before the bishop, he still did not believe. Then a portrait of Mary miraculously appeared on the blanket, and that convinced him. The church was built, and the Fiesta of Our Lady of Guadalupe became Mexico's leading religious festival.

1562: Peter Martyr Vermigli, a theologian with reform tendencies, died. He fled from Italy to England, but with the rise of Catholicism under Mary Tudor, he fled again, this time to Switzerland.

1917: Father Flanagan opened a home for poor boys. He insisted, "There is no such thing as a bad boy."

Deadlock Gave the Church Celestine V

The cardinals were deadlocked. They had been deadlocked for twenty-seven months, since the spring of 1292 when Pope Nicholas IV died. There were only twelve cardinals, and they were evenly divided between two factions of the Roman nobility. Neither side would give way, each hoping for the perks and power that would flow from having one of their number on the papal throne.

Then a message arrived from the mountains. Peter Murrone, the hermit founder of the Celestines, strict Benedictines, warned that God was angry with the cardinals. If they did not elect a pope within four months, the Lord would severely chastise the Church.

Eager for a way out of their deadlock, the cardinals asked themselves, Why not elect Peter himself? Finally the cardinals could agree. In a vote that they declared to be "miraculous" they unanimously chose Peter.

When three of the cardinals climbed to his mountain roost to tell Peter he had been chosen, the hermit was not happy. All of his life, he had tried to run away from people. Dressed like John the Baptist, he subjected himself to fasts, heavy chains and nights of prayer without sleep. But when the cardinals and his friend King Charles II of Naples insisted that he must accept the position for the good of the Church, Peter reluctantly agreed and took the name Celestine.

Charles II prompted Celestine to name a number of new cardinals—all of them from France and Naples, completely changing the makeup of the Church's leadership. Peter, who was too trusting, made many mistakes. A babe in political matters, he was used by everyone around him. The Vatican staff even sold blank bulls with his signature on them.

The business of the Church slowed to a crawl because he took too much time making decisions. Within weeks it became apparent he had to resign for the good of the Church. But could a pope resign? Guided by one of the cardinals, Benedetto Caetani, Celestine as pope issued a constitution that gave himself the authority to resign.

All sorts of rumors followed his resignation. Celestine had built himself a hut in the Vatican where he could live like a hermit. Supposedly Caetani thrust a reed through the wall of the hut and pretended he was the voice of God, ordering Celestine to resign. Since the hermit was undecided as to his proper course of action, this trick convinced him.

Celestine stepped down on this day in 1294, having actually reigned as pope for only three months. He was replaced by Caetani, who took the name Boniface VIII. Afraid that Celestine would become a rallying point for troublemakers, Boniface locked up the old man. He destroyed most of the records of Celestine's short time in office, but he could not unmake the cardinals.

Peter escaped and wandered in mountains and forests. He was recognized and recaptured when he tried to sail to Greece, his boat having been driven back by a tempest. The last nine months of his life he spent in prayer as a prisoner of Boniface, badly treated by his guards. When he died in 1296, rumor had it that Boniface had murdered him. He was about eighty-one years old. Pope Clement V declared Celestine a saint in 1313.

Bewildered Celestine V was tricked into stepping down. (Montor, Chevalier Artaud de. *Lives and Times of the Popes*. New York: Catholic Publication Society of America, 1911.)

Other Events

1304: Lucy, one of the earliest Christian saints to achieve popularity, was martyred. Apparently she was one of several Christians killed in the Diocletian persecution.

1124: Pope Calixtus II died. After defeating Emperor Henry V in battle, Calixtus was able to resolve the controversy between Church and state over investiture (rulers wanted to appoint bishops). He also made peace between England and France.

1698: The First Baptist Church of Philadelphia was formed.

1837: Father German, the heart of the Orthodox mission to the Kodiak of Alaska, died on this day. With him the mission ended for a time.

1895: Gustav Mahler's *Second Symphony*, "The Resurrection," was first performed in completion. "Rise again, my dust, after a brief rest—You were not born in vain," sang the artists. The performance, which took place in Berlin, was a triumph, and the work remains one of the masterpieces of religious composition. However, Mahler did not believe there really would be a judgment. The program notes declared, "There is no punishment and no reward. An overwhelming love illuminates our being."

Mahler's "Resurrection Symphony" went off well this day. (Mermsmann, Hans. *Moderne Musik Seit der Romantik*. Wildpark-Potsdam: Akademische Verlagsgesellschaft Athenaion M.B.H., 1927.)

The cruel death of Sir John Oldcastle. (Foxe, John, et al. *Foxe's Christian Martyrs of the World*. Chicago: Moody Press, n.d.)

December 14

Falstaff's Original Captured

One of William Shakespeare's most memorable characters is Falstaff, the companion of the youthful Prince Hal in his days of wild living before becoming King Henry V of England. However, Shakespeare didn't tell in his plays about Falstaff's later conversion to Christ and execution for following the teachings of John Wycliffe.

The real-life Falstaff was Sir John Oldcastle of Cowling Castle. Oldcastle was acquainted with the writings of Wycliffe and became a Lollard, as Wycliffe's followers were called. He had many copies of Wycliffe's writings made and circulated them throughout Canterbury, Rochester, London and Hertford. If any Lollard preacher was forbidden to preach or was arrested, Oldcastle protected him—and King Henry in turn protected his favorite.

The established clergy, however, told the king that Oldcastle was organizing a plot against the Church, the king and the royal family. They said he had secretly collected 20,000 men for battle at St. Giles in the Field. When the king and his soldiers went to St. Giles, they found only eighty people in a worship service. These, however, were either killed or captured; those who lived were compelled to confess under torture that Oldcastle was their ringleader.

In 1413, Oldcastle was put on trial by the ecclesiastical court. He refused to recognize the pope's authority, asserting that no pope should teach anything contrary to Scripture. The court demanded a confession from Oldcastle. He first confessed to God, saying:

> I confess to Thee, O God! and acknowledge that in my frail youth I seriously offended Thee by my pride, anger, intemperance, and impurity: for these offenses I implore thy mercy!

Then to the crowd he said, "I ask not your absolution: it is God's only that I need." When the sentence of death was read out, Oldcastle said, "It is well, though you condemn my body, you can do no harm to my soul by the grace of my eternal God." He was taken to the Tower of London, but he managed to escape before his execution and took refuge in Wales.

His freedom did not last, however. On this day in 1417, Oldcastle was recaptured. He was taken to London's St. Giles in the Field, suspended by chains over a slow fire and cruelly burned to death. He was the first martyr for Christ among England's nobility.

Thomas Tenison helped found the Society for the Propagation of the Gospel. (Carpenter, Edward. *Thomas Tenison, Archbishop of Canterbury: His Life and Times*. London: S.P.C.K., 1948.)

Other Events

872: Pope Adrian II died. He had refused the papacy twice before he finally accepted. Unsure of himself, he even turned to the antipope Anastasius for support. Adrian is said to have been the last married pope.

1591: The Spanish mystic and poet John of the Cross died. His religious poem "Dark Night of the Soul" is well-known, and his writings profoundly influenced Catholic and Protestant thought:

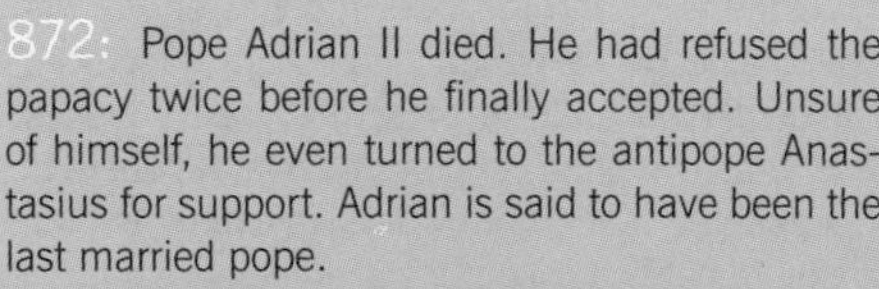

> A Christian should always remember that the value of his good works is not based on their number and excellence, but on the love of God which prompts him to do these things.

1715: Influential Anglican Thomas Tenison, one of the founders of the Society for the Propagation of the Gospel, died. He was unusually tolerant toward non-Anglicans for that day and drew non-conformists into the Church of England.

1922: "Toc H," a fellowship that ministers through social service, was chartered. Its name is from British signal code for "T.H.," which stood for Talbot House, a recreation and spiritual center developed during World War I in Belgium by chaplain P.T.B. Clayton, M.C.

Most Extraordinary Political Document for Religion

James Madison introduced the constitutional amendments that became the Bill of Rights. (Courtesy of the Christian History Institute archives.)

In 1787 a convention meeting in Philadelphia drafted what is usually recognized as the most extraordinary political document of history. The Constitution of the United States created a federal system with checks and balances on power. The world had never seen anything like it.

Despite its benefits, there was doubt it would be ratified by the individual states. Having so recently escaped one tyranny, the people did not want to subject themselves to another. The new Constitution was feared because, while it specified the rights of the new government and gave such rights as the writ of *habeas corpus*, it did not spell out several rights that the people felt it should. These could be inferred, but the majority of Americans felt safer having them in writing.

For the most part, those who were for a federal system were for the Constitution as it stood. But those who opposed a federal system wanted more guarantees of rights. Several state conventions asked for such a bill. Thomas Jefferson urged that they be given their wish. A "bill of rights is what the people are entitled to against every government on earth, general or particular, and what no just government should refuse, or rest on inference." When the first Congress convened under the United States' new Constitution, James Madison introduced several constitutional amendments. Congress passed ten of them by a two-thirds majority, and they became known as the Bill of Rights.

On this day in 1791, the United States Bill of Rights was ratified. It is significant to Church history because of a line in its first amendment: "Congress shall make no law respecting an establishment of religion, or prohibiting the free exercise thereof." This amendment was the result of long centuries of efforts by religious groups such as the Quakers and the Baptists to obtain religious liberty. Baptist leader Isaac Backus, for example, had proposed the following wording for a bill of rights:

> As God is the only worthy object of all religious worship, and nothing can be true religion but a voluntary obedience unto His revealed will . . . every person has an unalienable right to act in all religious affairs according to the full persuasion of his own mind, where others are not injured thereby.

The first amendment meant that the federal government of the United States would not establish a national Church, such as was common in many other nations. Anyone could worship as he or she pleased, and the federal government could not legitimately say "boo" except under special circumstances.

Federal civil rights are not obligatory for states, however. At the state level, established churches continued to exist for a while.

Many battles have been fought in the courts over just what this amendment does or does not mean. Today when those words are sometimes used as an excuse to forbid children to pray in school or read a Bible on school property, it is good to remember that the understanding of the generation who wrote the amendment was not that the government should oppose religion or deny it the same rights of expression enjoyed by other organizations, but rather that it should not impose a national religion nor stop people from engaging in their preferred form of worship.

Other Events

1634: Thomas Kingo was born in Slangerup, Denmark. He became a clergyman and eventually bishop of Odense. Kingo's hymns were called "the greatest miracle of the seventeenth century" by Nikolai Grundtvig, a prominent Church reformer and educator. These lines from "He That Believes and Is Baptized" are typical of Kingo's writing:

> He that believes and Is baptized
> Shall see the Lord's salvation;
> Baptized into the death of Christ,
> He is a new creation.

1683: Sir Isaak Walton died. He wrote *The Compleat Angler* but is important to Christian historians because he also penned affectionate biographies of five of his contemporaries, including the famed churchmen-poets John Donne and George Herbert; Robert Sanderson, the bishop of Lincoln; theologian Richard Hooker; and ambassador, educator and Christian poet Sir Henry Wotton.

1727: As his first official act as a bishop, Count Nikolaus von Zinzendorf ordained Peter Bohler. Bohler became one of the most influential Moravians in England and America. He was instrumental in leading John Wesley to a more profound experience of Christian faith.

1870: African-American Methodists from eight local conferences met in Jackson, Tennessee. After hearing opening remarks by Bishop Paine, the delegates founded a new church for African-American Methodists, calling it the Colored Methodist Episcopal Church. Its leaders noted that they were not breaking with the long-established Methodist Episcopal Church but merely forming a new branch of it.

1956: The Communist government of Poland relented from previous decisions and allowed religious instruction in schools on a voluntary basis.

Peter Bohler showed John Wesley the way to an assurance of salvation. (Townsend, W.J., H.B. Workman and George Eayrs, eds. *A New History of Methodism*, vol 1. London: Hodder and Stoughton, 1909.)

December

16

From Bible Burning to Gospel Preaching

Sundar Singh burned the Bible, then changed his mind and followed its Author. (Courtesy of the Christian History Institute archives.)

Bitter over the death of his mother, Sundar Singh blamed God. The fourteen-year-old boy formed a gang and threw filth on his Christian teachers. He mocked their Scriptures and interrupted class. Then he bought a Bible. On this day in 1903, he built a fire outside his house and, page by page, tore up the Scriptures and burned it.

For the next three days he was unhappy—so unhappy he could bear his misery no longer. Late on the third evening, he rose from bed and prayed, "O God, if there is a God, reveal yourself to me tonight." He said that otherwise "I planned to throw myself in front of the train which passed by our house." For seven hours Singh prayed. The next train was due at five in the morning.

Suddenly, the room filled with a glow. A man appeared, and a voice said, "How long will you deny me? I died for you; I have given my life for you." Singh saw the man's hands, pierced by nails. This could only be Christ! In that moment, the boy who had burned the Bible became a man who would endure anything for Christ. He fell to his knees with a wonderful sense of peace.

Singh was a Sikh. Sikhs had endured terrible persecution in their early history. Consequently, they were fiercely loyal to their faith. Conversion to Christianity was considered treachery. Every effort was made to woo Singh back. An uncle opened a cellar full of treasure and said it was Singh's if only he would return to Sikhism. A prince appealed to the boy's patriotism. The Christian mission was attacked. A boy who followed Singh was poisoned to death.

Singh's father alternately pleaded in tears with his son or raged in fury. Thinking marriage would change the boy's attitude, he ordered Singh to marry. Although such commands are law among Sikhs, Singh refused in Christ's name. Finally he was cast out. "We reject you forever. . . . I declare you are no more worthy to be called our son. . . . We shall forget you as if you had never been born." Hours later Singh experienced wrenching pain in his gut. His family had poisoned his last meal! A missionary-medic was able to save the young man's life. Singh rejoiced in his sufferings and later said, "When we have left this life, we will not have another chance to bear the cross for Christ."

Indian churches offered Singh a pulpit. Instead, dressed in the thin yellow robe of a holy man, he took to the road. Maybe Indians would listen if he came in a garb they understood. Many did. Even his father eventually converted to Christianity.

In the remote mountains of Tibet, souls were starved for the Word of God. But Buddhist monks wanted no part of Christianity because it would rob them of their income and influence. Before Singh's death, he traveled into the forbidden land about twenty times, despite intense suffering. In 1912, for example, he was beaten and thrown to die in a pit filled with rotting bodies in the Tibetan village of Lazar. His arm was broken, the pit was sealed above him, and only the grand lama had the key. The stench was unbearable. Three nights later, Singh heard the grate open. A shadowy figure lowered a rope and pulled him out. The next morning he boldly preached in the streets again. Furious, the grand lama seized Singh and asked who had helped him. Who had stolen the key? When the grand lama found the key still on his ring, he released Sundar Singh in terror.

Seventeen years later, in 1929, Singh turned his eyes to Tibet again. He had been sick. Worn down, he no longer possessed the strength and will of former years. Before he was fully recovered, he climbed again to Tibet. Nothing was ever heard of him again.

Charles the Bald, first of three emperors that Pope John VIII crowned. (Courtesy of the Christian History Institute archives.)

Other Events

345: Eusebius (not to be confused with historian Eusebius of Caesarea) became bishop of Vercelli, Italy. He was influential in having the Nicene Creed restored to the empire.

882: Pope John VIII died. He was forced to pay the Saracens tribute, but he crowned three emperors, beginning with Charles the Bald, continuing through Louis the Stammerer and concluding with Charles the Fat.

1811: A massive earthquake focused in New Madrid, Missouri, rocked the central United States. Many people believed it foretold the end of the world, and slaves rejoiced aloud that now their masters were "going to get it."

Was "Nosey" Parker Properly Consecrated?

Matthew Parker was consecrated archbishop of Canterbury on this day in 1559 at Lambeth, England. But was it a true consecration? To those who hold the theory of apostolic succession, the legitimacy of the Church of England may depend on the legitimacy of Matthew Parker, for he was the first Church of England archbishop after Mary Tudor's Catholic reign.

During Mary's reign, Parker prudently stayed out of sight. Mary had deprived him of the deanery of Lincoln. And little wonder: Parker was one of them—a reformer who had fallen for Martin Luther's teachings while at Cambridge. He had even served as chaplain to Anne Boleyn, the woman who had displaced Mary's mother as queen.

But times that change can change about again. Mary died, and Elizabeth restored the Protestant Church. She summoned Parker to become archbishop of Canterbury. With reluctance, he agreed. He knew himself to be more of a scholar than a Church leader. He was consecrated by four Anglican bishops who survived from the time of Edward VI.

Parker resisted change. He did not believe in democratic reforms. "God keep us from such a visitation as Knox has attempted in Scotland—the people to be orderers of things," he prayed. The Puritans, who wanted to move further from the Church of Rome, found Parker's conservatism distasteful. His relations with dissenters were not happy.

He spent much of his time at books, revising the *Thirty-Nine Articles* (the essential statement of Church of England beliefs) and issuing the Bishop's Bible, with its beautiful New Testament preface:

> These be the mysteries of our faith, these be the grounds of our salvation, these be thus written that we should believe them, and by our belief enjoy life everlasting. Once and in times past God diversely and many ways spoke unto the fathers by the prophets, but in these last days he has spoken unto us . . . by his own son, whom he has made heir of all things, whose dignity is such that he is the brightness of the father's glory, the very image of his substance, ruling all things by the word of his power.

Determined to discover the roots of the English Church apart from Rome, Parker combed through old manuscripts and published the results of his findings. He asked so many questions in his research that he was given the nickname "Nosey Parker."

Parker died in 1575. Thirty years later, a controversy erupted over his consecration. A book claimed that Parker's consecration had been flawed, not least because one of the bishops who placed hands on him had allegedly not been consecrated. Partisans of the Roman Church were quick to press these claims. A disturbed James I called his privy counsel. Research eventually settled the matter in favor of Parker and the Church of England. All four of the bishops had been properly consecrated, although one had lost his papers. Parker's own record of his consecration was unearthed and showed a proper ritual.

That was not the end of Parker's story, however. He seemed destined to be even more controversial in death than in life. During the Roundhead Rebellion against King Charles I, his body was dug up and thrown on a dung heap by Puritans who detested his memory.

Matthew Parker was destined to be even more controversial in death than in life. (Kennedy, W.M. *Archbishop Parker*. Makers of National History series. London: Sir Isaac Pitman & Sons, Ltd., 1908.)

Other Events

Annual: At the monastery of Fulda, monks of the ninth century listened to a reading of the life of Sturm, their founder, on this day each year.

1836: John Rippon, an English Baptist pastor, died. He wrote the hymn "How Firm a Foundation."

1843: Charles Dickens' *A Christmas Carol*, one of the most popular novelettes ever written, was published. Its theme of a stingy Scrooge versus kindly merrymakers became associated with the celebration of Christmas as no other literary work can claim to have done and has been freely imitated.

Charles Dickens created an enduring Christmas legend. (Crotch, Walter. *Charles Dickens, Social Reformer: The Social Teachings of England's Great Novelist*. London: Chapman & Hall, 1913.)

Evie Brand learned to paint as a young girl, loving John Joseph Turner's work. She painted into old age. (Wilson, Dorothy Clark. *Granny Brand: Her Story*. New York: Christian Herald Books, 1976. Used by permission of Paul Brand.)

December 18

Carrying On

Mission leaders sighed with relief when Evelyn Brand's mission years drew to a close. Years before, her husband, Jesse, and she had vowed to reach five mountain ranges of India with the gospel. But Jesse died four ranges short. Brand harped at wearisome length on the spiritual and medical needs of the five mountains. It was time for her to call it quits.

The staff gathered to bid their coworker good-bye. That's when Brand hit them with a shocker. She was retiring from the mission—retiring to take up independent work in the mountains. Warnings that she was too old fell on deaf ears. As far as she was concerned, life began at seventy.

Strictly speaking, life may begin a little sooner. Brand was born in England in 1879. Her father was well-to-do, and when she reached young womanhood, she cut a fine figure in plumed hats and frilled dresses. For all that, she was involved in mission support, street work and charities.

A trip overseas turned Brand's mind toward the needs of India. The arrival of a young missionary reinforced her decision to become a missionary. She found Jesse Brand too intense, but he seemed to look directly at her as he described the filth and squalor of India's mission field. His unspoken question was: Could she, a fashionable girl, handle such things? Yes, with God's help she could!

Assigned to Madras, she discovered that Jesse was there too, and she fell in love. Then she overheard a conversation: He was engaged. Shaking, she fled to her bathroom and poured cold water over herself. She had made a fool of herself! Her heart grew dry. Looking at India's flowers, blooming brilliantly in the dry season, she prayed, "Let me be like that, Lord, flowering best when life seems most dry and dead."

Language study took her to the hills. Jesse wrote to her. His engagement was off. Would she marry him? They would work the mountains together.

Her wedding day was no dream. Dressed in wedding white, she waited beside the litter in which she was to be carried. The bearers were chasing a wild pig. As thunder rumbled, others gathered. Heat wilted her dress. She was hoisted up and lurched along precipices. Thorns clutched her clothes. Rain turned the litter into a tub. When she dismounted to walk, she sank deep into mud holes. They lost their way in the dark.

Despite that rugged start, the Brands energetically taught the people better farming methods, treated the sick and built houses. They preached from village to village. But the people pulled back from Christianity. Local Hindu priests, fearful of lost influence and revenues, opposed the gospel. When Jesse died, Brand was reassigned to the plains.

Retirement meant liberation for Brand. Rejoicing, she fulfilled Jesse's dream. Just as in the old times, she rode a hill pony from village to village, camping, teaching and dispensing medicine. She rescued abandoned children. Despite broken bones, fevers and infirmities, the face that she turned upon the world was full of joy. "Praise God!" she exclaimed continually. She helped plant a mission work on each of the five ranges, and she added two more ranges to her sights.

While under treatment for torn ligaments, her mind failed. On this day in 1974, she died. Her body was taken back to the hills and laid beside Jesse's as a multitude wept. The woman who had been declared too old for India had carried on for twenty-four years, working to within seven days of her death.

Innocent VI. (Montor, Chevalier Artaud de. *Lives and Times of the Popes*. New York: Catholic Publication Society of America, 1911.)

Other Events

1352: Etienne Aubert was elected as Pope Innocent VI.

1555: John Philpot was burned for his Protestant views during the reign of England's Queen Mary Tudor.

1834: Emory College was chartered by Methodists in Georgia. It became Emory University many years later, just one of many notable educational establishments founded by Christians.

1902: An education act in Britain transferred control of Church schools to local powers.

1925: Edith Warner died from pleurisy and related complications after thirty-three years of service in Niger. She had served as an educator but also was the first white woman to set foot in areas of West Niger.

An Amazing Find in a Cave

On this day in 1947, a Bedouin stumbled across scrolls in pots in a cave. Thinking they might have some value, he placed them with Khalil Iskander, an antique dealer in Jerusalem. Iskander supposed they might be Syrian—valuable, but not immensely so. He consulted with a friend who agreed. The friend spoke to Orthodox Archbishop Athanasius Yeshua Samuel. Almost at once Samuel recognized the scrolls as sections of the Old Testament. Unable to suppress his excitement, he frantically made arrangements to purchase them.

Samuel showed the parchments to various experts. However, most of those who viewed them did not consider them highly significant. An exception was Father Boutris Sowmy, who was well-acquainted with the languages and declared the scrolls to be very old. He theorized that they were Essene manuscripts.

Months passed in which Samuel's efforts to learn the value of the scrolls were thwarted. He persisted, however, and contacted the American University of Beirut. The man he connected with was John Trever, who was not only a Bible student but was also trained in photographing old scrolls. Trever was intrigued and told Samuel to bring the manuscripts around. Father Sowmy conveyed them to Trever on February 19, 1948. Trever, the first American to see the scrolls, was intrigued. To him they looked valuable, but he did not know for sure.

He sought permission from Samuel to photograph the scrolls. He could not sleep as he waited. The next day, on February 20, 1948, Samuel's permission was forthcoming. The Orthodox archbishop was as keen as Trever to find out what the scrolls were worth. Trever began photographing at once. By Tuesday the pictures were on their way to the famed paleographer William F. Albright. On March 14 the answer came back: Albright congratulated the men on their find. The scroll was older than the Nash papyrus, he assured them, dating from probably 100 BC. "What an absolutely incredible find!" he wrote.

That it was. The whole world was soon electrified with the announcement of the discovery of the Dead Sea Scrolls. Their importance can hardly be overrated. Not only have they confirmed the accuracy of the Old Testament, but they have shed light on the years just before Christ's coming. We now know that much of Christ's message and many of his phrases were "in the air" before he was born.

Trever and his colleagues studied the scrolls the rest of that summer. Although E.L. Sukenik, an archaeology professor, recognized the value of other manuscripts from the caves a year earlier, and even risked his life trying to get pieces, Trever and his colleagues were the first to provide useful information to the world.

The original Dead Sea Scrolls were similar to this scroll from the Pentateuch. (Courtesy of the Christian History Institute archives.)

Other Events

821: Theodulf, poet, scholar, secretary of education and bishop of Orleans during Charlemagne's reign, was buried. He wrote hymns, among which his best remembered is "All Glory, Laud and Honor." After Charlemagne's death, Theodulf was accused of treason and imprisoned but eventually was pardoned in time to die a free man.

1789: The leaders of the French Revolution ordered the sale of 400 million livres worth of Church property. The revolutionary leaders were virulently anti-Christian and hated the Catholic Church for the long years of its ascendancy, years in which it had sometimes been as ruthless as the government in extracting wealth from the poor and tyrannizing the helpless.

1790: An interdenominational meeting opened in Philadelphia to create the First Day Society to strengthen Sunday observance.

1950: Bill Wallace, missionary surgeon to China, was taken captive in a predawn raid by the Communists and placed in a cell, where he was brutally interrogated as an American spy and finally murdered.

Robespierre, a Deist and leader of the French Revolution who was among those who ordered the sale of Church property. (Munro, Dana Carleton and Merrick Whitcomb. *The Middle Ages and Modern Europe*. New York: D. Appleton and Company, 1912.)

Edmund Grindal butted heads with Elizabeth I (shown here) as to where preaching could take place. (Pollard, Albert Frederick. *Thomas Cranmer and the English Reformation, 1489-1556*. Hamden, CT: Archon Books, 1905.)

December 20

Grindal Bucks His Queen

Edmund Grindal was once saved from instant death because he loved to read. As a youngster, he was so intent on improving himself that he took a book with him wherever he went. Walking in the woods one day, he had just tucked one of these books back into his breast pocket when an arrow sped out of nowhere, thumped into the book and quivered there. Thanks to his reading habit, Grindal was not killed on the spot. He matured to become one of the few men who dared to openly buck an order from Queen Elizabeth I.

Grindal's bold challenge to his queen would not come for many years, however. While studying at Cambridge, he sat under the teaching of Martin Bucer, a continental reformer who was closely acquainted with both Martin Luther and Ulrich Zwingli. Grindal became a Protestant and sought to imitate his teacher, who was notable for his holy and peaceful life. During the reign of Edward VI, Grindal held religious office at Westminster and was a chaplain to the king.

But upon the accession of Mary, whose intention to restore the Roman Church was no secret, Grindal fled overseas. While in Europe, he gathered material on the many martyrs whom Mary's reign had supplied. His notes became the basis of John Foxe's massive *Actes and Monuments* (now usually encountered in condensed versions entitled *Foxe's Book of Martyrs*).

With the death of Mary and the rise of Queen Elizabeth, Grindal returned to England, where he was made bishop of London. Eleven years later, he advanced to become archbishop of York. While in York, Grindal led teams of ministers throughout his archdiocese, teaching the reformed doctrine, establishing churches and placing in the pulpits men who showed evidence of genuine conversion experience. He cared less if a man had a university education than if he had the Holy Spirit. The result was genuine revival in York.

The archbishop of Canterbury, Matthew Parker, died in 1575. The following January, Elizabeth moved Grindal into England's highest Church office. He was in office not even a year before the crisis came. A form of preaching known as "prophesying" was in vogue, especially among Christians with Puritan sympathies. Two or three pastors would band together to speak on a chosen topic, questioning and critiquing each other. This method of presenting the gospel drew large crowds. Grindal himself had made heavy use of it in York.

Elizabeth feared that under the guise of such meetings, insurrections could gather. She ordered Grindal to suspend the practice. He could have complied, or he couldhave quietly ignored the queen. Instead, he sent her a long letter on this day in 1576. In it he refused to comply with her order. Christ commanded us to preach the gospel, he said. Church matters should be left to the Church. The archbishop reminded her that she too was mortal, although a great monarch.

Elizabeth was furious. She placed Grindal under house arrest. That she did not execute him was owing to his wide popularity and winsome spirit. He remained under arrest until his death, despite petitions from the other clergy that he be restored to his archdiocese. The queen did, however, send Grindal a heavy silver cup as a gesture of peace and allowed him to conduct some of his functions quietly. She was wise enough not to appoint anyone else in his place during his lifetime, even after he went blind and requested to be relieved of his duties.

Katie Luther in middle age. (McGiffert, Arthur Cushman. *Martin Luther, the Man and His Work*. New York: The Century Co., 1911.)

Other Events

1046: At the Synod of Sutri, Holy Roman Emperor Henry III deposed Benedict, Sylvester and Gregory, three rival claimants to the papacy, and placed his own man, Clement II, in the papal chair.

1157: Clement III was crowned pope. Unlike many churchmen, he protected Jews. Clement also organized the Third Crusade.

1511: Fray Antonio Montesinos preached a violent sermon against enslaving the Indians of the Indies. The message impelled Bartolomé de Las Casas to emancipate his Indian slaves and champion their cause both in the New World and at the court in Spain.

1550: Martin Luther's wife, Katie, died, saying, "I will stick to Christ like a burr."

1803: Samuel Hopkins, the first Congregationalist pastor to become an abolitionist, died on this day. He had studied under Jonathan Edwards but held non-traditional views on original sin and the atonement.

1934: Adelaide A. Pollard, an ascetic who taught in Nyack Missionary Training Institute in New York, died. She wrote the hymn "Have Thine Own Way, Lord."

The Man Born to Be King

The year was 1941. Britain was at war—and not just with Germany. At home, a firestorm of controversy roared around a solitary Christian writer.

The trouble began when the British Broadcast Corporation (BBC) announced that it would produce a series of twelve radio plays retelling the life of Christ. *The Man Born to Be King* was written by the scholar Dorothy L. Sayers, a member of the Church of England. At a press conference, she explained that in order to adapt the gospels to radio, she had invented characters and combined two or more Bible personages into one. To make the radio voices distinct, she sometimes used American slang or regional accents. For instance, Matthew says, "The fact is, Philip, you've been had for a sucker. You ought to keep your eyes skinned."

From the reaction, one would have thought that Sayers had burned a Bible in St. Paul's Cathedral. Before a single play was released, newspaper headlines screamed, "Blasphemy!" Atheists complained that Christians were being given free radio time for propaganda. Language lovers, who wanted to keep English "pure," griped, "Should children listen to such unwholesome, American slang?" The Lord's Day Observance Society said that using an actor to impersonate Christ bordered on blasphemy. "A sinful man presuming to impersonate the Sinless One! It detracts from the honor due to the Divine Majesty."

Prime Minister Winston Churchill found his office swamped with letters urging a ban on the plays. The archbishop of Canterbury, leading official of the Church of England, received a similar flood of requests. Sir Percy Hurd, a member of Parliament, raised a question about the plays in the House of Commons.

Despite all of the controversy, Sayers kept writing. Although she was best known as the creator of detective Lord Peter Wimsey, she was well-qualified to write Christian plays. She had already done two for Canterbury Cathedral, both of which were so good they ran for several weeks in London.

Sayers was also qualified as a Christian. Reared in the Church of England, she did not follow the path of the majority of intellectuals, who abandoned the Church. Although she had not lived a saintly life—she had an illegitimate son, for instance—neither had she renounced the faith. Others might have drifted from the creeds and denied the dogmas (if they ever held them), but Sayers increasingly turned to them as the only worldview that fit reality. Just how satisfying Christianity was for her became clear in 1938 when she wrote a Sunday editorial for the *Times*. "The Christian faith is the most exciting drama that ever staggered the imagination of man . . . and the dogma is the drama."

More and more, Sayers spoke out on behalf of Christianity. She accused religious leaders of being so careful to say nothing that would offend anyone that they said nothing worth saying at all. In her radio dramas she tried to present Christ's story with superb craftsmanship. This meant she even had to invent the form she used. The nearest equivalent was the cycle of Arthur legends.

The first play from *The Man Born to Be King* was broadcast on this day in 1941. Most listeners who contacted the BBC said they loved it. For many, the play raised morale by reminding them of their Christian roots. Sayers made Christ's life seem so real that people were forced to reconsider its meaning for themselves. The bishop of Winchester said the cycle was the greatest evangelical appeal made in the twentieth century. *The Man Born to Be King* was replayed often in Sayers' lifetime. She joked that if it became any more popular, bakers and fishmongers would demand advertising slots when it aired.

Sayers was not content to bask in her triumph. Before she died, she wrote another play, this one about Constantine, and made superb verse translations of Dante's *Divine Comedy* and *The Song of Roland*. She also wrote witty essays defending Christianity. A typical Sayers approach was to poke fun at the silliness of a certain kind of Bible criticism by soberly applying its techniques to Sherlock Holmes mysteries.

Christ in the temple, which was one of the scenes depicted in Dorothy Sayers' *The Man Born to Be King*. (Bell, Mrs. Arthur. *Saints in Christian Art*. London: George Bell, 1901-4.)

Other Events

1597: Peter Canisius, an energetic Dutch Jesuit who established the Catholic Counter-Reformation in Germany and Austria, died.

1620: The Pilgrims landed at Plymouth Rock.

1804: Benjamin Disraeli, who would convert from Judaism to Christianity and become the British prime minister, was born in London.

1807: John Newton, the parson who had been a slaver and wrote the hymn "Amazing Grace," died on this day.

1835: Oglethorpe University was chartered by Presbyterians in Georgia.

1896: Walter Lewis Wilson was converted. Years later he received a filling of the Holy Spirit and became a mighty man of God, winning many to Christ.

British Prime Minister Benjamin Disraeli converted from Judaism to Christianity. (Courtesy of the University of Texas collection of public domain portraits on the Web.)

John Hunt and his wife were forced to breathe the nauseating smell of roasting humans. (McLean, Archibald. *Epoch Makers of Modern Missions*. Cincinnati: Fleming H. Revell Co., 1912.)

The Hunts Arrive at Fiji's Cannibal Land

When John Hunt was a lad in the early 1800s, he believed that God heard prayers. He prayed for protection against the things that made him fearful—dogs, gypsies and thunder. As he grew older, he drifted from faith. His clumsiness was mocked. Handier farm boys taunted him as an idiot. He fell in with rough companions. At times he promised the Lord that he would change, but he did not keep his word.

Then Hunt got sick and death loomed before his eyes. It was no use making the Lord more promises. He fell to his knees and vowed to serve God then and there. When he recovered, he repeated his promise to godly neighbors, making himself accountable for spiritual growth. After that, he attended church, read the Bible and religious books in his spare time and addressed a local congregation. Friends encouraged him to preach, but he wasn't sure. He prayed earnestly to know what God expected him to do, until his last doubt vanished.

Untrained though Hunt was, God used him. He studied at night so as not to neglect his farm duties. His earnestness was apparent to all. Revival broke out when he attended a London institution. He began to think of mission work, and soon South Africa was his goal.

However, an appeal was made for workers in Fiji. Asked point blank to go, Hunt returned home much troubled—not for himself but for the girl he hoped to marry. Hanna Summers, in poor health, would have accompanied him to South Africa, where a measure of civilization prevailed. But Fiji? The Fijians were cannibals and completely savage. Thieves and liars to a man, they killed their sick and old, treated women as beasts of burden, robbed graves for food and strangled wives when their husbands died. But Hanna said she would go.

The couple sailed from England in 1838. They refused a lucrative offer to remain in Australia and sailed on to Fiji, arriving on the scene of their labors on this day in 1838. Although Hunt would master the language in short order, conversions were slow in coming. One cruel king threatened the Hunts with death if they closed their windows to keep out the smell of bodies roasting a short distance from their home.

Eventually, however, the situation began to improve. On one of the smaller islands, revival broke out. Many Fijians were transformed, and their faces shone with new hope. Hunt translated the New Testament into the native tongue for those converts. He was one of those men who could not rest long while there was work to be done. It is little wonder that he sickened. The islanders prayed for his recovery, offering God to take ten of them rather than him.

But Hunt was dying. He mourned over his inconsistencies, failures and backslidings. He prayed fervently for the salvation of the Fiji Islands. Suddenly he grew utterly calm. "You see a bright prospect before you," said someone.

"I see nothing but Jesus," exclaimed Hunt. He died, just thirty-three years old. Within fifty years of his landing, there was not a single person in the islands who openly professed the old heathen religion.

Dwight L. Moody, master soul-winner. (Thompson, C.L. *Times of Refreshing, Being a History of American Revivals with Their Philosophy and Methods*. Rockford: Golden Censer Co. Publishers, 1878.)

Other Events

1216: Pope Honorius III officially confirmed the Dominican order.

1560: Julian Hernandez was burned in Spain for heresy. His crime was possession of Protestant books.

1815: Revolutionary Mexican priest Jose Morelos was executed. A capable general, he issued Mexico's first constitution and killed Royalists.

1888: Isaac Hecker, the influential convert to Roman Catholicism who founded the order of Paulists in the United States and edited *Catholic World*, died.

1899: Dwight L. Moody, one of the most effective evangelists the United States ever produced, died on this day.

1906: Robert Rainy, influential leader of the Scottish Free Church who handled delicate negotiations to reunite the Free Church with the United Presbyterian Church in 1900, died.

Ivan the Terrible Lived Up to His Nickname

December 23

Czar Ivan IV of Russia was so noted for his cruelty that he is known in history as "Ivan the Terrible." Among his many atrocities was the murder of Philip of Moscow on this day in 1569.

Philip was born to a good Russian family in 1510 and named Fyodor Kolychev. The Kolychevs were active in government service, and Philip spent his youth at the court of the czar. One day while at church, he was convicted by Christ's warning that a man cannot serve two masters. Fearing that the court was keeping him from Christ, he fled the Russian capital and went north to the Solovetsky Monastery, just within the Arctic Circle on an island in the White Sea. It was a primitive place compared to the glitter of the capital.

There he was accepted into the monastery and given the name Philip. He became known for his piety, his intelligence and his sense of duty in following monastic rules. In 1547, the same year Ivan was crowned czar, Philip became the abbot of the monastery. His immense administrative abilities transformed the monastery into one of the great industrial complexes of the empire. Under Philip's administration, the monks cleared more fields for cultivation; established a dairy farm, a mill and a workshop for leather and fur clothes; built storage bins for the monastery's grain; developed a system of dams, reservoirs and canals to drain the swampland and bring water to the monastery; and built a hospital for pilgrims, new dormitories for the monks and a new cathedral. All of this agricultural and industrial labor was consecrated to God.

The czar was impressed with all of these works and appointed Philip metropolitan head of the Russian Church. Philip, however, opposed many of Ivan's policies and his mass executions. Ivan tried to intimidate Philip by beheading his cousin and sending the head to Philip sewn up in a leather bag. Philip asked himself, "Where is my faith if I am silent?" and he continued to speak out against the crazy czar.

He warned Ivan, "Your earthly rank has no control over death, which sinks its invincible teeth into everything. And remember that each person must answer for his own life." Ivan ignored the warning and continued his great massacres. To all of his other crimes he added this: He had Philip smothered in his prison cell on this day in 1569.

Philip's last moments. (Howe, Sonia E. *Some Russian Heroes, Saints, and Sinners: Legendary and Historical*. Philadelphia: J.B. Lippincott, 1917.)

Other Events

619: Boniface V was consecrated as pope. When a dispute arose as to which bishop in England was to exercise primacy over the island, he determined that the bishop of Canterbury was the head of the English Church. Boniface was known for his love of the clergy and his mild disposition.

1856: Tiyo Soga, an African Christian leader, was ordained in the Presbyterian Church. He became a powerful missionary to his own people.

1915: William H. Doane, who wrote many of our most beloved hymn tunes, including those to which we sing "More Love to Thee" and "I Am Thine, O Lord" to mention but two of many, died.

1950: Pope Pius XII declared in a radio broadcast that St. Peter's tomb had been found several feet below the altar of St. Peter's Basilica at the Vatican in Rome. The evidence proved to be seriously tainted by flaws in methodology.

Boniface V, known for his love and mildness. (Montor, Chevalier Artaud de. *Lives and Times of the Popes*. New York: Catholic Publication Society of America, 1911.)

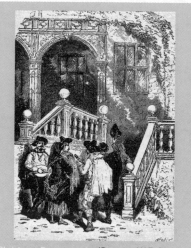

A Christmas Eve serenade. (Dawson, W.F. *Christmas, Its Origin and Associations, Together with Its Historical Events and Festive Celebrations During Nineteen Centuries*. London: Elliot Stock, 1902.)

December 24

How We Got Christmas Eve

Legend says that the outlaw Robin Hood, who gave to the poor what he robbed from the rich, died on this day, Christmas Eve, in 1247. It is, after all, only a legend, for some scholars doubt there ever was such a person. But Christmas Eve has a long and significant history.

In most countries with a Christian heritage, the birth of Christ came to be honored on December 25 as a religious celebration. Christmas means "Christ mass." Although the date is a guess, the tradition of observing it goes back to at least the fourth century. Under the influence of the Church, Christian traditions replaced pagan solstice festivals throughout Europe.

Often the more innocent pagan practices (such as bringing in a Yule log and decorating it with holly and the like) were carried over into the Christmas observance, transfigured with new meaning. For centuries, Christmas was celebrated not as a single day, but as a whole season, beginning with this day, December 24, Christmas Eve. Perhaps the practice of celebrating the eve is an echo from ancient Jewish reckoning carried over into the Church. Among most Jews, a day began at six in the evening and ran until six the following evening.

As Christmas observance spread throughout Europe and in lands colonized by Europeans, Christmas Eve was often celebrated with roaring fires, the telling of tales, happy feasting, drinking, dancing and sometimes clowning. Sir Walter Scott described the festive air in a poem:

> On Christmas Eve, the bells were rung;
> On Christmas Eve, the mass was sung.
> ...
> The damsel donned her kirtle sheen,
> the hall was dressed with holly green;
> ...
> All hail'd with uncontroll'd delight,
> And general voice the happy night
> That to the cottage, as the crown,
> Brought tidings of salvation down.

Things weren't always so pleasant, of course. On Christmas Eve in 1521, with the Reformation gaining steam in Germany, crowds rioted in Wittenberg. Andreas Carlstadt had given them both the bread and the wine at mass against the orders of Elector Frederick. Zealous for more "reformation," the mob smashed church lamps, out-sang the choir and intimidated priests.

Some say Martin Luther cut the first modern-day Christmas tree. The story may be apocryphal, but we know that on Christmas Eve in 1538, he was in a jolly mood, singing and talking about the Incarnation. Then he sighed, saying, "Oh, we poor men, that we should be so cold and indifferent to this great joy which has been given us."

However, others besides Luther would recognize Christmas Eve as special. In his memoirs, Sir John Reresby told how he invited his poor tenants for a feast on Christmas Eve in 1682.

During World War I, troops from both sides made their famous Christmas Truce on Christmas Eve in 1914, demonstrating once again the power for good inherent in the season. And on Christmas Eve in 1968, Apollo VIII astronauts James A. Lovell, William Anders and Frank Borman read Genesis 1 to a listening world while orbiting the moon.

Fyodor Dostoevsky was greatly influenced by the Bible. (Kaus, Otto. *Dostojewski zur Kritik der Personlichkeit*. München: R. Piper, 1916.)

Other Events

1541: Andreas Carlstadt, a Protestant reformer of Germany and a mystical precursor of the eighteenth-century Lutheran Pietists, died on this day. Somewhat unstable, he ran afoul of Martin Luther and worked with Ulrich Zwingli.

1784: At Baltimore, Francis Asbury formally organized the Methodist Episcopal Church in the United States.

1849: Dostoevsky started for the Omsk penal settlement to which he was condemned for joining a rebel plot. On the way, a woman thrust a Bible into his hands, and it began his turn toward Christ. Although Christian elements are strong in his writings, he suffered all his life from compulsive behaviors such as gambling.

1870: Albert Barnes, an American Presbyterian pastor and Bible expositor who precipitated a split in his church over the issue of salvation, died. He believed in a universal atonement (which many theologians do not accept), whereas old-school Presbyterians held that Christ died only for the elect.

1873: The Temperance Movement began when Eliza Thompson and seventy women prayed and sang in front of a saloon.

1933: The *Codex Sinaiticus*, sold by a cash-starved USSR, arrived in Britain.

DECEMBER 25

First Verifiable Christmas Celebration

This day is Christmas day (Christ's mass). But for the first 300 years of Christianity, it was not so. When was Christmas first celebrated? In an old list of Roman bishops, compiled in AD 354, these words appear for AD 336: "25 Dec.: *natus Christus in Betleem Judeae*." which means, "December 25th, Christ born in Bethlehem, Judea." This day in 336 is the first recorded celebration of Christmas.

For the first 300 years of the Church's existence, birthdays were not given much emphasis—not even the birth of Christ. The day on which a saint died was considered more significant than his or her birth, as it ushered him or her into the kingdom of heaven above. In the January 6 feast of Epiphany, Christ's baptism received more attention than his birthday.

No one knows for sure on what day Christ was born. Dionysus Exiguus, a sixth-century monk, was the first to date all of history from December 25, the year of our Lord 1. Other traditions gave dates as early as mid-November or as late as March. How did Christmas come to be celebrated on December 25? Cultures around the Mediterranean and across Europe observed feasts on or around December 25, marking the winter solstice. The Jews had a festival of lights; Germans had a Yule festival. Celtic legends connected the solstice with Balder, the Scandinavian sun god who was struck down by a mistletoe arrow. At the pagan festival of Saturnalia, Romans feasted and gave gifts to the poor. Drinking was closely connected with these pagan feasts. At some point, a Christian bishop probably adopted the day to keep his people from indulging in the old pagan festival.

Many of the pagan customs became associated with Christmas. Christian stories replaced the heathen tales, but the practices hung on. Candles continued to be lit. Kissing under the mistletoe remained common in Scandinavian countries. Over the years, gift exchanges became connected with the name of St. Nicholas, a real but legendary figure of fourth-century Lycia (a province of Asia). A charitable man, he threw gifts into homes.

Around the thirteenth century, Christians added one of the most pleasant touches of all to the Christmas celebration when they began to sing Christmas carols.

No one is sure just when the Christmas tree came into the picture. It almost certainly originated in Germany. The eighth-century English missionary St. Boniface, "Apostle to Germany," is supposed to have held up the evergreen as a symbol of the everlasting Christ. By the end of the sixteenth century, Christmas trees were common in Germany. Some say Martin Luther cut the first tree, took it home and decked it with candles to represent the stars. When the German court came to England, the Christmas tree came with them.

Puritans forbade Christmas, considering it too pagan. Governor Bradford actually threatened New Englanders with work, jail or fines if they were caught observing Christmas.

Wise men bring gifts to Christ and worship Him. (Dawson, W.F. *Christmas, Its Origin and Associations, Together with Its Historical Events and Festive Celebrations During Nineteen Centuries*. London: Elliot Stock, 1902.)

In Victorian England in 1843, Charles Dickens published his novelette *A Christmas Carol*. It became one of the most popular short works of fiction ever penned. Although the book is more a work of sentiment than of Christianity, it captures the Christmas spirit. The tightfisted grump, Ebenezer Scrooge, who exclaimed, "Humbug!" at the mention of Christmas, is contrasted with generous merrymakers such as his nephew, Fred, and with the struggling poor, symbolized by Bob Cratchit and Tiny Tim. The book's appeal to good works and charitable contributions virtually defined Christmas in English-speaking lands.

Whatever the ins and outs of Christmas, one thing is sure: We are still unwrapping the gift of God's Son—and what an incentive to generosity and joy that gift is!

OTHER EVENTS

496: Clovis of France was baptized with thousands of his followers. His wife, Clotilda, was instrumental in converting him.

597: Ethelbert of Kent was baptized by the missionary Augustine, an important event in the Christianization of southern England.

1185: Urban III was elected pope. He spent most of his brief pontificate in exile because of his insistence that the pope, not the Roman Senate, should govern the papal estates.

1541: Andreas Carlstadt, a reformer who first sided with Martin Luther and then against him, died. Carlstadt supposedly even plotted to do Luther physical harm. He disagreed with Luther on how Christ is present in the bread and the wine at Eucharist.

1909: Japanese evangelist Toyohiki Kagawa crossed the Higurashi Bridge to serve in the slums of Shinkawa. "Theology is but an appendix to love, and an unreliable appendix!" he said.

Clovis is baptized on Christmas day. (Baring-Gould, S. *Lives of the Saints*. Edinburgh: John Grant, 1914.)

Leo crowns Charles. (Bell, Mrs. Arthur. *Saints in Christian Art* London: George Bell, 1901-04.)

December 26

Waking to Charles the Great

On this day, a winter morning in 800, the people of Rome and much of Europe woke up with a Roman emperor on the throne for the first time in over 300 years. For on the day before—Christmas Day—a surprising and dramatic event had occurred: King Charles of France was kneeling in prayer before the altar of St. Peter's Basilica in Rome when Pope Leo III suddenly placed a golden crown on his head. The Roman people shouted three times, "To Charles Augustus, crowned by God, the great and pacific emperor of the Romans, life and victory!" Charles was revered by the pope and called "Emperor" and "Augustus," after the manner of the leaders of ancient Rome.

What had brought about this dramatic event 300 centuries after the fall of the Roman Empire in the West? The pope in Rome undoubtedly wanted to show his independence from the Greek Empire in Constantinople. Since the days of Constantine in the fourth century, the eastern part of the Roman Empire had authority over the whole, but it had been badly weakened in the West. In Charles, king of the Franks, the pope thought he had found a new Constantine who could be head of a revived Western empire as Constantine had been head of the Eastern empire.

Charles had become master of the French kingdom in 768. He used his great military might to forcibly bring the German tribes under his authority, requiring the people to be baptized and become Christians. His dominion stretched from the Baltic Sea to the British Channel to Rome itself. Charles worked diligently to provide a good, unified organization for his vast empire.

When King Charles returned to France after being crowned emperor by the pope, he made his subjects take a new oath to him as caesar. He had reestablished the old Roman empire on a Teutonic base. The coronation of Charles sparked much debate during the Middle Ages. At issue was the relationship between the Church and the government. Did this act show the pope's superior authority as giver of the empire to King Charles?

Charles didn't think so. He continued to rule as the divinely appointed protector of the Church, appointing bishops as well as counts to office. He was not only the first, but possibly even the greatest of the emperors who ruled from the eighth century through the nineteenth. In France, his very name was blended with his greatness, and he became known as Charlemagne—Charles the Great.

Christian businessman and philanthropist John Wanamaker displayed the first electric Christmas lights. (Wallace, Lew. *Living Leaders of the World*. Chicago: Hubbard Bros., 1889.)

Other Events

795: St. Leo III was elected pope. Five years later, the vigorous leader crowned Charlemagne as Holy Roman Emperor.

1767: Huguenot Marie Durand was released after thirty-eight years in prison. Her crime was having a Protestant minister as her brother.

1948: Cardinal Mindszenty was arrested. He scribbled a note to his mother:

> I have taken no part in any conspiracy of any kind. I shall not resign from my episcopal see. I shall not make a confession. But if despite what I now say you should read that I have confessed or resigned, and even see it authenticated by my signature, bear in mind that it will have been only the result of human frailty. In advance, I declare all such actions null and void.

On Feb 9, 1949, he was given a stiff sentence.

1968: The American Church historian Kenneth Scott Latourette, whose *History of the Expansion of Christianity* remains a notable achievement, died on this day.

The Sanctuary of Holy Wisdom Dedicated

Nothing like the new church of Constantinople had been seen before. Borrowing from several earlier architectural styles, Anthemius of Tralles and Isidorus of Miletus created the masterpiece of sixth-century Byzantium. Although they were not professional architects, Emperor Justinian chose them, presumably because they had helped construct some of his military works. At any rate, they applied mathematics to the structure in a manner that was new to architectural design. The result was a work of grace and beauty.

Because its dome was set upon a ring of closely spaced windows, the Hagia Sophia (Church of the Holy Wisdom) was so

> full of light and sunshine; you would declare that the place is not lighted by the sun from without, but that the rays are produced within itself, such an abundance of light is poured into this church.

Emperor Justinian had spared no expense to erect the masterpiece, which went up in the astonishing span of just five years. This was possible because Justinian lavished money on the enterprise. One source estimates he spent as much as 23 million gold *solidi* on the building (the equivalent of $25 billion* in today's purchasing power). On the decor alone, 40,000 pounds of silver were used.

When the emperor inspected the largely completed work just before its consecration, he was silent for a long time. His eyes scanned its contrasts of gold with blue, the alternation of vertical and horizontal marble slabs and the opposition of carven columns to curved arches. These created an interior beauty that made space seem to melt into space so that it was hard for the eye to gauge distances. "Solomon, I have surpassed you!" he murmured at last.

And in truth, no temple of antiquity had ever come close to the originality and magnificence of the Hagia Sophia. It had been made possible only by Justinian's zeal. At first it was simply called the Great Church, but later the name "Holy Wisdom" was applied to it.

On this day in 537, Patriarch Menas of Constantinople consecrated the architectural masterpiece. Eventually, a bridge linked the church directly to the nearby imperial palace. Six hundred religious workers served the building, in which important religious functions of the empire took place. According to the patriarchate of Constantinople, these workers included 80 priests, 150 deacons, 40 deaconesses, 60 subdeacons, 160 readers, 25 chanters and 75 doorkeepers.

The fabulous Hagia Sophia. (Wirth, Albrecht. *Der Balkan: Seine Länder und Völker in Geschichte, Kultur, Politik, Volkswirtschaft und Weltverkehr*. Stuttgart: Union Deutsche Verlagsgesellschaft, 1914.)

*This figure is arrived at through the following reasoning: A gold *solidus* was worth twenty-five silver *denarii*. A *denarius* was a day's wage for a common laborer. At a minimum wage of US$5.50 an hour, a *denarius* would be equivalent to $44 in buying power. The rest is multiplication.

Other Events

418: Pope St. Zosimus died. His fourteen-month pontificate served chiefly to reaffirm decrees against the Pelagians (after first declaring them Orthodox). He also became embroiled in a controversy with the Church of North Africa when he usurped their prescribed method of hearing appeals by African clergy.

1555: Johann Arndt was born in Ballenstedt, Germany. He became a Lutheran clergyman and put so much emphasis on the necessity of heart change for true Christian faith that he is sometimes described as the first Pietist.

1603: Thomas Cartwright, an English Presbyterian who publicly opposed the Church of England, which he said was not biblical, died. He was much loved by the common people wherever he went but had to flee England because of his views. He even landed in prison on occasion, but he died a free man with much honor.

1843: Benajah Caroll was born in Carrollton, Mississippi. Although his parents were devout Baptists, Caroll became a fanatical atheist as a result of reading books that attacked faith. One day, however, he heard a Methodist preacher challenge an audience to "make a practical, experimental test" of Christianity. Benajah agreed to try it and entered a woods on the way home and "had it out with the Lord." The result was that he became a notable Christian educator, writer and evangelist.

Pope St. Zosimus. He served for only fourteen months. (Montor, Chevalier Artaud de. *Lives and Times of the Popes*. New York: Catholic Publication Society of America, 1911.)

Edward the Confessor carried to his burial. (Baring-Gould, S. *Lives of the Saints*. Edinburgh: John Grant, 1914.)

December

28

England's Best-Known Abbey Dedicated

Westminster Abbey is the religious center for Britain's royalty. From William the Conqueror to Elizabeth II, all but one of Britain's kings and queens was crowned there. Westminster exudes history. It was founded by the last of the Saxon kings.

Even in legend, the abbey has been important. Sir Thomas Mallory placed Guenivere and Arthur at the abbey in one of his tales of the round table. Old tales say King Ebert of the East Saxons built a church there in the seventh century and that Mellitus, the first bishop of London, oversaw it, but the evidence for this is weak.

Our historical knowledge firms up with St. Dunstan, who founded (or took over) a monastery on the isle. A century later, Edward the Confessor, last of the Saxon kings to hold the English throne, constructed a great church on the spot. The story is a curious one.

Son of King Ethelred the Unready, Edward spent his youth in exile in Normandy because of struggles between the Danes and the Saxons for the English throne. Edward is said to have vowed to make a pilgrimage to Rome if he were restored to his native land and its throne. When this came about in 1041, through the help of Godwin, earl of Kent, Edward realized the impracticality of his vow and asked the pope to absolve Edward of it. Leo IX released him on the condition that he build an abbey in honor of St. Peter. Edward selected the isle of Thanet as the spot and built himself a palace nearby so that he could watch the work in progress.

The choir and transepts of Edward's famous chapel were dedicated on this day in 1065. Edward could not attend the ceremony because he was desperately ill. He died nine days later. A century after the dedication of Westminster Abbey, he was canonized (mostly for political reasons), and his remains were translated to the church.

Edward left the succession in doubt. Harold, son of Godwin, claimed that Edward had made the nation over to him on his deathbed. But William, duke of Normandy, said Edward had left the kingdom to him in his will. William won the contest.

On Christmas Day in 1066, William was crowned in the chapel that Edward built. Shouts of acclamation rang out, and soldiers, posted outside thought their duke was in danger. As a diversion, they set fire to neighboring buildings. The ceremony was hurriedly completed, and the audience rushed outside.

Present-day Westminster Abbey is not the same building that Edward erected. Henry III tore that down and rebuilt it. Edward's remains were transferred to this new building. The famous of England have been interred there ever since.

Other Events

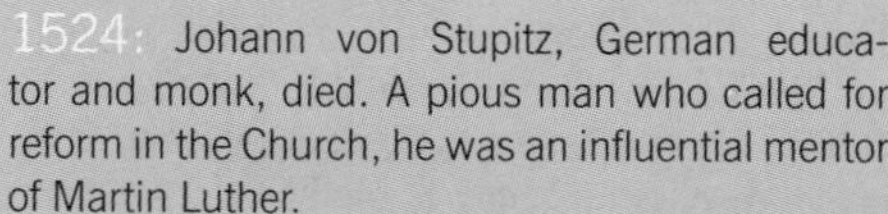

1524: Johann von Stupitz, German educator and monk, died. A pious man who called for reform in the Church, he was an influential mentor of Martin Luther.

1622: Francis de Sales, who said, "Nothing is so strong as gentleness, nothing so gentle as real strength," died.

1797: Charles Hodge was born in Philadelphia, Pennsylvania. A graduate of Princeton Theological Seminary, he became one of its most notable theologians and founded the magazine now known as *Princeton Review*. He prepared a three-volume *Systematic Theology* that influenced seminarians for over 100 years.

1838: Greensborough Female College was chartered in Greensborough, North Carolina, as a Methodist College. It became Greensboro College.

1948: Jacob DeShazzar, one of America's World War II Doolittle Raiders, returned to Japan to evangelize the country he had once bombed.

1973: *The Gulag Archipelago* was published in Paris. Its massive volumes documented Soviet oppression in its prison camps, where Solzhenitsyn had been incarcerated. In one of its most famous passages, Solzhenitsyn blessed the prison for having been in his life, explaining that there he had found God.

Francis de Sales. (Baird, Henry Martyn. *Theodore Beza: The Councilor of the French Reformation*. New York: G.P. Putnam's Sons, 1899.)

Fireworks in the Dark and a Conversion

The "Father of Modern Chemistry," Robert Boyle, was an outstanding seventeenth-century Christian. Though he is remembered as a founder of the Royal Society and for his scientific studies, especially his discovery of the law relating gas pressures to temperature and volume, Boyle himself considered his scientific studies simply one aspect of his Christian life and walk.

Born into a family of great wealth, even as a boy Boyle had a serious desire to live righteously in the world. In his own account of his boyhood, he gave himself the Greek name Philaretus, meaning "fond of virtue." On this day in 1640, when he was thirteen, Boyle had a conversion experience, which he later marked as the turning point of his life.

He recounted that at night he

> suddenly awoke in a fright by loud claps of thunder . . . and every clap was both preceded and attended with flashes of lightning so frequent and so dazzling, that Philaretus began to imagine them the sallies of that fire that must consume the world. The long continuance of that dismal tempest, when the winds were so loud, as almost drowned the noise of the very thunder, and the showers so hideous, as almost quenched the lightning, ere it could reach his eyes confirmed Philaretus in his apprehensions of the day of judgment's being at hand. Whereupon the consideration of his unpreparedness to welcome it, and the hideousness of being surprised by it in an unfit condition, made him resolve and vow, that if his fears were that night disappointed, all his future additions to his life should be more religiously and watchfully employed. The morning came, and a serene cloudless sky returned, when he ratified his determination so solemnly, that from that day he dated his conversion.

From that point on Boyle had a fixed determination to practice Christian piety—to study the Scriptures and the history of the Church and to consecrate his scientific work as a witness to God's creation. This was especially necessary as the pseudo-science of his day contradicted the Bible. He set out to find the truth and in the process discovered new scientific laws that nowhere disagreed with Scripture.

He had a passionate desire to see the gospel spread among the native populations of

Robert Boyle became a major figure in modern science when he could not reconcile existing theories with the Bible. (Evelyn, John. *Diary and Correspondence of John Evelyn*. London: Henry G. Bohn, 1859.)

Ireland, America and the Orient and became an active supporter of Christian missions. He wrote books and established lectureships to defend the truth of Christianity, but the strongest apologetic for Christianity he gave was his humble, upright and dedicated Christian life.

Other Events

1170: Four knights of England's King Henry II murdered the archbishop of Canterbury, Thomas á Becket.

1849: The words of the popular Christmas carol "It Came Upon a Midnight Clear" first appeared in print in *The Christian Register*, volume 28, number 52.

1851: In Boston, Massachusetts, Captain Thomas V. Sullivan organized the first US branch of the YMCA. While working with sailors, Sullivan saw the value of the Christian organization for providing them with activities other than the low pursuits so common among them when they entered port.

1876: Hymn writer P.P. Bliss died in a flaming train wreck in Ashtablua, Ohio. The train had plunged into a ravine when a trestle gave way. Ironically, on the night before Bliss is said to have sung "I'm Going Home Tomorrow." Among the hymns he wrote was "Hallelujah, What a Savior."

1932: Allen Yuan, who became an evangelical Church leader in China and spent many years in prison for his faith, was converted.

Hymn writer P.P. Bliss. (Thompson, C.L. *Times of Refreshing, Being a History of American Revivals with Their Philosophy and Methods*. Rockford: Golden Censer Co. Publishers, 1878.)

DECEMBER 30

Josephine Butler, Champion of Women

Josephine Butler sought out women who had suffered more than she had. (Hay-Cooper, L. *Josephine Butler and Her Work for Social Purity*. London: S.P.C.K., 1922.)

Six-year-old Eva Butler was excited—her mom and dad were home. She rushed to the staircase to greet her parents—and lost her footing. In front of her mother's horrified eyes, she fell over the banister onto the hard tile floor to her death. Josephine Butler would never erase that haunting sight from her memory. "It was pitiful to see her, helpless in her father's arms, her little drooping head resting on his shoulder and her beautiful golden hair all stained with blood, falling over his arm!" But rather than retire into a half-mad world of grief and nostalgia, Butler turned her attention outward. "[I] became possessed with an irresistible urge to go forth and find some pain keener than my own, to meet with people more unhappy than myself." She started to work with the prostitutes of Liverpool. Many had become street women out of desperation.

Butler was a beautiful upper-class woman, well-to-do, with many connections. She opened a home to reclaim lost women. As she learned more about their condition, she became increasingly indignant at the unfair laws of a system that refused women the right to vote. Women should not be denied the vote because they are different than men, she argued. They should be given the vote precisely for that reason, because their needs are different. She became a champion for women.

Butler, who had undergone a strong conversion experience as a teenager, needed the strength of faith in her lifelong battle for laws that were favorable to women. She took on the Contagious Diseases Acts that aimed to stop the spread of venereal disease. Under these laws, any woman in designated military towns could be forcibly inspected for venereal disease. The law was completely unfair. Men were not examined. Any woman, however pure, could be denounced to the authorities. Her reputation ruined, the woman might actually be forced into the sex trade. Butler declared:

> This legalization of vice, which is the endorsement of the "necessity" of impurity for man and the institution of slavery of woman, is the most open denial which modern times have seen of the principle of the sacredness of the individual being.

She warned that if a woman's rights could be stolen, so could anyone's.

When she stood up to speak against outrageous practices, Butler was slandered. Her enemies heckled and harassed her. They smeared her with dung. A mob smashed the windows of a hotel where she was staying, trying to get at her. They also threatened to set the building on fire. She fled through unfamiliar streets and hid behind piles of soap and candles in a shop. Another time, she hid in a hayloft while her opponents lit a fire to smoke her out. Her husband's college job was threatened, but he encouraged her to go on. When his wife sheltered fallen women in their home, he treated them like high-society ladies.

Far from retreating, Butler expanded her activities. "I felt very weak and lonely," she admitted. "But there was One who stood by me." She fought similar laws in Europe. In an age that tried to cover up sexual problems, she had the courage to address them openly. She fought against forced prostitution and appealed to governments not to license whorehouses. A government should never be in the sin business, she said.

While fighting government-sponsored prostitution, Butler always stood beside the prostitutes. If Christ forgave such women, so should we, she argued. She succeeded in getting some hateful laws repealed and helped rouse public sentiment to pass a bill that raised the age of consent from thirteen to sixteen.

Despite all of her hard work and efforts, however, Butler was largely forgotten by the time she died on this day in 1906.

Mrs. Gobat's child died in her arms in the Egyptian desert. (Pitman, E.R. *Lady Missionaries in Many Lands*. London: Pickering & Inglis, 1900.)

OTHER EVENTS

1845: The Gobats left Jaffa for Jerusalem. Mrs. Gobat had suffered tremendously as a missionary wife. One child died in her arms while they were crossing the desert.

1993: The Vatican and Israel signed a Fundamental Agreement. Israel had long sought recognition from the Vatican.

Morningstar of the Reformation Dies

When John Wycliffe, the "Morningstar of the Reformation," died of a stroke on this day in 1384, there would be no rest for his bones. Almost thirty years after his death, the Church Council of Constance condemned Wycliffe's teachings and ordered his bones to be disinterred and burned. But the burning of his bones would not end Wycliffe's influence.

Wycliffe had been a leading scholar at Oxford and a chaplain to the king of England. He had the boldness to speak out against the pope, the organizational hierarchy of the Roman Church and the corruption of the clergy in his day. He criticized not only the organization of the medieval Church but its theology as well. He believed the Church should return to the Scriptures. Pastors should live lives of simplicity and holiness, shepherding the flock the Lord had given them.

If the people in England were to know the truth, they must have the Word of God accessible for them to read in their own language. Under Wycliffe's direction, the entire Bible was translated into English for the first time. The translation was completed by Wycliffe's associates in 1395, eleven years after his death.

Wycliffe's principle opponent was Archbishop William Courtenay. Troubled by the fact that the common people loved Wycliffe, Courtenay called a local council to demonstrate that the whole English Church was united against the reformer. A terrifying earthquake struck just as the churchmen prepared to issue their condemnation. Burdened with guilty consciences, they fled. Courtnay convinced them the earthquake was Wycliffe's fault. The synod condemned Wycliffe's work.

Wycliffe's followers and the common people, however, insisted that the earthquake came from God as a judgment on the council. "They may have condemned Wycliffe," they said, "but God has condemned them!" The council became known as the "Earthquake Synod."

Though repeatedly condemned and burned by the authorities, copies of Wycliffe's Bible continued to bring the truth to England for over a century. It greatly influenced William Tyndale and the translators of the King James Version. Five hundred years after it was originally completed, Wycliffe's translation of John 3:36 still sounds familiar: "He that believeth in the son: hath everlasting life—but he that is unbelieveful to the same: shall not see everlasting life—but the wrath of God dwelleth on him."

John Foxe, in his book of martyrs, well described Wycliffe's influence when he said:

John Wycliffe, "Morningstar of the Reformation." (Courtesy of the Christian History Institute archives, Glimpses #78.)

> [T]hough they digged up his body, burnt his bones, and drowned his ashes, yet the Word of God and the truth of his doctrine, with the fruit and success thereof, they could not burn; which yet to this day . . . doth remain.

Other Events

1530: The German Protestant defense coalition known as the Schmalkald League was formed to resist efforts by Holy Roman Emperor Charles V to eradicate Lutheranism from Germany. Its formal agreement was not signed until the following year. Philip of Hesse was a key player in it.

1837: Australia's oldest Roman Catholic church, called the Church on the Hill, was ready for worship.

1892: Andrew Bonar, an influential Scottish Free Church leader, died. He visited Palestine in 1839 to inquire into the condition of Jews there.

1913: Harry Rimmer, scientist and Christian, was converted on this day. He was on the way home from a fight when he stopped to hear a preacher say, "Therefore if any may be in Christ, he is a new creature." Rimmer believed and became an evangelist.

1959: Patriarch Alexei of the Russian Orthodox Church excommunicated Ossipov, who had embraced materialist atheism.

Philip of Hesse, a key player in the Schmalkald league. (Tumbült, Georg. *Die Wiedertäufer: Die Socialen und Religiösen Bewegungen zur Zeit der Reformation*. Bielefeld: Leipzig, Velhagen & Klasing, 1899.)

Resources

Editors' Note: Many of the stories presented in this book have been used in previous Christian History Institute projects. The following list identifies the resources that have been most helpful in preparing *This Day in Christian History*. We hope this will assist readers who want to do further exploration into the events and people who have affected the history of Christianity and the Church.

Allen, John. *One Hundred Great Lives*. New York: Journal of Living, 1944.

Ammerman, Mark. *America: Built on Character, Founded on Faith*. Camp Hill, PA: Christian Publications, Inc., 2004.

Anderson, Gerald H. "Williams, John." *Biographical Dictionary of Christian Missions*. New York: Macmillan Reference USA; London: Simon & Schuster and Prentice Hall International, 1998.

Bainton, Roland H. *Here I Stand: A Life of Martin Luther*. New York: New American Library, 1950.

———. *Women of the Reformation in France and England*. Minneapolis: Augsburg Pub. House, 1973.

———. *Women of the Reformation in Germany and England*. Minneapolis: Augsburg Pub. House, 1973.

Baring-Gould, Sabine. *Lives of the Saints*. Edinburgh: John Grant, 1914.

"Catholic Online Saints," available online at: <http://www.catholic.org/saints/stindex.php>.

"Bartleby.com," available online at: <http://www.bartleby.com>.

Bede. *A History of the English Church and People*. Various editions.

Biblical Archaeology Review. Washington, DC. Various issues.

Blake, William D. *An Almanac of the Christian Church*. Minneapolis: Bethany House, 1987.

Blumenthal, Uta-Renate. *The Investiture Controversy: Church and Monarchy From the Ninth to the Twelfth Century*. Philadelphia: University of Pennsylvania Press, 1988.

Boreham, F.W. *Life Verses*. Grand Rapids: Kregel, 1994.

Bowie, Walter Russell. *Men of Fire: Torchbearers of the Gospel*. New York: Harper and Brothers, 1961.

Boxer, C.R. *Christian Century in Japan*. Berkeley: University of California Press, 1967.

Bradford, William. *Bradford's History of Plymouth Plantation*. New York: Scribner 1923.

Braght, Thieleman J. van. *The Bloody Theater of Martyrs Mirror of the Defenseless Christians Who Baptized Only Upon Confession of Faith, and Who Suffered and Died for the Testimony of Jesus, Their Saviour, From the Time of Christ to the Year A.D. 1660. Translated from the original Dutch or Holland Language from the Edition of 1660 by Joseph F. Sohm*. Available online at: <http://www.homecomers.org/mirror/head.htm>.

Brandenburg, Hans. *The Meek and the Mighty: The Emergence of the Evangelical Movement in Russia*. New York: Oxford University Press, 1977.

Brock, Sebastian P. and Susan Ashbrook Harvey. *Holy Women of the Syrian Orient*. Berkeley: University of California, 1987.

Brown, Theron and Hezekiah Butterworth. *Story of the Hymns and Tunes*. New York: American Tract Society, 1906.

Brusher, Joseph. *Popes Through the Ages*. Princeton, NJ: Van Nostrand, 1959. Available online at: <http://www.geocities.com/gvwrite/popes.htm>.

Burger, Delores T. *Women Who Changed the Heart of the City: The Untold Story of the City Rescue Mission Movement*. Grand Rapids: Kregel Publications, 1997.

Butler, Alban. *Lives of the Saints*. Various editions.

"Calendar of Saints O' the Day," available online at: <http://www.saintpatrickdc.org/ss/cal-ss.htm>.

Capper, W. Melville. *Some Great Christian Doctors*. London: Tyndale Press, 1960.

Carpenter, Humphrey. *The Inklings*. Boston: Houghton Mifflin, 1979.

Cathcart, William, ed. *The Baptist Encyclopedia*, 2 vols., rev. ed. Philadelphia: Louis H. Everts, 1883.

Catholic Encyclopedia. New York: Appleton, 1914.

"The Catholic Encyclopedia," available online at: <http://www.newadvent.org/cathen>.

Ceram, C.W. *Gods, Graves and Scholars: The Story of Archaeology*. Translated from the German by E.B. Garside and Sophie Wilkins. New York: Knopf, 1967.

Chadwick, Henry. *The Early Church*. Hammondsworth, Middlesex, England: Penguin, 1967.

"Christian Classics Ethereal Library," available online at: <http://www.ccel.org>.

"Christian Heroes," available online at: <http://www.christianheroes.com/>.

Christian History Magazine, Issues 1-80. Carol Stream, IL.

Commanger, Henry Steele. *Documents in American History*. New York: Appleton-Century-Crofts, 1963.

Cook, George. *History of the Reformation in Scotland. . . .* Edinburgh, 1811.

Copeland, Lewis. *The World's Great Speeches*. New York: Book League of America, 1942.

Cross, F.L. and E.A. Livingstone, eds. *The Oxford Dictionary of the Christian Church*. Oxford: Oxford University Press, 1997.

Current Biography. New York: H.W. Wilson. Various issues.

Curtis, A. Kenneth, Stephen J. Lang and Randy Petersen. *Dates with Destiny: The 100 Most Important Dates in Church History*. Tarrytown, New York: Revell, 1991.

"Cyberhymnal," available online at: <http://www.cyberhymnal.org>.

Daniel-Rops, Henri. *Heroes of God*. Garden City, NY: Doubleday, 1965.

Davies, Horton. *Great South African Christians*. Cape Town, NY: Oxford University Press, 1951.

Dawson, E.C. *Heroines of Missionary Adventure*. Philadelphia: Lippincott, 1909.

Dawson, W.F. *Christmas, Its Origin and Associations, Together with Its Historical Events and Festive Celebrations During Nineteen Centuries*. London: Elliot Stock, 1902.

Deen, Edith. *Great Women of the Christian Faith*. New York: Harper, 1959.

Deedy, John D. *Catholic Fact Book*. Chicago: T. More Press, 1986.

De Jong, Gerald F. *The Dutch Reformed Church in the American Colonies*. Grand Rapids: Eerdmans, 1978.

De Rosa, Peter. *Vicars of Christ: The Dark Side of the Papacy*. New York: Random House, n.d.

Dewar, Diana. *All for Christ: Some Twentieth-Century Martyrs*. Oxford, New York: Oxford University Press, 1980.

Dictionary of American Biography. New York: Scribner, 1958-1964.

Douglas, J.D., ed. *Who's Who in Church History*. London: Tyndale House.

Dowley, Tim, ed., et al. *Eerdman's Handbook to the History of Christianity*. Berkhamsted, Herts, England: Lion Publishing, 1977.

Drury, A.W. *History of the Church of the United Brethren in Christ*. Dayton, OH: United Brethren Press, 1931.

Duffield, Samuel Willoughby. *English Hymns: Their Authors and History*. New York: Funk & Wagnalls, 1888.

Dunney, Joseph Aloysius. *Church History in Light of the Saints*. New York: The Macmillan Company, 1944.

Durant, Will and Ariel. *The Story of Civilization*. New York: Simon and Schuster, n.d.

Dyke, Cornelius J. *An Introduction to Mennonite History: A Popular History of the Anabaptists and the Mennonites*. Scottsdale, PA: Herald Press, 1967.

Edwards, Tyron. *The New Dictionary of Thoughts: A Cyclopedia of Quotations*. Revised and enlarged by Catrevas and Jonathan Edwards. New York: Standard Book Co., 1949.

"Encyclopedia.com," available online at: <http://www.encyclopedia.com>.

Eusebius. *Ecclesiastical History*. Various editions.

Executive Committee of the International Sunday School Association. *Development of the Sunday School*. Boston: International Sunday School, 1905.

Finegan, Jack. *Handbook of Biblical Chronology*. Peabody, MA: Hendrickson, 1998.

Fisk, Samuel. *Forty Fascinating Conversion Stories*. Grand Rapids: Kregel, 1993.

Foster, Warren Dunham, ed. *Heroines of Modern Religion*. New York: Sturgis and Walton, 1913.

Foxe, John et al. *Foxe's Book of Martyrs*. Various editions.

Fremantle, Anne. *The Papal Encyclicals in their Historical Context*. New York: Mentor, 1956.

———. *The Protestant Mystics*. Boston: Little, Brown, 1964.

Frend, W.H.C. *The Early Church*. Philadelphia: Fortress Press, 1965.

Garrison, Webb. *Strange Facts About the Bible*. Nashville: Abingdon Press, 1968.

Gibson, George M. *The Story of the Christian Year*. Nashville: Abingdon Press, 1945.

Gillespie, Charles Coulston. *Dictionary of Scientific Biography*. New York: Scribner, 1970-1980.

Glimpses of People, Events, Life and Faith From the Church Across the Ages. Worcester, PA: Christian History Institute, 1986-present.

Gordon, Ernest. *Book of Protestant Saints*. Chicago: Moody, 1946.

Graves, Daniel. *Doctors Who Followed Christ*. Grand Rapids: Kregel, 1998.

———. *Scientists of Faith*. Grand Rapids: Kregel, 1996.

Gross, Ernie. *This Day in Religion*. New York: Neal-Schuman Publishers, 1990.

Haeussler, Armin. *The Story of Our Hymns: The Handbook of the Hymnal of the Evangelical and Reformed Church*. Saint Louis, MO: Eden Publishing, 1952.

"The Hall of Church History," available online at: <http://www.spurgeon.org/~phil/hall.htm>.

Harper, Howard V. *Days and Customs of All Faiths*. New York: Fleet Pub. Corp., 1957.

Harrison, E. Myers. *Heroes of Faith on Pioneer Trails*. Chicago: Moody Press, 1945.

Hastings, Adrian. *A History of African Christianity, 1950-1975*. Cambridge; New York: Cambridge University Press, 1979.

Hayne, David M., ed. *Dictionary of Canadian Biography*. Toronto: University of Toronto, 1969.

Headland, Isaac T. *Chinese Heroes*. New York: Eaton and Mains; Cincinnati: Jennings & Pye, 1902.

Henry, Carl F.H. *The Pacific Garden Mission*. Grand Rapids: Zondervan, 1942.

Hill, George H. *Airwaves to the Soul: The Influence and Growth of Religious Broadcasting in America*. Saratoga, CA: R & E Publishers, 1983.

Hillerbrand, Hans J., ed. in chief. *Oxford Encyclopedia of the Reformation*. New York: Oxford University Press, 1996.

Holder, Charles Frederick. *The Quakers in Great Britain and America: The Religious and Political History of the Society of Friends from the Seventeenth to the Twentieth Century*. New York: Nuner, 1913.

Hunter, Joseph. *Collections Concerning the Church or Congregation of Protestant Separatists Formed at Scrooby in North Nottinghamshire in the Time of King James I*. London: John Russell Smith, 1854.

Hutchinson, Ruth and Ruth Adams. *Every Day's a Holiday*. New York: Harper and Brothers, 1951.

Hutten, Kurt. *Iron Curtain Christians*. Minneapolis: Augsburg, 1967.

Ingpen, Robert R. *Encyclopedia of Events That Changed the World: Eighty Turning Points in History*. New York: Viking Studio Books, 1991.

Jacobs, Sylvia M. *Black Americans and the Missionary Movement in Africa*. Westport, CT: Greenwood Press, 1982.

Jedin, Hubert. *Ecumenical Councils of the Catholic Church*. Frieberg: Herder and Herder, 1960.

Johnston, Ken. *Story of New Tribes Mission*. Sanford, FL: New Tribes Mission, 1985.

Kennedy, James with Jerry Newcombe. *What if Jesus Had Never Been Born?* Nashville: Thomas Nelson, 1994.

Kidd, B.J. *Documents Illustrative of the Continental Reformation*. Oxford: The Clarendon Press, 1911.

"Kirchenlexicon," available online at: <http://www.bautz.de>.

Kleinsteuber, R. Wayne. *More than a Memory: The Renewal of Methodism in Canada*. Mississauga, Ontario: Light and Life Press, 1984.

Knowles, David. *Saints and Scholars: Twenty-Five Medieval Portraits*. Westport, CT: Greenwood Press, 1988.

Kunitz, Stanley. *American Authors, 1600-1900: A Biographical Dictionary of American Literature*. New York: H.W. Wilson Company, 1938.

———. *British Authors of the Nineteenth Century*. New York: H.W. Wilson Company, 1936.

Langer, William L. *An Encyclopedia of World History*. Boston: Houghton Mifflin, 1948.

Latourette, Kenneth Scott. *These Sought a Country*. New York: Harper, 1950.

Littell, Franklin H. *The Origins of Sectarian Protestantism*. New York: Macmillan, 1972.

Lockyer, Herbert. *All the Apostles of the Bible*. Grand Rapids: Zondervan, 1972.

Maus, Cynthia Peal. *The Church and the Fine Arts*. New York: Harper, 1959.

Mayr-Harting. Henry. *The Coming of Christianity to Anglo Saxon England*. University Park, PA: Pennsylvania State University Press, 1991.

Macartney, Clarence Edward. *Six Kings of the American Pulpit*. Philadelphia: Westminster Press, 1942.

Makers of Canada. London and Toronto: Oxford University Press, 1928.

McGrath, Alister E. *In the Beginning: The Story of the King James Bible and How It Changed a Nation, a Language, and a Culture*. New York: Doubleday, 2001.

McKilliam, A.E. *Chronicle of the Archbishops of Canterbury*. Cambridge, England: James Clarke & Co., 1913.

McLean, Archibald. *Epoch Makers of Modern Missions*. Cincinnati: Fleming H. Revell Co., 1912.

Mead, Frank S. *12,000 Religious Quotations*. Grand Rapids: Baker Book House, 1989.

———. *Handbook of Denominations in the United States*, 7th ed. Nashville: Abingdon, 1980.

"Medieval Sourcebook," available online at: <http://www.fordham.edu/halsall>.

Montor, Chevalier Artaud de. *Lives and Times of the Popes*. New York: Catholic Publication Society of America, 1911.

Moreau, A. Scott. *Evangelical Dictionary of World Missions*. Grand Rapids: Baker Books, 2000.

Morgan, Robert J. *On This Day*. Nashville: Thomas Nelson, 1997.

Morris, Joan. *The Lady Was a Bishop: The Hidden History of Women with Clerical Ordination and the Jurisdiction of Bishops*. New York: Macmillan, 1973.

Mullins, Mark M. *Christianity Made in Japan: A Study of Indigenous Movements.* Honolulu: University of Hawai'i Press, 1998.

Neill, Stephen. *A History of Missions*. The Pelican History of the Church: 6. Hammondsworth, Middlesex, England: Pelican, 1964.

New Catholic Encyclopedia. Prepared by an editorial staff at the Catholic University of America. New York: McGraw-Hill, 1967-79.

New Schaff-Herzog Encyclopedia of Religious Knowledge. Grand Rapids: Baker Book House, 1954.

Ninde, Edward S. *The Story of the American Hymn*. New York: Abingdon, 1921.

Obolensky, Dmitri. *Six Byzantine Portraits*. Oxford: Clarendon, 1988.

O'Brien, John A. *The American Martyrs*. New York: Appleton-Century-Crofts, 1953.

———. *Giants of the Faith: Conversions Which Changed the World*. Garden City, NY: Image Books, 1960.

Online Anglican Resources. *Biographical Sketches of Memorable Christians of the Past*. Available online at: <http://justus.anglican.org/ resources/bio/index.html>.

Ottosen, Knud. *A Short History of the Churches of Scandinavia*. Arhus, Denmark: Dept. of Church History, Universitetet, 1986.

Outerbridge, Leonard M. *The Lost Churches of China*. Philadelphia: Westminster Press, 1952.

Parkman, Francis. *The Jesuits in North America in the Seventeenth Century*. Boston: Little, Brown, and Company, 1897.

Perry, William Stevens. *The Episcopate in America*. New York: Christian Literature, 1895.

Pierce, Richard A., ed. and Colin Bearne, tr. *The Russian Orthodox Religious Mission in America 1794-1837: With Materials Concerning the Life and Works of the Monk German and Ethnographic Notes by Hieromonk Gedeon*. Kingston, Ontario: Limestone Press, 1978.

Pitman, E.R. *Lady Missionaries in Many Lands*. London: Pickering and Inglis, 1900.

Pollock, John. *The Cambridge Seven*. London: Intervarsity Fellowship, 1954.

———. *Victims of the Long March and Other Stories*. Waco, TX: Word Books, 1970.

Price, Carl F. *One Hundred and One Hymn Stories*. New York: Abingdon, 1923.

Raab, Clement. *The Twenty Ecumenical Councils of the Catholic Church*. Westminster, MD: Newman Press, 1959.

Reynolds, William J. *Companion to Baptist Hymnal*. Nashville: Broadman Press, n.d.

Runes, Dagobert. *Treasury of Philosophy*. New York: Philosophical Library, 1955.

"Scottish Preachers Hall of Fame," available online at: <http://www.newble.co.uk/hall/hallofame.html>.

Shelley, Bruce. *Church History in Plain Language*. Dallas: Word Publishing, 1996.

"Significant Scots," available online at: <http://www.electricscotland.com>.

Slosser, Gaius Jackson. Frank W. Caldwell, et al., contr. *They Seek a Country: The American Presbyterians, Some Aspects*. New York: Macmillan, 1955.

Smellie, Alexander. *Men of the Covenant*. New York: Revell, 1903.

Spinka, Matthew. *Jan Hus and the Czech Reform*. Hamden, CT: Archon Books, 1966.

Stephen, Leslie and Sidney Lee. London: , eds. *Dictionary of National Biography*. Oxford University Press, 1921-1996.

Stephenson, Carl and Frederick George Marcham, eds. and trans. *Sources of English Constitutional History: A Selection of Documents from A.D. 600 to the Present*. New York: Harper and Row, 1937.

Sutherland, Allan. *Famous Hymns of the World, Their Origin and Their Romance*. New York: Frederick A. Stokes Company, 1906.

"Sword of the Lord Biographies," available online at: <http://www.swordofthelord.com/biographies.htm>.

Synan, Vinson. *The Holiness-Pentecostal Tradition: Charismatic Movements in the Twentieth Century*. Grand Rapids: Eerdmans, 1997.

Tappert, Theodore G., ed. *Lutheran Confessional Theology in America*. New York: Oxford, 1972.

Tenney, Merrill C., ed. *Pictorial Bible Dictionary*. Nashville. Southwestern Co. 1972.

Tucker, Ruth A. and Walter Liefeld. *Daughters of the Church: Women and Ministry from New Testament Times to the Present*. Grand Rapids: Academie, 1987.

Vaughan, Alden T. *Encyclopedia of American Biography*. New York: Harper and Row, 1974.

Vincent, Benjamin. *Haydn's Dictionary of Dates*. New York: Putnam, 1911.

"Virtual American Biographics," available online at: <http://www.famousamericans.net>.

Whiting, Lilian. *Women Who Have Enobled Life*. Philadelphia: American Sunday School Union, 1915.

"Wholesome Words," available online at: <http://www.wholesomewords.org>.

Williams, George Huntston. *The Radical Reformation*. Philadelphia: Westminster Press, 1962.

Wintle, Justin. *Makers of Nineteenth-Century Culture, 1800-1914*. London: Routledge & Kegan Paul, 1982.

Wood, James E., ed. *Baptists and the American Experience*. Valley Forge, PA: Judson Press, n.d.

Wooding, Dan and Ray Barnett. *Uganda Holocaust*. Grand Rapids: Zondervan Pub. House, 1980.

Wylie, James A. *History of Protestantism*. Available online at: <www.whatsaiththescripture. com/Fellowship/James.A.Wylie.html>.

EDITORS' NOTE: The following is a list of the *major* subjects covered in *This Day in Christian History*. Therefore, not every instance of each word listed is noted, just the primary instance of each major subject.

Subject Index